AUTOCOURSE

The World's Leading Grand Prix Annual

HAZLETON PUBLISHING

winners

Jacques Villeneuve
1997 Formula One World Drivers' Champion

Rothmans Williams Renault
1997 Formula One World Constructors' Champion

Winning is everything

- it proves Castrol lubricants in competition

- it says Castrol is the **best** you can buy.

www.castrol.com

The technical partnership between Castrol and the Rothmans Williams Renault team has one goal - to win the Formula One World Championship ...and we have!

When the Rothmans Williams Renault team win - we all win. Castrol use the technology from racing to develop lubricants for the vehicles we all drive everyday.

OFFICIAL SUPPLIER
WILLIAMS GRAND PRIX

TECHNICAL SPONSOR
WILLIAMS GRAND PRIX

THE LUBRICANTS SPECIALIST

contents

AUTOCOURSE 1997-98
is published by
Hazleton Publishing Ltd,
3 Richmond Hill,
Richmond, Surrey
TW10 6RE.

Colour reproduction by
Barrett Berkeley Ltd, London.

Printed in England by
Butler and Tanner Ltd,
Frome, Somerset.

© Hazleton Publishing Ltd 1997.

ISBN: 1-874557-47-0

DISTRIBUTORS
UNITED KINGDOM
Biblios Ltd
Star Road
Partridge Green
West Sussex RH13 8LD
Telephone: 01403 710971
Fax: 01403 711143

NORTH AMERICA
Motorbooks International
PO Box 1
729 Prospect Ave.
Osceola
Wisconsin 54020, USA
Telephone: (1) 715 294 3345
Fax: (1) 715 294 4448

AUSTRALIA
Technical Book and
Magazine Co. Pty
295 Swanston Street
Melbourne
Victoria 3000
Telephone: (03) 9663 3951
Fax: (03) 9663 2094

NEW ZEALAND
David Bateman Ltd
PO Box 100-242
North Shore Mail Centre
Auckland 1330
Telephone: (9) 415 7664
Fax: (9) 415 8892

SOUTH AFRICA
Motorbooks
341 Jan Smuts Avenue
Craighall Park
Johannesburg
Telephone: (011) 325 4458/60
Fax: (011) 325 4146

FOREWORD *by Jacques Villeneuve* — 5

EDITOR'S INTRODUCTION — 6

THE TOP TEN DRIVERS OF 1997 — 15

COMPOUND INTEREST
Adam Cooper looks at the latest F1 tyre war — 35

THE WINNING HABIT
*Alan Henry pays tribute to Williams, constructors' champions
for a record-breaking ninth time* — 40

BLOND AMBITION
A profile of the 1997 World Champion by Eric Silbermann — 44

FORMULA 1 REVIEW
by Bob Constanduros, Maurice Hamilton and Alan Henry — 47

1997 GRANDS PRIX *by Alan Henry* — 97

1997 FORMULA 1 STATISTICS
compiled by David Hayhoe and Nick Henry — 244

FORMULA 3000 REVIEW *by Tom Alexander* — 246

FORMULA 3 REVIEW *by Jaimes Baker* — 248

GT RACING REVIEW *by Gary Watkins* — 250

TOURING CAR RACING REVIEW *by Paul Fearnley* — 252

AMERICAN RACING REVIEW *by Gordon Kirby* — 258

OTHER MAJOR 1997 RESULTS *compiled by David Hayhoe* — 273

acknowledgements

The Editor of AUTOCOURSE wishes to thank the following for their assistance in compiling the 1997-98 edition:
France: ACO, Fédération Française du Sport Automobile, FIA (Bernie Ecclestone, Max Mosley, Francesco Longanese-Cattani, Alistair Watkins and Charlie Whiting), Peugeot Sport (Jean-Claude Lefebvre), Prost F1 (Alain Prost, Sophie Sicot and Chris Williams), Renault Sport (Jean-Jacques Delaruwière, Bernard Dudot and Christine Marquilie); **Germany:** Formel 3 Vereinigung, Mercedes-Benz (Norbert Haug and Wolfgang Schattling); **Great Britain:** Arrows (Tom Walkinshaw, Daniele Audetto, John Barnard, Ann Bradshaw, Frank Dernie, Patricia Guerendel and Jackie Oliver), *Autocar*, Martin Brundle, Colin Burr, Timothy Collings, Bob Constanduros, Cosworth Engineering, Steve Cropley, John Fitzpatrick, Ford (Cliff Peters, Martin Whitaker, Ellen Kolby and Sabine Marcon), Peter Foubister, Mike Greasley, Maurice Hamilton, Brian Hart Ltd (Jane Brace and Brian Hart), Nick Henry, John Hogan, Ian Hutchinson, Ilmor Engineering (Mario Illien), Jordan Grand Prix (Gary Anderson, Giselle Davies, Eddie Jordan, Ian Phillips and Lindsay Haylett), McLaren International (Ron Dennis, Justine Blake, Anna Guerrier, Adrian Newey, Neil Oatley, Steve Nichols, Jo Ramirez and Peter Stayner), Stan Piecha, Dan Pratt, RAC MSA (Derek Tye), The Hon. Nigel Roebuck, Shell International, Eric Silbermann, Silverstone Circuits (Katie Tyler), Stewart Grand Prix (Jackie and Paul Stewart, Alan Jenkins and Stuart Sykes), Simon Taylor, Tyrrell Racing Organisation (Rupert Manwaring, Harvey Postlethwaite, Ben Taylor, Bob Tyrrell and Ken Tyrrell), Murray Walker, Professor Sid Watkins, Williams Grand Prix Engineering (Jane Gorard, Patrick Head, James Robinson, Dickie Stanford, Lindsay Morle, Ffiona Welford and Frank Williams), Eoin Young; **Italy:** Benetton Formula (Flavio Briatore, David Richards and Patrizia Spinelli), Commissione Sportiva Automobilistica Italiana, Scuderia Ferrari (Ross Brawn, Claudio Berro, Antonio Ghini and Jean Todt), Minardi Team (Giancarlo Minardi, Amanda Gadaselli and Renato Capucci); **Japan:** Bridgestone (James Penroso), Yamaha (Herbie Blash); **Switzerland:** Marlboro Motorsport (Agnès Carlier), Sauber (Gustav Büsing and Peter Sauber); **USA:** CART, Daytona International Speedway, Goodyear (Cal Lint, Ron Pike, Tony Shakespeare, Stu Grant and Dermot Bambridge), Indianapolis Motor Speedway, Indy Lights, NASCAR, Roger Penske, SportsCar.

photographs published in Autocourse 1997-98 have been contributed by:

Allsport/Michael Cooper/Clive Mason/Mark Thompson, Gérard Berthoud, Michael C. Brown, Diana Burnett, Paul-Henri Cahier, Ray Doblick, Lukas Gorys, *GP Photo*/Peter Nygaard, Darren Heath, W.P. Johnson/*At Speed Photographic*, Nigel Kinrade, *LAT Photographic*/Steve Tee/Martyn Elford/Charles Coates, Pamela Lauesen/*FOSA*, Dominique Leroy, *Steve Mohlenkamp Photography*, John Overton, *Publiracing Agency*/Manfred Giet, Michael Roberts, Matthias Schneider, *Shutterspeed Photografik*, Nigel Snowdon, *Sporting Pictures (UK) Ltd*, Sutton Motorsport Images/Keith Sutton/Mark Sutton, Bryn Williams.

publisher
RICHARD POULTER

editor
ALAN HENRY

managing editor
PETER LOVERING

art editor
STEVE SMALL

production manager
STEVEN PALMER

publishing development manager
SIMON MAURICE

business development manager
SIMON SANDERSON

sales promotion
CLARE KRISTENSEN

results and statistics
DAVID HAYHOE
NICK HENRY

f1 illustrations
IAN HUTCHINSON
NICOLA FOX

chief contributing photographers
ALLSPORT
DIANA BURNETT
PAUL-HENRI CAHIER
DARREN HEATH
LAT PHOTOGRAPHIC
PETER NYGAARD
MATTHIAS SCHNEIDER
NIGEL SNOWDON
SUTTON MOTORSPORT
IMAGES
BRYN WILLIAMS

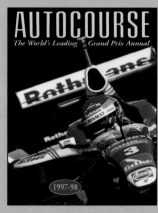

Dust-jacket photograph:
World Champion Jacques Villeneuve
in the Rothmans Williams-Renault
by Steve Mohlenkamp Photography

Title page photograph:
The controversial collision between
Michael Schumacher and Jacques
Villeneuve in the European Grand
Prix at Jerez that decided the
outcome of the drivers' championship
by Steve Tee/LAT Photographic

Moët Silver Trophy
1996 Winners :
Damon Hill
Williams Grand Prix
Renault.

MOËT & CHANDON. *Sao Paulo, Monaco, Silverstone, Hockenheim, Spa, Monza, Suzuka, Estoril ...*

MOËT
SILVER TROPHY
—FORMULA ONE—

foreword
by Jacques Villeneuve

Winning the FIA F1 World Championship only two seasons after taking the Indy car championship has obviously been enormously satisfying for me and, although I'm not a great racing historian, I gather I am the first driver to have taken the F1 title after only two full seasons of Grand Prix racing.

In many ways it has been a season of contrasts. We had a strong start and a strong finish, but in the middle of the year I think there were times when both myself and the Williams team made a few mistakes which could have cost us dearly in terms of results. Yet I am happy that we got everything together in the closing races of the year to launch a counter-attack which carried us to the championship crown.

I would like to thank all those who helped me achieve my ambition. Now I've got the taste for this F1 business, the next item on my personal agenda is working to retain the World Championship in 1998!

F1'S SLOW BURN

MANY F1 insiders would have wholeheartedly approved had Ferrari been able to celebrate its 50th anniversary by securing either the drivers' or constructors' World Championships. As things transpired, the team was not a sufficiently consistent scorer to fend off Williams in the battle for the constructors' title, and a down-to-the-wire shoot-out between Maranello's team leader Michael Schumacher and Williams star Jacques Villeneuve ended in tears with the German driver vilified in the European media for trying to ram Villeneuve out of the final race of the season.

As is now history, the move backfired dramatically on Schumacher, who will now be hoping that his third World Championship title will follow in due course next season. Yet for everyone who argues that Schumacher

is the Grand Diabolarch, the proven Bad Boy of contemporary F1, more moderate voices rightly point out that no other driver could have carried the Prancing Horse any closer to its first drivers' title since 1979.

Certainly the FIA World Motor Sports Council took a lenient view of Schumacher's alleged malfeasance. Despite expectations of draconian fines, possible race suspensions or even his starting the season with a negative points total, FIA President Max Mosley announced that he would be stripped of his second place in the championship and required to carry out some road safety campaign work on an FIA/European Union initiative in 1998.

Most observers regarded this as little more than a slap over the wrists, but Mosley explained it was intended as a

deterrent aimed at anybody who had a mind to transgress the rules in the future.

'It sends a message to all drivers at all levels of the sport that, if you do something you shouldn't do when the championship is at issue, you will be excluded from that championship,' he said. 'You cannot possibly gain anything by engaging in an illegitimate act.'

At the start of the season Ferrari President Luca di Montezemolo said it was the team's ambition to improve on its 1996 record of three wins. Schumacher duly obliged with five victories, so from that standpoint it was a case of Mission Accomplished. Perhaps the biggest sin of which Michael was guilty was actually raising Maranello's expectations so high that when the final disappointment arrived the sense of anti-climax and pain was even

more acutely felt. That, at least, he can easily be forgiven!

It was therefore left to Jacques Villeneuve to win the World Championship in only his second season of F1 driving. The 26-year-old former Indy car champion survived a wobbly mid-season slump to bounce back against the odds and take the title. Even exclusion from the Japanese Grand Prix for a trifling offence, a penalty that was admittedly self-induced, failed to ruffle his calm even though he went into the final race one point behind title favourite Schumacher.

If Villeneuve's irreverent non-conformity was hailed by some as a welcome breath of fresh air, the fact remains that the French-Canadian driver was the latest beneficiary of the Williams team's technical excellence. Like Nigel Mansell, Alain Prost and

Welcome to Marlboro Country. The threat of a ban on tobacco sponsorship and advertising within the European Union has emphasised F1's dependence on this controversial source of funding.

Damon Hill before him, Villeneuve was the throttle jockey who made full use of the equipment placed at his disposal, helping to assure the British team of its ninth constructors' championship in only 17 years. It was a remarkable, not to mention all-time-record, achievement.

There were other performances worth noting in 1997. The McLaren-Mercedes alliance scored its first three wins, returning Ron Dennis's team to the top step of the winner's rostrum for the first time in its post-Ayrton Senna era. Giancarlo Fisichella, Jarno Trulli and Alexander Wurz all signalled that there is another bright-eyed, highly promising generation of F1 stars waiting in the wings while Damon Hill goes into 1998 as Grand Prix racing's Senior Citizen following the retirement of the ever-popular Ger-

hard Berger, who rounded off his career with a hard-fought fourth place at Jerez, less than two seconds behind Mika Häkkinen's victorious McLaren.

Money continued to make the F1 wheels go round, of course, and the season was also marked by a potentially ugly confrontation between the sport's commercial czar Bernie Ecclestone and three of the competing teams, Williams, McLaren and Tyrrell.

Ecclestone started the year with the apparent intention of floating his F1 Holdings empire on the stock exchange, an exercise which would reputedly have enriched Bernie and his family to the tune of $2.5 billion. The success of such a flotation would depend to a degree on the effectiveness of Bernie's efforts to capitalise on the development of digital pay-TV channels across Europe and, in his role as the

FIA's Commercial Rights holder, he helped persuade seven of the competing teams to sign a revised Concorde Agreement which would guarantee them significantly enhanced income from television revenues.

The three dissident teams were not happy with this arrangement, claiming that the seven signatories had not fully understood the extent of the commercial rights they were signing away to Ecclestone. They stuck out for a better deal, which, by the season's end, it looked as though they were going to get. Ecclestone will be hoping that this finally clears the way for the successful flotation of his company.

The other great *cause célèbre* was the apparent lifting of the proposed UK tobacco advertising ban, but only as far as F1 was concerned. The recently elected Labour government may have pledged to ban all tobacco sponsorship in sport, but they had reckoned without the persuasive powers of Max Mosley and Bernie Ecclestone.

The FIA President made the very valid point that F1 with unfettered tobacco advertising would be beamed into British homes from the far corners of the world anyway, so why not agree to lifting the UK ban in exchange for an FIA organised global *reduction* in tobacco exposure in all international racing categories.

The Government accepted the deal, duly lapping up hints that British jobs would be lost if UK-based F1 teams found it necessary to decamp to the Pacific Rim in the event of Grand Prix racing moving away from Europe as a result of the EU tobacco restrictions. This seemed gullible in the extreme, but the FIA certainly did a brilliant sales pitch.

Coincidentally, it was revealed that Bernie Ecclestone had made a million-pound contribution to the Labour party earlier in 1997. This potentially embarrassing episode was resolved when Tony Blair and Labour's General Secretary Tom Sawyer decided to refer the matter to Sir Patrick Neill, the Public Standards watchdog. As a result it was decided that the best strategy would be to return the money to Mr E. in case the motives behind the donation were misunderstood.

Considering an even broader canvas, Ecclestone, the FIA and the F1 teams have developed a sophisticated culture of commercial interdependence over the past decade or more which would be almost impossible to unravel. Ultimately the divergent views held by the FIA Vice-President and certain of the competing teams will have to be reconciled. Even if it hurts.

Grand Prix racing may have its faults, but it is a whole lot better than any other international racing category. Admittedly, GT racing is enjoying something of a renaissance, thanks largely to the high-profile involvement of Mercedes-Benz and BMW. Formula 3000 is nicely stabilised as an effective F1 training ground, while CART and the Indy Racing League continue to pursue their own interests on the North American domestic scene. In that connection, CART is thriving while the IRL is determined to carve its own independent furrow, even if that means the Indy 500 becomes something of a secondary attraction in the process. The Biggest Race in the World, perhaps. But where are the drivers?

Yet from the viewpoint of sustained interest, the 1997 FIA Formula 1 World Championship offered a varied and absorbing menu, even though all the tempting side dishes could not disguise the fact that the main course – namely the racing itself – was slightly tasteless. More than ever, F1 has developed into an overly esoteric technical exercise with overtaking on most circuits the product of refuelling tactics rather than passing other cars on the track itself.

The FIA has attempted to address this problem with new rules for 1998. The cars will be narrower, awkward-looking, and run on grooved tyres. The theory is that there will be substantially less grip and that braking distances should open up considerably. Many competing teams, with the exception of Ferrari, feel these changes will offer no measurable improvement in terms of close competition.

With BMW and Honda having stated their firm intention of returning to the F1 fray, the commercial future of the sport has never looked better. Yet the question of quite how 'F1 Incorporated' would be operated as a public company still sends a frisson of apprehension down many a spine.

Bernie Ecclestone may yet float his company successfully. But what of the future? Will F1's business arm flourish as a publicly floated corporation? Or will it become a fertile breeding ground for commercial dissension? Nobody can be quite certain how it will work out.

Either way, F1 is entering uncharted waters which could lead to further massive expansion. There is no alternative but to trust in those on the bridge to keep it away from the corporate rocks.

Alan Henry
Tillingham, Essex
November, 1997

Photo: Darren Heath

7

Face your fears.

Live your dreams.

NO
FEAR

COMMITTED TO BE FIRST . . .

IN celebrating its 100th anniversary and its 100 per cent success in Formula 1 in 1997, Goodyear can reflect that its entire history encompasses the development and evolution of the automobile for the everyday motorist. The company's leading position in the automotive industry is supported by a commitment to engineering, research and development, and a long-term involvement in international motor racing.

The company is firmly established as number one in racing worldwide with a successful programme that encompasses Formula 1, Indy cars, stock cars, sports cars, sprints, drag racing and off-road racing.

Goodyear was founded in 1898 by 38-year-old Frank A. Seiberling in Akron, Ohio. He named the company 'Goodyear' in honour of Charles Goodyear who, almost 60 years earlier, had discovered vulcanisation, a process of 'cooking' gum rubber and sulphur to make a stable rubber end product.

Almost from the outset of motorised competition, Goodyear was quick to appreciate that lessons learned on the race track could feed back into the general tyre manufacturing process. Charlie Metz used Goodyear tyres on his Stutz to finish third in the Indianapolis 500 as early as 1913, although it was not until six years later that the world's largest tyre and rubber company became really serious about the world's largest motor race.

A major development effort by Goodyear engineers resulted in the production of tyres which helped competitors break the magic 100

mph barrier at Indianapolis in 1919. Howdy Wilcox, who qualified his Peugeot at 101.01 mph, won the race on Goodyear rubber at an average speed of 88.05 mph. Just to confirm the company's superiority, nine of the top ten finishers were on Goodyear rubber – and two went the distance without a tyre change, regarded as an almost unbelievable feat at the time!

GOODYEAR
100
1 9 9 8 - 1 9 9 8

Top: Howdy Wilcox, winner at Indianapolis in 1919, qualified his Peugeot at an average speed of 101.01 mph.
Right: Goodyear advertising from the early period.
Below: More than seven decades on, Goodyear still leading the way, as Jacques Villeneuve takes the victory in the 1997 Argentine Grand Prix and goes on to win the 1997 championship.

Thereafter, the company gradually scaled down its motor racing involvement and it dropped out of the sport in 1922. It was not until the early 1950s that Goodyear began to reconsider its attitude towards motor racing. Surveys conducted around that time indicated that Goodyear had a strong appeal to middle-aged and older customers, with its products having an image of dependability and reliability.

Yet the management decided it was time to develop a more dynamic corporate image. Thus was born the 'Go, Go Goodyear' advertising and promotional

campaigns and at the same time the company made a return to motor racing after an interval of over three decades.

In 1957, Goodyear appeared in the stock car racing arena and quickly established itself as a competitive force. By 1960, the company had furnished the winning tyre in the Daytona 500 in what is now the prestigious NASCAR Winston Cup Series championship trail. By 1962, Goodyear was the dominant NASCAR tyre supplier.

During this period Goodyear tyres appeared in Grand Prix racing for the first time. In 1960, Lance Reventlow, the millionaire son of Woolworth heiress Barbara Hutton, used Goodyear rubber for his lavishly over-ambitious F1 foray to Europe. Disappointingly, his front-engined Scarabs were a year or so behind the times. The rear-engined F1 revolution was in full swing and the cars proved to be a failure.

Although by now Goodyear was a proven competitor on the NASCAR trail, its first post-war foray onto the international racing scene came at Indianapolis in 1963. The 1961 Indy 500 winner A.J. Foyt was frustrated that Firestone had produced some special tyres for the trend-setting new Lotus-

GOOD〜YEAR
100
1 9 9 8 - 1 9 9 8

Top: Richard and Lee Petty, legends both in NASCAR, run together on the banking at Darlington in 1960.
Below left: One of America's finest, the great A.J. Foyt, was instrumental in bringing Goodyear to the Indianapolis Motor Speedway, winning the race in 1967 on Goodyears – the start of three decades of almost total tyre dominance in this legendary arena.
Below right: Richie Ginther, the pint-sized Californian who brought Goodyear its maiden Grand Prix victory in Mexico City in 1965.

Fords driven by Jim Clark and Dan Gurney, but at the same time declined to supply them for his own front-engined machine. Foyt urged Goodyear to begin an Indy tyre development programme and he won the first race of the 1964 season on Goodyears in Phoenix. Just three years later, Foyt would speed to victory in his Goodyear-shod Coyote to register the company's first Indy 500 win in over four decades. From 1972 onwards, Goodyear's total domination of the Indy 500 would remain unchallenged for almost a quarter of a century, with Goodyear marking its 300th Indy car victory in 1994 with Al Unser Jr at Vancouver, British Columbia.

In 1964, Goodyear established its international racing division in Wolverhampton, Great Britain, and an intensive programme of F1 competition would be sustained for the next 15 years from that location. In 1965, Goodyear struck up a partnership with both the Brabham and Honda F1 teams, Richie Ginther posting the company's maiden Grand Prix victory at Mexico City in what was the final race of the 1.5-litre Formula 1.

In 1966, Goodyear F1 contracts were signed with Gurney's new Eagle team, in addition to Brabham, but it was Jack Brabham who dominated the season, winning the French, British, Dutch and German Grands Prix to give Goodyear its first F1 World Championship. It was a success repeated the following year by Brabham's team-mate Denny Hulme. A new range of massive, square-shouldered tyres provided the vital interface between car and track surface.

In 1971, Goodyear's international sporting image received a further boost when the company entered into a partnership with Jackie Stewart and the Tyrrell team. Stewart's relationship with Goodyear, from both a promotional and a technical development standpoint, lasted for more than a decade after his retirement from racing at the end of the 1973 season.

It set the tone for the company's future relationships with front-line F1 drivers and teams over the years that followed, underpinning a level of support to the F1 World Championship in general which has displayed an unwavering consistency of commitment.

Goodyear was also the first company to introduce slick-treaded tyres into F1, these new covers making their debut in the 1971 French Grand Prix at Paul Ricard, a race won by Stewart's Tyrrell on his way to his first World Championship title achieved on Goodyear rubber. He would repeat this title success in 1973 before retiring from the cockpit.

In 1977, Niki Lauda marked a significant milestone in Goodyear's F1 racing involvement by posting the company's 100th Grand Prix victory at the wheel of his Ferrari at Hockenheim. At the Canadian Grand Prix in Montreal six years later, René Arnoux took this total to 150 wins and the 200th victory duly rolled up when Gerhard Berger won the 1987 Australian GP at Adelaide. Four years later there was even more celebrating when Ayrton Senna combined his first victory in his home Grand Prix – the Brazilian race at São Paulo's Interlagos circuit – with Goodyear's 250th win.

The company's victory tally continued to mount over the next few seasons, Damon Hill raising the total to 300 when he won the 1994 Spanish Grand Prix driving a Williams-Renault. In 1997, Goodyear has faced a determined challenge from a new rival, Bridgestone. It has responded to this competition by stepping up its technical development and has dominated the battle for the World Championship. In May, Jacques Villeneuve scored the company's 350th Grand Prix victory at Barcelona's Circuit de Catalunya, emphasising the depth of Goodyear's Formula 1 experience and its unrivalled winning pedigree.

The 1997 season proved to be a great success for Goodyear with every win, every pole position and all fastest laps being achieved on Eagle tyres. Ultimately Goodyear's championship tally was further increased by Williams-Renault and Jacques Villeneuve winning both the constructors' and drivers' World Championships.

Goodyear's commitment to the ever-changing technical challenges of Grand Prix tyre engineering will be sustained into 1998 when new regulations demand grooved dry weather tyres as part of a

Top: *Jack Brabham, Goodyear's first World Champion, winning the Dutch Grand Prix in 1966.* Left: *Jacques Villeneuve celebrates his win in the 1997 Spanish Grand Prix – Goodyear's 350th victory.*

package intended to reduce Grand Prix car lap speeds. Yet the company is confident that it will consolidate its proven track record of transferring advanced technology from its racing activities to its road car products.

'We are extremely proud of Goodyear's dominant F1 victory record against competition in 1997,' says Stu Grant, general manager of racing worldwide. 'We intend to remain victorious and are backing up that goal with an aggressive Eagle tyre development programme supported by major capital investments to support our excellent F1 teams in 1998 and beyond. We will deal with tyre rule changes and challenges in all series, knowing we have the best people on the job and that our technical centres in the US, Japan and Luxembourg are linked to share critical data.'

The conviction that the technical knowledge derived from participating in Formula 1 is relevant to the ordinary motorist is exemplified by Goodyear's latest-generation high-performance road tyre, the Goodyear Eagle F1. Unlike Formula 1 racing tyres, which are specifically developed for either dry or wet track conditions, tyres used by the everyday motorist require supreme versatility and dependability in all driving conditions. Consequently Goodyear's high-performance road tyres must provide high levels of dry weather grip and directional stability, combined with a tread design which efficiently evacuates the water to provide maximum performance in heavy rain.

Top: Goodyear Technical Center at Akron, Ohio, where the Eagle race tyres are produced. The intense development and testing of these tyres in the heat of competition brings swifter benefits to the ordinary motorist as technology is transferred from the track to the road.
Below: Steve Myers (left), director of racing tyre sales and marketing, with Stu Grant, general manager of racing worldwide.

'Much of what we learn with race tyres in terms of handling, cornering and overall response, we can transfer to the design of tyres that operate at lower speeds and in a less demanding environment,' explains Pierre Kummer, the company's director of tyre technology for Europe, based at Goodyear's Technical Centre in Luxembourg.

'For Goodyear, motor sport represents the ultimate testing environment. Only many years of experience, the most modern technology and the never-flagging enthusiasm of our engineers and researchers guarantee success.'

Walt Curtiss, director of the Akron Technical Center, says, 'It is no secret why design, development and manufacturing of Goodyear's Formula 1 race tyres are located at the Akron Tech Center. Proximity to core research, developing new technologies, the feedback from race tyre development and racing experience offer a synergy that benefits the consumer's street tyre and world-class race drivers on the track.

'This ability to get fast technology transfer in every area from manufacturing capability to high-tech computer-aided performance simulation keeps Goodyear on the leading edge in all arenas of competition.'

Stu Grant confirms the link between passenger and racing tyres. 'The customer is the ultimate beneficiary of our racing involvement,' he says. 'The leading edge technology developed in racing benefits all of the

company's tyre development programmes in one form or another.'

Of course, extensive experience in Formula 1 has confirmed Goodyear's view that the rewards of Grand Prix racing are evenly divided between commercial and technical benefits. It is a well established fact that brand awareness for Goodyear's products is enhanced if there is opposition from a rival manufacturer, as has been the case in all but ten of the 32 seasons the company has participated in Formula 1 racing. However, the continued success of Goodyear's high-performance road tyres, such as the Eagle F1, emphasises that the company continued to develop its product even though it enjoyed a monopoly tyre supply situation in Grand Prix racing over

Top: *Goodyear Eagle racing rain tyres for CART are tested under controlled track conditions.*
Left and above right: *Tyre engineers at work in just two of the motor sport arenas contested by Goodyear: CART and NASCAR.*
Below: *The enormously successful Goodyear Eagle F1 tyres, winners of more than 350 Grand Prix races and fitted to 1997's World Championship-winning car.*

tailored for the individual performance of one high-profile machine. The company's engineers continually fine-tune the delicate balance between tyre construction and rubber compounds to provide the best tyre for constantly changing Formula 1 racing vehicles. Grand Prix cars may evolve from year to year, but tyre designers focus one step ahead when it comes to optimising car/tyre performance.

In general terms, Goodyear's race tyre division balances the need to look months ahead with the immediate requirement to have subtly improved tyre performance at the next race on the calendar. There is always one carefully planned compound available for each individual race, which is supplemented by an optional compound, to ensure that every possible variation in track and weather conditions is confidently anticipated prior to each individual Grand Prix.

the five seasons prior to 1997 due to no other tyre company wishing to take up the challenge.

Looking ahead, Goodyear's racing department is confident that it will continue to produce a top-quality tyre which works well across the wide range of cars being supplied, and is not simply

'While the results of next weekend's race are certainly important, we are focused ahead,' says Stu Grant. 'I am optimistic and excited about the future. Racing helps inspire a winning spirit among members of our global Goodyear family. We are committed to be first, not second, in everything we do as a company.'

GOODYEAR'S 100 YEAR HISTORY

Goodyear is the leading competitor in many fields of motor sport worldwide. Its famous tyres have brought countless victories in such diverse motor sport disciplines as (clockwise from top left) Formula 1, CART, NHRA drag racing, the Indy Racing League, NASCAR Winston Cup and NASCAR Craftsman Truck racing.

FIA FORMULA ONE
WORLD CHAMPIONSHIP 1997

top ten

drivers

Chosen by the
Editor, taking into
account their racing
performances and
the equipment at
their disposal

photography by
Matthias Schneider

jacques
villeneuve

1

Date of birth: 9 April 1971

Team: Rothmans Williams Renault

Grand Prix starts in 1997: 17

World Championship placing: 1st

Wins: 7; Poles: 10; Points: 81

JACQUES Villeneuve won seven Grands Prix and came on strongly in the closing races of the year to clinch the World Championship. This was achieved despite a sometimes rather erratic second F1 season for the French-Canadian, who peppered a succession of splendid victories with some surprisingly elementary mistakes.

In some ways Villeneuve is a bundle of contradictions. Hugely talented, there are times when he seems to have deliberately cultivated the role of F1's most conspicuous dissident, a blond-tinted, high-grunge *enfant terrible* who marches to his own beat, no matter whether it makes his team uneasy or leaves him vulnerable to sanctions from officialdom.

Villeneuve kicked off the season as strong favourite for the World Championship. Eddie Irvine's cack-handed performance in Melbourne may have torpedoed Jacques's chances in the first race of the year, but he soon took command at the head of the championship points table with superb victories at Interlagos and Buenos Aires. Retirement at Imola was followed by a passive role in Williams's Monaco débâcle, but he bounced back to score possibly his best win of the year at Barcelona – where he was among only a handful of drivers who'd worked out how to conserve their tyres – before leaving his fans goggle-eyed with disbelief when he spun into the wall at Montreal.

This set the tone for a difficult few months which yielded good wins at Silverstone, the A1-Ring and the Nürburgring – plus a lucky first at Budapest – punctuated by lacklustre showings at Hockenheim, Spa and Monza.

Away from the cockpit he has not always been prudent in terms of his own self-interest. Describing the proposed 1998 F1 regulations as 'shit' caused him to be summoned to Paris to explain himself in front of the FIA during the run-up to the Canadian Grand Prix.

Moreover, the activation of a one-race ban which so scrambled his Japanese Grand Prix prospects was, at the end of the day, Villeneuve's cumulative reward for passing waved yellow flags on four occasions during the course of the season. In that respect, Jacques should have been a little more worldly wise.

Yet there is an appealing side to Jacques Villeneuve. Resolutely his own man, he displays a consistent determination to confront life exclusively on his own terms. This is admirable, as far as it goes. Yet even for one of the best drivers in the world, in the F1 pit lane it is a strategy strewn with potential pitfalls. As Jacques may now reflect, albeit with quiet satisfaction from his position

M **...Schumacher was on course for the undisputed number one slot in this list until** midway round lap 48 of the European Grand Prix. What followed next not only reminded us of Ayrton Senna's treatment of Alain Prost at Suzuka seven years ago, but also put an unfortunate retrospective gloss on Michael's own tangle with Damon Hill at Adelaide in 1994.

We subscribe to Jackie Stewart's view that there is a place for ethics in Grand Prix racing. Schumacher tarnished his image with this incident, and could count himself fortunate to get away with only the loss of his second place in this year's drivers' championship when he appeared in front of the FIA World Council.

Yet, technically, Michael remains the most complete driver in F1 today. The dazzling car control which earned him superb wet-weather victories in the Monaco and Belgian Grands Prix was only part of the equation. Apart from his talent behind the wheel, Michael ruled the Italian team with a psychological rod of iron, taking as much responsibility for technical and strategic decisions connected with car set-up and tyre choice before the start as he did for capitalising on those decisions once the race got under way.

Michael opened the season with a distant second place in the Australian Grand Prix where the Ferrari F310B's performance limitations seemed initially rather worrying. Fifth place at Interlagos was little more than a damage-limitation exercise and a rare driving error on the first corner at Buenos Aires, which saw him eliminated from the race in a tangle with Rubens Barrichello's Stewart, represented another setback. Then came the fight-back. A close second to Frentzen at Imola was followed by a brilliant wet-weather win at Monaco where Michael's ability to take the strategic initiative was demonstrated to brilliant effect.

Instead of just sitting on the starting grid in a state of suspended animation, Schumacher made sure he left his final acclimatisation lap to the very last moment in order to assess the track conditions. Armed with that knowledge, he selected the best available set-up option for the circumstances and won commandingly. That astute capacity to think on his feet was deployed again to great effect at Spa, where he was admittedly fortunate that the first few laps of the race were run behind the safety car, partly drying the track to the point where his choice of intermediate rubber proved perfectly suited to the conditions.

Michael Schumacher also has the intellectual capacity to sustain his edge when he is out of the cockpit. Jackie Stewart believes that the man who eventually eclipses him is perhaps not yet even in F1. He could be right.

Date of birth: 3 January 1969

Team: Scuderia Ferrari Marlboro

Grand Prix starts in 1997: 17

World Championship placing: Annulled

Wins: 5; Poles: 3; Points: 78

2

michael schumacher

mika
häkkinen

3

Date of birth: 28 September 1968

Team: West McLaren Mercedes

Grand Prix starts in 1997: 17

World Championship placing: 5th=

Wins: 1; Poles: 1; Points: 27

MIKA Häkkinen should have won at least four Grands Prix in 1997, possibly even more. Yet in his seventh year of F1, the likeable Finn looked as though he would finish the season unable to string together a winning performance. In the end, he scored his first victory in the final race of the season at Jerez, although inheriting it from the Williams team in acknowledgement of tacit assistance rendered earlier in the race was not the ideal way for him to break his duck. He deserved, and was capable of, something much better.

Häkkinen again consolidated his position as one of the McLaren team's all-time favourites, even though his luck, for the most part, remained as dismal as ever despite incontrovertible evidence that he had all the right credentials to get the job done.

It must have been very difficult for him to open the year watching from third place on the rostrum as team-mate David Coulthard celebrated the first win for the McLaren-Mercedes partnership.

Yet if Häkkinen ever felt dispirited or downhearted, he never let it show to the outside world. For public consumption he wore a mask of relaxed geniality for most of the time and, in the cockpit, always gave his best. Even so, despite all that accumulated experience, there were still moments when Häkkinen could display a raw heavy-handedness which was at variance with his natural skill. Charging out of the tunnel at Monaco straight into a second-lap accident at the chicane, which had originally been triggered by his team-mate, ranked as probably his most spectacular lapse of the season.

For Mika, Silverstone proved the turning point. Six laps from the end of the race, with Villeneuve's second-place Williams nailed to the tail of his silver McLaren-Merc, pundits were predicting that Jean Alesi in third place looked most likely to pick up this particular race win.

The implication was obvious: Villeneuve was on course to attempt an over-zealous passing manoeuvre and Häkkinen would implacably resist such advances. In the event, engine failure cost Mika his chance and deprived the fans of a grandstand finish. Yet the exuberant manner in which the Finn erupted from the cockpit, graciously to accept the plaudits of the crowd, signalled that here was a man who knew his Time had Come.

THERE were some less-than-obvious subtleties to David Coulthard's year which made it an extremely close call when it came to judging the affable Scot against his McLaren-Mercedes team-mate. Yet after three years of full-time F1, Coulthard certainly deserves his best-ever AUTOCOURSE Top Ten rating, even though I suspect he believes he had done enough to earn third place ahead of Häkkinen.

You can see his point of view. He triumphed in two races for the McLaren-Mercedes squad and was on course to win a third at Jerez until he bowed graciously to the requirements of team orders and dropped back behind Häkkinen. Yet the other side of the coin is that Coulthard's performance has been prone to more obvious peaks and troughs when assessed across the wider canvas of a 17-race season.

Coulthard took over the mantle of Britain's top F1 driver in 1997 from outgoing World Champion Damon Hill and was well qualified to do so. Blessed with a well-controlled temperament, David's range of outward emotions is always kept discreetly in check. When he wins, he never quite seems effusive, but that same Scottish reserve enables him to put a philosophical face on disappointment. Rather than shoot from the hip, he tends to count up to five before opening his mouth. Although his critics say this makes him appear rather bland, these qualities have generally proved to be assets rather than handicaps.

Coulthard finished fourth in the drivers' championship table (prior to Michael Schumacher's exclusion) only six points behind Williams number two Heinz-Harald Frentzen. Yet it was only in the last five races of the year that he really got into his stride, with a well-judged Monza win plus second places at the A1-Ring and Jerez really boosting his score. Yet had not victory in the Canadian GP slipped through his fingers due to technical problems at the last moment, he would easily have taken third place in the title battle behind Villeneuve and Schumacher, an achievement which would have dramatically boosted his perception from the touchlines.

Yet, by the same token, there were days when Coulthard could look quite average. He couldn't match Häkkinen's raw pace at Interlagos and his second-lap spin at Monaco was not the sort of mistake one would have expected from a driver of his innate skill. He had a handful of silly driving errors – and technical problems, to be fair – which lost him crucial time in free practice sessions, as well as seeming just a touch finicky when it came to getting the car balanced out to his taste in medium-speed corners.

When Coulthard drove well, he was outstanding. If he can string together rather more consistency in 1998, the battle for the World Championship could yet be fought out between the two McLaren-Mercedes team-mates.

Date of birth: 27 March 1971

Team: West McLaren Mercedes

Grand Prix starts in 1997: 17

World Championship placing: 3rd=

Wins: 2; Poles: 0; Points: 36

4

david
coulthard

jean
alesi

5

Date of birth: 11 June 1964

Team: Mild Seven Benetton Renault

Grand Prix starts in 1997: 17

World Championship placing: 3rd=

Wins: 0; Poles: 1; Points: 36

YET again, Jean Alesi had a roller-coaster season at the wheel of his Benetton-Renault. After he had run his car's tanks dry in the opening race of the year, simply through forgetting to come in for his scheduled refuelling stop despite near-hysterical warnings from his pit, one would not have been totally surprised if Flavio Briatore had sacked him on the spot. Yet this lapse represented the most negative end of the Alesi performance spectrum; in many other races, he was a convincing and highly competitive performer, even though that assured touch failed to yield him his second Grand Prix win.

Alesi still represents an emotional rag-bag of contradictions. Some days he can be sunny, relaxed, supremely confident. On others, he appears over-wound and nervous, like the proverbial cat on hot bricks. Under the circumstances, it seems amazing that he tied with David Coulthard to take fourth place (later to become third) in the drivers' championship, an achievement which genuinely reflected some very good races indeed.

After that initial disappointment, Jean took three or four races before getting into his stride. Sixth in Brazil and fifth at Imola kept him in play, but third in Spain – the second Goodyear runner home after winner Villeneuve and second-place man Panis's Bridgestone-shod Prost – was a just reward for a sensitive touch in terms of tyre utilisation on a day when many of his colleagues were blistering rubber left, right and centre.

Then came a strong second place in Canada, a hard-won fifth in France, where he helped Coulthard into a gravel trap on the final lap, and then a sure run to another slightly fortuitous second at Silverstone, temporary team-mate Alexander Wurz following in his wheel tracks to the chequered flag.

Alesi bagged the second pole position of his F1 career at Monza, where he led commandingly during the opening stages of the race, only to be leapfrogged by Coulthard's McLaren at his sole refuelling stop. After that, there was little he could do but settle for second place. He also drove well at the Nürburgring to extract six points from the Luxembourg GP, fending off a hard charge from Frentzen's Williams in the closing stages.

Alesi had a feisty personal relationship with team boss Briatore which seemed to deteriorate

EVEN Heinz-Harald must reflect on his first season in the cockpit of a Williams-Renault as something of a major disappointment. After the controversy surrounding the manner in which the team dispensed with Damon Hill's services, the mild-mannered German driver certainly delivered very much less than one might reasonably have expected had the reigning World Champion been kept on the payroll.

In fact, there were moments during the season when one could sense certain members of the Williams management were only stopping one syllable short of admitting that the whole thing had been a dreadful error of judgement. Yet by the end of the year Frentzen's initially faltering start had given way to a composure of sorts and the team finished the season guardedly confident that Heinz-Harald would be in a position to build on his shaky first campaign in 1998.

That said, the season started on a high note with the German newcomer leading for much of the Australian GP after team-mate Villeneuve was bundled off the road at the first corner thanks to the unexpected intervention of Eddie Irvine. Only a shattered brake disc in the closing moments of the race prevented his posting second place behind Coulthard and ahead of Michael Schumacher.

Frentzen's disappointment at finishing out of the points at Interlagos and an early technical retirement at Buenos Aires was accentuated by the fact that Villeneuve won both these races. Yet Heinz-Harald turned things round by scoring his first win in the San Marino GP, expertly fending off a late-race surge by the Ferraris of Schumacher and Irvine. He followed this up with an excellent pole position at Monaco, only for Williams to scramble its race strategy with an unaccountable decision to run slicks in the pouring rain.

After an excellent fourth in Canada and a heartening second at Magny-Cours, Frentzen then got bogged down in a mid-season slump. He messed up both the British and German Grands Prix with silly mistakes and had a possible victory in Hungary snatched from his grasp due to a failure of his on-car refuelling valve. Thereafter, things began to improve with a string of four successive third places from Spa onwards, topped off with a run to second place at Suzuka which clinched Williams's ninth constructors' championship.

Finally, at Jerez, Frentzen did his best to help Villeneuve in the opening phase of the race. Williams insiders say that Heinz-Harald is developing into a good team player. Next year, of course, could be his last chance.

Date of birth: 18 May 1967

Team: Rothmans Williams Renault

Grand Prix starts in 1997: 17

World Championship placing: 2nd

Wins: 1; Poles: 1; Points: 42

6

heinz-harald
frentzen

giancarlo
fisichella

7

Date of birth: 14 January 1973

Team: B&H Total Jordan Peugeot

Grand Prix starts in 1997: 17

World Championship placing: 8th

Wins: 0; Poles: 0; Points: 20

HAD this Top Ten been finalised after the Italian Grand Prix, it is likely that Fisichella would have been further up the order. Some say he should have been anyway, but the popular Italian's form slumped dramatically in the closing races of the season, perhaps due to a drop-off in the Jordan 197's performance, perhaps down to the driver. It is not clear.

What remains obvious is that Fisichella fully deserves a place in any Top Ten driver rating this season. Earlier in the year he demonstrated a style and consistency which quickly eclipsed team-mate Ralf Schumacher's unbridled speed. Giancarlo proved that there is more to F1 success than simply going quickly and, when the Jordan was fully dialled in, he certainly used it to great effect.

Understandably, Fisichella reacted badly when Ralf took him out of the Argentine Grand Prix in a thoughtlessly reckless overtaking manoeuvre. Yet it was Giancarlo who had the last laugh. Fourth at Imola was followed by a slightly frustrating, yet extremely mature, run to sixth in the rain at Monaco, then a storming third place at Montreal to score his first podium finish.

Fisichella showed a sure touch on high-speed circuits, always a good sign in a rising star. His pace at Hockenheim and Spa marked him out as a potential winner and his fourth place at Monza was equally impressive, with only Coulthard, Alesi and Frentzen ahead of him at the finish. Despite this, he admitted that he was rather disappointed and reckoned he could have got a place on the podium.

We will probably never know the convoluted detail of Eddie Jordan's contract to run Fisichella for 1997, an arrangement which ended up in the London High Court in a legal action with Benetton designed to clarify the situation. Jordan lost, as it subsequently transpired he expected to, with the result that Fisichella will drive a Benetton-Mecachrome next season alongside Alexander Wurz.

Fisichella has now served his F1 apprenticeship in some style and has proved he has the personal charisma to support his role as one of Grand Prix racing's most promising newcomers. One just hopes that David Richards's sure management hand will mitigate the inevitable stresses Fisichella will be subjected to driving as an Italian in an Italian team.

Four years at Jordan had left Rubens Barrichello just a touch stale, all agreed. Initial reaction to his recruitment by the Stewart-Ford team was a degree of surprise. On the face of it, the young Brazilian perhaps did not seem the obvious choice for this fledgling F1 operation.

However, Jackie and Paul Stewart were making their judgements from a different standpoint. They had seen Barrichello at first hand during his F3 and F3000 years when Paul Stewart Racing's entries were pitched against him. As a result, they reckoned he had just the right blend of youthful competitiveness balanced with sufficient experience. In fact, they probably struck just the right note.

Jordan insiders bade him farewell with mixed feelings. 'He's got what it takes inside of him, but we just can't quite figure how to extract it,' said one of their number thoughtfully. It was a perceptive observation. In the Stewart-Ford squad, Barrichello had sufficient accumulated experience to make a worthwhile contribution to the package. He scored points on only a single occasion, but when he did it was quite a performance.

Bridgestone's rain tyres might have been just the job for that Monaco Grand Prix monsoon, but Barrichello rose to the occasion in brilliant style to capitalise on his advantage and finish a magnificent second. This result really put the Stewart *équipe* on the map, here in Monaco where Jackie had won three times between 1966 and '73. When the team reflects on that historic moment, Barrichello will always be the man who deserves the credit.

There were other promising moments too. Third on the grid at Montreal was, in its own way, perhaps even more remarkable. There were also confident and competent runs in the Austrian and Luxembourg GPs, although the chance of a sixth place in the former event evaporated when Rubens slid off the road after being hounded into a mistake by a relentless Michael Schumacher's Ferrari.

Taken as a whole, Barrichello had a better year than his results indicated. But for technical failures, he could have easily doubled his points tally of six. Next season, he will be aiming to do that and more.

Date of birth: 23 May 1972

Team: Stewart Ford

Grand Prix starts in 1997: 17

World Championship placing: 13th

Wins: 0; Poles: 0; Points: 6

8

rubens
barrichello

eddie
irvine

9

Date of birth: 10 November 1965

Team: Scuderia Ferrari Marlboro

Grand Prix starts in 1997: 17

World Championship placing: 7th

Wins: 0; Poles: 0; Points: 24

EDDIE Irvine is close to making his own personal, albeit slightly eccentric mark in the F1 history books. He is embarking on his third year as a Ferrari number two paired alongside a dynamically talented team leader. He has held on to his drive despite an argument with Maranello over the size of his retainer, one race when he complained that his car was useless and firmly sticking to his practised mantra that the press corps are by and large a waste of space and know nothing about motor racing.

For many drivers in Ferrari history, such a strategy would have made about as much sense as tying the Hoover flex round your neck and kicking away the chair. Yet Irvine leads a charmed life, probably because his devil-may-care insolence has something of a following in F1 circles, together with the fact that he can drive well and – most crucially – benefits from the Michael Schumacher Good Housekeeping Seal of Approval.

Thankfully for him, the press know enough about F1 to have offered due acknowledgement for his splendid runs to third place at Imola and Monaco, and the common sense he showed in not risking his career with a *banzai* do-or-die effort to pass Jacques Villeneuve's Williams at Buenos Aires. Second place in Argentina, he rightly judged, was far more desirable than a trip to the employment exchange.

By the same token, Irvine clearly lives on a planet populated by one if he feels his first-corner antics at Melbourne were anything else but an own goal. But he more than atoned for that stupid lapse with his shrewd and disciplined support of Schumacher's World Championship bid at Suzuka where he relinquished his own chances of success to help the German ace take ten points from the penultimate round of the title chase.

Off-track, Irvine remains chirpy, chatty and unflustered by all the fuss. He is the quintessential F1 bachelor, as he admitted when he featured in a full-page interview in *Country Life*, on the face of it the most unlikely publication imaginable in which to read the thoughts of Grand Prix racing's self-styled Wild Child.

'Racing is just a small segment of what I want to achieve,' he told this bastion of English conservatism. 'I'll do three or four more years of F1, and then I'll just walk away, and go and see the world. I want to die saying, "I did it all." '

So now you know.

Date of birth: 25 June 1964

Team: Red Bull Sauber Petronas

Grand Prix starts in 1997: 17

World Championship placing: 10th

Wins: 0; Poles: 0; Points: 15

JOHNNY Herbert didn't really have the equipment to showcase his true talent in 1997, but when things went well he could be relied upon to be up there challenging for championship points, if not outright victory. He scored on six occasions, but probably did not manage enough to guarantee his front-line presence in F1 beyond the end of next season.

In many ways, it is a shame that one of the established top-line teams did not snap up Herbert's services after his 1995 season playing second fiddle to Michael Schumacher at Benetton. Many people regard him as more naturally talented than several names that appear ahead of him in this list, but his career path has never really recovered from that F3000 accident at Brands Hatch back in 1988.

That said, once Heinz-Harald Frentzen left the Sauber ranks at the end of 1996, Herbert was able to integrate himself much more effectively into the Swiss team. Peter Sauber may be one of the more formal and conservative members of the F1 community, but even he seems to have been won over by Johnny's effervescent personality. Shame is that this relationship has not been underpinned by more in the way of hard results.

Herbert believes he could have finished on the podium in Melbourne had he not been bundled off the road at the first corner as a result of Irvine's inside dive which pushed Villeneuve's Williams into his Sauber. But he made up for that disappointment with a good run to fourth place in Buenos Aires and was on course for another helping of points at Imola and Monaco until, respectively, electrical problems and a huge accident wrote him out of the equation.

Fifth places in Spain and Canada kept his motivation high and his sole podium finish came in Hungary with third place behind Villeneuve and Hill. But he also ran extremely well at Spa where he looked to have the measure of Frentzen's Williams for much of the distance and wound up finishing fifth on the road.

In many ways, Herbert's most impressive performance came at Monza after he was bundled off the track by the unthinking Ralf Schumacher's Jordan. Instead of hysterically running in five directions at once, Johnny simply delivered a mature and reasoned rebuke to his inexperienced colleague. He might have inwardly felt like punching the German driver, but his way certainly had more effect.

10

johnny
herbert

gerhard
berger

THE reader might conclude that there are some obvious names missing from this year's AUTOCOURSE Top Ten, Gerhard Berger and Damon Hill included. Berger scored one of the most impressive dry-weather victories of the season at Hockenheim and Hill's second place at the Hungaroring, after dominating much of the race in his Arrows-Yamaha, certainly reflected a great deal of credit on the 1996 World Champion.

Yet objectively, taken over a season, neither driver seemed to get the best from his machinery on a sufficiently consistent basis. Berger admittedly spent much time wrestling with recurrent sinus problems, missing three races as a result, but although he drove very well to finish second at Interlagos also peppered his year with a series of very average performances.

Hill also performed well on occasion, but the spat with Tom Walkinshaw at Silverstone reflected the fact that his motivation had been flagging in some early-season races. He also made a fist of overtaking Shinji Nakano's Prost at Imola, drove off the road on the first corner at Magny-Cours and was then outgunned by pay-driving teammate Pedro Diniz at Spa-Francorchamps. Spa, remember, not somewhere like the Hungaroring or Buenos Aires.

Olivier Panis was another who

damon

only just missed the Top Ten cut. He drove some storming races early in the season, carrying the Bridgestone flag to within shouting distance of victory in several races. Then came his terrible Montreal shunt, followed by a remarkable recovery which saw him back in the Prost cockpit before the end of the season. Like Hill, next year I would expect him to return to the Top Ten.

Ralf Schumacher was a disappointment. The more experience he gained, the more he over-drove and the less effective he became. By the end of the season his driving style seemed to verge on panic-stricken. Alexander Wurz subbed for Berger in three races, taking third at Silverstone behind Villeneuve and Alesi. He is a man worth watching, as indeed is Jarno Trulli, who cut his teeth with Minardi and then went on to lead the Austrian GP commandingly in a Prost-Mugen Honda.

Another worth a mention was Mika Salo, who ran non-stop at Monaco to gain Tyrrell's only points of the season, and may well blossom at Arrows next year alongside the increasingly accomplished Diniz. Jos Verstappen was unlucky at Tyrrell and Nakano less out of his depth than one might reasonably have expected, while Sauber number twos Nicola Larini, Gianni Morbidelli and Norberto Fontana were mere footnotes to the main proceedings.

celebrating the M-FACTOR

During its first quarter-century, BMW Motorsport GmbH has powered winners from Grands Prix to touring cars, via Le Mans. *Jeremy Walton* highlights an innovative BMW enterprise which returns to Grands Prix as the power behind Williams Grand Prix Engineering in the millennium.

REWIND 25 years back to 1972, and discover a 25-year-old Emerson Fittipaldi winning his first World Championship for Lotus. Then, as now, Britain exported its music to the world, but back then the headline act was the Rolling Stones rather than Oasis.

As spring 1972 slipped into summer, German motorsport was rocked by the news that the architects of Ford Cologne's competition success – Herren Jochen Neerpasch and Martin Braungart – were to migrate south to Bavaria.

The Munich-based management of BMW AG – energised by former fighter pilot Bob Lutz – decided to formalise their extended support of motorsport, forming a new 'company-within-a-company'. Not for BMW the usual big banker's draft for an outside specialist. BMW Motorsport continued to rely on in-house talent, particularly in engine design, to reap results.

There was also a BMW pedigree dating back 44 years for utilising production components wherever possible. This philosophy took BMW into Grands Prix, where in 1983 their Motorsport division took the first World Championship for the driver of a turbocharged car, utilising an iron production cylinder block.

From May 1972 BMW Motorsport GmbH was charged with the job of bringing honour to the whirling white and blue roundel badge. The infant company responded by hauling in two European Championships in its first season of racing, in 1973.

A European Formula 2 title came courtesy of Jean-Pierre Jarier, along with the first of many BMW Motorsport seasons wedded to March at Bicester. During the years 1973-84 the company erased previous painful memories of Formula 2, dominating the 2-litre category between 1973 and 1982.

BMW M12/7 Motorsport-engineered units generated an astounding 70 victories. As with all official BMW Motorsport entries, including the forthcoming Grand Prix unit, those 10,000 rpm fours were developed by a team under the leadership of born and bred Munich resident, Paul Rosche.

These were not easy F2 wins, for both Renault and Honda fielded effective pedigree racing V6s against the BMW four-cylinder. Yet the BMW motor's low weight and wide torque curve saw it win five Formula 2 Championships and inspire a sixth title. BMW cylinder blocks actually won 76 races, because a Schnitzer unit behind Jacques Laffite additionally won six races and the 1975 title.

Apart from Laffite and his agile Martini, those BMW M-Power Champions were all March-mounted. They were: Frenchmen Jean-Pierre Jarier (1973) and Patrick Depailler (1974), followed by Italy's Bruno Giacomelli in 1978. Switzerland's Marc Surer secured the title in 1979 and Corrado Fabi took the final honours, in 1982.

The Good News was that 1973's European Championship success could be translated into orders for racing hardware, establishing the 2-litre Formula 2 engine as the one to buy. Production of these hand-built Munich masterpieces finally exceeded 500, most producing over 300 bhp apiece.

Jean-Pierre Jarier *(below)* took the BMW-powered March to the 1973 European Formula 2 Championship. It was to be just the start of a long run of successes in this category, and paved the way for M-GmbH ultimately to take the step into Grand Prix racing.

Top: Classic car. Classic pose. Classic circuit. The Hans Stuck/Jacky Ickx BMW CSL in flight at the 1974 Nürburgring 1000 Km.

Above: CSL turbo, Seventies style. This car was dubbed the world's fastest painting, courtesy of artist Frank Stella's eye-catching livery.

Above right: The 1973 European Touring Car Champion Toine Hezemans in the CSL at the TT race at Silverstone.

Right: The shape of things to come. A flame-snorting BMW 320 at Brands Hatch in 1978. This shape and its successors were to become a mainstay of touring car racing for the next two decades.

Left: Nelson Piquet in the M1 ProCar. These exotic machines, driven by the stars of the day, proved an entertaining support to many Grands Prix during 1979 and 1980.

Motorsport at Munich took its second 1973 debut season European Championship with the magnificent CSL coupé. This former paragon of understated elegance was developed to sprout Braungart's rapidly developed wings, splitters and hoops. Rosche and company dialled in 375 M-power horses and an extra half-litre from the classic straight six. The boldly striped ensemble equally rapidly earned both the European title (the first of six) and the affectionate sobriquet 'Batmobile'.

Drivers of Niki Lauda's calibre drove CSLs for the factory-favoured Alpina team. Factory aces Hans Stuck, Chris Amon, champion Toine Hezemans and the inevitable Dieter Quester did most of the winning, once the factory got into its crushing stride.

Soon nicknamed M-GmbH , the main company offshoot expanded commercially at virtually competition speed: in the beginning there were eight employees and earnings equated to $130,000 a year. In 1991 employees were counted by the hundred at two Munich sites trading on a turnover of $445 million! Today some 450 employees yield a turnover of $528 million, so M-business is big business in a niche market that is unique to BMW.

There was sustained BMW AG investment in the M-badge as a commercial proposition: during the 1978/79 winter the parent company injected £1.3 million in the original Preussenstrasse site to allow separate production facilities for M-Power and M cars. By 1986 business justified a second site, Garching, on a suburban trading estate in north-western Munich.

Initially the M5 was a hand-built Motorsport machine, along with the M3 convertible, but demand in the 1990s has required that the new M5 be a production item for the main company, just as the M3 saloon has always been in all but its early convertible guise.

What did M-GmbH sell in the Seventies? Anything from a key fob to serious racing hardware was the short answer, but some services were supplied to outsiders...

Surviving staff smile when they recall the prototype installation of BMW diesel engines into large American Fords. Huge sedans would wobble around BMW's test track, accompanied by tell-tale clouds of smoke, as BMW employees tried to detect some signs of performance in the American knee-jerk reaction to petrol economy worries.

BMW Motorsport survived on this strange Ford contract and more obvious applications of its expertise without redundancies. The M-division also shows long-term loyalty to its driving force: recently retired Roberto Ravaglia, the world's most successful touring car driver, was with them for 14 years and BMW also retain links with their Grand Prix and ProCar title winner, Nelson Piquet. Dieter Quester has raced BMWs for more than 30 years and regularly appeared in 1997 USA M3s.

Another Seventies adjunct to the main competition programme created two separate branches to the central M-GmbH organisation, which have secured increasing prominence for the M-branding. Highest profile have been the M-prefixed cars: the original M1, two generations of M3 in five bodies, the M5 in four body shapes, two generations of M535i and the much-loved M635CSi, dubbed the M6 in the USA.

A further offshoot of pioneering Motorsport labour was BMW Individual, a phenomenally successful commercial division which tailors non-production specifications to one in twenty customer orders.

Beginning as a VIP service to contracted star drivers, BMW Motorsport constructed increasingly sophisticated road cars. They featured unobtainable combinations of the mainstream product: the 5-series was the usual victim, growing 3- to 3.3-litre versions of BMW's sibilant straight six at a time when production was restricted to the smaller 528i.

Between the drivers and motor-sport mechanics, further advances in suspension and braking specification brewed, alongside racier steering wheels and clinging front seats to remind the contractees of their day jobs. These special product developments were particularly interesting to the main BMW AG set-up for their production potential, as Motorsport employed numerous production parts on a mix-and-match basis from elsewhere in the main company range.

The first M-car was the 1978-81 M1, but a larger engined 5-series (M535i) was in serial production by April 1980 and would found a line of ever-faster M5s. The latter peaked with the Frankfurt announcement in 1997 of a 400 bhp V8 version to replace ever-larger (3.8-litre) descendants of the 3.5-litre BMW racing six cylinders.

The marvellous M1, literally a Supercar, made the best of a bad job. A BMW contract had been assigned to Lamborghini and Italian subcontractors, with the idea of competing against Porsche in the ill-fated FIA Group 5 'Silhouette' Championship. Delays scotched that Group 5 race plan.

Thus the mid-engined M1 needed an exotic one-make race series to demonstrate its competition merits. ProCar was conceived by Neerpasch, in association with Bernie Ecclestone and Max Mosley, to support most major 1979-80 European Grands Prix.

Instead of the M1 attributes of 277 bhp and 162 street mph, ProCars proffered 470 bhp and 192 mph – and they made champions of then Brabham team-mates, Niki Lauda and Nelson Piquet.

As an individual competition car, the M1 came too late to offer Porsche consistent opposition. However, in the USA the charismatic Red Lobster team, with drivers Kenper Miller/David Cowart, demolished all their IMSA GTO class opposition for 1981. They also set new records for the number of category wins recorded in a season.

BMW also resorted to even wilder versions of the CSL: as the old warrior went out of production in 1975, it was fielded as the official factory car in America. Hans Stuck proved it could win at IMSA level and BMW netted the 1976 Daytona 24 Hours (a shortened race that foggy year) with ex-pat Briton Brian Redman on the team.

The most powerful BMW racing saloon to date, and the ultimate car/driver alliance for spectators, was the pairing of Ronnie Peterson and a monstrous CSL, one carrying the clout of a 3.2-litre twin-turbo six. The result was enough power – boost was *lowered* for 'only' 750 bhp! – to challenge even 'SuperSwede's' fabled reflexes, munching Silverstone's main straight at 178 mph in 1976...

At Dijon and Le Mans (it led...briefly!) the Peterson turbo CSL appeared in the graph paper design of American inventor/artist Frank Stella, part of a series of four American 'Art Cars' that BMW had backed since 1975. Contributing artists included Andy Warhol, and the sixth-placed M1 he decorated for 1979 recorded BMW's best overall result at Le Mans prior to the 1995 McLaren-BMW victory. Later, BMW extended the Art concept internationally and included road cars, as well as a 1993 M3 racing prototype.

A radically reworked 3-series was a predictable 1977-78 class (but not overall) winner in Group 5 trim, when it carried a 305 bhp Formula 2 motor. It sold strongly to privateers at £30,000 a copy. However, the 1977-79 need for 3-series speed in the domestic German Championship, and American national racing, led to a brace of very different turbocharged four-cylinders...and on to Formula 1 power.

Paul Rosche recalled, 'The M12/7 four-cylinder engine was developed in turbocharged form first for saloon car racing, and then – as the M12/13 series – for Grands Prix. So our Formula 2 experience in the single-seaters was important to us, as were the developments we made with McLaren (North America) and Schnitzer in saloon car racing.'

Left: The dart-shaped Brabham BT52-BMW which propelled Nelson Piquet to the 1983 World Championship.

Below: The four-cylinder turbocharged Formula 1 engine.

Centre: Rosche in conference with Piquet.

Below far left: Piquet was still competitive in 1984, taking two Grand Prix wins.

Bottom left: The BMW powerplant in situ.

Bottom right: Gerhard Berger scored BMW's last Grand Prix win in the turbo era with his Benetton in 1986.

The rock on which so much power would be built was the production iron block four, carefully aged to simulate 100,000 km (62,000 miles) and externally lightened. Schnitzer and other German specialists used 1.4 turbocharged litres to achieve German class success – former German journalist Harald Ertl won the 1978 title in a 410 bhp Schnitzer 3-series – while the American programme used 2-litre turbos that achieved over 600 bhp.

The German 1.4-litre programme and its short-stroke motors had most relevance to BMW's increasing Formula 1 aspirations, for Grand Prix operated a 1.5-litre turbo equivalency formula. Rosche remembered, 'The Schnitzer car of 1978 was interesting for us, so we got behind the 1979 GS Tuning 320 for Markus Hottinger.' This Jagermeister orange fireball won on its sixth outing and deployed a massive 610 bhp from its BMW Motorsport-supplied 1.4 turbo four.

Technically, it looked as though BMW had cracked open a path to Grand Prix success at low cost, for the motors used a tremendous amount of the uprated hardware found in their proven Formula 2 design.

Grand Prix life could never be that simple, though. A rugged course in character-building politics awaited Rosche and new BMW Motorsport manager Dieter Stappert for, in March 1980, Munich had signed to supply Brabham with the F1 power units.

By October 1980 Brabham-BMW had completed the first test runs at Silverstone with a unit rated at 557 bhp at 9500 rpm in the back of a converted BT49. The same British venue saw Nelson Piquet officially record the fourth-fastest time and more than 190 mph at the Grand Prix in July 1981.

As on so many subsequent occasions the engine was not raced, which tested the durability of the Paul Rosche-Gordon Murray working relationship immediately. It took some world class diplomacy from Dieter Stappert, public pressure from BMW management and a winter full of

often explosive testing before the M12/13 unit was deemed ready for trial by Grand Prix.

That was at the January 1982 South African GP. Piquet's second-fastest practice time was encouraging, but not a reliable guide to race form. Piquet slid off after four laps and Brabham number 2, Riccardo Patrese, also retired. Not an auspicious start, but better than the three races which intervened before its next event!

Prevailing Grand Prix politics had played a part and the BMW unit was not raced again until the Belgian GP of May 1982. Belgium's bumpy Zolder circuit gave Brabham-BMW its first World Championship point for Piquet's sixth, but it was obvious that the motor's peaky power required soothing if it was to succeed on North America's tight street circuits.

America strained the BMW-Brabham alliance as Piquet failed to qualify on the Detroit doorstep of Motown. 'No Pain, No Gain' – but this was more like a prolonged torture session. There were enormous risks for BMW in the prestige market should the motor continue to misbehave.

BMW's board kept their nerve and, just a week later, were rewarded with their first victory! Deploying leading edge Bosch technology to monitor and manage their motor, BMW went into the record books with a win in the restarted Canadian GP of June 1982.

There were no more GP wins that season for BMW, but some compensation in the achievement of three pole positions and a brand new Gordon Murray design for 1983: the bold and beautiful Brabham BT52.

Bold because it was born with a pioneering pit-stop role, and because the crash-tested Brabham-BMW (another first) compensated for the loss of ground effect with almost 60 per cent of the weight shifted aft. It was beautiful in its arrow-inspired clean lines and looked a winner from the Brazilian opening round to the close of play in Murray's native South Africa.

Looking back in the summer of 1997 Gordon Murray commented, 'That was a very special moment...winning the championship with one driver and the race with the other. And that BMW beat Renault to the title, the first for a turbo car, for just a fraction of what the French were spending. That just made our Kyalami satisfaction complete, especially as I was on home turf.'

There should have been a lot more winning in 1984, and another world title. Brabham-BMW's undoubted pace saw Piquet pick up eight pole positions, but he only took two victories, in Canada and Detroit.

The root cause of BMW's previously unpublicised problems lay with a German supplier, but the consequent component change came too late to add another title. Subsequent seasons of ever-tightening legislation to lower turbo boost ensured that the four-cylinder would be uncompetitive against its V6 opposition, though it was still a quick proposition.

In 1987 a Benetton B186 rated at 900 race bhp and driven by Teo Fabi recorded 0-100 mph in 4.8 seconds in trials for *Road & Track* magazine. However, the figures enthusiasts remember for the BMW Motorsport 1.5-litre turbo are those for qualifying specials.

Paul Rosche recalled, 'The truth was that we were only brave enough to see the maximum of 1200 horsepower on our test bed at Preussenstrasse...' A pause for a quiet chuckle before Rosche grinned: 'As 1200 was the maximum on the scale, there was no point in going on. Besides, we were all scared what would happen if it exploded!'

From 1983 onwards BMW supplied Grand Prix engines for cars apart from Brabham, including Arrows (1984-86, then as Megatron BMW for 1987/88); ATS (1983-84) and Ligier (1987). Benetton's single 1986 season deploying Munich works motors was most significant: they scored the only GP win outside Brabham, but also the last M-Power GP victory, when Gerhard Berger won in Mexico.

Overall the BMW M12/13 Formula 1 motor took nine Grand Prix wins, all but two recorded by Nelson Piquet. An excellent 14 pole positions were seized, with 11 coming from the Brazilian.

The faithful BMW CSL went on winning long after its production death. The Batmobile dropped only one European Touring Car title between 1973 and 1979. The CSL and Alpina/BMW were responsible both for Jaguar's non-winning run in its first assault on the European series (1976-77), and for sustaining the driving and business career ambitions of one Tom Walkinshaw. 'Mr TWR' returned to make sure Jaguar did become winners in the Eighties. You can take sportsmanship too far...!

BMW were so successful in the 1980s European Touring Car Championship that almost any of their cars – with varying support from Motorsport – appeared capable of netting the title for a variety of drivers, whatever the prevalent formula.

In 1980 the Group 2 smallest BMW, a 320, did the job to record the first of three successive Drivers' titles for Helmut Kelleners. Subsequent Euro Championships were racked up in the Group 2 BMW 635 coupé (1981), while the change to Group A in 1982 failed to stop either BMW or Kelleners winning, this time in an Eggenberger 528i four-door.

The Group A era saw the stiffest opposition to BMW in the European Championship. TWR fielded Mazda rotaries, Rover V8s and Jaguar V12s during the Eighties, with the two British marques regular outright winners. Volvo developed their superquick 240 turbos, and GM-Holden allowed their mighty V8s to roam beyond Australia.

BMW Motorsport did not have the best products in the BMW showroom armoury to face this onslaught of touring car power, for their national sporting organisation, ADAC, would permit no rule-bending on homologation numbers. That meant the 635 coupé relied on its 12-valve engine at 285 reliable race horsepower, rather than redeveloping the 24-valve M635i, which gave 286 bhp on the street...and could yield 400 bhp in competition trim.

Nevertheless, BMW acquired the 1983 title with a Schnitzer-run BMW Motorsport 635CSi and – after an FIA recount – the same combination also conquered in 1986. For 1987 Ford became the threat, via turbocharged Cosworth power for the Sierra.

BMW Motorsport retaliated, designing both road and racing versions of the M3, a 3-series with production-based modifications that allowed BMW to meet turbo power with a normally aspirated 2.3-litre engine. The 200 bhp road version of the M3, under a team led by Thomas Ammerschlager (now engineering future products for BMW AG), was an enormous commercial success for the M-brand. They sold over 17,100 saloons – including 600 of the final 2.5-litre Sport Evo M3 – and almost 1000 M3 convertibles, these latter hand made at Motorsport.

Although the track version of the M3 was enormously successful, it utilised a lot of production technology. It was raced to victory in the German Championship twice, in 1987 and 1989, with full catalytic converter cleansing. The M3 also built on BMW's advanced Seventies work, featuring ABS braking in Nineties competition.

The M3 captured the only World Touring Car title for Drivers, too, when Roberto Ravaglia won in 1987, as well as the two final European Championships and national titles literally all around the world. The M3 was so versatile that Prodrive even resurrected an obsolete BMW tradition and made simple rear drive into a rally winner. Prodrive M3s won a World Championship round (Corsica) in the Eighties 4x4 turbo era – and national titles in France, Spain and Belgium.

The arrival of the 2-litre Super Touring car racing formula in Britain and the rest of the world also saw BMW switching 3-series models for competition and commerce. The M-people constructed over 85 racing E36 four-door saloons between 1992 and 1996 – and a few coupés for the 1992 British season, won by Tim Harvey.

BMW Motorsport-backed 'Threes' have won 2-litre titles in most countries that cater for the category, literally from Japan (Steve Soper, 1995) to Australia, via Britain. Here Joachim Winkelhock's 1993 Autotrader title was the third successive UK Championship win for BMW Motorsport-backed hardware.

The M3 became a six-cylinder (initially a 3 litre, now 3.2), but neither its sales rate nor its appetite for motorsport success have diminished. After winning the 1993 German national ADAC Championship with Johnny Cecotto in a 325 bhp version, the M3 transferred its competition affections to its biggest sales market: the USA.

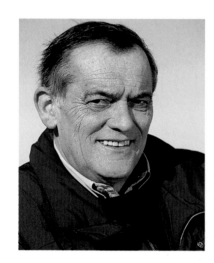

Right: Joachim Winkelhock, a hugely popular driver in the Super Touring class, won championships for BMW in both Great Britain and Germany.

Below: Two BMWs head the pack as they thunder down to Eau Rouge at the start of the 1997 Spa 24 Hours race. The winning car (front right) was handled by Marc Duez, Eric Helary and Didier de Radigues.

Veteran preparation and race management specialist Thomas H. Milner, ironically working out of the old Jaguar Group 44 premises in Virginia, took the six-cylinder M3 on as an IMSA GT class racer in 1995 for Preparation Technology Group (PTG). Strongly backed by BMW North America, Milner persisted in adversity, as had Rosche and Murray in Grand Prix racing in the Eighties.

A consistently winning race reward materialised for the 380-400 bhp PTG M3s in 1996, taking the company's first national IMSA title since the early Eighties. PTG and BMW established such a strong winning streak that they enjoyed the marketing-led luxury of constructing four-door M3 winners, as well as the original coupés.

The McLaren BMW V12 F1 supercar was drawn by Gordon Murray as the ultimate road driving machine – not a racer. The F1 three-seater re-established a Murray working relationship with Rosche and BMW Motorsport at Preussenstrasse, after Gordon had scanned the world for possible power plants. Murray set strict size, power and weight parameters that only BMW Motorsport could meet. They rapidly developed a 627 bhp V12 of 6.1 litres which exceeded Murray's requirement for 100 bhp a litre.

Some one hundred McLaren-BMW F1s were built, including the racing prototype that made history in a winning Le Mans debut in 1995. Persuasion from privateers Thomas Bscher

Top right: The classic BMW M3 road car which met the aspirations of many driving enthusiasts in the late Eighties and early Nineties.

Centre right: 'Smokin' Jo' Winkelhock, a superstar in touring cars and one of the most popular drivers in motorsport.

Above: BMWs compete successfully all over the globe. A Valvoline-backed M3 heads into the night at the 1997 Daytona 24 Hours.

Above: Over the past three seasons, the McLaren-BMW F1 GTR has been a massive success. Since its competition debut in 1995 the F1, designed initially as the ultimate road car by Gordon Murray *(above right),* has helped to breathe new life into GT racing and prompted other major manufacturers to enter this class of the sport and battle for honours.

Right: Back to the future! Nelson Piquet, his 1983 World Championship-winning Brabham-BMW, and Karl-Heinz Kalbfell at the official announcement of BMW's return to Grand Prix racing with Williams in the year 2000.

and Ray Bellm converted the McLaren into a racing winner of the BPR Global Cup in both 1995 and 1996, and it also commandeered the Japanese GT Championship of 1996.

That contract to supply the S70 M-Power 12 also led BMW to forge closer links with Britain. Rosche and Murray headed the Bracknell- and McLaren-based UK offshoot of M-GmbH: BMW Motorsport Ltd.

The British end tackled all touring car development work outside the engine bay for the 1996-97 seasons. Motorsport Ltd also further developed the 'long tail' McLaren for the 1997 FIA GT Championship, a series BMW and McLaren led for much of 1997 with a lower-weight-break (6-litre) version of the V12.

Although the GT programme has proved an unexpectedly successful triumph for the converted McLaren supercar, all attention is now centred on BMW Motorsport's new alliance with Williams. The aim is a Le Mans specification open sports car and 'other projects at the highest level of motor racing'. For this reason BMW Motorsport Ltd will move 'near the Williams facility in order to enable the two companies to work closely together', according to the September 1997 formal announcement about the BMW Williams Grand Prix engine.

Paul Rosche confirmed that the Preussenstrasse building, creative home to all these victorious engines, is already resounding to the birth cries of the first V10 BMW motors. As the best compromise between torque and power, the V10 has proven ability.

Led by Rosche, BMW Motorsport engineers will explore the V10's potential in private until late 1998, when the first BMW V10s will be installed in a Williams chassis. The 1999 season will see a full year of track and bench testing, with BMW Williams pursuing M-Power's second world title in the year 2000 season, and beyond.

It's been a rewarding first 25 years, but BMW Motorsport anticipate that the twenty-first century will hold even greater competitive and commercial prizes than did the twentieth century.

COMPOUND INTEREST

by Adam Cooper

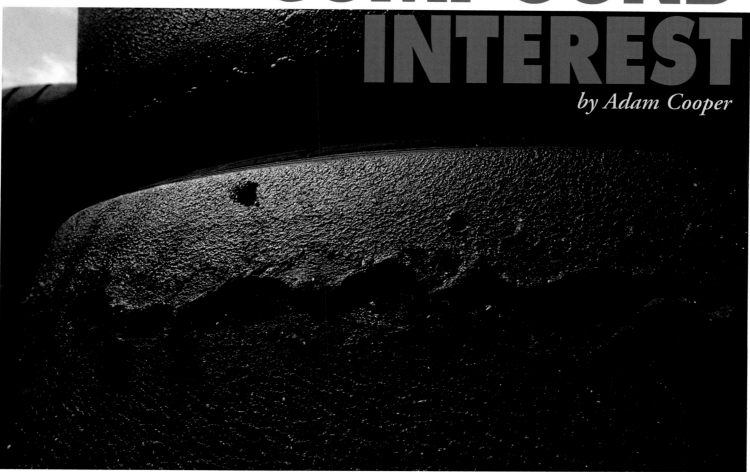

Darren Heath

Q UESTION: What connects the 1991 season-closing Australian GP in Adelaide with the 1997 opener in Melbourne? Answer: Five seasons of comfortable monopoly for the Goodyear Tire and Rubber Co.

A week can be a long time in motor racing, and the half a decade which spanned the withdrawal of Pirelli and the arrival of Bridgestone seemed like a very long time indeed. During that period of Goodyear domination tyres became an issue only when the FIA toyed with their dimensions. In 1997, tyres were among the main topics of paddock conversation, and at times the subject seemed as hard to comprehend as Bernie Ecclestone's flotation plans.

This renewed focus on tyres suited Goodyear just fine, for no company likes to invest so much and be taken for granted. Competition makes people sit up and take notice of your product. If you win, then you gain far more than if you're a sole supplier. But if you lose, then you stand to lose big time.

Goodyear did a lot of winning in 1997, and the bare statistics suggest that Bridgestone's challenge was successfully repelled. But Goodyear had all the top teams in its armoury, and anything other than a clean sweep would have given cause for concern.

'In spite of the threat of Bridgestone the history books will show that Goodyear have won every race,' says Benetton technical director Pat Symonds. 'That sounds pretty dominant, but the reality is not quite like that, because of course Bridgestone were amazingly unlucky to lose Hungary, and there have been many occasions when their tyre has looked superior to the Goodyear. But the Goodyears are on the better cars, so it hasn't been a straight fight . . .'

Damon Hill's last-lap heartache in Hungary wasn't Bridgestone's only tilt at success, for the Prost team could so easily have scored the company's first win early in the season. Olivier Panis could have won in Argentina had he not been claimed by an early hydraulic

Above: The blisters disfiguring Heinz-Harald Frentzen's tyres provide graphic confirmation that the intensity of the battle between Goodyear and Bridgestone allows little margin for error.

Bridgestone's first season in Formula 1 yielded no wins – but they came mighty close in Hungary.

Bryn Williams

leak, and Spain too might have gone the Frenchman's way had he lost less time in traffic early on.

After that race I asked Jacques Villeneuve who he considered his main opposition for the remainder of the season; 'Schumacher and Panis,' was his reply. But at the very next race in Canada Olivier was sidelined by injury. We can only guess at what a fit Panis might have achieved for Bridgestone, but rookie Jarno Trulli's magnificent performance at the head of the field in Austria gave some indication. Yet again a mechanical failure saved Goodyear's blushes.

After a brief appearance in the Japanese GPs of 1976-77, Bridgestone had been toying with an entry into F1 for years. In the early Eighties the company dominated European F2, and by the end of the decade a modest F1 testing programme was under way in Japan, latterly using ex-works Tyrrell

chassis. Drivers from the local F3000 series were engaged for the testing, including Heinz-Harald Frentzen.

F1 ambitions were put on hold after the company acquired Firestone in a massively expensive deal. When the time came to consider a high-profile racing programme, Indy cars got priority, and the rejuvenated American brand name was employed. Firestone hired a team and undertook a serious testing programme during 1994, went racing the following year, and won its first CART title in 1996. All this was done with considerable input from Japan.

Success Stateside enabled Bridgestone to nominate 1997 for its entry into F1. An exclusive deal with Arrows saw the company test with the team throughout '96, following the successful Indy practice by running at circuits shortly after races wherever possible. Results were encouraging, and the Bridgestone con-

nection was instrumental in Hill's decision to join Arrows.

Prost (then Ligier) and Minardi also signed up for the first racing season, together with new boys Stewart and Lola, although the latter would last for but one race. Everyone else agreed multi-year deals with Goodyear.

Bridgestone made its presence felt as early as the Melbourne opener, when Panis qualified ninth and finished fifth. But it was his performance in Brazil which made people sit up and take notice; by going for one stop while the Goodyear opposition made two, he scored a solid third place. A podium in its second race was a stunning result for the Japanese company.

Surprisingly it was the Stewart team which first went one better when Rubens Barrichello was a brilliant runner-up in the Monaco rain. Panis and Hill added seconds in Spain and Hungary.

Bridgestone's impact was not con-

fined to the occasional giant-killing drive by one of its customers.

The tyre war was the major factor in tumbling lap times; at Suzuka, the race's fastest lap was cut by 5.1s in 12 months! Cars were quicker under braking and acceleration, and round the corners.

The new rules gave teams the choice between the 'prime' and 'option' tyres before qualifying, at which point they'd be committed for the rest of the weekend. That created a massive headache.

'It's had a very fundamental effect on the way we've operated this year,' says Symonds, 'there's no doubt about that. Of all the various decisions you have to take over the weekend, like how do you set your car up, how you approach practice and qualifying, what strategy do you use in the race, probably the most important decision is which tyres do you run.

'A great deal of your practice session

Black magic. Providing the vital interface between car and track, tyres are a critical component of any racing package. Millions spent on hi-tech engine and chassis development will be pointless if the power cannot be transmitted to the road effectively.

Overleaf: The Bridgestone engineers have learned a lot during their first season in Formula 1 and will be hoping to build on that experience in 1998.
Photo: Diana Burnett

being better than the softer compound; it was all about how a team prepared its race tyres during the weekend, and how the driver looked after them early in the race. Villeneuve's victory in Spain was all about tyres; the team had carefully stored and cured them after Friday's practice.

'Before the race we laughed when we saw Ferrari on new tyres,' explained Jacques. 'There was just no way. With all the testing we had done at Barcelona, I knew the tyres were on an edge. It was important not to push them too hard, to not get the temperature in them too hard at the beginning. At the beginning of the race I was just staying in front of Michael, not really pushing.

After two or three laps, once I felt that I'd brought the tyres in comfortably, I pushed a bit, and got a small lead. Michael pushed a bit harder and completely destroyed his tyres. That's what I knew was going to happen . . .'

Tyres contributed to an unpredictable formbook; for example, the grid positions of Benetton's Gerhard Berger varied between pole and 18th.

'This year we've had a problem with our car on a specific type of circuit and a specific type of tyre,' says Symonds, 'that's a soft tyre, on a low-grip circuit. Our real nightmare is that we couldn't test on any circuit like that. We could only test at Magny-Cours, Silverstone, Monza, Jerez, Barcelona – all of them are hard-tyre, high-loading circuits.'

Like Benetton, Ferrari also found that its form was better on the circuits where Goodyear had brought its hardest compound.

'We had a tyre in Suzuka that we've always done well on, and you could see the difference,' says Ross Brawn. 'It's the tyre we had at Magny-Cours, and Silverstone. It's a tyre that suits our car, and gives us a much more consistent balance. The [softer] tyres we had in Austria and the Nürburgring were not what we wanted. It's always a bit of a compromise situation. Goodyear are in a difficult position, because they're having to provide a tyre that's for the general good of the teams.

'The test programmes are offered to all the top teams. It's up to them whether they've got the time and the capacity to do them. And then they try and draw a conclusion from the results. We've had to use tyres that Williams and McLaren have done some work on, they've had to use tyres that we've done some work on. That's the situation when you've got four top teams on Goodyear.'

The testing situation is extremely complicated; it's difficult enough trying to perfect a car over a season without changing tyres being a factor. However, the tyres didn't change as much as you might think.

'Goodyear have tried very hard,' says Symonds, 'and they've certainly done more development than we've seen for many years. But we went to Jerez in October and ran exactly the same tyre that we tested on in February. Things have gone full circle, and a lot of this development has been up blind alleys and in wrong directions, and we've come back to our starting point.

'It's not easy to track it all the time. You often have limited testing on the tyres – even on those occasions when you go to a circuit that you're about to race on, there will often be only a limited number of tyres that are going to be used at the race available for testing, because of production difficulties. Just like with the chassis you can test something at one circuit and think, "Yes, we've made a step forward," and you go to another circuit and that step forward can be a zero improvement, or even a step backwards.

'We tested one of the major construction changes at Barcelona just before the race there – together with the other top teams, we definitely felt it was an improvement. We re-tested those tyres against an earlier tyre at Magny-Cours, and there was no doubt that the earlier tyre was better there! Now those were clear-cut, quite accurate tests. But they gave totally different answers. Of course when you're going to a circuit that you've never tested on, you can get it wrong . . .'

One final point. Much was made about the problems Bridgestone might face on circuits at which the company had not been able to test. However, generally its teams were more competitive at such venues. Was that because Bridgestone went the conservative route on circuits where it had tested extensively, and gambled a bit more at places it didn't know? Whatever, perhaps we won't see the true picture until Bridgestone lands one of Goodyear's top teams.

'I think we have felt the problem maybe more than almost any other Goodyear runner,' says Tyrrell's Harvey Postlethwaite. 'But because they've got all the major teams, they've been looking good in all the races. They've been winning the battles, but I've got a feeling that they may lose the war.'

Feelin' groovy

IF tyres were news in 1997, it was nothing compared to what will happen next season; grooved rubber will be a whole new ball game for drivers, teams and suppliers.

Goodyear and Bridgestone introduced their prototype grooved tyres early in the season, and both undertook extensive testing programmes with their contracted teams. Inevitably this proved a distraction to the main business of the year; Williams and McLaren gave the job to test drivers Jean-Christophe Boullion and Nick Heidfeld. For those used to standard '97 cars, the narrow-track interim machines proved a rude shock. Johnny Herbert's reaction after his first run in a Sauber was typical: 'That was the worst car I've ever driven. It was twitchy, unstable, oversteered and understeered . . .'

That was in October, so you can imagine how difficult it was for the first drivers to try the new tyres.

'We feel confident that we are making progress,' says Goodyear's Perry Bell. 'Certainly it does require a different approach from what we've been used to in the past. The biggest issue that we're struggling with is consistency. In the past with slicks you had a more stable package, and we're seeing some fluctuation in lap times from new tyres to used tyres.'

Ferrari did less work with grooved rubber than most other top teams, and at season's end Ross Brawn admitted that he didn't know what to expect come 1998.

'I wish I knew the answer. We've done a bit of testing with the current car, but it's too early to say. Not enough work has been done. We'll test some tyres in December which Goodyear feel will be the tyres we start the season with, and then we can make a judgement.

'It's going to be a chicken-and-egg situation – what sort of tyre is going to work, and how it's going to work. We don't know what geometry we need, for instance, we don't really know what weight distribution we need. These are all questions we're going to have to answer as quick as we can at the beginning of the season. I think the biggest difficulty everyone faces is how to police the grooved tyre laws.'

Most parties agreed that it would not be practical to have a situation where all grooves had to be carefully inspected after a race. Instead tyres would be passed fit before a race, as Bell explains: 'The FIA was concerned that someone would develop a tyre that would wear the grooves off in the very early stages of a race, and then operate as a slick. But we've shown them that it's not a very viable alternative and it's not going to happen.'

Watch this space . . .

is devoted to evaluating the two tyres that are available, to try to make the best decision. Sometimes it's easy, more often it will be difficult, as there won't be much difference. But this year "not much difference" can make a massive difference in your grid position.

'You can think, "OK, I know this tyre is going to be a better race tyre, but this other one is going to be 0.3s quicker," and that can be the difference between being fifth and 15th on the grid. So it really has affected the way we've gone racing, and on occasions, notably Spain, Canada and Hungary, it's actually turned into a disaster – it's totally screwed up a race . . .'

Benetton was not the only team affected by blistering in those three events, which revealed there was far more to the black art of tyres than anyone suspected. It wasn't simply a question of the Goodyears faring worse than the Bridgestones, or harder tyres

"WORLD'S BEST EVER SLR CAMERA"
EISA EUROPEAN CAMERA AWARD

"GRAND WINNER"
POPULAR SCIENCE USA

"BEST SLR 97/98"
TIPA EUROPEAN PHOTO-VIDEO AWARD

"HIGHEST-CLASS SLR MODEL OF OUR TIME"
CAMERA GRAND PRIX JAPAN

THE WORLD PRESS HAS SPOKEN.

15 INDEPENDENT PHOTOGRAPHY JOURNALS
FROM THE WHOLE OF EUROPE
BELONG TO THE EUROPEAN IMAGING & SOUND
ASSOCIATION, WHOSE TRADE JOURNALISTS
COMPRISE THE JURY FOR THE
EUROPEAN CAMERA AWARD.

FROM SWEDEN TO GREECE, THE
29 PHOTOGRAPHY JOURNALS BELONGING
TO THE TECHNICAL IMAGE PRESS
ASSOCIATION WERE UNANIMOUS: THE
NIKON F5 IS THE NO. 1 AMONG
SLR CAMERAS.

THE AMERICAN SCIENCE MAGAZINE
POPULAR SCIENCE SOUGHT OUT THE
100 BEST PRODUCTS OF 1996.
IN THE PHOTOGRAPHY CATEGORY IT
WAS THE NIKON F5.

JAPAN'S LEADING PHOTOGRAPHY MAGAZINES,
PHOTO EDITORS AND REPRESENTATIVES
OF THE PHOTO JOURNALISTS' ASSOCIATION
HAVE BEEN AWARDING THE CAMERA GRAND PRIX
FOR 14 YEARS. IN 1997,
IT WENT AGAIN TO NIKON. FOR THE F5.

F5 3 YEAR WORLDWIDE WARRANTY

Phone 0800 230 220 (Eire 01800 409 282)
http://www.klt.co.jp/nikon

STEP AHEAD. **Nikon**

THE WINNING HABIT

by Alan Henry

'WE respect Ferrari, admire McLaren, but there is a genuine affection in the paddock for Frank Williams, Patrick Head and their racing team.' So said one seasoned F1 insider at Suzuka as the Williams team stood poised on the verge of a record-breaking ninth constructors' World Championship, just 20 years after Frank had reinvented his racing team as Williams Grand Prix Engineering.

The Constructors' Cup was inaugurated in 1958, and Williams now tops the table of winners. Chasing them into the 1998 season will be Ferrari on eight titles, McLaren on seven and Tyrrell and Benetton with one each.

The others to have made their mark are now long gone: Lotus (seven), Cooper and Brabham (two), with Vanwall, BRM and Matra on one apiece.

Francis Owen Garbett Williams has come a long way since he was born on Tyneside on 16 April 1942. From an early age he was mad about cars, obsessive even. And that obsessive nature has been the powerhouse of his ambition ever since. From minorleague racing driver, to wheeler-dealing in second-hand single-seaters, to F1 team owner, Williams has been driven by a wide-eyed, unstinting enthusiasm for the sport which originally snared him at the age of twenty.

Yet 20 years ago, nobody would have believed it possible. After wrestling to say afloat as an F1 owner with a succession of uncompetitive racing cars operated on a precarious financial shoestring, Williams sold out to the Austro-Canadian oil man Walter Wolf. His reasoning was simple. 'They'll be Walter's cars, but everybody in the business who matters will know that it is Frank who runs the team,' he rationalised.

It didn't take long for Williams to tire of his role as what amounted to a highly paid *aide-de-camp* to Walter Wolf. In 1977, he set up shop again in his own right, starting from scratch

with a private March 761 and a young Belgian pay-driver, Patrick Neve. Far more crucial was the decision to recruit Patrick Head as his chief designer. The young engineer had been working alongside Harvey Postlethwaite on the Wolf-Williams project and now felt that he was ready for the challenge of becoming a senior designer in his own right.

Head's primary role would be to design Williams Grand Prix Engineering's very first F1 car, the FW06. Compact, agile and bankrolled by Frank's new cache of Saudi Arabian sponsors, this new machine began to put Williams seriously on the map in

Paul-Henri Cahier

the end of that season and then to around 80 at the time of the first factory move. By the time the team moved into its current base at Grove, near Wantage, in 1996 the workforce had expanded to around 250.

Head's F1 designs quickly became respected as robust and impeccably engineered, if slightly conservative. 'In the early part of my career I got cured of any idea of being egotistical from an engineering standpoint,' he would say. 'By that I mean in the sense that one might say, "I'm going to prove to the world that my conceptual ideas are better than anybody else's."

'I think that attitude came about because I saw the damage that can be done to a company if one person over-indulges himself in conceptual ideas that don't work.'

That philosophy served Williams well through the Honda years with the team taking the constructors' championship again in 1986 and '87 and Nelson Piquet also posting the company's third drivers' title in the latter season. A premature breach with Honda led to a bleak 1988 season marking time with Judd V8 power, an absence of wins resulting in Nigel Mansell switching to Ferrari at the end of the year.

But Williams bounced back, forging an engine-supply deal with Renault at the start of 1989 which is set to endure through to the end of 1999, albeit next year under the Mecachrome banner on a purely commercial basis. The Williams-Renault partnership has yielded World Championships for Nigel Mansell (1992), Alain Prost (1993), Damon Hill (1996) and, most recently, Jacques Villeneuve.

Patrick Head believes that this has been the key to the Williams team's sustained success. 'I think continuity and stability have been major factors contributing to our level of achievement,' he says. 'In terms of staff, in terms of sponsors and in terms of engine partnerships. The engine partnership with Renault has been particularly important. I don't know of any team which has been obliged to change engines every couple of years really having a great deal of success.

'I think we also have a clarity of purpose which is understood by everyone who works for us in the company. I think they understand that Frank, and myself to a secondary degree, are not simply here wanting to make money. They know that we want to succeed and win races, make no mistake.'

Jackie Stewart, himself a newcomer in the role of F1 team owner, marvels at the Williams team's successes. 'What Frank has achieved is remark-

able,' he says. 'When you've worked that hard to get there, you're not going to let it go. He's more determined than ever.

'Think about it. If you were a tetraplegic like Frank, and you had one thing in your life that you could do better than anybody in the whole damn' world, you'd be pretty focused, because there wouldn't be a lot in your life that allows you the privilege of excelling like that.

'I also take my hat off to Patrick Head, because his continuing commitment is almost more remarkable than Frank's. Patrick has other options. He could be sailing, perhaps every day if he could. He has a life outside of racing, yet here he is now, still the best engineer of racing cars in the world and has been for some considerable time now.'

Frank's paralysis, the legacy of a road accident in southern France eleven years ago, has certainly produced a personal resilience which he has been able to harness as something of a psychological asset in dealing with difficult situations. In particular, he has been able to conceal the pain stemming from the knowledge that Ayrton Senna – a driver he lionised – was killed at the wheel of a Williams in the 1994 San Marino Grand Prix.

It is ironic that Senna should have been one of the few drivers viewed in a sentimental light by the British team owner. Williams gave Ayrton his first F1 test in 1983 and the two men talked frequently on the phone for years before they finally got together to do a deal in the summer of 1993. It was a brutally short-lived partnership, but the photographs of Senna both in Frank's factory office suite and the team's motorhome serve as a poignant reminder of what they might have achieved together.

Yet at the end of the day, the statistics say it all for Frank Williams and his team. Since 1973 – when Frank technically became an F1 constructor for the first time – his cars have contested 379 races with 103 wins, a strike rate of 27.1 per cent.

Key rivals McLaren have appeared in 460 races since 1966 with 107 wins, a strike rate of 23.2 per cent. Old hands Ferrari, who have raced in 587 Grands Prix since 1950, have 113 wins to their credit, a strike rate of 19.2 per cent.

More to the point, with a BMW engine partnership scheduled to come on stream from the start of the 2000 season, it is fair to predict that Frank Williams, Patrick Head and their team have not finished yet. By any means.

1978. Alan Jones challenged for the lead at Long Beach before developing fuel system problems, but despite this disappointment the team had got a taste for life at the front of the F1 field. There would be no stopping them now.

The 1978 season was dominated by Colin Chapman's ground-effect Lotus 79s. Working out of a small industrial unit in Station Road, Didcot, Head would then process the Lotus concept a stage further with the epochal Williams FW07. Stiffer and stronger than the Lotus 79, this second-generation ground-effect challenger was used by Clay Regazzoni to post the team's

first F1 victory in the 1979 British Grand Prix. It would carry Alan Jones to the World Championship the following year and still be winning races at the end of 1981.

The FW07 set the tone perfectly for what was to follow. Williams was relentless in his quest for adequate funding to allow Head free rein to develop his design concepts. By the time Williams GP Engineering moved into bespoke premises on Didcot's Basil Hill Road in 1984, the team had cemented a long-term engine partnership with Honda.

The workforce had also grown from 18 people at the start of 1979 to 45 by

In 1997, Dave Morris rode his Chrysalis BMW F650 to a convincing victory in the single-cylinder class at the Isle of Man TT. To experience

1sTT.

BMW's superior engine technology for yourself, race round to your nearest BMW dealer.

The Ultimate Riding Machine

ON Sunday in Jerez, before Michael Schumacher made his conversion from Saint in the making to Satan incarnate, there was a body of opinion in the paddock which maintained that, even if Jacques Villeneuve took the title, the German was actually more deserving of the crown. What arrant nonsense! The two men were streets ahead of the rest, slogged it out over 17 rounds and when the dust settled, literally as it happened, Villeneuve emerged victorious, with more points and seven wins to Schumacher's five. The best man won.

Taking the Formula 1 World Championship at only his second attempt, having been runner-up to Damon Hill in 1996, Villeneuve could also lay claim to a triple crown which he shares with the legendary Mario Andretti: the Formula 1 and Indy car titles and victory in the Indy 500. So why these rumblings that he was less than deserving of the title? No doubt it has something to do with the manner of his arrival on the Grand Prix scene. The Indy car series has always been sneered at by the F1 *cognoscenti* and here was this young upstart with the famous surname joining our school and instantly becoming teacher's pet as well as getting the best toy to play with, in the shape of the Williams FW18. His Melbourne debut, where he started from pole and almost won, was seen as something of an embarrassment to the established order, rather than the confirmation of a prodigious new talent. To make matters worse, Jacques resisted all attempts at comparing him to his father. No victories were dedicated to Gilles; scoring more wins than Villeneuve Senior apparently meant little and racing in Montreal on the Circuit Gilles Villeneuve was nothing special, 'because he did not design the track'.

Frank Williams did not care. He had found himself a racer and that was all that mattered. For a team, there is nothing more satisfying than discovering in the winter that next year's car is quick straight out of the box, and in Villeneuve, Williams had a driver who met the same criteria. It is worth reflecting that the 26-year-old Canadian has driven in only 33 Grands Prix, winning 11 of them. Of the 22 drivers who raced in 1997, just six have fewer starts to their credit and none of this half-dozen has won a race.

Villeneuve underwent a sea change over the 1996/97 winter with the realisation that he now wore the mantle of number one driver at Williams. Previously the team had been built around Damon Hill and before him a string of drivers whose ideas on car set-up were in line with the Patrick Principle of car design. This was Jacques's chance to pull the team his way and end up with a Villeneuve car as opposed to a Patrick Head one. Hence the very pub-

lic outbursts at not being allowed to set up the car the way he wanted. You could be forgiven for thinking that Villeneuve and his engineer Jock Clear pore over chicken entrails before tweaking the toe-in, but the truth is far simpler: Villeneuve prefers a car that turns on a sixpence, has plenty of oversteer and is uncomfortable to drive on the limit. It is a view he shares with the likes of Schumacher and Häkkinen, both noted for their pure speed and car control. The set-up slanging match between driver and designer was actually far less hostile than it appeared on the surface. For both parties it provided an insurance policy against future problems. If Villeneuve failed on the track, Williams could point to the fact he would not listen to sound advice, whereas if he capitulated to the team's opinion and did not win, then the Canadian could claim his driving style was hampered. For a 26-year-old to pit his wits against the most experienced technical director in the sport and to stick to his guns defines a man who has the courage of his convictions and is self-confident in the extreme; a characteristic we would see demonstrated on the track on several occasions in '97. Frank, Patrick and Jacques might not be quite as enamoured of one another as the Beverley Sisters, but there is certainly a two-way traffic of respect.

Respect is not part of Villeneuve's baggage when it comes to speaking his mind and he suffered the consequences when he locked horns with the FIA over the 1998 technical regulations. Having tried the prototype version of next year's Williams, the Canadian was not at all impressed with the narrow wheelbase and grooved tyres, accusing the FIA of turning Formula 1 into a circus. Worse still, he suggested that if any driver other than Senna had died at Imola in 1994, then we would not be facing a future of Mickey Mouse tracks and Noddy cars. It did not help his cause that his choice of language, in English, French and Italian, all of which he speaks like a native, was peppered with vocabulary that can only be expressed as asterisks and exclamation marks in polite society. The FIA responded by dragging him back across the Atlantic from Canada, just days before his home Grand Prix. He got away with a reprimand, but the true punishment came the following Sunday afternoon in Montreal, when he made a simple mistake at the end of the first lap, burying the nose of his Williams into an advertising panel, which ironically urged tourists to visit Quebec! Whatever he said at the time, the row, the pressure and the jet-lag had got to him.

That was just one of several mistakes committed by Villeneuve and the team this year. The season-opener in

Melbourne was another race where the Canadian saved a few bob in fuel and tyre bills, as he got no further than the first corner after the almost traditional coming-together with Eddie Irvine's Ferrari: an accident which might have been avoided with a better start and a bit more experience. He redeemed himself in Brazil, and in Argentina took his second win on the trot; trots being the right word to describe the unpleasant medical condition which saw him spend more time in the Buenos Aires toilets than on the track.

His European season got off to an inauspicious start, with a gearbox problem in Imola and then that ridiculous decision to start on slicks in the Monaco downpour. Here, his lack of experience worked against him. Whereas Schumacher delayed his exploratory lap of the track until fifteen minutes before the start, Villeneuve left the Williams garage as soon as the pit lane opened. Sat on the grid for a full half-hour, in the shelter of the trees and tall buildings, with an umbrella over his head, he was in a world of his own and Williams must take the blame for this one. In Spain, he made his third win of the season look easy, but arriving in Magny-Cours for the French race, Villeneuve once again managed to destabilise his own situation. Firstly, he was whingeing about not having free rein in his car set-up, and secondly he declared that Olivier Panis's Canadian accident was nothing serious and two broken legs was an acceptable risk in this sport. He might have been right, but remember we were in France at the time. The *coup de grâce* came when he declared that if he died in a race, he would not want it stopped! While this all made excellent copy, the F1 press corps was having to delve into the Hairdressers' Handbook to describe Villeneuve's appearance. He had dyed his hair blond! Forget tyre choice and gear ratios – was Jacques's hair strawberry or peroxide? The psychoanalysts had a field day, suggesting he was cracking under the strain. Truth was, Jacques fancied a change and realised full well that the tonsorial tint would create shock waves in the stuffy middle-aged environment that is Formula 1. For a man who is so camera-shy that he even wears his helmet to go to the toilet, it certainly made him the centre of attention, unlike his performance in the race, where he only finished fourth.

The British GP proved that Villeneuve is as tenacious as a terrier. Parked in the pit lane for 33 seconds thanks to a recalcitrant wheel nut, he never gave up and was there to pick up the trophy when Häkkinen's McLaren expired. After spinning off in Germany, he lucked into another win in Budapest. In Belgium, Williams lost him the race with another bad tyre

choice. It is no secret that Ferrari did not want Schumacher to start on intermediate tyres, but with seven years' experience behind him, the German insisted on his choice. Villeneuve, still not an expert on wet conditions, merely took advice from his engineers and catastrophically started on full wets. A lacklustre fifth at Monza was followed by two wins in one week in the Austrian and Luxembourg Grands Prix, which effectively clinched the title for

BLOND AMBITION

by Eric Silbermann

him. Next came the compelling if contrived final two races. Villeneuve's move on Schumacher in Jerez was risky, but he said he preferred to take the risk rather than tug round in second place and lose. It is typical of a man whose only interest is in driving a racing car as quickly as possible. He draws more satisfaction from winning a good scrap for a minor placing than from dominating a race unchallenged.

Villeneuve might have a relaxed attitude to life but the championship was desperately important to him in terms of his career. On a personal level, he claims it means little as he is happy with life as it is. Although a millionaire, he does not share his fellow drivers' enthusiasm for the conspicuous trappings of wealth. With his scruffy clothes and owlish glasses, he looks more like the college nerd than a

sporting superstar. Not for him the expensive leather briefcase and the flashy car. An old blue rucksack holds the books and CDs he brings to the races, along with the all-important contact lens cleaning kit, while his preferred method of transport is a restored '51 Chevy pickup truck. While his look and demeanour might infuriate the sponsors, he is far more representative of his age than his perfectly

polished peers and as such will be a great ambassador for the sport as we head for the next millennium.

Rest assured, he will still be around then, as he has admitted he now wants a second title. I do not think Villeneuve will be at the peak of his powers for another two years yet, which is good news for us, if rather depressing for Michael Schumacher and the rest of the pack.

Undefeated champion

Johnny Mowlem, 1997 champion: 17 races, 17 wins

AFN are used to being first. First to import Porsche cars into the UK, where they are still the largest Porsche dealership group. And first for Porsche drivers who want results.

So well done Johnny Mowlem for being the Porsche Cup's first undefeated champion, an achievement worthy of a place in the Guinness Book of Records. Congratulations to Eurotech for preparing the unbeatable car. And thank you to the whole support team and sponsors, Comet, Mobil Oil, Moving Shadow and Allport.

PORSCHE

FORMULA 1 REVIEW

Darren Heath

CONTRIBUTORS

Bob Constanduros • *Maurice Hamilton* • *Alan Henry*

F1 ILLUSTRATIONS

Ian Hutchinson

DAMON HILL

PEDRO DINIZ

Team manager John Walton *(right)* faced the task of forging a cohesive unit from the disparate elements that made up the restructured team.

Bottom: Tom Walkinshaw *(right)* outlines his ambitious plans to newly appointed technical director John Barnard at the Spanish Grand Prix.

Far right: Final adjustments are made to Damon Hill's car in preparation for another qualifying attempt. The World Champion's reputation was inevitably eroded during a bitterly disappointing season with the underpowered Arrows.

WHEN Tom Walkinshaw announced that he had signed the new World Champion, Damon Hill, to drive for his Arrows team in 1997, he predicted that they could win two or three races. Many mocked the suggestion and, in the first half of the season, his prediction looked like pie-in-the-sky. Even the arrival of John Barnard was not going to bring about that kind of miracle. Nor, indeed, did a very public rebuke from Walkinshaw for Hill at the British Grand Prix.

Yet two races later, everyone watched Hill and his Arrows lead for lap after lap at the Hungarian Grand Prix, jaws dropping in astonishment. Was Arrows, one race short of its 300th outing, finally going to win a race? We all know the answer, but the point had been made. Tom's prediction really hadn't been that far-fetched.

This had been the first year in which Arrows had been fully based at Leafield rather than Milton Keynes, run by Tom Walkinshaw with co-owner and team founder Jackie Oliver not even attending all the races. However, the relocation also meant that there was an extraordinary mix of per-

sonnel – a few men from the old Milton Keynes team, people recruited from various TWR operations, some who had left Ligier with Tom Walkinshaw in the spring of 1996 and others from outside the company altogether. In this respect, Arrows in 1997 was actually a newer team than Stewart Grand Prix.

There was also a less publicised reason for the subsequent débâcle during the first part of the season: the quality of some of the components on the Frank Dernie-designed A18 was not up to standard. Also a factor was the late development of bottom-end modifications to the Yamaha V10 by John Judd's Engine Developments company, big-end failures having cost Tyrrell dearly the previous season with the result that Yamaha's C-spec engine featured a new crank and oil system from the beginning of the year.

One aspect of the car's design which was most unusual was the stiffening 'pontoon' which extended rearwards over the engine to add to the rear end's torsional rigidity. It was not cal-

culated to make changes to the airbox a straightforward task, however.

The car was launched in early January, but was not to run for the first time for another ten days, and then only spasmodically for weeks after that. 'The general quality of the parts was not fantastic, because they were rushed and late,' admitted one team member, 'so we were having to use parts that shouldn't have been on the car. The car was also riddled with little snags: gearbox, hydraulics, suspension problems, parts that didn't fit.' It was scarcely tested before Australia, certainly not for any reasonable length of time.

Hill didn't even manage to start the first race and, two races later, a leaked fax suggested that Walkinshaw already had contingency plans to push forward the team's engineering department. John Barnard, released by Ferrari now that it had brought its engineering in-house at Maranello, would move to Arrows with around half a dozen of his engineers and designers and Frank Dernie quietly left.

'I needed someone different to work

with more modern techniques and a much more detailed application of the engineering,' explained Walkinshaw. 'If you are going to lead a team of 30 or 40 engineers, you've also got to be a good manager.'

As Barnard was heading towards Arrows, and Dernie prepared to quit, the team finally got down to some reasonable testing and began to develop the car. One race after Barnard joined, Hill posted his first Grand Prix finish of the year in Canada and team-mate Pedro Diniz recorded his second finish. From then on, Hill saw the chequered flag on almost every occasion, even if Diniz didn't.

Just as Dernie had been able to do little about Alan Jenkins's FA17 the previous season, so Barnard did nothing major to Dernie's A18. 'We started off by re-calculating the suspension loads and made the wishbones again to ensure adequate safety,' said Barnard. 'The first thing was to ensure reliability and then we looked at performance. We introduced a new airbox intake, which was a good step forward, and changed the cooling around. At Silverstone, we worked on a new approach to the set-

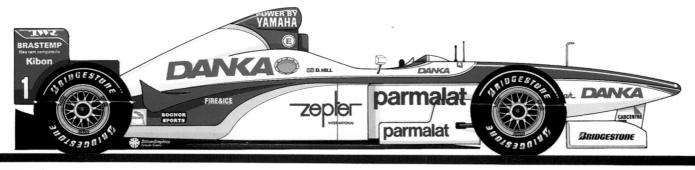

ARROWS A18-YAMAHA

Sponsors: Danka, Zepter, Parmalat, Brastemp, Remus

Team Principal: Tom Walkinshaw **Technical Director:** John Barnard **Team Manager:** John Walton **Chief Mechanic:** Les Jones

ENGINE **Type:** Yamaha OX11A/C and OX11A/D **No. of cylinders/vee angle:** V10 (72°) **Sparking plugs:** NGK **Electronics:** Zytek **Fuel:** Petroscience **Oil:** Elf

TRANSMISSION **Gearbox:** Arrows/Xtrac six-speed longitudinal semi-automatic **Driveshafts:** Arrows **Clutch:** AP (either hand- or foot-operated)

CHASSIS **Front suspension:** double wishbones, pushrod **Rear suspension:** double wishbones, pushrod **Suspension dampers:** Dynamics **Wheel diameter:** front: 13 in. rear: 13 in. **Wheel rim widths:** front: 12 in. rear: 13.7 in. **Wheels:** BBS **Tyres:** Bridgestone **Brake pads:** Carbone Industrie **Brake discs:** Carbone Industrie **Brake calipers:** Brembo **Steering:** Arrows **Radiators:** Secan, Marston **Fuel tanks:** ATL **Battery:** FIAMM **Instruments:** Arrows/PI Research

DIMENSIONS **Wheelbase:** 118.1 in./3000 mm **Track:** front: 65.0 in./1650 mm rear: 63.0 in./1600 mm **Gearbox weight:** 130.1 lb/59 kg **Formula weight:** 1322.8 lb/600 kg including driver **Fuel capacity:** 24.2 gallons/110 litres

Jacques Villeneuve's excellent working partnership with race engineer Jock Clear was a crucial factor in their championship triumph.

Below: Villeneuve found himself under intense pressure in Canada, where he carried the burden of the home crowd's expectations. Pushing too hard in his efforts to stay in touch with Michael Schumacher's Ferrari, he slid out of the race on the second lap.

Diana Burnett

Paul-Henri Cahier

down as title favourite with fine wins at Interlagos and Buenos Aires, with Frentzen following up by beating Schumacher's Ferrari fair and square at Imola. Then came Monaco, and the Williams plot started to come unravelled.

Frentzen qualified superbly on pole with Villeneuve in third place, only for the team to make the incomprehensible decision to start on slicks, even though a cursory glance at the TV monitors revealed that the track was soaking for much of its length. The team justified its choice by saying its 'weather forecasters' were confident that it would be nothing more than a short, sharp shower. In fact, it turned out to be a short, sharp shock for the team when the prospect of another dominant victory was squandered.

Thereafter, things became unpredictable for Williams. Villeneuve produced a brilliantly astute win at Barcelona where he seemed to be one of only a handful of drivers who understood how to get the best out of

their Goodyear tyres, but he followed that up with a second-lap spin into the wall at Montreal and a huge practice accident at Magny-Cours.

Patrick Head does not need reminding of this mid-season slump. 'It's not right to go round thrashing our backs with birch twigs saying, "Woe, woe and thrice woe," but equally we had our disappointments this season.

'Last year we did not change the car too much, but this season we have actually made quite a lot of changes during the season. For example, we have made a lot of suspension members; in common with a number of other teams, we have had some structural problems with the lower rear wishbones, which have been redesigned a couple of times.

'In terms of actually developing the car, we've obviously done a pretty big job introducing a new electronic brake balance system. We were originally planning a more sophisticated system with a view to 1998, but half-way

through the year a very rapid job was done on an adequate, but less sophisticated system than we originally planned, and that was raced at Monza for the first time.

'Another aspect of the car's performance which is worth noting is that the FW19 is perhaps not quite as good under braking, having excessive pitch sensitivity. This means that it isn't a car which you can slap rain tyres onto without a complete set-up change, because some of the protection we have been putting into the car against that pitch sensitivity is to run it stiffer.'

Yet perhaps not quite as stiff as Jacques Villeneuve would have liked. During the course of the season the team's number one driver and technical director would seem to have been at odds over details of car set-up, Head tending towards the view that the Canadian could extract even more performance from the FW19 with a softer set-up.

'It may be that Jacques is better

than he looks because he is making the car hard work for himself setting it up the way he wants,' said Patrick after the Luxembourg GP at the Nürburgring.

After a disappointing fourth place in the French GP – where Frentzen finished second – Villeneuve bounced back to win commandingly at Silverstone, but the FW19s proved difficult to balance in low-downforce trim at Hockenheim, which turned out to be the worst race of the year with both drivers making silly errors which cost them a finish. At about this time Villeneuve was also making noises to the effect that Williams was spending a little too much time concentrating on its 1998 narrowtrack prototype at the expense of continued development on the FW19.

He may have been right. A rather disappointing pre-French GP test at Magny-Cours galvanised Williams into refocusing on the current car's development programme, resulting in a longer-wheelbase development being

RENAULT LAGUNA

IT'S ALL WORKED OUT BEAUTIFULLY ON ROAD AND TRACK

BTCC 1997 TRIPLE CHAMPIONS

WINNERS OF THE DRIVERS', MANUFACTURERS' AND TEAMS' CHAMPIONSHIPS

RENAULT

For more information about the Renault Laguna, call Renault Freephone 0800 52 51 50

Nigel Snowdon

A superbly judged win in the Spanish Grand Prix *(left)* provided evidence of Jacques Villeneuve's increasing maturity. New team-mate Heinz–Harald Frentzen *(below)* scored his first Grand Prix win at Imola but, somewhat disappointingly, was unable to add to it.

Team manager Dickie Stanford *(centre left)* was once again a regular visitor to the podium to collect the trophy awarded to the winning constructor.

Bottom left: Seemingly deaf to the entreaties of technical director Patrick Head, Villeneuve stubbornly pursued his own ideas on car set-up.

readied for the Austrian GP in September. In conjunction with Renault, Williams also produced a torque control system which was raced from Hungary onwards. Of course, Renault's engine development programme continued apace to its customary high standard, with a slightly higher-revving RS9A version available for the French GP, followed by an even more powerful RS9B which was used only in qualifying for the remainder of the season.

Diana Burnett

Nigel Snowdon

Diana Burnett

good race meeting, and then went to the next test and said, "No, I don't want that, switch it off." And we haven't run it very much since.'

So, all in all, it was the same old Williams team in 1997. Still vulnerable to coming unstuck when it came to race tactics, still rather intolerant of its drivers' shortcomings, the latter per-

Overall, it was hard to place any question marks against the Williams team's achievements during the course of 1997. However, from the touchlines, it was difficult to conclude that Frentzen had been anything else than a disappointment. He took a long time to get to grips with the Williams FW19, eventually explaining that crucial changes to the differential set-up had been the key to his turn-round of form at Imola.

Yet Patrick Head says this is not the case. 'I think there is a certain amount of nonsense talked in this business about drivers saying that cars are not set up the way they like,' he says trenchantly.

'We were certainly doing things with the diff to try and help the car on corner entry, but that had been available to Heinz-Harald right from the first moment he stepped into the car. He knew of its availability.

'In talking to him about the areas in which he had the biggest problems, we said, "Why don't you use this?" and he said, "Well, OK, I'll try it at Imola." He told us that was much better, had a

haps understandable after Villeneuve blasted past a waved yellow flag at Suzuka to earn himself a one-race suspension that might have had a decisive influence on the outcome of the drivers' championship battle. In fact, Jacques survived the final race at Jerez to finish the season as the fourth Williams driver in six seasons to take the title.

Yet, overwhelmingly, Williams again demonstrated their remarkable ability to build superbly competitive and reliable racing cars which are more than capable of taking the lion's share of the victory laurels.

Next year, when Williams will be paying a reputed £13 million for 'customer' Mecachrome engines as a device to keep Renault's F1 involvement alive, comes the real test as F1's top team prepares the run-up to its new partnership with BMW which is scheduled for the start of the 2000 season.

Alan Henry

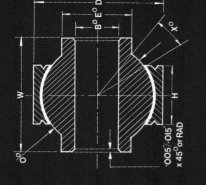

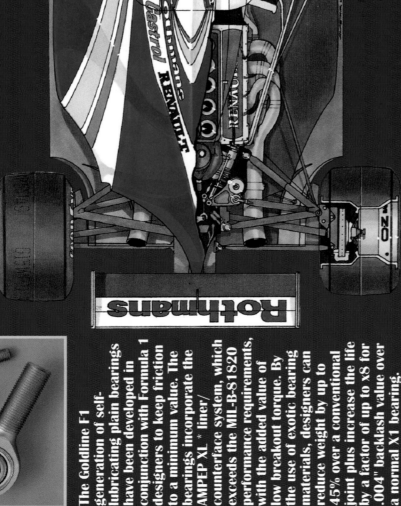

Diana Burnett

Diana Burnett

Michael Schumacher's win in the Japanese Grand Prix (right) set up an epic win-or-bust confrontation with Jacques Villeneuve in the final round at Jerez.

MICHAEL SCHUMACHER

EDDIE IRVINE

AT the start of the season, Ferrari faced another potentially disruptive programme with the technical hub of the operation reverting to Maranello after its UK-based design office was sold to previous chief designer John Barnard.

Presiding over this latest sea change was Maranello's new technical director, Ross Brawn, who switched from a similar position at Benetton together with colleague Rory Byrne. Race team direction was again in the capable hands of Jean Todt with the entire effort focused on helping Michael Schumacher offer a robust World Championship challenge to mark the famous Italian company's 50th anniversary.

As an indication of just what Michael Schumacher means to Ferrari, from the start of this season the Commendatore's old office building within the Fiorano test track had been converted to provide a flat and gymnasium for the German ace so that he has his own private accommodation whenever he visits Maranello.

After an investment of around $60 million over three seasons, it made obvious sense for the Prancing Horse to cosset its prime investment. Yet at the

launch of the 1997 F1 Ferrari F310B, company president Luca di Montezemolo raised his sights only marginally. This year, said Luca, four race wins is the aim. The title bid would take yet another year to materialise.

Schumacher clearly felt the same way. 'We expect reliability, we hope to win more races than we did,' he predicted, 'but to be honest, I think we won't really be able to win the championship until 1998.'

Historians did not need reminding that this would be getting precariously close to the 20th anniversary of Jody Scheckter winning Ferrari its previous drivers' title in 1979. To some, the current regime had at least provided stability and a sense of steady progression. Others found themselves thinking that the promise of jam tomorrow has gone on just a little too long.

'This is a fairly conventional, standard F1 car upon which we tried different things with some surprises,' said John Barnard before his departure from the team.

'I feel very comfortable with this

new car and it should be reliable, which is another reason why we have continued using the same gearbox for now. Easy to drive, stable and consistent are the qualities we have looked for in this car for 1997.'

Barnard's design also favoured lower cockpit sides. The previous year's high-sided cockpit configuration caused problems with the efficiency of the engine airbox, forcing Schumacher and teammate Eddie Irvine to cant their heads to one side on the straights in an effort to compensate. The new car's garish livery reflected considerably increased Marlboro sponsorship with continued additional backing from Shell, Pioneer, Asprey, Goodyear and Telecom Italia.

Paolo Martinelli's engine department had worked hard to develop an EV2 version of the 75-degree V10, 40-valve engine which the team initially hoped would be fully reliable after two months' testing prior to the first race in Melbourne on 9 March. In fact, for a variety of reasons, it would not be raced for the first time until the French Grand Prix at the end of June.

Perhaps surprisingly, Ferrari comfortably exceeded Montezemolo's predictions. Although Williams would scoop the constructors' championship, Schumacher carried the battle for the drivers' crown to the very last race of the season. It was more than even he expected at the start of the year.

To start with, Barnard's early departure from the equation left the new design team with the challenge of coaxing the best out of a car which they had not originally conceived. Inevitably, this gave rise to an element of inspired guesswork.

'Rory is chief designer, but I work quite closely with him and have a reasonable influence on what sort of a car we end up with,' said Brawn. 'I understand the process of optimisation, how what decisions we make on weight distribution and the general configuration of the car affect its performance, so I know how we arrive at those decisions.

'On the other hand, with John's car, it is fairly different from what I'm used to: different weight distribution, different geometry and I don't know how John has arrived at those things. So we had a lot of unknowns and uncertainties, a lot

FERRARI F310B

Sponsors: Marlboro, Shell, Asprey, Pioneer, Telecom Italia

Team Principal: Jean Todt **Technical Director:** Ross Brawn **Team Manager:** Stefano Domenicali **Chief Mechanic:** Nigel Stepney

ENGINE **Type:** Ferrari 046 and 046/2 **No. of cylinders/vee angle:** V10 (75°) **Sparking plugs:** Champion **Electronics:** Magneti Marelli **Fuel:** Shell **Oil:** Shell

TRANSMISSION **Gearbox:** Ferrari seven-speed transverse semi-automatic **Driveshafts:** Ferrari **Clutch:** Sachs (hand-operated)

CHASSIS **Front suspension:** double wishbones, pushrod **Rear suspension:** double wishbones, pushrod **Suspension dampers:** Ferrari/Sachs **Wheel diameter: front:** 13 in.

rear: 13 in. **Wheels:** BBS **Tyres:** Goodyear **Brake pads:** Carbone Industrie **Brake discs:** Carbone Industrie **Brake calipers:** Brembo **Steering:** Ferrari (power-assisted)

Radiators: Secan **Fuel tanks:** ATL **Battery:** Magneti Marelli **Instruments:** Magneti Marelli

DIMENSIONS **Formula weight:** 1322.8 lb/600 kg including driver

BEEF

**SUPERBIKE STYLE
MAGNESIUM ENGINE CASES**

**IN-FLIGHT INFORMATION
ZX-9R STYLE**

**ZX-9R POWERPLANT -
BIG, BRASH AND BRUTAL**

**LIME GREEN ZX-9R -
WE HAD TO DIDN'T WE?**

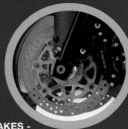

**RACE BRED BRAKES -
A ZX-9R TRADEMARK**

ZX-6R

tuck-in behind screen

end - I'm in LOVE !

cuts in - 4th...oops!   *6th top gear*

TWO YEAR WARRANTY.

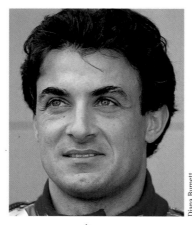
Diana Burnett

Lukas Gorys

Sutton Motorsport Images

JEAN ALESI

GERHARD BERGER

ALEXANDER WURZ

WHEN the new Benetton B197 was launched at a typically extrovert media bash at London's Planet Hollywood, then team chief Flavio Briatore expressed the view that the car would realistically be battling for third place in this year's F1 pecking order behind Ferrari and Williams.

As things turned out, Briatore was right on the money. It was certainly a candid prediction, but backed up by initial testing results which had displayed enormous promise in the month separating the day the car first ran and its official unveiling.

It might have seemed an almost painfully frank assessment of Benetton's potential, but Briatore always shoots from the hip. 'Ferrari is strong, Michael Schumacher we know is the best driver and after that I would expect Williams to be there as usual,' he said. He was right on that one as well.

Despite what was seen as a guarded vote of confidence in both his drivers, Gerhard Berger and Jean Alesi started out absolutely determined to prove that the latest B197, from the new design team directed by Pat Symonds and Nick Wirth, could be a championship contender. The emphasis was

on an evolutionary development of the previous year's car, which both drivers had found difficulty getting the best out of. With subtly revised aerodynamics and suspension detailing, first signs for the B197 during testing at Jerez looked very promising.

Symonds admits that it was necessary to undergo a process of mental recalibration when it came to designing the 1997 car.

'Losing Michael [Schumacher at the end of 1995] was a major disappointment,' he said. 'In retrospect we had underestimated the effect of the discontinuity. Because we'd worked with Michael over many years, we'd forgotten what it took to get settled in with a new driver. I think we realised that very early on; it takes a while to get to know your drivers, to get to know what's wanted.

'That procedure carried on throughout 1996, but you get to the point where you've gone as far as you can with a design and you've got your ideas for the next one. So this car [the B197] is very much tailored to the '96/97 drivers.'

Symonds also admitted that there were some very specific areas of the B196 design which needed addressing when it came to the new car, throwbacks to the pointy, oversteering set-up which Schumacher relished.

'I don't really want to go into details of what they were – but there were limitations we'd reached in the design,' he said. 'You tend to evolve your set-ups towards a particular driver, and then you find you've reached the end of the road and you need to take the fundamental design more in that direction rather than just the set-up.'

The new Benetton owed much of its concept to Symonds's long-time colleague Rory Byrne, who went off to join previous Benetton technical director Ross Brawn at Ferrari. It featured double wishbone/pushrod suspension all round with twin dampers at the rear and the facility for a triple damper set-up at the front, while Symonds replaced the seven-speed gearbox with a six-speed unit for reasons of reduced weight and improved packaging.

Berger opened the season on an up-

beat note with fourth place at Melbourne followed by a spirited chase into second place behind Villeneuve's Williams at Interlagos. By contrast, Alesi kicked off his programme with a bizarre lapse in Australia, running his B197's tank dry on the circuit after repeatedly ignoring signals to come in for fuel and tyres.

This was not calculated to provoke the most sympathetic response from Briatore and the day ended with Alesi close to tears after a vigorous bawling-out from his employer. To many observers, this was the start of a slippery slope in terms of the personal relationship between the two men.

Yet as the year unfolded, the Benetton B197 settled down to produce a consistent sequence of top-six results, but only a single win when Berger delivered an outstanding performance to triumph in the German Grand Prix at Hockenheim. Apart from that, the season could best be remembered as a year of close calls and near-misses.

'I know we've had our ups and downs,' explains Symonds, 'but this

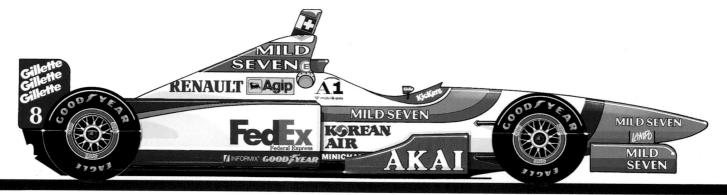

BENETTON B197-RENAULT

Sponsors: Mild Seven, Agip, FedEx, Akai, Korean Air, Gillette

Team Principals: Alessandro Benetton, Flavio Briatore/David Richards **Technical Director:** Pat Symonds **Team Manager:** Joan Villadelprat **Chief Mechanic:** Mick Ainsley-Cowlishaw

ENGINE Type: Renault RS9, RS9A and RS9B **No. of cylinders/vee angle:** V10 (71°) **Sparking plugs:** Champion **Electronics:** Magneti Marelli **Fuel:** Agip **Oil:** Agip

TRANSMISSION Gearbox: Benetton six-speed longitudinal semi-automatic **Driveshafts:** Benetton **Clutch:** AP

CHASSIS Front suspension: double wishbones, pushrod, triple damper **Rear suspension:** double wishbones, pushrod, twin damper **Suspension dampers:** Bilstein

Wheel diameter: front: 13 in. rear: 13 in. **Wheel rim widths:** front: 12 in. rear: 13.7 in. **Wheels:** BBS **Tyres:** Goodyear **Brake pads:** Carbone Industrie

Brake discs: Carbone Industrie **Brake calipers:** Brembo **Steering:** Benetton (power-assisted) **Radiators:** Secan **Fuel tanks:** ATL **Battery:** Benetton

Instruments: Benetton

DIMENSIONS Wheelbase: 114.2 in./2900 mm **Track:** front: 66.5 in./1690 mm rear: 63.2 in./1605 mm **Formula weight:** 1333.8 lb/605 kg including driver

Fuel capacity: 28.6 gallons/130 litres

Bryn Williams

Gerhard Berger made an
encouraging start to the
season, scoring points in
each of the first three
races and setting fastest
lap in Argentina *(pictured)*,
but ill health blighted
what seems likely to have
been his last year in F1.

£18,340* ON THE ROAD. (PIT CREW NOT INCLUDED.)

It shouldn't come as a surprise if this Vectra looks familiar. After all, not only is it identical to every other car in the Vectra SRi V6 Challenge, it also comes off the same production line as the model you'll find in our showrooms. Both versions have the same Lotus prepared chassis; both have a powerful 2.5l V6 24valve engine. But of course, it would be ridiculous for us to suggest that you could buy the exact car shown for £18,340. The drivers in The Challenge have to put up with a racing version. They don't get air-conditioning, traction control, driver's airbag, remote central locking, electronic engine immobilizer, electric windows or ABS fitted as standard on theirs. But they do get some very attractive stickers.

VECTRA *SRi V6 Challenge*  **VAUXHALL**

Prodrive boss David Richards *(right)* faces a considerable challenge as he attempts to restore the Benetton team's fortunes.

With the departure of Ross Brawn and Rory Byrne, Pat Symonds *(centre right)* and Nick Wirth *(far right)* assumed responsibility for the development of the B197.

Below right: Alexander Wurz shone during his three-race stint as Gerhard Berger's understudy, securing a permanent drive for 1998 in the process.

Flavio Briatore *(below)* has guided Benetton to great success and helped change the face of Formula 1.

year's chassis has certainly been a machine which the drivers preferred to last year's. With the possible exception of Austria, I think the problems were very much down to how we could make the tyres work on the low-grip circuits.

'With that exception, when we could get the car onto a circuit where we could get some load into it, then we could make the tyres work. Unfortunately many of our problems arose at the early circuits – Melbourne, Buenos Aires, Imola and Monaco, all tracks we can't test at – the ones where it is very difficult to get the car loaded up and the tyres utilised properly.

'This has been our problem with our cars for a considerable amount of time. I think you've only got to look back to 1994/95 with Michael when we were winning an awful lot of races, but we didn't actually get so many pole positions. Our qualifying wasn't as good as our racing. So I would say that our design philosophy over the years has evolved in a way that we make a car which is very kind to its tyres. So in a race, it is a good package, because it looks after its tyres. But in qualifying, when the tyres need to be used more vigorously, it has been a problem.'

Nevertheless, Symonds believes that

the team has started to get some clues as to how it can handle this tyre temperature issue to the benefit of future Benetton designs. 'If I could spend a week testing at Melbourne or Buenos Aires, I think we could learn a bit more about our problem,' he said, 'but that's basically the reason behind our ups and downs.'

Of the team's two regular drivers, Alesi was the more consistent. Second places in the Canadian, British, Italian and Luxembourg Grands Prix helped boost his points total to the point that he was challenging Frentzen for third place in the drivers' points table going into the final race of the season.

Jean also gained the second pole position of his career at Monza, leading commandingly in the opening stages of the race only to be leapfrogged by Coulthard's McLaren at the refuelling stop, as the team expected. With a bigger fuel tank than the Benetton, Coulthard was able to start with more fuel and therefore needed to take on less when he made his stop. The McLaren's advantage was almost preordained, in that respect, reflects Symonds. Not that this made it any less frustrating for the team!

Yet it was Berger's victory at Hockenheim which really propelled Benetton into the headlines. Starting from pole, Gerhard's B197 was absolutely the class of the field from start to finish. Yet it was a rare high moment for the Austrian, who retired from racing at the end of a season bedevilled by sinus problems which forced him to miss three races in the run-up to Hockenheim, not to mention having to cope with the tragic death of his father in an air crash.

During Berger's absence, Alexander Wurz was drafted in from his testing duties to stand in for his fellow Austrian. He did a splendid job to shadow Alesi home and finish third at Silverstone, a performance which helped cement himself a full-time job on the race team in 1998.

'When you look back on the season, Jean has brought in quite a lot of points for Benetton,' says Symonds. 'He keeps bringing in the prizes and, this year, he has driven some really rather good races. In Barcelona and Canada, for example, he quickly sorted out how to get the best out of the tyres and at Monza, of course, he was battling against that fundamental problem posed by the McLaren. I think he has done a good, consistent job.

'As for Gerhard, I think he has suffered from his health problems an awful lot more than people have realised. It's a matter of history that he had those three races off, but maybe it should have happened earlier, because I think he was suffering quite badly from Argentina onwards without anybody – himself included – quite realising how much it was taking out of him.

'I think that ruined what was potentially a fantastic season for Gerhard. After that pre-season testing I thought, "Wow, the guy has got a new lease of life," and would be pretty successful. I don't think he showed his full potential until he came back at Hockenheim. I think it was a great shame. If you took away that health problem, he had every chance of retiring on a very high note, and I just wish he could have done.'

Symonds and the Benetton engineering team seem almost self-conscious in their assertion that 1997 was generally disappointing, although on paper it certainly looks rather better than that.

With the colourful Briatore bowing out of F1 at the end of the season, his place taken by Prodrive boss David Richards, the Enstone-based team is now confident of opening a new phase in its history. Now follows a big push to get up alongside Williams and Ferrari for 1998.

Alan Henry

67

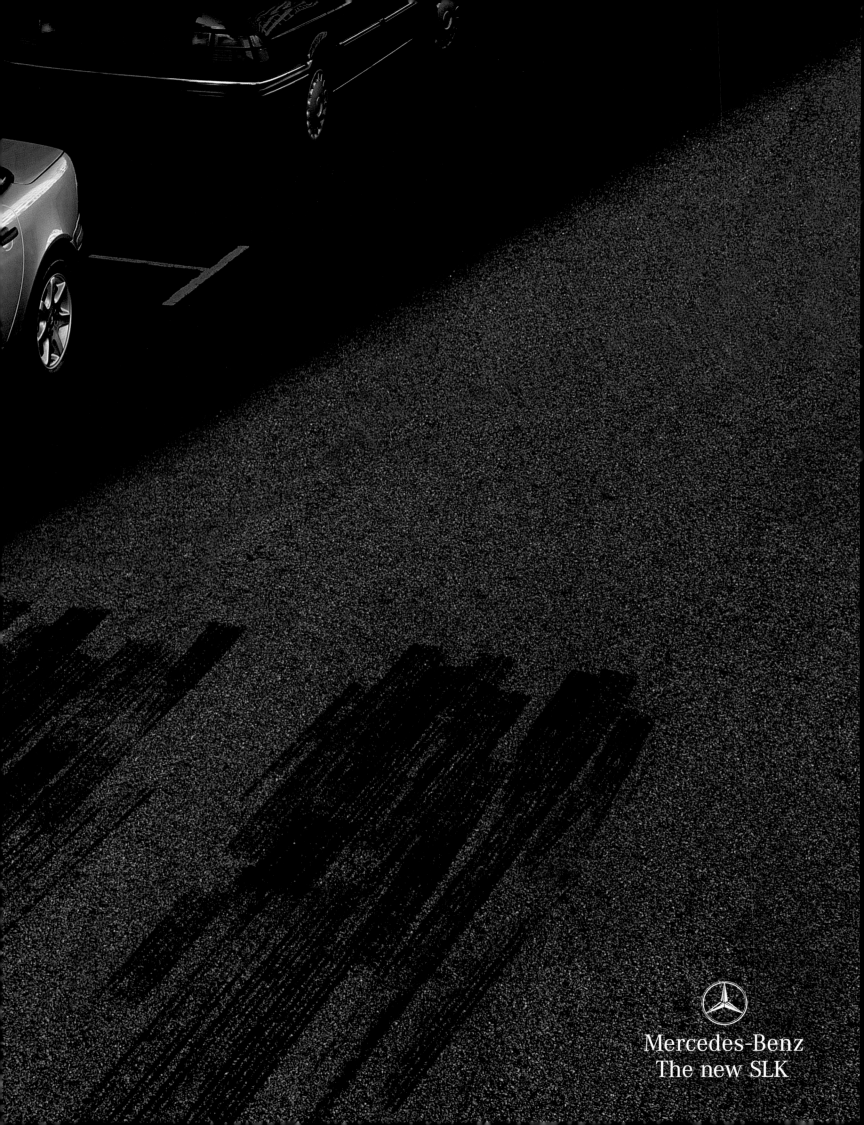

Mercedes-Benz
The new SLK

9 McLAREN 10

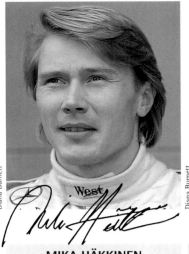

Diana Burnett

MIKA HÄKKINEN

Diana Burnett

DAVID COULTHARD

Scotland's David Coulthard gave the McLaren-Mercedes alliance its first win in Australia and added a second in Italy, but it could have been more.

Bottom right: Mika Häkkinen's utter dominance at the Nürburgring was nullified by engine failure but the Finn was to enjoy better fortune at Jerez.

McLAREN bounced back as F1 front-runners in 1997, finishing the season back where they were in 1993 as contenders that none of their opposition could afford to ignore. They started the season well with David Coulthard's victory in the Australian GP, but it was not until the second half of the year that the team finally consolidated its position as potential pacesetters on a wide variety of differing circuits. Coulthard scored his second win at Monza and the year was topped off with a 1-2 success in the European Grand Prix at Jerez where Mika Häkkinen led the Scot home to post his long-overdue first F1 victory.

The striking new McLaren MP4/12-Mercedes was originally unveiled at breakfast time on Tuesday, 14 January at the team's Woking factory, neatly decked out in the smart orange livery which the team had first used in the 1960s. This was a neat promotional device, enabling the new car to be shown without taking the gloss off a lavish, multi-million-dollar launch of the team's new sponsorship deal with West cigarettes, staged at London's Alexandra Palace to the accompaniment of live entertainment from the Spice Girls and Jamiroquai.

The new McLaren had been completed just after six o'clock on the morning of its preliminary unveiling and four hours later was already being loaded into a transporter which was shipped, together with its own tow van, direct from Luton to Jerez in a giant Ilyushin cargo jet in preparation for David Coulthard's first test at the Spanish track.

The MP4/12 was a totally new machine with several imaginative design innovations as well as incorporating features such as a rear impact zone, collapsible steering column, reduced winglet area and suspension components of restricted aspect ratio designated by the new 1997 F1 technical regulations.

Power came from a further revised Mercedes-Benz FO110E 75-degree V10 engine developed by Ilmor Engineering. 'This is another major evolution from the specification which we used in the final race of last season,' explained Ilmor boss Mario Illien.

'It involves a new block design which we decided on both for performance and installation reasons. The inlet system has been completely redesigned and it is also marginally lighter. We have enhanced the power output, but how much better it is in terms of driveability will only be established once the car starts testing, although indications from the dynamometer suggest that we have certainly made improvements.'

From the outset, McLaren MD Ron Dennis was cautiously optimistic about prospects for the new car, hinting that some significant aerodynamic improvements had been found as a result of the intensive wind tunnel testing completed over the winter.

'We know that we have made quantifiable gains in the wind tunnel,' said Dennis, 'but I would be surprised if all the other teams haven't made corresponding improvements. The only thing we don't know is where they are starting from. That said, I think attempting to evaluate the qualities of the opposition is pretty much a waste of time. We just have to concentrate on developing the best car that we can.' That they certainly did.

Pre-season testing proved very promising and Coulthard's run to victory in the first race of the season equally well merited, although admittedly made easier by the fact that both Williams drivers failed to complete the distance.

Yet there was a frustrating inconsistency about the MP4/12's performance in the opening races of the season, and while Häkkinen seemed more able to adapt his driving style to accommodate any incipient handling imbalance, Coulthard's track record of never being at his best when his mount shows any degree of rear-end instability continued as a feature of the 1997 season.

On the other hand, McLaren quickly displayed great resourcefulness when it came to planning its refuelling strategies. For example, at Buenos Aires, where the MP4/12 was not at its best in qualifying trim on the harder of Goodyear's two tyre compounds, a one-stop strategy with a long opening stint helped translate Häkkinen's 17th place on the grid into fifth place at the chequered flag.

It was a strategy which worked well for the team again later in the year at Silverstone, although most outsiders believed that the McLaren management

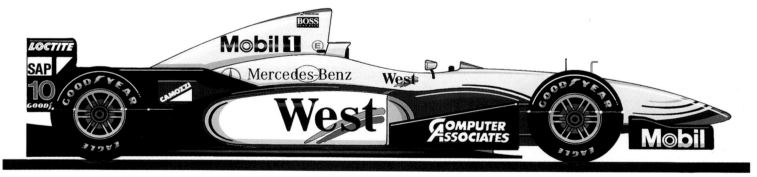

McLAREN MP4/12-MERCEDES

Sponsors: West, Mobil, Loctite, SAP, Camozzi, Computer Associates, Boss, Sun, British Aerospace

Team Principal: Ron Dennis **Technical Director:** Adrian Newey **Team Manager:** Dave Ryan **Chief Mechanic:** Mike Negline

ENGINE **Type:** Mercedes-Benz FO110E and FO110F **No. of cylinders/vee angle:** V10 (75° and 72°) **Sparking plugs:** NGK **Electronics:** TAG Electronics **Fuel:** Mobil **Oil:** Mobil

TRANSMISSION **Gearbox:** McLaren six-speed longitudinal semi-automatic **Driveshafts:** McLaren **Clutch:** Sachs (hand-operated)

CHASSIS **Front suspension:** double wishbones, pushrod-operated inboard coil spring/damper **Rear suspension:** double wishbones, pushrod-operated inboard coil spring/damper

Suspension dampers: Penske/McLaren **Wheel diameter:** front: 13 in. rear: 13 in. **Wheel rim widths:** front: 11.75 in. rear: 13.7 in. **Wheels:** Enkei

Tyres: Goodyear **Brake pads:** Hitco, Carbone Industrie **Brake discs:** Hitco, Carbone Industrie **Brake calipers:** AP **Steering:** McLaren **Radiators:** Calsonic

Fuel tanks: ATL **Battery:** GS **Instruments:** TAG Electronics

DIMENSIONS **Wheelbase:** 118.7 in./3015 mm **Track:** front: 66.6 in./1692 mm rear: 63.5 in./1612 mm **Formula weight:** 1322.8 lb/600 kg including driver

Fuel capacity: 28.6 gallons/130 litres

Paul-Henri Cahier

SUCCESS.
IT'S A
MIND
GAME.

The McLaren design team can boast a formidable array of talent with Adrian Newey *(far left)* joining respected figures such as Neil Oatley *(left)*.

Below: Triumvirate. Mario Illien, Norbert Haug and Ron Dennis are finally close to attaining the goals they set themselves when their partnership was first created.

Bottom: McLaren enjoyed a return to the glory days at Melbourne when David Coulthard scored the team's first win since the 1993 Australian Grand Prix.

Photos: Diana Burnett and Nigel Snowdon

should have told a brake-troubled David Coulthard to move out of the path of his faster team-mate early in the race. Had it not been for the knock-on effect of a sticking wheel nut which caused Villeneuve's Williams to be stationary for 33.1s at its first refuelling stop, Häkkinen would never have been in a position to surge through into the lead after Villeneuve made his second stop.

Nevertheless, once ahead, Häkkinen used the opportunity as a shop-window to display the full competitive edge of the McLaren-Mercedes wares, only for his hopes of victory to be cruelly dashed by engine failure a mere six laps from the chequered flag.

By this stage, McLaren was using the all-new F-spec version of the FO110 engine which had first broken cover at Barcelona, helping propel

Coulthard's MP4/12 to third place on the grid. The new engine, reputedly developing in excess of 740 bhp at over 16,000 rpm despite a somewhat peaky torque curve, eventually made its race debut at Montreal where Coulthard drove superbly to keep his first set of tyres in good shape, staying out to lead after a single scheduled refuelling stop.

After Schumacher's Ferrari made a second stop, Coulthard had such a commanding advantage that the team rightly judged there was sufficient time in hand to make a precautionary second stop as one of the McLaren's tyres had developed a blister. Unfortunately at that stop a problem with the clutch actuation system negated all chances of a well-deserved victory.

Reflecting objectively on the 1997

season, McLaren should have won at least seven Grands Prix. David Coulthard drove beautifully to post his second win of the season at Monza, slick pit work by the mechanics and possibly the benefit of a slightly larger fuel tank enabling him to vault ahead of Jean Alesi's Benetton come refuelling time. But McLaren should also have won at Montreal, Silverstone, the A1-Ring, the Nürburgring and, arguably, Suzuka, where Häkkinen was crucially wrong-footed by Eddie Irvine's Ferrari in the opening stages of the race.

Engine failures, including problems with oil system aeration and bottom-end failures, overshadowed the season. 'Although we had our share of engine failures, we won at Monza with the latest F-spec engine and might well

have scored a 1-2 there without Mika's tyre problem,' said Norbert Haug, the Mercedes-Benz motorsport manager.

'We finished David in second place at Zeltweg after Mika stopped. You cannot say this is a complete 100 per cent unreliability problem, but we hope that we have now resolved these problems. But as far as our progress is concerned related to speed and lap times, this is quite promising and satisfying.'

Throughout the season, both McLaren and Mercedes stinted nothing when it came to extending themselves in the interests of enhancing their competitive pitch. On the chassis design side, the team scored a coup in securing Adrian Newey's services as technical director, one of his first contributions reflected by the introduction of a new front wing at the Austrian Grand Prix which enhanced the MP4/12's front-end bite.

McLaren also sought early clarification from the FIA as to whether engine revs could be used as an additional input parameter for throttle operation, a move which many saw as an attempt to establish whether or not rivals Ferrari were using such a torque-modulating device.

The team duly developed its own system which offered a slight improvement in the Mercedes V10's driveability, yet their most ingenious development was a secondary braking system which was the subject of much speculation and interest from other teams and the media. The system was, however, confirmed by the FIA to be entirely legal and may have been imitated by leading rival teams.

McLaren also deployed its resources to include an intensive programme of development testing in preparation for next year's narrow-track, grooved-tyre F1 regulations. It was first to field a development car to the new specification, the testing of which was largely entrusted to German F3 contender Nick Heidfeld.

As far as next year's driver line-up is concerned, McLaren opted for continuity and security by renewing its deals with Mika Häkkinen and David Coulthard. Ron Dennis would like to see the two men who have shared the trials and tribulations involved in the team's renaissance finally share in the benefits.

In that connection, many F1 insiders believe Damon Hill should have bitten Dennis's hand off at the first hint of a possible deal. In 1997, McLaren re-established itself as a winning force. In 1998, it could well take over as F1's pacesetters.

Alan Henry

Nigel Snowdon

Symbols of

Quality Parts & Workmanship   *plus*   Nationwide Guarantee

*E*xcellence

plus   Friendly & local to you   =   ALL OF THESE

You don't have to look far for quality servicing and repairs. There's at least one
Unipart Car Care Centre near you, part of a UK network of expert independent
garages all backed by a nationwide guarantee.
To find details of your nearest, just call free on: 0800 20 20 20
or you'll find us on the internet http://carcare.unipart.co.uk

UNIPART

11

12

JORDAN

Diana Burnett

RALF SCHUMACHER

Diana Burnett

GIANCARLO FISICHELLA

Slick work by the well-drilled Jordan pit crew helped Giancarlo Fisichella establish a reputation as a star in the making. Having served his apprenticeship with the Silverstone-based team, the young Italian will be expected to win races for Benetton in 1998.

JORDAN, in their seventh season of F1, failed yet again to win a Grand Prix. So, what's new?

In truth, a significant amount. For the first time, Jordan were a force to be reckoned with. They were reasonably consistent (in other words, no more inconsistent than any other team) and, on a good day, in with a shout of victory. An overdue expansion programme within the technical department provided the back-up Gary Anderson needed. For once the technical director was able to see his usual workmanlike product develop rather than stand still, as it had in previous years.

Perhaps Anderson's most significant achievement was persuading Eddie Jordan to open his cheque book and start writing. It probably hurt EJ to allocate a cool £5 million for toys he would be unable to play with, but the benefit soon became apparent. The team opened their own 40 per cent wind tunnel on the site of the former facility owned by March at Brackley while, back at the Silverstone HQ, a gearbox test rig and, most important, a seven-post chassis test rig were installed.

For the first time, Jordan arrived at each race with the car boasting some

further development, no matter how small. Better than that, the telecommunication link with the seven-post rig meant, more often than not, that the car could be improved for the all-important 60 minutes of qualifying on Saturday afternoon. It was not uncommon to find a Jordan-Peugeot in the first six; the lower reaches of the top ten would be considered a major disappointment. In addition, the good work would be continued into the race, Jordan scoring more points than ever before.

'One of my main objectives,' says Anderson, 'was to get the structure of the company big enough to get rid of the unreliability problems and have a development programme running at the same time. We had to have the team strong enough to be able to do both jobs. During the year we've had probably four major updates – an active diff being one. It was very important to be able to achieve that. You can't just be a team going racing; you've got to have something going on behind the scenes.'

To help achieve his goal, the workforce was expanded to 130. As ever, Anderson could have done with even more people but, in the end, the budget, reasonable though it was, had to be the limiting factor. Benson and Hedges, now into their second year of sponsorship, really went to town with one of the most striking and imaginative colour schemes seen in F1, the muddy gold of 1996 being replaced by a bold yellow, complete with an eye-catching serpent on the nose which proved to be the most highly publicised logo of the season. No one quite knew what the serpent was for, but that mattered little judging by the unease it spread among tobacco rivals with their more staid corporate schemes.

As ever, Jordan Grand Prix was forcing the pace. For the first time, the team held an all-singing, all-dancing new-car launch in London. At the time, it appeared to be no more than a colourful stick with which to beat themselves when they failed to deliver, particularly in the light of a controversial choice of drivers.

Rubens Barrichello, after a four-year F1 apprenticeship with the team, had decided that the time had come to move on. Martin Brundle's 12-month tenure at Jordan had hardly been a success, the two sides somehow failing to click. Damon Hill took a look and, making a decision he would regret in private, if not in public, the World Champion opted for Arrows in 1997.

That left Jordan in something of a quandary. They had already caused a minor stir by signing Ralf Schumacher on the strength of his victory in the 1996 Formula Nippon Championship, but very little else – apart from some attractive backing which might come with the family name, of course. Now the team seemed set on a suicidal course by choosing Giancarlo Fisichella, a young Italian whose experience had been limited to eight outings with the Minardi team. Individually, the novices had plenty of promise. Collectively, they did not appear to be what Jordan needed during a season when nothing less than front-running performances were expected. 'We'll see,' said Eddie Jordan. 'But I tell you what. It'll be very interesting. There'll be some fireworks.' Indeed there were.

JORDAN 197-PEUGEOT

Sponsors: Benson & Hedges, Total, Hewlett Packard, MasterCard, Excalibur, s.Oliver

Team Principal: Eddie Jordan **Technical Director:** Gary Anderson **Team Manager:** Jim Vale **Chief Mechanic:** Tim Edwards

ENGINE Type: Peugeot A14 **No. of cylinders/vee angle:** V10 (72°) **Sparking plugs:** NGK **Electronics:** TAG Electronics **Fuel:** Total **Oil:** Total

TRANSMISSION Gearbox: Jordan seven-speed longitudinal semi-automatic **Driveshafts:** Jordan **Clutch:** Jordan (hand-operated)

CHASSIS Front suspension: double wishbones, pushrod **Rear suspension:** double wishbones, pushrod **Suspension dampers:** Jordan/Penske **Wheels:** OZ **Tyres:** Goodyear

Brake pads: SEP **Brake discs:** SEP **Brake calipers:** Brembo **Steering:** Jordan (power-assisted) **Radiators:** Secan **Fuel tanks:** ATL **Instruments:** Jordan/TAG Electronics

DIMENSIONS Wheelbase: 116.1 in./2950 mm **Track:** front: 66.9 in./1700 mm rear: 63.7 in./1618 mm **Gearbox weight:** 114.6 lb/52 kg **Chassis weight (tub):** 110.2 lb/50 kg

Formula weight: 1322.8 lb/600 kg including driver **Fuel capacity:** 31.9 gallons/145 litres

Additional funding enabled Gary Anderson *(right)* to restructure the team's technical department and acquire an array of state-of-the-art technological aids. Team boss Eddie Jordan *(far right)* was quickly reassured that his cash had been invested wisely.

Below: Ralf Schumacher and Giancarlo Fisichella sandwich the Ferrari of Eddie Irvine. While the Italian made impressive progress during the season, his team-mate appeared to lose his way after a confident beginning.

In Argentina, Schumacher was so desperate to overtake Fisichella that he bundled his team-mate off the road and almost took himself out in the process. But the point was, they were running in the top three at the time. It took some stern words from the boss to bring some law and order and, from that point on, there was much to be said for having two precocious and talented youngsters on the books, particularly when they finished on the podium three times. That said, there was the undeniable feeling that Jordan could have made it to the top of the rostrum with, say, Damon Hill on board.

'I'll admit that I'm disappointed we didn't win a race,' says Anderson. 'There's been maybe three or four races where we should have had a good shot but, one way or another, we managed to beat ourselves. And I mean the team as a whole when I say that. It's all very well saying we didn't have a driver who knows how to win, the drivers were too young, and all that sort of thing. But I think Giancarlo came on very well; certainly, his mental stabil-

ity has been as good as any Italian I have ever seen. I would have no reservations about seeing Giancarlo in the lead on the first lap because I don't think he would do anything silly and you would expect him still to be there at the last corner. You can't say that about a lot of drivers – and I'm not just talking about the young guys.

'Having two new drivers was very good for us even though, in the natural course of events, you knew one of them would be left behind. The only surprise was that it was Ralf who suffered. Ralf has probably more confidence in his ability than Giancarlo has in his but the difference was that Giancarlo was prepared to work at it.

'Ralf had to do it on the first lap and, as a result, he ended up over-driving. No matter what you do, you have to respect the grip level of the track and the car and drive to the maximum of that. If you go beyond that, you lose tenths at every corner by sliding wide and, because you realise the mistake, you add to the problem by trying to make up for it elsewhere. Ralf has tremendous poten-

tial; he's incredibly quick. He just needs to come at it with a bit more patience.'

Having perhaps seen the error of his ways, Hill will join the team for 1998 and play his part in helping Jordan make the adjustment from Peugeot to Mugen Honda. The three-year relationship with the French firm has been successful enough – 'they have done a fine job,' says Anderson – but there is the underlying feeling that Peugeot could have done even more. Conservatism has ruled much of the decision-making. Peugeot have refused to race an engine which has been an improvement for fear of blowing it up, a principle which goes against Anderson's instincts as an out-and-out racer.

'If you are going racing, you've got to go out on a limb from time to time,' he says. 'F1 should be technology at the limit and yet we were running the least revs of any V10 in the pit road. In fact, we were actually running less revs in 1997 than we were two years ago! Peugeot's way of running a reliability programme is to reduce the revs rather than fixing the problem.

'Okay, the V10 had very good power at the top end but there was a power hiccough down the range. They didn't seem to move forward. For instance, we ran the same engine at Hockenheim as we did at Monaco. I don't believe you should do that. The attitude seems to be: 'power is power'. Well, it's not quite like that. There is always something which can be done – different trumpets or exhaust systems, for example – just to make a difference. I have to say, I'm looking forward to the change in philosophy in 1998.

'In fact,' concludes Anderson, 'I'm pleased there is a major change to the regulations for next year because we're much stronger now as a company. We've got a very good Research and Development programme and we will come up with some good ideas. As always, the big teams will be hard to beat but I think we are now ready to mix it with them.'

Maurice Hamilton

design that
bitessss

The graphic design for the Benson and Hedges Jordan 197 and supporting team activity was created by Light & Coley, one of the UK's leading design consultancies.

Specialising in creative and effective graphic design through all media, Light & Coley has a "bigger picture" understanding of communications, not a narrow appreciation of a single channel. The results speak for themselves.

Contact: James Sanderson or Antony Wolfson

Telephone ++ 44 171 381 6644 or Fax ++ 44 171 381 2833 or e-mail jsanders@lightcoley.co.uk

LIGHT & COLEY

14
PROST
15

OLIVIER PANIS

Diana Burnett

JARNO TRULLI

Diana Burnett

SHINJI NAKANO

Diana Burnett

ALAIN Prost's acquisition of Ligier was the source of much good news in 1997. There was, of course, the change of ownership and name, allegedly at a cost of approximately £5.25 million, an obviously worthwhile investment as blue-chip companies rushed to become associated with France's national F1 team now led by one of the country's all-time heroes.

There was also a much-improved car which proved so promising in testing, followed by a succession of points-scoring results – including second in Spain – before Olivier Panis broke both his legs in an accident in Canada.

There the good news might have ended, but stand-in Jarno Trulli proved an absolute revelation, finishing fourth in Germany and then leading brilliantly in his last race in Austria. A week later, Panis made a great comeback with sixth place in the Luxembourg GP and even written-off team-mate Shinji Nakano had his moments, the Japanese out-qualifying Trulli in Italy, having scored his first World Championship point in Canada. After Panis's great win at Monaco the previous year, the team's progress continued in 1997, albeit under a different name.

That victory, however popular, revealed the first glimpse of a driver who deserves much greater recognition. His influence on the car's design over the winter of 1996/97 should not be underestimated, nor should his role as inspirational team leader. That was duly acknowledged by his new team chief when Prost confirmed that Panis would be re-signed for 1998. On the track, Panis discovered another new overtaking place at Monaco and single-mindedly came back after an accident from which lesser drivers might never have returned.

Panis was already hard at work on the 1997 car as lawyers worked to transfer the legal ownership of Ligier from Flavio Briatore to Alain Prost. 'I spent a lot of time at Magny-Cours over the winter with Loïc Bigois [who took over the role of chief designer from Frank Dernie],' explained the French driver. 'Last year's cars had a lot of problems with braking, locking up the rear wheels. It was very difficult on quick circuits, so this year's car was the work of last winter to solve those problems.'

'The weight distribution last year was very much biased towards the rear, so the car understeered under acceleration. This year's car had much more of a [weight] bias towards the front, in order to have a more "pointy" front end to eliminate this understeer problem. There was also a new Honda engine with a lower centre of gravity.

'The first time I stepped into this year's car, all the problems we had last year had been 90–100 per cent eliminated. There were places where it was less good in qualifying, but that was perhaps a result of the tyre war.'

The team duly emerged as Bridgestone's number one runner and worked hard to develop their products. But while they led the Bridgestone thrust, there was a feeling that the Japanese company might have been less conservative in the choice of tyres they made available. 'Wear was not a problem,' continued Panis, 'so we could have taken more of a risk on occasions.

'During the year we have tried to improve the pitch control and shock absorbing of the car. Last year we had

lots of problems on bumpy tracks, but I think we reacted well to them. We tested at Barcelona and Jerez as Magny-Cours is so smooth.'

The combination of Panis's input, Bigois's interpretation and the work of Bridgestone and Honda bore immediate fruit, causing the Goodyear teams to glance warily over their shoulders. Even the team's boss was impressed. When Panis followed up his fifth place in Australia with a third in Brazil, thereby confirming the progress made in improving the car's performance on bumpy circuits, Prost was moved to admit that 'the quality of work in this team never ceases to amaze me'.

At the same time, he also praised the input from both Bridgestone and Honda. The latter had already introduced a new version of their MF301HA engine at the start of the year, significantly lower thanks to a modified oil scavenging system but also offering another 500 rpm and weighing less.

Reliability was a little suspect, however, but generally only with Nakano's

PROST JS45-MUGEN HONDA

Sponsors: Gauloises Blondes, Canal+, Alcatel, PlayStation, Bic

Team Principal: Alain Prost **Technical Director:** Loïc Bigois **Team Manager:** Cesare Fiorio **Chief Mechanic:** Robert Dassaud

ENGINE   Type: Mugen Honda MF301HA and MF301HB **No. of cylinders/vee angle:** V10 (72°) **Sparking plugs:** NGK **Electronics:** Mugen Honda **Fuel:** Elf **Oil:** Elf

TRANSMISSION   Gearbox: Prost six-speed transverse semi-automatic **Driveshafts:** Prost **Clutch:** AP (either hand- or foot-operated)

CHASSIS   Front suspension: double wishbones, pushrod, twin or triple damper **Rear suspension:** double wishbones, pushrod, twin damper **Suspension dampers:** Showa

Wheels: BBS **Tyres:** Bridgestone **Brake pads:** Carbone Industrie **Brake discs:** Carbone Industrie **Brake calipers:** Brembo **Steering:** Prost **Radiators:** Secan

Fuel tanks: ATL **Battery:** FIAMM **Instruments:** Prost

DIMENSIONS   Wheelbase: 115.5 in./2935 mm **Track: front:** 66.6 in./1693 mm **rear:** 63.3 in./1608 mm **Formula weight:** 1322.8 lb/600 kg including driver

Fuel capacity: 33.0 gallons/150 litres

Bryn Williams

Olivier Panis looked likely to add to his win at Monaco in 1996 before his dreadful accident in Canada interrupted his season.

Right: All eyes are on the timing screen as Jarno Trulli, race engineer Humphrey Corbett and the rest of the Prost team monitor the efforts of the opposition.

Four-times World Champion Alain Prost *(below right)* confirmed that he remains as ambitious as ever during his first season as a team owner.

Japanese novice Shinji Nakano *(below far right)* stuck to his guns and performed respectably in difficult circumstances.

Following his switch from Minardi, Trulli *(bottom)* lost no time in confirming that he is a man with a big future.

Nigel Snowdon

car. Panis retired from second place in Argentina due to a tiny crack in a weld causing a hydraulic leak and this was his only retirement in the first half of the season prior to the suspension failure which caused his accident in Canada. Nakano followed up his finishes in the first two races with a succession of retirements, mainly due either to on-circuit incidents or engine problems.

All this prompted Honda to introduce their B-specification engine at Magny-Cours which was intended as a more reliable version of the original V10. Work on improving car balance with driveability continued throughout the year, as did improvements to ignition and mixture mapping.

Trulli, however, confirmed the team's continuing reputation for supplying a reliable car. He finished every race except for the last one, Austria, which he had been leading. By this stage Honda had introduced its C-spec engine in Belgium which marked a big step forward with a different intake configuration, but the retirement at the A1-Ring was caused by poor piston quality, which continued in the following races.

The 'S' – for Suzuka – specification embraced two types of engine: a low-friction version with more top-end power for qualifying, plus a race version which was intended to be more reliable but which, embarrassingly, still suffered from piston problems at home in Japan.

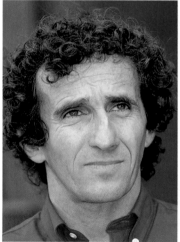

Nigel Snowdon & Diana Burnett

By this stage it had been announced that Peugeot and Mugen Honda would swap teams in 1998, so the continuity that the French team had enjoyed for three years would cease. Peugeot co-operation began in the early summer – giving rise to one incident of alleged information shar-

ing – so the atmosphere could never really be ideal.

This mood was compounded by Hirotoshi Honda's insistence that his protégé Nakano should stay with the team even though Prost wanted to drop him. Against this unsettling background, the Japanese driver did a more than passable job.

Overall, Alain Prost's first year as a team boss suggested a huge desire to make progress – and quickly. Happily, he had the finance to do so as his own fame secured sponsors such as Bic, Canal+, Alcatel and Sony PlayStation to join Gauloises on the flanks of the blue cars.

At the same time, he wanted to make changes, including relocating the team to a new base in Paris. However, along the way he had to relearn some of the rudiments of racing: that a team is a cohesive unit which reacts badly to disruption, that sometimes you have to take a driver to secure an engine and that driver negotiation is not always straightforward.

But that may be a story for 1998 when the path of the Prost star in the ascendant could well cross those of the Big Four.

Bob Constanduros

Darren Heath

Diana Burnett

Diana Burnett

Nigel Snowdon

Left, left to right: Technical co-ordinator Gabriele Tredozi and team manager Frédéric Dhainaut again played influential roles as Giancarlo Minardi battled to move the team that bears his name off the back row of the starting grids.

Below: Tarso Marques leads team-mate Ukyo Katayama at Jerez. Despite his inexperience and the Minardi's uncompetitiveness, the Brazilian *(below centre)* showed occasional promise.

Jarno Trulli *(bottom)* quickly proved that he belongs in Grand Prix racing and was soon whisked off to replace the injured Olivier Panis at Prost.

Nigel Snowdon

Champion. 'I want to know what I can get from the car.'

He was slower than Katayama only in the first race at Melbourne, thereafter always qualifying quicker. Indeed, his two ninth places in Australia and Argentina were the team's best of the year. The Italian also starred in Canada.

Meanwhile, Katayama had his moments. It had been a challenge for the team to take on the Japanese driver and it took him time to adapt to their language and culture. He did at least finish almost half his races, but retired from a third of them due to incidents and it was perhaps significant – and honest – that he decided to retire from F1 once the season was out. If he had

faults, said the team, it was that when he had a car that was good, he messed it up. Crashing off the start line at Silverstone was a case in point.

When Trulli left, his place was taken by Tarso Marques, the Brazilian driver who had tackled the two South American races for the team 15 months before. After his Bridgestone testing experience during the intervening period, the team hoped that he would show a little more maturity.

In theory, several factors should have seen Minardi move up a gear and, correspondingly, up the grid in 1997. In practice, apart from the first couple of races, they went nowhere, and languished at the back of the grid

Diana Burnett

with Tyrrell, the other V8 team. An unresponsive chassis did not help.

The state of play in F1 is highlighted by the team: 'The level of the game is now very competitive. Recently we've had 20 cars covered by 2.5s. That's good. We need a competitive F1, but from a small team's viewpoint it is disappointing. If we make progress, so do the other teams.

'Since last year F1 has become a better package – and we're happy to be last in this F1. But we're still working hard to make someone else last!'

Bob Constanduros

Nigel Snowdon

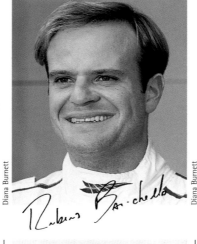

The undoubted highlight of the Stewart team's creditable debut season in Formula 1 was Rubens Barrichello's magnificent second place at Monaco.

P ERHAPS the bravest decision was to start completely from scratch. Jackie and Paul Stewart chose not to take over an existing team – Arrows, for example, was on the market at the time of initial planning in early 1996 – and effectively buy into Formula 1. Instead, they opted for the 'clean sheet of paper' approach. They would serve their time even though that meant doing the full season in 1997, finishing second in the most glamorous race of all, and not earning a single penny for their troubles. Not a brass farthing. Not even an extra paddock pass.

Such is the true cost of battling your way into Grand Prix racing while being outside the protective umbrella held tightly by Bernie Ecclestone with the connivance of the FIA. Hardship could rain down and there would not be the slightest offer of shelter. That's the point, of course. You first have to prove that you can survive before being allowed in with the sharks. If nothing else, Stewart Grand Prix showed they can swim strongly and with a good deal more grace than some of their opponents can muster. The arrival of this team has been as impressive as any in the past decade.

RUBENS BARRICHELLO

You could tell that from the moment the lone piper escorted everyone to their places at the launch of the SF1. This was a thoroughly professional event matched by the car itself. The Stewarts had chosen wisely when Alan Jenkins was selected to establish the technical department and pen a car to accept the Ford Zetec-R V10. Jenkins's vast experience, coupled with an unflappable demeanour and wry Liverpudlian humour, was perfect for the mammoth job in hand as he literally began with an empty room at the Stewart headquarters in Milton Keynes.

The product which emerged was shaped to a great extent by ex-Williams aerodynamicist Eghbal Hamidy, the clean lines of the SF1 being untrammelled by identification for multifarious two-bit sponsors.

Apart from wearing tartan trousers in the pit lane, Jackie also broke new ground by introducing the HSBC financial institution and the tourist board from Malaysia as the prime backers alongside Ford, with additional support from Texaco and Sanyo.

JAN MAGNUSSEN

And that was it. The budget seemed sufficient at the time. The intense competitiveness of F1 would prove otherwise half-way through the season as Stewart felt the effects of, among other things, not being able to afford a separate test team.

There was much work to be done. Apart from learning about the set-up, there was tyre testing for Bridgestone and, more important perhaps, the need to put serious miles on the Ford V10 in its latest guise, of which there were many. The plethora of developments – from the Project 5, which had been used by Sauber at the end of 1996, through to the P9 – was brought about by the realisation that the P5 would not, in the words of one Ford executive, 'pull the skin off a rice pudding'. Added to which, it was proving wholly unreliable, a charge which had not often been levied by the Swiss team the previous year. If it was clear that there were faults on both sides, the initial problem was getting Stewart and Cosworth to agree on that score.

While Cosworth worked night and

day as they set about a major overhaul of their systems, Stewart gave some thought to the gearbox and the integral oil tank which appeared to be contributing to some of the mechanical grief. While that could be cured by a suitable revision, Cosworth were saddled with the handicap of having the only V10 in the paddock with chain-drive to the camshafts. Thanks to the lack of testing, they also had to cope with doing most of the development at the races – and the spectacular public failures which frequently ensued.

Silverstone was the worst weekend by far, a succession of blow-ups relegating the cars to the back of the grid. It also marked a turning point as the successful integration of Stewart and Cosworth personnel began to pay off. In Belgium, Ford and Cosworth finally felt that they had an engine which was a match for the car. Which was saying something.

From the moment that Rubens Barrichello had qualified 11th for the first race, it was clear that the SF1 was basically a competitive proposition. He underscored that by taking fifth on the grid in Argentina and a highly impressive third-fastest time in Canada. But it

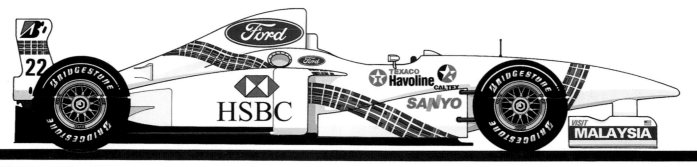

STEWART SF1-FORD

Sponsors: HSBC, Ford, Government of Malaysia, Texaco, Sanyo

Team Principals: Jackie and Paul Stewart **Technical Director:** Alan Jenkins **Team Manager:** David Stubbs **Chief Mechanic:** David Redding

ENGINE Type: Ford Zetec-R **No. of cylinders/vee angle:** V10 (72°) **Sparking plugs:** Champion **Electronics:** Visteon **Fuel:** Texaco **Oil:** Havoline

TRANSMISSION Gearbox: Stewart/Xtrac six-speed longitudinal semi-automatic **Driveshafts:** Xtrac **Clutch:** AP (hand-operated)

CHASSIS Front suspension: double wishbones, pushrod **Rear suspension:** double wishbones, pushrod **Suspension dampers:** Stewart/Penske **Wheel diameter:** front: 13 in. rear: 13 in. **Wheel rim widths:** front: 12 in. rear: 13.75 in. **Wheels:** BBS **Tyres:** Bridgestone **Brake pads:** Carbone Industrie **Brake discs:** Carbone Industrie **Brake calipers:** AP **Steering:** Stewart **Radiators:** Secan/IMI **Fuel tanks:** ATL **Battery:** FIAMM **Instruments:** Visteon

DIMENSIONS Gearbox weight: 143.3 lb/65 kg **Chassis weight (tub):** 88.2 lb/40 kg **Formula weight:** 1322.8 lb/600 kg including driver **Fuel capacity:** 28.6 gallons/130 litres

Diana Burnett

In opting to build a new team from scratch, Jackie and Paul Stewart set themselves a daunting challenge but emerged with the foundations of future success firmly in place.

The Stewart-Fords shone in Austria, with Rubens Barrichello *(below)* running in second place ahead of Jacques Villeneuve in the early stages of the race.

Bottom: Jan Magnussen struggled to adapt to the demands of Formula 1 in the first half of the season and it was only in the last few races of the year that the young Dane began to show the form promised by his glittering F3 career.

was in the wet at Monaco that Barrichello really shone and gave the stunned team six points for second place. Then it was back to reality two weeks later in Spain where the drivers had their worst qualifying performances of the season – and this on the only circuit where serious pre-season testing had been carried out. Welcome to the black art of Formula 1.

While it was unusual to see Barrichello in the rear quarter of the grid, that had become familiar territory for his team-mate. Jan Magnussen was a major disappointment during the first half of the season but then he began to get to grips with the car and F1 and suddenly kicked in at the A1-Ring in September. Just in time to save his place. Magnussen's faltering progress was one of the many aspects which Jackie Stewart had to take care of during his first season as an F1 entrant.

'To be so competitive was ahead of all expectations,' said Stewart. 'But the failure to find reliability was an enormous disappointment because I really felt we could have finished in the top six on more than one occasion. Silverstone was so bad it was laughable but I was actually more depressed following a race such as Monza where we just weren't competitive – and that I couldn't accept. I just thought, where are we going here? This is ridiculous.

'But I will say that the team has been fantastic. Everyone has adopted the right attitude and the energy level has been incredibly high. This first year, with the six points at Monaco, has been something to cherish. I have absolutely no regrets.'

The fact is that Stewart Grand Prix not only survived their first season, they did it with unobtrusive style. If you ignore the tartan trousers, that is.

Maurice Hamilton

COSWORTH

CASTINGS

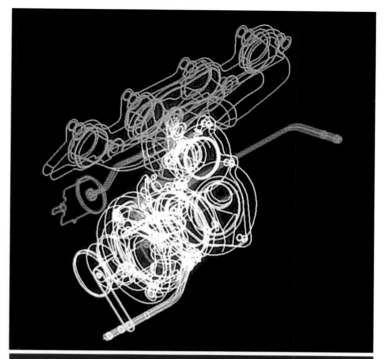

ENGINEERING

MANUFACTURING

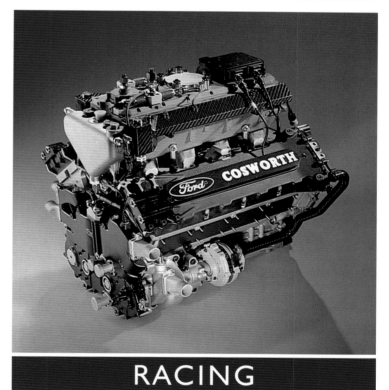

RACING

WORLD CLASS WORLD WIDE

COSWORTH
A Vickers company

COSWORTH   ST. JAMES MILL ROAD   NORTHAMPTON   NN5 5JJ   UK.   TELEPHONE: +44 (0) 1604 732100   FACSIMILE: +44 (0) 1604 732113

VINCENZO SOSPIRI

RICARDO ROSSET

Below: Eric Broadley's determined attempts to establish Lola in F1 ultimately resulted in the veteran engineer losing control of the company he founded.

Below left: Melbourne witnessed a brief and inglorious beginning and the effective end of another of Grand Prix racing's expensive follies.

LOLA Cars founder Eric Broadley decided to take the plunge and run a works F1 team for the first time in 1997. It was a decision which would end in financial catastrophe, not only for the Grand Prix team itself but also for the company he had run for over three decades. By the end of the year, Broadley was gone from the firm, its ownership passed to long-time racer Martin Birrane, the owner of Dublin's Mondello Park cir-

cuit, and the F1 operation was a distant memory.

With apparently lavish sponsorship from MasterCard, the new Lola was unveiled in late February at a smart London hotel. Even then it was clear that the project faced an uphill struggle. Drivers Ricardo Rosset and Vincenzo Sospiri went into battle using

leased Zetec-R V8 engines similar to those which had powered Michael Schumacher to his 1994 World Championship, but with the promise of Al Melling's bespoke V10 coming on line later in the season.

The new Lola T97/30 was a straightforward chassis design using Lola's own six-speed transverse gearbox. 'Unlike the common practice in F1, which places emphasis on one designer, Lola's approach has been to utilise specialist skills in a design team for the new car,' said Broadley. 'We have used a lot of wind tunnel work, currently with the one at Cranfield, but we are also constructing our own facility on-site here at Huntingdon.'

Despite Broadley's rather plaintive prediction that 'we want to be the fastest Bridgestone runner and collect a point or two this season', the whole project was a disaster from the moment Rosset and Sospiri predictably missed the 107 per cent qualifying cut at Melbourne.

The team duly arrived at Interlagos for the second race, but was called home prior to the start of practice.

Promised sponsorship had not yet arrived and Broadley decided to withdraw rather than become further in debt. It was a desperately sad end to what was, in truth, an ill-judged project in the first place.

Alan Henry

LOLA T97/30–FORD

Sponsors: MasterCard, Pennzoil	
Team Principal: Eric Broadley **Technical Director:** Eric Broadley **Team Manager:** Ray Boulter **Chief Mechanic:** Dave Luckett	
ENGINE **Type:** Ford Zetec-R **No. of cylinders/vee angle:** V8 (75°)	
TRANSMISSION **Gearbox:** Lola six-speed transverse semi-automatic **Driveshafts:** Lola **Clutch:** AP	
CHASSIS **Front suspension:** double wishbones, pushrod, inboard spring damper **Rear suspension:** double wishbones, pushrod, inboard spring damper	
Suspension dampers: Koni **Wheels:** OZ **Tyres:** Bridgestone **Brake pads:** Carbone Industrie, AP **Brake discs:** Carbone Industrie, AP **Brake calipers:** AP	
Steering: Lola **Radiators:** Serck, Marston **Fuel tanks:** Premier	
DIMENSIONS **Formula weight:** 1322.8 lb/600 kg including driver	

IF YOU CAN'T MAKE IT TO THE VECTRA V6 CHALLENGE YOU CAN ALWAYS SEE ONE IN THE HIGH STREET.

For a free 48 hour test drive of a Vectra,* contact your local dealer.

(Call 0345 400 800 for details.)

At Vauxhall, we think winning a motor race should be more about a driver's skill and not about the extra technical "gadgets" in his car. That's why we set up the V6 Challenge, in which every competitor drives a top of the range Vectra SRi V6. However, not only are these race cars identical to each other, they also come off the same production line as the road-going model you'll find in our showrooms. Both versions have the same Lotus prepared chassis; both have a powerful 2.5 V6 24valve engine. But that's where the similarity stops.

That's because the model you can buy also has ABS, traction control and air conditioning – all fitted as standard. And what's more, yours won't be covered in stickers.

VECTRA *SRi V6 Challenge*    **VAUXHALL**   * Not this one, of course.

When you need all the
PERFORMANCE
you can get

When you're spending £50 million in a season. When 220 mph still may not be enough. Whenever performance is everything, which spark plug do you choose? Champion. Over 340 Grand Prix wins. World Champion yet again in 1997, bringing the total to a remarkable 21 World Championships. Chosen by more Formula 1 teams than any other spark plug. And by you, if you care how your car performs.

Nothing performs like a Champion

1997 GRANDS PRIX

AUSTRALIAN GRAND PRIX	98
BRAZILIAN GRAND PRIX	108
ARGENTINE GRAND PRIX	116
SAN MARINO GRAND PRIX	124
MONACO GRAND PRIX	132
SPANISH GRAND PRIX	142
CANADIAN GRAND PRIX	150
FRENCH GRAND PRIX	160
BRITISH GRAND PRIX	168
GERMAN GRAND PRIX	178
HUNGARIAN GRAND PRIX	186
BELGIAN GRAND PRIX	194
ITALIAN GRAND PRIX	204
AUSTRIAN GRAND PRIX	212
LUXEMBOURG GRAND PRIX	220
JAPANESE GRAND PRIX	228
EUROPEAN GRAND PRIX	236

AUSTRALIAN
grand prix

COULTHARD

M. SCHUMACHER

HÄKKINEN

BERGER

PANIS

LARINI

In qualifying for the 1996 Australian Grand Prix, Damon Hill had battled for pole position with his new Williams-Renault team-mate Jacques Villeneuve. Twelve months on, the new World Champion spent practice and qualifying re-adjusting to life away from the front of the F1 starting grid. It was a set of circumstances with which he was previously only fleetingly acquainted in 1992 when he drove a handful of races in an old Brabham before being promoted to the Williams ranks.

To bracket his new Arrows-Yamaha in the same tail-end category would have been an extreme exaggeration. Yet Hill, running on Bridgestone tyres, could not better 13th-fastest time in Friday free practice, 2.5s slower than Michael Schumacher's Ferrari, on a day punctuated by a gearbox breakage and a quick spin.

'In all honesty, I think that if we can qualify two and a half seconds away from the front of the grid, that would be a good result for us right now,' said Hill thoughtfully.

Schumacher kept his F1 rivals guessing as to the real potential of his new F310B by setting the fastest time in sweltering conditions at Albert Park, ending the day 0.4s ahead of arch-rival and compatriot Heinz-Harald Frentzen's Williams-Renault.

Schumacher's time was achieved on soft-compound rubber and a light fuel load, a combination offering better grip and enhanced straightline speed. Frentzen, who was having his first outing as Hill's successor in the Williams ranks, was running on harder tyres with a heavier fuel load as his team experimented with other aspects of their car's performance.

'I don't know how much fuel the others were running,' said Schumacher. 'Maybe we had less than them, so that coming first today is a meaningless prize.

'But in general the car performed better than I expected. Our main problem with last year's car was turn-in oversteer, and understeer on the exit of the corners. We no longer appear to have this difficulty and the car is undoubtedly better.'

Jean Alesi wound up third on Friday in his Benetton with championship favourite Jacques Villeneuve fourth in the other Williams, what should have been his fastest lap of the day spoiled when he found himself inadvertently blocked behind the slow Lola-Ford of Italian newcomer Vincenzo Sospiri.

This all pointed to a continuation of the Williams team's five-year domination when the starting signal was given. It also heralded the beginning of the first tyre war since 1991 with the arrival of the Japanese Bridgestone company to pitch its products against Goodyear, F1's most experienced ever tyre maker.

Come Saturday qualifying and the situation proved decisively different. Villeneuve was in the driving seat almost from the outset. Coulthard set the ball rolling with a 1m 31.531s, but Jacques quickly asserted himself with a stunning 1m 30.505s, demonstrating the unruffled confidence of a man who could seemingly do no wrong.

Ferrari alone had opted for the harder of the two Goodyear compounds available, the new regulations requiring that the drivers make their choices prior to Saturday qualifying – and then live with that decision through to the end of the race. Nevertheless, a 1m 31.803s from the German driver suggested that the new Ferrari was not far from the mark in terms of absolute track performance.

Frentzen got into his stride gently. Yet moments after he turned a 1m 32.763s for seventh-fastest time, Villeneuve went round in 1m 29.369s – 2.162s quicker than anybody else had managed up to that point. He was also 3.3s quicker than his new team-mate, a fact which must have called for a degree of stoicism from Damon Hill's successor.

'The car was great, very driveable on the edge,' recounted Villeneuve after securing the fourth pole position of his career. 'You can get it very sideways and control it well. While I wouldn't say it necessarily feels particularly nice, it obviously feels a lot nicer than the others.'

With two minutes of the session to go, out came the red flag

after Gerhard Berger inadvertently pushed Nicola Larini's Sauber into the wall, much to the detriment of the Swiss machine. In many such circumstances, the stewards might well have called it a day there and then, but with several key runners poised to complete their fastest laps the track was re-opened for a spine-tingling two-minute blast.

Allowing for the 'out' lap, just a single flying lap now remained to all the competitors and they all crowded out of the pit lane in one massive nose-to-tail bunch. For Frentzen, these final moments represented salvation. Having lost his first run in traffic, he had then tried to press on for another quick lap, which used up his first set of tyres. He tried again, made changes to the set-up, and then found his efforts thwarted by the red flag. For the final two-minute stint, he fitted fresh tyres and slammed round to record a 1m 31.123s, good enough to join Villeneuve on the front row.

Schumacher was well satisfied with third on the grid, two places ahead of Eddie Irvine. Michael reported that his F310B seemed to lose more time than expected during the slightly hotter conditions early in the session and he also ran out of fuel just after taking the chequered flag. Irvine, whose car required an engine change between sessions on Saturday, made some slight aerodynamic adjustments which he felt slightly improved his car's set-up.

It was a measure of McLaren's competitiveness that Coulthard and Häkkinen were slightly disappointed to end up in fourth and sixth places respectively. Mika was 0.6s up on what promised to be his best lap when he caught Magnussen's Stewart and lost crucial tenths, while Coulthard understeered wide on a corner after being 0.2s up at the first split.

Immediately behind Mika came Johnny Herbert, the Briton feeling upbeat and optimistic about the driveability and set-up of his Sauber C16. He had been fifth until the last-minute spurt, but even so was well satisfied. Larini lost time on his second set after being held up by one of the Minardis, then fell foul of Berger in the accident which stopped the session. Gerhard was suitably apologetic, but the F1 returnee had to face the start from 13th place on the grid.

In the Benetton camp, there was much head-scratching as Alesi and Berger emerged in eighth and tenth, neither driver able to get his B197's tyres up to working temperature. This was later rectified for the race after Nick Wirth confessed to 'a massive mistake' in set-up, believed to be excessively low ride height.

A similar lack of grip bugged both Jordans, Ralf Schumacher and Fisichella managing no better than 12th and 14th respectively, allowing Panis's Prost and Barrichello's Stewart to impress as the best-qualifying Bridgestone runners in ninth and 11th positions.

By contrast, Jan Magnussen lost a great raft of time early in qualifying when his Stewart developed a major water leak and he finished the session 1.5s slower than Rubens, a distant 19th on the grid, one place behind Salo's Tyrrell-Ford.

Katayama and Trulli qualified their Minardis just 0.4s apart, sandwiching Nakano's Prost, while Hill scrambled to squeeze in ahead of Verstappen's Tyrrell in 20th place. Hill's real problems had started on Saturday morning when his Arrows stopped out on the circuit. Since he couldn't select neutral, the session was red-flagged to a halt and the team were thereafter visited by a succession of officials checking that the car's clutch release system would work.

Somehow all this fiddling about damaged a seal in the system, so when the mechanics fired up Hill's car about ten minutes prior to the start of qualifying, the clutch would not engage. He switched to the spare car, wrongly set up as it transpired, and had to muscle his way into the race in a series of lurid twitches. It wasn't quite what he had been expecting.

Consolation for Arrows at least came in the form of Diniz being allowed into the race, even though he had failed to make the 107 per cent cut-off, since the stewards judged him well capable of lapping competitively. That was more than could be said for either of the untested Lola-Fords, both of which missed the grid by miles.

Michael Schumacher opened his championship challenge with a dogged second place after an unplanned fuel stop had ended his chances of victory.

Below left: Rubens Barrichello gave the ambitious new Stewart team some early encouragement with 11th place on the grid and also ran well in the race before retiring with engine trouble.

SO David Coulthard had to dye his hair silver after all! The Scot had made a deal with Mercedes-Benz motorsport manager Norbert Haug that he would sport the company's traditional racing livery if he scored his first victory at the wheel of a McLaren-Merc, but only a handful of committed believers would have wagered that Coulthard would see off both Williams and Ferrari in the first race of the year.

Just as the 1996 season had closed with victory for a British driver when Damon Hill clinched his championship crown, so Coulthard carried aloft his former team-mate's fallen standard in the first race of the new campaign. It was Coulthard's second Grand Prix victory and the first for McLaren in 50 races, since the revered Ayrton Senna blitzed the pack at Adelaide at the end of 1993.

Coulthard's success admittedly came

Paul-Henri Cahier

after Jacques Villeneuve – who had celebrated the first anniversary of his F1 debut with another stunning pole position 1.7s ahead of the pack – was rowed out of the equation in a first-corner collision. Yet to describe the Scot's win as lucky would be unfair. His MP4/12 was a consistent front-runner throughout the race, led more laps than any of the opposition and saw off firm challenges from both Michael Schumacher and Heinz-Harald Frentzen in the closing stages of the contest.

Coulthard was followed home by Schumacher's Ferrari F310B and Mika Häkkinen in the second McLaren, a result which catapulted Ron Dennis's team into a commanding constructors' championship lead. In a remarkable reversal of recent form, neither of the dominant Williams-Renaults made it to the finish, new boy Frentzen spinning out of second place when an

overtaxed brake disc exploded with three laps left to run.

Hill's debut outing for Arrows ended before it had started when his Arrows A18 suffered a malfunctioning throttle sensor and ground to a halt on the warm-up lap, rounding off a difficult weekend during which it had briefly looked as though he might struggle to make the 107 per cent qualifying cut.

At the start Villeneuve had squandered his qualifying advantage by making a poor getaway from pole position, allowing Frentzen to accelerate straight into an immediate lead – and out of trouble. Villeneuve moved in behind his team-mate, but as the Williams duo moved over to the left to take the racing line into the first right-hander Eddie Irvine found it impossible to resist the temptation of an inside dive in a bid for glory.

Unfortunately the Ulsterman came in too quickly on a tight line, locked

up on the dust and elbowed both Jacques and Johnny Herbert's Sauber-Petronas into the gravel trap on the outside of the corner. 'It was just three into one,' he said. 'It was my corner. I don't feel guilty about it, but everybody has their own opinion. People assume if you have tyre smoke, you're out of control.' That, of course, was his critics' very point.

'I let the clutch slip too much at the start,' admitted Villeneuve, 'but I was still OK in second or third place. Then Eddie just braked far too late on the inside of me. I just ended up pushing Johnny off because Eddie was pushing me off.'

Irvine remained resolutely unabashed by the incident, shrugging aside his responsibility for the pile-up. This was not a standpoint which cut much ice with the frustrated Herbert, who graphically recalled how Irvine's indiscipline had similarly

wiped him out at the first corner of the '94 Italian GP.

'The idiot screwed it up again,' said Johnny. 'It just annoys me that he won't admit that he's done anything wrong. I just wish he would sometimes think what he's doing.' At least Irvine failed to profit from his over-ambitious move, having cut his left-front tyre against Villeneuve's right front wing end plate and rolled to a standstill on the exit of the turn.

All this drama allowed Frentzen to get away comfortably at the head of the field, the German driver completing the opening lap already a couple of seconds ahead of Coulthard, with Schumacher third followed by Häkkinen, Alesi, Berger, Panis, Larini, Ralf Schumacher, Fisichella and Barrichello.

Acute concern about brake wear levels had prompted Williams to opt for a two-stop strategy and, with most

Photos: Paul-Henri Cahier

of its rivals taking the one-stop view, Frentzen duly pulled away commandingly in the opening stages. With six laps completed Frentzen was 10.5s in front and the German was 17.6s ahead by lap 13 with Coulthard and Schumacher in tight formation behind, and Häkkinen a further 7.1s back in fourth.

The problem facing Williams was the added grip provided by the latest generation of soft-compound Goodyear rubber and the team had only one type of brake disc available at this race. They tried to counter the problem by running larger cooling ducts but this, and their one-stop strategy, was not quite sufficient to keep them out of trouble.

After a dozen or so laps, Häkkinen in turn was being caught by the two Benettons and at the same time Panis was steadily making ground on Alesi and Berger, with the result that by lap 15 these four contenders were running pretty well nose to tail. By this time Ralf Schumacher and Jos Verstappen had joined the list of casualties, the Jordan pirouetting into a gravel trap on the second lap due to a driveshaft joint problem, while Verstappen

plunged off the road after a run-in with Katayama's Minardi.

On lap 15, the second Jordan went missing as Fisichella attempted to repass Barrichello's Stewart and also flew into a gravel trap, rounding off a bitterly disappointing outing for the Silverstone-based team.

At the end of lap 18, Frentzen made his first scheduled pit stop, dropping to third behind Coulthard and Schumacher, and at the same time Panis came in, dropping from seventh to ninth. Coulthard and Schumacher were now left circulating in first and second places, barely half a second apart, with the Scot displaying admirable resilience to any challenge the Ferrari ace seemed able to throw at him.

Panis's first stop promoted Larini's Sauber to seventh, but when the Italian came in at the end of lap 28 the Prost moved back to head the chase for sixth place. On lap 30 Berger came in for fuel, dropping to seventh, Schumacher brought the Ferrari in on lap 31, dropping from second to fifth, and then the Benetton pit prepared itself for Alesi's scheduled arrival.

What followed was the most remarkable episode of the entire weekend. Totally embroiled in his chase of Häkkinen, Jean repeatedly ignored his pit signals to come in, climbing briefly to second when Coulthard and Häkkinen made their routine single stops on laps 33 and 34. Despite Benetton chief designer Nick Wirth literally being hung over the pit wall by his legs in a final attempt to attract Alesi's attention, Jean pressed on into lap 35 only to run out of fuel on the circuit.

'I am obviously extremely disappointed,' he later commented in a crestfallen mood. 'I had a very good start and was having a very good race. I lost radio contact with the team and did not realise that it was time for me to come into the pits for refuelling. I came to a stop, and it was a terrible feeling to waste the race for such a silly reason.'

Flavio Briatore controlled his annoyance when it came to commenting publicly about his driver's latest *faux pas*. 'It's a pity for Jean,' he noted wryly. Behind closed doors he was less understanding and Alesi finished the

afternoon in tears, having been told his fortune in the most singularly direct and uncompromising manner.

Coulthard's refuelling stop allowed Frentzen to surge past into an 18.7s lead which he duly expanded to 26 seconds before it was time for him to make his second stop at the end of lap 40. It was touch and go whether he would be able to retain his lead, but his strategy went out of the window when the Williams mechanics had a problem removing the right-rear wheel. He was stationary for 16.4s as a result and resumed a frustrated third behind Coulthard and Schumacher.

David now led the race by a couple of seconds with Frentzen a further five seconds back, but the Williams now clearly the quickest car on the circuit. Gradually Frentzen eased himself closer to the Ferrari, but it was one thing making up ground on his old rival, clearly quite another finding the opportunity to duck past – particularly in a situation where the Williams brakes were so marginal.

Yet on lap 51 another wild card was

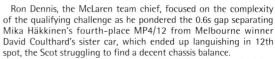

At the end of Friday's free practice session at Interlagos, it seemed as though the Williams team had reapplied its familiar stranglehold to the sharp end of the Formula 1 business. The day ended with Heinz-Harald Frentzen just pipping Jacques Villeneuve to fastest time over the punishingly bumpy Interlagos circuit.

Yet with the crucial hour-long battle for qualifying positions reserved for Saturday afternoon, Friday's practice sessions have increasingly become unpredictable and misleading barometers of form.

Third fastest in this first session was Jean Alesi's Benetton, although the Frenchman's efforts to atone for running his car out of fuel in Melbourne were dented when he spun into the pit wall, damaging the front suspension and rear wing.

Johnny Herbert's Sauber wound up fourth fastest, only 0.7s away from Frentzen's Williams, while Australian GP winner David Coulthard was a cautious eighth in his McLaren-Mercedes. This put him only one place ahead of Damon Hill's Arrows, the World Champion ending the day in a remarkably upbeat mood despite spinning off during the morning session when his throttle stuck open.

Yet come Saturday afternoon, in qualifying trim with a low fuel load, Frentzen couldn't get the FW19 to his liking and began to over-drive, a strategy which simply heightened his dilemma on a day when a wafer-thin 1.1s covered the first ten cars on the grid. Later it was found that his car had a duff left-front damper, increasing his frustration and sense of desperation. But it couldn't alter the fact that he ended the session a dismal eighth on the grid.

Frentzen's difficulties graphically illustrated the new challenge involved in selecting a race tyre after Saturday free practice and then matching it to the best possible chassis set-up for both qualifying and the race.

The gap separating Frentzen from Villeneuve was only 0.9s, but that was enough to put Jacques on pole position by 0.5s from Michael Schumacher's Ferrari F310B. Jacques did his pole-winning best of 1m 16.004s only 17 minutes into the hour-long session, thereafter switching to the spare FW19 after his race machine developed a water leak.

'The spare car was set up for Heinz and it took a while to get it ready for me,' he later explained. 'The set-ups for the race and qualifying were not exactly the same, but it was OK.' Not that Jacques need have worried, because Schumacher Senior simply couldn't get close.

Michael was one of several drivers who found themselves slightly wrong-footed when the red flag came out with ten minutes of the session left after Giancarlo Fisichella crashed his Jordan quite heavily into the tyre barriers at the bottom of the hill before the left-hander which leads onto the start/finish straight.

Just as in Melbourne, this left time for just a single flying lap for all those competitors who wanted to give it a go before it was time for the chequered flag to be shown. As things transpired, Pedro Diniz was the only driver to improve his time during that final sprint, moving up to 16th place on the grid.

Schumacher was not too disappointed. 'To be honest, I am surprised that the gap between Jacques and I is so small,' he grinned. 'The car has actually behaved better over the bumps than I expected. We have made significant progress with the chassis set-up since yesterday.'

His team-mate Eddie Irvine was markedly less satisfied with 14th place on the grid. Both Ferrari drivers had opted for the harder of the two available Goodyear compounds prior to qualifying and Eddie felt he couldn't really 'lean' sufficiently hard on the car without losing front- or rear-end grip. 'But it works better with a heavier fuel load, which is encouraging for the race,' he added.

In the Benetton camp set-up changes on the B197s since Australia had improved things considerably. Slightly raised ride height made for a more impressive showing at Interlagos and, despite a spin, Gerhard Berger qualified third on 1m 16.644s. Jean Alesi was back in sixth place, slightly disappointed about his absolute performance, but content at least to have had a trouble-free run.

Ron Dennis, the McLaren team chief, focused on the complexity of the qualifying challenge as he pondered the 0.6s gap separating Mika Häkkinen's fourth-place MP4/12 from Melbourne winner David Coulthard's sister car, which ended up languishing in 12th spot, the Scot struggling to find a decent chassis balance.

'When you have a grid as compacted as this, the tyre is doing most of the work,' he said. 'The potential of the cars becomes clear as more laps come off the tyres. Our strategy so far has really been to work hard on the car in the condition in which it is going to race, and the requirements of the car in that condition are different from those needed to optimise the qualifying performance.

'Sometimes you just get it wrong and end up going too far towards a race set-up when you need to be closer to its qualifying requirements.'

Behind Häkkinen, Olivier Panis's Prost lined up in an impressive fifth place, a particularly satisfying performance after his Mugen V10 broke during the morning's free practice session and the team had to install a fresh unit for qualifying.

Despite his qualifying accident, Fisichella did well to take seventh place only 0.2s behind Alesi, but Ralf Schumacher was extremely disappointed not to have bettered tenth place. The young German lost valuable time with hydraulic fluid leaks on both Friday and Saturday morning, then finished the qualifying hour in a very angry mood. Ironically, his best lap had been spoilt by the red flags signalling his team-mate's accident and he then accused Irvine of blocking him.

In ninth place, only 0.1s behind Frentzen, Damon Hill could have been forgiven for a wry smile of satisfaction after his efforts in the Arrows A18. It was the pay-off for a weekend which had started on a lurid note when a sticking throttle propelled him into a gravel trap in Friday free practice. Modifications to the engine airbox and general improvements in the A18's set-up paid off with a grid position which lifted the spirits of the entire team.

Hill, team-mate Diniz, Magnussen, Coulthard and Frentzen all had at least one of their flying laps during qualifying disallowed because they had strayed across the white line delineating the entrance to the pit lane on the fast left-hander before the start/finish line. Thankfully, none of these penalties affected the overall grid position.

Stewart-Ford boss Jackie Stewart had promised a top-of-the-range Rolex wristwatch to whichever of his drivers first qualified in the top ten. Rubens Barrichello came close, but was eventually bumped back to 11th by Ralf Schumacher.

'I tried like hell on my last flying lap,' said Rubens. 'The car was on the limit, but the time just didn't come – I was a bit disappointed when I saw it.' Both he and team-mate Jan Magnussen had a revised Ford Zetec-R V10, revving to 16,700 rpm, available for qualifying, but the young Dane had a roll bar failure on Friday and generally struggled to get the best out of his SF1, trailing in 20th place.

The best Sauber's Johnny Herbert could manage in qualifying was a disappointing 13th overall. 'For some reason we just couldn't find the form we had this morning,' he shrugged. 'The car felt nervous under braking and over the bumps, and I couldn't maintain the rhythm in my driving. It's very confusing, especially as I was initially as quick as Michael this morning.'

Team-mate Nicola Larini was left down in 19th place, handicapped by too much rearward brake bias, which pitched him into a spin. 'With my lack of experience, I feel I'm making too many mistakes trying to push hard to make up the deficit,' he said.

Behind Irvine came Shinji Nakano's Prost in 15th place, then Diniz and the cool Jarno Trulli's Minardi, just ahead of team-mate Ukyo Katayama. Behind Larini and Magnussen the two Tyrrell 025s lined up together on the last row of the grid, Jos Verstappen getting the better of Mika Salo on this occasion.

have a driveshaft problem. Herbert took the spare Sauber C16, Fisichella the spare Jordan, Ferrari mechanics shoehorned Irvine into Schumacher's spare F310B and everybody lined up to try getting through the first corner again.

At the restart it was Ukyo Katayama's turn to have problems, the Japanese driver stalling his Minardi and eventually joining in several laps down. At the head of the field it was Schumacher who again just squeezed into the first corner ahead, but Villeneuve was all over him like a rash and, as they came up the hill to complete the opening lap, Jacques just pulled out and surged past the Ferrari as if it was standing still.

In third place was Häkkinen's McLaren pursued by Berger, Alesi,

DIARY

Ford reveals that it will make customer Zetec-R V10 engines available to other teams from the start of 1998, although Stewart Grand Prix will retain superior specification unit as the designated works Ford runner.

Provisional 'agreement to reach an agreement' ending the Williams, Tyrrell and McLaren teams' position as non-signatories to the 1997 Concorde Agreement reached at meetings behind closed doors over the Brazilian GP weekend. Resolution of this long-running problem would give the three entrants a share in the enhanced television revenues already enjoyed by the other seven signatories.

Benetton tipped to be close to an agreement to use Mecachrome-prepared Renault V10 engines for the 1998 and '99 F1 championship seasons.

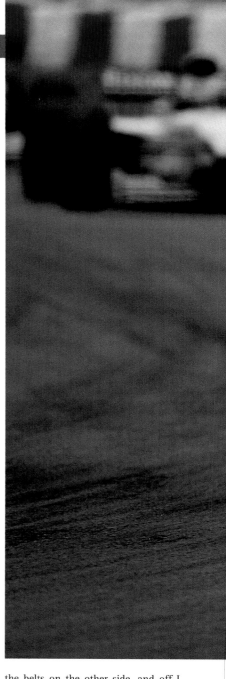

Damon Hill leads David Coulthard and the Jordan-Peugeots of Giancarlo Fisichella and Ralf Schumacher. A single-stop strategy helped the World Champion work his way up to fourth place in the first half of the race.

Lola reaches the end of the F1 road

THE Lola F1 team withdrew from the 1997 World Championship after only a single race where neither of its Ford V8-engined cars driven by Ricardo Rosset and Vincenzo Sospiri managed to qualify. The team's T97/30s were already in the paddock at Interlagos, together with all the necessary personnel, when word came from England that they were to pack up and return home as quickly as possible.

Cash-flow difficulties were at the root of the problem and it seems that Eric Broadley acted promptly – some suggested prematurely – to prevent costs running out of control in the absence of sufficient immediate sponsorship.

'We have met every manufacturing deadline asked of us so far,' said Broadley, 'but the demands of the ongoing programme must be matched by our funding streams and this was just not forthcoming presently.'

Lola's F1 backing was scheduled to be generated from a complex promotion involving a fan club for MasterCard holders. However, the time and complexity involved in establishing this meant that Lola faced delays in receiving its sponsorship payments. Broadley felt this was unacceptable and instead chose to pull the plug on what had become his pet project.

Tentative plans were subsequently mooted in an effort to get the Lola F1 operation back on the road in time for the San Marino GP at Imola, with both Sospiri and Rosset attempting to raise the necessary backing. Yet the harsh facts of the matter were that once Lola had missed the Brazilian GP, they were effectively dead in the water as far as the FIA World Championship was concerned.

If they could not afford to continue racing, it was difficult to imagine how they would be able to meet the $500,000 per car fine imposed by the FIA on any team which missed even a single race.

briefly back into second place, but the Ferrari came in – together with brother Ralf and race leader Villeneuve – at the end of lap 26.

Jacques had been 23 seconds ahead by this point in the race and the Williams crew managed to get him back into the fray still nursing a 1.3s advantage over Panis, whose durable Bridgestones enabled him to run a one-stop strategy and stay out until half-distance before making his sole pit visit.

Hill, meanwhile, was doing much the same, gradually moving up to fourth place by lap 27 as the faster Goodyear-shod cars in front of him progressively made their first refuelling stops. He was privately surprised that Coulthard, next in line behind him, hadn't been able to coax his McLaren close enough to the Arrows to make any sort of overtaking bid. 'I really think he should have been able to do that,' said Damon later.

Even less impressed with Coulthard's performance was Giancarlo Fisichella, the Italian irked by the way in which the McLaren driver had squeezed him towards the pit wall on a couple of occasions as he attempted to slingshot the Jordan ahead. Tellingly, both Jordans immediately lapped 1.5s quicker when Coulthard peeled off for his first refuelling stop!

Lumbering along behind Fisichella and Ralf Schumacher was Frentzen, simply unable to make any worthwhile progress in the Williams, while Irvine was having an excruciatingly painful ride in the second Ferrari F310B owing to an ill-fitting harness.

He duly made his first stop on lap 24, dropping from 11th to 16th, but finally came back in 11 laps later to see if something could be done to alleviate his discomfort.

'I had to jump into Michael's [spare] car after the first-corner shunt and the mechanics changed most things, but the belts didn't fit,' he explained.

'We could only get one belt done up, so I was moving around a lot at the start of the race. It got to the stage that it was really painful. I didn't realise, but at one stage, I came on the radio and told them that it was becoming very difficult and that I might be coming into the pits.

'I forgot to switch the radio off, and when I was braking, I was screaming my head off, I was in so much pain, and I didn't realise they were all in the pits listening to me. They must have thought I was having orgasms or something, at the excitement of the race. But that wasn't the case.

'The belts were too short for me, so we had to come in and do up one of

the belts on the other side, and off I went again. It was the worst pain I think I've ever had.'

Panis also stopped on lap 35, the Prost resuming in seventh place. Villeneuve now led by 13.9s from Berger, Häkkinen was third and Hill – who was to stop three laps later – fourth. Then came Michael Schumacher's Ferrari, Alesi and Panis.

Damon's stop dropped him to 13th place, then Häkkinen came in at the end of lap 39, slipping back to eighth. With 40 laps completed Villeneuve was running about 12 seconds ahead, but after Jacques and Gerhard made their second stops – on laps 45 and 48 respectively – the Benetton really began to make inroads into Jacques's advantage.

Admittedly, with only 25 laps left to run, Villeneuve was in a position to dictate the race and didn't have to take any unnecessary risks. But Berger was right on form and piled on the pressure as the race ran out to its conclusion. Jacques later admitted that he was braking a few metres early in the closing stages – he reported that his final set of tyres was 'pretty bad' – and things might have been very tight if Gerhard had been a little closer.

At the end of the day, Villeneuve kept control to win by 4.19s, but

Panis, Hill, Coulthard, the Jordans of Fisichella and Ralf Schumacher, Herbert and Barrichello. By the end of the second lap Villeneuve had opened a 1.1s advantage over Schumacher's Ferrari, and the Canadian was 2.2s ahead on lap three and a decisive 3.7s in front by the end of lap five.

On lap four, Berger burst ahead of Häkkinen and settled down to nibble away at the second-place Ferrari which was only 0.5s in front of his Benetton. Alesi and Panis now moved onto Häkkinen's tail, while Hill's seventh-placed Arrows was storming along at the head of a six-car train comprising Coulthard, the two Jordans, Frentzen and Herbert, with Barrichello and Irvine not far behind in the next two places.

Villeneuve looked pretty confident at the head of the pack, but, as he later admitted, he was not without his problems. 'The brakes were very soft throughout the whole race,' he explained. 'Compared with the warm-up, the rear brakes were somehow locking up quite a lot, and I had to adapt to that. Apart from that, there was nothing major.'

By the end of lap nine, Berger had successfully hauled his Benetton tight onto Schumacher's tail. He took a couple of runs at the Ferrari in an effort to

get by coming past the pits, finally making it stick at the start of lap 12. But by now he was almost ten seconds down on Villeneuve and faced an uphill struggle if he was going to be in a position to make a bid for the lead.

On lap 16 Diniz spun off and was unable to continue, while at the end of that same lap Barrichello came limping into the pits with the spare Stewart, worried that there was something wrong at the rear of the car.

'I had been running well,' said the Brazilian, 'but I had to let Frentzen and Herbert go past on the straight. I was hanging on until I started feeling the problem with the rear suspension, and after a few laps I thought it was better to stop and check.' Close examination revealed that a toe-link bracket had broken in the right-rear suspension, so he undid his belts and the car was pushed away.

Next time round, Sauber brought Herbert's C16 in for a tactically astute early first stop which had the effect of vaulting him from 12th to eighth place at the end of lap 29, by which time most of his immediate rivals had made their first refuelling stops.

Coulthard came in on lap 21, Berger and Larini on lap 22, Alesi on lap 23 and Häkkinen and Irvine on lap 24. Berger's first stop allowed Schumacher

Darren Heath

Berger's morale had been boosted substantially by his late-race charge. 'Until now, the Williams has still been ahead,' he said. 'This race shows the difference in performance between our cars a little better. I had rather the same problem with tyres in the middle of the race that Jacques had. It was fine in the end, but seven or eight laps from the finish there was a problem with back-markers – Damon and two others – and it was difficult to overtake them.

'It was one of those situations where you can't take risks everywhere because you don't want to lose second place. But on the other hand, the only way to try for first place was to put pressure on Jacques. I tried my best, but I just couldn't do it.'

If second place for Benetton – backed up by Alesi coming home sixth – was a cause for celebration, Olivier Panis's third place in the Prost-Mugen Honda was every bit as impressive a performance from the French team. At the chequered flag, Panis was only 15.8s behind Villeneuve and 11.6s behind Berger. It also confirmed that Bridgestone's relentless F1 progress was being maintained.

The French driver was delighted with the performance of his tyres, but paid tribute to new team owner Alain Prost, the four-times World Champion,

who concluded that a single-pit stop strategy was the best way of producing a good result.

'Alain is a great champion,' said Panis. 'He has lots of experience at every circuit and with many cars. I settled the car set-up with my engineer, and when we were discussing strategy it was Alain who pushed for one stop.

'I pushed for it, too, because the tyre wear figures were fantastic, both in qualifying and again in the warm-up on race morning.'

Hill, whose Arrows-Yamaha ran as high as fourth before making its single pit stop only to retire with four laps left when a terminal oil leak triggered an engine bay fire, echoed Panis's sentiments. 'The Bridgestone performance is very encouraging,' he said. 'At this stage they are taking things quite conservatively, I suspect, because they naturally do not want to be seen to have any obvious problems.

'On Sunday the tyres were almost hard enough to go a full distance on a single set of rubber. But when we get back to Europe I think they might be a little more ambitious. I am very optimistic.'

Häkkinen's fourth place for McLaren was less than the Finn had been expecting. Mika found his tyre performance deteriorating and made an early second stop on lap 39 – about six laps

or so before most of his immediate rivals. That left him struggling for grip in the closing miles of the race and he only just squeezed home 0.69s ahead of Schumacher's fifth-place Ferrari.

Nevertheless, Mika's performance at least ensured that McLaren retained the constructors' championship points lead for the moment, although Coulthard's tenth place was extremely disappointing.

Schumacher's Ferrari had rejoined the race seventh after its second refuelling stop on lap 45, but the F310Bs were running with a touch too much aerodynamic downforce, thereby compromising their straightline speed, and he could only make up further ground when his rivals ahead made their own stops.

'Our biggest problem was a lack of mechanical grip,' he reported. 'Just as I expected, our tyres did not maintain their performance level over the whole race and I had a job getting past Hill [after Michael's first stop] as his tyres were still in top condition.'

Alesi was at least happy to have kept his nose clean following the Melbourne débâcle where he ignored signals to come in for a refuelling stop. Behind the Benetton, Johnny Herbert's Sauber had been steadily making ground, but as its fuel load went down the Englishman found it handling

more nervously over the bumps and had to settle for seventh.

'The car was pretty good on full tanks,' said Herbert, 'and thanks to the team reading the development of the race so well, and changing the pit stop strategy accordingly, then doing some great pit work, I managed to get past all the cars that were ahead of me in our bunch early in the race.'

Fisichella drove well to eighth place but Frentzen seemed to have no answers to his distinctly average performance in the second Williams. Ninth place was simply not good enough, even allowing for the fact that he was grappling with sticking gearchange paddles in the closing stages of the race.

Behind Coulthard's tenth-place McLaren, Larini's Sauber headed home Trulli's Minardi, Salo, Nakano, Verstappen and Irvine – the Ulsterman happy that the nightmare had ended.

Jacques Villeneuve had certainly put Williams back in familiar territory with the team's first win of the season. Apart from that first-corner slip, Jacques finished the day looking every inch the World Championship favourite. Yet Benetton and Prost had both signalled that the season might not be quite the easy ride for Williams that some commentators had predicted. Not quite.

GRANDE PREMIO DO
BRASIL
28–30 MARCH 1997
INTERLAGOS

Race distance: 72 laps, 192.024 miles/309.024 km

Race weather: Humid, overcast

FIA FORMULA 1 WORLD CHAMPIONSHIP

ROUND 2

AUTODROMO JOSE CARLOS PACE, INTERLAGOS, SÃO PAULO

SUBIDA DO LAGO — CURVA DO SOL — DESCIDA DO SOL — BICO DE PATO — MERGULHO — PINHEIRINHO — FERRA DURA — SUBIDA DOS BOXES

CIRCUIT LENGTH: 2.667 MILES/4.292 KM

Pos.	Driver	Nat.	No.	Entrant	Car/Engine	Tyres	Laps	Time/Retirement	Speed (mph/km/h)
1	Jacques Villeneuve	CDN	3	Rothmans Williams Renault	Williams FW19-Renault RS9 V10	G	72	1h 36m 06.990s	119.865/192.905
2	Gerhard Berger	A	8	Mild Seven Benetton Renault	Benetton B197-Renault RS9 V10	G	72	1h 36m 11.180s	119.778/192.765
3	Olivier Panis	F	14	Prost Gauloises Blondes	Prost JS45-Mugen Honda MF301HA V10	B	72	1h 36m 22.860s	119.537/192.376
4	Mika Häkkinen	SF	9	West McLaren Mercedes	McLaren MP4/12-Mercedes FO110E V10	G	72	1h 36m 40.023s	119.183/191.807
5	Michael Schumacher	D	5	Scuderia Ferrari Marlboro	Ferrari F310B 046 V10	G	72	1h 36m 40.721s	119.169/191.784
6	Jean Alesi	F	7	Mild Seven Benetton Renault	Benetton B197-Renault RS9 V10	G	72	1h 36m 41.010s	119.163/191.774
7	Johnny Herbert	GB	16	Red Bull Sauber Petronas	Sauber C16-Petronas V10	G	72	1h 36m 57.902s	118.816/191.217
8	Giancarlo Fisichella	I	12	B&H Total Jordan Peugeot	Jordan 197-Peugeot A14 V10	G	72	1h 37m 07.629s	118.618/190.898
9	Heinz-Harald Frentzen	D	4	Rothmans Williams Renault	Williams FW19-Renault RS9 V10	G	72	1h 37m 22.392s	118.319/190.416
10	David Coulthard	GB	10	West McLaren Mercedes	McLaren MP4/12-Mercedes FO110E V10	G	71		
11	Nicola Larini	I	17	Red Bull Sauber Petronas	Sauber C16-Petronas V10	G	71		
12	Jarno Trulli	I	21	Minardi Team	Minardi M197-Hart 830 V8	B	71		
13	Mika Salo	SF	19	Tyrrell	Tyrrell 025-Ford ED4 V8	G	71		
14	Shinji Nakano	J	15	Prost Gauloises Blondes	Prost JS45-Mugen Honda MF301HA V10	B	71		
15	Jos Verstappen	NL	18	Tyrrell	Tyrrell 025-Ford ED4 V8	G	70		
16	Eddie Irvine	GB	6	Scuderia Ferrari Marlboro	Ferrari F310B 046 V10	G	70		
17	Damon Hill	GB	1	Danka Arrows Yamaha	Arrows A18-Yamaha OX11A/C V10	B	68	Engine fire	
18	Ukyo Katayama	J	20	Minardi Team	Minardi M197-Hart 830 V8	B	67		
	Ralf Schumacher	D	11	B&H Total Jordan Peugeot	Jordan 197-Peugeot A14 V10	G	52	Electrics	
	Rubens Barrichello	BR	22	Stewart Ford	Stewart SF1-Ford Zetec-R V10	B	16	Suspension	
	Pedro Diniz	BR	2	Danka Arrows Yamaha	Arrows A18-Yamaha OX11A/C V10	B	15	Spun off	
DNS	Jan Magnussen	DK	23	Stewart Ford	Stewart SF1-Ford Zetec-R V10	B	0	Accident at first start	
DNP	Vincenzo Sospiri	I	24	Mastercard Lola F1 Team	Lola T97/30-Ford Zetec-R V8	B			
DNP	Ricardo Rosset	BR	25	Mastercard Lola F1 Team	Lola T97/30-Ford Zetec-R V8	B			

Fastest lap: Villeneuve, on lap 28, 1m 18.397s, 122.465 mph/197.089 km/h (record on new lap length).

Previous lap record: Michael Schumacher (F1 Benetton B194-Ford V8), 1m 18.455s, 123.315 mph/198.457 km/h (1994).

B – Bridgestone   G – Goodyear

Grid order	1	2	3	4	5	6	7	8	9	10	11	12	13	14	15	16	17	18	19	20	21	22	23	24	25	26	27	28	29	30	31	32	33	34	35	36	37	38	39	40	41	42	43	44	45	46	47	48	49	50	51	52	53	54	55	56
3 VILLENEUVE	3	3	3	3	3	3	3	3	3	3	3	3	3	3	3	3	3	3	3	3	3	3	3	3	3	3	3	3	3	3	3	3	3	3	3	3	3	3	3	3	3	3	3	3	3	3	8	8	8	3	3	3	3	3	3	3
5 M. SCHUMACHER	5	5	5	5	5	5	5	5	5	5	5	8	8	8	8	8	8	8	8	8	8	8	5	5	5	14	14	14	14	14	14	14	14	8	8	8	8	8	8	8	8	8	3	3	3	8	8	8	8	8	8	8	8	8	8	8
8 BERGER	9	9	9	8	8	8	8	8	8	8	8	5	5	5	5	5	5	5	5	5	5	9	14	14	5	8	8	8	8	8	8	8	8	14	9	9	9	9	5	5	5	5	7	14	14	14	14	14	14	14	14	14	14	14	14	14
9 HÄKKINEN	8	8	8	9	9	9	9	9	9	9	9	9	9	9	9	9	9	9	9	9	9	14	9	8	8	1	1	1	1	1	9	9	9	1	1	5	5	7	7	7	7	7	5	7	4	9	9	9	9	9	9	9	9	9	9	9
14 PANIS	7	7	7	7	7	7	7	7	7	7	7	7	7	7	7	7	7	7	7	7	7	8	1	4	9	9	9	9	1	1	1	1	5	5	7	7	14	14	14	14	14	4	9	5	5	5	5	5	5	5
7 ALESI	14	14	14	14	14	14	14	14	14	14	14	14	14	14	14	14	14	14	14	14	14	8	1	11	4	9	5	5	5	5	5	5	5	5	7	14	14	16	4	4	4	9	5	4	7	7	7	7	7	7
12 FISICHELLA	1	1	1	1	1	1	1	1	1	1	1	1	1	1	1	1	1	1	1	1	12	4	9	5	7	7	7	7	7	7	14	14	16	4	16	9	9	9	9	5	7	16	16	16	16	16	16	16	16
4 FRENTZEN	10	10	10	10	10	10	10	10	10	10	10	10	10	10	10	10	10	10	10	10	12	12	12	11	9	7	7	4	16	16	16	16	16	16	16	10	9	9	12	12	12	16	16	16	4	4	4	4	4	4
1 HILL	12	12	12	12	12	12	12	12	12	12	12	12	12	12	12	12	11	11	11	4	7	11	16	10	10	10	10	10	10	10	10	1	4	10	12	17	17	1	1	1	12	12	12	12	12
11 R. SCHUMACHER	11	11	11	11	11	11	11	11	11	11	11	11	11	11	11	11	4	4	7	12	16	10	10	11	11	11	11	11	11	11	12	12	17	16	16	1	10	10	12	12	1	1	1	1	10	10
22 BARRICHELLO	16	16	4	4	4	4	4	4	4	4	4	4	4	4	4	4	4	17	6	6	15	10	15	11	4	4	4	4	4	4	4	11	17	1	1	1	12	10	10	10	10	10	10	1
10 COULTHARD	22	4	16	16	16	16	16	16	16	16	16	16	16	16	16	16	17	7	10	17	15	15	16	16	16	4	4	4	4	4	1	10	10	12	11	11	11	11	11	11	11	17	17	17
16 HERBERT	4	22	22	22	22	22	22	22	22	22	22	22	22	17	16	6	6	6	15	21	16	10	21	11	21	12	15	15	15	17	17	17	1	11	11	11	11	11	11	17	17	17	21	21	21
6 IRVINE	21	6	6	6	6	6	2	2	2	2	2	2	2	17	6	6	15	15	15	21	16	21	17	17	17	17	17	17	15	15	19	19	19	19	19	21	21	21	21	21	21	21	19	19	19
15 NAKANO	6	2	2	2	2	2	6	6	6	17	17	17	2	15	21	21	21	16	10	10	17	12	12	21	21	21	21	19	19	21	21	21	19	19	18	18	19	19	19	19	15	15	15
2 DINIZ	2	17	17	17	17	17	17	17	6	6	6	21	18	18	16	16	10	17	7	6	6	6	6	6	21	18	18	18	18	18	18	15	15	15	5	6	15	18	18	18
21 TRULLI	17	21	15	15	15	15	15	15	15	15	15	15	19	19	19	19	19	18	18	18	15	15	15	15	15	15	15	15	6	6	15	15	6	6	6	6
20 KATAYAMA	15	15	21	21	21	21	21	21	21	21	21	22	18	16	7	7	18	19	19	19	19	18	18	18	18	18	6	6	18	18	6	18	18	18	20	20
17 LARINI	19	19	19	19	19	19	19	19	19	19	19	19	18	20	20	20	20	20	20	20	20	20	20	20	20	20	20	20	20	20	20	20	20
23 MAGNUSSEN	18	18	18	18	18	18	18	18	18	18	18	18	18	18	20
18 VERSTAPPEN	20	20	20	20	20	20	20	20	20	20	20	20	20	20
19 SALO																																												Pit stop											

STARTING GRID

5 **M. SCHUMACHER** Ferrari	3 **VILLENEUVE** Williams
9 **HÄKKINEN** McLaren	8 **BERGER** Benetton
7 **ALESI** Benetton	14 **PANIS** Prost
4 **FRENTZEN** Williams	12 **FISICHELLA** Jordan
11 **R. SCHUMACHER** Jordan	1 **HILL** Arrows
10 **COULTHARD** McLaren	22 **BARRICHELLO** Stewart
6 **IRVINE** Ferrari	16 **HERBERT** Sauber
2 **DINIZ** Arrows	15 **NAKANO** Prost
20 **KATAYAMA** Minardi	21 **TRULLI** Minardi
23 **MAGNUSSEN*** Stewart	17 **LARINI** Sauber
19 **SALO** Tyrrell	18 **VERSTAPPEN** Tyrrell

* did not take restart

TIME SHEETS

QUALIFYING

Weather: Sunny and hot

Pos.	Driver	Car	Laps	Time
1	Jacques Villeneuve	Williams-Renault	9	1m 16.004s
2	Michael Schumacher	Ferrari	11	1m 16.594s
3	Gerhard Berger	Benetton-Renault	10	1m 16.644s
4	Mika Häkkinen	McLaren-Mercedes	10	1m 16.692s
5	Olivier Panis	Prost-Mugen Honda	12	1m 16.756s
6	Jean Alesi	Benetton-Renault	10	1m 16.757s
7	Giancarlo Fisichella	Jordan-Peugeot	10	1m 16.912s
8	Heinz-Harald Frentzen	Williams-Renault	10	1m 16.924s
9	Damon Hill	Arrows-Yamaha	12	1m 17.090s
10	Ralf Schumacher	Jordan-Peugeot	11	1m 17.175s
11	Rubens Barrichello	Stewart-Ford	12	1m 17.259s
12	David Coulthard	McLaren-Mercedes	11	1m 17.262s
13	Johnny Herbert	Sauber-Petronas	12	1m 17.409s
14	Eddie Irvine	Ferrari	11	1m 17.527s
15	Shinji Nakano	Prost-Mugen Honda	10	1m 17.999s
16	Pedro Diniz	Arrows-Yamaha	12	1m 18.095s
17	Jarno Trulli	Minardi-Hart	12	1m 18.336s
18	Ukyo Katayama	Minardi-Hart	11	1m 18.557s
19	Nicola Larini	Sauber-Petronas	11	1m 18.644s
20	Jan Magnussen	Stewart-Ford	12	1m 18.773s
21	Jos Verstappen	Tyrrell-Ford	11	1m 18.885s
22	Mika Salo	Tyrrell-Ford	9	1m 19.272s

FRIDAY FREE PRACTICE

Weather: Sunny and hot

Pos.	Driver	Laps	Time
1	Heinz-Harald Frentzen	29	1m 17.506s
2	Jacques Villeneuve	30	1m 17.829s
3	Jean Alesi	27	1m 18.000s
4	Johnny Herbert	30	1m 18.261s
5	Gerhard Berger	22	1m 18.437s
6	Ralf Schumacher	30	1m 18.479s
7	Michael Schumacher	30	1m 18.488s
8	David Coulthard	28	1m 18.818s
9	Damon Hill	27	1m 18.978s
10	Mika Häkkinen	23	1m 19.271s
11	Giancarlo Fisichella	30	1m 19.326s
12	Olivier Panis	30	1m 19.408s
13	Mika Salo	30	1m 19.546s
14	Pedro Diniz	27	1m 19.573s
15	Rubens Barrichello	25	1m 19.613s
16	Ukyo Katayama	25	1m 19.963s
17	Jos Verstappen	29	1m 20.076s
18	Shinji Nakano	30	1m 20.520s
19	Jarno Trulli	29	1m 20.521s
20	Eddie Irvine	14	1m 20.787s
21	Nicola Larini	16	1m 21.120s
22	Jan Magnussen	20	1m 21.864s

SATURDAY FREE PRACTICE

Weather: Sunny and hot

Pos.	Driver	Laps	Time
1	Jacques Villeneuve	26	1m 16.030s
2	Mika Häkkinen	27	1m 16.205s
3	Gerhard Berger	28	1m 16.517s
4	Jean Alesi	26	1m 16.588s
5	Heinz-Harald Frentzen	25	1m 16.611s
6	Michael Schumacher	30	1m 16.720s
7	David Coulthard	27	1m 16.820s
8	Ralf Schumacher	15	1m 16.833s
9	Rubens Barrichello	28	1m 17.148s
10	Giancarlo Fisichella	30	1m 17.192s
11	Damon Hill	26	1m 17.490s
12	Johnny Herbert	26	1m 17.587s
13	Eddie Irvine	28	1m 17.635s
14	Pedro Diniz	30	1m 17.795s
15	Nicola Larini	28	1m 17.934s
16	Jarno Trulli	21	1m 18.043s
17	Olivier Panis	14	1m 18.089s
18	Mika Salo	27	1m 18.181s
19	Shinji Nakano	24	1m 18.283s
20	Ukyo Katayama	26	1m 18.318s
21	Jos Verstappen	29	1m 18.473s
22	Jan Magnussen	23	1m 18.630s

WARM-UP

Weather: Sunny and hot

Pos.	Driver	Laps	Time
1	Jacques Villeneuve	14	1m 17.421s
2	Mika Häkkinen	11	1m 17.642s
3	Olivier Panis	14	1m 17.800s
4	Johnny Herbert	18	1m 17.843s
5	Heinz-Harald Frentzen	15	1m 17.866s
6	Damon Hill	15	1m 17.973s
7	Jean Alesi	12	1m 18.034s
8	David Coulthard	14	1m 18.313s
9	Michael Schumacher	17	1m 18.316s
10	Gerhard Berger	10	1m 18.358s
11	Giancarlo Fisichella	17	1m 18.563s
12	Ralf Schumacher	16	1m 18.630s
13	Rubens Barrichello	16	1m 18.743s
14	Eddie Irvine	11	1m 18.879s
15	Mika Salo	15	1m 19.088s
16	Jarno Trulli	20	1m 19.102s
17	Ukyo Katayama	11	1m 19.218s
18	Jan Magnussen	12	1m 19.282s
19	Nicola Larini	14	1m 19.401s
20	Shinji Nakano	15	1m 19.406s
21	Pedro Diniz	12	1m 19.664s
22	Jos Verstappen	14	1m 19.690s

RACE FASTEST LAPS

Weather: Humid, overcast

Driver	Time	Lap
Jacques Villeneuve	1m 18.397s	28
Ralf Schumacher	1m 18.441s	29
Gerhard Berger	1m 18.509s	25
Giancarlo Fisichella	1m 18.611s	39
Mika Häkkinen	1m 18.618s	34
Heinz-Harald Frentzen	1m 18.707s	30
Nicola Larini	1m 18.730s	48
Jean Alesi	1m 18.754s	25
Michael Schumacher	1m 18.773s	44
David Coulthard	1m 18.925s	35
Johnny Herbert	1m 19.008s	19
Olivier Panis	1m 19.094s	57
Eddie Irvine	1m 19.275s	41
Shinji Nakano	1m 19.657s	39
Damon Hill	1m 19.910s	41
Ukyo Katayama	1m 19.960s	42
Jarno Trulli	1m 20.105s	55
Jos Verstappen	1m 20.274s	43
Mika Salo	1m 20.376s	61
Pedro Diniz	1m 20.406s	10
Rubens Barrichello	1m 20.788s	14

Lap chart

57	58	59	60	61	62	63	64	65	66	67	68	69	70	71	72	
3	3	3	3	3	3	3	3	3	3	3	3	3	3	3	3	1
8	8	8	8	8	8	8	8	8	8	8	8	8	8	8	8	2
14	14	14	14	14	14	14	14	14	14	14	14	14	14	14	14	3
9	9	9	9	9	9	9	9	9	9	9	9	9	9	9	9	4
5	5	5	5	5	5	5	5	5	5	5	5	5	5	5	5	5
7	7	7	7	7	7	7	7	7	7	7	7	7	7	7	7	6
16	16	16	16	16	16	16	16	16	16	16	16	16	16	16	16	
4	4	4	4	4	4	4	12	12	12	12	12	12	12	12	12	
12	12	12	12	12	12	12	4	4	4	4	4	4	4	4	4	
10	10	10	10	10	10	10	10	10	10	10	10	10	10	10	10	
1	1	1	1	1	1	1	1	1	1	1	1	17	17	17	17	
17	17	17	17	17	17	17	17	17	17	17	1	21	21	21		
21	21	21	21	21	21	21	21	21	21	21	19	19	19			
19	19	19	19	19	19	19	19	19	19	19	15	15	15			
15	15	15	15	15	15	15	15	15	15	15	15	18				
18	18	18	18	18	18	18	18	18	18	18	6	6				
6	6	6	6	6	6	6	6	6	6							
20	20	20	20	20	20	20	20	20	20	20						

CHASSIS LOG BOOK

1	Hill	Arrows A18/3
2	Diniz	Arrows A18/2
	spare	Arrows A18/1
3	Villeneuve	Williams FW19/4
4	Frentzen	Williams FW19/3
	spare	Williams FW19/3
5	M. Schumacher	Ferrari F310B/174
6	Irvine	Ferrari F310B/173
	spare	Ferrari F310B/172
7	Alesi	Benetton B197/5
8	Berger	Benetton B197/4
	spare	Benetton B197/3
9	Häkkinen	McLaren MP4/12/2
10	Coulthard	McLaren MP4/12/3
	spare	McLaren MP4/12/1
11	R. Schumacher	Jordan 197/3
12	Fisichella	Jordan 197/2
	spare	Jordan 197/1
14	Panis	Prost JS45/3
15	Nakano	Prost JS45/2
	spare	Prost JS45/1
16	Herbert	Sauber C16/3
17	Larini	Sauber C16/2
	spare	Sauber C16/1
18	Verstappen	Tyrrell 025/2
19	Salo	Tyrrell 025/3
	spare	Tyrrell 025/1
20	Katayama	Minardi M197/3
21	Trulli	Minardi M197/2
22	Barrichello	Stewart SF1/2
23	Magnussen	Stewart SF1/3
	spare	Stewart SF1/1
24	Sospiri	Lola T97/30/3
25	Rosset	Lola T97/30/2
	spare	Lola T97/30/1

POINTS TABLES

Drivers

1 =	David Coulthard	10
1 =	Jacques Villeneuve	10
3	Gerhard Berger	9
4	Michael Schumacher	8
5	Mika Häkkinen	7
6	Olivier Panis	6
7 =	Nicola Larini	1
7 =	Jean Alesi	1

Constructors

1	McLaren	17
2 =	Williams	10
2 =	Benetton	10
4	Ferrari	8
5	Prost	6
6	Sauber	1

FOR THE RECORD

50th Grand Prix start

Heinz-Harald Frentzen

Eddie Irvine

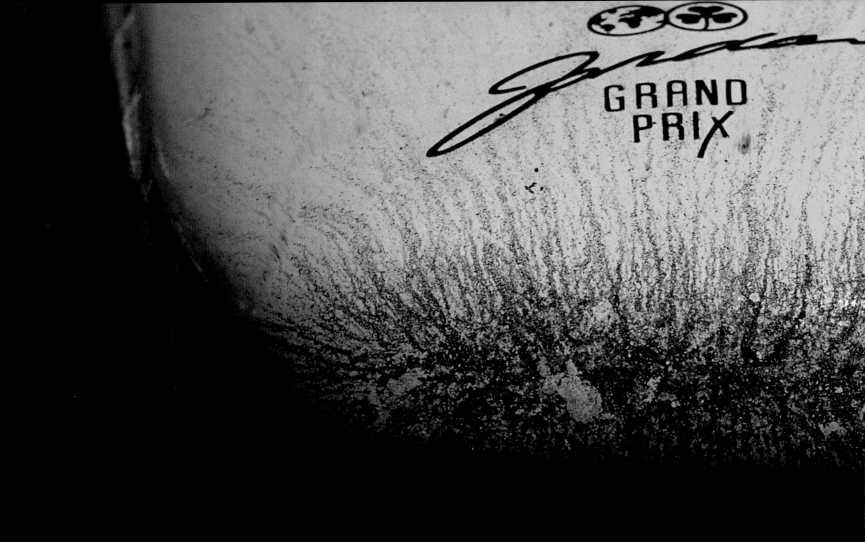

ARGENTINE
grand prix

VILLENEUVE

IRVINE

R. SCHUMACHER

HERBERT

HÄKKINEN

BERGER

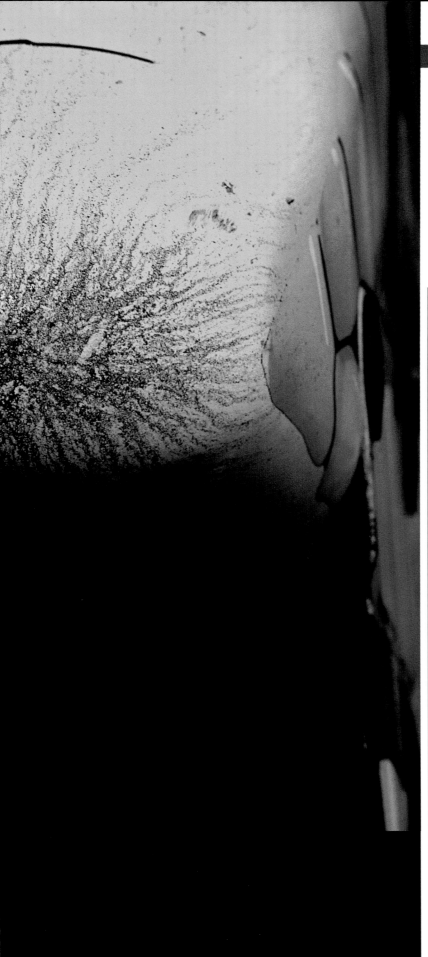

While the Jordan team demonstrated its potential with a podium finish for Ralf Schumacher, Jacques Villeneuve *(below left)* confirmed his status as the man to beat with his second consecutive victory.

JACQUES Villeneuve completed his South American tour by scoring his second victory of the season in the Argentine Grand Prix at Buenos Aires, but if he had thought he'd had a fight on his hands at Interlagos, it was kids' stuff compared with what he was to face in the third round of the '97 World Championship battle. This time he not only had to withstand the pressure of Eddie Irvine's Ferrari breathing down his neck in the closing stages but, just like Damon Hill the previous year, also had to battle against the effects of a severe stomach bug which he simply couldn't shake off throughout the race weekend.

Nevertheless, the French-Canadian emerged victorious by the oh-so-slender margin of 0.9s after a performance straight out of the mould of his late father Gilles, the dynamic Ferrari star who was killed practising for the 1982 Belgian Grand Prix and whose record of six GP victories he thereby equalled.

Villeneuve felt so drained and dehydrated following the race morning warm-up that he cancelled all his promotional activities and rested up in order to revive himself for the gruelling 72-lap event.

'It was a tough race,' said Villeneuve afterwards. 'The only problem with the car came when the gear lever was getting stuck just after my first refuelling stop, but I also blistered a front tyre in the closing stages and Eddie was certainly quicker than us towards the end.'

For the last ten laps of the race the Williams and Ferrari were seldom more than a second apart, Irvine trying every trick in the book to pressure his exhausted rival, while shrewdly mindful that any last-minute trip into the gravel trap would be another black mark against him after two disastrous outings in the first two races of the season.

Yet Villeneuve demonstrated a resilience and strength apparently at odds with his dehydrated physical state. He ran as gently as he dared, stoically retaining his advantage in the closing stages of this epic contest.

In their wake the Jordan team celebrated its 100th Grand Prix with Ralf Schumacher storming through to a superb third place, surviving an earlier collision with team-mate Giancarlo Fisichella, while Johnny Herbert's Sauber just edged out Mika Häkkinen's McLaren-Mercedes to take fourth place by 0.4s.

Irvine's performance was a timely morale-booster and represented his first points finish of the season. He made a great start and picked up the Maranello gauntlet after Michael Schumacher had rammed Rubens Bar-richello's Stewart at the first corner, triggering a multi-car pile-up which also eliminated David Coulthard's McLaren against Ralf Schumacher's Jordan.

Having qualified superbly on pole position ahead of team-mate Heinz-Harald Frentzen, Jacques made a terrific getaway and led the sprint down towards the first corner. Frentzen was slower away from second spot on the grid and had Michael Schumacher literally tracking his every move as they sped towards the first turn, so much so that the Ferrari driver swerved so violently at Panis's Prost that the Frenchman was obliged to edge virtually off the track to avoid a collision.

All hell was let loose at the first corner. Michael was out on the spot and his hopes of being able to take the spare F310B for the restart were dashed when the safety car was deployed rather than the event being red-flagged – even though one slightly confused official did in fact briefly display a red flag, a mix-up which resulted in a $10,000 fine for the race organisers.

Trying to avoid the mayhem, Coulthard removed his McLaren's left-front wheel against Ralf Schumacher's Jordan, Magnussen's Stewart hit Larini's Sauber and Berger indulged in a brief bout of autocrossing. Barrichello amazingly managed to resume, and was able to make two shrewdly judged pit stops for repairs without losing a lap to the safety car. The first time he came in for a new nose section, the second time for fresh rear tyres and a wing adjustment.

On lap three the safety car was withdrawn and Villeneuve immediately pulled out a 1.3s lead over Frentzen with Panis third from Irvine, Fisichella and Hill. Unfortunately for Williams, any chance of a 1-2 result was thwarted on lap six when Heinz-Harald rolled to a halt out on the circuit when the drive disengagement mechanism – used to engage neutral in the event of a stricken car needing to be moved from a hazardous position – accidentally activated itself due to the malfunction of a seal in the pressure bottle at the heart of the system.

Frentzen's demise left Panis's Prost with a clear run at the leading Williams. On lap seven the Frenchman was 1.0s behind and for several laps thereafter Olivier, who was on a two-stop strategy as opposed to Villeneuve's three-stop plan, kept pace with the leading Williams. Even so, once Jacques got into a consistent rhythm he began to ease away from the Mugen-engined machine.

Photos: Darren Heath

117

Below: Former Grand Prix star Carlos Reutemann takes a closer look at the action via the massive telephoto lens of Paul-Henri Cahier's Canon.

Right: Jordan's Ralf Schumacher made amends for pushing his team-mate Giancarlo Fisichella out of the race by scoring his first podium finish at only his third attempt.

Below right: Undismayed by the uncompetitiveness of their V8-powered Tyrrells, Mika Salo and Jos Verstappen enjoy their moment in the spotlight during the pre-race drivers' parade.

BUENOS AIRES QUALIFYING

The latest chapter in Jacques Villeneuve's process of undermining the morale of his new Williams team-mate Heinz-Harald Frentzen began in Friday free practice at Buenos Aires when he sliced a whopping 1.4s off the German driver's best time achieved earlier in the session.

Frentzen's apparent discomfiture on the notoriously bumpy circuit was subsequently heightened as he slumped to an eventual seventh place, outgunned in the closing moments of the session by Rubens Barrichello's Stewart, Olivier Panis's Prost, Gerhard Berger's Benetton, Michael Schumacher's Ferrari and the Jordan of Giancarlo Fisichella.

Villeneuve's performance was made even more outstanding by the fact that he was suffering from a serious stomach upset. Although Frentzen was also grappling with the effects of flu, the disparity between the performance of the two Williams drivers served to endorse – superficially, at least – an ever-increasing body of paddock opinion that ditching Damon Hill was one of Frank Williams's most spectacular errors of judgement.

In fact, Frentzen was far more comfortable in the car than he had been at Interlagos a couple of weeks earlier. After the Brazilian race, he had flown back to England for a detailed technical post-mortem on his race performance with both Patrick Head and his race engineer Tim Preston.

'We discussed various solutions in setting up my car,' he explained. 'There was a big question mark as to why I was not adapting to the car in the way I wanted to and I think we have now made progress on this front.' As things turned out during qualifying, Frentzen's optimism was not altogether misplaced.

On another topic altogether, Frank Williams declined to comment on rumours that he had already re-signed Villeneuve for the 1998 season. 'There is no rush,' he said. 'He has a two-year contract which expires at the end of this season and we have an option on his services. I don't want to talk about drivers at the moment.' In fact, the team had quietly taken up its option and Villeneuve's position at Williams seemed secure for at least another 18 months.

This coincided with Rothmans confirming the extension of its title sponsorship of the Williams team through to the end of 1998, thereby guaranteeing the funds to meet Villeneuve's financial aspirations.

Lukas Gorys

Qualifying took place in bright and sunny conditions with Schumacher's Ferrari making the initial running on 1m 26.011s. This turned out to be a somewhat tentative yardstick, for Villeneuve was soon into the swing of things, shrugging aside his digestive problems to post a 1m 25.235s a few moments later.

Among the opposition, Ralf Schumacher proved highly impressive with the Jordan 197 – on his first run he was 0.1s inside Villeneuve's time to the first timing split, ending the lap with fourth-fastest time on 1m 26.334s.

Then Olivier Panis showed what the Prost JS45 could do, turning second-fastest time with a 1m 25.491s, prompting Villeneuve to move the goalposts quite dramatically on his second run with a 1m 24.747s. Then Frentzen steeled himself for a big effort, ducking inside Panis's best to record a 1m 25.417s.

With 15 minutes of the session left, Villeneuve settled the issue with a 1m 24.473s with Frentzen also improving further to 1m 25.271s, thereby ensuring himself second place in the final grid order.

The sheer ferocity of F1's latest tyre war could be judged from the fact that Villeneuve's pole-winning time was 5.9s inside the fastest 1996 qualifying time established by Damon Hill. More impressively, even Pedro Diniz – 22nd and last on the grid in his Arrows – managed a qualifying time 1.4s quicker than the British driver could manage in 1996.

'It's unbelievable,' said Hill. 'With last year's best car I wouldn't have even made the cut this year. The track and car improvements probably contribute about a second and a half a lap – the rest comes from the tyres.'

The performance of Panis and Barrichello again underscored the potential challenge to Goodyear's domination by the Bridgestone newcomers. In particular, Alain Prost's face broke into a broad grin as Panis slammed round to qualify third, while Rubens Barrichello gave a further boost to the credibility of Jackie Stewart's fledgling team with an excellent run to fifth place on the grid.

Prior to qualifying, all four Bridgestone teams opted for the softer of the two available compounds, while Jordan, Benetton and McLaren chose the harder of Goodyear's available rubber – a move which appeared increasingly shrewd as the temperature edged relentlessly towards the 30 degree mark on race morning.

In fourth and seventh places came the two Ferraris of Michael Schumacher and Eddie Irvine. Neither driver had managed to improve on his times set early in the session, but Irvine at least reported that the car felt better than he had originally anticipated.

'This morning I got some of my settings slightly wrong, but I did succeed in reducing the rear-end instability,' he said. 'I still have a little mid-corner understeer, but with more fuel on board the car feels balanced and easy to drive.'

Barrichello had originally transferred to the spare Stewart SF1 after his race car developed an oil system problem, but that was duly rectified and he switched back to his original chassis to post fifth-fastest time. Qualifying a Stewart-Ford in the top ten for the first time also earned him a bonus – a new Rolex Daytona wristwatch from team owners Jackie and Paul Stewart.

Magnussen, meanwhile, had suffered an oil leak and a blown engine during the morning and did a single qualifying run at the start of the afternoon session in the spare before relinquishing it to Rubens so that the Brazilian could post a time early in the session. When Barrichello switched back to his race car, the spare was vacated for the Danish driver's use for the remainder of qualifying.

Sixth and ninth were the two Jordan-Peugeots of Ralf Schumacher and Giancarlo Fisichella, two excellent performances by EJ's young lions. Ralf's only slip was a spin on the first lap of his opening run, while he later caught a yellow flag and, like several others, felt he could have gone even quicker if the track temperature hadn't been so high towards the end of the session. Fisichella was privately a little disappointed not to have been quicker, but it was a good enough effort nevertheless.

Behind Irvine, eighth place on the grid fell to Johnny Herbert's Sauber. The British driver was satisfied that his car's handling balance had been improved immeasurably over the bumps. 'This car is better than an eighth-place qualifier,' he insisted.

Team-mate Nicola Larini spent the session making up for a spin during the morning's free practice session and wound up 14th in the final line-up. 'The car felt quite good, so I am happy enough with what I managed to do in the circumstances,' he said.

Benetton and McLaren had a simply hellish time in qualifying. Both opted for Goodyear's harder-compound rubber and, despite front suspension revisions, Jean Alesi and Gerhard Berger could only manage 11th and 12th places on the grid. David Coulthard managed to squeeze in ahead of them to take tenth place for McLaren, but Mika Häkkinen spun off early in the spare MP4/12 and switched back to his race car, which he could only coax to 17th-fastest time.

Damon Hill did a reasonable job qualifying his Arrows-Yamaha 13th. 'I don't think we could have expected to do better,' he said. 'We need more horsepower and downforce to be able to compete more strongly on circuits like this.'

In the Tyrrell camp, both 025s were transformed into the most distinctive cars on the circuit by the incorporation of two small winglets on stalks fitted either side of the cockpit in the quest for further enhanced downforce. Jos Verstappen made the most of the sole uprated Cosworth ED4 V8 on hand for this race, qualifying a worthwhile 16th, three places ahead of team-mate Mika Salo.

Sandwiching the Finn were Jarno Trulli's Minardi (18th) and Shinji Nakano's Prost (20th), with Ukyo Katayama's Minardi sharing the final row of the grid with Pedro Diniz in the second Arrows-Yamaha.

By lap 16 he was a comfortable 6.4s ahead of Panis with Irvine third ahead of Fisichella, Herbert, Ralf Schumacher, the fast-starting Hill and Alesi. Unfortunately, by then the Prost driver was in trouble. A hydraulic fluid radiator began leaking and he rolled to a halt with loss of pressure midway round lap 19.

'It's a shame, because the car worked very well,' he reflected. 'I was full of confidence, because the speed was there. When Michael touched me the suspension was bent and a tyre was going down slowly, but it would have been no problem to last the race. I think it was certainly possible that we would have won; the car was quick and the strategy was good.'

Meanwhile, there had been trouble in the battle for seventh place. Alesi had gradually whittled down Hill's advantage to the point where, going into lap 18, the Benetton driver took the incomprehensible decision to attempt overtaking the World Champion down the outside on the run towards the first corner.

He just didn't have the speed necessary to make it stick. Not that this de-

Bryn Williams

Sutton Motorsport Images

terred Jean from trying. Having nosed ahead of the Arrows on the outside line, he chopped across, his right-rear wheel hit Damon's left-front and they both half-spun. Both continued in the same order, but now in 10th and 11th places after a close-running queue comprising Diniz, Verstappen, Häkkinen and the impressive Barrichello nipped by during their *pas de deux*.

On lap 21 Villeneuve came in for his first refuelling stop. The Williams was stationary for just 7.5s and squeezed back into the race 0.9s ahead of Irvine's Ferrari, which was scheduled to make only two stops. Herbert came in from third place for a 7.6s stop, resuming in fifth behind Jordan duo Fisichella and Ralf Schumacher. Barrichello, now eighth, also came in for fuel and fresh tyres.

On lap 23 Irvine made his first refuelling stop (7.3s) and two laps later Barrichello stopped out on the circuit with loss of hydraulic pressure, a bitterly disappointing end to a race which he reckoned would have seen him finish in the top three, despite that first-corner drama.

Darren Heath

On lap 25 came the most controversial single episode of the afternoon when Ralf Schumacher's exuberance boiled over and the young German driver took team-mate Giancarlo Fisichella out of the race with a wildly optimistic overtaking manoeuvre.

'In the fast corner before the back straight, he [Fisichella] missed his line and in the next hairpin I thought he made a space,' said Schumacher. 'I tried to overtake him, but he closed the door. I tried to go over the grass, but I touched him. It happened, but it's a shame.'

Gary Anderson's engineering team certainly seems to build sturdy racing cars. Schumacher's Jordan had already survived one impact when he was rammed by Coulthard at the first corner. The machine now successfully withstood the coming-together with Fisichella, although Ralf reported that

the power steering system packed up soon afterwards.

On the same lap, Nicola Larini's Sauber had a problem with its refuelling rig which meant that he was stationary for an agonising 37.5s. That put him well down the field so he spent the rest of the afternoon playing catch-up and his race eventually ended on lap 65 when Magnussen's Stewart shut the door on him and he spun off as a result.

This was Magnussen's second brush with the Italian Sauber driver, the Dane having lost his Stewart's nose section against the Ferrari-engined car on the opening lap.

'There was a lot of hassle at the start,' said Jan. 'I was pushed onto the grass, came back on, then half a lap later I tried to get a good exit out of the last corner to be able to pass Larini

down the straight. But in the middle of the corner he just slowed right down, I clipped him and took my nose off, so I had to come in for a new front wing.'

By the time of their second encounter, Magnussen was approaching the end of a race in which he had been initially bugged by serious understeer. 'It gradually got better, but from lap 61 I was seeing the oil pressure light and eventually it [the engine] just let go,' he shrugged.

Up at the front of the pack, Villeneuve now found himself grappling with a slight technical problem. After his first refuelling stop he found difficulty changing gear. 'The gear lever was getting stuck and it was really difficult to change gears,' he explained. 'Sometimes it was soft and sometimes it shifted by itself. That was giving me some problems, so I slowed down a bit

until I realised that Ralf and Eddie were doing less stops than me and that gave us a hard time.'

On lap 34, Ralf Schumacher brought his Jordan in from second place for its sole refuelling stop, dropping to sixth, which immediately became fifth when Alesi came in next time round. Further back, Hill's Arrows had retired from eighth place when its Yamaha V10 expired abruptly out on the circuit.

Villeneuve came in for his second refuelling stop (7.9s) at the end of lap 38, dropping to second behind Irvine. The Ferrari driver then enjoyed a stint in the lead through to lap 44 when he made his second and final pit visit, accelerating back into the race in second place only 2.9s ahead of the hard-charging Ralf Schumacher's Jordan.

At this point Ralf realised that, had he pushed a bit harder after his pit stop,

Eddie Irvine *(left)* finished less than a second behind the winning Williams of Jacques Villeneuve, having resisted the temptation to risk everything in a desperate bid to pass the dehydrated French-Canadian.

Barnard to design new F1 Arrows

THE terms of an apparent contract for John Barnard to join the Arrows-Yamaha F1 team as technical director were leaked to the *Sun* newspaper in London over the Argentine GP weekend, causing a degree of embarrassment and ire to team boss Tom Walkinshaw while he was 5000 miles away from his UK base.

The news came at a time when Arrows was lobbying hard to take over the Mugen Honda engine contract currently in place with the Prost team for 1998, possibly dropping the Mugen identification to reflect expanded involvement from the Japanese car maker, whose engines dominated F1 for the second half of the 1980s.

Barnard's new deal, apparently signed the previous month, provides for him to eventually relocate the former Ferrari Design & Development operation at TWR's Leafield, Oxfordshire, headquarters.

'A lot of it is correct, but some of it isn't,' said Barnard from his home in Surrey. 'It certainly was not leaked from my end. You could say that I am pretty flabbergasted.'

The newspaper report stated that Barnard had paid Maranello £800,000 for Ferrari Design & Development, the Italian team's UK design studio, and then sold it on to Arrows for £1.7 million. His contract with Arrows was said to provide for a £350,000 annual salary, first class air travel for the races and a company car. Arrows was also tipped to pay Barnard's company a monthly fee of £250,000 for him to design and develop the new F1 machine.

Walkinshaw commented: 'It is no secret that we are talking to Mugen Honda, Yamaha and Mecachrome about possible engine options for next season. We will be investigating how this leak occurred, but I think I have quite a clear idea.'

mechanics did not join Eddie Jordan in the pit wall celebrations. Speculation that this was due to an ongoing dispute over bonus payments was quickly denied, the team instead explaining that the last time a Jordan was running in third place on the final lap had been in Hungary two years previously where Rubens Barrichello ground to a halt 100 metres from the line. That unhappy memory, they said, was now buried with a successful outcome to the team's 100th Grand Prix appearance.

Johnny Herbert's Sauber-Petronas ran among the leading bunch and eventually finished fourth, squeezing home by a length from Mika Häkkinen's McLaren and Gerhard Berger's Benetton. The British driver was slowed by a faulty master switch cutting the engine every time he bumped a kerb. 'That is the only quick way round here,' he said, 'but I had to stop using them and this cost me time as a result.'

Benetton and McLaren to some extent both made up for their disappointing qualifying performances, Häkkinen and Berger running strongly during the race, with Gerhard managing to post the fastest lap of the afternoon as he sprinted up onto Häkkinen's tail in the closing stages.

'This was the hardest race so far this season,' said Berger. 'I got involved in the [first-corner] accident and basically started the race from the very back. I tried to keep a steady pace and take out the pressure, always thinking that it was important to try and get one or two points. My fastest lap proves once again that the car is competitive, but we obviously have a problem in qualifying and have to work hard in that direction.'

Häkkinen also drove extremely well, using a single-stop strategy to move up from his lowly 17th-place starting position. In reality, it was the only solution after his disappointing qualifying performance, but the Finn exploited these difficult circumstances to the best advantage possible.

Alesi came home seventh ahead of Mika Salo and Jarno Trulli with Magnussen classified tenth, although he actually stopped running with six of the race's 72 laps still to go.

Williams finished the day still the class of the field, but many observers wondered just where Michael Schumacher would have been running at the chequered flag had his Ferrari F310B not succumbed to that first-corner shunt.

Given the precarious state of his stomach, Jacques Villeneuve must have been very glad that it had.

he might well have been able to stay ahead of Irvine when the Ferrari emerged from its second stop. As things transpired, Eddie proved to have the measure of the Jordan driver. By lap 47 he was 3.9s ahead, and the gap grew to 6.0s on lap 49 and 6.7s on lap 50.

However, Schumacher hadn't finished yet. By lap 56 he had trimmed the Ferrari's advantage to 4.9s and, with Irvine simultaneously closing on the leading Williams, a really close finish between the first three cars was now in serious prospect.

By lap 63 Irvine was only 0.9s behind Villeneuve and looking for any opportunity to pass. But Jacques had the edge in terms of straightline speed, so there just wasn't going to be any realistic chance. Unless he made a mistake.

On lap 69 Irvine seemed closer than ever, but there was still no gap. 'On the straight he just disappeared,' said Eddie afterwards. 'I think I had more downforce than he had and the Williams is anyway a very efficient car aerodynamically. I was on the rev-limiter half-way down the straight, so there wasn't much chance to overtake him unless I did a do-or-die, and it probably isn't the time to do this at the moment.'

Despite locking a front wheel under braking for the final corner, Villeneuve just made it to the chequered flag with less than a second to spare while the confident Schumacher crossed the line just 11 seconds further back, confirming his position as one of F1's most exciting new talents by taking a podium finish in only his third GP outing.

The surviving Jordan crossed the finishing line to an underwhelming greeting from the team personnel. The

GRAN PREMIO
MARLBORO
DE ARGENTINA
11–13 APRIL 1997
BUENOS AIRES

Race distance: 72 laps, 190.542 miles/306.648 km

Race weather: Dry, hot and sunny

FIA FORMULA 1 WORLD CHAMPIONSHIP

ROUND **3**

AUTODROMO OSCAR ALFREDO GALVEZ, BUENOS AIRES

ASCARI
OMBÚ
ESSES
SENNA'S S
CONFITERIA CURVE
HAIRPIN
CURVE 1

CIRCUIT LENGTH: 2.646 MILES/4.259 KM

Pos.	Driver	Nat.	No.	Entrant	Car/Engine	Tyres	Laps	Time/Retirement	Speed (mph/km/h)
1	Jacques Villeneuve	CDN	3	Rothmans Williams Renault	Williams FW19-Renault RS9 V10	G	72	1h 52m 01.715s	102.001/164.155
2	Eddie Irvine	GB	6	Scuderia Ferrari Marlboro	Ferrari F310B 046 V10	G	72	1h 52m 02.694s	101.986/164.131
3	Ralf Schumacher	D	11	B&H Total Jordan Peugeot	Jordan 197-Peugeot A14 V10	G	72	1h 52m 13.804s	101.818/163.860
4	Johnny Herbert	GB	16	Red Bull Sauber Petronas	Sauber C16-Petronas V10	G	72	1h 52m 31.634s	101.549/163.428
5	Mika Häkkinen	SF	9	West McLaren Mercedes	McLaren MP4/12-Mercedes FO110E V10	G	72	1h 52m 32.066s	101.542/163.417
6	Gerhard Berger	A	8	Mild Seven Benetton Renault	Benetton B197-Renault RS9 V10	G	72	1h 52m 33.108s	101.527/163.392
7	Jean Alesi	F	7	Mild Seven Benetton Renault	Benetton B197-Renault RS9 V10	G	72	1h 52m 48.074s	101.303/163.031
8	Mika Salo	SF	19	Tyrrell	Tyrrell 025-Ford ED4 V8	G	71		
9	Jarno Trulli	I	21	Minardi Team	Minardi M197-Hart 830 V8	B	71		
10	Jan Magnussen	DK	23	Stewart Ford	Stewart SF1-Ford Zetec-R V10	B	66	Engine	
	Nicola Larini	I	17	Red Bull Sauber Petronas	Sauber C16-Petronas V10	G	63	Spun off	
	Pedro Diniz	BR	2	Danka Arrows Yamaha	Arrows A18-Yamaha OX11A/C V10	B	50	Engine	
	Shinji Nakano	J	15	Prost Gauloises Blondes	Prost JS45-Mugen Honda MF301HA V10	B	49	Engine	
	Jos Verstappen	NL	18	Tyrrell	Tyrrell 025-Ford ED4 V8	G	43	Fuel pressure	
	Ukyo Katayama	J	20	Minardi Team	Minardi M197-Hart 830 V8	B	37	Spun off	
	Damon Hill	GB	1	Danka Arrows Yamaha	Arrows A18-Yamaha OX11A/C V10	B	33	Engine	
	Giancarlo Fisichella	I	12	B&H Total Jordan Peugeot	Jordan 197-Peugeot A14 V10	G	24	Collision with R. Schumacher	
	Rubens Barrichello	BR	22	Stewart Ford	Stewart SF1-Ford Zetec-R V10	B	24	Hydraulics	
	Olivier Panis	F	14	Prost Gauloises Blondes	Prost JS45-Mugen Honda MF301HA V10	B	18	Hydraulic leak	
	Heinz-Harald Frentzen	D	4	Rothmans Williams Renault	Williams FW19-Renault RS9 V10	G	5	Clutch	
	Michael Schumacher	D	5	Scuderia Ferrari Marlboro	Ferrari F310B 046 V10	G	0	Collision with Barrichello	
	David Coulthard	GB	10	West McLaren Mercedes	McLaren MP4/12-Mercedes FO110E V10	G	0	Collision with R. Schumacher	

Fastest lap: Berger, on lap 63, 1m 27.981s, 108.286 mph/174.269 km/h (record).

Previous lap record: Jean Alesi (F1 Benetton B196-Renault V10), 1m 29.413s, 106.551 mph/171.478 km/h (1996).

B – Bridgestone   G – Goodyear

Grid order																																																									
	1	2	3	4	5	6	7	8	9	10	11	12	13	14	15	16	17	18	19	20	21	22	23	24	25	26	27	28	29	30	31	32	33	34	35	36	37	38	39	40	41	42	43	44	45	46	47	48	49	50	51	52	53	54	55	56
3 VILLENEUVE	3	3	3	3	3	3	3	3	3	3	3	3	3	3	3	3	3	3	3	3	3	3	3	3	3	3	3	3	3	3	3	3	3	3	3	6	6	6	6	6	6	6	3	3	3	3	3	3	3	3	3	3	3	3	3	3
4 FRENTZEN	4	4	4	4	14	14	14	14	14	14	14	14	14	14	14	14	14	6	6	6	6	12	11	11	11	11	11	11	11	11	11	11	11	11	6	3	3	3	3	6	6	6	6	6	6	6	6	6	6	6	6	6	6	6	6	6
14 PANIS	14	14	14	14	14	6	6	6	6	6	6	6	6	6	6	6	12	12	16	12	12	11	6	6	6	6	6	6	6	6	6	16	16	16	16	9	11	11	11	11	11	11	11	11	11	11	11	11	11	11	11	11	11	11	11	11
5 M. SCHUMACHER	6	6	6	6	6	12	12	12	12	12	12	12	12	12	12	12	16	16	12	11	11	6	16	16	16	16	16	16	16	16	16	9	9	9	9	11	16	16	16	16	16	16	16	16	16	16	16	16	16	16	16	16	16	16	16	16
22 BARRICHELLO	12	12	12	12	12	1	11	11	11	16	16	16	16	16	16	16	11	11	11	16	16	16	9	9	9	9	9	9	9	9	9	7	11	11	11	11	6	9	9	9	9	9	9	9	9	9	9	9	9	9	9	9	9	9	9	9
11 R. SCHUMACHER	1	1	1	1	1	16	11	16	16	16	11	11	11	11	11	11	11	11	2	2	2	2	18	2	2	2	7	7	7	7	7	7	11	8	7	7	7	7	7	7	7	7	7	7	7	7	7	7	7	7	7	7	7	7	7	8
6 IRVINE	16	23	16	16	16	11	16	1	1	1	1	1	1	1	1	1	1	18	18	18	18	2	9	7	7	2	2	8	8	8	8	8	7	18	18	18	18	18	18	18	8	8	8	8	8	8	8	8	8	8	8	8	8	8	7	7
16 HERBERT	11	16	11	11	11	7	7	7	7	7	7	7	7	7	7	7	18	9	9	22	9	9	7	1	1	8	8	2	2	1	1	18	18	8	8	8	8	8	23	17	23	23	23	23	23	23	23	23	23	23	23	23	23	23	23	23
12 FISICHELLA	7	11	7	7	7	2	2	2	2	2	2	2	2	2	2	9	22	22	9	7	7	1	8	8	1	1	1	1	2	2	23	23	23	23	23	23	23	17	17	17	21	21	21	21	21	21	21	21	21							
10 COULTHARD	2	7	2	2	18	18	18	18	18	18	18	18	18	22	1	1	7	1	1	8	17	19	19	18	18	18	18	21	21	21	21	19	19	19	17	21	21	19	19	19	19	19	19	19	19											
7 ALESI	18	2	18	18	18	9	9	9	9	9	9	9	9	9	9	1	7	7	8	23	19	18	18	23	23	23	23	19	19	19	19	17	17	17	19	19	19	15	15	2	17	17	17	17	17											
8 BERGER	20	18	9	9	9	20	20	20	20	22	22	22	22	22	7	8	8	8	23	17	18	23	23	21	21	21	21	20	17	17	17	17	21	21	21	21	15	15	15	2	2	17														
1 HILL	9	9	20	20	20	21	21	21	21	20	8	8	8	8	8	23	23	23	19	19	21	21	21	19	19	19	19	17	20	20	20	15	15	15	15	15	2	2	2	17	17															
17 LARINI	21	20	21	21	21	8	8	8	22	21	21	23	23	23	23	23	19	19	17	21	15	20	20	20	20	20	20	15	15	15	15	2	2	2	2	2																				
23 MAGNUSSEN	19	21	19	19	8	19	22	22	8	8	19	19	20	19	19	19	17	17	22	15	20	15	15	15	15	15	15	2	2	2																										
18 VERSTAPPEN	8	19	8	8	19	22	19	19	19	23	19	20	19	20	17	17	21	21	21	21	20	17	17	17	17	17	17	17																												
9 HÄKKINEN	17	8	17	17	22	17	17	17	23	23	23	21	17	17	20	21	15	15	15	15	15																																			
21 TRULLI	15	17	15	15	17	15	15	15	17	17	21	21	21	21	15	20	20	20	20	20																																				
19 SALO	23	15	22	22	15	23	23	23	15	15	15	15	15	15	15	15	20	20																																						
15 NAKANO	22	22	23	23	23																																																			
20 KATAYAMA																																																									
2 DINIZ																																																									

Pit stop (shaded)
One lap behind leader (lighter shaded)

STARTING GRID

	3 **VILLENEUVE** Williams
4 **FRENTZEN** Williams	
	14 **PANIS** Prost
5 **M. SCHUMACHER** Ferrari	
	22 **BARRICHELLO** Stewart
11 **R. SCHUMACHER** Jordan	
	6 **IRVINE** Ferrari
16 **HERBERT** Sauber	
	12 **FISICHELLA** Jordan
10 **COULTHARD** McLaren	
	7 **ALESI** Benetton
8 **BERGER** Benetton	
	1 **HILL** Arrows
17 **LARINI** Sauber	
	23 **MAGNUSSEN** Stewart
18 **VERSTAPPEN** Tyrrell	
	9 **HÄKKINEN** McLaren
21 **TRULLI** Minardi	
	19 **SALO** Tyrrell
15 **NAKANO** Prost	
	20 **KATAYAMA** Minardi
2 **DINIZ** Arrows	

57	58	59	60	61	62	63	64	65	66	67	68	69	70	71	72	
3	3	3	3	3	3	3	3	3	3	3	3	3	3	3	3	1
6	6	6	6	6	6	6	6	6	6	6	6	6	6	6	6	2
11	11	11	11	11	11	11	11	11	11	11	11	11	11	11	11	3
16	16	16	16	16	16	16	16	16	16	16	16	16	16	16	16	4
9	9	9	9	9	9	9	9	9	9	9	9	9	9	9	9	5
8	8	8	8	8	8	8	8	8	8	8	8	8	8	8	8	6
7	7	7	7	7	7	7	7	7	7	7	7	7	7	7	7	
23	23	23	23	23	23	23	23	23	23	19	19	19	19	19		
21	19	19	19	19	19	19	19	19	19	21	21	21	21	21		
19	21	21	21	21	21	21	21	21	21							
17	17	17	17	17	17	17	17									

FOR THE RECORD

First Grand Prix points
Ralf Schumacher

TIME SHEETS

QUALIFYING

Weather: Dry, hot and sunny

Pos.	Driver	Car	Laps	Time
1	Jacques Villeneuve	Williams-Renault	12	1m 24.473s
2	Heinz-Harald Frentzen	Williams-Renault	12	1m 25.271s
3	Olivier Panis	Prost-Mugen Honda	11	1m 25.491s
4	Michael Schumacher	Ferrari	10	1m 25.773s
5	Rubens Barrichello	Stewart-Ford	12	1m 25.942s
6	Ralf Schumacher	Jordan-Peugeot	11	1m 26.218s
7	Eddie Irvine	Ferrari	11	1m 26.327s
8	Johnny Herbert	Sauber-Petronas	12	1m 26.564s
9	Giancarlo Fisichella	Jordan-Peugeot	11	1m 26.619s
10	David Coulthard	McLaren-Mercedes	11	1m 26.799s
11	Jean Alesi	Benetton-Renault	12	1m 27.076s
12	Gerhard Berger	Benetton-Renault	10	1m 27.259s
13	Damon Hill	Arrows-Yamaha	12	1m 27.281s
14	Nicola Larini	Sauber-Petronas	11	1m 27.690s
15	Jan Magnussen	Stewart-Ford	12	1m 28.035s
16	Jos Verstappen	Tyrrell-Ford	11	1m 28.094s
17	Mika Häkkinen	McLaren-Mercedes	9	1m 28.135s
18	Jarno Trulli	Minardi-Hart	12	1m 28.160s
19	Mika Salo	Tyrrell-Ford	11	1m 28.224s
20	Shinji Nakano	Prost-Mugen Honda	12	1m 28.366s
21	Ukyo Katayama	Minardi-Hart	12	1m 28.413s
22	Pedro Diniz	Arrows-Yamaha	12	1m 28.969s

FRIDAY FREE PRACTICE

Weather: Hot but cloudy

Pos.	Driver	Laps	Time
1	Jacques Villeneuve	29	1m 25.755s
2	Rubens Barrichello	24	1m 26.693s
3	Olivier Panis	23	1m 26.983s
4	Gerhard Berger	30	1m 27.017s
5	Michael Schumacher	30	1m 27.052s
6	Giancarlo Fisichella	29	1m 27.129s
7	Heinz-Harald Frentzen	30	1m 27.169s
8	Johnny Herbert	24	1m 27.702s
9	Ralf Schumacher	30	1m 27.823s
10	Jean Alesi	22	1m 27.979s
11	Eddie Irvine	28	1m 28.137s
12	David Coulthard	27	1m 28.163s
13	Damon Hill	26	1m 28.932s
14	Nicola Larini	29	1m 29.153s
15	Jos Verstappen	29	1m 29.302s
16	Mika Häkkinen	27	1m 29.426s
17	Mika Salo	20	1m 29.893s
18	Shinji Nakano	30	1m 30.069s
19	Jan Magnussen	30	1m 30.376s
20	Ukyo Katayama	10	1m 30.546s
21	Pedro Diniz	22	1m 30.727s
22	Jarno Trulli	14	1m 31.269s

SATURDAY FREE PRACTICE

Weather: Hot and sunny

Pos.	Driver	Laps	Time
1	Heinz-Harald Frentzen	27	1m 24.874s
2	Jacques Villeneuve	30	1m 25.704s
3	Michael Schumacher	30	1m 26.359s
4	Ralf Schumacher	29	1m 26.455s
5	Johnny Herbert	28	1m 26.494s
6	Gerhard Berger	25	1m 26.703s
7	Olivier Panis	30	1m 26.772s
8	Giancarlo Fisichella	29	1m 26.789s
9	Jean Alesi	22	1m 26.835s
10	Rubens Barrichello	23	1m 27.229s
11	Jos Verstappen	27	1m 27.423s
12	Eddie Irvine	25	1m 27.468s
13	David Coulthard	30	1m 27.496s
14	Mika Salo	28	1m 27.768s
15	Shinji Nakano	27	1m 27.885s
16	Mika Häkkinen	25	1m 28.086s
17	Ukyo Katayama	29	1m 28.600s
18	Damon Hill	21	1m 28.654s
19	Jan Magnussen	10	1m 28.710s
20	Pedro Diniz	16	1m 28.853s
21	Nicola Larini	11	1m 29.118s
22	Jarno Trulli	29	1m 29.140s

WARM-UP

Weather: Sunny and hot

Pos.	Driver	Laps	Time
1	Jacques Villeneuve	11	1m 27.425s
2	Heinz-Harald Frentzen	9	1m 27.438s
3	Rubens Barrichello	14	1m 27.605s
4	Giancarlo Fisichella	15	1m 27.748s
5	Olivier Panis	18	1m 27.824s
6	Jean Alesi	14	1m 27.941s
7	Michael Schumacher	13	1m 27.957s
8	Nicola Larini	11	1m 28.052s
9	Ralf Schumacher	16	1m 28.252s
10	David Coulthard	14	1m 28.451s
11	Johnny Herbert	16	1m 28.459s
12	Mika Häkkinen	14	1m 28.464s
13	Eddie Irvine	10	1m 28.601s
14	Damon Hill	14	1m 28.737s
15	Jarno Trulli	15	1m 28.842s
16	Gerhard Berger	11	1m 29.083s
17	Jos Verstappen	15	1m 29.269s
18	Pedro Diniz	15	1m 29.341s
19	Shinji Nakano	14	1m 29.490s
20	Jan Magnussen	14	1m 29.920s
21	Ukyo Katayama	14	1m 29.920s
22	Mika Salo	12	1m 30.045s

RACE FASTEST LAPS

Weather: Dry, hot and sunny

Driver	Time	Lap
Gerhard Berger	1m 27.981s	63
Jacques Villeneuve	1m 28.028s	54
Ralf Schumacher	1m 28.382s	56
Nicola Larini	1m 28.410s	46
Eddie Irvine	1m 28.473s	63
Jean Alesi	1m 18.827s	33
Olivier Panis	1m 29.090s	8
Mika Häkkinen	1m 29.076s	58
Johnny Herbert	1m 29.296s	62
Jos Verstappen	1m 29.541s	43
Jan Magnussen	1m 29.834s	48
Shinji Nakano	1m 29.865s	40
Rubens Barrichello	1m 29.913s	23
Mika Salo	1m 29.931s	62
Giancarlo Fisichella	1m 30.278s	19
Jarno Trulli	1m 30.593s	53
Damon Hill	1m 30.649s	23
Pedro Diniz	1m 31.111s	42
Heinz-Harald Frentzen	1m 31.832s	5
Ukyo Katayama	1m 31.869s	29

CHASSIS LOG BOOK

1	Hill	Arrows A18/3
2	Diniz	Arrows A18/2
	spare	Arrows A18/1
3	Villeneuve	Williams FW19/1
4	Frentzen	Williams FW19/2
	spare	Williams FW19/3
5	M. Schumacher	Ferrari F310B/174
6	Irvine	Ferrari F310B/173
	spare	Ferrari F310B/172
7	Alesi	Benetton B197/5
8	Berger	Benetton B197/4
	spare	Benetton B197/3
9	Häkkinen	McLaren MP4/12/2
10	Coulthard	McLaren MP4/12/3
	spare	McLaren MP4/12/1
11	R. Schumacher	Jordan 197/3
12	Fisichella	Jordan 197/2
	spare	Jordan 197/1
14	Panis	Prost JS45/3
15	Nakano	Prost JS45/2
	spare	Prost JS45/1
16	Herbert	Sauber C16/3
17	Larini	Sauber C16/2
	spare	Sauber C16/1
18	Verstappen	Tyrrell 025/2
19	Salo	Tyrrell 025/3
	spare	Tyrrell 025/1
20	Katayama	Minardi M197/3
21	Trulli	Minardi M197/2
22	Barrichello	Stewart SF1/2
23	Magnussen	Stewart SF1/3
	spare	Stewart SF1/1

POINTS TABLES

Drivers

1	Jacques Villeneuve	20
2 =	David Coulthard	10
2 =	Gerhard Berger	10
4	Mika Häkkinen	9
5	Michael Schumacher	8
6 =	Eddie Irvine	6
6 =	Olivier Panis	6
8	Ralf Schumacher	4
9	Johnny Herbert	3
10 =	Nicola Larini	1
10 =	Jean Alesi	1

Constructors

1	Williams	20
2	McLaren	19
3	Ferrari	14
4	Benetton	11
5	Prost	6
6 =	Sauber	4
6 =	Jordan	4

SAN MARINO

grand prix

Lukas Gorys

- FRENTZEN
- M. SCHUMACHER
- IRVINE
- FISICHELLA
- ALESI
- HÄKKINEN

Bryn Williams

Heinz-Harald Frentzen explains to the world's press that his first Grand Prix win 'is like oil on my soul'. Michael Schumacher seems not to share his taste in poetry.

Frentzen's measured drive to victory *(below left)* gave an answer to those who had suggested that Frank Williams had made a calamitous mistake by signing him.

THE fact of the matter was that Heinz-Harald Frentzen had not won a motor race for almost four years. His previous visit to the winner's circle was at a round of the Japanese Formula 3000 championship in 1993, during a self-inflicted exile from the European stage he must have thought might never end.

Yet at Imola's Autodromo Enzo e Dino Ferrari, Heinz-Harald was finally rewarded with the pay-off for just over three seasons of F1 endeavour when he won the San Marino Grand Prix on his fourth outing at the wheel of a Williams FW19. Having dominated the closing stages of the event in a controlled and disciplined style, Frentzen came home 1.2s ahead of Michael Schumacher's Ferrari F310B to head the first 1-2

achieved by German drivers during the 47-season history of the official World Championship.

Even more importantly, Imola subtly changed the light in which the genial Frentzen was regarded in the F1 pit lane. After seemingly losing his way in at least two of the first three races, the former Sauber driver displayed the mettle necessary to operate as a front-line contender. 'This is like oil on my soul,' said Heinz-Harald with understandable emotion.

Moreover, with team-mate Jacques Villeneuve failing to finish due to a gearbox electronics problem, Frentzen also strengthened his position in the championship points table. Yet this was no lucky victory. He was ahead of Villeneuve when the other Williams retired and held off Schumacher with

just the right blend of aggression and confidence.

'I thought I was scheduled to come in for my first stop before Jacques,' said Frentzen. 'But then I saw both Michael and Jacques going in before me, so this was my chance to press hard and I just got out ahead.

'In the closing stages I was worried about the brakes as I didn't want the same thing to happen to me again that happened in Melbourne [a brake disc exploded close to the finish when he was running second]. But Michael was pushing quite hard and I could not save the brakes as much as I hoped to.'

Schumacher and team-mate Eddie Irvine underlined the strength of the Ferrari challenge with second and third places. Michael reported that his chassis set-up was fantastic, the result slightly better than he'd expected.

Both he and Frentzen – whose former girlfriend Corinna Michael married a couple of years ago – were pretty ruthless when it came to dealing with each other on the circuit. Michael nearly put 'HH' off the road on the opening lap, but Frentzen paid him back by blocking him out to keep the lead after his first refuelling stop. Neither seemed particularly irked, apparently regarding it as all part of the fun.

Immediately prior to the start, Benetton driver Gerhard Berger was presented with a silver salver on the grid to commemorate his 200th Grand Prix start. This little celebration understandably went unnoticed by the Arrows team, for whom Berger had driven his first full F1 season in 1985. Damon Hill's Arrows A18 had developed an oil leak and the reigning World Champion suffered the frustration of starting from the pit lane in the spare car.

Meanwhile Jarno Trulli's Minardi was also in trouble, suffering from a gearbox hydraulic pump failure which prevented him from even taking his place on the final grid. The weather was overcast after a short rain shower, which seemed likely to be repeated, but the track was virtually dry as the cars took up positions and everybody opted for slicks.

With Villeneuve and Frentzen together on the front row, there was the promise of high jinks as the pack sprinted towards the Tamburello chicane on the opening lap. In fact, Jacques made a copybook getaway and Schumacher managed to squeeze his Ferrari ahead of the second Williams as they went into the first turn.

On the short straight down to the Villeneuve chicane, Frentzen pulled

out to have a shot at passing his old rival, but Michael was having none of it and almost drove him off the road in a move so blatant as to raise muted gasps from the massed ranks in the press room. It was just the sort of stunt which Ayrton Senna used to pull on Alain Prost in days gone by.

At the end of the opening lap Villeneuve was 0.4s ahead of Schumacher's Ferrari and a gap was already opening to Frentzen, who had the impressive Ralf Schumacher's Jordan keeping pace on his tail. Herbert was next ahead of Panis, Irvine and Fisichella.

By the end of the second lap Schumacher was still hanging on to Villeneuve, but Frentzen was dropping slightly further back and increasingly seemed to have his work cut out fending off Ralf S. in the Jordan. Midway round the third lap, Magnussen, who had made some last-minute set-up changes to his Stewart-Ford, found his car bottoming out on the approach to Acque Minerali and spun ignominiously into the gravel trap.

On lap five Berger's celebrations gave way to acute disappointment when he too spun off for good at Acque Minerali. 'I had a bad start because my car, for some reason, went into neutral and I lost a few places,' he shrugged.

'Then I felt something was strange with the car which I had already experienced during the morning's warm-up. In fact, I had switched to the spare car during the warm-up, but decided to use my own car for the race. It was very strange.'

By lap eight Ralf Schumacher's initial spurt seemed to have ended, the Jordan driver now dropping away from the leading bunch as his overtaxed front tyres left him with a touch too much understeer.

Lap 11 produced plenty of action. Frentzen, shaping up to challenge Schumacher's Ferrari for second place, almost hit the back of the Italian car going into the tricky downhill Rivazza double left-hander. From the in-car camera shots, it certainly looked as though Michael backed off early, leaving Frentzen to sort out the ensuing moment, which lost him several lengths to his rival.

Damon Hill was also getting extremely frustrated, boxed in as he was by Shinji Nakano's Prost. On lap 12 he attempted to dive inside the journeyman Japanese driver on the tight essbend just before the pits, but the two cars made smart contact and were eliminated on the spot.

'I tried to pass Nakano, but he just

Giancarlo Fisichella earned his first points of the season with a fourth-place finish that provided further vindication of Eddie Jordan's controversial decision to place his faith in youth.

Bottom right: It was a dismal weekend on home ground for Jarno Trulli. Having qualified on the penultimate row of the grid, the Italian was unable to start after his Minardi suffered a hydraulic failure.

Bryn Williams

turned in on me,' said Hill. 'I had too much to make up after starting from the pit lane. I was getting held up badly by the guys ahead of me and could see I was losing time. It was going to be a very difficult job getting a result today, anyway.' As it transpired, the only result Damon managed to post was a one-race suspended ban 'for causing an avoidable accident'.

Five laps later Ralf Schumacher's Jordan slowed and limped into the pits after losing a driveshaft retention nut. This promoted Herbert to fourth, but the Sauber-Petronas driver lasted only one lap more before his car stopped abruptly out on the circuit.

'It was looking quite good in my 100th Grand Prix,' reflected Johnny later. 'But just as I was thinking that, the car cut out going into Piratella and

I coasted down the hill towards Acque Minerali. There had been a slight hiccup and then everything cut, including the dashboard display, so I suspect it was an electrical problem. I tried to reset the system, but it wouldn't.'

Further back, Olivier Panis was now in trouble with the Prost. He had started the race confident that a one-stop strategy would be the ideal choice and ran a comfortable sixth in the opening stages, even pulling away slightly from Irvine's Ferrari. Then, after about ten laps, he realised that he was in trouble.

'I was aware that something had deteriorated at the rear of the car, it suddenly became a major handful and the tyres began to wear quite quickly,' he explained. 'That obviously put paid to our strategy.' On lap 20 Panis came in for the first of two stops, driven by the

need for fresh Bridgestones. Only later would the Prost team identify his problem as a failed damper.

On lap 17, Villeneuve's advantage over the Schumacher Ferrari had suddenly shrunk from 3.3s to 1.8s as his Williams demonstrated the first signs of the gearchange glitch which would lead to its retirement. But at this stage the problem seemed an isolated drama and Jacques eased open his advantage to 4.0s on lap 21, but it was back down again to 1.6s next time round as he lapped Ukyo Katayama's Minardi.

Then came the first spate of refuelling stops. At the end of lap 24 Michael brought the Ferrari in for a 9.4s stop, resuming third behind the Williams duo. Then Villeneuve arrived for a 10.1s stop on lap 26 and Frentzen, seeing his team-mate enter the pit lane, piled on the pressure for a

really quick lap before coming in for an 11.1s stop next time round.

By the time Frentzen was accelerating back down the pit lane, Schumacher's Ferrari was crossing the start/finish line at full blast and Michael aimed up the inside of the Williams, intent on taking the lead into the Tamburello chicane. But Heinz-Harald was having none of it. Paying back his old sparring partner for blocking him on the opening lap, Frentzen moved gently across to squeeze Schumacher and keep him back in second place.

Villeneuve now found himself down in third place, so Frentzen confidently stretched his advantage over Schumacher. By lap 40 the Williams was 5.7s ahead and, four laps later, Heinz-Harald came in for his second stop. That allowed Schumacher ahead momentarily,

Practice and qualifying at Imola saw Heinz-Harald Frentzen really getting to grips with the Williams FW19 for the first time. At the previous week's Barcelona test he had experimented with a revised differential set-up which now allowed him to pitch the car into the corners with a much less severe transition between understeer and oversteer as he moved on and off the throttle.

Patrick Head was quick to remind everyone that this was no major technical breakthrough. 'This technical option has been available since the start of the season,' he said. Nevertheless, Frentzen wore a more convincing smile than at any time since joining the team. Moreover, his new-found speed had certainly caused Villeneuve to pay very serious attention.

The trend was sustained through Saturday's hour-long qualifying session. Giancarlo Fisichella's Jordan set a cracking pace from the start, but then Villeneuve got into his stride to produce a 1m 24.783s, Michael Schumacher's Ferrari bettered it with 1m 24.283s and then Jacques came back with 1m 24.216s.

Then it was Frentzen's turn to go ahead. On his first run he was 0.05s ahead at the first timing split and wound up with a 1m 23.911s. Next time round he rubbed home the point by improving further to 1m 23.738s.

At one point during the session Frentzen headed a German 1-2-3 at the head of the timing screens as the Schumacher brothers – Michael just leading Ralf's Jordan – banged in second- and third-fastest times. But Villeneuve's relegation to fourth place lasted no more than a couple of minutes. With 28 minutes of the session remaining, he redressed the balance with a 1m 23.586s and vaulted back to the top of the list.

Nor had he finished. By the end of the session Villeneuve had trimmed his time to 1m 23.303s – 3.6s inside Schumacher's 1996 pole time – to beat Frentzen by 0.3s. Yet such was the exuberance of the two Williams drivers that they both ended the day receiving $5000 fines and one-race bans – suspended for two races – after ignoring yellow flags indicating that Shinji Nakano's Prost was beached over the kerb at Acque Minerali.

Interestingly, Frentzen was getting through the fast flick before this corner without lifting, a feat Villeneuve never quite managed. But at the end of the afternoon, Jacques strung together three perfect timed sectors to keep intact his uninterrupted 1997 pole position qualifying record.

'It was the closest battle this year,' said Villeneuve, 'it was very stressful – and very interesting. Here the tyres are performing well: it is amazing how much grip we get. This track is now a lot of fun, just because of the extra speed we are getting from the tyres.'

Villeneuve also admitted that he'd been worried about Frentzen's pace in the morning. He had lost time when a throttle coupling deep in the vee of the Renault engine caused trouble, with the result that they had to rush through some of the set-up adjustments.

'We also had a leaking water radiator, so we couldn't do all the work we needed to do,' he added. 'I was a little worried because the car didn't feel as good as it had done in previous races. But I improved it during qualifying: the chemistry which I have got going now with my engineer Jock Clear and the rest of the team is pretty good.'

The fourth round of the World Championship was also something of a *tour de force* for Goodyear on a weekend when Ferrari president Luca di Montezemolo had described the Akron company as a 'sleeping giant'.

'Goodyear needs to wake up,' said the Ferrari supremo. 'I think it has fallen asleep and needs to be shaken up. But I have no doubt that we shall be able to recuperate.' As things transpired, Goodyear more than rose to the occasion at Imola and, come the race, not a single Bridgestone runner would make it into the top six.

Schumacher's Ferrari wound up third on the grid, its driver reporting that he felt a little more confident about its race set-up despite a touch too much understeer for his taste at the two Rivazza left-handers. Eddie Irvine was also handicapped by excessive understeer and could not improve on ninth place in the final grid order. After qualifying, it was decided that the team would defer the race debut of its more driveable, but slightly thirstier, 'Step 2' engines until Monaco or Barcelona at the earliest.

With only 17 minutes of the session left, Olivier Panis vaulted his Bridgestone-shod Prost through to fourth place on the grid, the Frenchman a little upset because he believed that Schumacher's Ferrari had slightly balked him on his final run while on its cooling-down lap. Panis was none the less upbeat and optimistic, in contrast to team-mate Nakano, who lost a lap early in the session checking out his newly installed Mugen engine and eventually qualified 18th, well off the pace.

The Jordan camp was understandably ecstatic after Ralf Schumacher and Giancarlo Fisichella qualified side by side on the third row of the grid. Moreover, the team privately believed they could have been even better placed had they not encountered traffic at crucial moments during their runs.

'I am satisfied with my fifth place,' said Schumacher, 'although I am cross with myself for making a mistake at the first chicane when I was on my third run on the first set of tyres.' Fisichella was equally positive, hoping against hope that he might manage a rostrum finish in front of his home crowd. It certainly seemed far from a tall order.

Johnny Herbert's Sauber-Petronas was seventh, the Englishman reporting that his car felt much better over the bumps after he'd reverted to the chassis settings he first used on Friday. By contrast, Nicola Larini had to be content with 12th place after switching to the spare car as his race machine's engine seemed down on power. Then, on his second flying lap, he lost time behind Verstappen's Tyrrell.

McLaren drivers Mika Häkkinen and David Coulthard had to be content with eighth and tenth places on the grid, the MP4/12s again proving difficult to balance out in qualifying configuration. Benetton had much the same trouble with their B197s, Gerhard Berger and Jean Alesi having to settle for 11th and 14th – the latter only 0.02s ahead of Damon Hill's Arrows A18. The problems Benetton confidently believed it had solved at the recent Barcelona test had certainly not been eliminated.

In 13th and 16th places came the two Stewart-Fords of Rubens Barrichello and a much-improved Jan Magnussen. Both cars ran in qualifying with the new Spec 6 version of the Ford Zetec-R V10 engines, but Rubens's developed a high-speed misfire which forced him to switch to the spare which was fitted with an early Spec 5 unit. There was no such luxury available for his team-mate.

Hill, meanwhile, could count himself lucky to have qualified 15th. He spun off on the first flying lap of his second run, then dashed back to the pits to take the spare car, in which team-mate Pedro Diniz had already done his first run while an engine change was completed in his race chassis. 'Unfortunately the handling balance of the spare was a bit different, so I couldn't get the most out of it,' shrugged Damon. 'It's a bit disappointing.'

Diniz finished the day in 17th ahead of Nakano, Salo, Trulli, Verstappen and Katayama.

but the Ferrari driver, having been wrong-footed into locking up a tyre by Nicola Larini's dawdling Sauber, duly made his second stop next time round.

Lap 40 also marked the end of Villeneuve's race. The gearbox electronics on his Williams had gone haywire, the change mechanism developing a mind of its own, and he pulled into the pit lane for good.

Further back, David Coulthard had been doing a good job with the McLaren MP4/12, moving up to fourth place on lap 25. On a one-stop strategy, he made his sole refuelling stop on lap 35 without losing a place. This was followed by an unwelcome ripple of excitement in the McLaren pit when Mika Häkkinen, running fifth, came in unexpectedly for his stop after sliding into the gravel trap at Rivazza while lapping Mika Salo's Tyrrell.

Above: Damon Hill emerges from the remains of his Arrows after his collision with the Prost of Shinji Nakano *(right)*. Frustrated at his inability to find a way past the Japanese novice, the World Champion attempted a desperate overtaking move that put both cars out of the race.

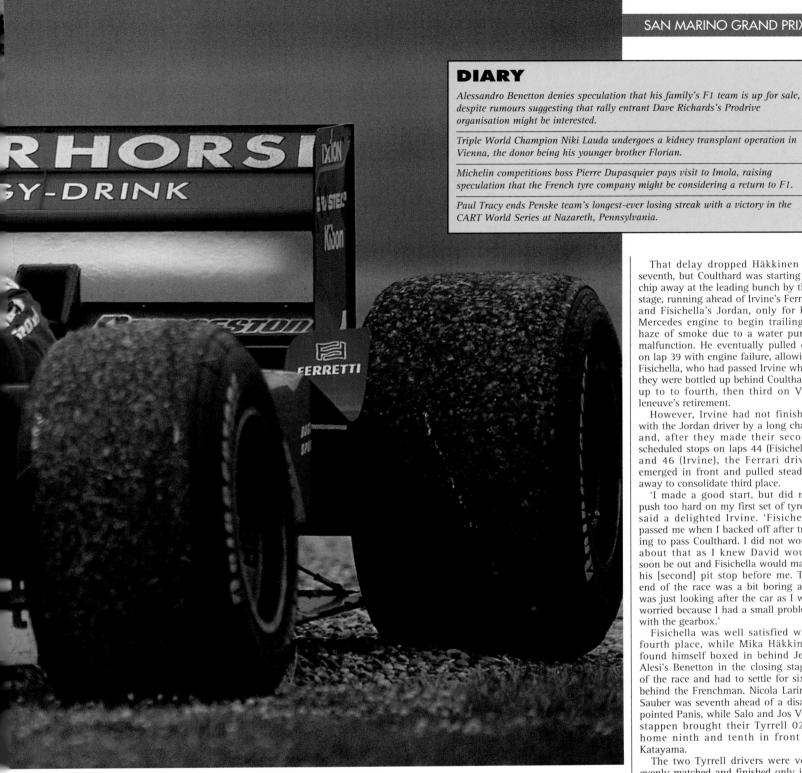

That delay dropped Häkkinen to seventh, but Coulthard was starting to chip away at the leading bunch by this stage, running ahead of Irvine's Ferrari and Fisichella's Jordan, only for his Mercedes engine to begin trailing a haze of smoke due to a water pump malfunction. He eventually pulled off on lap 39 with engine failure, allowing Fisichella, who had passed Irvine when they were bottled up behind Coulthard, up to to fourth, then third on Villeneuve's retirement.

However, Irvine had not finished with the Jordan driver by a long chalk and, after they made their second scheduled stops on laps 44 (Fisichella) and 46 (Irvine), the Ferrari driver emerged in front and pulled steadily away to consolidate third place.

'I made a good start, but did not push too hard on my first set of tyres,' said a delighted Irvine. 'Fisichella passed me when I backed off after trying to pass Coulthard. I did not worry about that as I knew David would soon be out and Fisichella would make his [second] pit stop before me. The end of the race was a bit boring as I was just looking after the car as I was worried because I had a small problem with the gearbox.'

Fisichella was well satisfied with fourth place, while Mika Häkkinen found himself boxed in behind Jean Alesi's Benetton in the closing stages of the race and had to settle for sixth behind the Frenchman. Nicola Larini's Sauber was seventh ahead of a disappointed Panis, while Salo and Jos Verstappen brought their Tyrrell 025s home ninth and tenth in front of Katayama.

The two Tyrrell drivers were very evenly matched and finished only just over six seconds apart, albeit two laps down on the leaders. Both made a single refuelling stop, Jos only relinquishing his advantage when his Cosworth V8 didn't rev cleanly as he was accelerating back into the fray. 'It was always going to be a difficult race for us,' he pondered, 'but I think we did as well as we could have hoped for.'

For the Williams team it had been a good day, their 1997 tally now standing at three wins out of four races. But the whole Ferrari squad was delighted with second and third places, which moved them ahead of McLaren into second place in the constructors' championship stakes.

'Tomorrow we will start testing at Fiorano in preparation for Monaco,' said Ferrari sporting director Jean Todt. As events were subsequently to prove, this work would be to very good effect.

Newey confirmed for McLaren

THE McLaren F1 team received a major boost during the week prior to the San Marino Grand Prix when it was formally confirmed that Adrian Newey, for six years the chief designer for the World Championship-winning Williams team, would join its staff as technical director on 1 August 1997.

As part of a deal which underlined that the services of a top designer are every bit as important as having the best driver, it was being speculated that Newey would collect a £2 million annual pay cheque. If so, it was regarded by many in the pit lane as a blue-chip investment which McLaren also clearly believes will be worth every penny if he can help produce a World Championship challenger for 1998.

One of the most highly regarded aerodynamic engineers in F1, Newey had been involved in a contractual dispute with Williams since the previous November over the terms of his existing contract, which was not due to expire until 1999. He claimed that the team had breached his agreement with them by not consulting him over the replacement of Damon Hill with the German driver Heinz-Harald Frentzen. It is also believed that he did not feel he was being accorded sufficient acknowledgement

for his part in the Williams team's spectacular run of success since he contributed to his first design for the team – the FW14 – back in 1991.

Since being 'rested' by Williams, Newey had been sitting at home on his full Williams salary – believed to be around £700,000 a year – while a solution to the problem was worked out by the parties' lawyers. Williams had originally issued a writ against their chief designer and a court case was pending until McLaren reached a financial settlement with its key rival.

Newey originally made his name as an Indy car designer with the now defunct March team in the mid-1980s, switching to Formula 1 in 1989 with Leyton House and then being recruited by Williams in time for the 1991 season. Every Williams car built since then has benefited from Newey's sure aerodynamic touch.

However, one rival designer expressed doubts as to whether Newey would transform McLaren overnight. 'F1 doesn't always work that way,' he noted. 'The great strength that Williams enjoyed was the partnership between Adrian and Patrick Head. I think some people may have also underestimated Patrick's contribution to the equation.'

17° GRAN PREMIO DI
SAN MARINO

25–27 APRIL 1997

IMOLA

Race distance: 62 laps, 189.906 miles/305.660 km

Race weather: Sunny and bright

FIA™ FORMULA 1 WORLD CHAMPIONSHIP

ROUND
4

IMOLA – AUTODROMO DINO E ENZO FERRARI
CIRCUIT LENGTH: 3.063 MILES/4.930 KM

Pos.	Driver	Nat.	No.	Entrant	Car/Engine	Tyres	Laps	Time/Retirement	Speed (mph/km/h)
1	Heinz-Harald Frentzen	D	4	Rothmans Williams Renault	Williams FW19-Renault RS9 V10	G	62	1h 31m 00.673s	125.212/201.509
2	Michael Schumacher	D	5	Scuderia Ferrari Marlboro	Ferrari F310B 046 V10	G	62	1h 31m 01.910s	125.183/201.463
3	Eddie Irvine	GB	6	Scuderia Ferrari Marlboro	Ferrari F310B 046 V10	G	62	1h 32m 19.016s	123.441/198.659
4	Giancarlo Fisichella	I	12	B&H Total Jordan Peugeot	Jordan 197-Peugeot A14 V10	G	62	1h 32m 24.061s	123.328/198.478
5	Jean Alesi	F	7	Mild Seven Benetton Renault	Benetton B197-Renault RS9 V10	G	61		
6	Mika Häkkinen	SF	9	West McLaren Mercedes	McLaren MP4/12-Mercedes FO110E V10	G	61		
7	Nicola Larini	I	17	Red Bull Sauber Petronas	Sauber C16-Petronas V10	G	61		
8	Olivier Panis	F	14	Prost Gauloises Blondes	Prost JS45-Mugen Honda MF301HA V10	B	61		
9	Mika Salo	SF	19	Tyrrell	Tyrrell 025-Ford ED4 V8	G	60		
10	Jos Verstappen	NL	18	Tyrrell	Tyrrell 025-Ford ED4 V8	G	60		
11	Ukyo Katayama	J	20	Minardi Team	Minardi M197-Hart 830 V8	B	59		
	Pedro Diniz	BR	2	Danka Arrows Yamaha	Arrows A18-Yamaha OX11A/C V10	B	53	Hydraulics	
	Jacques Villeneuve	CDN	3	Rothmans Williams Renault	Williams FW19-Renault RS9 V10	G	40	Gear selection	
	David Coulthard	GB	10	West McLaren Mercedes	McLaren MP4/12-Mercedes FO110E V10	G	38	Engine	
	Rubens Barrichello	BR	22	Stewart Ford	Stewart SF1-Ford Zetec-R V10	B	32	Engine	
	Johnny Herbert	GB	16	Red Bull Sauber Petronas	Sauber C16-Petronas V10	G	18	Electrics	
	Ralf Schumacher	D	11	B&H Total Jordan Peugeot	Jordan 197-Peugeot A14 V10	G	17	Driveshaft	
	Shinji Nakano	J	15	Prost Gauloises Blondes	Prost JS45-Mugen Honda MF301HA V10	B	11	Collision with Hill	
	Damon Hill	GB	1	Danka Arrows Yamaha	Arrows A18-Yamaha OX11A/C V10	B	11	Collision with Nakano	
	Gerhard Berger	A	8	Mild Seven Benetton Renault	Benetton B197-Renault RS9 V10	G	4	Spun off	
	Jan Magnussen	DK	23	Stewart Ford	Stewart SF1-Ford Zetec-R V10	B	2	Spun off	
DNS	Jarno Trulli	I	21	Minardi Team	Minardi M197-Hart 830 V8	B	0	Hydraulics	

Fastest lap: Frentzen, on lap 42, 1m 25.531s, 128.936 mph/207.503 km/h (record).

Previous lap record: Damon Hill (F1 Williams FW18-Renault V10), 1m 28.931s, 123.051 mph/198.032 km/h (1996).

B – Bridgestone   G – Goodyear

Grid order	1	2	3	4	5	6	7	8	9	10	11	12	13	14	15	16	17	18	19	20	21	22	23	24	25	26	27	28	29	30	31	32	33	34	35	36	37	38	39	40	41	42	43	44	45	46	47	48
3 VILLENEUVE	3	3	3	3	3	3	3	3	3	3	3	3	3	3	3	3	3	3	3	3	3	3	3	3	3	4	4	4	4	4	4	4	4	4	4	4	4	4	4	4	4	4	4	5	4	4	4	4
4 FRENTZEN	5	5	5	5	5	5	5	5	5	5	5	5	5	5	5	5	5	5	5	5	5	5	5	5	4	4	3	5	5	5	5	5	5	5	5	5	5	5	5	5	5	5	5	4	5	5	5	5
5 M. SCHUMACHER	4	4	4	4	4	4	4	4	4	4	4	4	4	4	4	4	4	4	4	4	4	4	4	4	5	5	5	3	3	3	3	3	3	3	3	3	3	3	3	3	12	12	12	6	6	6	6	6
14 PANIS	11	11	11	11	11	11	11	11	11	11	11	11	11	11	11	11	16		6	6	6	6	6	6	10	10	10	10	10	10	10	10	10	10	10	10	10	10	12	12	6	6	6	12	12	12	12	12
11 R. SCHUMACHER	16	16	16	16	16	16	16	16	16	16	16	16	16	16	16	16	6	12	12	12	12	12		9	9	9	9	9	9	9	9	9	6	6	6	12	6	6	7	7	7	7	7	7	7			
12 FISICHELLA	14	14	14	14	14	14	14	14	14	14	14	14	14	14	14	14	12	14	10	10	10	10	10	7	7	7	7	7	7	7	6	6	12	12	12	6	7	7	9	9	9	9	9	9	9			
16 HERBERT	6	6	6	6	6	6	6	6	6	6	6	6	6	6	6	6	14	10	9	9	9	9	9	6	6	6	6	6	6	6	12	12	9	7	7	7	9	9	17	17	17	17	17	17	17			
9 HÄKKINEN	12	12	12	12	12	12	12	12	12	12	12	12	12	12	12	12	10	9	7	7	7	7	12	12	12	12	12	12	12	7	7	7	9	9	9	17	17	14	14	14	14	14	14			
6 IRVINE	10	10	10	10	10	10	10	10	10	10	10	10	10	10	10	10	9	7	17	17	17	17	22	22	22	22	22	22	22	14	17	17	17	17	14	14	19	19	19	19	19	19	19			
10 COULTHARD	9	9	9	9	9	9	9	9	9	9	9	9	9	9	9	9	7	17	14	22	22	22	14	14	14	14	14	14	14	17	14	14	14	14	2	2	18	18	18	18	18	18	18			
8 BERGER	7	7	7	7	7	7	7	7	7	7	7	7	7	7	7	7	17	22	22	14	14	14	17	17	17	17	17	17	17	2	2	2	2	2	19	19	2	2	2	2	2	2	2			
17 LARINI	22	22	22	22	22	22	22	22	22	22	22	17	17	17	17	17	22	18	18	18	18	18	18	18	18	19	19	19	19	19	19	19	18	18	20	20	20	20	20	20						
22 BARRICHELLO	17	17	17	17	17	17	17	17	17	17	17	22	22	22	22	22	18	19	19	19	19	19	19	19	19	19	2	2	18	18	18	18	18	20	20													
7 ALESI	2	2	2	2	2	2	2	2	2	2	2	2	2	2	2	19	2	2	2	2	2	2	2	2	2	2	18	18	20	20	20	20	20	20													
1 HILL	23	23	18	18	18	18	18	18	18	18	18	18	18	18	18	18	2	20	20	20	20	20	20	20	20	20	20	20																				
23 MAGNUSSEN	18	18	19	19	19	19	19	19	19	19	20																																					
2 DINIZ	19	19	15	15	15	15	15	15	15	15	15	20	20	20	20	20	20																															
15 NAKANO	15	15	8	8	1	1	1	1	1	1	1																																					
19 SALO	8	8	20	20	20	20	20	20	20	20																																						
21 TRULLI	20	20	1	1																																												
18 VERSTAPPEN	1	1																																														
20 KATAYAMA																																																

Pit stop

One lap behind leader

STARTING GRID

3 **VILLENEUVE** Williams	**4** **FRENTZEN** Williams
5 **M. SCHUMACHER** Ferrari	**14** **PANIS** Prost
11 **R. SCHUMACHER** Jordan	**12** **FISICHELLA** Jordan
16 **HERBERT** Sauber	**9** **HÄKKINEN** McLaren
6 **IRVINE** Ferrari	**10** **COULTHARD** McLaren
8 **BERGER** Benetton	**17** **LARINI** Sauber
22 **BARRICHELLO** Stewart	**7** **ALESI** Benetton
1 **HILL*** Arrows	**23** **MAGNUSSEN** Stewart
2 **DINIZ** Arrows	**15** **NAKANO** Prost
19 **SALO** Tyrrell	**21** **TRULLI**** Minardi
18 **VERSTAPPEN** Tyrrell	**20** **KATAYAMA** Minardi

* started from pit lane

** did not start

49	50	51	52	53	54	55	56	57	58	59	60	61	62	●
4	4	4	4	4	4	4	4	4	4	4	4	4	4	1
5	5	5	5	5	5	5	5	5	5	5	5	5	5	2
6	6	6	6	6	6	6	6	6	6	6	6	6	6	3
12	12	12	12	12	12	12	12	12	12	12	12	12	12	4
7	7	7	7	7	7	7	7	7	7	7	7	7	7	5
9	9	9	9	9	9	9	9	9	9	9	9	9	9	6
17	17	17	17	17	17	17	17	17	17	17	17	17		
14	14	14	14	14	14	14	14	14	14	14	14	14		
19	19	19	19	19	19	19	19	19	19	19	19	19		
18	18	18	18	18	18	18	18	18	18	18	18			
2	2	2	2	2	20	20	20	20	20	20				
20	20	20	20	20										

TIME SHEETS

QUALIFYING
Weather: Bright and warm

Pos.	Driver	Car	Laps	Time
1	Jacques Villeneuve	Williams-Renault	11	1m 23.303s
2	Heinz-Harald Frentzen	Williams-Renault	12	1m 23.646s
3	Michael Schumacher	Ferrari	11	1m 23.955s
4	Olivier Panis	Prost-Mugen Honda	12	1m 24.075s
5	Ralf Schumacher	Jordan-Peugeot	11	1m 24.081s
6	Giancarlo Fisichella	Jordan-Peugeot	11	1m 24.596s
7	Johnny Herbert	Sauber-Petronas	12	1m 24.723s
8	Mika Häkkinen	McLaren-Mercedes	12	1m 24.812s
9	Eddie Irvine	Ferrari	12	1m 24.861s
10	David Coulthard	McLaren-Mercedes	12	1m 25.077s
11	Gerhard Berger	Benetton-Renault	11	1m 25.371s
12	Nicola Larini	Sauber-Petronas	11	1m 25.544s
13	Rubens Barrichello	Stewart-Ford	12	1m 25.579s
14	Jean Alesi	Benetton-Renault	10	1m 25.729s
15	Damon Hill	Arrows-Yamaha	11	1m 25.743s
16	Jan Magnussen	Stewart-Ford	8	1m 26.192s
17	Pedro Diniz	Arrows-Yamaha	11	1m 26.253s
18	Shinji Nakano	Prost-Mugen Honda	12	1m 26.712s
19	Mika Salo	Tyrrell-Ford	12	1m 26.852s
20	Jarno Trulli	Minardi-Hart	12	1m 26.960s
21	Jos Verstappen	Tyrrell-Ford	10	1m 27.428s
22	Ukyo Katayama	Minardi-Hart	11	1m 28.727s

FRIDAY FREE PRACTICE
Weather: Bright and warm

Pos.	Driver	Laps	Time
1	Eddie Irvine	25	1m 25.981s
2	Michael Schumacher	28	1m 25.997s
3	Gerhard Berger	25	1m 26.259s
4	Jean Alesi	30	1m 26.382s
5	Jacques Villeneuve	25	1m 26.499s
6	David Coulthard	29	1m 26.549s
7	Heinz-Harald Frentzen	28	1m 26.600s
8	Rubens Barrichello	25	1m 26.679s
9	Olivier Panis	28	1m 26.779s
10	Nicola Larini	29	1m 26.831s
11	Johnny Herbert	29	1m 26.842s
12	Mika Häkkinen	19	1m 27.184s
13	Damon Hill	26	1m 27.334s
14	Giancarlo Fisichella	9	1m 27.612s
15	Ralf Schumacher	13	1m 28.091s
16	Jan Magnussen	25	1m 28.177s
17	Shinji Nakano	30	1m 29.021s
18	Mika Salo	23	1m 29.087s
19	Pedro Diniz	21	1m 29.117s
20	Jos Verstappen	17	1m 29.736s
21	Ukyo Katayama	16	1m 29.974s
22	Jarno Trulli	17	1m 30.820s

SATURDAY FREE PRACTICE
Weather: Sunny and warm

Pos.	Driver	Laps	Time
1	Heinz-Harald Frentzen	27	1m 23.477s
2	Jacques Villeneuve	25	1m 23.739s
3	Giancarlo Fisichella	29	1m 24.325s
4	Olivier Panis	29	1m 24.586s
5	Ralf Schumacher	29	1m 24.626s
6	Eddie Irvine	26	1m 24.719s
7	Johnny Herbert	30	1m 24.766s
8	Mika Häkkinen	28	1m 24.980s
9	Michael Schumacher	27	1m 24.982s
10	Gerhard Berger	26	1m 25.027s
11	Jean Alesi	22	1m 25.586s
12	Rubens Barrichello	21	1m 25.586s
13	Nicola Larini	24	1m 25.650s
14	Jan Magnussen	27	1m 25.791s
15	Damon Hill	26	1m 26.034s
16	David Coulthard	12	1m 26.226s
17	Mika Salo	25	1m 27.004s
18	Pedro Diniz	23	1m 27.042s
19	Jos Verstappen	25	1m 27.383s
20	Shinji Nakano	17	1m 27.709s
21	Jarno Trulli	26	1m 27.970s
	Ukyo Katayama		No time

WARM-UP
Weather: Bright and warm

Pos.	Driver	Laps	Time
1	Heinz-Harald Frentzen	11	1m 48.505s
2	Eddie Irvine	10	1m 48.528s
3	Olivier Panis	13	1m 48.547s
4	David Coulthard	12	1m 48.605s
5	Michael Schumacher	12	1m 49.160s
6	Ralf Schumacher	11	1m 50.483s
7	Jan Magnussen	11	1m 50.556s
8	Jacques Villeneuve	10	1m 50.727s
9	Rubens Barrichello	7	1m 50.754s
10	Giancarlo Fisichella	13	1m 50.807s
11	Damon Hill	9	1m 50.824s
12	Ukyo Katayama	11	1m 50.994s
13	Jos Verstappen	12	1m 51.094s
14	Jean Alesi	12	1m 51.315s
15	Mika Häkkinen	11	1m 51.772s
16	Johnny Herbert	11	1m 51.904s
17	Nicola Larini	10	1m 51.953s
18	Pedro Diniz	10	1m 52.171s
19	Shinji Nakano	8	1m 52.581s
20	Gerhard Berger	11	1m 52.927s
21	Mika Salo	13	1m 53.344s
22	Jarno Trulli	11	1m 53.771s

RACE FASTEST LAPS
Weather: Sunny and bright

Driver	Time	Lap
Heinz-Harald Frentzen	1m 25.531s	42
Michael Schumacher	1m 25.537s	61
Jacques Villeneuve	1m 25.997s	21
David Coulthard	1m 26.067s	33
Giancarlo Fisichella	1m 26.620s	23
Nicola Larini	1m 26.753s	43
Mika Häkkinen	1m 26.791s	29
Eddie Irvine	1m 26.811s	45
Jean Alesi	1m 27.091s	30
Ralf Schumacher	1m 27.217s	17
Johnny Herbert	1m 27.594s	17
Rubens Barrichello	1m 27.741s	28
Pedro Diniz	1m 27.793s	45
Olivier Panis	1m 28.064s	27
Mika Salo	1m 28.189s	32
Jos Verstappen	1m 28.886s	54
Damon Hill	1m 29.237s	8
Ukyo Katayama	1m 29.554s	59
Shinji Nakano	1m 30.554s	11
Gerhard Berger	1m 33.513s	8
Jan Magnussen	1m 36.710s	2
Jarno Trulli	No time	

CHASSIS LOG BOOK

1	Hill	Arrows A18/3
2	Diniz	Arrows A18/2
	spare	Arrows A18/1
3	Villeneuve	Williams FW19/4
4	Frentzen	Williams FW19/5
	spare	Williams FW19/3
5	M. Schumacher	Ferrari F310B/174
6	Irvine	Ferrari F310B/173
	spare	Ferrari F310B/172
7	Alesi	Benetton B197/5
8	Berger	Benetton B197/4
	spare	Benetton B197/3
9	Häkkinen	McLaren MP4/12/2
10	Coulthard	McLaren MP4/12/4
	spare	McLaren MP4/12/1
11	R. Schumacher	Jordan 197/3
12	Fisichella	Jordan 197/4
	spare	Jordan 197/1
14	Panis	Prost JS45/3
15	Nakano	Prost JS45/2
	spare	Prost JS45/1
16	Herbert	Sauber C16/1
17	Larini	Sauber C16/2
	spare	Sauber C16/3
18	Verstappen	Tyrrell 025/2
19	Salo	Tyrrell 025/3
	spare	Tyrrell 025/1
20	Katayama	Minardi M197/3
21	Trulli	Minardi M197/2
22	Barrichello	Stewart SF1/2
23	Magnussen	Stewart SF1/3
	spare	Stewart SF1/1

POINTS TABLES

Drivers

1	Jacques Villeneuve	20
2	Michael Schumacher	14
3 =	David Coulthard	10
3 =	Gerhard Berger	10
3 =	Mika Häkkinen	10
3 =	Heinz-Harald Frentzen	10
3 =	Eddie Irvine	10
8	Olivier Panis	6
9	Ralf Schumacher	4
10 =	Johnny Herbert	3
10 =	Giancarlo Fisichella	3
10 =	Jean Alesi	3
13	Nicola Larini	1

Constructors

1	Williams	30
2	Ferrari	24
3	McLaren	20
4	Benetton	13
5	Jordan	7
6	Prost	6
7	Sauber	4

FOR THE RECORD

First Grand Prix win

Heinz-Harald Frentzen

First Grand Prix points

Giancarlo Fisichella

200th Grand Prix start

Gerhard Berger

100th Grand Prix start

Johnny Herbert

MONACO

grand prix

M. SCHUMACHER

BARRICHELLO

IRVINE

PANIS

SALO

FISICHELLA

In dauntingly treacherous conditions, Michael Schumacher drove with inch-perfect precision and absolute commitment to score an utterly dominant triumph.

Monaco unquestionably produced the most dramatic qualifying session of the season so far. With the latest 'Step 2' version of Maranello's V10 engine fitted to his Ferrari F310B, Michael Schumacher set the ball rolling with a first-run best of 1m 18.235s. Villeneuve opened his bidding with a 1m 19.373s, but it soon became clear that this was to be far from an easy run for the Canadian or his team-mate Heinz-Harald Frentzen.

Even so, Frentzen *(below)*, despite struggling slightly for front-end grip, motivated himself magnificently to duck under Villeneuve's best with a 1m 19.053s. The previous year, Jacques had been really struggling on his debut on this confined street circuit, both in terms of car set-up and overall familiarisation, but this time he was sharper and more focused, doggedly refusing to relinquish the prospect of a starting position on the front row of the grid.

With only eight minutes left the World Championship points leader launched a final assault on pole position. It certainly looked pretty promising. He was 0.2s up at the first split, stopping the clocks at 1m 18.583s, despite a big moment on the final corner which caused him to ease off the throttle for a split-second. Keeping his nerve, he set off on another lap, but paid the price of his over-exuberance by tapping the guard rail at Ste Devote, which eventually caused him to pull off just before the tunnel.

This was the crucial turning-point for Frentzen. Having changed his FW19's chassis set-up after the morning's free practice session, he now took a big gamble and made another minor change. It gave him fractionally more positive front-end bite and he took full advantage of that extra edge.

It enabled him to produce a simply terrific lap. Frentzen was 0.3s up at the first timing split, 0.2s at the second. Even though the Williams's performance advantage seemed to fade perceptibly through the final leg of the lap around the swimming pool, Frentzen kept everything under control to emerge with a best time of 1m 18.216s. It was the first pole position of his F1 career and over two seconds faster than Michael Schumacher's '96 pole time, an achievement explained at least in part by the fact

that the approach to the swimming pool esses had been slightly eased and opened out.

It also enabled him to breathe a personal sigh of relief. Heinz-Harald had arrived in Monaco fresh from his first F1 victory at Imola, only for Thursday's free practice session, which saw Johnny Herbert's Sauber impressively quickest, to end on a bruising note when he bounced his FW19 into the wall coming through the tricky right-hander before the pits.

The fact that he made such an elementary error of judgement beneath the steely gaze of Williams technical director Patrick Head only added to the German driver's nervousness. 'This is a very unsatisfactory position to be in,' said Head as he examined the badly damaged front end of Frentzen's chassis. It was a chilling understatement, to say the least. By Saturday evening, Head confessed that pole position meant Frentzen had atoned for his earlier transgression.

Schumacher made a last-ditch effort to salvage the situation for Ferrari, but couldn't quite make sense of the fact that he was unable to reproduce his earlier time. 'I was quite surprised,' he later admitted. 'I couldn't match it. The temperature crept up by about six degrees during the course of the session, but on the other hand the grip improved as more rubber went down. I seemed to have too much understeer on the slower corners.'

By contrast, Eddie Irvine was very disappointed to end up 15th fastest, reporting that his car's handling just did not feel the same as it did during the morning.

'The afternoon was a total mystery to me,' he explained, 'although I already had problems with understeer during the morning. I was

very slow coming out of all the corners as I had to wait for the front end to bite.

'On this track it is impossible to make up a few places at the start, so tomorrow will be a hard race. But our car is reliable, so hopefully I can bring home a couple of points for the team.' As things transpired, Irvine would do rather better than he had predicted.

The irrepressible Jordan duo scarcely put a wheel wrong, Giancarlo Fisichella raising the team's hopes by qualifying fourth. The Italian privately believed that he might possibly have ended up third but for a slight mistake coming past the swimming pool. On the other hand, Ralf Schumacher was disappointed not to have improved upon sixth place on the grid, his best lap thwarted when he came up behind Nicola Larini's Sauber.

McLaren would have been front row contenders had not Häkkinen clipped a barrier, breaking a steering arm, and then ploughed straight into the opposite barrier on a lap which looked set to earn him third place on the grid. Coulthard split the two Jordans, but the Scot still complained that nagging understeer was costing him crucial tenths. Häkkinen took the spare McLaren to finally qualify eighth.

On Saturday morning, Johnny Herbert spun his Sauber into the barrier at Mirabeau and the team had to work flat out to fit a new gearbox, rear suspension, wing and undertray, which left him spending much of the qualifying session sorting out a decent chassis set-up. Under the circumstances, seventh place on the grid, 0.6s faster than the 11th-placed Larini, was a pretty respectable effort.

Benetton had a dismal time in qualifying, once more unable to generate adequate tyre temperature while running a light fuel load. Jean Alesi managed to salvage ninth place on the grid, but Gerhard Berger was consigned to the outer darkness in 17th spot after wrecking his race car against the swimming pool barrier on Saturday morning and being obliged to qualify the spare B197.

Goodyear had produced new dry compounds and constructions for Monaco, and it showed. With little firm data for this one-off street circuit, Bridgestone was always going to be fighting something of a rearguard action at this race, their best qualifier being Rubens Barrichello's Stewart

in tenth place on the grid. Team-mate Jan Magnussen was back in 19th place on his first visit to Monaco, feeling that he was losing time particularly through the Casino Square section of the circuit.

Olivier Panis never quite got his Prost working as well as he would have liked and 12th place on the grid was a big disappointment for the 1996 winner. He just squeezed in ahead of Damon Hill's Arrows-Yamaha, the World Champion reckoning that he was just about all the potential he could unlock from his machine. 'It's just a question of needing more power and more downforce,' he explained succinctly.

Mika Salo managed a worthy 14th place with the Tyrrell-Ford, admitting that he was right on the limit all the way round his best lap, finishing up slightly disappointed not to have pipped Hill at the end. Meanwhile Jos Verstappen touched the guard rail coming out of the swimming pool complex, broke a steering arm and slammed into the opposite barrier, doing the right side of the 025 chassis a power of no good.

He ran back to the pits and took over the spare, which was set up for Salo, but could only qualify in last place on the grid. 'Taking an unfamiliar spare car at short notice is always difficult,' he admitted, 'but to do that when you are qualifying at Monaco requires a big effort just to get into the race!'

Behind Irvine's 15th-place Ferrari came an upbeat Pedro Diniz in the other Arrows, a dejected Berger and Jarno Trulli's Minardi. Separating Magnussen from Verstappen were the Japanese contingent, with Ukyo Katayama's Minardi getting the better of Shinji Nakano's Prost, the latter quite clearly out of his depth in this highly competitive environment.

Despite losing part of his front wing, Mika Salo earned a couple of precious points for Tyrrell with a gritty non-stop drive to fifth place.

FIFTY years to the day after Franco Cortese drove the first sports Ferrari in its maiden race outing at Piacenza, Michael Schumacher celebrated the Prancing Horse's competition half-century in fairy-tale fashion with a magnificent victory in a rain-soaked Monaco Grand Prix through the treacherous streets of the Mediterranean Principality.

With rain falling steadily at the start of the race, Schumacher tried both his Ferrari F310Bs in the final pre-start warm-up, opting for an intermediate chassis set-up and Goodyear's intermediate rubber option. He was 6.6s ahead on the opening lap, then stretched his advantage to 11.5, 15.7, 16.7 and 22.1s the next four times round.

This spectacular opening spurt was more than sufficient to put the outcome of the race beyond reasonable doubt. At his sole refuelling stop at the end of lap 32, Schumacher switched to a set of Goodyear's 1996-specification 'quattro' full rain tyres, although by this stage he had comfortably eclipsed all his fellow Goodyear runners, many of whom had opted for the latest hand-cut vee-pat-

Pamela Lauesen/FOSA

tern '97 rain tyre which didn't offer quite the same level of grip.

Even a momentary lapse of attention which caused him to steer up the escape road at Ste Devote on lap 53 when he judged he was approaching fractionally too fast to make the corner safely failed to jeopardise the overwhelming magnitude of Schumacher's domination. He finished the fifth round of the championship chase – flagged when it reached the two hour mark – just over 53s ahead of the admirably driven Stewart-Ford of Rubens Barrichello, but the margin could have been even bigger because Michael rolled off his pace so that team-mate Eddie Irvine would not have to complete an extra lap for his hard-won third place.

If Schumacher did receive any assistance, then it was from the Williams team. Heinz-Harald Frentzen qualified superbly on pole position, thereby atoning for a shunt during Thursday practice which brought a disapproving frown to the face of technical director Patrick Head, but then the team made the almost incomprehensible decision

to start him and third-place qualifier Jacques Villeneuve on slick rubber.

'We thought about putting one car on intermediates just to be conservative,' shrugged James Robinson, Williams's senior operations director. 'But we then thought it wasn't worth it, because the information we had suggested it would dry quite quickly. A bad call by me, you might say, but then that's the unpredictability of Monaco.'

McLaren took similar professional weather forecasting advice that the 'shower' would last no more than half an hour (although where they thought they would be running after 30 minutes on slicks in the rain is not clear) but David Coulthard opted for intermediates, unlike Mika Häkkinen. Either way, it turned out to be a disaster for both these high-profile operations.

By the time the pack plunged out of Casino Square and slithered towards Mirabeau on the opening lap, Schumacher's Ferrari was already ten lengths ahead of Giancarlo Fisichella's Jordan and the Italian finished the opening lap 6.6s adrift in second place.

Then came Ralf Schumacher's Jordan, the floundering Frentzen, Barrichello's Bridgestone-shod Stewart, Johnny Herbert's Sauber, Coulthard, Olivier Panis, Villeneuve, Häkkinen and Jean Alesi's Benetton.

Alesi nipped ahead of Häkkinen second time round, but all hell broke loose under braking for the chicane when Coulthard spun and stalled, the rest of the pack anchored up and Mika bounced off the right-hand guard rail into the back of the Frenchman's Benetton.

Alesi survived unscathed, but Häkkinen skidded to a halt minus his left-front corner. Both McLarens were out of the battle scarcely three minutes into the race.

Yet that was only the beginning of it. Alesi straight-lined the chicane, then almost stopped, causing Eddie Irvine to brake hard in the other Ferrari. Damon Hill hit the back of his old F3000 rival, glanced a passing Tyrrell and the World Champion's Arrows slithered to a halt at the side of the track.

'The first lap was absolutely extraordinary,' recalled Damon later. 'It

was so slippery, we were going very slowly and everybody was trying like mad to pass everyone else. They were going round the outside, the inside – I went round Loews hairpin with four cars abreast.

'Unfortunately on this circuit you need a bit of luck, and while I thought that once I'd got through the first corner I would be OK, that just wasn't with us today.'

As the race settled down and the Williams duo fell away, Barrichello slipped into focus as the second star of the race. On lap two he pushed ahead of Frentzen to take fourth place, then he moved up to third on lap five after Ralf Schumacher half-spun at Loews and let the Stewart driver through.

On lap six both Barrichello and Ralf Schumacher nipped ahead of Fisichella to take second and third places, even though Rubens was by now over 20 seconds behind the leading Ferrari. Villeneuve had already made his first stop for wet tyres at the end of lap three, but Frentzen soldiered gallantly on until the end of lap five before making his stop. Heinz-Harald resumed in 16th

DIARY

The McLaren team denies that it has made an offer to Damon Hill for the 1998 season.

BMW board reported to have given green light for F1 return. A formal announcement is expected in September.

McLaren test driver Nick Heidfeld dominates Monaco F3 supporting race from start to finish in his Bertram Schafer team Dallara.

Former F3000 champion Vincenzo Sospiri, left without a drive following the collapse of the Lola Formula 1 team, qualifies on front row of the grid for the Indianapolis 500.

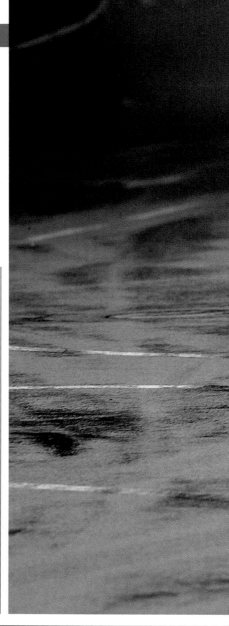

Johnny Herbert was lucky to emerge unscathed from a spectacular crash at Ste Devote. After the Sauber struck the barrier on the left of the track, its front wing became trapped beneath the car, which careered on towards a second heavy impact *(right)*.

Eddie Irvine *(below left)* added to Ferrari's delight with a disciplined drive to third place from 15th on the starting grid.

Below right: A disconsolate Ralf Schumacher prepares to face Eddie Jordan after spinning out of third place.

immediately behind Jarno Trulli's Minardi, soon picking up a place when the young Italian slid into the tyres at Mirabeau.

By lap ten Schumacher's Ferrari was 28.1s ahead and sweeping through Casino Square by the time second-place man Barrichello accelerated out of Rascasse and onto the start/finish straight. Herbert's Sauber was now holding a strong fifth place, but this was the lap which saw the Englishman's departure from the race in vividly spectacular fashion.

'The conditions hadn't been too bad,' he explained, 'but I was having trouble getting the power down and the car was twitchy on the straight. Starting the tenth lap I was flat in fifth on the pit straight when a bump flicked me into the barrier on the left-hand side going towards Ste Devote, and then the car was thrown across at almost undiminished speed and hit the barrier on the outside of the corner almost head-on. That was it.'

Continuing the carnage, Gerhard Berger slid straight on at Mirabeau, removing his Benetton's nose section and trickling round to the pits for re-

pairs. This little drama dropped him from 10th to 15th.

On lap 11 the field was further depleted when Ralf Schumacher spun off at Casino Square, promoting Panis to fourth place ahead of Irvine and Mika Salo, the Tyrrell driver by now firmly on course for something of an economy-run performance as the team was aiming to squeeze its V8-engined machine through the race without a single refuelling stop.

Schumacher Senior appeared to be revelling in the appalling conditions, kicking out the tail of his Ferrari on the slower corners just for the hell of it. Everybody else seemed to be poised on a precarious knife-edge of control by comparison.

On lap 12 Barrichello ran over the chicane kerbing, losing another two seconds to the leader. Two laps later Irvine did the same for the second time in the race and on lap 15 Villeneuve suffered the ultimate indignity when the leading Ferrari stormed through to lap his Williams on the climb towards Massenet. However, by this stage Jacques had already swiped a barrier and he came limping in to retire soon afterwards.

'We had data telling us that it would dry after 20 to 30 minutes, so we decided to keep the dry set-up and the slicks,' said Villeneuve as he looked back on the Williams team's disastrous day.

'But it started raining [even] more, so the slicks were useless, so we stopped and changed to intermediate tyres, but with the dry set-up the car was difficult to drive and at one point, just before Michael overtook me, I hit the guard rail. I continued for a few laps, but the rear of the car was too damaged to go on.'

So the dramas continued. On lap 17, Alesi's Benetton snapped into a pirouette at Portier. He successfully spin-turned the machine, then stalled the engine. By lap 20 Schumacher's Ferrari was 30.7s ahead with Barrichello a comfortable second and Fisichella now under intense pressure from Panis in their squabble over third place. Irvine was running fifth ahead of Salo, but the Tyrrell driver was beginning to close on the second Ferrari, non-stop strategy or not.

By lap 29 Schumacher had stretched his lead to an amazing 40.6s, so by the time he came into the

Sutton Motorsport Images

pits for his sole refuelling stop at the end of lap 32 there was no question of his advantage being jeopardised. He resumed with 23.4s still in hand over Barrichello while Panis nipped inside Fisichella to take third at the swimming pool on lap 34, quickly followed by Irvine, and the sole surviving Jordan duly made its refuelling stop at the end of the following lap.

Panis pitted on lap 37, followed by Barrichello two laps later. It wasn't enough for the Stewart driver's second place to be endangered, but Irvine stayed out until lap 45 before coming in for fuel and tyres and this was sufficient to keep him ahead of the Prost driver.

Further back, Jan Magnussen was doing an impressive job with the other Stewart-Ford and pulled past Fisichella to take sixth place on lap 38. Unfortunately the young Dane was not to be rewarded with his first F1 championship points.

'After my first pit stop, coming out of the tunnel and braking into the chicane, I locked up and went straight over the kerb, which took my front wing off,' he recalled. 'Ten laps later it happened again, but this time I knew I should not go across the kerb.' This delay would eventually drop him back to seventh place.

With 39 laps completed, Frentzen's bitter agony finally ended when he bounced his undriveable FW19 into the guard rail at the chicane. The

Pamela Lauesen/FOSA

Williams rout was now complete and all that remained was to watch Michael Schumacher reel off the laps to complete one of the single most impressive performances of his glittering F1 career.

Suddenly, on lap 53 there was Schumacher in the escape road at Ste Devote. Everybody gasped, but it was a false alarm. 'I locked the front wheels,' he later explained, 'and although I might have got round the corner, I decided not to risk it and took the escape road. There was no problem.'

The two hour mark eventually came up as Schumacher was completing his 62nd lap, 16 short of the originally scheduled race distance.

Michael chose to ease back so that Irvine, who'd only had a quick splash of fuel at his late stop, did not have to cover another lap. But there was no real problem; it was merely a precautionary measure.

Ferrari's delight was certainly further enhanced by Irvine's splendid run through from 15th on the grid to third at the chequered flag, but their satisfaction was as nothing compared with the unbridled joy in the Stewart-Ford camp as Rubens Barrichello came home a brilliant third on only the team's fifth Grand Prix outing, posting the best finish so far for Bridgestone in the process.

'I have never been happier in my entire racing career,' said Stewart, 'not from a race victory or a World Championship, not even here at Monaco. I've never been second at Monaco, but I'd much rather our team's car finished second here than win the race myself.

'Monaco is the jewel in the crown of Grand Prix racing. Rubens drove fantastically well. He really put it together superbly, apart from one slight error at the chicane, but apart from that it was all we could hope for. The Stewart-Ford team has certainly achieved its first podium finish much earlier than we could have ever expected.'

It was an upbeat ending to a weekend which had started with rumours that Stewart was taking legal opinions as to where it stands with motor racing's governing body, the FIA, in terms of television income and prize money.

'We are asking for legal advice about our position *vis-à-vis* the Concorde Agreement and our membership of our group,' he admitted. 'I cannot comment any further than that because I do not know the position.'

Although the Stewart team is new to F1 this year, Jackie feels that it should be entitled to a share of the TV income as it is as much part of the show as any other. There had also been tension between Stewart and FIA Vice-President Bernie Ecclestone when the team's motorhome was the only one denied access to the main F1 pad-

Rubens Barrichello put the disappointments of the last couple of seasons behind him with a splendid second place for Stewart-Ford.

Below: While Jackie Stewart and his son Paul are understandably elated at their team's achievement, Rubens looks back on his day's work with quiet satisfaction.

in too much understeer, but he held off a counter-attack from Fisichella to equal his best-ever F1 finish.

'I think that's what you call thinking on your feet,' he grinned. 'I didn't make a good start on the slippery outside of the track and was maybe a bit too careful going into the first corner. But then about half-way through the race I realised what the team was trying to do, so we reduced the fuel mix and revs and I started coasting through the corners to stay off the power.

'It was great thinking, but I wasn't sure I was going to make it. My tyres were completely shot and when it started raining again I lost all grip and was lucky not to hit the wall.'

His team-mate Jos Verstappen made a single stop for fuel and tyres on lap 41, finishing eighth behind Magnussen despite a spin. Berger and Ukyo Katayama's Minardi completed the list of finishers, two laps down like Verstappen.

Yet for all the meritorious performances down the field, the day overwhelmingly belonged to the dynamic Michael Schumacher. It also served as a reminder that Ferrari can no longer be discounted as a consistent performer. Five races into the championship and the red cars from Maranello had yet to record a retirement due to mechanical failure.

Just like the good old days, in fact.

Mosley defends new F1 rules

FIA President Max Mosley used his annual Monaco press conference to deliver a robust defence of the new F1 regulations which will see narrower chassis running on grooved slicks from the start of the 1998 season.

Rejecting comments from Jacques Villeneuve to the effect that the cars will not be fun to drive under the new rules, Mosley commented: 'When he stated that because racing cars slow down more rapidly on big tyres, and therefore crash with less energy, he was demonstrably wrong.

'And when he claimed that slower drivers would find it easier on grooved tyres to stay close to the most skilled drivers, all the evidence is to the contrary. Indeed, if you believe that, you wipe out the history of motorsport. In effect, Jacques suggests that all racing drivers were mediocre until he came along . . .'

Mosley made it clear there was no question of back-tracking on the new rules, even though Ferrari now appeared to be the only team which wished them to go through. He said that the prime consideration should be to keep the lid on F1 car performance in order to retain the remaining classic corners, such as Eau Rouge at Spa-Francorchamps. 'If we don't, we will be left with nothing but go-kart tracks,' he claimed.

Mosley also made the point that the issue as to whether the racing is dull or not was not part of the FIA's consideration of these topics. 'The only reason for the changes to the rules is safety,' he insisted.

'We are trying to retain lap times and cornering speeds more or less in the same area as they were in 1996. The second consideration is to make the chassis safer in the event of a crash. Under the revised 1998 rules, the driver will have more room, more crash resistance, more roll-over security, better fuel tank security, indeed greater security all round.

'The public's interest in the racing has been of no consideration in introducing these rules.'

dock at Monaco and sited in an overflow position some distance away.

Irvine was well satisfied with third place while Olivier Panis admitted after finishing fourth that he had 'rarely driven such a tough race at the wheel of such a difficult car to drive. Despite the problems we had since the beginning of the weekend, we finally established a good set-up for the dry – then it rained, but I started the race on the same settings.'

Inspired driving from Salo allied to that imaginative non-stop Tyrrell team strategy yielded a well-deserved fifth place and two valuable championship points. An early coming-together cost the Finn part of a front wing, resulting

Bryn Williams

GRAND PRIX DE
MONACO
8–11 MAY 1997
MONTE CARLO

Race distance: 62 laps, 129.704 miles/208.692 km
(reduced from 69 laps; race stopped at two hours)

Race weather: Wet and cloudy

FIA FORMULA 1 WORLD CHAMPIONSHIP

ROUND 5

MONACO – MONTE CARLO GRAND PRIX CIRCUIT

STE DEVOTE
MONTÉE DE BEAU RIVAGE
MIRABEAU
TABAC
NOUVELLE CHICANE
LOEWS
VIRAGE DU PORTIER
VIRAGE ANTHONY NOGHES
TUNNEL
LA RASCASSE

CIRCUIT LENGTH: 2.092 MILES/3.366 KM

Pos.	Driver	Nat.	No.	Entrant	Car/Engine	Tyres	Laps	Time/Retirement	Speed (mph/km/h)
1	Michael Schumacher	D	5	Scuderia Ferrari Marlboro	Ferrari F310B 046 V10	G	62	2h 00m 05.654s	64.787/104.264
2	Rubens Barrichello	BR	22	Stewart Ford	Stewart SF1-Ford Zetec-R V10	B	62	2h 00m 58.960s	64.311/103.498
3	Eddie Irvine	GB	6	Scuderia Ferrari Marlboro	Ferrari F310B 046 V10	G	62	2h 01m 27.762s	64.056/103.089
4	Olivier Panis	F	14	Prost Gauloises Blondes	Prost JS45-Mugen Honda MF301HA V10	B	62	2h 01m 50.056s	63.861/102.775
5	Mika Salo	SF	19	Tyrrell	Tyrrell 025-Ford ED4 V8	G	61		
6	Giancarlo Fisichella	I	12	B&H Total Jordan Peugeot	Jordan 197-Peugeot A14 V10	G	61		
7	Jan Magnussen	DK	23	Stewart Ford	Stewart SF1-Ford Zetec-R V10	B	61		
8	Jos Verstappen	NL	18	Tyrrell	Tyrrell 025-Ford ED4 V8	G	60		
9	Gerhard Berger	A	8	Mild Seven Benetton Renault	Benetton B197-Renault RS9 V10	G	60		
10	Ukyo Katayama	J	20	Minardi Team	Minardi M197-Hart 830 V8	B	60		
	Heinz-Harald Frentzen	D	4	Rothmans Williams Renault	Williams FW19-Renault RS9 V10	G	39	Accident	
	Shinji Nakano	J	15	Prost Gauloises Blondes	Prost JS45-Mugen Honda MF301HA V10	B	36	Spun off	
	Nicola Larini	I	17	Red Bull Sauber Petronas	Sauber C16-Petronas V10	G	24	Accident	
	Jean Alesi	F	7	Mild Seven Benetton Renault	Benetton B197-Renault RS9 V10	G	16	Spun off	
	Jacques Villeneuve	CDN	3	Rothmans Williams Renault	Williams FW19-Renault RS9 V10	G	16	Accident damage	
	Ralf Schumacher	D	11	B&H Total Jordan Peugeot	Jordan 197-Peugeot A14 V10	G	10	Accident	
	Johnny Herbert	GB	16	Red Bull Sauber Petronas	Sauber C16-Petronas V10	G	9	Accident	
	Jarno Trulli	I	21	Minardi Team	Minardi M197-Hart 830 V8	B	7	Accident	
	David Coulthard	GB	10	West McLaren Mercedes	McLaren MP4/12-Mercedes FO110E V10	G	1	Spun off	
	Mika Häkkinen	SF	9	West McLaren Mercedes	McLaren MP4/12-Mercedes FO110E V10	G	1	Collision with Alesi	
	Damon Hill	GB	1	Danka Arrows Yamaha	Arrows A18-Yamaha OX11A/C V10	B	1	Collision with Irvine	
	Pedro Diniz	BR	2	Danka Arrows Yamaha	Arrows A18-Yamaha OX11A/C V10	B	0	Spun off	

Fastest lap: M. Schumacher, on lap 26, 1m 53.315s, 66.447 mph/106.937 km/h (record on revised circuit).

Previous lap record: Michael Schumacher (F1 Benetton B194-Ford V8), 1m 21.076s, 91.821 mph/147.772 km/h (1994).

B – Bridgestone   G – Goodyear

Grid order	1	2	3	4	5	6	7	8	9	10	11	12	13	14	15	16	17	18	19	20	21	22	23	24	25	26	27	28	29	30	31	32	33	34	35	36	37	38	39	40	41	42	43	44	45	46	47	48
4 FRENTZEN	5	5	5	5	5	5	5	5	5	5	5	5	5	5	5	5	5	5	5	5	5	5	5	5	5	5	5	5	5	5	5	5	5	5	5	5	5	5	5	5	5	5	5	5	5	5	5	5
5 M. SCHUMACHER	12	12	12	12	12	22	22	22	22	22	22	22	22	22	22	22	22	22	22	22	22	22	22	22	22	22	22	22	22	22	22	22	22	22	22	22	22	22	22	22	22	22	22	22	22	22	22	22
3 VILLENEUVE	11	11	11	11	22	11	11	11	11	11	11	12	12	12	12	12	12	12	12	12	12	12	12	12	12	12	12	12	12	12	12	12	14	14	14	6	6	6	6	6	6	6	6	6	6	6	6	6
12 FISICHELLA	4	22	22	22	11	12	12	12	12	12	14	14	14	14	14	14	14	14	14	14	14	14	14	14	14	14	14	14	14	14	14	14	12	6	6	14	14	14	14	14	14	14	14	14	14	14	14	14
10 COULTHARD	22	16	16	16	16	16	16	16	16	6	6	6	6	6	6	6	6	6	6	6	6	6	6	6	6	6	6	6	6	6	6	6	6	19	19	19	19	19	19	19	19	19	19	19	19	19	19	19
11 R. SCHUMACHER	16	14	14	14	14	14	14	14	14	6	19	19	19	19	19	19	19	19	19	19	19	19	19	19	19	19	19	19	19	19	19	19	19	12	12	12	23	23	23	23	23	23	23	23	23	23	23	23
16 HERBERT	10	4	4	6	6	6	6	6	6	19	7	7	7	7	7	7	23	23	23	23	23	23	23	23	23	23	23	23	23	23	23	23	23	23	23	12	12	12	12	12	12	12	23	23	23			
9 HÄKKINEN	14	3	6	19	19	19	19	19	19	7	23	23	23	23	23	18	18	18	18	18	18	18	18	18	18	18	18	18	18	18	18	18	18	18	18	18	18	18	18	18	18	18	18	18	18	18	18	18
7 ALESI	3	7	19	4	7	7	7	7	7	23	18	18	18	18	18	18	20	4	4	4	4	4	4	4	4	4	4	4	4	4	4	4	4	4	4	4	4	4	20	8	8	8	8	8	8	8	8	8
22 BARRICHELLO	9	6	7	7	8	8	8	8	8	18	20	20	20	4	20	4	20	20	20	20	20	20	20	20	20	20	20	20	20	20	20	20	20	20	20	8	20	20	20	20	20	20	20	20	20			
17 LARINI	7	19	8	8	23	23	23	23	23	8	15	15	15	15	15	15	15	15	15	15	15	15	15	15	15	15	15	15	15	15	15	15	15	15	8	8												
14 PANIS	6	8	23	23	18	18	18	18	15	15	15	15	15	3	3	3	8	8	8	8	8	8	8	8	8	8	8	8	8	8	8	8																
1 HILL	1	23	18	18	20	20	20	20	20	4	3	3	3	15	15	15	17	17	17	17	17	17	17	17																								
19 SALO	8	18	21	21	15	15	15	15	15	3	8	8	8	8	8	8																																
6 IRVINE	19	21	20	20	21	21	21	4	4	8	17	17	17	17	17	17																																
2 DINIZ	18	20	15	15	4	4	4	3	3	17																																						
8 BERGER	21	15	17	3	3	3	3	17																																								
21 TRULLI	23	17	3	17	17	17	17																																									
23 MAGNUSSEN	20																																															
20 KATAYAMA	15																																															
15 NAKANO	17																																															
18 VERSTAPPEN																																																

Pit stop
One lap behind leader

5		4
M. SCHUMACHER		FRENTZEN
Ferrari		Williams
12		3
FISICHELLA		VILLENEUVE
Jordan		Williams
11		10
R. SCHUMACHER		COULTHARD
Jordan		McLaren
9		16
HÄKKINEN		HERBERT
McLaren		Sauber
22		7
BARRICHELLO		ALESI
Stewart		Benetton
14		17
PANIS		LARINI
Prost		Sauber
19		1
SALO		HILL
Tyrrell		Arrows
2		6
DINIZ		IRVINE
Arrows		Ferrari
21		8
TRULLI		BERGER
Minardi		Benetton
20		23
KATAYAMA		MAGNUSSEN
Minardi		Stewart
18		15
VERSTAPPEN		NAKANO
Tyrrell		Prost

49	50	51	52	53	54	55	56	57	58	59	60	61	62	
5	5	5	5	5	5	5	5	5	5	5	5	5	5	1
22	22	22	22	22	22	22	22	22	22	22	22	22	22	2
6	6	6	6	6	6	6	6	6	6	6	6	6	6	3
14	14	14	14	14	14	14	14	14	14	14	14	14	14	4
19	19	19	19	19	19	19	19	19	19	19	19	19	19	5
12	12	12	12	12	12	12	12	12	12	12	12	12	12	6
23	23	23	23	23	23	23	23	23	23	23	23	23		
18	18	18	18	18	18	18	18	18	18	18	18			
8	8	8	8	8	8	8	8	8	8	8	8			
20	20	20	20	20	20	20	20	20	20	20	20			

FOR THE RECORD

First Grand Prix points

Stewart Ford

First Grand Prix pole position

Heinz-Harald Frentzen

50th Grand Prix start

Nicola Larini

TIME SHEETS

QUALIFYING

Weather: Dry, hot and sunny

Pos.	Driver	Car	Laps	Time
1	Heinz-Harald Frentzen	Williams-Renault	12	1m 18.216s
2	Michael Schumacher	Ferrari	11	1m 18.235s
3	Jacques Villeneuve	Williams-Renault	11	1m 18.583s
4	Giancarlo Fisichella	Jordan-Peugeot	12	1m 18.665s
5	David Coulthard	McLaren-Mercedes	12	1m 18.779s
6	Ralf Schumacher	Jordan-Peugeot	11	1m 18.943s
7	Johnny Herbert	Sauber-Petronas	12	1m 19.105s
8	Mika Häkkinen	McLaren-Mercedes	12	1m 19.119s
9	Jean Alesi	Benetton-Renault	9	1m 19.263s
10	Rubens Barrichello	Stewart-Ford	12	1m 19.295s
11	Nicola Larini	Sauber-Petronas	12	1m 19.468s
12	Olivier Panis	Prost-Mugen Honda	12	1m 19.626s
13	Damon Hill	Arrows-Yamaha	12	1m 19.674s
14	Mika Salo	Tyrrell-Ford	12	1m 19.694s
15	Eddie Irvine	Ferrari	12	1m 19.723s
16	Pedro Diniz	Arrows-Yamaha	12	1m 19.860s
17	Gerhard Berger	Benetton-Renault	11	1m 20.199s
18	Jarno Trulli	Minardi-Hart	12	1m 20.349s
19	Jan Magnussen	Stewart-Ford	11	1m 20.516s
20	Ukyo Katayama	Minardi-Hart	12	1m 20.606s
21	Shinji Nakano	Prost-Mugen Honda	12	1m 20.961s
22	Jos Verstappen	Tyrrell-Ford	11	1m 21.290s

THURSDAY FREE PRACTICE

Weather: Cloudy and warm

Pos.	Driver	Laps	Time
1	Johnny Herbert	30	1m 21.188s
2	Michael Schumacher	29	1m 21.330s
3	Jacques Villeneuve	29	1m 21.445s
4	Giancarlo Fisichella	29	1m 21.463s
5	Gerhard Berger	29	1m 21.573s
6	Mika Häkkinen	30	1m 21.675s
7	Heinz-Harald Frentzen	28	1m 21.885s
8	Ralf Schumacher	28	1m 21.939s
9	Damon Hill	30	1m 21.962s
10	Jean Alesi	22	1m 22.010s
11	David Coulthard	30	1m 22.020s
12	Eddie Irvine	30	1m 22.072s
13	Rubens Barrichello	26	1m 22.370s
14	Nicola Larini	28	1m 22.383s
15	Pedro Diniz	27	1m 22.622s
16	Jos Verstappen	30	1m 23.056s
17	Olivier Panis	27	1m 23.096s
18	Mika Salo	29	1m 23.483s
19	Jan Magnussen	27	1m 23.810s
20	Jarno Trulli	29	1m 25.178s
21	Shinji Nakano	30	1m 25.530s
22	Ukyo Katayama	6	1m 39.353s

SATURDAY FREE PRACTICE

Weather: Sunny and warm

Pos.	Driver	Laps	Time
1	Heinz-Harald Frentzen	29	1m 18.370s
2	Giancarlo Fisichella	26	1m 18.560s
3	Jacques Villeneuve	29	1m 18.612s
4	Mika Häkkinen	27	1m 18.748s
5	Jean Alesi	30	1m 18.950s
6	David Coulthard	23	1m 19.192s
7	Michael Schumacher	27	1m 19.265s
8	Ralf Schumacher	27	1m 19.380s
9	Eddie Irvine	28	1m 19.563s
10	Gerhard Berger	24	1m 19.788s
11	Pedro Diniz	26	1m 19.947s
12	Damon Hill	28	1m 20.287s
13	Rubens Barrichello	24	1m 20.338s
14	Nicola Larini	29	1m 20.459s
15	Mika Salo	30	1m 20.516s
16	Jan Magnussen	23	1m 20.764s
17	Johnny Herbert	18	1m 20.976s
18	Jos Verstappen	15	1m 21.124s
19	Jarno Trulli	29	1m 21.849s
20	Shinji Nakano	28	1m 21.923s
21	Olivier Panis	13	1m 22.008s
22	Ukyo Katayama	30	1m 22.076s

WARM-UP

Weather: Bright and warm

Pos.	Driver	Laps	Time
1	Mika Häkkinen	16	1m 21.480s
2	Jacques Villeneuve	16	1m 21.657s
3	Olivier Panis	15	1m 21.683s
4	Heinz-Harald Frentzen	14	1m 21.794s
5	Michael Schumacher	15	1m 21.843s
6	David Coulthard	17	1m 22.141s
7	Johnny Herbert	15	1m 22.233s
8	Giancarlo Fisichella	16	1m 22.555s
9	Gerhard Berger	14	1m 22.974s
10	Ukyo Katayama	14	1m 22.982s
11	Eddie Irvine	12	1m 23.322s
12	Jos Verstappen	13	1m 23.334s
13	Jean Alesi	15	1m 23.349s
14	Mika Salo	13	1m 23.380s
15	Ralf Schumacher	13	1m 23.442s
16	Rubens Barrichello	15	1m 23.453s
17	Damon Hill	15	1m 23.561s
18	Pedro Diniz	17	1m 23.776s
19	Jarno Trulli	18	1m 23.875s
20	Nicola Larini	12	1m 23.958s
21	Jan Magnussen	11	1m 24.035s
22	Shinji Nakano	17	1m 24.656s

RACE FASTEST LAPS

Weather: Wet and cloudy

Driver	Time	Lap
Michael Schumacher	1m 53.315s	26
Ralf Schumacher	1m 53.430s	10
Rubens Barrichello	1m 53.495s	10
Heinz-Harald Frentzen	1m 53.504s	22
Eddie Irvine	1m 54.202s	48
Giancarlo Fisichella	1m 54.806s	9
Mika Salo	1m 54.968s	22
Jos Verstappen	1m 55.045s	23
Jacques Villeneuve	1m 55.218s	14
Jan Magnussen	1m 55.303s	27
Olivier Panis	1m 55.309s	18
Jean Alesi	1m 55.451s	9
Johnny Herbert	1m 55.840s	8
Gerhard Berger	1m 55.841s	8
Ukyo Katayama	1m 56.101s	24
Shinji Nakano	1m 56.906s	19
Nicola Larini	1m 56.940s	19
Jarno Trulli	2m 00.038s	7
David Coulthard	2m 11.201s	1
Mika Häkkinen	2m 15.786s	1
Damon Hill	2m 17.648s	1

CHASSIS LOG BOOK

1	Hill	Arrows A18/3
2	Diniz	Arrows A18/2
	spare	Arrows A18/1
3	Villeneuve	Williams FW19/4
4	Frentzen	Williams FW19/5
	spare	Williams FW19/3
5	M. Schumacher	Ferrari F310B/177
6	Irvine	Ferrari F310B/173
	spare	Ferrari F310B/172
7	Alesi	Benetton B197/5
8	Berger	Benetton B197/4
	spare	Benetton B197/3
9	Häkkinen	McLaren MP4/12/2
10	Coulthard	McLaren MP4/12/3
	spare	McLaren MP4/12/1
11	R. Schumacher	Jordan 197/3
12	Fisichella	Jordan 197/4
	spare	Jordan 197/1
14	Panis	Prost JS45/3
15	Nakano	Prost JS45/2
	spare	Prost JS45/1
16	Herbert	Sauber C16/1
17	Larini	Sauber C16/2
	spare	Sauber C16/3
18	Verstappen	Tyrrell 025/2
19	Salo	Tyrrell 025/3
	spare	Tyrrell 025/1
20	Katayama	Minardi M197/3
21	Trulli	Minardi M197/2
22	Barrichello	Stewart SF1/2
23	Magnussen	Stewart SF1/3
	spare	Stewart SF1/1

POINTS TABLES

Drivers

1	Michael Schumacher	24
2	Jacques Villeneuve	20
3	Eddie Irvine	14
4 =	David Coulthard	10
4 =	Gerhard Berger	10
4 =	Mika Häkkinen	10
4 =	Heinz-Harald Frentzen	10
8	Olivier Panis	9
9	Rubens Barrichello	6
10 =	Ralf Schumacher	4
10 =	Giancarlo Fisichella	4
12 =	Johnny Herbert	3
12 =	Jean Alesi	3
14	Mika Salo	2
15	Nicola Larini	1

Constructors

1	Ferrari	38
2	Williams	30
3	McLaren	20
4	Benetton	13
5	Prost	9
6	Jordan	8
7	Stewart	6
8	Sauber	4
9	Tyrrell	2

Peter Nygaard/GP Photo

DIARY

McLaren boss Ron Dennis argues against having more than 17 races on the F1 calendar, hinting that it might be necessary for top-line entrants to run two separate teams in order to reduce pressure on personnel.

Ford reveals plans for Cosworth to build a brand-new V10 F1 engine for the 1998 World Championship season.

Mugen Honda management express disapproval that Alain Prost has let Peugeot engineers examine one of the Japanese company's V10 engines at the F1 team's Magny-Cours headquarters.

John Willment, one of the leading lights in Ford's emergence as a competition force in the 1960s, dies at the age of 68.

SPANISH
grand prix

VILLENEUVE
PANIS
ALESI
M. SCHUMACHER
HERBERT
COULTHARD

FIA WORLD CHAMPIONSHIP • ROUND 6

Jacques Villeneuve opted to make only two pit stops and by the end of the race his Goodyear tyres were badly worn, but he was still able to maintain a comfortable advantage over the Bridgestone-shod Prost of Olivier Panis *(behind)*.

Bottom: Jean Alesi leads the Ferrari of Michael Schumacher and David Coulthard's McLaren on his way to an encouraging third place for Benetton.

JACQUES Villeneuve regained the World Championship points lead with a well-judged victory in the Spanish Grand Prix at Barcelona's Circuit de Catalunya, a tactically astute success in which his aspirations were immeasurably aided when Michael Schumacher catapulted his Ferrari through into second place on the exit of the first corner after making a brilliant start from seventh on the grid.

Schumacher had started the weekend aware that there was precious little chance of repeating his Monaco victory of a fortnight earlier. Testing had confirmed that his Ferrari F310B simply wasn't at home on the long, constant-radius curves of the Barcelona track. With that in mind, he opted to make as much ground as he could in the opening moments of the race, running on brand-new, unscrubbed tyres and a light fuel load.

Villeneuve instantly worked out what he was up to. 'I knew from testing that Michael would have trouble with his tyres and would have to do three stops,' said the Williams driver. 'We opted for a two-stop strategy which I knew would be risky on my own tyres, but on a three-stop strategy you have to drive like a maniac to keep the lead all the time.'

By the time Schumacher made his first stop for fuel and tyres at the end of lap 14, Villeneuve was already 16 seconds ahead and the battle, such as it was, was effectively at an end.

With tyre wear problems also handicapping David Coulthard's McLaren, which ran third in the opening stages, Olivier Panis steadily worked his way through the field to finish a strong second in the Bridgestone-shod Prost-Mugen Honda. It was the best dry-weather result to date for the Japanese tyre company in its first F1 season – matching Rubens Barrichello's performance in the rain at Monaco – and stood as Panis's best finish of the year, moving the Frenchman into third place in the championship.

At the start of the final parade lap, Gerhard Berger stalled his Benetton and needed a push-start. He took up position at the back of the grid, but got a second chance when Ralf Schumacher did the same as the field lined up to take the start. This meant that the Benetton driver was permitted to take his original grid position, but Schumacher Junior had to start from the back of the pack. The race distance was reduced by a single lap to compensate for the additional parade lap.

Coulthard came swooping through to challenge for the lead on the run to the first corner, but Villeneuve sat it out with him and the McLaren driver found himself edged up on the kerb. That lost him just enough momentum for Schumacher's Ferrari to get through into second place a couple of corners later.

At the end of the opening lap Villeneuve led by 0.4s with Coulthard keeping pace behind the Ferrari in third place. Already a gap was opening to Alesi's Benetton, Häkkinen, Frentzen, Herbert, Berger, Fisichella and Salo. For the first few laps Schumacher kept the Ferrari tight on Villeneuve's tail, but it wasn't long before his new tyres lost grip quite dramatically, so by lap five Jacques was already starting to ease away with a 1.5s cushion.

By lap nine a big queue had built up behind Schumacher's Ferrari, but Villeneuve was away on his own some 8.7s ahead after making 3.1s on the previous lap alone. Clearly Michael would have to stop soon. On lap 14 Coulthard overtook the Ferrari and they both immediately came in for their first stop, elevating Alesi to second place, now 21.6s behind the leading Williams.

Berger also stopped on lap 14, dropping from ninth to 15th, while Häkkinen, briefly promoted to third place, came in next time round, resuming in ninth. Heinz-Harald Frentzen, who'd made a poor start from second place on the grid, made his stop on lap 16 and dropped from third to 11th.

Damon Hill's Arrows had moved up to sixth place when it stopped in front

Paul-Henri Cahier

Michael Roberts

Left: Easing the tension? Jacques Villeneuve wrings his hands as he prepares to make another qualifying run.

Right: A close thing. Michael Schumacher narrowly avoids a collision with the Benetton of Gerhard Berger as he accelerates away after making a pit stop.

Jean Alesi underlined the Benetton team's worryingly erratic 1997 form by posting fastest time in Friday's free practice session, lapping 0.2s faster than pre-race favourite Jacques Villeneuve's Williams.

'We are pleased to have established that we can use the same chassis set-up as we tried in last week's test where we covered a lot of miles,' said Alesi. 'Now we must maintain this position in qualifying and, hopefully, in the race.'

Despite this, the Italian team has been bruised by false hopes in the past and took a cautiously low-key attitude towards its achievement. None of its number needed any reminding that the team's last victory had been achieved in Japan two years earlier when the dynamic Michael Schumacher was their number one driver.

'I would certainly not say that our problems have been solved,' said Pat Symonds, the Benetton technical director. 'On circuits like Barcelona, which has a high-grip track surface, we seem to have less of a problem than we do on more slippery surfaces. The problem can be solved and we have several ideas.'

Symonds spoke in the knowledge that few firm conclusions can be reached on the strength of a single free practice session. Benetton had been struggling to work their tyres up to optimum operating temperatures during the crucial hour-long qualifying sessions. They were now hoping for more success in mastering this complex technical conundrum on Saturday afternoon.

Meanwhile, Villeneuve and Williams arrived in the confident knowledge that they had been consistently quick at every test session held at the Barcelona track this year and few in the pit lane would have bet against the Canadian driver taking pole position even though he was not totally satisfied with his car's handling.

'Compared to the testing we have done, the car was very difficult to drive and we have had to adjust it a lot,' he said. Mention of Williams's Monaco débâcle, where both cars started the race on slicks in the rain, was certainly unwelcome. Yet Jacques clearly regarded the Spanish race as a not-to-be-missed opportunity to grasp back the championship lead from Michael Schumacher and the Ferrari team on a circuit which the German driver believed from the outset would suit his car much less than most.

Come qualifying, of course, Villeneuve got everything firmly back under control, keeping intact the Williams team's 1997 record of qualifying on pole at every race. Jacques pipped team-mate Frentzen by 0.266s on his final run, despite reporting that he had too much understeer on his first three runs. On his fourth, everything clicked and he rammed home his advantage at the end of the lap.

Frentzen was quite satisfied with second place, although he felt he had a touch too much oversteer on his final run, but the real tale of qualifying was the performance of the all-new Mercedes FO110F engine in the two McLaren MP4/12s. The new powerplant had not originally been scheduled for its debut until Hockenheim, but Mario Illien's crew at Ilmor Engineering had pulled out all the stops to ready it for qualifying at Barcelona.

The new Merc engine was reputed to offer 775 bhp – 25 bhp up on the Renault V10s – and David Coulthard and Mika Häkkinen harnessed it to good effect, qualifying third and fifth. Add to that a small package of aerodynamic changes, including new front wings and extended barge boards, and both McLaren drivers started the race in confident mood, even though they reverted to the earlier-specification engine on Sunday morning.

'I think we have a chance to score a podium finish,' said Coulthard. 'The car's balance is much better and tyre wear lower as a result.' Subsequent events would reveal that perhaps he had spoken too soon.

In the Benetton camp, Alesi posted fourth-fastest time and expressed himself happy with the performance of the B197. He encountered traffic on his second set when he reckoned he was on course for his best time but, despite being worried that he would be unable to reproduce this effort, gained a second-row position on his third run. His team-mate Gerhard Berger had to be content with sixth-fastest time, having been hit by a tear-off helmet visor on his first run and later admitting to making a mistake on his last.

Meanwhile, a spectacular failure of one of the latest 'Step 2' type 046 engines in his race chassis forced Michael Schumacher to take over the spare Ferrari F310B for his qualifying run, which eventually earned him seventh place in the grid line-up. Eddie Irvine battled with poor balance initially, then switched to a different rear wing which made the car more stable but at the expense of straightline speed. He qualified 11th.

Jordan drivers Giancarlo Fisichella and Ralf Schumacher qualified eighth and ninth; their cars handled well, but were just too slow. Johnny Herbert's Sauber was tenth, the Englishman alone among the Goodyear runners in finding it difficult to generate decent tyre temperatures, which made life particularly difficult through the slow corners.

Nicola Larini's place in the Sauber team was taken by Ferrari test driver Gianni Morbidelli, the two men exchanging their roles. The newcomer started his weekend on a worrying note when he lost control on cold tyres coming out of the pits during Friday free practice, spearing straight across the track at right angles into the opposite barrier. Mercifully nobody was coming down the start/finish straight at the time and the car survived its unscheduled excursion with remarkably little damage.

On Saturday Morbidelli qualified 13th, only 0.2s slower than Panis's Prost, which the Frenchman reported didn't want to turn into the corners as crisply as he had hoped. Mika Salo's Tyrrell was 14th, the Finn encouraged by the performance of the latest Cosworth ED5 V8 despite coming out late due to a throttle sensor problem which necessitated the removal of his car's gearbox.

Damon Hill was moderately satisfied with 15th place on the grid, happy to be less than a second away from Panis's best in the contest to be the fastest Bridgestone runner, but Rubens Barrichello – 17th in the line-up – was very much less than amused to find his Ford V10-engined Stewart slower than the fastest V8-engined Tyrrell. Even so, he reckoned that his car was handling well enough.

Shinji Nakano's Prost qualified 16th behind Hill, while Jarno Trulli did well to claim 18th place in the Minardi-Hart, just ahead of Tyrrell's Jos Verstappen, who had to use the Cosworth ED4-powered spare car for his first run while the installation of the more powerful ED5 in his race car was completed in the team's garage.

Katayama's Minardi, Pedro Diniz's Arrows and Jan Magnussen's Stewart completed the grid, the Dane very disappointed – and slightly bewildered – after being quicker than Barrichello in Friday's free practice sessions.

of the pits with sudden loss of oil pressure after 18 laps. Even so, the World Champion was far from totally disheartened.

'I think the performance of the car was quite good today,' he concluded. 'We were going to be in good shape for the race, I think, and had a two-stop strategy planned. But we were let down again by poor reliability.'

On lap 20 Villeneuve made his first routine stop in 8.3s, dropping behind Alesi only to regain the lead next time round when the Benetton driver dropped to fifth at his own first refuelling stop.

This left Coulthard second, the McLaren driver steadying Villeneuve's advantage at 3.5s, with Panis now third ahead of Häkkinen. By lap 25 Villeneuve was 3.8s ahead, but Coulthard still looked a force to be reckoned with, although he was already telling his pit over the radio that his second set of tyres was feeling very inconsistent.

On lap 29 Coulthard came in earlier than originally planned for his second stop (7.9s), having begged to be allowed in earlier but been told that he would have to stay out for at least a couple more laps. This dropped David from second to third, but had more worrying knock-on effects for the Scot, who made a third stop at the end of lap 40 – and then faced the task of making his final set last through another 24 laps to the chequered flag. It was a more than difficult task.

'Like most teams, high levels of tyre wear and degradation forced us into a three-stop strategy,' said McLaren boss Ron Dennis. 'For reasons that at this stage we do not understand, the second and third sets proved extremely inconsistent, not only making life very difficult for the drivers, but also forcing us into earlier second stops than we had planned.'

With 37 laps completed, Rubens Barrichello's Stewart dropped out from 11th place with engine failure after a race which had contrasted dramatically with his run to second place in the rain at Monaco.

'I stopped because my engine started to make the same noise that I had heard in the race at Imola,' he shrugged. 'I didn't have the straightline speed to overtake people and basically I needed to start a bit closer to the front.'

By lap 40, Villeneuve effectively had it in the bag. He was 14.2s ahead of Alesi with Panis moving up to third place after Coulthard's third stop. Alesi and Panis made their second stops on laps 43 and 44 respectively, allowing Schumacher's Ferrari back to second,

Michael Cooper/Allsport

Darren Heath

then on lap 46 Michael momentarily went back into the lead after Villeneuve made his second stop, only to come in for the Italian car's third stop at the end of the lap. Michael then resumed in fourth place.

The hard-driving Panis almost lost his second place when he came up to lap Eddie Irvine's Ferrari with nine laps left to run. This immediately allowed Alesi's Benetton and Schumacher's Ferrari to pull right onto the Frenchman's tail. Nobody seriously suggested that Irvine was responding to any Ferrari instructions to assist Schumacher's cause, but the Northern Irish driver was given a ten-second stop–go penalty for blocking. After the race was over, Panis did not stint in his criticism of the Ferrari driver.

'It was just incredible trying to overtake Eddie,' he said, 'and it is very difficult to speak with this man, even though he obviously saw the blue [overtaking] flags. But perhaps he didn't see them, or maybe he has a problem with his eyes.'

Being held up in close traffic also resulted in a secondary problem for Panis, who was painfully aware of his oil temperature gauge flickering ominously each time he got close to another car. Once ahead of Irvine, however, Panis pulled away to consolidate his position and finished the race without any further difficulties.

Irvine, as one might have expected, remained stoically unrepentant. 'I am upset about my penalty,' he said. 'I saw the flag, but as Jos Verstappen and I had a car to pass in front of us, I assumed they were for him.'

Alesi's Benetton eventually held off Schumacher's Ferrari across the line by 5.4s to take third place while Johnny Herbert's Sauber sliced in front of Coulthard's McLaren on the last lap to take fifth place.

'I had seen that David was locking up his front brakes going into the sharp hairpin,' said Herbert. 'On the last lap we went side by side into the corner before that, because I was deliberately trying to make him push too hard and overshoot the hairpin. That's what he did and I'm really pleased to come through from tenth to fifth without anybody ahead of me dropping out.'

Villeneuve could not contain his satisfaction over this decisive Williams victory. 'After the stupidity of Monaco, it is especially good to have won here,' he said. 'Barcelona is where we did almost all our winter testing, but when we came here for the race we had different tyres and the car didn't feel as good.'

Outside the top six, Häkkinen took seventh place ahead of Frentzen, although Williams technical director Patrick Head was quick to absolve the German driver of any blame for this poor performance. 'Useless set-up; de-

stroyed its tyres,' he shrugged. 'Not Heinz's fault.'

For Frentzen, who has a reputation for being easy on tyres, it was an abject disappointment. 'I couldn't really push at all today,' he shrugged. 'I had very good tyre wear all through the weekend, but then for some reason in the race my rear tyres blistered quickly. I don't know how, because I really didn't push too hard.'

Jordan also had a simply dismal day with Fisichella fading to ninth and Ralf Schumacher's engine failing when he was running down in 13th place on lap 51. Berger finished tenth, his tyres dreadfully blistered despite running a chassis set-up very similar to Alesi's, while Jos Verstappen's Tyrrell headed home the delayed Irvine, Magnussen, Morbidelli and Trulli.

Verstappen was well pleased with both his own performance and the potential of the Cosworth ED5 V8 he was

Understandably concerned, David Coulthard, Giancarlo Fisichella, Michael Schumacher and Jean Alesi wait for news following a major accident involving Olivier Panis. The race had been red-flagged to a halt and the cars abandoned on the start/finish straight *(below left)*.

Far left: A medical team led by Professor Watkins attend to the luckless Olivier Panis, who suffered two broken legs in the crash.

Left: The shattered remains of the Frenchman's Prost bear witness to the severity of the impact.

MICHAEL Schumacher emphasised that he is not only the best driver of his generation but also one of the luckiest when he emerged from the Canadian Grand Prix at Montreal with Ferrari's second victory of the year at the end of a race flagged to a halt with 15 of its 69 scheduled laps left to run.

The cause of this early finish was a disastrous 140 mph accident involving Olivier Panis's Prost which left the French driver hospitalised with serious leg injuries. Had the race gone its full distance, even the combination of Schumacher's dazzling driving talent and the latest aerodynamic revisions to the Ferrari F310B would probably not have been enough to guarantee him victory.

In terms of pure performance and race strategy, he was simply out-performed by David Coulthard's McLaren-Mercedes, which looked to have the race in the bag until clutch troubles intervened at a fateful, final tyre stop.

The Scot had driven a brilliantly disciplined race – the first for the latest Mercedes FO110F-spec V10 engine – to keep his first set of tyres in immaculate condition through to his sole scheduled pit stop on lap 40 – well beyond half-distance. However, a precautionary second stop to change blistered rubber 12 laps later produced unexpected clutch problems which prevented him from retaining his advantage.

At almost the same moment, Panis slammed into a tyre wall after losing control on a flat-out, fourth-gear 145 mph right-hander on the return leg of the circuit. The car initially snapped into an oversteering slide, brushing the inside wall with its nose, before catapulting into the tyre-protected barrier on the opposite side of the circuit.

The front end of the car was ripped open by the ensuing impact and the driver was wrestled from the shattered wreckage of his car with both legs broken. This sad episode resulted in the safety car being deployed for the second time in the afternoon, and the race was then red-flagged to a halt with results being declared at the end of lap 54. It was later concluded that the car had suffered a rear suspension breakage, almost certainly caused when the Prost driver brushed a barrier earlier in the race.

However, the manner in which Panis was manhandled out of the cockpit before the arrival of FIA medical delegate Professor Watkins added to the unfortunate Frenchman's discomfort and inevitably raised immediate questions as to whether this was the sort of treatment which should be expected in response to a major F1 accident.

Had Coulthard stayed out for just another lap, rather than responding to the fact that Schumacher had brought the Ferrari in for an unscheduled (third) stop on the previous lap, the Scot would have won. But David was more concerned with Panis's plight than his own disappointment.

'Clearly, Olivier had a very big accident, and maybe we need to look at increasing the amount of tyres at that point on the circuit,' he noted, 'because something in the impact has allowed the car to take a severe enough shunt to split the front of the chassis. It is very unusual to see that with a modern F1 car.

'This is not a particularly difficult corner. It is fairly straightforward. It is no more dangerous here than at Monaco, and I don't class Monaco as a particularly dangerous circuit. Clearly, if you make a mistake there, you hit the wall, but we all know that an initial impact at a shallow angle is pretty safe. The worry is when you have a head-on impact. Maybe that's what split Olivier's car.'

It also turned out to be a painful weekend for the Williams team. Pre-race favourite Jacques Villeneuve qualified second, then spun off on the last corner of the second lap as he tried too hard to keep up with Schumacher, leading the race for Ferrari. Team-mate Heinz-Harald Frentzen was also out of luck, blistering his first set of tyres and being forced to make a premature first pit stop.

Schumacher had produced a simply wondrous lap to edge out Villeneuve from pole position on the final lap of qualifying and the Ferrari driver made perfect use of his advantage to accelerate into an immediate lead as the pack jostled into the first tight left-hander.

Further back, Panis knocked the wing off Häkkinen's McLaren, Eddie Irvine running into the debris and spinning into immediate retirement. On the exit of the corner Panis also side-swiped Magnussen's Stewart out of the contest, the Frenchman trailing round to the pits for repairs.

Schumacher had completed the opening lap 1.4s ahead of Villeneuve, the French-Canadian ace being willed on by the enthusiastic 120,000-strong crowd. Unfortunately the occasion proved too much for him. Coming into the final ess-bend to complete lap two, Villeneuve allowed the Williams to slide a little off-line as he swung into the first right-hander.

In a flash the rear end was sliding wildly out of control. He tried to slam

MONTREAL QUALIFYING

In bright and sunny conditions, Villeneuve's Williams was hard on the pace from the start of Saturday afternoon's hour-long qualifying session. As Damon Hill's problems continued with a first-corner spin in the opening moments of the session, Jacques opened the bidding with a brisk 1m 19.418s.

Hill later recounted how his Arrows's Yamaha engine had stalled when he pulled for first gear in order to continue. He spent the rest of the session in the spare car, never getting a traffic-free lap and ending up 15th. 'It was actually one of the worst-ever qualifying sessions I can remember,' he said firmly.

It was half an hour into the session before anybody improved on Villeneuve's time, Ralf Schumacher taking his Jordan round in 1m 19.249s, followed quickly by Frentzen, who was the first to dip below the 1m 19s barrier with a 1m 18.947s.

Over the following twenty minutes, the leading contenders progressively chipped their way down through the 1m 18s bracket. Michael Schumacher did 1m 18.661s, then Villeneuve came back with 1m 18.746s and Coulthard signalled what was to come in the race with a 1m 18.669s.

Schumacher Senior raised the stakes even further with a dramatic 1m 18.159s then, with ten minutes to go, Villeneuve seemed to have the final answer with a 1m 18.108s. Five minutes later, Alexander Wurz, the promising Austrian who was subbing for Gerhard Berger (ruled out by a troublesome sinus infection), crashed his Benetton into the retaining wall on the exit of the final ess-bend and the car ended up in a pile of debris sitting in the middle of the circuit in front of the pits. The session was red-flagged with five minutes still left to run.

'Salo's Tyrrell was about 18 seconds in front of me at the time,' explained Wurz, 'and he went off onto the grass and put dust on the circuit. I was the first one there, went through the corner normally and, by the time I tried to catch the oversteer, I had gone round so fast that I was more or less already in the wall!'

After the damaged car was cleared away, the field scrambled out for a last-minute blast. Rubens Barrichello evened out every slip, slide and lurch of his dramatically low-downforce Stewart-Ford to clinch a remarkable third place on the grid, but Villeneuve seemed confident that pole was in the bag.

Yet Michael Schumacher had one more surprise up his sleeve. The chequered flag was already waving at the start/finish line as his Ferrari burst into view onto the pit straight, stopping the clocks at a superb 1m 18.095s. Ferrari came to Canada with a revised airbox and rear-end aerodynamic improvements, including a tighter 'waisting' of the bodywork ahead of the rear wheels. Villeneuve could certainly look forward to a fight on his hands come Sunday's race.

'I am happy,' grinned Schumacher contentedly, 'especially as the team put in a big effort to improve my F310B and these modifications contributed to my getting pole position. I hope that, as has been the case since the start of the season, my car will be better in the race than in qualifying.'

For his third run of the afternoon, Michael had used the spare car so that his engineers could check out a suspected problem in the high-pressure hydraulic system on his race car. Once this had been completed, he switched back to his race chassis for his successful assault on pole position.

For his part, Villeneuve remained philosophical. 'This is not the best circuit for the Williams,' he noted, 'but the car is good on full tanks and at least this is a track on which you can pass.'

Behind Villeneuve, Barrichello was understandably delighted with the performance of his Stewart SF1, even though the uprated P6 version of the Zetec-R Ford V10 engine was still short on power.

'Our car is very strong aerodynamically,' explained Rubens, 'so we can afford to run with very low downforce and it is still steady under braking.' By contrast, his team-mate Jan Magnussen had a frustrating time and could not better 21st place on the grid after grappling with understeer and heavy traffic.

Heinz-Harald Frentzen wound up fourth in the other Williams FW19, having lost time running into his qualifying lap too close to Nakano's Prost, while Coulthard could count himself fortunate to emerge fifth fastest after suffering an engine failure during the morning, then being late out for qualifying after the replacement V10 developed a slight fuel leak. On his second qualifying run his car suffered an engine problem out on the circuit, so he ran back to take the spare, which he found was understeering too much.

Mika Häkkinen, by contrast, was disappointed not to have improved on ninth-fastest time, his best lap ruined when he came upon Wurz's crashed Benetton coming out of the final corner. The two McLarens were thus separated in the grid order by the Jordans of Giancarlo Fisichella and Ralf Schumacher, plus Jean Alesi's Benetton.

Alesi suffered a broken gear which prevented him from improving on his first-run time and that, together with Wurz's accident, added up to a bleak day for the Benetton squad. Even so, the Austrian new boy did well to claim 11th place just behind Olivier Panis's Prost, the Frenchman emerging in a disappointed mood after finding one of the Tyrrells in his path on his best lap.

Eddie Irvine could not understand why he was unable to improve on 12th-fastest time, reporting that he had been quicker on worn rubber in the morning's free practice session than he could manage on new rubber in the afternoon. He was just ahead of Johnny Herbert, whose Sauber was behaving inconsistently over the bumps, and a delighted Jos Verstappen, for whom 14th place represented his best qualifying position of the season so far. His team-mate Mika Salo complained that he was unable to find a clear lap and wound up 17th as a result, Hill and his Arrows-Yamaha team-mate Pedro Diniz splitting the Tyrrell pair in the final order.

Shinji Nakano's Prost took 19th place behind Gianni Morbidelli, the Italian reporting that his Sauber lacked grip, while the Minardis of Jarno Trulli and Ukyo Katayama sandwiched the hapless Jan Magnussen at the back of the grid.

Villeneuve's maverick streak upsets FIA

I N the run-up to the Canadian race, motor racing's governing body took a critical view of the crude language used by Jacques Villeneuve to criticise its proposed rule changes for 1998 during an interview in the German magazine *Der Spiegel*. As a direct result, Villeneuve received a reprimand when he was summoned to appear before the FIA's World Council on the Wednesday prior to his home race.

An official FIA bulletin stated: 'The World Motor Sport Council stressed to Jacques Villeneuve [who had called the new rules "shit"] that he had not been summoned to appear before the Council because of his opinions but because he had expressed them in offensive terms. The Council was clear that everyone is entitled to the free expression of their opinion, but in a dignified and responsible manner.

'Jacques Villeneuve acknowledged the view of the World Motor Sport Council and declared that his words had been inappropriate but had probably been mistranslated by the journalist.

'The World Motor Sport Council gave Jacques Villeneuve a reprimand, with a warning that, should he commit a similar offence in the future, the World Motor Sport Council would regard it with the utmost severity.'

The World Championship leader was thus faced with an additional return trans-Atlantic flight, but he diplomatically tugged his forelock and accepted his reprimand from the sport's masters before returning to his home turf to be feted as a national hero by the Canadian fans and media alike.

Montreal's *Gazette* newspaper decided it would support the hometown hero by wading into FIA President Max Mosley on Villeneuve's behalf: 'By calling such an ill-timed meeting, Mosley emerges from the affair covered in infamy and looking for all the world like a petty tyrant on a power trip.'

Villeneuve finished the episode unbowed, saying that the penalty would not stop him speaking his mind. 'I haven't been asked to change my views,' he insisted. 'Just my language.'

on corrective steering lock, but the situation was beyond salvation. The Williams half-spun into the outside wall, deranging its left-front wheel as it did so. There was nothing left for Villeneuve but to release his seat harness and walk away, punching his helmet in disbelief that he could have made so elementary an error.

Villeneuve's early departure from the race was a body-blow for the capacity crowd. Jacques later admitted that he'd been a little anxious over the speed at which Schumacher's Ferrari was pulling away in the early stages of the race. The Williams team's telemetry revealed that he came into the ess-bend before the pits 10 km/h faster than at any time during practice. From then on, his fate was sealed.

This unforeseen drama left Schumacher nursing a 1.8s lead over Giancarlo Fisichella's Jordan, Jean Alesi's Benetton and the McLaren-Mercedes of David Coulthard. At the end of lap four Damon Hill headed for the pits, the World Champion's frustrating season continuing in familiar vein. He had lost a lot of ground at the start when he too ran over debris at the first corner. 'I had to make an extra stop because I wasn't sure whether a wheel vibration had been related to that contact with the wing,' he explained. He dropped from 14th to 18th – and last – as a result.

Then on lap seven Schumacher sustained what could have been a disastrous setback. Ukyo Katayama's Minardi piled into the barrier on the fast back leg of the circuit when its throttle jammed open, obliging the organisers to send out the safety car while the damaged machine was removed from the edge of the circuit. Hill used the cover of the pace car to make a second stop at the end of lap eight which meant that he continued for a few laps more as tail-end Charlie. This drama also cost Schumacher his four-second lead over Fisichella, so when the green flag signalled the restart two laps later he had to produce that initial effort all over again. For the next five laps the young Italian driver kept pace with the leading Ferrari, but gradually Schumacher asserted his superiority and eased open a 3.4s advantage by the end of lap 20.

The field was further depleted on lap 15 when Ralf Schumacher's Jordan plunged off the circuit under braking for the first left-hander while running fifth, close behind Alesi and Coulthard. Ralf just got too close to the edge of the circuit and was 'sucked' into the barrier, the Peugeot-engined machine slamming into the end of the tyres at

DIARY

Bernie Ecclestone confirms in Canada that the ongoing dispute between himself and the teams over the share they would get from the flotation of his company F1 Holdings would not affect its stock market launch.

Renault technical director Bernard Dudot denies rumours that he has finalised a deal to join the Prost Grand Prix operation for 1998.

Jackie Stewart calls for a more detailed and analytical approach to the implementation of new technical regulations in F1.

Lebanon reveals plans to host a World Championship Grand Prix by the end of the century.

Greg Moore wins CART street race in Detroit after former Grand Prix stalwarts Mauricio Gugelmin and Mark Blundell run out of fuel on the last lap.

Right: Benetton's Jean Alesi maintained his good form with second place, while new boy Alexander Wurz *(bottom)*, deputising for Gerhard Berger, showed admirable maturity on his debut after an unfortunate crash during qualifying.

Overleaf: Ralf Schumacher was fortunate to escape injury when his Jordan plunged into the guard rail at high speed before striking the end of the tyre barrier.

seemingly undiminished speed. Thankfully, the young German was able to walk away without a scratch and the chassis emerged in a repairable state.

The Williams team's prospects had taken another dive when Heinz-Harald Frentzen made an unexpectedly early first pit stop on lap ten in order to change badly blistered tyres. The German driver had qualified fourth and could reasonably have been expected to pick up where Villeneuve had left off. Now this premature delay dropped him back to 17th and last place behind Hill, but he buckled down and began picking off the midfield runners in a bid to salvage his race.

Meanwhile, Rubens Barrichello's impressive qualifying form with the Stewart-Ford had evaporated once the race got under way, the Brazilian making a slow start to complete the opening lap in eighth place. Next time round he had been passed by the Benetton of debu-

tant Alexander Wurz and was struggling to keep ahead of the two Tyrrells of Verstappen and Salo, a task made doubly hard by the fact that he was loaded down with fuel for a one-stop race and was grappling with a slightly damaged front wing which he'd brushed against the back of Coulthard's McLaren going into the first turn.

Within a few laps the Tyrrell twins were all over the hapless Stewart. Despite Rubens taking some pretty unhelpful lines under braking for both the hairpin and the ess-bend before the pits, Verstappen got through into seventh place on lap 12 and Salo followed suit four laps later, Herbert's Sauber pushing the Brazilian back to ninth place on lap 17.

On lap 25 Fisichella and Alesi came in for their first pit stops together, but the Frenchman's Benetton just got out ahead of the Jordan, the pair rejoining the race behind Schumacher, Coulthard and Wurz, who dropped back to sixth when he called at the pits on the following lap.

On lap 28 Schumacher made a 7.6s refuelling stop while Coulthard set fastest race lap in 1m 19.954s. The Scot now went into the lead and it was a measure of just what a good job he had done of conserving his first set of tyres that he was able to trim that to 1m 19.635s – the quickest lap of the afternoon – on lap 37.

Meanwhile Barrichello retired with a sixth gear problem after 33 laps, but not before he had incurred a ten-second

stop-go penalty for overtaking Mika Salo's Tyrrell under a yellow flag.

Coulthard stayed out until the end of lap 40 before dodging in for tyres and fuel. That put Schumacher back in front, but the Ferrari was in for its second stop at the end of lap 44, resuming in second place. McLaren's strategy now seemed set to pay off as Coulthard went back into the lead, but badly blistered tyres meant that he had to follow Schumacher's example and make an unplanned extra stop, returning to the pits on lap 52. With only 17 laps left to run, the McLaren's engine stalled and Coulthard's gallant effort was over.

On the same lap as he pitted, Panis's accident brought out the safety car once again and, as soon as the gravity of the situation was appreciated, the race was stopped and results declared with Schumacher back in the lead.

Coulthard was philosophical about the outcome, his disappointment in some way mitigated by the knowledge

Paul-Henri Cahier

that the latest Mercedes FO110F engine, being raced here for the first time, had made the McLaren MP4/12 a genuinely winning proposition.

'Earlier in the race I had a three-lap period during which I had a down-change problem,' said Coulthard. 'I mentioned it over the radio, but nothing showed on the telemetry. The car was very good under braking and I thought I would be able to keep Michael out to the finish, but we decided to make an extra stop when he came in.

'I put the car into first gear and it stalled. We started it up again, but the reset mechanism went haywire and it shot up to peak revs. We shut it down again and tried for a third time; when it was cool, I managed to start it off the jack. The rest, as they say, is history.'

Alesi was delighted to have finished second and Fisichella out of his mind with joy at having posted his first podium finish for third. 'I am so happy,' he gushed. 'This was my target for the

season, so it is fantastic. The race went very well without incidents, just some slight blistering on my second set.'

For Frentzen, who had made a second stop on lap 32, fourth place was extremely frustrating. When the race was finally red-flagged to a halt, he found himself sitting behind Schumacher, Alesi and Fisichella in the queue of cars on the start/finish line. Inwardly he and his team knew that he had a good chance of winning the race had it been restarted over the balance of the distance. But that was not to be and he had to settle for three hard-fought championship points.

'The second set of tyres was perfect – no problems – and I felt that I could push hard to the end,' he shrugged. 'I feel I could have got through to the end on one set of tyres and that is disappointing to know.'

Herbert, who had taken the spare Sauber C16 for the race, was equally frustrated to have ended up fifth.

'What a disappointing race,' he said. 'Our strategy was perfect, and everything was going well until I rejoined after my sole pit stop.

'I worked hard at keeping everything nice and smooth, but the pit lane speed-limiter somehow turned itself off and I was given a stop–go penalty. Without that, maybe I could have been second.'

Just to add to his dismay, team-mate Morbidelli ran into the back of him on the final lap of the race behind the safety car, ripping off his rear wing. 'Just at that moment I was looking down trying to adjust the brake balance,' explained the Italian. 'I am sorry!'

Shinji Nakano's Prost completed the top six – an indication, perhaps, of the punishing toll which had been exacted on the front-runners – while the luckless Coulthard restarted in time to be classified seventh. Diniz and Hill trailed home in eighth and ninth for Arrows

with Morbidelli the last car running and the luckless Panis classified 11th.

Wurz's fine top-six run in the Benetton ended with gearbox failure while both Tyrrells wilted after their initially promising spurt, Salo with engine trouble and Verstappen with gearbox problems. Neither Minardi made it to the flag.

The immediate aftermath of the race was a nervous time for Ferrari, for a report from the FIA technical delegate Charlie Whiting suggested that Schumacher had in fact used 31 tyres during the course of the weekend – three more than is permitted under the current regulations.

Once the officials had examined the tyre records of Ferrari engineer Stefano Domenicali and the tyre marking officials' records, it was decided that there were inconsistencies in those records such as to raise a doubt over their accuracy. Under the circumstances, no action was taken.

Ferrari could breathe again.

GRAND PRIX
PLAYER'S
DU CANADA
13–15 JUNE 1997
MONTREAL

Race distance: 54 laps, 148.338 miles/238.734 km
(reduced from 69 laps following an accident)

Race weather: Dry, hot and sunny

FIA FORMULA 1 WORLD CHAMPIONSHIP

ROUND 7

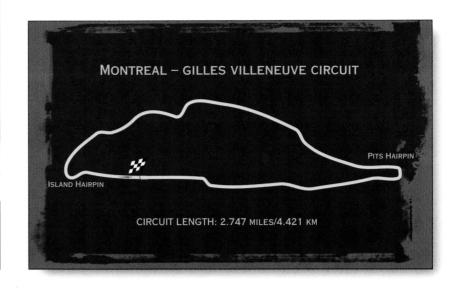

MONTREAL – GILLES VILLENEUVE CIRCUIT

PITS HAIRPIN

ISLAND HAIRPIN

CIRCUIT LENGTH: 2.747 MILES/4.421 KM

Pos.	Driver	Nat.	No.	Entrant	Car/Engine	Tyres	Laps	Time/Retirement	Speed (mph/km/h)
1	Michael Schumacher	D	5	Scuderia Ferrari Marlboro	Ferrari F310B 046 V10	G	54	1h 17m 40.646s	114.583/184.404
2	Jean Alesi	F	7	Mild Seven Benetton Renault	Benetton B197-Renault RS9 V10	G	54	1h 17m 43.211s	114.520/184.302
3	Giancarlo Fisichella	I	12	B&H Total Jordan Peugeot	Jordan 197-Peugeot A14 V10	G	54	1h 17m 43.865s	114.504/184.276
4	Heinz-Harald Frentzen	D	4	Rothmans Williams Renault	Williams FW19-Renault RS9 V10	G	54	1h 17m 44.414s	114.491/184.255
5	Johnny Herbert	GB	16	Red Bull Sauber Petronas	Sauber C16-Petronas V10	G	54	1h 17m 45.362s	114.467/184.217
6	Shinji Nakano	J	15	Prost Gauloises Blondes	Prost JS45-Mugen Honda MF301HA V10	B	54	1h 18m 17.347s	113.688/182.963
7	David Coulthard	GB	10	West McLaren Mercedes	McLaren MP4/12-Mercedes FO110F V10	G	54	1h 18m 18.399s	113.662/182.922
8	Pedro Diniz	BR	2	Danka Arrows Yamaha	Arrows A18-Yamaha OX11A/C V10	B	53		
9	Damon Hill	GB	1	Danka Arrows Yamaha	Arrows A18-Yamaha OX11A/C V10	B	53		
10	Gianni Morbidelli	I	17	Red Bull Sauber Petronas	Sauber C16-Petronas V10	G	53		
11	Olivier Panis	F	14	Prost Gauloises Blondes	Prost JS45-Mugen Honda MF301HA V10	B	51	Accident	
	Mika Salo	SF	19	Tyrrell	Tyrrell 025-Ford ED5 V8	G	46	Engine	
	Jos Verstappen	NL	18	Tyrrell	Tyrrell 025-Ford ED5 V8	G	42	Air valve	
	Alexander Wurz	A	8	Mild Seven Benetton Renault	Benetton B197-Renault RS9 V10	G	35	Transmission	
	Rubens Barrichello	BR	22	Stewart Ford	Stewart SF1-Ford Zetec-R V10	B	33	Gearbox	
	Jarno Trulli	I	21	Minardi Team	Minardi M197-Hart 830 V8	B	32	Engine	
	Ralf Schumacher	D	11	B&H Total Jordan Peugeot	Jordan 197-Peugeot A14 V10	G	14	Accident	
	Ukyo Katayama	J	20	Minardi Team	Minardi M197-Hart 830 V8	B	5	Accident	
	Jacques Villeneuve	CDN	3	Rothmans Williams Renault	Williams FW19-Renault RS9 V10	G	1	Spun off	
	Eddie Irvine	GB	6	Scuderia Ferrari Marlboro	Ferrari F310B 046 V10	G	0	Spun off	
	Mika Häkkinen	SF	9	West McLaren Mercedes	McLaren MP4/12-Mercedes FO110F V10	G	0	Collision damage	
	Jan Magnussen	DK	23	Stewart Ford	Stewart SF1-Ford Zetec-R V10	B	0	Accident	

Fastest lap: Coulthard, on lap 37, 1m 19.635s, 124.185 mph/199.856 km/h (record).

Previous lap record: Jacques Villeneuve (F1 Williams FW18-Renault V10), 1m 21.916s, 120.727 mph/194.291 km/h (1996).

B – Bridgestone   G – Goodyear

Grid order	1	2	3	4	5	6	7	8	9	10	11	12	13	14	15	16	17	18	19	20	21	22	23	24	25	26	27	28	29	30	31	32	33	34	35	36	37	38	39	40	41	42
5 M. SCHUMACHER	5	5	5	5	5	5	5	5	5	5	5	5	5	5	5	5	5	5	5	5	5	5	5	5	5	5	5	5	10	10	10	10	10	10	10	10	10	10	10	10	5	5
3 VILLENEUVE	3	12	12	12	12	12	12	12	12	12	12	12	12	12	12	12	12	12	12	12	12	12	12	12	10	10	10	5	5	5	10	5	5	5	5	5	5	5	10	10	10	
22 BARRICHELLO	12	7	7	7	7	7	7	7	7	7	7	7	7	7	7	7	7	7	7	7	7	7	7	7	8	7	7	7	7	7	7	7	7	7	7	7	7	7	7	7	7	7
4 FRENTZEN	7	10	10	10	10	10	10	10	10	10	10	10	10	10	10	10	10	10	10	10	10	10	10	7	12	12	12	12	12	12	12	12	12	12	12	12	12	12	12	12	12	
10 COULTHARD	10	4	4	4	4	11	11	11	11	11	11	11	11	11	8	8	8	8	8	8	8	8	8	12	16	16	16	16	16	16	16	16	16	16	16	16	16	16	16	16	16	
12 FISICHELLA	4	11	11	11	11	4	4	4	4	8	8	8	8	18	18	18	18	18	18	18	18	19	19	8	8	8	8	4	8	8	8	8	4	4	4	4	4	4	4	4	4	
11 R. SCHUMACHER	11	8	8	8	8	8	8	8	22	22	18	18	18	22	19	19	19	19	19	19	19	16	16	4	4	4	4	8	18	18	18	18	18	18	18	18	18	18	18	18	14	
7 ALESI	22	22	22	22	22	22	22	22	18	18	22	22	22	19	22	16	16	16	16	16	16	18	18	18	18	18	18	18	4	4	4	4	19	14	14	14	14	14	18	
9 HÄKKINEN	8	18	18	18	18	18	18	18	19	19	19	19	19	16	16	22	22	22	22	22	22	4	4	4	19	19	19	19	19	19	19	19	14	19	1	1	19	19	19	
14 PANIS	18	19	19	19	19	19	19	19	16	16	16	16	16	2	2	2	2	2	2	4	22	2	2	2	2	2	2	2	2	2	2	15	1	19	19	15	15	15	
8 WURZ	19	16	16	16	16	16	16	16	2	2	2	2	2	14	14	14	14	17	17	2	2	17	17	17	17	17	17	17	17	14	14	14	1	15	15	15	2	2	2	
6 IRVINE	16	2	2	2	2	2	2	2	17	17	17	17	21	17	17	17	21	21	21	17	21	21	21	21	21	21	21	21	15	15	15	2	2	2	17	17	
16 HERBERT	2	21	21	21	21	21	21	21	21	21	14	14	17	21	21	21	4	21	21	21	15	15	15	15	15	15	14	14	1	1	1	17	17	17	17	1	
18 VERSTAPPEN	21	1	1	17	17	17	17	17	17	14	21	21	21	15	15	15	15	15	15	15	1	1	1	14	14	14	14	15	15	17	17	17	
1 HILL	1	17	17	15	15	15	15	15	15	15	15	15	15	1	1	4	1	1	1	1	14	14	14	1	1	1	1	1	22				
2 DINIZ	20	20	15	20	20	14	14	14	14	1	1	1	1	4	4	1	14	14	14	14	4	22	22	22	22	22	22	22	22	22		
19 SALO	17	15	20	14	14	1	1	1	1	4	4	4	4																	
17 MORBIDELLI	15	14	14	1	1																						
15 NAKANO	14																										
21 TRULLI																											
23 MAGNUSSEN																											
20 KATAYAMA																											

Pit stop
One lap behind leader

STARTING GRID

	5
3	**M. SCHUMACHER**
VILLENEUVE	Ferrari
Williams	
	22
4	**BARRICHELLO**
FRENTZEN	Stewart
Williams	
	10
12	**COULTHARD**
FISICHELLA	McLaren
Jordan	
	11
7	**R. SCHUMACHER**
ALESI	Jordan
Benetton	
	9
14	**HÄKKINEN**
PANIS	McLaren
Prost	
	8
6	**WURZ**
IRVINE	Benetton
Ferrari	
	16
18	**HERBERT**
VERSTAPPEN	Sauber
Tyrrell	
	1
2	**HILL**
DINIZ	Arrows
Arrows	
	19
17	**SALO**
MORBIDELLI	Tyrrell
Sauber	
	15
21	**NAKANO**
TRULLI	Prost
Minardi	
	23
20	**MAGNUSSEN**
KATAYAMA	Stewart
Minardi	

TIME SHEETS

QUALIFYING

Weather: Dry, hot and sunny

Pos.	Driver	Car	Laps	Time
1	Michael Schumacher	Ferrari	11	1m 18.095s
2	Jacques Villeneuve	Williams-Renault	12	1m 18.108s
3	Rubens Barrichello	Stewart-Ford	12	1m 18.388s
4	Heinz-Harald Frentzen	Williams-Renault	11	1m 18.464s
5	David Coulthard	McLaren-Mercedes	8	1m 18.466s
6	Giancarlo Fisichella	Jordan-Peugeot	12	1m 18.750s
7	Ralf Schumacher	Jordan-Peugeot	11	1m 18.869s
8	Jean Alesi	Benetton-Renault	10	1m 18.899s
9	Mika Häkkinen	McLaren-Mercedes	9	1m 18.916s
10	Olivier Panis	Prost-Mugen Honda	11	1m 19.034s
11	Alexander Wurz	Benetton-Renault	10	1m 19.286s
12	Eddie Irvine	Ferrari	12	1m 19.503s
13	Johnny Herbert	Sauber-Petronas	11	1m 19.622s
14	Jos Verstappen	Tyrrell-Ford	10	1m 20.102s
15	Damon Hill	Arrows-Yamaha	12	1m 20.129s
16	Pedro Diniz	Arrows-Yamaha	12	1m 20.175s
17	Mika Salo	Tyrrell-Ford	10	1m 20.336s
18	Gianni Morbidelli	Sauber-Petronas	12	1m 20.357s
19	Shinji Nakano	Prost-Mugen Honda	12	1m 20.370s
20	Jarno Trulli	Minardi-Hart	10	1m 20.370s
21	Jan Magnussen	Stewart-Ford	9	1m 20.491s
22	Ukyo Katayama	Minardi-Hart	11	1m 21.034s

FRIDAY FREE PRACTICE

Weather: Warm and overcast

Pos.	Driver	Laps	Time
1	Heinz-Harald Frentzen	26	1m 20.289s
2	Giancarlo Fisichella	18	1m 20.416s
3	Jacques Villeneuve	26	1m 20.552s
4	Jean Alesi	21	1m 20.624s
5	Olivier Panis	26	1m 20.727s
6	Johnny Herbert	30	1m 20.876s
7	Ralf Schumacher	22	1m 20.930s
8	Eddie Irvine	23	1m 20.987s
9	Michael Schumacher	18	1m 21.201s
10	Rubens Barrichello	27	1m 21.269s
11	Alexander Wurz	29	1m 21.215s
12	Mika Häkkinen	24	1m 21.372s
13	Gianni Morbidelli	26	1m 21.415s
14	David Coulthard	21	1m 21.468s
15	Pedro Diniz	30	1m 21.777s
16	Mika Salo	28	1m 21.848s
17	Damon Hill	18	1m 22.460s
18	Jos Verstappen	20	1m 22.550s
19	Ukyo Katayama	26	1m 22.708s
20	Shinji Nakano	29	1m 22.930s
21	Jan Magnussen	25	1m 23.826s
22	Jarno Trulli	22	1m 24.131s

SATURDAY FREE PRACTICE

Weather: Bright and warm

Pos.	Driver	Laps	Time
1	Michael Schumacher	28	1m 18.034s
2	Olivier Panis	26	1m 18.514s
3	Jean Alesi	30	1m 18.563s
4	Giancarlo Fisichella	27	1m 18.651s
5	Eddie Irvine	28	1m 18.829s
6	Rubens Barrichello	19	1m 18.833s
7	Heinz-Harald Frentzen	25	1m 18.871s
8	Johnny Herbert	27	1m 18.883s
9	Jacques Villeneuve	25	1m 18.953s
10	Mika Häkkinen	23	1m 19.053s
11	David Coulthard	20	1m 19.087s
12	Alexander Wurz	28	1m 19.189s
13	Gianni Morbidelli	29	1m 19.366s
14	Ralf Schumacher	29	1m 19.540s
15	Mika Salo	26	1m 19.744s
16	Jos Verstappen	25	1m 19.812s
17	Jarno Trulli	28	1m 19.929s
18	Damon Hill	30	1m 19.957s
19	Jan Magnussen	18	1m 20.084s
20	Shinji Nakano	30	1m 20.089s
21	Pedro Diniz	6	1m 20.366s
22	Ukyo Katayama	26	1m 21.134s

WARM-UP

Weather: Very hot and sunny

Pos.	Driver	Laps	Time
1	Olivier Panis	19	1m 19.477s
2	David Coulthard	17	1m 19.594s
3	Giancarlo Fisichella	18	1m 19.645s
4	Jean Alesi	15	1m 19.727s
5	Mika Häkkinen	16	1m 19.829s
6	Ralf Schumacher	18	1m 19.854s
7	Jacques Villeneuve	11	1m 19.940s
8	Johnny Herbert	15	1m 20.457s
9	Michael Schumacher	13	1m 20.489s
10	Heinz-Harald Frentzen	15	1m 20.507s
11	Mika Salo	14	1m 20.863s
12	Jan Magnussen	10	1m 20.903s
13	Rubens Barrichello	11	1m 20.929s
14	Alexander Wurz	17	1m 20.989s
15	Jos Verstappen	13	1m 21.005s
16	Eddie Irvine	15	1m 21.469s
17	Jarno Trulli	12	1m 21.516s
18	Gianni Morbidelli	15	1m 21.802s
19	Shinji Nakano	17	1m 21.850s
20	Pedro Diniz	14	1m 22.110s
21	Ukyo Katayama	13	1m 22.359s
22	Damon Hill	14	1m 22.721s

RACE FASTEST LAPS

Weather: Dry, hot and sunny

Driver	Time	Lap
David Coulthard	1m 19.635s	37
Heinz-Harald Frentzen	1m 19.997s	49
Michael Schumacher	1m 20.171s	27
Jean Alesi	1m 20.679s	50
Johnny Herbert	1m 20.709s	33
Olivier Panis	1m 20.945s	47
Giancarlo Fisichella	1m 21.013s	27
Alexander Wurz	1m 21.048s	25
Mika Salo	1m 21.622s	24
Jos Verstappen	1m 21.902s	21
Shinji Nakano	1m 22.077s	48
Rubens Barrichello	1m 22.366s	26
Ralf Schumacher	1m 22.372s	26
Pedro Diniz	1m 22.434s	34
Damon Hill	1m 22.435s	6
Gianni Morbidelli	1m 22.659s	32
Jarno Trulli	1m 22.712s	29
Ukyo Katayama	1m 24.294s	5
Jacques Villeneuve	1m 28.356s	1

CHASSIS LOG BOOK

1	Hill	Arrows A18/3
2	Diniz	Arrows A18/2
	spare	Arrows A18/1
3	Villeneuve	Williams FW19/4
4	Frentzen	Williams FW19/5
	spare	Williams FW19/3
5	M. Schumacher	Ferrari F310B/177
6	Irvine	Ferrari F310B/176
	spare	Ferrari F310B/175
7	Alesi	Benetton B197/5
8	Wurz	Benetton B197/4
	spare	Benetton B197/3
9	Häkkinen	McLaren MP4/12/6
10	Coulthard	McLaren MP4/12/3
	spare	McLaren MP4/12/1
11	R. Schumacher	Jordan 197/3
12	Fisichella	Jordan 197/4
	spare	Jordan 197/1
14	Panis	Prost JS45/3
15	Nakano	Prost JS45/2
	spare	Prost JS45/1
16	Herbert	Sauber C16/1
17	Morbidelli	Sauber C16/2
	spare	Sauber C16/3
18	Verstappen	Tyrrell 025/2
19	Salo	Tyrrell 025/3
	spare	Tyrrell 025/1
20	Katayama	Minardi M197/3
21	Trulli	Minardi M197/2
	spare	Minardi M197/1
22	Barrichello	Stewart SF1/2
23	Magnussen	Stewart SF1/3
	spare	Stewart SF1/1

POINTS TABLES

Drivers

1	Michael Schumacher	37
2	Jacques Villeneuve	30
3	Olivier Panis	15
4	Eddie Irvine	14
5 =	Heinz-Harald Frentzen	13
5 =	Jean Alesi	13
7	David Coulthard	11
8 =	Gerhard Berger	10
8 =	Mika Häkkinen	10
10	Giancarlo Fisichella	8
11	Johnny Herbert	7
12	Rubens Barrichello	6
13	Ralf Schumacher	4
14	Mika Salo	2
15 =	Nicola Larini	1
15 =	Shinji Nakano	1

Constructors

1	Ferrari	51
2	Williams	44
3	Benetton	23
4	McLaren	21
5	Prost	16
6	Jordan	12
7	Sauber	8
8	Stewart	6
9	Tyrrell	2

Lap Chart

43	44	45	46	47	48	49	50	51	52	53	54	
5	10	10	10	10	10	10	10	10	10	5	5	1
10	5	5	5	5	5	5	5	5	7	7	7	2
7	7	7	7	7	4	4	4	7	12	12	12	3
12	12	4	4	4	7	7	7	12	4	4	4	4
4	4	12	12	12	12	12	12	4	16	16	16	5
16	16	16	16	16	16	16	16	15	15	15	15	6
14	14	14	14	14	14	14	14	14	10	10	10	
19	19	19	19	15	15	15	15	15	2	2		
15	15	15	15	2	2	2	2	2	1	1		
2	2	2	2	1	1	1	1	1	17	17		
1	1	1	1	17	17	17	17	17				
17	17	17	17									

FOR THE RECORD

First Grand Prix start
Alexander Wurz

First Grand Prix point
Shinji Nakano

FIA WORLD CHAMPIONSHIP • ROUND 8

FRENCH
grand prix

M. SCHUMACHER

FRENTZEN

IRVINE

VILLENEUVE

ALESI

R. SCHUMACHER

Nevers Magny-Cours Circuit Nevers Magny-Cours

Tennis fans might have been praying for the sun to emerge at Wimbledon, but Rubens Barrichello and Damon Hill ended Friday practice at the Circuit de Nevers with their fingers firmly crossed that the dank, grey skies would continue delivering their periodic downpours, at least through to the end of Sunday afternoon.

'I'm doing my rain dance,' admitted World Champion Hill at the end of the Friday morning session, having set second-fastest time up to that point behind the Brazilian's Stewart-Ford. Hill's Arrows-Yamaha might have been a ponderous piece of equipment in the dry, but when the track was wet, he stood to benefit from the same Bridgestone rain tyres which had helped clinch Barrichello's splendid second place at Monaco.

However, such dreams were cruelly transient. By the end of the afternoon the track had dried out sufficiently for top Goodyear user Michael Schumacher's Ferrari F310B to emerge quickest on slick tyres ahead of the consistently impressive Giancarlo Fisichella at the wheel of the Jordan-Peugeot. Barrichello faded to tenth, Hill to 13th, but with the promise of more unsettled weather ahead, the battle was far from resolved.

'The sessions went well and I think we switched to slicks at about the right time,' said Hill. 'But when it was wet, I believe the Bridgestones were superior and their performance was very consistent. The conditions changed throughout the sessions and this was a very good exercise for us to try all the different types of tyres.'

Come Saturday qualifying, Schumacher and Ferrari rammed home the message that their form was improving by leaps and bounds with every race. Using the 'Step 2' version of the 046 V10 engine, Michael performed brilliantly to button up the 16th pole position of his career and the 120th for the team with a best lap of 1m 14.548s. Ferrari had a new front wing which was certainly giving Eddie Irvine reassuringly enhanced consistency when turning into the corners, but Schumacher was unsure precisely how much this had contributed to his pole time.

'Something we didn't do before coming here was to test this new front wing,' he explained. 'We just stuck it on the car and I don't know how much it is worth. It will give something, but I don't know how much. I am surprised that we gained pole because I am a second quicker than we managed during testing and I was struggling with understeer through the two long corners after the pits.'

Eddie Irvine wound up fifth fastest on 1m 14.860s, reporting that he had been slightly balked by Giancarlo Fisichella's Jordan on what would have been his best run. He was happy with his car, but reckoned he might have made the second row of the grid given a clear run.

In Schumacher's wake, Heinz-Harald Frentzen and Jacques Villeneuve emerged second and fourth fastest. Frentzen was only 0.2s away from Michael's best despite complaining that his car lost grip towards the end of the session and being forced to abandon his final run with loss of fuel pressure. Like the Benetton squad, both Williams drivers had a slightly revised RS9A version of the Renault V10 available for this race, offering an operational increment of 400 rpm.

During the Saturday morning session Jacques lost control after clipping a kerb going into one of the high-speed ess-bends, slamming his FW19 into the tyre barrier. That left the Williams lads facing a lunchtime rebuild with the tattered machine requiring new wings, bodywork, suspension wishbones and rear wing support beam. While the crew put the last few finishing touches to the car, Jacques did a couple of runs in the spare chassis but preferred his original car, in which he set his best time of 1m 14.800s despite losing ground through the second and third sectors of the lap.

Meanwhile, Jordan's Ralf Schumacher rounded off a German 1-2-3 grand slam to line up on the inside of the second row. Ralf reported that he felt much happier after fuel system problems had been rectified, but team-mate Fisichella finished the day in an extremely disappointed mood, his car apparently unable to generate adequate tyre temperatures and the Italian facing an 11th-place grid position as a result.

Since Canada, lots of behind-the-scenes negotiation had resulted in Minardi's Jarno Trulli being transferred into the Prost line-up to take over the position vacated by the injured Olivier Panis and the young Italian did a good job to qualify sixth fastest, despite losing time in the final corner of his best run when he momentarily found the steering wheel slipping through his hands. The Prost team's comparative mastery of its 'home' track was further emphasised by the fact that Shinji Nakano managed to qualify the second Mugen Honda-engined car in 12th place.

'If I had not made a mistake through the final corner of my last flying lap, perhaps I might have been able to gain a place or two on the grid,' said an apologetic Trulli.

The Benetton-Renaults proved closely matched, but Alexander Wurz again impressed to qualify seventh, 0.3s faster than team-mate Jean Alesi. Wurz complained of a slight braking inconsistency while the veteran Frenchman reported that he was acutely disappointed about his car's lack of balance.

'I really have very little to say,' shrugged Jean. 'It has been a very frustrating weekend because I have never managed to feel satisfied with the car. I am particularly sorry to have disappointed my public here in Magny-Cours, where they have been so supportive.'

David Coulthard qualified his McLaren-Mercedes in ninth position, despite losing about 0.3s when he ran over some debris going into what proved to be his quickest lap. 'It is very frustrating,' he confessed. 'We did a 15.2s, but it should have been a 14.9s. But that would have been the best we could manage.'

For his part, Mika Häkkinen spun at the ess-bend before the pits, then fell back on the spare MP4/12, which took some time to ready as the cockpit was set up for Coulthard. He did not get out quickly enough to complete another flying lap before the end of the session and had to be content with tenth place on the grid.

'Towards the end of the session, I hit a kerb too hard and lost the back end,' said Mika. 'Then I stalled the engine which meant that I had to run back to the pits and change to the spare. Unfortunately, I didn't get out onto the circuit in time to put in a quick lap.'

Rubens Barrichello's Stewart SF1 took 13th place behind Nakano, the Brazilian setting his best time on the last of his four runs, having briefly tried the spare car for comparative purposes on his third.

'I'm not too unhappy with the way the session went,' said Rubens. 'We were working hard to cure a little too much understeer on my race car and we went the right way for that.'

All told, the day had not turned out too badly, for Barrichello's Saturday morning free practice session was interrupted by the need to complete an engine change due to an oil pressure problem. Team-mate Jan Magnussen also did a respectable job to line up 15th fastest, equalling his best qualifying position of the season thus far.

'I set my fastest time on my first set of tyres, even though we were working with the brake balance and I locked up the fronts a little at one point,' he explained.

Johnny Herbert struggled with traction problems and could only split the Stewarts with his Sauber-Petronas, 14th place on the grid being far less than he had hoped for at Magny-Cours. In 16th place, Pedro Diniz just managed to out-qualify Damon Hill by 0.2s after the World Champion locked up his Arrows's rear brakes, spun and had to take over the spare A18.

Jos Verstappen and Mika Salo took 18th and 19th places for Tyrrell, neither driver having much grip and Jos also suffering an engine failure. Completing the top 20 was Norberto Fontana, the young Argentine driver standing in for Gianni Morbidelli in the second Sauber after the regular driver had broken an arm during pre-race testing at Magny-Cours. Finally, the last row of the grid was composed of the two Minardi-Harts with Tarso Marques taking over from the promoted Trulli.

Right: While Jacques Villeneuve's comments regarding Olivier Panis's accident caused a stir, his new hair colouring was far more shocking!

Below left: Sibling rivalry. Michael and Ralf Schumacher qualified in first and third places respectively. Heinz-Harald Frentzen completed a trio of German drivers at the front of the grid.

There is a better class of cleaner in the F1 pit lane. Jackie Stewart helps sweep away the aftermath of a practice downpour.

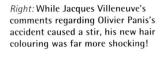

MICHAEL Schumacher underlined the fact that Ferrari had become a seriously consistent competitive force, no longer needing lashings of luck to steer a path to the F1 winner's circle, when he drove to an outstanding victory in the French Grand Prix at Magny-Cours.

It was his third win in four races and his characteristic poise was not even vaguely ruffled when a heavy shower turned the track surface into a treacherous skating rink in the closing stages of the 72-lap event. Moreover, Schumacher, who raced the 046/2 version of Ferrari's V10 engine for the first time, stayed out on slicks to the very end, even a momentary slide into a gravel trap hardly denting his advantage. His 23-second victory over Heinz-Harald Frentzen's Williams boosted his points total to 47, Michael finishing the day 14 points ahead of pre-season favourite Jacques Villeneuve, who managed to scramble his Williams home in fourth place.

'It was always going to be a two-stop strategy and we stuck to that,' said Schumacher afterwards. 'Apart from my trip into the gravel I was able to control the race throughout. We opted for a compromise chassis set-up which worked surprisingly well in the dry. In the closing stages I knew that intermediate tyres would be the best choice, but I kept looking at the sky and decided that it was only going to be a shower. So I stayed out to the end on my slicks.'

Schumacher's continued insistence at the pre-race press conference that he did not expect his car to be particularly competitive on this circuit proved nothing more than repetitive gamesmanship. Even his younger brother Ralf, who finished the race sixth for Jordan, suggested that it was time the Ferrari star laid off that particular theme.

Frentzen admitted that he simply could not believe the speed at which Schumacher had pulled away from his Williams in the opening stages of the race. 'I am happy with the result today,' he added, 'because I was desperate for points. But I was astonished by the speed of Michael – I thought he was on a three-stop strategy, because he was pushing like hell at the beginning.'

Eddie Irvine drove a beautifully disciplined race to take third place, but he was almost caught out by a final lunge from Villeneuve's Williams on the very last corner. Jacques instead spinning wildly into the pit lane entrance. In his anxiety to get back into the fray, the Canadian briefly drove against the traffic before spin-turning his Williams back onto the circuit almost under the

Paul-Henri Cahier

nose of Jean Alesi's Benetton, which he beat across the line into fourth place by a scant second. Unsurprisingly, the race stewards invited him for an audience after the race, but no sanction was imposed.

Jacques had run off the pace in fourth place during the opening stages of the race, his wet–dry compromise chassis set-up erring further to the full-wet end of the scale than his team-mate's. That meant that he was slow for much of the day, but a late switch to wet tyres with the onset of that final rain shower enabled him to gobble up Irvine's advantage in the closing stages.

World Champion Damon Hill, who had won this race in 1996 for Williams as commandingly as Schumacher would twelve months later, qualified a dismal 17th and compounded his disappointment by sliding through a gravel trap at the first turn, coming in for a new nose section to be fitted at the end of the opening lap. Thereafter the Arrows-Yamaha ran slowly and reliably through to finish 12th and last, three laps behind Schumacher's winning Ferrari. 'I am pleased that we've got a finish in,' he shrugged, 'and the car was running OK during the race. That was progress, I suppose, because I got pushed out onto the gravel at the first corner and the race was a shambles.'

His season so far had been much the same. Even the loyal and even-tempered Hill looked as though his patience with the Arrows-Yamaha package was running out.

The race morning warm-up had taken place in breezy conditions with

Villeneuve shrugs aside Panis injuries

OLIVIER Panis, who suffered serious leg injuries in the Canadian Grand Prix, returned home to France on the Tuesday prior to his home race and gave a press conference via a television link from his recuperation centre in Brittany to the Prost team's headquarters at Magny-Cours on the eve of first practice.

Panis was upbeat and optimistic about his prospects for a quick recovery, but it was left to Williams driver Jacques Villeneuve to ruffle some more F1 feathers by expressing the view that, quite honestly, he did not regard breaking both legs as a terribly big deal and felt that some of his colleagues were being disingenuous with their expressions of concern.

'If you think about it, two broken legs is nothing very bad,' he said with an almost cheerful insouciance. 'That happens to everybody in their lifetime. How many skiers hurt themselves like that in winter? So just relax a little bit.

'Olivier was having a great season and it's terrible that it has happened to him at this point, because he was going forward with big leaps in his career, but even when your legs are weak, you can still come back in a race car.

'If you see an accident like that happen and straight afterwards you go to the podium, you are bound to have the impression that the accident is worse than it was in reality. I understand that. With the money we make, we know the risks we take. The risks are ten times less than they were a few years back and we make ten times more money, so we have nothing to complain about.'

This standpoint rather startled Villeneuve's friend David Coulthard, who rightly pointed out that the last time he saw a driver lying at the side of the circuit it was Ayrton Senna at Imola. 'Jacques is entitled to his opinion, but I was genuinely upset at Montreal,' he said.

Meanwhile, Panis remained confident for the future. 'I am now recuperating well and we're starting to prepare for my return to the cockpit. I must take time, because I want to come back 150 per cent fit so that I am competitive right away and can give my best. My aim is to be World Champion, and I will be.'

rain falling steadily. The Ferraris of Irvine and Schumacher topped the timing sheets ahead of Rubens Barrichello, Mika Häkkinen, David Coulthard and Ralf Schumacher. Villeneuve was already a little cautious. 'The car felt average,' he shrugged. 'Really, the conditions were so inconsistent that it was impossible to do any meaningful work on the car.'

By the time the cars lined up to take the start, the track conditions were totally dry. But cloud scudding across

the sky hinted at the ever-present possibility of a rain shower, or more. And so it was to prove.

Giancarlo Fisichella had switched to the spare Jordan at the last moment due to engine failure, while Tarso Marques stalled his Minardi on the final parade lap, but the Brazilian continued to take up his last-place qualifying position. Nobody was surprised when Schumacher's Ferrari settled into an immediate lead once the starting signal was given. As the pack fanned out

through the Estoril right-hander and out onto the back straight, Frentzen, Irvine and Ralf Schumacher took up station behind the Ferrari, but Villeneuve neatly outbraked the Jordan driver as they went into the Adelaide hairpin to take over fourth place.

By the end of the opening lap Schumacher was already 0.8s ahead of Frentzen, who, in turn, was 1.2s clear of Irvine, Villeneuve, Ralf Schumacher, Coulthard, Häkkinen, Jarno Trulli (substituting for Olivier Panis in the Prost line-up), Jean Alesi, Alexander Wurz and Shinji Nakano. After the rest of the pack had gone through, Hill trailed into the pits for a replacement nose cone to be fitted, watched by an exasperated Arrows team chief Tom Walkinshaw from the pit wall.

Completing his fifth lap, Marques suffered an engine failure in his Minardi as he accelerated past the pits, while two laps later Nakano's exuberant efforts to keep pace with the leading bunch came to a premature end when the Japanese driver spun off the road.

By lap ten Schumacher's Ferrari was a confident 6.9s ahead of Frentzen while Villeneuve's initial threat to Irvine's third place had seemingly steadied. Coulthard and Häkkinen were now both crowding Ralf Schumacher's Jordan while the cool Trulli was fending off both Benettons, Wurz seemingly content to follow in Alesi's wheeltracks for the moment.

Further back down the order, Diniz, whose Arrows was on a one-stop schedule, was managing to keep pace with Jos Verstappen's Tyrrell. However, when he tried to overtake the Dutchman on lap 12 the two cars collided

163

DIARY

Niki Lauda attends Magny-Cours race, his first appearance at an F1 event since recovering from a kidney transplant.

Ulsterman Dino Morelli sustains serious leg injuries in F3000 accident at the Nürburgring. The race was abandoned after only four laps with victory going to Brazil's Ricardo Zonta.

Damon Hill describes as 'pure fantasy' speculation that he might leave the Arrows team mid-season and switch to the Prost squad.

Ford indicates that it is prepared to supply its Zetec-R V10 engines on a customer basis in 1998.

Nigel Mansell declines invitation to drive in Porsche Supercup event supporting the British Grand Prix at Silverstone.

and Diniz emulated his team-mate Hill by trailing in for a replacement nose section to be fitted. Three laps later, Verstappen's race came to an end when his throttle stuck open, the Tyrrell bounding across a gravel trap and coming to rest firmly embedded in a tyre barrier.

On lap 19, Häkkinen's McLaren slowed suddenly and dropped from seventh place, pulling up out on the circuit with a broken engine. Three laps later Schumacher's Ferrari came in for its first refuelling stop, the Italian machine stationary for 8.0s before accelerating back into the fray in second place behind Frentzen. At the same moment, Alesi came in from eighth place for a 10.9s first refuelling stop.

On the following lap Frentzen (8.3s) and Irvine (8.4s) made their first stops, the Williams driver's return to the race being momentarily delayed when he had to wait for the Ferrari to pull in ahead of him. The net result was that Schumacher completed lap 24 with a 9.0s lead over Villeneuve with Frentzen, Ralf Schumacher and Irvine next up.

On lap 25 it was the turn of Villeneuve and Ralf Schumacher to make their first refuelling stops, the Williams resuming in fourth place and the Jordan in sixth. By lap 30, Michael Schumacher's Ferrari had opened its lead over Frentzen to 16.3s with Villeneuve again eating into Irvine's third-place advantage, having trimmed it from 11 seconds immediately after the pit stops to 7.7s.

Further back, the Stewart-Fords of Magnussen and Barrichello had moved up to 12th and 13th by lap 25, but there was trouble ahead for both men. After making his single scheduled refuelling stop on lap 30, Magnussen found his brakes locking up with alarming frequency. The problem was caused by a broken right-front cooling duct which caused terminal overheating and he was forced to retire after 34 laps. For his part, Rubens was running 12th when his car suffered an engine failure three laps later.

'The car felt fine,' he explained, 'and while the engine was still down a little [on speed], it was a lot less so than before, so that was encouraging. After my pit stop I just had to go for it, and really I was having quite a good race in terms of recuperation.'

By lap 35 Schumacher's advantage had steadied at 12.8s over Frentzen, Irvine, Villeneuve and Ralf Schumacher. Fisichella surrendered sixth place when he came in for a 10.8s refuelling stop with the spare Jordan, allowing Coulthard, Wurz and Alesi to lead the rest of the pack.

The first signs of a rain shower had already started to brush the circuit when Schumacher brought the Ferrari in for its second (9.5s) stop on lap 46, but he fitted another set of slicks and charged back into the fray in second place, only 1.8s behind Frentzen, who came in for his own second refuelling stop (8.1s) two laps later. Frentzen also gambled by continuing on slicks, even though the clouds were darkening ominously by this stage of the race.

On lap 60 the heavens opened and rain began to fall really heavily, Coulthard and Ralf Schumacher scuttling into the pits next time round and resuming on intermediates. On the following lap Schumacher's Ferrari had a brief off-track moment exiting the Estoril right-hander, but Michael gathered it all up and continued as though nothing had happened.

Meanwhile, Coulthard's return to the contest soon saw him back in fifth place and lapping seven seconds quicker than Villeneuve's fourth-place Williams, so on lap 67 the Canadian rushed in for a final switch to intermediates, as did Irvine's Ferrari. Eddie got back into the race in third place, but Villeneuve managed to hold sixth behind Coulthard and Ralf Schumacher, and only fractionally ahead of Alesi's hard-charging Benetton.

By lap 70, Coulthard, Ralf Schumacher, Villeneuve and Alesi were absolutely nose-to-tail as they braked for the Adelaide hairpin, Jacques just nipping past the Jordan to take fifth. The Canadian continued to attack and on the following lap he repassed Coulthard, who was promptly relegated to sixth place by Schumacher. However, the young German immediately spun at the following 180-left, resuming in seventh behind Coulthard and Alesi.

Coming down to complete his last lap, Michael Schumacher allowed his brother's Jordan to unlap itself, giving Ralf the chance to profit from any late retirements, before taking the chequered flag to win by 23.537s from Frentzen. As Villeneuve made his abortive bid for third place and spun, Coulthard, who had gone into the final lap heading for fifth place, ended the

afternoon stuck in a gravel trap after Alesi's Benetton drove straight into the back of him and rammed him off the circuit. Villeneuve recovered to claim fourth place ahead of Alesi, Ralf Schumacher taking sixth thanks purely to the fact that he was able to complete that final tour and overtake the gravel-bound Coulthard.

'It was totally unacceptable,' said Coulthard indignantly. 'I would go and have a word with him, but I don't think there would be any point. He wouldn't take any notice.'

Schumacher was hard pressed to conceal his delight over his third victory of the season. 'My predictions for the race were wrong,' he confessed, 'and this was a convincing win. There were no mistakes in the car's set-up, nor in our strategy, as we planned two stops and stuck to that. In the final part of the race, I was just watching to see what Frentzen would do.'

Heinz-Harald had no more shots left in his locker, but was pleased to gain the six points which came with second place. Irvine was a satisfied third, Villeneuve a frustrated fourth. Alesi described fifth place as the 'best result I could have hoped for', while Ralf Schumacher was simply happy to have scored his first point since Argentina.

'This race was run under very difficult circumstances,' he shrugged, 'especially in the last few laps. We could not stay out on slicks, so I came in for intermediates. But then it dried out and things became slippery – it was like driving on soap. I was really lucky to get that extra lap from Michael – I owe him one, or perhaps this is his birthday present for me tomorrow!'

The fuming Coulthard was classified seventh ahead of Herbert, whose Sauber's set-up only really came into its own when the rain began falling seriously. He was comfortably ahead of the ninth-placed Jordan of Fisichella, the Italian struggling throughout as the spare car was not fitted with the latest differential and proved difficult to drive. Trulli, Katayama and the stoic Hill completed the list of finishers, Wurz having spun off in his Benetton and Mika Salo's Tyrrell succumbing to engine failure.

For the Ferrari team not only had this success extended Schumacher's World Championship points lead over arch-rival Jacques Villeneuve, but Irvine's contribution to the party had also enhanced their lead in the constructors' title race.

By his own admission, Michael was also now thinking for the first time that a third title might be a realistic possibility.

Heinz-Harald Frentzen gave his confidence a lift by outpacing team-mate Jacques Villeneuve, but couldn't match Michael Schumacher in the race and had to be satisfied with second place.

Right: Argentina's Norberto Fontana, drafted into the Sauber team in place of the injured Gianni Morbidelli, endured a difficult Grand Prix baptism.

GRAND PRIX DE FRANCE

27–29 JUNE 1997

NEVERS MAGNY-COURS

Race distance: 72 laps, 190.008 miles/305.814 km

Race weather: Warm and overcast, rain at end

ROUND
8

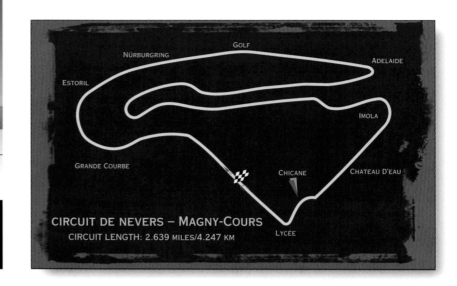

CIRCUIT DE NEVERS – MAGNY-COURS
CIRCUIT LENGTH: 2.639 MILES/4.247 KM

Pos.	Driver	Nat.	No.	Entrant	Car/Engine	Tyres	Laps	Time/Retirement	Speed (mph/km/h)
1	Michael Schumacher	D	5	Scuderia Ferrari Marlboro	Ferrari F310B 046/2 V10	G	72	1h 38m 50.492s	115.351/185.639
2	Heinz-Harald Frentzen	D	4	Rothmans Williams Renault	Williams FW19-Renault RS9A V10	G	72	1h 39m 14.029s	114.894/184.905
3	Eddie Irvine	GB	6	Scuderia Ferrari Marlboro	Ferrari F310B 046/2 V10	G	72	1h 40m 05.293s	113.913/183.326
4	Jacques Villeneuve	CDN	3	Rothmans Williams Renault	Williams FW19-Renault RS9A V10	G	72	1h 40m 12.276s	113.781/183.113
5	Jean Alesi	F	7	Mild Seven Benetton Renault	Benetton B197-Renault RS9A V10	G	72	1h 40m 13.227s	113.763/183.084
6	Ralf Schumacher	D	11	B&H Total Jordan Peugeot	Jordan 197-Peugeot A14 V10	G	72	1h 40m 20.363s	113.628/182.867
7	David Coulthard	GB	10	West McLaren Mercedes	McLaren MP4/12-Mercedes FO110F V10	G	71	Collision with Alesi	
8	Johnny Herbert	GB	16	Red Bull Sauber Petronas	Sauber C16-Petronas V10	G	71		
9	Giancarlo Fisichella	I	12	B&H Total Jordan Peugeot	Jordan 197-Peugeot A14 V10	G	71		
10	Jarno Trulli	I	14	Prost Gauloises Blondes	Prost JS45-Mugen Honda MF301HB V10	B	70		
11	Ukyo Katayama	J	20	Minardi Team	Minardi M197-Hart 830 V8	B	70		
12	Damon Hill	GB	1	Danka Arrows Yamaha	Arrows A18-Yamaha OX11A/C V10	B	69		
	Mika Salo	SF	19	Tyrrell	Tyrrell 025-Ford ED5 V8	G	61	Engine	
	Alexander Wurz	A	8	Mild Seven Benetton Renault	Benetton B197-Renault RS9A V10	G	60	Spun off	
	Pedro Diniz	BR	2	Danka Arrows Yamaha	Arrows A18-Yamaha OX11A/C V10	B	58	Spun off	
	Norberto Fontana	RA	17	Red Bull Sauber Petronas	Sauber C16-Petronas V10	G	40	Spun off	
	Rubens Barrichello	BR	22	Stewart Ford	Stewart SF1-Ford Zetec-R V10	B	36	Engine	
	Jan Magnussen	DK	23	Stewart Ford	Stewart SF1-Ford Zetec-R V10	B	33	Brakes	
	Mika Häkkinen	SF	9	West McLaren Mercedes	McLaren MP4/12-Mercedes FO110F V10	G	18	Engine	
	Jos Verstappen	NL	18	Tyrrell	Tyrrell 025-Ford ED5 V8	G	15	Stuck throttle	
	Shinji Nakano	J	15	Prost Gauloises Blondes	Prost JS45-Mugen Honda MF301HB V10	B	7	Spun off	
	Tarso Marques	BR	21	Minardi Team	Minardi M197-Hart 830 V8	B	5	Engine	

Fastest lap: M. Schumacher, on lap 37, 1m 17.910s, 122.025 mph/196.380 km/h.

Lap record: Nigel Mansell (F1 Williams FW14B-Renault V10), 1m 17.070s, 123.355 mph/198.521 km/h (1992).

B – Bridgestone   G – Goodyear

Grid order	1 2 3 4 5 6 7 8 9 10 11 12 13 14 15 16 17 18 19 20 21 22 23 24 25 26 27 28 29 30 31 32 33 34 35 36 37 38 39 40 41 42 43 44 45 46 47 48 49 50 51 52 53 54 55 56
5 M. SCHUMACHER	5 5 5 5 5 5 5 5 5 5 5 5 5 5 5 5 5 5 5 5 5 5 5 4 5 5 5 5 5 5 5 5 5 5 5 5 5 5 5 5 5 5 5 5 5 5 4 5 5 5 5 5 5 5 5 5
4 FRENTZEN	4 4 4 4 4 4 4 4 4 4 4 4 4 4 4 4 4 4 4 4 4 4 4 5 3 3 4 4 4 4 4 4 4 4 4 4 4 4 4 4 4 4 4 4 4 5 4 4 4 4 4 4 4 4 4 4
11 R. SCHUMACHER	6 6 6 6 6 6 6 6 6 6 6 6 6 6 6 6 6 6 6 6 6 6 6 4 4 6 6 6 6 6 6 6 6 6 6 6 6 6 6 6 6 6 6 3 3 3 3 3 3 3 6 6 6 6
3 VILLENEUVE	3 3 3 3 3 3 3 3 3 3 3 3 3 3 3 3 3 3 3 3 3 3 3 11 6 3 3 3 3 3 3 3 3 3 3 3 3 3 3 3 3 3 3 6 6 6 6 6 6 6 3 3 3 3
6 IRVINE	11 11 11 11 11 11 11 11 11 11 11 11 11 11 11 11 11 11 11 11 11 11 11 6 11 14 14 14 14 14 11 11 11 11 11 11 11 11 11 11 11 11 11 11 11 11 11 11 11 11 11 11 11 11 10 10 10
14 TRULLI	10 10 10 10 10 10 10 10 10 10 10 10 10 10 10 10 10 10 10 10 10 10 10 14 14 11 11 11 11 11 10 10 10 10 10 10 10 10 10 10 10 10 10 10 10 10 8 7 7 7 11 11 11
8 WURZ	9 9 9 9 9 9 9 9 9 9 9 9 9 9 9 9 9 9 9 9 14 14 14 8 12 12 12 12 12 12 10 10 10 12 8 8 8 8 8 8 8 8 8 8 8 8 7 8 14 10 7 7 7
7 ALESI	14 14 14 14 14 14 14 14 14 14 14 14 14 14 7 7 7 8 8 12 10 10 10 10 10 8 8 8 8 8 7 7 7 7 7 7 7 7 7 7 7 7 7 10 14 10 8 8 8
10 COULTHARD	7 7 7 7 7 7 7 7 7 7 7 7 7 7 8 8 8 7 12 10 8 8 8 8 8 7 7 7 7 14 14 14 14 14 14 14 14 14 14 14 14 14 10 12 12 12 12 12
9 HÄKKINEN	8 8 8 8 8 8 8 8 8 8 8 8 8 8 8 12 12 12 12 7 7 7 7 7 7 7 7 14 14 14 14 14 12 12 12 12 12 12 12 12 12 12 12 12 12 12 8 14 14 14 16
12 FISICHELLA	15 15 15 15 15 15 12 12 12 12 12 12 12 12 16 16 16 16 16 16 16 16 16 16 16 16 16 16 16 16 16 16 19 19 19 19 19 19 19 19 19 19 19 19 16 16 16 16 14
15 NAKANO	12 12 12 12 12 12 16 16 16 16 16 16 16 16 23 23 23 23 23 23 23 23 23 22 22 22 22 22 22 22 19 19 19 19 19 19 16 16 16 16 16 16 16 16
22 BARRICHELLO	16 16 16 16 16 16 23 23 23 23 23 23 23 23 22 22 22 22 22 22 22 22 22 19 19 19 19 19 20 20 20 20 20 20 20 20 20 20 20 20 20 20 20 20
16 HERBERT	23 23 23 23 23 23 22 22 22 22 22 22 22 22 19 19 19 19 19 19 19 19 23 20 20 20 20 2 1 1 2 2 2 2 2 2 2 2 2 1 1 1 1
23 MAGNUSSEN	22 22 22 22 22 22 18 18 18 18 18 18 18 18 19 19 20 20 20 20 20 20 20 20 20 23 2 2 1 2 2 1 1 1 1 1 1 1 1 1 2 2 2
2 DINIZ	18 18 18 18 18 18 2 2 2 2 2 2 2 2 20 17 17 17 17 17 17 17 17 2 1 1 17 17 17
1 HILL	2 2 2 2 2 19 19 19 17 17 20 20 17 17 17 17 17 17 17 17 2 1 1 17 17 17
18 VERSTAPPEN	19 19 19 19 19 19 17 17 17 20 20 17 17 2 2 2 1 1 1 1 1 1 2 2 2
19 SALO	17 17 17 17 17 17 17 20 20 20 20 2 2 2 2 1 1 1
17 FONTANA	20 20 20 20 20 20 20 1 1 1 1 1 1 1 1
20 KATAYAMA	21 21 21 21 21 1 1
21 MARQUES	1 1 1 1 1

Pit stop
One lap behind leader

STARTING GRID

	5
4	M. SCHUMACHER
FRENTZEN	Ferrari
Williams	
	11
3	R. SCHUMACHER
VILLENEUVE	Jordan
Williams	
	6
14	IRVINE
TRULLI	Ferrari
Prost	
	8
7	WURZ
ALESI	Benetton
Benetton	
	10
9	COULTHARD
HÄKKINEN	McLaren
McLaren	
	12
15	FISICHELLA
NAKANO	Jordan
Prost	
	22
16	BARRICHELLO
HERBERT	Stewart
Sauber	
	23
2	MAGNUSSEN
DINIZ	Stewart
Arrows	
	1
18	HILL
VERSTAPPEN	Arrows
Tyrrell	
	19
17	SALO
FONTANA	Tyrrell
Sauber	
	20
21	KATAYAMA
MARQUES	Minardi
Minardi	

FOR THE RECORD

First Grand Prix start

Norberto Fontana

TIME SHEETS

QUALIFYING

Weather: Cloudy and bright

Pos.	Driver	Car	Laps	Time
1	Michael Schumacher	Ferrari	9	1m 14.548s
2	Heinz-Harald Frentzen	Williams-Renault	11	1m 14.749s
3	Ralf Schumacher	Jordan-Peugeot	11	1m 14.755s
4	Jacques Villeneuve	Williams-Renault	12	1m 14.800s
5	Eddie Irvine	Ferrari	11	1m 14.860s
6	Jarno Trulli	Prost-Mugen Honda	12	1m 14.957s
7	Alexander Wurz	Benetton-Renault	12	1m 14.986s
8	Jean Alesi	Benetton-Renault	12	1m 15.228s
9	David Coulthard	McLaren-Mercedes	11	1m 15.270s
10	Mika Häkkinen	McLaren-Mercedes	9	1m 15.339s
11	Giancarlo Fisichella	Jordan-Peugeot	12	1m 15.453s
12	Shinji Nakano	Prost-Mugen Honda	12	1m 15.857s
13	Rubens Barrichello	Stewart-Ford	12	1m 15.876s
14	Johnny Herbert	Sauber-Petronas	12	1m 16.018s
15	Jan Magnussen	Stewart-Ford	12	1m 16.149s
16	Pedro Diniz	Arrows-Yamaha	12	1m 16.536s
17	Damon Hill	Arrows-Yamaha	11	1m 16.729s
18	Jos Verstappen	Tyrrell-Ford	11	1m 16.941s
19	Mika Salo	Tyrrell-Ford	12	1m 17.256s
20	Norberto Fontana	Sauber-Petronas	12	1m 17.538s
21	Ukyo Katayama	Minardi-Hart	12	1m 17.563s
22	Tarso Marques	Minardi-Hart	12	1m 18.280s

FRIDAY FREE PRACTICE

Weather: Heavy rain at first, then drying

Pos.	Driver	Laps	Time
1	Michael Schumacher	20	1m 18.339s
2	Giancarlo Fisichella	30	1m 19.838s
3	Mika Häkkinen	23	1m 20.014s
4	Ralf Schumacher	23	1m 20.020s
5	Jacques Villeneuve	30	1m 20.225s
6	Heinz-Harald Frentzen	28	1m 20.469s
7	Jos Verstappen	23	1m 21.512s
8	Jean Alesi	15	1m 21.742s
9	Johnny Herbert	25	1m 22.206s
10	Rubens Barrichello	26	1m 23.232s
11	Ukyo Katayama	30	1m 23.469s
12	Shinji Nakano	29	1m 23.839s
13	Damon Hill	30	1m 24.494s
14	Tarso Marques	30	1m 24.535s
15	Mika Salo	30	1m 25.449s
16	Pedro Diniz	26	1m 26.108s
17	David Coulthard	25	1m 27.460s
18	Norberto Fontana	30	1m 27.905s
19	Jarno Trulli	29	1m 29.600s
20	Eddie Irvine	17	1m 31.193s
21	Alexander Wurz	17	1m 31.943s
22	Jan Magnussen	13	1m 34.357s

SATURDAY FREE PRACTICE

Weather: Dry and warm

Pos.	Driver	Laps	Time
1	Jacques Villeneuve	19	1m 14.596s
2	Heinz-Harald Frentzen	20	1m 14.987s
3	Eddie Irvine	22	1m 15.184s
4	Michael Schumacher	22	1m 15.313s
5	David Coulthard	26	1m 15.443s
6	Giancarlo Fisichella	29	1m 15.452s
7	Shinji Nakano	29	1m 15.858s
8	Alexander Wurz	20	1m 15.885s
9	Jarno Trulli	28	1m 16.162s
10	Ralf Schumacher	14	1m 16.232s
11	Mika Häkkinen	24	1m 16.243s
12	Jean Alesi	13	1m 16.320s
13	Johnny Herbert	30	1m 16.523s
14	Rubens Barrichello	21	1m 16.609s
15	Jos Verstappen	26	1m 16.941s
16	Jan Magnussen	14	1m 17.008s
17	Mika Salo	29	1m 17.085s
18	Pedro Diniz	28	1m 17.174s
19	Norberto Fontana	28	1m 17.263s
20	Damon Hill	26	1m 17.280s
21	Tarso Marques	27	1m 18.109s
22	Ukyo Katayama	7	1m 19.469s

WARM-UP

Weather: Rain, breezy

Pos.	Driver	Laps	Time
1	Eddie Irvine	13	1m 30.456s
2	Michael Schumacher	11	1m 31.613s
3	Rubens Barrichello	15	1m 31.986s
4	Mika Häkkinen	13	1m 32.307s
5	David Coulthard	12	1m 32.369s
6	Ralf Schumacher	14	1m 32.573s
7	Jacques Villeneuve	13	1m 32.916s
8	Heinz-Harald Frentzen	13	1m 33.314s
9	Alexander Wurz	14	1m 33.789s
10	Norberto Fontana	13	1m 33.910s
11	Jan Magnussen	8	1m 33.972s
12	Damon Hill	13	1m 34.061s
13	Giancarlo Fisichella	4	1m 34.284s
14	Johnny Herbert	13	1m 34.425s
15	Jarno Trulli	16	1m 34.514s
16	Jean Alesi	13	1m 34.697s
17	Tarso Marques	9	1m 34.786s
18	Mika Salo	11	1m 35.174s
19	Ukyo Katayama	12	1m 35.569s
20	Shinji Nakano	12	1m 35.929s
21	Pedro Diniz	11	1m 36.257s
22	Jos Verstappen	11	1m 37.212s

RACE FASTEST LAPS

Weather: Warm and overcast, rain at end

Driver	Time	Lap
Michael Schumacher	1m 17.910s	37
Heinz-Harald Frentzen	1m 18.136s	46
Jacques Villeneuve	1m 18.649s	27
Alexander Wurz	1m 18.684s	35
Rubens Barrichello	1m 18.781s	27
Eddie Irvine	1m 19.029s	20
Jean Alesi	1m 19.055s	27
Ralf Schumacher	1m 19.225s	27
Giancarlo Fisichella	1m 19.225s	34
David Coulthard	1m 19.317s	37
Jarno Trulli	1m 19.417s	32
Norberto Fontana	1m 19.849s	35
Jan Magnussen	1m 19.912s	32
Mika Häkkinen	1m 20.153s	14
Mika Salo	1m 20.385s	31
Damon Hill	1m 20.434s	42
Ukyo Katayama	1m 20.534s	26
Pedro Diniz	1m 20.557s	55
Shinji Nakano	1m 20.662s	7
Johnny Herbert	1m 20.845s	40
Jos Verstappen	1m 22.034s	15
Tarso Marques	1m 22.325s	4

CHASSIS LOG BOOK

1	Hill	Arrows A18/3
2	Diniz	Arrows A18/4
	spare	Arrows A18/1
3	Villeneuve	Williams FW19/4
4	Frentzen	Williams FW19/5
	spare	Williams FW19/3
5	M. Schumacher	Ferrari F310B/177
6	Irvine	Ferrari F310B/173
	spare	Ferrari F310B/175
7	Alesi	Benetton B197/5
8	Wurz	Benetton B197/2
	spare	Benetton B197/3
9	Häkkinen	McLaren MP4/12/6
10	Coulthard	McLaren MP4/12/4
	spare	McLaren MP4/12/3
11	R. Schumacher	Jordan 197/5
12	Fisichella	Jordan 197/4
	spare	Jordan 197/1
14	Trulli	Prost JS45/3
15	Nakano	Prost JS45/2
	spare	Prost JS45/1
16	Herbert	Sauber C16/5
17	Fontana	Sauber C16/6
	spare	Sauber C16/3
18	Verstappen	Tyrrell 025/4
19	Salo	Tyrrell 025/3
	spare	Tyrrell 025/1
20	Katayama	Minardi M197/3
21	Marques	Minardi M197/2
	spare	Minardi M197/1
22	Barrichello	Stewart SF1/2
23	Magnussen	Stewart SF1/1
	spare	Stewart SF1/3

POINTS TABLES

Drivers

1	Michael Schumacher	47
2	Jacques Villeneuve	33
3	Heinz-Harald Frentzen	19
4	Eddie Irvine	18
5 =	Olivier Panis	15
5 =	Jean Alesi	15
7	David Coulthard	11
8 =	Gerhard Berger	10
8 =	Mika Häkkinen	10
10	Giancarlo Fisichella	8
11	Johnny Herbert	7
12	Rubens Barrichello	6
13	Ralf Schumacher	5
14	Mika Salo	2
15 =	Nicola Larini	1
15 =	Shinji Nakano	1

Constructors

1	Ferrari	65
2	Williams	52
3	Benetton	25
4	McLaren	21
5	Prost	16
6	Jordan	13
7	Sauber	8
8	Stewart	6
9	Tyrrell	2

Lap Chart

57	58	59	60	61	62	63	64	65	66	67	68	69	70	71	72	
5	5	5	5	5	5	5	5	5	5	5	5	5	5	5	5	1
4	4	4	4	4	4	4	4	4	4	4	4	4	4	4	4	2
6	6	6	6	6	6	6	6	6	6	6	6	6	6	6	6	3
3	3	3	3	3	3	3	3	3	3	10	10	10	10	3	3	4
10	10	10	10	10	10	7	10	10	10	10	11	11	3	10	7	5
11	11	11	11	7	10	10	11	11	11	11	3	3	11	7	11	6
7	7	7	7	11	11	11	7	7	7	7	7	7	7	11		
8	8	8	8	12	12	16	16	16	16	16	16	16	16			
12	12	12	12	16	16	16	12	12	12	12	12	12	12			
16	16	16	16	19	14	14	14	14	14	14	14	14				
14	19	19	19	14	20	20	20	20	20	20	20	20				
19	14	14	14	20	1	1	1	1	1	1	1					
20	20	20	20	1												
1	1	1	1													
2	2															

FIA WORLD CHAMPIONSHIP • ROUND 9

BRITISH

grand prix

VILLENEUVE
ALESI
WURZ
COULTHARD
R. SCHUMACHER
HILL

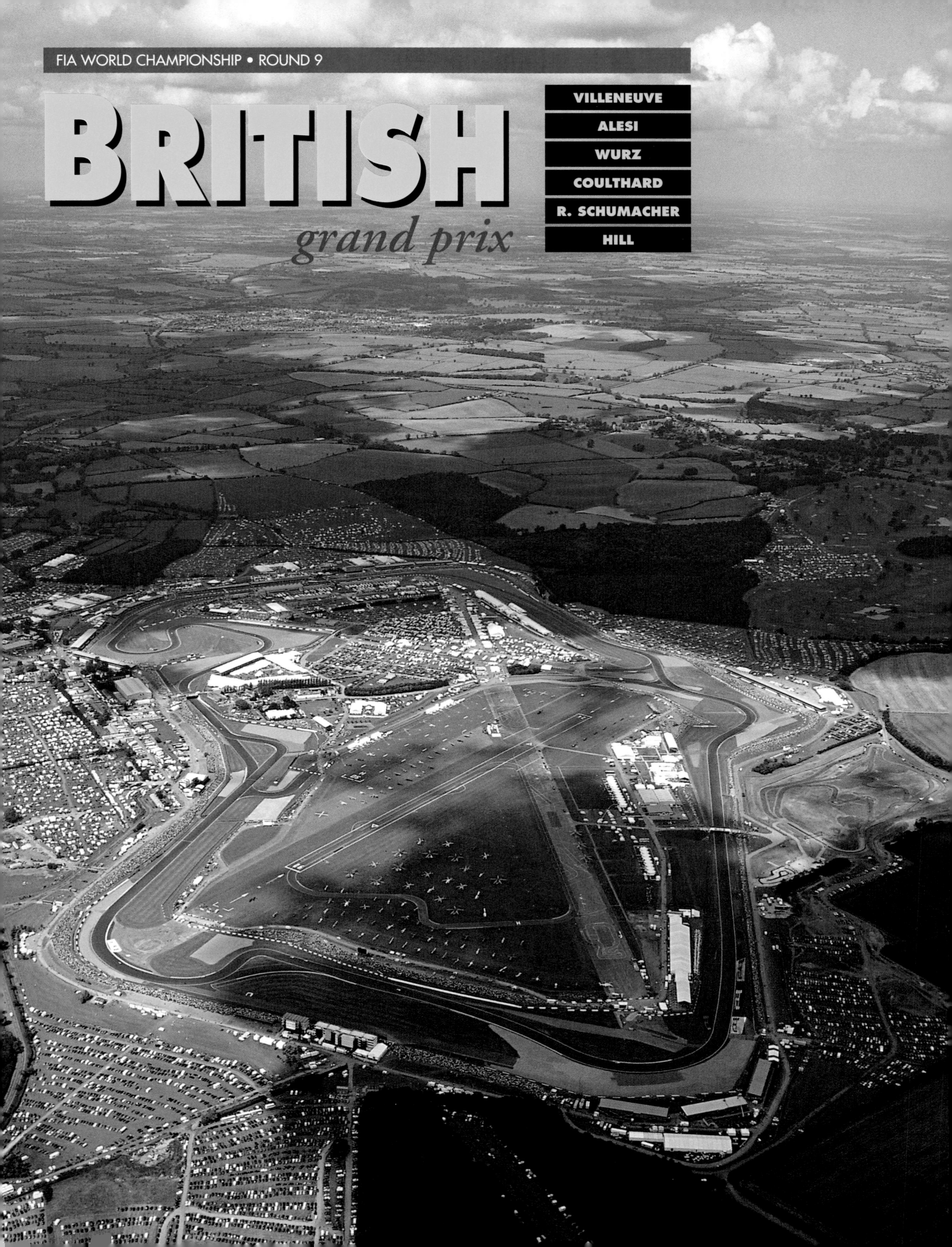

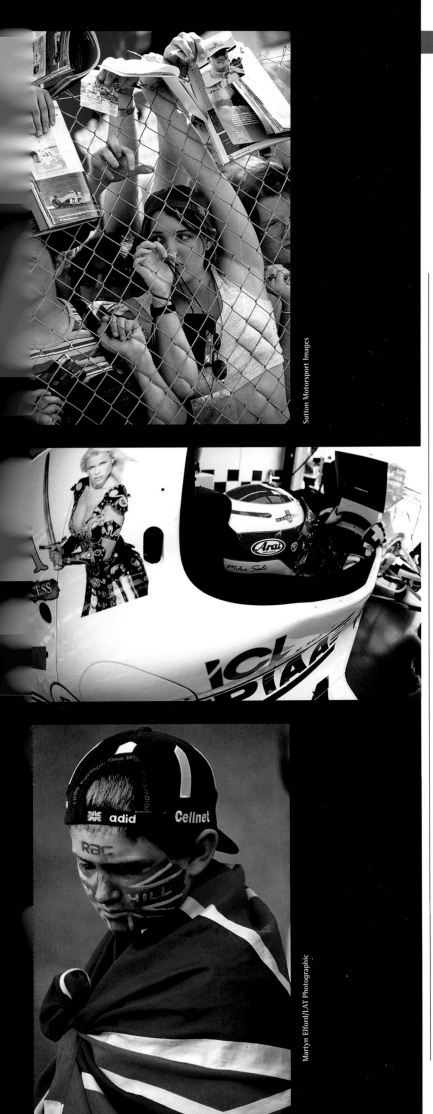

Sights of Silverstone '97.
Main photo: The circuit had been remodelled once again with the intention of making it more challenging. In this aerial view the former wartime airfield looks almost picturesque as it nestles in the rolling English countryside.
Left: Ardour undimmed by the wire fence separating them from their heroes, fans wait devotedly in the hope of getting an autograph.
Below left: 'Melinda, Warrior Princess' proved to be no talisman for Mika Salo but livened up the Tyrrell's livery all the same.
Bottom: Damon Hill's sixth place must have delighted this staunch supporter.

Sutton Motorsport Images

Martyn Elford/LAT Photographic

JACQUES Villeneuve scored the Williams team's 100th World Championship F1 victory in the British Grand Prix at Silverstone, eighteen years to the very race after Clay Regazzoni had recorded Frank's maiden F1 success on the same circuit. The Canadian achieved this notable landmark for the team after what had seemed likely to be an uphill struggle ended with all the lucky breaks going his way.

Michael Schumacher lost the lead when his Ferrari suffered its first retirement of the season due to technical problems, but Villeneuve was not assured of victory until just over six laps from the chequered flag, when Mika Häkkinen's McLaren MP4/12, leading by a couple of lengths and seemingly on course for the Finn's first F1 victory, suffered a Mercedes engine failure and rolled to a halt at the Abbey chicane.

Villeneuve reckoned he had a trick or two up his sleeve and could have outfumbled the Finn in the closing moments of the race. Häkkinen felt differently and it was absolutely characteristic of Frank Williams's admiration for a real racer that after the finish he was among the very first to congratulate Mika on his splendid drive.

Certainly, it was shaping up to be a grandstand finish. Villeneuve, who had run a two-stop strategy and was therefore on fresher rubber, was flexing his muscles for a last-ditch challenge. Encouraged by the sight of a blister on the McLaren's left-rear tyre, he was planning a *banzai* outbraking manoeuvre. It was just a shame that the capacity 90,000-strong crowd was deprived of what might have been a riveting shoot-out.

'I was going to make a move on him a couple of laps after he broke,' said Villeneuve. 'I was confident that I was going to be able to get by, because he was sliding more and more, although it would have been very difficult.'

Race day started on an upbeat and optimistic note for the Williams squad with Jacques Villeneuve and Heinz-Harald Frentzen having qualified on the front row of the grid, but the team's prospects began to unravel even before the starting signal had been given.

The first problem occurred as Frentzen accelerated too quickly up to his grid position, braked hard and then fumbled the cockpit procedure to put the car in neutral, with the result that he stalled the engine. The start was aborted and the embarrassed German driver had to take the restart from the back of the grid, becoming the latest competitor to suffer this penalty for disrupting the schedule.

At the restart, Villeneuve accelerated cleanly away into the lead ahead of Schumacher's Ferrari and the McLarens of David Coulthard and Häkkinen, while further back in the pack Minardi's Ukyo Katayama got caught out on the dust as he accelerated away from the grid, losing grip as he changed into second gear and pirouetting into the pit wall.

Meanwhile Frentzen was already picking off the tail-enders, but the German came unstuck at Becketts as he went swooping round the outside of Jos Verstappen's Tyrrell, running over the Ford-engined car's nose wing and spinning the Williams into the gravel. Frentzen was out on the spot while Verstappen trailed round to the pits for repairs.

As the leaders completed the opening lap, the vulnerable position of Katayama's stricken Minardi resulted in the organisers deploying the safety car, which the pack duly caught after two laps at racing speeds. At the end of lap four, the field was unleashed again and the serious racing resumed.

Villeneuve and Schumacher immediately began to edge away at the head of the crocodile and, with ten laps completed, were 9.4s ahead of Coulthard and Häkkinen. The Scot was already suffering slight brake locking problems with his McLaren which left Häkkinen feeling extremely frustrated, for not only was Johnny Herbert's Sauber close behind but Ralf Schumacher's Jordan, Eddie Irvine, Jean Alesi and Giancarlo Fisichella were also closing hard.

By lap 15 the leading duo were 18 seconds ahead as Hill brought the Arrows-Yamaha in for its first scheduled stop (13.1s), which dropped him from 12th to 18th. Four laps later Villeneuve and Schumacher had expanded their advantage to 27.2s over their pursuers. On lap 21 Schumacher brought the Ferrari in for a brisk 7.1s first refuelling stop, resuming in second place, while a lap later it was Villeneuve's turn.

Unbeknown to anyone outside the Williams team, Jacques had been grappling with major handling problems almost from the start. 'Somehow, the left-front wheel became loose, so it was very difficult to drive the car,' he explained. 'I thought I had a problem with the power steering, or that the suspension was breaking, because I had to turn the steering wheel through about ten degrees more than usual in order to turn the car.'

When he finally came into the pits, Villeneuve was stationary for an apparently disastrous 33.1s and he rejoined

It used to be the case that Williams could rightly consider Silverstone's fast, sweeping curves as their own unchallenged stamping ground. Yet with McLaren edging up alongside Ferrari as potential winning forces, it took brisk comments from Frank Williams himself going into the British Grand Prix weekend to counter Jacques Villeneuve's recently expressed concerns that the team was spending too much time developing next year's car at the expense of this year's.

'There are a lot of good reasons why Ferrari are presently ahead of Williams [in the championship],' said Williams. 'Jacques, however, comes to the factory insufficiently frequently to evaluate what has been going on there, so some of his remarks were not particularly accurate. However, there is a small element of truth in some of what he's saying.'

Ferrari looked strong from the outset, Michael Schumacher keen to notch up Maranello's first British GP victory since Alain Prost in 1990. During the previous week of intensive testing, he had coaxed and polished the chassis set-up of the Ferrari F310B to the point where it displayed a hitherto unimaginable high-speed poise through the 140 mph swerves which abound at this one-time RAF airfield.

Yet Villeneuve was up to the job, edging his team-mate out of a pole-position start on his final run, aided by the track temperature dropping slightly in the closing moments of the session. 'On my second and third runs, I made a mistake,' he admitted, 'but then I saw Heinz's time and I went for it. It all worked out in the end.'

Frentzen's 1m 21.732s was just over a tenth away from Villeneuve's best and the German driver admitted that he thought he'd got the job done. 'I'm pretty disappointed not to have taken pole,' he admitted. 'I did my final run eight minutes before the end after making some drastic set-up changes which improved the car. I still had slightly higher track temperatures, but I don't know if it made a difference because I had a traffic-free run this time.'

Objectively, Mika Häkkinen had the ability and equipment to have made pole position. Along with Tyrrell, Sauber and Minardi, McLaren opted for the softer of the two available tyre compounds, which certainly helped. It could have been risky if the race day weather had duplicated Friday's torrid conditions, but it was cooler on Sunday and Mika was confident he had the job under control.

Early in the session the Finn had a huge moment right on the limit at Copse Corner, but survived to make a serious assault on pole position later on. It certainly looked good enough for pole. Häkkinen was 0.3s up at the first timing split, but then got balked by slower traffic. Under the circumstances third place was a touch disappointing, but it was three places ahead of team-mate David Coulthard. The Scot spun off into a gravel trap on Friday morning and never quite caught up the crucial time lost by this excursion.

Fourth and fifth were the brothers Schumacher. Michael was quite satisfied to have qualified fourth, but admitted he was losing time through the last sector of the lap, which pointed to a small set-up problem. He was certainly suffering slightly through the slower corners.

Ralf Schumacher had hoped for something better than a third-row starting position. 'We might have expected a little bit more after all the test sessions we have done here, but the other teams have closed up a little and I am happy to be fifth,' he said. 'The understeer problems have improved and the car is running well, so I hope to win more points tomorrow.'

By contrast, team-mate Giancarlo Fisichella was disappointed not to have improved on tenth place due to traffic on his second run and acknowledged mistakes on his next two. Coulthard qualified sixth ahead of Eddie Irvine, the Ulsterman having a big fright on his first quick lap when he hit a hare, historically a Silverstone hazard to be avoided. 'I was forced to pit to check over the car and change the tyres,' he explained.

'My car had a tendency to wash out in the middle of the corners. We put more downforce on, but as I was short of time I was not able to check what effect this had before going for a quick lap. I think the race will be very tough, as it will be difficult to maintain a very quick pace.'

In eighth place, Alexander Wurz performed beautifully to out-qualify his Benetton team-mate Jean Alesi by three places. 'At the beginning of the session it was hard work as there was not much grip,' he said, 'but the track was a lot better on the second run.' Meanwhile Alesi was briskly dismissive of his car's performance. 'I am not satisfied,' he said. 'It is very disappointing and frustrating.'

The two Benettons were separated by Johnny Herbert's Sauber and Fisichella. 'The car is good here,' said Herbert. 'We made a small step forward again today and are closer [to the pace], but there is still work to do. My only problem was a spin this morning when I went a bit wide and got a wheel on the kerb at Copse. Fortunately the car spun to the right, not to the left where the wall was, as I was doing 247 km/h at the time!'

Damon Hill could have been forgiven for reflecting nostalgically about the good old days when he used to start from the front row of the grid in front of his home crowd in a Williams-Renault. Hill qualified his Arrows in 12th place which, in reality, was good enough with a Yamaha V10 struggling to make the 700 bhp barrier. Hill had also completed some beneficial set-up improvements after productive discussions with the team's new technical director John Barnard.

'I am reasonably pleased with today,' said Hill. 'Given the set-backs we have had, the problems we have had, and the pressure that has been put on the team this weekend, I think we can be pleased with that qualifying result. We are only 1.6s away from pole and, given the resources of the other teams, I think that is very reasonable.'

Behind Hill, Jarno Trulli lined up 13th in his Prost-Mugen Honda, only one place ahead of team-mate Shinji Nakano. 'I don't think we really got the best out of the car this afternoon,' said Trulli. 'We were significantly quicker here in private testing, and when things gradually started to come right in qualifying, I think it was a bit late.'

Behind Nakano came Jan Magnussen in the fastest Stewart-Ford. The Dane did all three of his runs in his own race car with a P7-spec engine, but by the time circumstances dictated he hand it over to team-mate Rubens Barrichello, it was already losing power. On Barrichello's first run in his own race chassis, he had an engine problem which caused him to stop out on the circuit. He then switched to the spare car, fitted with a P6 engine and with its cockpit set up for Magnussen, but after his second run of the afternoon had to abandon it when heat from the exhaust system caused the undertray to catch fire in the pit garage.

'By the time I switched to Jan's race car at the very end of the session, there was clearly a problem with the engine or its oil system,' he shrugged, 'so I had to stop going into Stowe second time round.' He qualified last and it was no consolation when he found himself promoted to 21st when Norberto Fontana had his times disallowed for missing the pit lane weight check, pushing his Sauber back to last place in the line-up.

Splitting the two Stewart-Fords were Pedro Diniz in 16th place, the Brazilian struggling to find a balance, Mika Salo's Tyrrell, Ukyo Katayama's Minardi, Jos Verstappen's Tyrrell and the Minardi of Tarso Marques. Both the Tyrrell drivers reported that their cars handled well enough, but there was no possibility of competing with such a significant power deficit. In the Minardi camp, Katayama and Marques complained of poor chassis balance, but were happy with the Bridgestone tyre performance.

Below left: The real Melinda Messenger's assets adorned the Jordan, providing the massed ranks of photographers with an unmissable photocall!

Right: Mika on the edge. The Finn saw a possible first Grand Prix win snatched from his grasp when his McLaren suffered an engine failure just over six laps from the finish.

Jacques Villeneuve inherited the victory and also scored the Williams team's 100th World Championship win.

in a distant seventh place. Any realistic prospect of a win now seemed to have been completely wiped out. Subsequent detailed examination of the car revealed that the little screws which attach the disc bell to the hub appeared not to have been fully tightened and that the wheel was not properly seated as a result.

Schumacher was now left with a comfortable lead over the two McLarens, Mika now pressing David extremely hard. Despite the fact that a long traffic jam had built up behind the two Mercedes-engined cars, the McLaren management declined to give Coulthard instructions to move over and let his faster team-mate go through. Under the circumstances, it was a questionable strategy.

By lap 26 things were getting so tight that Häkkinen was having to drive defensively to prevent Fisichella's Jordan, now in fourth place, from diving inside his McLaren. The pressure was relieved next time round as the Italian driver came in for a routine refuelling stop, but the logjam was finally broken when Coulthard locked a brake once too often and Mika nipped through as they exited the Vale and turned through Club.

Once ahead, Häkkinen simply flew away in second place, leaving Coulthard to make his sole refuelling stop (9.3s) at the end of lap 30. That left the order Schumacher, Häkkinen, Alesi, Alexander Wurz, the steadily recovering Villeneuve, Herbert, Irvine and Ralf Schumacher.

On lap 33 Häkkinen made his sole refuelling stop in 9.9s, resuming in eighth place, just ahead of Coulthard. If McLaren's pre-race strategy was now to unfold successfully, he would have to keep going hard to make up ground as the cars in front of him made their second stops.

Yet in what might eventually have come to be regarded as the turning point of the season, Ferrari's challenge fell apart and the two scarlet cars from Maranello succumbed to their first technical failures of the season. Schumacher, who seemed set for his fourth win of the year, succumbed to a left-rear wheel bearing failure just after a precautionary stop to check an obvious problem at the end of lap 37. Häkkinen was now sixth.

'What happened was a shame,' said Schumacher with masterly understatement. 'I am not too disappointed as I was comfortably in the lead when it occurred. Williams has a slight advantage in qualifying trim, but we are competitive in the race. Technical problems happen to other teams as well. That is racing.'

Bryn Williams

Steven Tee/LAT Photographic

Darren Heath

DIARY

Jordan confirm two-year deal to run Mugen Honda engines in 1998 and '99 in addition to co-sponsorship from MasterCard.

Gerhard Berger, who missed the British Grand Prix as he struggled to recover from sinus problems, receives another personal blow when his father Johann is killed in a light-aircraft accident.

FIA denies that it has opened the door to traction control by another name after issuing a clarification of the rule relating to the control systems for F1 electronic throttles in response to a request from the McLaren team. This enabled engine revs to be used as an additional control parameter in an effort to smooth out the engine's torque characteristics.

Team Lotus boss David Hunt announces plans for the famous F1 team to return to the World Championship stage in 1999.

Previous spread: Jean Alesi is tracked by Benetton team-mate Alexander Wurz. The young Austrian had made the most of the opportunity presented by Gerhard Berger's unfortunate absence.

Right: David Coulthard inspects his rear tyres at the finish. Brake problems blunted the Scot's challenge and he had to be content with fourth place.

Below right: In only his third F1 race, Alexander Wurz took a richly merited place on the podium alongside team-mate Jean Alesi and race winner Jacques Villeneuve.

Meanwhile, Johnny Herbert was being reminded of the painful truth behind that sentiment. The 1995 British GP winner had been enjoying a good run, holding fifth place through to his first refuelling stop at the end of lap 17 and then climbing back to fourth before stopping again at the end of lap 38. Häkkinen took over the position, moving up to third when Ralf Schumacher brought the Jordan in for its second refuelling stop on lap 42.

Having made his second stop, Herbert was now grappling with terminal technical problems. The Sauber's gearchange mechanism developed a gremlin and, in any case, a cut tyre meant that he had to come back in next time round. Then the gearchange went totally haywire and he was in for a third time to have the steering wheel changed in case the selector paddles were the cause of the electronic fault. They weren't, so he called it a day for good at the end of lap 42.

By now Irvine was up to second behind Villeneuve and he followed the Williams in for their second refuelling stops at the end of lap 44, at which point Häkkinen sailed past into the lead. As Irvine accelerated back into the contest his right-hand driveshaft broke and he rolled to a halt at the end of the pit lane.

The fact that Häkkinen went ahead as the race entered its closing stages did not come as a surprise as he had been hard on the pace throughout the weekend. Now all that preparation and tactical acuity seemed poised to deliver him the pay-off.

Häkkinen completed lap 45 with 5.8s in hand over Villeneuve only to get stuck behind Trulli as he lapped the Italian's Prost. By the end of lap 47 Villeneuve had trimmed the McLaren's advantage to 2.8s and the battle was seriously on. For the next five laps the two cars circulated in nose-to-tail formation before Mika's engine expired and he pulled off at Abbey, the Finn acknowledging the sympathetic applause of the crowd by throwing his gloves into the packed spectator enclosure.

In the Benetton camp, for once Jean Alesi managed to produce a disciplined and clean-cut performance, coming home second ahead of the dutiful, yet none the less highly impressive, Alexander Wurz. The young Austrian spent the entire race shadowing Alesi's every move, never putting a foot wrong to score a podium finish in only his third Grand Prix.

'I am relieved, not just for me but also for the team,' said Alesi afterwards. 'We have been having problems in qualifying which means that we cannot

Hill and Walkinshaw in Silverstone breach

DAMON Hill's relationship with the Arrows F1 team was shaken up quite dramatically at Silverstone over the British GP weekend as team chief Tom Walkinshaw told the press that the reigning World Champion should pull his finger out and start earning his £4.5 million retainer.

Walkinshaw's frustration with the team's poor season to date boiled over as he targeted Hill for much of his criticism. 'His performances speak for themselves,' he said. 'I think it's quite obvious to anyone who has been watching the team closely that we are not satisfied. None of us are.

'We're not happy with Damon's performances and nor should he be happy with them either. He is one of the fastest drivers around and we recruited him to drive the team on, to lead the team, not for us to have to motivate him. We have the right to expect him to show he is the lead driver in the team.'

Walkinshaw also said that he regarded the Arrows A18's natural qualifying position as tenth place on the grid. Hill eventually lined up 12th for the Silverstone race, only 1.6s away from Villeneuve's pole-winning Williams.

Hill responded to this outburst with a guarded dignity. 'It has certainly taken the shine off my British Grand Prix weekend,' he admitted. 'I am aware that there are problems which do have a bearing on making a comfortable environment for a driver.'

Damon was referring to the fact that on the very first occasion he drove the Arrows A18 in a test at Silverstone its nose section flew off, and the car has also suffered suspension breakages. 'I have had worse criticism from other team managers in the past,' he added. 'Tom is entitled to put a rocket up the backside of his drivers whenever he wants to.' It was clear, however, that taking such action in public left Damon and his manager Michael Breen wearing distinctly fixed expressions.

By the end of the weekend rumours were circulating to the effect that Damon had put a £7.5 million price tag on his services for 1998. His name was being mentioned as a possible candidate for McLaren, Sauber and even Ferrari, where Michael Schumacher strenuously denied rumours that he had vetoed the possibility of Damon replacing Eddie Irvine.

said; 'I could have been second or third as we changed our strategy to a single stop and I was running ahead of both Benettons.' He made his scheduled stop on lap 27 and then came in again on lap 54 to atone for his driving error.

The biggest cheer of the afternoon was reserved for the luckless Shinji Nakano, but only when the Japanese driver's Mugen V10 expired spectacularly. The shriek from the crowd signalled that Damon Hill's Arrows-Yamaha had thus been promoted to sixth place and was on course for its first championship point of the season.

Hill, who had been slightly taken aback by team chief Tom Walkinshaw's outspoken criticism, was praying for a wet race. In the soaking race morning warm-up, he had set fastest time on Bridgestone intermediates. In the dry, the truth was that he was lucky to finish with a point due to the high rate of mechanical attrition among the quicker runners. But it was a minor triumph nevertheless.

Outside the points, the frustrated Fisichella could manage only seventh, mentally kicking himself for his earlier lapse. Prost's Jarno Trulli was a slightly disappointed eighth ahead of the steady Norberto Fontana's Sauber, Tarso Marques in the Minardi and Nakano's Prost.

Not a single Ford-propelled runner made it to the chequered flag, both Stewarts and both Tyrrells succumbing to engine trouble. Yet the fact that Jan Magnussen got to within seven laps of the finish with the latest-spec Project 7 Zetec-R V10 in his Stewart, barely a week after this new engine first ran on the test bed, at least offered a sliver of hope to Cosworth at a very depressing moment.

On the other hand, Rubens Barrichello was understandably frustrated that, even using an earlier Project 6 version of the V10 running at reduced revs, he was unable to make the finish. As for the Tyrrells, both Cosworth Ford ED5 V8s let go at almost the same moment.

Villeneuve's win hung in the balance for an hour or so after the chequered flag as he was summoned before the stewards for not maintaining the correct distance from the safety car, an AMG Mercedes 320CLK driven by former British F3 Champion Oliver Gavin. In the event, it was decided not to impose any penalty more serious than a one-race suspended ban on Villeneuve, leaving the Williams team to reflect with pleasure on that 100th Grand Prix victory. By any standards, it was a momentous milestone.

be in a good position at the start. But we are able to compromise for the race and a one-stop strategy worked for us.'

Wurz was equally satisfied, admitting that he had been looking for an opportunity to overtake his team-mate as they were lapping slower cars. 'But in the end, after the pit stop and when the situation became clear, I decided to hold back by myself,' he explained.

'At the beginning of the race I was struggling with the car because it had a lot of fuel on board and was oversteering. But when the fuel ran down, and after the first stop, the car was in very good shape on its second set of tyres.'

Jordan, for whom Ralf Schumacher had raised hopes by qualifying fifth, rather disappointed on their home turf. Ralf lost some places at the start and nearly ran over his mechanics at his second stop, wasting valuable seconds in the pit lane. He was only 0.6s behind Coulthard's fourth-placed McLaren at the chequered flag. Team-mate Giancarlo Fisichella had managed to find a way past both Benettons in the opening laps, but scuppered his chances with a big slide into the gravel at Copse which meant an extra stop for fresh tyres.

'I am very angry with myself,' he

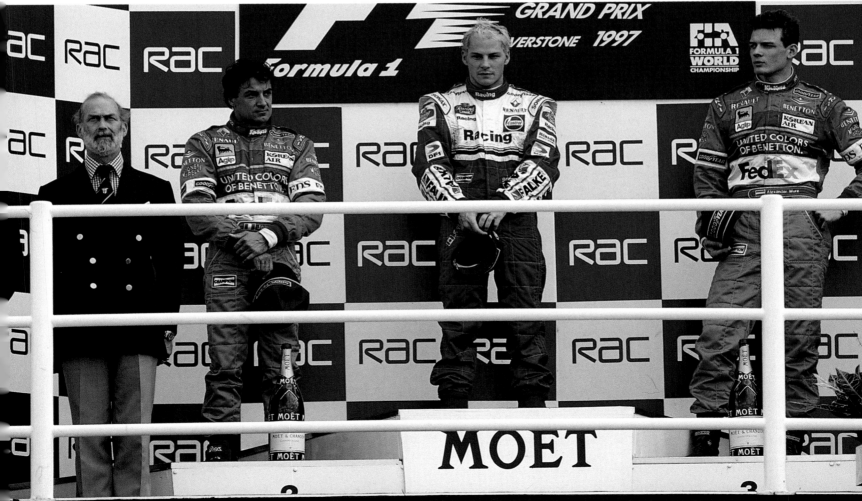

THE RAC BRITISH GRAND PRIX

11–13 JULY 1997

SILVERSTONE

Race distance: 59 laps, 188.437 miles/303.260 km

Race weather: Dry, hot and sunny

FIA FORMULA 1 WORLD CHAMPIONSHIP

ROUND 9

SILVERSTONE – GRAND PRIX CIRCUIT

CIRCUIT LENGTH: 3.194 MILES/5.140 KM

COPSE · MAGGOTTS · CHAPEL · HANGAR STRAIGHT · BROOKLANDS · PRIORY · BRIDGE · THE VALE · STOWE CORNER · WOODCOTE · LUFFIELD · ABBEY CURVE · CLUB CORNER

Pos.	Driver	Nat.	No.	Entrant	Car/Engine	Tyres	Laps	Time/Retirement	Speed (mph/km/h)
1	Jacques Villeneuve	CDN	3	Rothmans Williams Renault	Williams FW19-Renault RS9A V10	G	59	1h 28m 01.665s	128.439/206.703
2	Jean Alesi	F	7	Mild Seven Benetton Renault	Benetton B197-Renault RS9A V10	G	59	1h 28m 11.870s	128.191/206.304
3	Alexander Wurz	A	8	Mild Seven Benetton Renault	Benetton B197-Renault RS9A V10	G	59	1h 28m 12.961s	128.164/206.261
4	David Coulthard	GB	10	West McLaren Mercedes	McLaren MP4/12-Mercedes FO110F V10	G	59	1h 28m 32.894s	127.684/205.488
5	Ralf Schumacher	D	11	B&H Total Jordan Peugeot	Jordan 197-Peugeot A14 V10	G	59	1h 28m 33.545s	127.668/205.462
6	Damon Hill	GB	1	Danka Arrows Yamaha	Arrows A18-Yamaha OX11A/D V10	B	59	1h 29m 15.217s	126.675/203.864
7	Giancarlo Fisichella	I	12	B&H Total Jordan Peugeot	Jordan 197-Peugeot A14 V10	G	58		
8	Jarno Trulli	I	14	Prost Gauloises Blondes	Prost JS45-Mugen Honda MF301HB V10	B	58		
9	Norberto Fontana	RA	17	Red Bull Sauber Petronas	Sauber C16-Petronas V10	G	58		
10	Tarso Marques	BR	21	Minardi Team	Minardi M197-Hart 830 V8	B	58		
11	Shinji Nakano	J	15	Prost Gauloises Blondes	Prost JS45-Mugen Honda MF301HB V10	B	57	Engine	
	Mika Häkkinen	SF	9	West McLaren Mercedes	McLaren MP4/12-Mercedes FO110F V10	G	52	Engine	
	Jan Magnussen	DK	23	Stewart Ford	Stewart SF1-Ford Zetec-R V10	B	50	Engine	
	Jos Verstappen	NL	18	Tyrrell	Tyrrell 025-Ford ED5 V8	G	45	Engine	
	Eddie Irvine	GB	6	Scuderia Ferrari Marlboro	Ferrari F310B 046/2 V10	G	44	Driveshaft	
	Mika Salo	SF	19	Tyrrell	Tyrrell 025-Ford ED5 V8	G	44	Engine	
	Johnny Herbert	GB	16	Red Bull Sauber Petronas	Sauber C16-Petronas V10	G	42	Transmission	
	Michael Schumacher	D	5	Scuderia Ferrari Marlboro	Ferrari F310B 046/2 V10	G	38	Wheel bearing	
	Rubens Barrichello	BR	22	Stewart Ford	Stewart SF1-Ford Zetec-R V10	B	37	Engine	
	Pedro Diniz	BR	2	Danka Arrows Yamaha	Arrows A18-Yamaha OX11A/D V10	B	29	Engine	
	Heinz-Harald Frentzen	D	4	Rothmans Williams Renault	Williams FW19-Renault RS9A V10	G	0	Collision with Verstappen	
	Ukyo Katayama	J	20	Minardi Team	Minardi M197-Hart 830 V8	B	0	Spun off	

Fastest lap: M. Schumacher, on lap 34, 1m 24.475s, 136.109 mph/219.047 km/h (record on revised circuit).

Previous lap record: Jacques Villeneuve (F1 Williams FW18-Renault V10), 1m 29.288s, 127.068 mph/204.497 km/h (1996).

B – Bridgestone   G – Goodyear

Grid order	1	2	3	4	5	6	7	8	9	10	11	12	13	14	15	16	17	18	19	20	21	22	23	24	25	26	27	28	29	30	31	32	33	34	35	36	37	38	39	40	41	42	43	44	45	46
3 VILLENEUVE	3	3	3	3	3	3	3	3	3	3	3	3	3	3	3	3	3	3	3	3	3	3	3	5	5	5	5	5	5	5	5	5	5	5	5	5	5	5	5	3	3	3	3	3	3	9	9
4 FRENTZEN	5	5	5	5	5	5	5	5	5	5	5	5	5	5	5	5	5	5	5	5	5	5	5	10	10	10	10	10	9	9	9	9	9	9	7	7	8	8	6	6	6	6	6	6	3	3
9 HÄKKINEN	10	10	10	10	10	10	10	10	10	10	10	10	10	10	10	10	10	10	10	10	10	10	10	9	9	9	9	9	10	10	7	7	7	8	8	3	3	8	11	11	11	9	9	9	7	7
5 M. SCHUMACHER	9	9	9	9	9	9	9	9	9	9	9	9	9	9	9	9	9	9	9	9	9	9	12	12	12	12	7	7	7	8	8	8	8	3	3	16	16	16	9	9	9	11	7	7	8	8
11 R. SCHUMACHER	16	16	16	16	16	16	16	16	16	16	16	16	16	16	16	16	11	11	11	11	11	12	7	7	7	8	8	8	3	3	16	16	6	6	11	7	7	7	7	8	8	10	10			
10 COULTHARD	11	11	11	11	11	11	11	11	11	11	11	11	11	11	11	11	6	6	6	6	6	7	8	8	8	12	3	3	10	16	16	16	6	7	11	9	8	8	8	8	10	10	11	11		
6 IRVINE	6	6	6	6	6	6	6	6	6	6	6	6	6	6	6	12	12	12	12	12	8	3	3	3	3	3	16	16	16	6	6	6	11	11	9	7	15	15	10	10	11	11	12	12		
8 WURZ	7	7	7	7	7	7	7	7	7	7	12	12	12	12	12	7	7	7	7	7	11	16	16	16	16	16	6	6	6	11	11	11	9	9	9	7	15	10	10	15	12	12	12	15	15	
16 HERBERT	8	8	8	12	12	12	12	12	12	8	8	8	8	8	8	8	8	8	8	8	6	2	6	6	6	6	11	11	11	15	15	15	15	15	15	10	12	12	15	15	15	1	1			
12 FISICHELLA	12	12	12	8	8	8	8	8	8	8	8	8	8	8	8	16	15	15	15	15	2	6	11	11	11	11	12	15	10	10	10	10	10	10	10	12	16	16	16	1	1	1	1			
7 ALESI	15	15	15	15	15	15	15	15	15	15	15	15	15	15	15	15	2	2	2	2	16	11	15	15	15	12	12	12	12	12	12	12	12	12	5	1	1	1	23	23	14	17	17			
1 HILL	1	1	1	1	1	1	1	1	1	1	1	1	1	1	1	14	14	17	16	16	15	15	1	1	1	1	1	1	1	1	1	1	1	1	1	14	14	17	23	14	14	23	23	23		
14 TRULLI	14	14	14	14	14	14	14	14	14	14	14	14	14	14	2	2	14	17	19	19	1	1	2	2	2	2	23	14	14	14	14	14	14	14	1	17	23	14	17	17	17	21	21			
15 NAKANO	23	23	23	23	23	23	23	23	23	23	23	23	2	2	17	17	16	19	1	1	21	23	23	23	23	2	2	17	17	17	17	17	17	17	19	14	17	19	19	19	19	18				
23 MAGNUSSEN	2	2	2	2	2	2	2	2	2	2	2	2	22	19	19	1	21	23	14	14	14	14	14	14	14	22	22	22	22	22	19	23	19	19	21	21										
2 DINIZ	19	19	19	19	19	22	22	22	22	22	22	22	21	17	17	21	19	21	21	23	14	17	17	17	17	23	19	19	19	19	23	21	21	21	18	18										
19 SALO	22	22	22	22	22	19	19	17	17	17	17	2	23	19	1	1	23	14	14	21	22	22	22	19	23	23	23	23	23	23	21	18	18	18	16											
20 KATAYAMA	21	17	17	17	17	17	19	19	19	19	19	21	1	18	23	14	17	22	22	21	21	21	21	21	21	21	21	21	18																	
18 VERSTAPPEN	17	21	21	21	21	21	21	21	21	21	18	18	18	23	22	22	18	18	18	18	18	18	18	19	18	18	18	18																		
21 MARQUES	18	18	18	18	18	18	18	18	18	18	18	18	18	23	23	22	18	18	18	19	19	19	19	19	19	19	18																			
22 BARRICHELLO																																														
17 FONTANA																																														

Pit stop
One lap behind leader

STARTING GRID

3 VILLENEUVE Williams	4 FRENTZEN* Williams
9 HÄKKINEN McLaren	5 M. SCHUMACHER Ferrari
11 R. SCHUMACHER Jordan	10 COULTHARD McLaren
6 IRVINE Ferrari	8 WURZ Benetton
16 HERBERT Sauber	12 FISICHELLA Jordan
7 ALESI Benetton	1 HILL Arrows
14 TRULLI Prost	15 NAKANO Prost
23 MAGNUSSEN Stewart	2 DINIZ Arrows
19 SALO Tyrrell	20 KATAYAMA Minardi
18 VERSTAPPEN Tyrrell	21 MARQUES Minardi
22 BARRICHELLO Stewart	17 FONTANA** Sauber

* started from back of grid
** qualifying times disallowed

47	48	49	50	51	52	53	54	55	56	57	58	59	
9	9	9	9	9	9	3	3	3	3	3	3	3	1
3	3	3	3	3	7	7	7	7	7	7	7	7	2
7	7	7	7	7	8	8	8	8	8	8	8	8	3
8	8	8	8	8	10	10	10	10	10	10	10	10	4
10	10	10	10	10	10	11	11	11	11	11	11	11	5
11	11	11	11	11	15	15	15	15	15	1	1		6
12	12	12	12	12	12	1	1	1	1	12			
15	15	15	15	15	1	12	12	12	12	14			
1	1	1	1	1	14	14	14	14	17				
14	14	14	14	14	17	17	17	17	21				
17	17	17	17	17	21	21	21	21					
23	23	23	23	21	21								
21	21	21	21										

FOR THE RECORD

First Grand Prix points
Alexander Wurz

50th Grand Prix start
David Coulthard

TIME SHEETS

QUALIFYING

Weather: Dry, hot and sunny

Pos.	Driver	Car	Laps	Time
1	Jacques Villeneuve	Williams-Renault	12	1m 21.598s
2	Heinz-Harald Frentzen	Williams-Renault	11	1m 21.732s
3	Mika Häkkinen	McLaren-Mercedes	8	1m 21.797s
4	Michael Schumacher	Ferrari	12	1m 21.977s
5	Ralf Schumacher	Jordan-Peugeot	12	1m 22.277s
6	David Coulthard	McLaren-Mercedes	11	1m 22.279s
7	Eddie Irvine	Ferrari	12	1m 22.342s
8	Alexander Wurz	Benetton-Renault	12	1m 22.344s
9	Johnny Herbert	Sauber-Petronas	12	1m 22.368s
10	Giancarlo Fisichella	Jordan-Peugeot	11	1m 22.371s
11	Jean Alesi	Benetton-Renault	11	1m 22.392s
12	Damon Hill	Arrows-Yamaha	11	1m 23.271s
13	Jarno Trulli	Prost-Mugen Honda	12	1m 23.366s
14	Norberto Fontana*	Sauber-Petronas	12	1m 23.790s
15	Shinji Nakano	Prost-Mugen Honda	11	1m 23.887s
16	Jan Magnussen	Stewart-Ford	10	1m 24.067s
17	Pedro Diniz	Arrows-Yamaha	12	1m 24.239s
18	Mika Salo	Tyrrell-Ford	12	1m 24.478s
19	Ukyo Katayama	Minardi-Hart	12	1m 24.553s
20	Jos Verstappen	Tyrrell-Ford	12	1m 25.010s
21	Tarso Marques	Minardi-Hart	12	1m 25.154s
22	Rubens Barrichello	Stewart-Ford	4	1m 25.525s

* times disallowed

FRIDAY FREE PRACTICE

Weather: Dry, warm and sunny

Pos.	Driver	Laps	Time
1	Mika Häkkinen	28	1m 22.935s
2	Jacques Villeneuve	30	1m 23.266s
3	Heinz-Harald Frentzen	27	1m 23.327s
4	Johnny Herbert	30	1m 23.581s
5	Jean Alesi	23	1m 23.785s
6	Giancarlo Fisichella	27	1m 23.883s
7	Michael Schumacher	27	1m 24.132s
8	Alexander Wurz	27	1m 24.203s
9	Eddie Irvine	23	1m 24.424s
10	Jarno Trulli	30	1m 24.946s
11	Ralf Schumacher	17	1m 24.948s
12	Jan Magnussen	28	1m 25.136s
13	David Coulthard	12	1m 25.360s
14	Mika Salo	27	1m 26.035s
15	Shinji Nakano	29	1m 26.270s
16	Ukyo Katayama	18	1m 26.446s
17	Norberto Fontana	30	1m 26.640s
18	Rubens Barrichello	15	1m 26.785s
19	Pedro Diniz	30	1m 26.797s
20	Damon Hill	30	1m 26.810s
21	Tarso Marques	28	1m 27.066s
22	Jos Verstappen	16	1m 27.923s

SATURDAY FREE PRACTICE

Weather: Dry, warm and sunny

Pos.	Driver	Laps	Time
1	Mika Häkkinen	27	1m 22.000s
2	Jacques Villeneuve	24	1m 22.063s
3	Michael Schumacher	29	1m 22.586s
4	David Coulthard	24	1m 22.712s
5	Giancarlo Fisichella	29	1m 22.962s
6	Heinz-Harald Frentzen	25	1m 23.022s
7	Johnny Herbert	29	1m 23.131s
8	Alexander Wurz	24	1m 23.161s
9	Rubens Barrichello	26	1m 23.577s
10	Jean Alesi	24	1m 23.607s
11	Eddie Irvine	15	1m 23.614s
12	Ralf Schumacher	26	1m 23.647s
13	Shinji Nakano	27	1m 23.823s
14	Damon Hill	27	1m 23.871s
15	Jarno Trulli	15	1m 24.172s
16	Norberto Fontana	29	1m 24.181s
17	Jan Magnussen	20	1m 24.181s
18	Ukyo Katayama	29	1m 24.716s
19	Pedro Diniz	26	1m 24.961s
20	Mika Salo	29	1m 25.015s
21	Jos Verstappen	26	1m 25.195s
22	Tarso Marques	28	1m 25.725s

WARM-UP

Weather: Wet, gradually drying

Pos.	Driver	Laps	Time
1	Damon Hill	12	1m 38.031s
2	Eddie Irvine	13	1m 38.061s
3	Jacques Villeneuve	13	1m 38.507s
4	Michael Schumacher	11	1m 38.670s
5	Johnny Herbert	16	1m 38.707s
6	Jean Alesi	14	1m 38.876s
7	Giancarlo Fisichella	11	1m 38.993s
8	Mika Häkkinen	13	1m 39.074s
9	Jan Magnussen	8	1m 39.498s
10	Norberto Fontana	14	1m 39.693s
11	Heinz-Harald Frentzen	11	1m 39.756s
12	David Coulthard	12	1m 39.846s
13	Rubens Barrichello	9	1m 39.868s
14	Mika Salo	11	1m 40.652s
15	Jos Verstappen	12	1m 41.039s
16	Alexander Wurz	12	1m 41.489s
17	Pedro Diniz	10	1m 41.751s
18	Ukyo Katayama	14	1m 41.781s
19	Shinji Nakano	12	1m 41.920s
20	Ralf Schumacher	7	1m 42.261s
21	Tarso Marques	13	1m 43.088s
22	Jarno Trulli	14	1m 43.612s

RACE FASTEST LAPS

Weather: Dry, hot and sunny

Driver	Time	Lap
Michael Schumacher	1m 24.475s	34
Jacques Villeneuve	1m 25.082s	42
Eddie Irvine	1m 25.236s	43
Ralf Schumacher	1m 25.872s	35
Mika Häkkinen	1m 25.988s	38
Giancarlo Fisichella	1m 26.119s	57
Johnny Herbert	1m 26.232s	34
Jean Alesi	1m 26.260s	50
Alexander Wurz	1m 26.429s	51
Damon Hill	1m 26.471s	57
David Coulthard	1m 26.475s	57
Jarno Trulli	1m 26.610s	57
Shinji Nakano	1m 26.778s	24
Pedro Diniz	1m 27.111s	25
Jan Magnussen	1m 27.586s	32
Norberto Fontana	1m 27.783s	17
Rubens Barrichello	1m 27.877s	35
Mika Salo	1m 28.053s	35
Tarso Marques	1m 29.100s	32
Jos Verstappen	1m 29.137s	25

CHASSIS LOG BOOK

1	Hill	Arrows A18/5
2	Diniz	Arrows A18/3
	spare	Arrows A18/4
3	Villeneuve	Williams FW19/4
4	Frentzen	Williams FW19/5
	spare	Williams FW19/3
5	M. Schumacher	Ferrari F310B/177
6	Irvine	Ferrari F310B/173
	spare	Ferrari F310B/175
7	Alesi	Benetton B197/5
8	Wurz	Benetton B197/4
	spare	Benetton B197/3
9	Häkkinen	McLaren MP4/12/6
10	Coulthard	McLaren MP4/12/7
	spare	McLaren MP4/12/3
11	R. Schumacher	Jordan 197/6
12	Fisichella	Jordan 197/4
	spare	Jordan 197/1
14	Trulli	Prost JS45/3
15	Nakano	Prost JS45/2
	spare	Prost JS45/1
16	Herbert	Sauber C16/5
17	Fontana	Sauber C16/6
	spare	Sauber C16/3
18	Verstappen	Tyrrell 025/4
19	Salo	Tyrrell 025/3
	spare	Tyrrell 025/1
20	Katayama	Minardi M197/4
21	Marques	Minardi M197/2
	spare	Minardi M197/1
22	Barrichello	Stewart SF1/2
23	Magnussen	Stewart SF1/3
	spare	Stewart SF1/1

POINTS TABLES

Drivers

1	Michael Schumacher	47
2	Jacques Villeneuve	43
3	Jean Alesi	21
4	Heinz-Harald Frentzen	19
5	Eddie Irvine	18
6	Olivier Panis	15
7	David Coulthard	14
8 =	Gerhard Berger	10
8 =	Mika Häkkinen	10
10	Giancarlo Fisichella	8
11 =	Johnny Herbert	7
11 =	Ralf Schumacher	7
13	Rubens Barrichello	6
14	Alexander Wurz	4
15	Mika Salo	2
16 =	Nicola Larini	1
16 =	Shinji Nakano	1
16 =	Damon Hill	1

Constructors

1	Ferrari	65
2	Williams	62
3	Benetton	35
4	McLaren	24
5	Prost	16
6	Jordan	15
7	Sauber	8
8	Stewart	6
9	Tyrrell	2
10	Arrows	1

Darren Heath

GERMAN
grand prix

BERGER

M. SCHUMACHER

HÄKKINEN

TRULLI

R. SCHUMACHER

ALESI

FIA WORLD CHAMPIONSHIP • ROUND 10

Gerhard Berger's first Grand Prix win for three years could scarcely have been achieved at a more significant moment for the Austrian veteran and, as he sprayed the celebratory Moët on the winner's rostrum, he must have felt that he had proved a point to those who had written him off.

T HE outcome of the German Grand Prix at Hockenheim left almost everybody in F1 with a broad grin on their face. Gerhard Berger, international motor racing's senior citizen, marked his return from a three-race break caused by sinus problems in the best way imaginable. He qualified on pole position and then walked away with the race in dominant style to post the first victory for the Benetton-Renault squad since Michael Schumacher moved to Ferrari at the end of 1995.

It was a success which left the 37-year-old Austrian dealing with a tangle of mixed emotions. The win came less than three weeks after the death of Berger's father Johann, the driving force behind his career and his number one fan, in a light-aircraft accident in the Tyrol. It also followed closely on Benetton's decision not to continue with Berger in 1998, although at least Flavio Briatore had the sensitivity to let Gerhard make the announcement that he would not be staying with the team himself.

Berger finished the race 17.5s ahead of Michael Schumacher's Ferrari F310B, the German driver thereby extending his championship lead to ten points over Silverstone winner Jacques Villeneuve. The Canadian spun off while occupying fifth place with 12 of the race's 45 laps left to run after jousting wheel to wheel with Jarno Trulli's Prost and there were strong words exchanged between the two men afterwards.

Villeneuve's failure to finish capped the worst weekend in recent memory for the Williams team after Heinz-Harald Frentzen had retired at the end of the opening lap with damaged suspension following a first-corner collision with Eddie Irvine's Ferrari.

'I have experienced big emotions throughout the weekend,' said Berger after apparently cold-shouldering Briatore as he climbed the victory podium. 'This has been special for me, very special. I have to say I am happy for myself today, but also for the team.

'It really was time to give something back to them. After Michael [Schumacher] left at the end of 1995, it was difficult to change to another area, so I am very happy for them all. We have come close several times, but today takes away some of the pressure. I hope I gave them what they deserved.'

He also joked that he had struck a blow for F1's older generation. 'The younger drivers still have to practise a little bit,' he said.

Berger, a veteran of 203 Grand Prix starts over almost 14 seasons, had been in a class of his own throughout qualifying, taking pole position with exuberant aplomb during Saturday's hour-long qualifying session. He then never looked back as he sped to the tenth victory of his career and his first since winning in Germany for Ferrari three years earlier.

The race had looked likely to be a real treat for the capacity Hockenheim crowd. With Michael Schumacher's Ferrari clearly destined to be a contender from the second row, the fans could reasonably expect a German – or at least a German-speaking – driver to be in the thick of the action from the very start.

There were some nervous moments in the run-up to the race as, about 40 minutes before the start, heavy rain began to fall. Thankfully it soon stopped and conditions dried out sufficiently for every competitor to run on slick rubber from the outset.

Berger was absolutely determined not to squander the golden opportunity afforded by pole position. He made a cracking getaway to beat Giancarlo Fisichella's Jordan to the first turn with Schumacher's Ferrari right behind. Meanwhile, Irvine came storming through from the fifth row of the grid, getting on the inside of Frentzen's Williams into the first corner.

His left-rear wheel made contact with the right-front wheel of Frentzen's FW19 on the exit of the right-hander. Both men dropped to the tail of the pack and came limping into the pits long after the pack had chased through behind Berger at the end of the opening lap. At the back of the field, meanwhile, Tarso Marques hadn't even got as far as the first turn, his Minardi suffering transmission failure on the grid.

Mechanics immediately fell on the two cars, fitting fresh tyres, but further examination revealed that both had sustained terminal damage and they were quickly pushed away. The bodywork on Irvine's Ferrari ahead of the left-rear wheel was very badly damaged and a brief fire was quickly extinguished before he climbed from the cockpit.

'I was on the outside and Irvine came on the inside,' said Frentzen. 'We drove round the corner together, but when I accelerated out I had no place to go, and the only way to have avoided an accident was to go out onto the grass. I couldn't go on the dirt at that stage to leave Eddie on the track, so we collided.'

In the ensuing mêlée immediately behind this duo, Villeneuve braked hard and Coulthard's McLaren touched one of the Canadian's rear wheels, dislodging its nose cone. He trailed round slowly, but momentarily slid off the road as he made for the pits, spin-turning his way back onto the track and then giving the car a full-throttle start once he was pointing in the right direction.

By the time the McLaren received its fresh nose section, Coulthard had – taking into account the parade lap and start proper – completed four racing starts in about as many minutes. Small wonder that when he accelerated back into the race the clutch decided that it had endured enough for one day.

Meanwhile, by the end of the opening lap Berger led by 1.8s from Fisichella, Michael Schumacher, Mika Häkkinen, Jean Alesi, Villeneuve, Trulli, Rubens Barrichello, Johnny Herbert, Ralf Schumacher (kicking himself for squandering a decent grid position with an appalling start) and Damon Hill.

Berger was certainly not hanging about. On lap three he had stretched his advantage to 3.6s, but Fisichella was still doing a magnificent job holding off Schumacher's Ferrari. Already a gap was opening to Häkkinen, who had Alesi close behind, while Villeneuve had his hands full fending off Trulli and Ralf Schumacher was lining up to take Barrichello next time round.

On lap eight, Hill took Herbert's Sauber for tenth place coming into the stadium, leaving Johnny to hold off the on-form Pedro Diniz, who was next up in the queue. Pedro was clearly getting a little excited and, anxious to keep pace with Damon, was carried away by his own exuberance as he braked for the Clark chicane on lap nine, locking

HOCKENHEIM QUALIFYING

Ralf and Michael Schumacher ended the first day of practice – held for much of the time on a patchily damp track surface – in first and second places on the timing screens, an apparently dream-like situation for the Hockenheim promoters, who were already guaranteed a capacity crowd for the remainder of the weekend.

Both men timed their best runs to coincide with a brief spell when the circuit was completely dry, and the fact that Ralf ended his day with the Jordan firmly planted against a tyre barrier after spinning off at the Senna chicane was neither here nor there. The nationalistic crowd regarded this setback as no more than a trifling footnote to the day's proceedings.

Hockenheim offers a daunting challenge to driver skill and mechanical durability. Technically, it requires low-downforce trim for the straights combined with enough grip to handle the surprisingly slow corners – only the right-hander into the stadium is negotiated at more than 100 mph. Yet achieving this sort of balance proved unexpectedly difficult for F1's most seasoned old hands at Williams.

'Basically, the balance of our car has not been very good with low wing settings,' said Patrick Head after Heinz-Harald Frentzen had only managed to scrape onto the third row of the starting grid.

'We've got some ideas as to what's wrong, but not necessarily things we can do here.' Just 24 hours later, as the team surveyed the debris of possibly its worst collective race performance of the decade, Head just shrugged and smiled. 'What can one say?' he mused. 'Nothing sensible, certainly.'

Meanwhile, at the front of the pack, Gerhard Berger was a man with a mission. Some people might have written him off as a has-been, doubting whether he would ever regain his form after his enforced lay-off. Yet he simply took qualifying by its throat and hurled the Benetton B197 round to clinch pole position. 'There's nobody braver than Gerhard,' smiled Martin Brundle approvingly. Even so, it was a close call for the veteran Austrian.

Peter Nygaard

Eight minutes into the session, he took fastest time away from Mika Häkkinen's McLaren with a 1m 42.086s. Then half an hour later Giancarlo Fisichella – ironically one of the players indirectly responsible for Gerhard's departure from Benetton – slammed round in 1m 41.896s, literally only seven seconds after Gerhard had raised the stakes with 1m 41.873s.

Inwardly Berger knew that was all he could extract from the car, but he couldn't resist two more runs just to see if another sliver of time could somehow be shaved off. On his third run, he flat-spotted a tyre, ran wide on the final right-hander before the pits and aborted the lap. On his final run he spun at the Sachskurve hairpin, an excursion which might have cost the flying Häkkinen a crack at pole position had not the Finn straight-lined the Senna chicane a few seconds earlier.

Fisichella's bid for glory was exhilarating in the extreme. The Jordan 197 showed itself to be particularly good under sustained braking from 210 mph and Fisichella actually added a touch more downforce before achieving his best time.

In practice and qualifying the Jordans sported small aerofoils on either side of their raised noses – not a totally new F1 development, but one which designer Gary Anderson clearly believes unlocks the possibility of promising developments in terms of aerodynamic performance. The Jordan technical director was not forthcoming regarding these appendages, but it was believed that they offered more flexibility in terms of front wing settings and also helped to reduce the cars' pitch sensitivity. This latest accessory certainly seemed to work, although Ralf Schumacher eventually faded to seventh on the grid after an increasingly erratic performance marked by dramatic over-driving throughout the session.

In the McLaren camp, the latest Mercedes F-spec engines continued to be quick, but fragile. Running at over 17,000 rpm for over 70 per cent of this 6.8-km circuit is a technically precarious affair at the best of times, Häkkinen and team-mate David Coulthard suffering an engine breakage apiece on Friday and Saturday respectively.

Nevertheless, Mika continued to exude the same relaxed confidence which had been apparent at Silverstone, where his MP4/12 had succumbed to engine failure while leading only six laps from the end of the British GP. The latest engines had successfully completed several race-distance runs at Monza prior to the German round, so the team was keeping its fingers crossed.

Häkkinen ultimately lined up third ahead of Michael Schumacher's Ferrari F310B, the championship leader spending much of his time fine-tuning his chassis set-up with subtly different levels of downforce. Under the circumstances, to be only 0.3s away from pole position on such a long lap was a pretty respectable achievement.

In fifth and ninth places, Heinz-Harald Frentzen and Jacques Villeneuve were certainly not satisfied with the performance of their Williams-Renaults. Both were short of straightline speed, so much so that Villeneuve decided to take Heinz-Harald's spare FW19 for qualifying. It was a little better on the straights, but no benefit through the corners.

Alesi was uncomplaining about his sixth place on the grid, but Ralf Schumacher was very disappointed with seventh, three rows behind team-mate Fisichella. 'My last run was very good,' he said, 'but I missed the apex of the first corner and lost four-tenths. The engine also did not seem to be as strong this afternoon, which did not help either.'

David Coulthard frankly admitted that he didn't get the best out of his McLaren-Mercedes, qualifying eighth fastest, 0.6s behind Häkkinen's sister car. Then came Villeneuve, with a rather frustrated Eddie Irvine tenth in the second Ferrari.

'My car wouldn't ride the kerbs as well as the others and you have to do that to get a good qualifying lap,' said Irvine. 'I also still have some understeer on the exit of the corners, and the fact I did not test much at Monza recently means it took me a while to get the right balance for this high-speed track.'

In 11th place, Jarno Trulli's Prost just pipped Rubens Barrichello's Stewart for the distinction of being the fastest Bridgestone runner. 'I was happy with the balance of the car going into qualifying,' said Trulli, 'so we just really made detail changes to the rear wing set-up during the session itself. I was quick through the stadium part of the circuit, but each time we tried to revert to less downforce I found myself with problems trying to brake for the three chicanes.'

Barrichello, who had been delayed in the garage before the first run when the fire extinguisher accidentally went off in the cockpit of his car before he climbed in, did three runs and set his best time on the second. Both Stewart drivers used the latest development Project 7 version of the Ford Zetec-R V10 engine for qualifying and Rubens believed he could have qualified in the top ten had Marques not spun his Minardi in front of him when he was 0.3s up on his final run.

Team-mate Jan Magnussen ended up a very respectable 15th despite raising the ride height of his car after it had been bottoming out excessively on his first run.

Damon Hill's Arrows-Yamaha wound up 13th fastest, which was a quite respectable performance on a circuit which places such an overwhelming premium on engine power. 'We had good mechanical balance and that is very much the key to this place as we don't run a lot of downforce,' he explained. 'I expected we would have difficulty getting into the top 15, given the level of horsepower we have at the moment, so I am not at all disappointed with that.' His team-mate Pedro Diniz lined up 16th after engine problems obliged him to take the spare A18.

Yet if the Arrows team felt moderately optimistic, the mood in the Sauber-Petronas garage was very much more depressed. Johnny Herbert could not improve on 14th place and was simply not satisfied. 'It has been very disappointing today, for we weren't able to carry over the speed we'd shown at the Monza test last week,' he reflected. 'I went off at the Ostkurve this morning, which didn't help, but we really struggled to find a set-up that could get the power down coming out of the chicanes and in the stadium. I just couldn't get enough traction.'

Shinji Nakano's Prost was 17th ahead of Norberto Fontana's Sauber, the young Argentine driver unable to work out a decent set-up for Hockenheim, while the Tyrrell-Fords of Mika Salo and Jos Verstappen completed the top 20, neither having any problems – apart from the limitations of Cosworth V8 power on this ultra-fast track.

Much the same applied to the Minardi-Hart drivers, Tarso Marques and Ukyo Katayama, who completed the final row of the grid.

Above: **Jacques Villeneuve's girlfriend, Sandrine, is caught in an almost saintly pose as she watches the Canadian bid for pole position.**

Above left: **Move over, big brother is coming through! Michael Schumacher dives his Ferrari inside Ralf's Jordan during practice.**

Right: **So you think being a Grand Prix photographer is glamorous, do you?**

DIARY

Honda President Nobuhiko Kawamoto confirms that the Japanese company will eventually return to F1 as a fully fledged engine supplier.

F1 teams reject suggestions that engine manufacturers should be obliged to supply a minimum of two competitors.

Emerson Fittipaldi, attending Hockenheim for a Mercedes-Benz demonstration, admits that he may return to racing in the GT category.

Britain's Jamie Davies heads F3000 championship table after finishing third in Hockenheim supporting race.

Alex Zanardi wins US 500 at Michigan to take CART points lead from Paul Tracy.

Photos: Paul-Henri Cahier

Jarno Trulli survived a collision with Jacques Villeneuve to claim fourth place for the Prost team.

Below left: Giancarlo Fisichella drove magnificently before a puncture ended his chances of a rostrum finish. Michael Schumacher gives the little Italian a lift back to the pits after damage to an oil cooler had forced him to abandon the Jordan out on the circuit.

up his brakes and running into the back of the Swiss machine. Both drivers were out on the spot.

'I did a good start and managed to overtake some people, which I was pleased with as I was running a one-pit-stop strategy,' explained Diniz. 'It is a shame the accident happened with Johnny. I was very close to him when I braked, locked the rear wheels and slid into him.'

On lap 11 Hill made his first refuelling stop and resumed in 15th place, but Berger was still piling on the pressure at the front of the field, now running some 9.5s ahead of the opposition. Alesi was the first of the front-runners to stop for fuel, coming in on lap 16 for a 7.3s pit visit which dropped him from fifth to ninth. Next time round Berger came in for his first stop, resuming in fourth place behind Fisichella, Schumacher's Ferrari and Häkkinen, although he lost no time in moving ahead of the Finn once more.

Michael stayed out until lap 22 when he made what he thought was going to be his sole refuelling stop. The Ferrari was stationary for 9.7s and resumed in fifth place.

Fisichella, staying out even longer, now led by 1.8s from Berger, but then the Jordan driver came in for his sole refuelling stop at the end of lap 24. He was stationary for 8.3s before rejoining the race in second place, just ahead of Alesi and Schumacher, who were now running in close company. Fifth was Häkkinen, having made his sole stop on lap 21, with Villeneuve coming under pressure from Trulli in sixth.

On lap 28, Berger was just coming up to lap Jan Magnussen's Stewart-Ford, which was running in 11th place, when the Dane's Ford V10 engine blew up spectacularly. The episode cost Gerhard the best part of five seconds.

'I thought I had lost the race,' he said. 'I almost had to stop because I could not see. I thought I would not be able to get ahead after my final pit stop, but I was very surprised that I was only just behind Giancarlo Fisichella when I came back into the race.'

That second stop came at the end of lap 34, Gerhard just nipping back into the fray on Fisichella's tail. But Giancarlo immediately made a slight mistake at the Ostkurve, losing speed out onto the following straight, which allowed Gerhard to slipstream back into the lead as they went down to the Senna chicane.

Lap 34 also saw Villeneuve's demise. Jacques misjudged the right-hander out of the stadium, allowing Trulli's Prost to tow up onto his tail.

The young Italian darted for the inside, but Villeneuve moved across on him. So Trulli went to the outside, pulling level and slightly ahead as they went into the braking area for the Clark chicane. Villeneuve found himself squeezed towards the inside and spun off into the gravel.

On lap 39, Fisichella's Jordan suffered a left-rear tyre failure as he braked for the right-hander into the stadium. He kept the car under control, but sadly spun over a kerb as he limped round the final turn into the pit lane. He kept the engine running and got to the pits, where a replacement wheel was fitted. He resumed, but the excursion had damaged an oil cooler and he retired for good a little over a lap later. It was a cruel reward for a brilliant performance.

As if that wasn't enough, Schumacher's Ferrari suddenly appeared at the end of the pit lane, in for a quick 'splash and dash'. Amazingly, he squeezed back into the race just ahead of Häkkinen's McLaren. 'It was fuel, nothing more,' he shrugged. 'There had been a problem with the rig at the first stop and they did not get enough in the car to go the whole distance.'

Now it was just a question of Berger reeling off the laps to the chequered flag, mindful of the fact that his engine had failed in the same race in 1996 with just over two laps to go. Yet this time there was to be no such disappointment. The Benetton B197 never missed a beat and Gerhard pounded home 17.52s ahead of Schumacher.

Gerhard was elated, Michael simply well satisfied. For Ferrari, although Irvine had dropped out at the end of the opening lap, Schumacher had again exceeded the apparent capability of his F310B, which was using the earlier-spec 046/1 engine in the interests of durability. He was also troubled by the apparent failure of his gearbox to select fifth from half-distance onwards, so it was a fine effort.

Häkkinen, perhaps slightly lacklustre, held off Trulli for third place by 2.3s. Ralf Schumacher was fifth while Alesi, who had an unscheduled trip up a chicane escape road on lap 25, had to content himself with sixth and the final point of the afternoon.

Shinji Nakano's Prost was seventh ahead of Hill, the British driver satisfied with the performance of the Arrows-Yamaha on this very fast circuit and happy that the Japanese V10 had run reliably once again. Norberto Fontana's Sauber and Jos Verstappen's Tyrrell were the only other runners to make the finish, but the luckless Fisichella was officially classified 11th.

Berger to quit Benetton

Steven Tee/LAT Photographic

DESPITE dominating the German Grand Prix from pole position through to the finish, F1 veteran Gerhard Berger confirmed he would be leaving the Benetton team at the end of the season.

The 37-year-old Austrian's official announcement came only two days after Benetton's decision to take up its option on Giancarlo Fisichella for 1998. Benetton had paid Jordan $1 million to run the young Italian this season and it was being speculated that he would be partnered by the young Austrian, Alexander Wurz, in next year's Benetton squad, thereby ensuring that Jean Alesi joins Berger on the driver market.

'I will not drive for Benetton in 1998,' said Berger. 'It is not the team, nor its performance level. I had a [personal] two-year plan when I joined them last year and I will have completed that.

'There are a few things [available] outside F1, but I just have to see what happens over the next three or four races, but I don't want to be a team boss and I am not worried about money at this stage of my career. I want to keep in F1, but it doesn't necessarily have to be with a team that is winning at the moment.' Berger's name had been linked with McLaren, but insiders believed he was most likely to obtain a berth with Sauber if he continued in F1.

Meanwhile, Benetton boss Flavio Briatore expressed his enthusiasm for Fisichella. 'Giancarlo has been on loan to Jordan this season,' he said. 'We have been impressed by his performances and had no hesitation in exercising our option so he can drive for us next year. We think he has a very bright future.'

Fisichella said he was delighted to be driving for Benetton next season, but insisted this would not blunt his determination to do well for Jordan in the remaining eight races of the year.

'I am very pleased that I will be driving for an Italian team,' he said. 'The people at Jordan have been great and I will do my best for the rest of the season.'

It was speculated that Alesi's strong Japanese connections – in particular, his second wife, Kumiko, who is a leading TV personality – could mark him out for the vacant Mugen Honda-engined Jordan in 1998.

GROSSER MOBIL 1 PREIS VON DEUTSCHLAND

25–27 JULY 1997

HOCKENHEIM

Race distance: 45 laps, 190.782 miles/307.035 km

Race weather: Dry, hot and sunny

ROUND 10

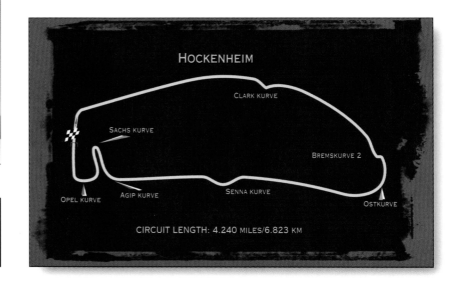

HOCKENHEIM

CLARK KURVE
SACHS KURVE
BREMSKURVE 2
OPEL KURVE   AGIP KURVE   SENNA KURVE   OSTKURVE

CIRCUIT LENGTH: 4.240 MILES/6.823 KM

Pos.	Driver	Nat.	No.	Entrant	Car/Engine	Tyres	Laps	Time/Retirement	Speed (mph/km/h)
1	Gerhard Berger	A	8	Mild Seven Benetton Renault	Benetton B197-Renault RS9A V10	G	45	1h 20m 59.046s	141.348/227.478
2	Michael Schumacher	D	5	Scuderia Ferrari Marlboro	Ferrari F310B 046 V10	G	45	1h 21m 16.573s	140.840/226.660
3	Mika Häkkinen	SF	9	West McLaren Mercedes	McLaren MP4/12-Mercedes FO110F V10	G	45	1h 21m 23.816s	140.631/226.324
4	Jarno Trulli	I	14	Prost Gauloises Blondes	Prost JS45-Mugen Honda MF301HB V10	B	45	1h 21m 26.211s	140.562/226.213
5	Ralf Schumacher	D	11	B&H Total Jordan Peugeot	Jordan 197-Peugeot A14 V10	G	45	1h 21m 29.041s	140.481/226.082
6	Jean Alesi	F	7	Mild Seven Benetton Renault	Benetton B197-Renault RS9A V10	G	45	1h 21m 33.763s	140.345/225.864
7	Shinji Nakano	J	15	Prost Gauloises Blondes	Prost JS45-Mugen Honda MF301HB V10	B	45	1h 22m 18.768s	139.066/223.806
8	Damon Hill	GB	1	Danka Arrows Yamaha	Arrows A18-Yamaha OX11A/C V10	B	44		
9	Norberto Fontana	RA	17	Red Bull Sauber Petronas	Sauber C16-Petronas V10	G	44		
10	Jos Verstappen	NL	18	Tyrrell	Tyrrell 025-Ford ED5 V8	G	44		
11	Giancarlo Fisichella	I	12	B&H Total Jordan Peugeot	Jordan 197-Peugeot A14 V10	G	40	Oil cooler	
	Jacques Villeneuve	CDN	3	Rothmans Williams Renault	Williams FW19-Renault RS9A V10	G	33	Spun off	
	Rubens Barrichello	BR	22	Stewart Ford	Stewart SF1-Ford Zetec-R V10	B	33	Engine	
	Mika Salo	SF	19	Tyrrell	Tyrrell 025-Ford ED5 V8	G	33	Clutch	
	Jan Magnussen	DK	23	Stewart Ford	Stewart SF1-Ford Zetec-R V10	B	27	Engine	
	Ukyo Katayama	J	20	Minardi Team	Minardi M197-Hart 830 V8	B	23	Out of fuel	
	Johnny Herbert	GB	16	Red Bull Sauber Petronas	Sauber C16-Petronas V10	G	8	Collision with Diniz	
	Pedro Diniz	BR	2	Danka Arrows Yamaha	Arrows A18-Yamaha OX11A/C V10	B	8	Collision with Herbert	
	David Coulthard	GB	10	West McLaren Mercedes	McLaren MP4/12-Mercedes FO110F V10	G	1	Transmission	
	Heinz-Harald Frentzen	D	4	Rothmans Williams Renault	Williams FW19-Renault RS9A V10	G	1	Collision with Irvine	
	Eddie Irvine	GB	6	Scuderia Ferrari Marlboro	Ferrari F310B 046 V10	G	1	Collision with Frentzen	
	Tarso Marques	BR	21	Minardi Team	Minardi M197-Hart 830 V8	B	0	Transmission	

Fastest lap: Berger, on lap 9, 1m 45.747s, 144.331 mph/232.278 km/h (record).

Previous lap record: David Coulthard (F1 Williams FW16-Renault V10), 1m 46.211s, 143.700 mph/231.264 km/h (1994).

B – Bridgestone   G – Goodyear

Grid order / lap chart

```
Grid order      1  2  3  4  5  6  7  8  9 10 11 12 13 14 15 16 17 18 19 20 21 22 23 24 25 26 27 28 29 30 31 32 33 34 35 36 37 38 39 40 41 42 43 44 45 ●
 8 BERGER       8  8  8  8  8  8  8  8  8  8  8  8  8  8  8  8  8  8  8  8  8  8  8  8  8  8  8  8  8  8  8  8  8  8  8  8  8  8  8  8  8  8  8  8  8  1
12 FISICHELLA  12 12 12 12 12 12 12 12 12 12 12 12 12 12 12 12 12 12  5  5  5  5  5  8  8 12 12 12 12 12 12 12 12 12 12 12 12  5  5  5  5  5        2
 9 HÄKKINEN     5  5  5  5  5  5  5  5  5  5  5  5  5  5  5  5  5  9  8  8  8  5 14  7  7  7  7  7  7  5  5  5  5  5  5  5  5  9  9  9  9  9  9  9  9  3
 5 M. SCHUMACHER 9  9  9  9  9  9  9  9  9  9  9  9  9  9  9  9  9  8  9  9 14 14  7 14  5  5  5  5  7  9  9  9  9  9  9  9 14 14 14 14 14 14 14      4
 4 FRENTZEN     7  7  7  7  7  7  7  7  7  7  7  7  7  7  7  3  3  3  3  9  7  5  5  9  9  9  9  9  3  3  3 14 14 14 14 11 11 11 11 11 11 11         5
 7 ALESI        3  3  3  3  3  3  3  3  3  3  3  3  3  3  3 14 14 14 11 11  9  9  3  3  3  3  3  3 14 14 14 11 11 11 11 11 12  7  7  7  7  7  7      6
11 R. SCHUMACHER 14 14 14 14 14 14 14 14 14 14 14 14 14 14 14 11 11 11  3  9  3 14 14 14 14 14 11 11 11  7  7  7  7  7  7 12 15 15 15 15 15
10 COULTHARD   22 22 22 11 11 11 11 11 11 11 11 11 11 11 11 22  7  7  7  7  3 11 11 11 11 11 11 11  7  7  7 15 15 15 15 15 15  1  1  1  1
 3 VILLENEUVE  16 11 11 22 22 22 22 22 22 22 22 22 22 22  7 22 15 15 15 22 22 22 22 22 22 22 22 22  1  1  1  1  1  1 17 17 17 17
 6 IRVINE      11 16 16 16 16 16 16  1  1  1  1 23 23 23 23 15 15 22 22 22 15 15 15 15 15 15 15 15 15 17 17 17 17 17 17 18 18 18 18
14 TRULLI       1  1  1  1  1  1  1 16 23 23 23 17 15 15 15 23 19 19 17 17 17 23 23 23 23  1  1  1  1  1  1 18 18 18 18 18 18
22 BARRICHELLO 23 23 23  2  2  2 17 17 15 15 19 19 17 17 17 17 19 19 19 17 17 23 23  1  1  1 17 17 17 17 17
 1 HILL         2  2  2 23 23 23 23 23 15 19 19 17 17 17 17 17  1  1 23  1  1 17 19 19 19 19 19 19 19
16 HERBERT     17 17 17 17 17 17 17 17 19 19 19 18  1  1  1  1  1 23 23  1 19 19 20 19 19 17 17 18 18 18 18 18 18
23 MAGNUSSEN   19 15 15 15 15 15 15 15 18 18 18  1 18 18 18 18 20 20 20 20 20 20 19 18 18 18 18
 2 DINIZ       15 19 19 19 19 19 19 19 20 20 20 20 20 20 20 18 18 18 18 18 18 18
15 NAKANO      18 18 18 18 18 18 18 18
17 FONTANA     20 20 20 20 20 20 20 20
19 SALO        10
18 VERSTAPPEN   4
21 MARQUES      6
20 KATAYAMA
```

Pit stop

One lap behind leader

STARTING GRID

8 **BERGER** Benetton	12 **FISICHELLA** Jordan
9 **HAKKINEN** McLaren	5 **M. SCHUMACHER** Ferrari
4 **FRENTZEN** Williams	7 **ALESI** Benetton
11 **R. SCHUMACHER** Jordan	10 **COULTHARD** McLaren
3 **VILLENEUVE** Williams	6 **IRVINE** Ferrari
14 **TRULLI** Prost	22 **BARRICHELLO** Stewart
1 **HILL** Arrows	16 **HERBERT** Sauber
23 **MAGNUSSEN** Stewart	2 **DINIZ** Arrows
15 **NAKANO** Prost	17 **FONTANA** Sauber
19 **SALO** Tyrrell	18 **VERSTAPPEN** Tyrrell
21 **MARQUES** Minardi	20 **KATAYAMA** Minardi

TIME SHEETS

QUALIFYING

Weather: Dry, hot and sunny

Pos.	Driver	Car	Laps	Time
1	Gerhard Berger	Benetton-Renault	10	1m 41.873s
2	Giancarlo Fisichella	Jordan-Peugeot	12	1m 41.896s
3	Mika Häkkinen	McLaren-Mercedes	10	1m 42.034s
4	Michael Schumacher	Ferrari	11	1m 42.181s
5	Heinz-Harald Frentzen	Williams-Renault	12	1m 42.421s
6	Jean Alesi	Benetton-Renault	10	1m 42.493s
7	Ralf Schumacher	Jordan-Peugeot	12	1m 42.498s
8	David Coulthard	McLaren-Mercedes	10	1m 42.687s
9	Jacques Villeneuve	Williams-Renault	12	1m 42.967s
10	Eddie Irvine	Ferrari	12	1m 43.209s
11	Jarno Trulli	Prost-Mugen Honda	12	1m 43.226s
12	Rubens Barrichello	Stewart-Ford	10	1m 43.272s
13	Damon Hill	Arrows-Yamaha	12	1m 43.361s
14	Johnny Herbert	Sauber-Petronas	12	1m 43.660s
15	Jan Magnussen	Stewart-Ford	10	1m 43.927s
16	Pedro Diniz	Arrows-Yamaha	10	1m 44.069s
17	Shinji Nakano	Prost-Mugen Honda	12	1m 44.112s
18	Norberto Fontana	Sauber-Petronas	12	1m 44.552s
19	Mika Salo	Tyrrell-Ford	12	1m 45.372s
20	Jos Verstappen	Tyrrell-Ford	12	1m 45.811s
21	Tarso Marques	Minardi-Hart	12	1m 45.942s
22	Ukyo Katayama	Minardi-Hart	12	1m 46.499s

FRIDAY FREE PRACTICE

Weather: Dry, then torrential rain, then drying

Pos.	Driver	Laps	Time
1	Ralf Schumacher	7	1m 46.196s
2	Michael Schumacher	12	1m 46.322s
3	Johnny Herbert	22	1m 46.517s
4	Rubens Barrichello	16	1m 46.526s
5	Norberto Fontana	19	1m 46.706s
6	Pedro Diniz	17	1m 46.873s
7	Shinji Nakano	19	1m 47.143s
8	Mika Häkkinen	14	1m 47.386s
9	Damon Hill	16	1m 47.542s
10	Eddie Irvine	19	1m 47.594s
11	Jos Verstappen	22	1m 47.720s
12	Jan Magnussen	8	1m 47.769s
13	Jarno Trulli	24	1m 47.784s
14	Gerhard Berger	18	1m 47.887s
15	Jean Alesi	8	1m 48.455s
16	Jacques Villeneuve	21	1m 48.639s
17	David Coulthard	16	1m 48.648s
18	Heinz-Harald Frentzen	19	1m 48.958s
19	Giancarlo Fisichella	14	1m 49.010s
20	Tarso Marques	18	1m 49.563s
21	Mika Salo	17	1m 49.831s
22	Ukyo Katayama	22	1m 51.058s

SATURDAY FREE PRACTICE

Weather: Sunny and warm

Pos.	Driver	Laps	Time
1	Ralf Schumacher	26	1m 42.987s
2	Mika Häkkinen	22	1m 42.989s
3	Jean Alesi	19	1m 43.257s
4	Giancarlo Fisichella	24	1m 43.349s
5	Gerhard Berger	21	1m 43.428s
6	David Coulthard	20	1m 43.579s
7	Michael Schumacher	26	1m 43.628s
8	Heinz-Harald Frentzen	26	1m 43.646s
9	Rubens Barrichello	19	1m 44.096s
10	Jacques Villeneuve	22	1m 44.291s
11	Jarno Trulli	30	1m 44.328s
12	Shinji Nakano	28	1m 44.741s
13	Damon Hill	13	1m 44.875s
14	Norberto Fontana	30	1m 44.927s
15	Eddie Irvine	20	1m 44.988s
16	Johnny Herbert	17	1m 45.082s
17	Jan Magnussen	22	1m 45.446s
18	Pedro Diniz	20	1m 45.454s
19	Mika Salo	25	1m 45.983s
20	Jos Verstappen	28	1m 46.548s
21	Ukyo Katayama	25	1m 46.569s
22	Tarso Marques	17	1m 46.800s

WARM-UP

Weather: Wet, but drying

Pos.	Driver	Laps	Time
1	Jacques Villeneuve		1m 45.006s
2	Damon Hill		1m 45.347s
3	Giancarlo Fisichella		1m 45.403s
4	Heinz-Harald Frentzen		1m 45.483s
5	Gerhard Berger		1m 45.497s
6	Ralf Schumacher		1m 45.782s
7	David Coulthard		1m 46.138s
8	Mika Häkkinen		1m 46.258s
9	Norberto Fontana		1m 46.376s
10	Jean Alesi		1m 46.448s
11	Pedro Diniz		1m 46.477s
12	Jarno Trulli		1m 46.560s
13	Shinji Nakano		1m 46.655s
14	Michael Schumacher		1m 46.662s
15	Rubens Barrichello		1m 46.797s
16	Johnny Herbert		1m 46.919s
17	Eddie Irvine		1m 47.502s
18	Tarso Marques		1m 47.775s
19	Mika Salo		1m 48.420s
20	Jos Verstappen		1m 49.418s
21	Jan Magnussen		1m 50.058s
22	Ukyo Katayama		1m 50.614s

RACE FASTEST LAPS

Weather: Dry, hot and sunny

Driver	Time	Lap
Gerhard Berger	1m 45.747s	9
Jean Alesi	1m 45.917s	20
Ralf Schumacher	1m 46.127s	24
Giancarlo Fisichella	1m 46.274s	34
Damon Hill	1m 46.560s	10
Michael Schumacher	1m 46.603s	43
Jarno Trulli	1m 46.733s	23
Mika Häkkinen	1m 46.831s	9
Jacques Villeneuve	1m 47.044s	24
Rubens Barrichello	1m 47.074s	28
Norberto Fontana	1m 47.908s	27
Shinji Nakano	1m 47.939s	24
Jan Magnussen	1m 48.189s	14
Pedro Diniz	1m 48.836s	5
Johnny Herbert	1m 49.184s	3
Mika Salo	1m 49.611s	25
Jos Verstappen	1m 50.159s	4
Ukyo Katayama	1m 50.161s	22
David Coulthard	2m 22.236s	1
Heinz-Harald Frentzen	3m 13.699s	1
Eddie Irvine	2m 16.256s	1

CHASSIS LOG BOOK

1	Hill	Arrows A18/5
2	Diniz	Arrows A18/4
	spare	Arrows A18/3
3	Villeneuve	Williams FW19/4
4	Frentzen	Williams FW19/5
	spare	Williams FW19/3
5	M. Schumacher	Ferrari F310B/177
6	Irvine	Ferrari F310B/173
	spare	Ferrari F310B/175
7	Alesi	Benetton B197/2
8	Berger	Benetton B197/4
	spare	Benetton B197/3
9	Häkkinen	McLaren MP4/12/5
10	Coulthard	McLaren MP4/12/7
	spare	McLaren MP4/12/
11	R. Schumacher	Jordan 197/6
12	Fisichella	Jordan 197/4
	spare	Jordan 197/1
14	Trulli	Prost JS45/3
15	Nakano	Prost JS45/2
	spare	Prost JS45/1
16	Herbert	Sauber C16/5
17	Fontana	Sauber C16/6
	spare	Sauber C16/3
18	Verstappen	Tyrrell 025/4
19	Salo	Tyrrell 025/1
	spare	Tyrrell 025/3
20	Katayama	Minardi M197/4
21	Marques	Minardi M197/2
	spare	Minardi M197/1
22	Barrichello	Stewart SF1/1
23	Magnussen	Stewart SF1/3
	spare	Stewart SF1/2

POINTS TABLES

Drivers

1	Michael Schumacher	53
2	Jacques Villeneuve	43
3	Jean Alesi	22
4	Gerhard Berger	20
5	Heinz-Harald Frentzen	19
6	Eddie Irvine	18
7	Olivier Panis	15
8 =	David Coulthard	14
8 =	Mika Häkkinen	14
10	Ralf Schumacher	9
11	Giancarlo Fisichella	8
12	Johnny Herbert	7
13	Rubens Barrichello	6
14	Alexander Wurz	4
15	Jarno Trulli	3
16	Mika Salo	2
17 =	Nicola Larini	1
17 =	Shinji Nakano	1
17 =	Damon Hill	1

Constructors

1	Ferrari	71
2	Williams	62
3	Benetton	46
4	McLaren	28
5	Prost	19
6	Jordan	17
7	Sauber	8
8	Stewart	6
9	Tyrrell	2
10	Arrows	1

FOR THE RECORD

First Grand Prix points

Jarno Trulli

VILLENEUVE

HILL

HERBERT

M. SCHUMACHER

R. SCHUMACHER

NAKANO

HUNGARIAN

grand prix

So near and yet so far away. The pit board tells the story as Damon Hill's Arrows flashes into frame.
Photo: Lukas Gorys

Johnny Herbert ran strongly throughout in the Sauber-Petronas, working his way up the order to take a well-deserved third place at the flag.

HUNGARORING QUALIFYING

One thing on which most rival teams could depend was Michael Schumacher's continuing presence as a competitive front-runner throughout the weekend. The German driver seemed able to respond at will to any challenge from the opposition, confidently pulling out another couple of tenths each time somebody edged close to his time.

Under the circumstances, it was therefore almost a relief for the other drivers to watch as Schumacher spun his Ferrari onto the grass in the closing stages of Friday free practice, a rare mistake which at least proved that he was human like the rest of them.

Schumacher, who was using a brand-new, lighter F310B chassis with a slightly enlarged fuel tank – developed in order to eliminate the possibility of having to make emergency additional fuel stops, as he did in both the Australian and German Grands Prix – ended Friday 0.2s faster than David Coulthard's McLaren-Mercedes.

After a week of intensive testing at Barcelona, the Williams-Renault team arrived in Hungary feeling significantly more confident than when they had left Hockenheim a couple of weeks earlier. Heinz-Harald Frentzen posted fourth-fastest Friday time with Jacques Villeneuve, handicapped by over-stiff front suspension and a touch of understeer, down in 11th place.

Come Saturday qualifying, Schumacher was again the class of the field, bagging the 17th pole position of his career on 1m 14.672s ahead of Villeneuve's Williams while McLaren's Mika Häkkinen (below) had to be content with fourth place behind the remarkable Damon Hill.

'We were on pole position from the beginning, and we never gave it away,' grinned Schumacher. 'I have to say that I made a slight mistake on my fastest lap. I should have done it slightly better. I was waiting until the end, to see what Häkkinen and Jacques were going to do, before deciding whether to go for another run. Obviously it wasn't necessary.'

After qualifying second, Villeneuve admitted that the team had made a huge improvement to his car overnight. 'A front row spot is one better than I managed last year,' he grinned.

Hill, meanwhile, could not have been happier. After originally predicting that a top ten qualifying position would have been satisfactory, to end up third was a real bonus. 'I'm surprised,' he admitted, 'but I always thought it was possible to go quicker, so I put the hammer down and went for it. It was one of the best laps of my life.'

On the face of it, this performance from Hill and Arrows took a bit of believing. In fact it was a combination of Damon's astute setting-up ability, excellent grip from Bridgestone's rubber and an improvement in the power output from the latest D-spec Yamaha V10. Add that to the fact that the Hungaroring is not a power circuit and Hill was able to make hay while the sun shone.

Häkkinen, meanwhile, did a good job to qualify fourth ahead of Eddie Irvine's Ferrari and Frentzen in the second Williams, but his McLaren team-mate Coulthard wound up eighth after spinning on his final run. The Scot looked like a man under pressure. In seventh and ninth places, Benetton's Gerhard Berger and Jean Alesi were troubled by extreme tyre wear, having opted for the softer of the available Goodyear compounds.

Completing the top ten was Johnny Herbert, the British driver moderately happy with the feel of his Sauber C16. 'The car seemed to perform a little bit better today,' he agreed, 'but again it was more a matter of fiddling with minor things, trying to find that bit extra. I reached a plateau after my second run and the performance curve just flattened out, but the balance was good.'

Behind him, Rubens Barrichello used Bridgestone's softer compound to post 11th-fastest time in his Stewart-Ford, while Jarno Trulli found himself struggling with lack of grip in 12th place. 'I don't understand what happened this afternoon,' said the young Italian. 'We were expecting much better. Both yesterday and this morning I had a good, nicely balanced car and was up there with the fastest. Then, this afternoon, I suddenly found myself struggling to find any grip.'

His team-mate Shinji Nakano broadly echoed those sentiments from 16th place on the grid, the Japanese driver admitting that he was 'expecting better', having been slowed by a slight misfire in the middle of his third flying lap and then grappled with too much oversteer in the closing moments of the session.

In 13th and 14th places came the Jordan-Peugeots of Giancarlo Fisichella and Ralf Schumacher. Both men had experienced blistering problems with Goodyear's softer tyre compound, so joined Frentzen in the minority who opted for the harder rubber.

'The upside may be that the hard tyres will be to our advantage in the race tomorrow,' shrugged Fisichella, 'but the car certainly felt nervous today.' Ralf Schumacher experienced a small fire on his race car at the start of qualifying which forced him to switch to the spare 197 chassis, set up for Fisichella.

'This was a disappointment for us, as I expected to be in the top six,' said Ralf. 'Although I improved a little in the spare car, it was impossible to make a real impact.'

Behind the slower of the two Jordans, Gianni Morbidelli's Sauber lined up just ahead of Nakano. The Italian driver – back in action after missing three races with a broken arm – picked up more grip as the session progressed and was happy to report he had managed to reduce his car's understeer during the course of the afternoon.

In 17th place Jan Magnussen found his Stewart-Ford struggling on hard-compound Bridgestones, but he squeezed in ahead of Jos Verstappen in the faster of the two Tyrrell-Fords. 'I got just about the perfect lap on my third run and I don't think there was much more we could have done today,' said the Dutchman. 'The car was handling well and we made some small adjustments which also helped.'

Mika Salo ended the session 21st fastest, having inadvertently blocked Villeneuve on his second lap of the session, after which the Williams driver paid him back next time round. 'It's not the same if you do it deliberately,' mused Salo. 'It ruined our schedule, because it meant that after 25 minutes I only had one run left and the track was getting better all the time. We also had mid-corner understeer all weekend which was enough to prevent me getting on the power earlier. That is certainly costing me some time.'

Splitting the two Tyrrells were Pedro Diniz in the second Arrows-Yamaha and Ukyo Katayama's Minardi, while the final place in the line-up fell to Tarso Marques in the other Hart V8-engined machine.

Michael Roberts

DAMON Hill came within two miles of upending the F1 form book in the most spectacular manner possible when his Arrows-Yamaha lost victory in a breathtaking Hungarian Grand Prix on the final lap after dominating the race virtually from the start.

Having qualified a splendid third, the 36-year-old World Champion took the lead from Michael Schumacher's Ferrari F310B going into the first corner at the start of the 11th lap. It was almost as if reality had been suspended as Hill pulled relentlessly away into the distance, amassing a 28-second lead before being slowed dramatically by hydraulic problems which allowed Jacques Villeneuve's Williams-Renault to charge past on the final lap.

Hill survived to finish second ahead of fellow Brit Johnny Herbert's Sauber-Petronas, with Schumacher's Ferrari fading to fourth. It was a result which swung the World Championship pendulum back in Villeneuve's direction, the Canadian finishing the afternoon only three points behind the Ferrari driver in the closely contested title race.

'I was just on the point of winding down for the last few laps,' said Hill, 'but then with three laps to go I had trouble with the car's throttle operation, but this was an indication of a problem with the hydraulics.

'Then the gears started playing up as well, so I wasn't able to change gear or use the throttle. At one point I was stuck in second gear, then in third, and after that it was a case of the throttle working when it liked. I have to say that we are really pretty pleased with second place, although I would have loved to have won this race. I am very, very pleased with that.'

Hill's magnificent exhibition of driving prowess came at a crucial moment in the season, reminding everybody of his quality and consistency behind the wheel just as the driver transfer market became active in preparation for 1998. It was a performance which also emphatically underlined the capricious and unpredictable nature of Formula 1. Only two races had passed since Hill was being briskly criticised by Arrows chief Tom Walkinshaw for not pulling his weight and motivating the team in a manner commensurate with his £5 million retainer.

Yet there was nothing magic about this apparent transformation in form. At the Hungaroring, Bridgestone's rubber did not blister like its Goodyear opposition and Hill had the expertise and savvy to set up the Arrows to make the best possible use of the tyres available to him. He then drove the car with characteristic precision, coming within shouting distance of celebrating the fourth anniversary of his first F1 win with a 22nd career victory.

It was therefore singularly appropriate that the most spontaneous praise came from his former employer Frank Williams. 'Damon drove superbly well,' he said. 'Grands Prix are not won by people who cruise around. He drove brilliantly.'

Having qualified in pole position, Schumacher compromised his race chances with an uncharacteristic slip during the Sunday morning warm-up. He rode the kerb too fast on a high-speed ess-bend, momentarily launching his new lightweight Ferrari into the air, and it landed askew, damaging the underside of the monocoque beyond immediate repair. This meant that he had to switch back to one of the original-spec F310Bs for the race, although this would turn out to be the least of his problems.

At the start, Schumacher took full advantage of the cleaner racing line ahead of his Ferrari to accelerate into the lead on the sprint to the first corner, Villeneuve's Williams predictably getting bogged down on the dusty right-hand side of the circuit. Hill followed Schumacher through, but for a second it looked as though Eddie Irvine might slip his Ferrari past on the inside of the Arrows. However, Damon moved gently across to the right to cover his position as they braked for the first turn.

Further back in the pack all hell was let loose with three different drivers having individual accounts of what appeared to be two separate incidents. Going into the first corner, Jan Magnussen's Stewart made contact with Gianni Morbidelli's Sauber, the incident delaying the Sauber driver but eliminating the young Dane from the contest.

'I went into the first corner on the outside of Nakano,' said Magnussen. 'I was following Trulli going in and half-way through the corner somebody came out and his front wheel went between my front and rear wheels. It damaged the bodywork and there were also some other steering problems. I could not hold the steering wheel in the fast corners – it wanted to go straight.'

Magnussen trailed round to the pits and eventually retired with five laps completed. In fact, it was Morbidelli's Sauber with which he had collided. Needless to say, Gianni saw the situation from a different viewpoint. 'Magnussen tried to overtake me on the outside, but touched my left-rear wheel, and we both lost time going straight on,' he said.

'I had a quick pit stop as a result, and then after three laps I felt something odd in the engine and a warning light came on in the dashboard display. After seven laps I could not continue.'

Darren Heath

Right: The blisters on Jacques Villeneuve's tyres give an indication of the difficulties experienced by many of the Goodyear runners in Hungary. The Canadian was unable to match the pace of Damon Hill's flying Arrows and it was only the heartbreaking problems that befell the World Champion in the closing laps of the race that allowed him to mount the top step of the podium (bottom right).

At the next corner, the Arrows of Pedro Diniz and the two Minardis somehow contrived to run into each other, but the rest of the pack was stringing out into its race order, Schumacher's Ferrari howling into view at the end of the opening lap already 1.7s ahead of Hill, who in turn had another 1.3s in hand over Irvine. Mika Häkkinen was fourth from Villeneuve, Heinz-Harald Frentzen, David Coulthard and Herbert.

Diniz later reflected: 'I made a good start but the two Minardis did a *kamikaze* manoeuvre trying to overtake me, and put all three of us off the track at the second corner. It was a shame, as this made me lose some positions and the car was quite good from the beginning.'

Initially it looked as though Schumacher would steadily pull away, but within five laps his first set of Goodyears began blistering badly. The problem was shared by team-mate Irvine, who made a quick 7.3s stop at the end of lap seven, dropping from third to the tail of the field.

By lap nine it was clear that Schumacher was in quite serious trouble, the Ferrari slowing now to the point that Hill, Häkkinen's McLaren and the Williams duo, Villeneuve and Frentzen, were closing in to make it a five-way contest. Michael was so troubled by lack of grip that Hill was able to dive inside the Ferrari, outbraking it cleanly into the first corner at the start of lap 11, coming round next time with an amazing 2.6s lead.

On lap 13 Häkkinen's McLaren rolled to a halt out on the circuit with hydraulic problems and, a lap later, Schumacher brought the Ferrari in for a 6.0s first tyre stop, resuming in 12th. This now left Hill 8.6s ahead of Villeneuve with Frentzen picking up the pace dramatically in third place.

Coulthard was now fourth ahead of Herbert, Jean Alesi, Jarno Trulli, Rubens Barrichello and the two Jordans of Giancarlo Fisichella and Ralf Schumacher. Yet Frentzen's pace was already marking him out as the unsung hero of the race. Between laps 15 and 24, when Hill's lap times varied from 1m 19.744s to 1m 21.405s, Frentzen recorded times ranging between 1m 18.372s and 1m 20.933s. During that time the Williams driver closed the gap to the leading Arrows from 11.5s to 7.2s, proving that his choice of the harder Goodyear compound had been absolutely correct.

On lap 24 Villeneuve made his first stop (11.0s), dropping from second to fourth, and when Hill came in a lap later, his Arrows stationary for 8.9s,

Frentzen went storming through into the lead, completing lap 26 some 19 seconds ahead of the Englishman.

Frentzen now looked as though he might have the race in the palm of his hand. Yet more cruel disappointment was waiting in store for the man who had replaced Hill in the Williams-Renault line-up.

Coming down the pit straight to start his 29th lap, Frentzen's FW19 appeared to shed a small piece of debris. Marshals recovered it from the track, subsequently showing it to the Williams team, who immediately identified it as part of the sleeve of the car's refuelling valve, which had somehow vibrated loose and flown off the car.

Meanwhile, Frentzen pressed on, oblivious to the fact his FW19 was spurting great gouts of flame as fuel slopped out and ran back over the engine cover in the corners. He was due in anyway next time round for his first refuelling stop, so there was an element of confusion when he rolled to a halt in front of the garage.

The mechanics went to work on the car as usual – apart from the refueller, who took one look at the car-mounted nozzle and shook his head in disbelief. Meanwhile, Patrick Head was urging him to get on with it and it took a few seconds before the seriousness of the situation was fully appreciated. There was nothing more to be done and the car had to be withdrawn on the spot.

'It was looking good for me,' shrugged Frentzen, 'and I would have been able to push hard right to the end with the tyres we had chosen.' The same lap also saw the retirement of Barrichello's Stewart.

'It is a real pity,' he shrugged. 'I had overtaken both Benettons and several other people, then something happened to the engine. I could have been in the points today!'

All this left Hill leading by 12.2s from Villeneuve, who was running just ahead of Coulthard's McLaren-Mercedes. Then came a gap to Michael Schumacher, who would make his second stop from fourth place on lap 33, Herbert, Irvine, Fisichella, Trulli, Shinji Nakano and Ralf Schumacher.

After Schumacher Senior's Ferrari resumed after its second stop, Michael found himself down in fifth place and challenged hard by Fisichella's Jordan. Meanwhile Hill extended his advantage to 15 seconds on lap 39 as Villeneuve lost three seconds lapping Diniz's Arrows.

On lap 43, Fisichella finally steeled himself to get closer than ever to Schumacher's Ferrari going into the first turn. But Michael was keeping a watchful eye on his right-hand mirror and also braked later than ever, the Ferrari twitching absolutely on the limit. Giancarlo's bid simply didn't work under the circumstances, the result being that he spun and stalled.

This left Nakano to take over in sixth place ahead of Ralf Schumacher and Irvine. On lap 50 the second-place stalemate was broken when Coulthard made his second refuelling stop (7.0s), followed in by Herbert's Sauber from fourth place (7.5s). Coulthard resumed in third, but next time round the pit lane became extremely busy as Hill, Villeneuve and both Schumacher brothers came in.

Damon accelerated back into the fray without his lead being threatened, but it was touch-and-go for Villeneuve, as Coulthard was flashing down the pit straight by the time the Williams cleared the speed-restricted pit lane. In many ways it was a defining moment: Coulthard should have forced his way through into second place, but Jacques just made it to the right-hander before him and the McLaren driver concluded that discretion was the better part of valour. Wisely, perhaps.

By lap 65 Hill was 31 seconds ahead of Villeneuve but on the next lap Coulthard rolled to a halt with alternator failure. Herbert was now a lonely third with the Schumacher brothers, Irvine and Nakano in tight formation. With only eight laps left to run, Damon seemed set to pull off one of the most remarkable F1 successes in recent history.

Yet three laps from the finish, everything started to go wrong. 'I came out of the chicane and the throttle wouldn't shut when I lifted off,' he recalled. 'I thought that was a bit strange – maybe it was my foot – then about three or four corners later it wouldn't change gear properly.'

The Arrows almost rolled to a halt on a couple of occasions as the gearbox began to malfunction, leaving him first jammed in second gear, then in third. Coming out of the third turn on the last lap, Villeneuve's Williams had the stricken Arrows in its sights and the Canadian driver swooped past into the lead, using the grass at the edge of the track as he did so.

Amazingly, Hill struggled round to

finish second, still 11 seconds ahead of Herbert's Sauber-Petronas. 'If someone said to me, "Do you feel as though you lost a win or won a second place today?" I must say second is a good result, but when you are running at the front and expected a win, it is a little disappointing,' he said.

'The throttle went on the blink completely and a few times the car just stopped, so I was really amazed to get to the end.'

Villeneuve admitted that he was lucky to win, but that he was delighted to do so in a successful quest to erode Michael Schumacher's advantage in the championship points table. With six of the season's 17 races left to run, he now trailed Schumacher by only three points.

'The team told me when Damon's lap times began slowing down, so I started pushing again,' he said. 'As I came towards him, he started going left and right, so I just went on the grass and passed him.'

Michael Schumacher finished fourth, fending off a firm challenge from his brother Ralf's Jordan, which finished less than a second behind in fifth place.

'At the end of the race my brother was quicker than me, and if I had not been fighting for the title I could have let him pass,' said Michael. 'I hoped that Hill would win, as he deserved to and also because it would have helped me in the championship [by pushing Villeneuve back to second place].'

Irvine's hopes of sixth place ended on the final lap when his Ferrari was pushed off the road by Nakano's Prost, which went through to inherit the final championship point of the afternoon.

Trulli was seventh while Berger trailed home a dejected eighth, classified ahead of Irvine, Katayama and Alesi. Both Benetton drivers had had a bad afternoon. Gerhard reported that his first set of tyres blistered quickly, and although the second and third sets were more normal, there was no way he could push at all.

'Towards the end, I got stuck behind a Minardi for six or seven laps, but at that point it did not really matter,' he explained. Alesi concluded that a two-stop strategy was simply the wrong way to go, he, too, finding it difficult to get the best out of his car.

Villeneuve was happy to accept what, by any standards, was a fortuitous victory. Yet he was generous in his praise for Hill's efforts. 'He was worth a win today,' he said of his former Williams team-mate. 'He drove really well, and was flying. It's a shame for him.'

Masterly understatement indeed.

Michael Roberts

Former rival salutes Hill's return to the front

TV television commentator Martin Brundle offered a generous tribute to Damon Hill's efforts in the aftermath of the World Champion's run to second place in the Hungarian Grand Prix.

'That was a great drive by any standards,' said the former F1 driver and Le Mans winner, who had been invited by Benetton to shake down the team's cars at Silverstone in preparation for the Hungarian race.

'Damon must have gained enormous satisfaction from it bearing in mind that here was a reigning World Champion who had made a controversial choice of team, then stood up in the winter and predicted that he would win another Grand Prix this season, to the accompaniment, it must be said, of a certain amount of sniggering,' said Brundle.

'Yet it was a bitter-sweet moment. If he'd won, it would have been a classic victory which everybody would have talked about for ages. He's won 20 Grands Prix, so really second place doesn't mean that much to him. It would have gone down in history as a great win – the first for Arrows, the first for Bridgestone, the first for Yamaha – which he certainly deserved.

'It is easy to say, well, he was on Bridgestones and they worked better than the opposition. But where were the other Bridgestone runners? Where was his team-mate?

'That, for me, puts it all in perspective.'

MARLBORO
MAGYAR NAGYDIJ
8–10 AUGUST 1997
HUNGARORING

Race distance: 77 laps, 189.851 miles/305.536 km

Race weather: Dry, hot and sunny

FORMULA 1 WORLD CHAMPIONSHIP

ROUND **11**

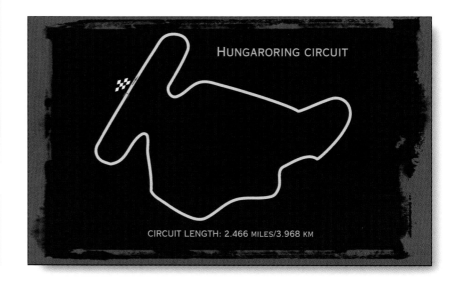

HUNGARORING CIRCUIT

CIRCUIT LENGTH: 2.466 MILES/3.968 KM

Pos.	Driver	Nat.	No.	Entrant	Car/Engine	Tyres	Laps	Time/Retirement	Speed (mph/km/h)
1	Jacques Villeneuve	CDN	3	Rothmans Williams Renault	Williams FW19-Renault RS9A V10	G	77	1h 45m 47.149s	107.680/173.295
2	Damon Hill	GB	1	Danka Arrows Yamaha	Arrows A18-Yamaha OX11A/D V10	B	77	1h 45m 56.228s	107.526/173.047
3	Johnny Herbert	GB	16	Red Bull Sauber Petronas	Sauber C16-Petronas V10	G	77	1h 46m 07.594s	107.334/172.738
4	Michael Schumacher	D	5	Scuderia Ferrari Marlboro	Ferrari F310B 046/2 V10	G	77	1h 46m 17.650s	107.165/172.466
5	Ralf Schumacher	D	11	B&H Total Jordan Peugeot	Jordan 197-Peugeot A14 V10	G	77	1h 46m 17.864s	107.161/172.460
6	Shinji Nakano	J	15	Prost Gauloises Blondes	Prost JS45-Mugen Honda MF301HB V10	B	77	1h 46m 28.661s	106.981/172.169
7	Jarno Trulli	I	14	Prost Gauloises Blondes	Prost JS45-Mugen Honda MF301HB V10	B	77	1h 47m 02.701s	106.413/171.256
8	Gerhard Berger	A	8	Mild Seven Benetton Renault	Benetton B197-Renault RS9A V10	G	77	1h 47m 03.558s	106.399/171.233
9	Eddie Irvine	GB	6	Scuderia Ferrari Marlboro	Ferrari F310B 046/2 V10	G	76	Collision with Nakano	
10	Ukyo Katayama	J	20	Minardi Team	Minardi M197-Hart 830 V8	B	76		
11	Jean Alesi	F	7	Mild Seven Benetton Renault	Benetton B197-Renault RS9A V10	G	76		
12	Tarso Marques	BR	21	Minardi Team	Minardi M197-Hart 830 V8	B	75		
13	Mika Salo	SF	19	Tyrrell	Tyrrell 025-Ford ED5 V8	G	75		
	David Coulthard	GB	10	West McLaren Mercedes	McLaren MP4/12-Mercedes FO110F V10	G	65	Alternator	
	Jos Verstappen	NL	18	Tyrrell	Tyrrell 025-Ford ED5 V8	G	61	Pneumatic leak	
	Pedro Diniz	BR	2	Danka Arrows Yamaha	Arrows A18-Yamaha OX11A/D V10	B	53	Alternator	
	Giancarlo Fisichella	I	12	B&H Total Jordan Peugeot	Jordan 197-Peugeot A14 V10	G	42	Spun off	
	Heinz-Harald Frentzen	D	4	Rothmans Williams Renault	Williams FW19-Renault RS9A V10	G	29	Fuel valve	
	Rubens Barrichello	BR	22	Stewart Ford	Stewart SF1-Ford Zetec-R V10	B	29	Engine	
	Mika Häkkinen	SF	9	West McLaren Mercedes	McLaren MP4/12-Mercedes FO110F V10	G	12	Hydraulics	
	Gianni Morbidelli	I	17	Red Bull Sauber Petronas	Sauber C16-Petronas V10	G	7	Engine	
	Jan Magnussen	DK	23	Stewart Ford	Stewart SF1-Ford Zetec-R V10	B	5	Collision damage	

Fastest lap: Frentzen, on lap 25, 1m 18.372s, 113.256 mph/182.269 km/h.

Lap record: Nigel Mansell (F1 Williams FW14B-Renault V10), 1m 18.308s, 113.349 mph/182.418 km/h (1992).

B – Bridgestone   G – Goodyear

Grid order	1 2 3 4 5 6 7 8 9 10 11 12 13 14 15 16 17 18 19 20 21 22 23 24 25 26 27 28 29 30 31 32 33 34 35 36 37 38 39 40 41 42 43 44 45 46 47 48 49 50 51 52 53 54 55 56 57 58 59 60
5 M. SCHUMACHER	5 5 5 5 5 5 5 5 5 1 1 1 1 1 1 1 1 1 1 1 1 1 1 4 4 4 4 1 1 1 1 1 1 1 1 1 1 1 1 1 1 1 1 1 1 1 1 1 1 1 1 1 1 1 1 1 1 1 1 1
3 VILLENEUVE	1 1 1 1 1 1 1 1 1 5 5 5 3 3 3 3 3 3 3 3 3 4 4 1 1 1 3 3 3 3 3 3 3 3 3 3 3 3 3 3 3 3 3 3 3 3 3 3 3 3 3 3 3 3 3 3 3 3 3 3
1 HILL	6 6 6 6 6 9 9 9 9 9 9 3 4 4 4 4 4 4 4 4 4 3 16 16 3 3 3 10 10 10 10 10 10 10 10 10 10 10 10 10 10 10 10 10 10 10 10 10 10 10 10 10 10 10 10 10 10 10 10 10
9 HÄKKINEN	9 9 9 9 9 3 3 3 3 3 3 4 10 10 10 10 10 10 10 10 10 10 3 3 10 10 10 5 5 5 5 16 16 16 16 16 16 16 16 16 16 16 16 16 16 16 16 16 5 6 6 6 6 6 16 16 16 16
6 IRVINE	3 3 3 3 3 4 4 4 4 16 16 16 16 16 16 16 16 16 16 16 10 10 12 5 5 16 16 16 16 5 5 5 5 5 5 5 5 5 5 5 5 5 5 5 11 16 16 16 16 16 5 5 5 5
4 FRENTZEN	4 4 4 4 4 10 10 10 10 10 10 16 5 7 7 7 7 7 7 14 14 14 14 5 12 16 6 6 6 6 12 12 12 12 12 12 12 15 15 15 15 15 15 11 6 6 6 16 16 16 16 16 5 5 5 5
8 BERGER	10 10 10 10 10 10 16 16 16 16 16 7 7 14 14 14 14 14 14 22 22 22 12 15 15 16 6 12 12 12 12 6 15 15 15 15 15 15 15 11 11 11 11 11 6 6 6 16 16 15 11 11 11 15 15 15
10 COULTHARD	16 16 16 16 16 7 7 7 7 7 7 14 14 22 22 22 22 22 22 12 12 12 15 5 16 6 12 14 14 14 15 15 15 14 14 14 14 11 11 11 6 6 6 6 15 15 15 15 15 11 15 15 6 6 6
7 ALESI	7 7 7 7 7 6 9 14 14 14 22 22 12 12 12 12 12 12 7 11 11 22 14 6 14 14 15 15 15 14 14 11 11 11 11 14 14 14 14 14 14 7 7 7 7 14 14 14 14 14 14 14 14 14
16 HERBERT	8 8 8 8 8 14 22 22 22 12 12 11 11 11 11 11 11 11 11 15 15 5 6 14 22 22 11 11 11 11 11 11 6 6 6 6 6 6 7 7 7 20 20 14 14 14 7 2 2 20 8 8 8 8 8
22 BARRICHELLO	14 14 14 14 14 14 22 12 12 12 12 12 15 15 15 15 15 15 15 5 5 11 22 22 11 11 7 7 7 7 7 7 7 7 7 20 20 14 8 8 8 2 20 20 8 20 20 20 20 20 20
14 TRULLI	22 22 22 22 22 22 22 12 11 11 11 11 11 15 5 5 5 5 5 5 5 7 6 11 11 11 11 18 18 18 18 18 18 2 2 2 2 2 20 20 14 8 8 2 2 20 20 20 8 7 7 7 7 7 7
12 FISICHELLA	12 12 12 12 12 12 12 11 15 15 15 8 8 8 8 6 6 6 6 6 7 8 7 7 7 2 2 2 2 2 2 20 20 20 20 20 8 8 2 2 20 20 20 8 7 7 18 18 18 18 18 18
11 R. SCHUMACHER	11 11 11 11 11 11 11 11 15 8 8 8 8 18 18 6 6 8 8 8 8 8 8 7 18 18 20 20 20 20 20 20 20 18 8 8 8 8 18 18 18 18 18 18 18 18 18 21 21 21 21 21 21
17 MORBIDELLI	15 15 15 15 15 15 15 18 18 18 18 20 20 6 20 20 20 20 21 21 18 18 18 18 2 2 2 8 8 8 8 8 8 18 18 18 18 18 21 21 21 21 21 21 21 21 21 21 19 19 19 19 19 19
15 NAKANO	18 18 18 18 18 18 20 18 20 20 20 19 6 20 19 21 21 18 18 18 2 2 2 2 20 20 19 19 19 19 19 19 19 19 19 19 19 19 19 19 19 19 19 19 19 19 19
23 MAGNUSSEN	20 20 20 20 20 18 20 19 19 19 19 6 19 19 21 21 19 18 18 2 2 19 20 19 21 21 21 21 21 21 21 21 21
18 VERSTAPPEN	19 19 19 19 19 19 19 21 21 21 21 21 21 18 18 18 2 2 19 20 19 19 19 8 8 8
2 DINIZ	21 21 21 21 21 21 21 2 2 2 2 6 2 2 2 2 19 19 20 20 21 21 21 21 21 21
20 KATAYAMA	2 2 2 2 2 2 2 6 6 6 6 6 2
19 SALO	17 17 17 17 17 17 17 17
21 MARQUES	23 23 23 23 23

Pit stop

One lap behind leader

STARTING GRID

5 **M. SCHUMACHER** Ferrari	3 **VILLENEUVE** Williams
1 **HILL** Arrows	9 **HÄKKINEN** McLaren
6 **IRVINE** Ferrari	4 **FRENTZEN** Williams
8 **BERGER** Benetton	10 **COULTHARD** McLaren
7 **ALESI** Benetton	16 **HERBERT** Sauber
22 **BARRICHELLO** Stewart	14 **TRULLI** Prost
12 **FISICHELLA** Jordan	11 **R. SCHUMACHER** Jordan
17 **MORBIDELLI** Sauber	15 **NAKANO** Prost
23 **MAGNUSSEN** Stewart	18 **VERSTAPPEN** Tyrrell
2 **DINIZ** Arrows	20 **KATAYAMA** Minardi
19 **SALO** Tyrrell	21 **MARQUES** Minardi

61 62 63 64 65 66 67 68 69 70 71 72 73 74 75 76 77	
1 1 1 1 1 1 1 1 1 1 1 1 1 1 1 1 3	1
3 3 3 3 3 3 3 3 3 3 3 3 3 3 3 3 1	2
10 10 10 10 10 16 16 16 16 16 16 16 16 16 16 16 16	3
16 16 16 16 16 5 5 5 5 5 5 5 5 5 5 5 5	4
5 5 5 5 5 11 11 11 11 11 11 11 11 11 11 11 11	5
11 11 11 11 11 6 6 6 6 6 6 6 6 6 6 6 15	6
15 15 15 15 6 15 15 15 15 15 15 15 15 15 15 15 14	
6 6 6 6 15 14 14 14 14 14 14 14 14 14 14 14 8	
14 14 14 14 14 8 8 8 8 8 8 8 8 8 8 8	
8 8 8 8 8 20 20 20 20 20 20 20 20 20 20 20	
20 20 20 20 20 7 7 7 7 7 7 7 7 7 7	
7 7 7 7 7 21 21 21 21 21 21 21 21 21 21	
21 21 21 21 21 19 19 19 19 19 19 19 19 19 19	
18 19 19 19 19	
19	

TIME SHEETS

QUALIFYING

Weather: Dry, hot and sunny

Pos.	Driver	Car	Laps	Time
1	Michael Schumacher	Ferrari	11	1m 14.672s
2	Jacques Villeneuve	Williams-Renault	11	1m 14.859s
3	Damon Hill	Arrows-Yamaha	12	1m 15.044s
4	Mika Häkkinen	McLaren-Mercedes	10	1m 15.140s
5	Eddie Irvine	Ferrari	11	1m 15.424s
6	Heinz-Harald Frentzen	Williams-Renault	12	1m 15.520s
7	Gerhard Berger	Benetton-Renault	9	1m 15.699s
8	David Coulthard	McLaren-Mercedes	11	1m 15.705s
9	Jean Alesi	Benetton-Renault	12	1m 15.905s
10	Johnny Herbert	Sauber-Petronas	12	1m 16.138s
11	Rubens Barrichello	Stewart-Ford	12	1m 16.138s
12	Jarno Trulli	Prost-Mugen Honda	12	1m 16.297s
13	Giancarlo Fisichella	Jordan-Peugeot	12	1m 16.300s
14	Ralf Schumacher	Jordan-Peugeot	12	1m 16.686s
15	Gianni Morbidelli	Sauber-Petronas	12	1m 16.766s
16	Shinji Nakano	Prost-Mugen Honda	12	1m 16.784s
17	Jan Magnussen	Stewart-Ford	12	1m 16.858s
18	Jos Verstappen	Tyrrell-Ford	12	1m 17.095s
19	Pedro Diniz	Arrows-Yamaha	12	1m 17.118s
20	Ukyo Katayama	Minardi-Hart	12	1m 17.232s
21	Mika Salo	Tyrrell-Ford	11	1m 17.482s
22	Tarso Marques	Minardi-Hart	11	1m 18.020s

FRIDAY FREE PRACTICE

Weather: Sunny and bright

Pos.	Driver	Laps	Time
1	Michael Schumacher	16	1m 17.583s
2	David Coulthard	24	1m 17.810s
3	Jarno Trulli	29	1m 17.848s
4	Heinz-Harald Frentzen	26	1m 17.884s
5	Damon Hill	14	1m 18.161s
6	Ralf Schumacher	21	1m 18.368s
7	Rubens Barrichello	21	1m 18.565s
8	Giancarlo Fisichella	29	1m 18.686s
9	Eddie Irvine	17	1m 18.734s
10	Johnny Herbert	28	1m 18.796s
11	Jacques Villeneuve	29	1m 18.805s
12	Jan Magnussen	19	1m 18.856s
13	Gerhard Berger	24	1m 18.923s
14	Jos Verstappen	30	1m 19.346s
15	Jean Alesi	18	1m 19.358s
16	Ukyo Katayama	30	1m 19.521s
17	Gianni Morbidelli	29	1m 19.567s
18	Pedro Diniz	21	1m 20.002s
19	Mika Salo	29	1m 20.106s
20	Mika Häkkinen	21	1m 20.176s
21	Shinji Nakano	30	1m 20.414s
22	Tarso Marques	22	1m 20.707s

SATURDAY FREE PRACTICE

Weather: Warm, light overcast

Pos.	Driver	Laps	Time
1	Heinz-Harald Frentzen	25	1m 15.431s
2	Jacques Villeneuve	24	1m 15.500s
3	Mika Häkkinen	21	1m 15.839s
4	David Coulthard	27	1m 15.998s
5	Michael Schumacher	26	1m 16.032s
6	Jarno Trulli	30	1m 16.175s
7	Jean Alesi	25	1m 16.205s
8	Eddie Irvine	24	1m 16.274s
9	Ralf Schumacher	27	1m 16.343s
10	Gerhard Berger	29	1m 16.373s
11	Damon Hill	28	1m 16.556s
12	Johnny Herbert	30	1m 16.739s
13	Shinji Nakano	29	1m 16.841s
14	Pedro Diniz	19	1m 17.117s
15	Rubens Barrichello	22	1m 17.129s
16	Ukyo Katayama	26	1m 17.605s
17	Giancarlo Fisichella	14	1m 17.757s
18	Jan Magnussen	16	1m 17.864s
19	Jos Verstappen	27	1m 18.025s
20	Gianni Morbidelli	23	1m 18.043s
21	Mika Salo	27	1m 18.087s
22	Tarso Marques	11	1m 19.912s

WARM-UP

Weather: Hot and dry

Pos.	Driver	Laps	Time
1	Michael Schumacher	16	1m 16.996s
2	Jacques Villeneuve	14	1m 17.393s
3	Mika Häkkinen	15	1m 17.579s
4	Heinz-Harald Frentzen	15	1m 17.614s
5	Pedro Diniz	18	1m 17.696s
6	Eddie Irvine	14	1m 17.781s
7	Gerhard Berger	13	1m 17.875s
8	Ukyo Katayama	15	1m 17.890s
9	Damon Hill	12	1m 17.953s
10	Johnny Herbert	15	1m 18.050s
11	Jarno Trulli	17	1m 18.114s
12	Shinji Nakano	13	1m 18.499s
13	Gianni Morbidelli	12	1m 18.632s
14	Jean Alesi	9	1m 19.013s
15	Rubens Barrichello	9	1m 19.122s
16	Giancarlo Fisichella	16	1m 19.145s
17	David Coulthard	10	1m 19.246s
18	Jos Verstappen	14	1m 19.332s
19	Ralf Schumacher	10	1m 19.673s
20	Jan Magnussen	13	1m 20.154s
21	Mika Salo	9	1m 20.432s
22	Tarso Marques	15	1m 20.778s

RACE FASTEST LAPS

Weather: Dry, hot and sunny

Driver	Time	Lap
Heinz-Harald Frentzen	1m 18.372s	25
Jacques Villeneuve	1m 19.066s	15
Giancarlo Fisichella	1m 19.366s	37
Eddie Irvine	1m 19.527s	44
Damon Hill	1m 19.648s	13
Ralf Schumacher	1m 19.651s	48
Michael Schumacher	1m 19.684s	28
Gerhard Berger	1m 19.923s	52
Shinji Nakano	1m 20.003s	26
Mika Häkkinen	1m 20.161s	4
Pedro Diniz	1m 20.317s	46
David Coulthard	1m 20.329s	19
Jean Alesi	1m 20.573s	57
Johnny Herbert	1m 20.606s	28
Ukyo Katayama	1m 20.672s	46
Jarno Trulli	1m 21.074s	71
Gianni Morbidelli	1m 21.167s	4
Rubens Barrichello	1m 21.409s	23
Mika Salo	1m 21.578s	67
Jan Magnussen	1m 21.628s	3
Jos Verstappen	1m 21.676s	43
Tarso Marques	1m 21.874s	45

CHASSIS LOG BOOK

1	Hill	Arrows A18/5
2	Diniz	Arrows A18/4
	spare	Arrows A18/3
3	Villeneuve	Williams FW19/4
4	Frentzen	Williams FW19/5
	spare	Williams FW19/3
5	M. Schumacher	Ferrari F310B/178
6	Irvine	Ferrari F310B/173
	spare	Ferrari F310B/175
7	Alesi	Benetton B197/2
8	Berger	Benetton B197/4
	spare	Benetton B197/3
9	Häkkinen	McLaren MP4/12/5
10	Coulthard	McLaren MP4/12/6
	spare	McLaren MP4/12/3
11	R. Schumacher	Jordan 197/6
12	Fisichella	Jordan 197/4
	spare	Jordan 197/1
14	Trulli	Prost JS45/3
15	Nakano	Prost JS45/2
	spare	Prost JS45/1
16	Herbert	Sauber C16/3
17	Morbidelli	Sauber C16/6
	spare	Sauber C16/5
18	Verstappen	Tyrrell 025/4
19	Salo	Tyrrell 025/1
	spare	Tyrrell 025/3
20	Katayama	Minardi M197/4
21	Marques	Minardi M197/2
	spare	Minardi M197/1
22	Barrichello	Stewart SF1/2
23	Magnussen	Stewart SF1/3
	spare	Stewart SF1/1

POINTS TABLES

Drivers

1	Michael Schumacher	56
2	Jacques Villeneuve	53
3	Jean Alesi	22
4	Gerhard Berger	20
5	Heinz-Harald Frentzen	19
6	Eddie Irvine	18
7	Olivier Panis	15
8 =	David Coulthard	14
8 =	Mika Häkkinen	14
10 =	Ralf Schumacher	11
10 =	Johnny Herbert	11
12	Giancarlo Fisichella	8
13	Damon Hill	7
14	Rubens Barrichello	6
15	Alexander Wurz	4
16	Jarno Trulli	3
17 =	Mika Salo	2
17 =	Shinji Nakano	2
19	Nicola Larini	1

Constructors

1	Ferrari	74
2	Williams	72
3	Benetton	46
4	McLaren	28
5	Prost	20
6	Jordan	19
7	Sauber	12
8	Arrows	7
9	Stewart	6
10	Tyrrell	2

Michael Roberts

BELGIAN
grand prix

M. SCHUMACHER

FISICHELLA

FRENTZEN

HERBERT

VILLENEUVE

BERGER

FIA WORLD CHAMPIONSHIP • ROUND 12

For the first time in Grand Prix history, the race was started behind a pace car. Jacques Villeneuve, Michael Schumacher and the rest of the field dutifully follow the Mercedes C230K, handled with great skill by former British F3 Champion Oliver Gavin, around the treacherous circuit. On the podium after the race *(left)*, Michael smiles contentedly as he reflects on his overwhelming victory, well aware that the decision to use the safety car in this way had played into his hands.

SPA QUALIFYING

Left: Pedro Diniz qualified a stunning eighth fastest, lining up one place ahead of team-mate Damon Hill, and went on to outshine the World Champion in the race.

Mika Häkkinen *(below left)* was left winded when his McLaren suffered a suspension breakage at nearly 200 mph on Saturday morning and smashed into the plastic barriers at Les Combes.

While Ferrari's Ross Brawn *(below right)* keeps an eye on Michael Schumacher's qualifying efforts, Satoru Nakajima *(bottom right)* looks for signs of progress at Tyrrell, where he fills the role of sporting director.

ASTUTE tyre choice and the benefit of the first three laps of the Belgian Grand Prix being run at reduced speed on a near-flooded track behind the safety car enabled Michael Schumacher to deliver yet another dominant performance at Spa-Francorchamps, his third straight victory at this, one of the most demanding and charismatic circuits on the World Championship trail.

It was also Schumacher's fourth victory of the season, propelling him 12 points clear of arch-rival Jacques Villeneuve, who trailed home sixth after a tactically disastrous race for the Williams-Renault squad.

After qualifying third, Schumacher held off from making a final decision as to which car set-up he would use until he had completed a final pre-race reconnaissance lap after a torrential rain shower doused the circuit just 20 minutes before the scheduled start time.

As his key rivals sat on the grid with full rain tyres, Michael switched at the last moment to the spare, heavier F310B with a light fuel load, the latest 046/2 engine and a medium wet/dry chassis set-up, rather than his new lightweight chassis which had been prepared for dry conditions and which he had also taken on an earlier reconnaissance lap.

Even so, the track was still far too wet for the intermediate tyres he had opted for to seriously come into their own, but the decision to start the race at reduced speed behind Oliver Gavin in the Mercedes C230K safety car gave Schumacher another crucial three laps' respite during which the track dried out sufficiently for him to capitalise on his audacious choice of set-up.

'When I saw the sun coming out as I sat on the starting grid, I smiled to myself and thought I had made the right decision,' he said. 'I made some last-minute adjustments to the wing settings on the grid, but I would certainly have been in trouble without those early laps behind the safety car before the track began to dry a little.'

Rather less astute was the Ferrari driver's younger brother Ralf, who ventured out onto his first reconnaissance lap on slicks, paying the price for this over-confidence by crashing his Jordan-Peugeot at Blanchimont.

He was then faced with the challenge of jogging the best part of a mile back to the pits to take over the spare 197. By that time the grid had been closed, so he started on full wets from the pit lane. Jarno Trulli was another in trouble, his Prost failing to fire up on the grid due to waterlogged

Friday's free practice session was all about wet-weather performance as the rain poured down in typical Spa style. This enabled Rubens Barrichello's Stewart and Damon Hill's Arrows to demonstrate again the potential of Bridgestone's rain tyres by posting third- and fourth-fastest times behind the Benettons of Gerhard Berger and Jean Alesi.

Berger and Alesi had set their times earlier in the session when the track conditions were at their least wet. Both used Goodyear rubber, the development of which attracted obliquely subtle criticism from both Ferrari drivers, Michael Schumacher and Eddie Irvine, who set fifth- and 14th-fastest times respectively.

'I am reasonably happy with today's session,' said Schumacher, who needed no lessons about car control in the wet. 'But if these conditions persist for the race, tyre choice will be the determining factor. Goodyear have brought types of tyre here which work well in two conditions, whereas the other supplier [Bridgestone] seems to have an advantage in a third type of track condition.'

Schumacher was referring to the effectiveness of Bridgestone's full-wet rubber, used when the track conditions are saturated. He was clearly nervous that Goodyear might be lagging slightly behind and wasn't reluctant to speak his mind.

Happily for the Goodyear contingent, Saturday's weather was much better. In humid and overcast conditions, the track surface was wet from the start of free practice, but steadily dried out during the 90-minute session. This was red-flagged to a halt on no fewer than three occasions, the worst incident being when Mika Häkkinen's McLaren MP4/12 suffered a rear suspension failure at almost 200 mph approaching Les Combes.

The car's left-rear lower suspension toe-link control rod suffered a structural failure with the result that this corner of the car virtually disintegrated, the wheel flying off as well for good measure. The McLaren slewed wildly out of control before slamming head-on into a plastic barrier in the escape road. Although he lay down to recover immediately after climbing from the cockpit, the Finn was only winded and was soon back in the paddock after a precautionary check over in the circuit medical centre.

The session was also stopped when Jarno Trulli spun and stalled his Prost out on the circuit with the car unable to be released from gear, then again when Gianni Morbidelli's Sauber glanced the pit wall exiting the final chicane.

Jacques Villeneuve was in superb form throughout qualifying, planting his Williams FW19 on pole position 0.3s ahead of Alesi's Benetton. 'The car was really good in the dry,' he enthused. 'We had only 45 minutes of dry testing [in the morning], but from the first lap of qualifying the car was great.

'The track was very grippy at the start of the session – grippier than this morning – but towards the end when the sun picked up, it started to become a little bit slippery. Whatever the weather is tomorrow, I think we have a very strong car.'

Alesi was also well satisfied with the feel of his Benetton, but Schumacher was certainly struggling with the Ferrari. He seemed unable to work out a decent handling balance with his latest lightweight chassis and switched to the earlier-spec spare to qualify third. Yet the fact that he was only 0.843s away from pole on this challenging 4.329-mile track said a great deal for his grit and determination.

Giancarlo Fisichella did an excellent job to qualify fourth ahead of the bruised Häkkinen and Ralf Schumacher in the other Jordan. The young German was forced to switch to the spare car after suffering

engine problems on his third set of tyres, finding that his replacement machine understeered too much, especially in the left-hand corners.

Frentzen just got lost with his Williams set-up, causing a few more raised eyebrows in the paddock and frustration among his crew. The sight of a Williams-Renault sitting on the fourth row of the grid alongside an Arrows-Yamaha – and one driven by Pedro Diniz, at that – was certainly rather hard to explain.

It had been a difficult afternoon for Frentzen. On his third run he understeered onto the kerb at Les Combes and crashed his race chassis, switching to the spare car for the rest of the session.

'However, it was set up for Jacques,' he explained, 'and when I went out there was too much traffic, so I did not have an opportunity to attack on my last outing.'

All in all, it was a bad day for second drivers. While Diniz pipped Damon Hill to eighth place on the grid, this was a marginal advantage probably caused by the fact that Damon risked running too little wing angle late in the session and paid the price accordingly. But to have both Arrows-Yamahas qualifying in the top ten on this fast circuit was no mean achievement.

In the McLaren-Mercedes camp, David Coulthard was unhappy with the balance of his MP4/12, qualifying five places behind Häkkinen in tenth place. Gerhard Berger had a rear sus-

pension pick-up point breakage on his Benetton coming past the pits, after which he had to limp round the entire lap before he could take over the spare car. 'No grip and no balance,' was his crisp verdict on the latter machine, having slipped to 15th in the grid order.

In 11th place, Johnny Herbert was struggling with a number of minor problems in the Sauber-Petronas. On his first run he found the race car bottoming a bit too much through Eau Rouge, but after the ride height was raised he was troubled with a worrying vibration through the chassis. He switched to the spare car and was balked by Tarso Marques's Minardi, so that was the end of that. Team-mate Morbidelli wound up 13th, not bad considering he had lost much of the morning free practice session.

Jarno Trulli was a disappointed 14th, separated from Prost team-mate Shinji Nakano by Berger's Benetton, both men struggling to work out a decent chassis balance.

In 17th place, Eddie Irvine had been suffering rotten luck virtually from the start of practice. He was excluded from Friday free practice after beaching his Ferrari over the 'Bus Stop' chicane after a spin, having received outside assistance to get it going again. On Saturday he grappled first with oversteer, then understeer. All three qualifying runs were fraught with problems, consigning him to a ninth-row start.

Rubens Barrichello did well to qualify 12th for Stewart-Ford, but Jan Magnussen was struggling slightly six places further back. His fleeting moment of glory would come during the race. Meanwhile, Ford's other runner, Tyrrell, benefited from further modified ED5 V8 engines, but on this fast circuit the modest power increment was nowhere near enough. Mika Salo qualified 19th but Jos Verstappen dumped his car in the gravel at Rivage on his third flying lap, and although the spare 025 was set up for him, by the time he returned to the pits the session was all but over.

That meant that the Dutchman shared the final row of the grid with Marques's Minardi, the other Hart-engined car of Ukyo Katayama qualifying 20th in a session blighted by clutch problems.

Mark Thompson/Allsport

Michael Cooper/Allsport

Sporting Pictures (UK)

197

Photos: Paul-Henri Cahier

electrics, after which he switched to the spare and started a lap down.

Meanwhile, one man going out to the starting grid with mixed feelings was McLaren's Mika Häkkinen, who lined up in fifth place. The previous day a routine check of a fuel sample taken from his car had revealed that it did not match the gas chromatograph 'fingerprint' which had been lodged by the team prior to the race.

McLaren was fined $25,000 and Häkkinen's time was disallowed, seemingly consigning him to the back of the grid. But the team lodged an appeal and Mika duly took up his place on the third row, but with the prospect of his entrant having to account for its actions in front of an FIA Court of Appeal. He was keeping his fingers crossed.

Of all the drivers out on the circuit, the one under the greatest pressure was Gavin as he led the pack round in a ball of spray, mindful that he needed to lap quickly enough to keep the F1 drivers comfortable without flinging his machine off the glisteningly slippery road. He did a fine job, averaging well over 70 mph on his quickest lap a few yards ahead of Villeneuve.

In his wake, potential problems were already in the pipeline. Häkkinen's McLaren slid off the road on the opening lap, the Finn losing his place in the grid order to the Williams of Heinz-Harald Frentzen and Pedro Diniz's Arrows. Mika then regained his fifth place just before the safety car pulled off at the end of lap three, allowing the pack to be unleashed.

This was in contravention of Article 157 of the F1 Sporting Code, which forbids overtaking while the safety car is out on the circuit, a slip which would later attract a protest from the Williams team. As things turned out, there was even worse in store for Häkkinen and the McLaren squad.

As Gavin peeled off into the pits, Villeneuve immediately sprang into a 1.5s lead from Alesi and Michael Schumacher, but the Ferrari ace was now in his element as a dry line began to appear all round the circuit.

At the end of lap four, Schumacher aimed confidently down the inside of Alesi's Benetton going into La Source. For a split-second it looked as though Jean might be considering a counter-attack, but he wisely thought twice.

Another brilliant performance from the fast-maturing Giancarlo Fisichella brought Jordan second place.

Bottom: Jacques Villeneuve discusses the prospects for the race with Patrick Head. Williams misjudged the changing track conditions and the Canadian had to be satisfied with a sixth-place finish.

The Ferrari was past, sailing away through Eau Rouge in hot pursuit of Villeneuve's Williams.

By the time they reached Les Combes, Schumacher had the Ferrari right on Villeneuve's tail and, as they braked for the downhill Rivage right-hander, Michael had no compunction about going off-line to relieve Jacques and the Williams team of their lead.

Alesi was still third at the end of the lap, but next time round Fisichella swept round the outside of him at Les Combes to take the position while Schumacher came through to complete lap six an amazing 16.9s ahead.

By this time Villeneuve was seriously thinking in terms of intermediates, asking the Williams pit over the radio where he was likely to resume if he came in at the end of the lap. 'Probably 16th, so stay out,' came the reply after a quick calculation. Yet, despite this, without warning Jacques appeared in the pit lane at the end of lap six for a hurried stop which immediately dropped him to 18th.

At first glance, it looked as though he'd been forced into overshooting the 'Bus Stop' chicane under pressure from Fisichella, but Jacques would later deny this. Even so, it was a major setback to his challenge as he had to come in again for slicks, and fuel, at the end of lap 11, which dropped him back to 15th again.

Lap seven saw Alesi make his first refuelling stop, dropping from fourth to 15th, while next time round both Frentzen and Barrichello came in to make the change to slicks.

This left Schumacher 28.42s ahead of Fisichella, but this advantage expanded to 41.86s ahead of Häkkinen's McLaren when the Italian brought the Jordan in for slicks and refuelling at the end of lap ten. At the same time, Hill made a disastrous call for intermediates, unlike teammate Pedro Diniz, who waited another two laps before bringing his Arrows in for slicks.

On lap 12 Häkkinen straight-lined the ess-bend at Les Combes before bringing the second-place McLaren in for a 6.1s stop, switching to slicks before resuming in fourth behind Alesi and Fisichella. This left Schumacher's Ferrari over a minute ahead of the pack, allowing Michael to make an 8.1s stop to fit slicks at the end of lap 14, Alesi still trailing by 40 seconds when the Ferrari accelerated back into the fray.

Now the order was Schumacher, Alesi, Fisichella, Häkkinen, Herbert, Coulthard and Frentzen. Unfortunately Coulthard's weekend would finish on a

Hill and McLaren fail to strike a deal

DESPITE persistent rumours that the Mercedes-Benz board would have delighted in a partnership between McLaren and Damon Hill, the 1996 World Champion proved unable to strike a deal with Ron Dennis after weeks of speculation and anticipation.

After preliminary negotiations fell through, McLaren and Mercedes confirmed at Spa that they would be retaining the services of Mika Häkkinen and David Coulthard *(below)* for 1998. For his part, Hill felt that the team had been guilty of bad faith and a certain lack of seriousness in terms of the proposal which was put to him.

'I would like to clarify the recent speculation regarding the possibility of me driving for McLaren-Mercedes,' said Hill. 'There were negotiations over recent weeks, during which time an offer to drive for the team in 1998 was made. After consideration of the terms of the offer I felt I was left with no alternative but to reject it.

'It did not accord with what I had previously been led to believe from our prior negotiations, and I did not consider that it demonstrated a serious commitment to me as a driver from McLaren-Mercedes.'

Hill's seriousness of purpose was sounded out by initial offers of a $2 million (£1.4 million) retainer to be supplemented by a $1 million (£700,000) bonus for every win he scored up to a specified maximum.

Perhaps unsurprisingly, Hill immediately rejected this as a derisory offer, frankly doubting that McLaren was serious, and feeling that his status in the F1 community called for a larger up-front payment. He remained unshaken in his belief that he was worth more on the strength of his proven ability to string together sufficient sustained success to win a World Championship title.

This cut no ice with the pragmatic Dennis, who clearly felt that recruiting Adrian Newey – ironically the man credited for much of the performance advantage displayed by Hill's title-winning Williams FW18 last year – as the team's technical director could give his cars the sort of edge Hill enjoyed when he won the championship.

The memory of Nigel Mansell's abortive foray in a McLaren-Mercedes two years earlier also haunts Dennis's memory. He needed to establish whether or not Hill was still committed and hungry to win.

Sources close to McLaren hinted that the team in fact never entered into detailed negotiations with Hill. The financial terms offered seemed to be non-negotiable, as if McLaren were testing the 1996 World Champion's seriousness of purpose. Häkkinen and Coulthard were offered similar packages.

The McLaren boss would not be drawn into a war of words with Hill over their failure to reach an agreement. 'Our press release says it all,' he said, referring to the bulletin announcing the decision to retain Coulthard and Häkkinen.

Diana Burnett

Panis to stay with Prost

OLIVIER Panis made a welcome return to the F1 community at Spa, the Frenchman now walking unaided after a remarkable recovery from the two broken legs he sustained when he crashed his Prost-Mugen Honda during the Canadian Grand Prix in June.

As a boost to his morale, Alain Prost announced that his fellow Frenchman had signed a new contract to race with the team at least until the end of 1999.

'To my eyes, Olivier represents a cornerstone of the team,' said Prost. 'He proved this behind the wheel early in the season, and this was later confirmed during his absence because we have missed his experience.'

The Prost team also announced a three-year extension of its title sponsorship deal with La Seita, the privatised company which used to hold a monopoly of tobacco sales in France, under its Gauloises Blondes banner.

Photos: Mark Thompson/Allsport

disappointing note midway round lap 20 when he lost control, pressing a little too strongly on slicks, having been overtaken by Frentzen's Williams for sixth place three laps earlier.

'I had been quite happy with the first part of the race until my intermediate tyres started to go off,' he reflected later. 'I was pushing a little too hard and mounted a kerb with my left-front tyre, which pitched me into a spin and out of the race.'

Alesi made his second stop on lap 23, dropping from second to fifth and allowing Fisichella and Häkkinen back into second and third places. The young Italian was driving with enormous maturity and precision, and although Häkkinen began cutting into his second-place advantage Fisichella never looked like being ruffled or losing his composure.

Lap 22 had seen Ralf Schumacher's misery end as he spun off again, hitting the guard rail hard on the right-hander after Les Combes, the German driver possibly wondering why his early-season promise had evaporated so disappointingly in the second half of the campaign.

On lap 24 Frentzen made his second stop, dropping from fourth to seventh, having been locked in a battle with Herbert for many laps, the Sauber driver eventually having to let him past but not without showing great spirit before doing so.

Schumacher Senior made his second stop without fuss on lap 29, resuming 47.9s ahead of Fisichella as Häkkinen also came in for a second time. Lap 31 saw Fisichella (7.0s), Herbert (7.4s) and Villeneuve (7.9s) make their second stops, but next time round Alesi came back in for a third time, unnerved by a strange feeling of instability at the rear of his Benetton. It was later discovered that some bolts securing the Jabroc plank beneath the car – which makes it conform with the stepped undertray regulations – had worked loose, causing the diffuser to trail on the ground and wear away.

By lap 34 the order was Schumacher, Fisichella, Häkkinen, Frentzen and Herbert with Villeneuve stalking Alesi for sixth place, the Canadian getting his Williams into a lurid 'tank slapper' as he hurtled up the hill from Eau Rouge next time round. On lap 36 he finally got ahead of the Benetton and a bewildered Alesi duly made a fourth stop at the end of lap 38 in a vain bid to sort out the problem.

With Schumacher now beyond reach at the head of the pack, the remaining interest centred on Häkkinen's continued efforts to close on

Fisichella and Frentzen's inroads into the surviving McLaren's advantage. On lap 38 it was 7.1s/2.0s and by lap 41 6.5s/1.4s. Yet as Schumacher completed his commanding victory, rolling off his pace to cross the line a mere 26.75s ahead of the Jordan, the order behind the winning Ferrari remained unchanged to the chequered flag.

For Eddie Jordan's team, Fisichella had done a simply brilliant job. 'We've still got to achieve our first win,' said Jordan, the man who gave Michael Schumacher his first F1 chance in this same race six years ago. 'But with Michael on his current form, I don't know how we're going to do it.

'I think we would have been in with a real chance of winning had the track not dried out so quickly, but Giancarlo drove brilliantly and it was a fitting finish to a difficult weekend.

'But Michael has yet again proved beyond doubt he is, dare I say it, probably the greatest racing driver of all time.'

Häkkinen's run to his third top-three finish of the season was a deserved reward after a troubled time in practice. Yet, as things turned out, he would not keep his hard-won third place. Both Williams drivers had started on full-wet chassis settings, so fourth and sixth, split by Herbert's Sauber, was the best they could manage, particularly as Jacques made one stop more than necessary.

Gerhard Berger worked out a decent race set-up and drove consistently quickly all afternoon to take seventh ahead of Pedro Diniz, who collided with Eddie Irvine's Ferrari on the last lap at Les Combes. The Arrows survived to take eighth, but Irvine's mount moved no further and he had to settle for 11th, the two antagonists separated by Alesi and Gianni Morbidelli's Sauber in the final order.

Mika Salo drove well to take 12th ahead of Stewart's Jan Magnussen, the Dane having excelled on a drying track with wet tyres and a high-down-force set-up in the early stages. Despite removing a gurney flap at one pit stop, he had too much downforce when conditions became really dry and faded to 13th at the end.

Meanwhile, Damon Hill's weekend in the Arrows also ended unproductively, the World Champion being classified 14th after coming into the pits on the last lap with a loose wheel-securing nut, which could neither be removed nor tightened. It compounded the problems caused by his earlier, premature first pit stop and brought his day to a close in particularly disappointing fashion.

The right way. Michael Schumacher once again proved the master of Spa. A combination of tactical acuity, incomparable skill and a dash of good fortune gave him a crushing victory.

The wrong way. Younger brother Ralf *(right)* crashed his Jordan at Blanchimont on a pre-race reconnaissance lap and was obliged to run almost a mile back to the pits, eventually taking the start from the pit lane in the spare car.

BELGIAN
GRAND PRIX
22–24 AUGUST 1997
SPA-FRANCORCHAMPS

Race distance: 44 laps, 190.498 miles/306.577 km

Race weather: Wet, then sunny and warm

FIA™
FORMULA 1
WORLD
CHAMPIONSHIP

ROUND 12

SPA-FRANCORCHAMPS

LES COMBES
MALMEDY
KEMMEL
EAU ROUGE
RAIDILLON
POUHON
RIVAGE
LA SOURCE
"BUS STOP"
FAGNES
BLANCHIMONT
STAVELOT

CIRCUIT LENGTH: 4.329 MILES/6.968 KM

Pos.	Driver	Nat.	No.	Entrant	Car/Engine	Tyres	Laps	Time/Retirement	Speed (mph/km/h)
1	Michael Schumacher	D	5	Scuderia Ferrari Marlboro	Ferrari F310B 046/2 V10	G	44	1h 33m 46.717s	121.881/196.149
2	Giancarlo Fisichella	I	12	B&H Total Jordan Peugeot	Jordan 197-Peugeot A14 V10	G	44	1h 34m 13.470s	121.304/195.221
DQ	Mika Häkkinen	SF	9	West McLaren Mercedes	McLaren MP4/12-Mercedes FO110F V10	G	44	1h 34m 17.573s	121.216/195.079
3	Heinz-Harald Frentzen	D	4	Rothmans Williams Renault	Williams FW19-Renault RS9A V10	G	44	1h 34m 18.864s	121.189/195.035
4	Johnny Herbert	GB	16	Red Bull Sauber Petronas	Sauber C16-Petronas V10	G	44	1h 34m 25.742s	121.042/194.798
5	Jacques Villeneuve	CDN	3	Rothmans Williams Renault	Williams FW19-Renault RS9A V10	G	44	1h 34m 28.820s	120.976/194.692
6	Gerhard Berger	A	8	Mild Seven Benetton Renault	Benetton B197-Renault RS9A V10	G	44	1h 34m 50.458s	120.516/193.952
7	Pedro Diniz	BR	2	Danka Arrows Yamaha	Arrows A18-Yamaha OX11A/D V10	B	44	1h 35m 12.648s	120.047/193.198
8	Jean Alesi	F	7	Mild Seven Benetton Renault	Benetton B197-Renault RS9A V10	G	44	1h 35m 28.725s	119.711/192.656
9	Gianni Morbidelli	I	17	Red Bull Sauber Petronas	Sauber C16-Petronas V10	G	44	1h 35m 29.299s	119.699/192.637
10	Eddie Irvine	GB	6	Scuderia Ferrari Marlboro	Ferrari F310B 046/2 V10	G	43	Collision with Diniz	
11	Mika Salo	SF	19	Tyrrell	Tyrrell 025-Ford ED5 V8	G	43		
12	Jan Magnussen	DK	23	Stewart Ford	Stewart SF1-Ford Zetec-R V10	B	43		
13	Damon Hill	GB	1	Danka Arrows Yamaha	Arrows A18-Yamaha OX11A/D V10	B	42	Wheel nut	
14	Ukyo Katayama	J	20	Minardi Team	Minardi M197-Hart 830 V8	B	42	Engine	
15	Jarno Trulli	I	14	Prost Gauloises Blondes	Prost JS45-Mugen Honda MF301HB V10	B	42		
	Jos Verstappen	NL	18	Tyrrell	Tyrrell 025-Ford ED5 V8	G	25	Spun off	
	Ralf Schumacher	D	11	B&H Total Jordan Peugeot	Jordan 197-Peugeot A14 V10	G	21	Accident	
	David Coulthard	GB	10	West McLaren Mercedes	McLaren MP4/12-Mercedes FO110F V10	G	19	Spun off	
	Tarso Marques	BR	21	Minardi Team	Minardi M197-Hart 830 V8	B	18	Spun off	
	Rubens Barrichello	BR	22	Stewart Ford	Stewart SF1-Ford Zetec-R V10	B	8	Spun off	
	Shinji Nakano	J	15	Prost Gauloises Blondes	Prost JS45-Mugen Honda MF301HB V10	B	5	Spun off	

Fastest lap: Villeneuve, on lap 43, 1m 52.692s, 138.314 mph/222.596 km/h.

Lap record: Alain Prost (F1 Williams FW15C-Renault V10), 1m 51.095s, 140.424 mph/225.990 km/h (1993).

B – Bridgestone   G – Goodyear

Grid order	1	2	3	4	5	6	7	8	9	10	11	12	13	14	15	16	17	18	19	20	21	22	23	24	25	26	27	28	29	30	31	32	33	34	35	36	37	38	39	40	41	42	43	44	
3 VILLENEUVE	3	3	3	5	5	5	5	5	5	5	5	5	5	5	5	5	5	5	5	5	5	5	5	5	5	5	5	5	5	5	5	5	5	5	5	5	5	5	5	5	5	5	5	1	
7 ALESI	7	7	7	7	3	12	12	12	12	9	9	9	7	7	7	7	7	7	7	7	7	7	7	12	12	12	12	12	12	12	12	12	12	12	12	12	12	12	12	12	12	12	12	2	
5 M. SCHUMACHER	5	5	5	5	7	7	9	9	9	12	2	2	12	12	12	12	12	12	12	12	12	12	12	9	9	9	9	9	9	7	7	7	9	9	9	9	9	9	9	9	9	9	9	9	
12 FISICHELLA	12	12	12	12	12	9	7	10	10	10	16	23	23	9	9	9	9	9	9	9	9	9	9	4	7	7	7	7	7	16	16	4	4	4	4	4	4	4	4	4	4	4	4	3	
9 HÄKKINEN	4	9	9	9	9	4	4	2	2	23	7	9	16	16	16	16	16	16	16	4	4	4	16	16	16	16	16	3	3	4	16	16	16	16	16	16	16	16	16	16	16	16	16	4	
11 R. SCHUMACHER	9	4	4	4	4	2	10	16	16	16	10	12	16	10	10	10	4	4	4	16	16	16	3	3	3	3	3	9	16	7	7	7	3	3	3	3	3	3	3	3	5				
4 FRENTZEN	2	2	2	2	10	2	1	1	1	17	16	10	4	4	4	10	10	10	8	8	8	8	4	4	4	4	4	2	8	3	3	7	7	7	8	8	8	8	8	6					
2 DINIZ	1	1	1	1	1	1	1	23	23	23	18	1	1	8	8	8	8	8	3	3	3	3	18	6	6	6	2	2	3	8	6	8	6	6	6	8	6	6	6	6	6	2			
1 HILL	10	10	10	10	10	3	16	8	17	17	12	17	8	1	18	18	18	18	3	18	18	18	18	6	2	2	2	6	3	2	6	8	8	8	6	2	2	2	2	7					
10 COULTHARD	16	16	16	16	16	22	17	8	17	19	4	3	3	3	18	6	6	6	6	2	8	8	8	6	6	6	2	6	7	7	7	7	17												
16 HERBERT	22	22	22	22	22	22	23	22	18	7	3	8	18	3	1	2	2	2	8	19	19	19	17	17	17	17	17	19	19	17	17	17	17	17	17										
22 BARRICHELLO	17	17	17	17	17	17	17	4	21	21	21	4	2	2	2	6	6	6	2	19	19	19	19	19	23	23	17	17	19	19	19	19	19	17	17	19	19	19	19	19	19	19			
17 MORBIDELLI	8	8	8	8	23	23	8	18	7	3	1	18	3	6	19	19	19	19	19	23	23	23	23	17	17	23	23	23	23	23	23	23	23	23	23	23	23								
14 TRULLI	15	15	15	23	8	8	21	21	3	20	8	21	6	19	6	17	17	17	17	17	17	17	1	1	1	1	1	1	1	1	1	1	1	1	1	1	1								
8 BERGER	6	6	6	6	6	6	7	20	8	4	3	17	7	23	23	23	11	11	20	20	20	20	20	20	20	20	20	20	20	20	20	20	20	20											
15 NAKANO	23	23	23	15	15	21	20	20	4	4	20	6	19	23	1	21	11	11	11	20	1	1	1	14	14	14	14	14	14	14	14	14	14	14	14	14									
6 IRVINE	19	19	19	19	19	20	18	3	19	6	6	19	21	21	21	6	20	1	14	14	14																								
23 MAGNUSSEN	20	20	20	20	21	19	3	19	11	11	19	20	20	20	20	20	20	1	14	14																									
19 SALO	21	21	18	21	20	18	19	6	6	19	11	11	11	11	11	11	1	1	14																										
20 KATAYAMA	18	18	21	18	18	11	11	14	14	14	14	14	14	14	14	14	14																												
18 VERSTAPPEN	11	11	11	11	11	11	14	14	14																																			
21 MARQUES	14	14	14	14	14																																							

Pit stop
One lap behind leader

All results and data © FIA 1997

Pamela Lausen/FOSA

STARTING GRID

7 ALESI Benetton	3 VILLENEUVE Williams
12 FISICHELLA Jordan	5 M. SCHUMACHER Ferrari
11 R. SCHUMACHER* Jordan	9 HÄKKINEN McLaren
2 DINIZ Arrows	4 FRENTZEN Williams
10 COULTHARD McLaren	1 HILL Arrows
22 BARRICHELLO Stewart	16 HERBERT Sauber
14 TRULLI* Prost	17 MORBIDELLI Sauber
15 NAKANO Prost	8 BERGER Benetton
23 MAGNUSSEN Stewart	6 IRVINE Ferrari
20 KATAYAMA Minardi	19 SALO Tyrrell
21 MARQUES Minardi	18 VERSTAPPEN Tyrrell

* started from pit lane

TIME SHEETS

QUALIFYING

Weather: Hot, dry and sunny

Pos.	Driver	Car	Laps	Time
1	Jacques Villeneuve	Williams-Renault	11	1m 49.450s
2	Jean Alesi	Benetton-Renault	11	1m 49.759s
3	Michael Schumacher	Ferrari	11	1m 50.293s
4	Giancarlo Fisichella	Jordan-Peugeot	12	1m 50.470s
5	Mika Häkkinen	McLaren-Mercedes	11	1m 50.503s
6	Ralf Schumacher	Jordan-Peugeot	10	1m 50.520s
7	Heinz-Harald Frentzen	Williams-Renault	11	1m 50.656s
8	Pedro Diniz	Arrows-Yamaha	12	1m 50.853s
9	Damon Hill	Arrows-Yamaha	12	1m 50.970s
10	David Coulthard	McLaren-Mercedes	9	1m 51.410s
11	Johnny Herbert	Sauber-Petronas	11	1m 51.725s
12	Rubens Barrichello	Stewart-Ford	12	1m 51.916s
13	Gianni Morbidelli	Sauber-Petronas	7	1m 52.094s
14	Jarno Trulli	Prost-Mugen Honda	12	1m 52.274s
15	Gerhard Berger	Benetton-Renault	11	1m 52.391s
16	Shinji Nakano	Prost-Mugen Honda	11	1m 52.749s
17	Eddie Irvine	Ferrari	11	1m 52.793s
18	Jan Magnussen	Stewart-Ford	11	1m 52.886s
19	Mika Salo	Tyrrell-Ford	11	1m 52.897s
20	Ukyo Katayama	Minardi-Hart	10	1m 53.544s
21	Jos Verstappen	Tyrrell-Ford	7	1m 53.725s
22	Tarso Marques	Minardi-Hart	12	1m 54.505s

FRIDAY FREE PRACTICE

Weather: Wet and overcast

Pos.	Driver	Laps	Time
1	Gerhard Berger	14	2m 06.802s
2	Jean Alesi	8	2m 07.371s
3	Rubens Barrichello	21	2m 08.238s
4	Damon Hill	23	2m 08.372s
5	Michael Schumacher	21	2m 09.272s
6	David Coulthard	15	2m 09.288s
7	Johnny Herbert	18	2m 09.772s
8	Jarno Trulli	24	2m 09.772s
9	Pedro Diniz	16	2m 10.153s
10	Ukyo Katayama	20	2m 10.231s
11	Shinji Nakano	24	2m 10.272s
12	Mika Häkkinen	14	2m 10.413s
13	Heinz-Harald Frentzen	18	2m 10.914s
14	Eddie Irvine	17	2m 10.993s
15	Giancarlo Fisichella	16	2m 11.093s
16	Gianni Morbidelli	18	2m 11.262s
17	Jacques Villeneuve	25	2m 11.706s
18	Tarso Marques	17	2m 11.778s
19	Jan Magnussen	22	2m 12.545s
20	Ralf Schumacher	14	2m 12.750s
21	Mika Salo	15	2m 13.256s
22	Jos Verstappen	14	2m 14.048s

SATURDAY FREE PRACTICE

Weather: Damp, drying quickly

Pos.	Driver	Laps	Time
1	Jacques Villeneuve	25	1m 50.407s
2	Jean Alesi	21	1m 50.947s
3	Heinz-Harald Frentzen	23	1m 51.179s
4	Giancarlo Fisichella	24	1m 51.625s
5	Gerhard Berger	21	1m 52.057s
6	Damon Hill	20	1m 52.402s
7	Michael Schumacher	17	1m 52.562s
8	David Coulthard	20	1m 52.604s
9	Ralf Schumacher	26	1m 52.562s
10	Rubens Barrichello	19	1m 52.688s
11	Mika Salo	27	1m 53.929s
12	Johnny Herbert	20	1m 53.977s
13	Ukyo Katayama	16	1m 54.150s
14	Shinji Nakano	21	1m 54.299s
15	Gianni Morbidelli	16	1m 54.310s
16	Tarso Marques	16	1m 54.521s
17	Jan Magnussen	19	1m 54.608s
18	Jos Verstappen	24	1m 54.799s
19	Jarno Trulli	15	1m 55.895s
20	Pedro Diniz	12	1m 56.360s
21	Mika Häkkinen	7	2m 06.429s
22	Eddie Irvine	13	2m 07.786s

WARM-UP

Weather: Dry, hot and sunny

Pos.	Driver	Laps	Time
1	Jacques Villeneuve		1m 52.415s
2	Ralf Schumacher		1m 52.619s
3	Johnny Herbert		1m 52.626s
4	Jean Alesi		1m 52.637s
5	Damon Hill		1m 53.366s
6	Gerhard Berger		1m 53.631s
7	Pedro Diniz		1m 53.657s
8	Jarno Trulli		1m 53.760s
9	Heinz-Harald Frentzen		1m 53.777s
10	David Coulthard		1m 53.848s
11	Giancarlo Fisichella		1m 53.999s
12	Mika Häkkinen		1m 54.282s
13	Gianni Morbidelli		1m 54.448s
14	Ukyo Katayama		1m 54.570s
15	Michael Schumacher		1m 54.593s
16	Tarso Marques		1m 54.868s
17	Jos Verstappen		1m 54.895s
18	Shinji Nakano		1m 55.202s
19	Mika Salo		1m 55.588s
20	Jan Magnussen		1m 55.695s
21	Eddie Irvine		1m 55.993s
22	Rubens Barrichello		1m 56.062s

RACE FASTEST LAPS

Weather: Wet, then sunny and warm

Driver	Time	Lap
Jacques Villeneuve	1m 52.692s	43
Johnny Herbert	1m 53.615s	44
Gerhard Berger	1m 53.649s	43
Pedro Diniz	1m 53.652s	42
Heinz-Harald Frentzen	1m 53.874s	43
Damon Hill	1m 54.074s	41
Mika Häkkinen	1m 54.175s	43
Giancarlo Fisichella	1m 54.688s	39
Gianni Morbidelli	1m 54.818s	39
Jarno Trulli	1m 55.152s	37
Eddie Irvine	1m 55.290s	29
Michael Schumacher	1m 55.340s	41
Jean Alesi	1m 55.348s	30
Ukyo Katayama	1m 55.413s	41
Jan Magnussen	1m 55.726s	41
Mika Salo	1m 56.919s	43
Ralf Schumacher	1m 57.784s	16
David Coulthard	1m 59.169s	16
Jos Verstappen	1m 59.409s	16
Tarso Marques	2m 02.753s	16
Rubens Barrichello	2m 16.804s	5
Shinji Nakano	2m 19.161s	5

CHASSIS LOG BOOK

1	Hill	Arrows A18/5
2	Diniz	Arrows A18/4
	spare	Arrows A18/3
3	Villeneuve	Williams FW19/4
4	Frentzen	Williams FW19/5
	spare	Williams FW19/3
5	M. Schumacher	Ferrari F310B/179
6	Irvine	Ferrari F310B/173
	spare	Ferrari F310B/175
7	Alesi	Benetton B197/2
8	Berger	Benetton B197/4
	spare	Benetton B197/3
9	Häkkinen	McLaren MP4/12/7
10	Coulthard	McLaren MP4/12/6
	spare	McLaren MP4/12/5
11	R. Schumacher	Jordan 197/6
12	Fisichella	Jordan 197/5
	spare	Jordan 197/1
14	Trulli	Prost JS45/3
15	Nakano	Prost JS45/2
	spare	Prost JS45/1
16	Herbert	Sauber C16/3
17	Morbidelli	Sauber C16/6
	spare	Sauber C16/5
18	Verstappen	Tyrrell 025/4
19	Salo	Tyrrell 025/3
	spare	Tyrrell 025/1
20	Katayama	Minardi M197/4
21	Marques	Minardi M197/2
	spare	Minardi M197/1
22	Barrichello	Stewart SF1/2
23	Magnussen	Stewart SF1/3
	spare	Stewart SF1/1

POINTS TABLES

Drivers

1	Michael Schumacher	66
2	Jacques Villeneuve	55
3	Heinz-Harald Frentzen	23
4	Jean Alesi	22
5	Gerhard Berger	21
6	Eddie Irvine	18
7	Olivier Panis	15
8 =	David Coulthard	14
8 =	Mika Häkkinen	14
8 =	Johnny Herbert	14
8 =	Giancarlo Fisichella	14
12	Ralf Schumacher	11
13	Damon Hill	7
14	Rubens Barrichello	6
15	Alexander Wurz	4
16	Jarno Trulli	3
17 =	Mika Salo	2
17 =	Shinji Nakano	2
19	Nicola Larini	1

Constructors

1	Ferrari	84
2	Williams	78
3	Benetton	47
4	McLaren	28
5	Jordan	25
6	Prost	20
7	Sauber	15
8	Arrows	7
9	Stewart	6
10	Tyrrell	2

Results and points tables reflect the outcome of the FIA Court of Appeal hearing in Paris on Wednesday 3 September.

ITALIAN
grand prix

- COULTHARD
- ALESI
- FRENTZEN
- FISICHELLA
- VILLENEUVE
- M. SCHUMACHER

The outcome of the race was effectively settled when the McLaren pit crew sent David Coulthard back into the race narrowly ahead of Jean Alesi's Benetton after the pair had made their sole refuelling stops on lap 32.
Photo: Michael Cooper/Allsport

DIARY

Movie star Sylvester Stallone puts in an appearance at Monza where it is announced that he will star in a major Hollywood film centred on Grand Prix racing which could be in the cinemas as early as 1999.

Mika Häkkinen and the McLaren team lose their appeal against the verdict that illegal fuel had been used during qualifying for the Belgian GP, in which the Finn finished third on the road. The FIA Court of Appeal doubled the McLaren fine from $25,000 to $50,000 in addition to excluding the car from the results.

Alex Zanardi clinches the PPG CART World Series title with a third place at Laguna Seca. The race is won by his Ganassi Reynard-Honda team-mate Jimmy Vasser with Mark Blundell's PacWest Reynard-Mercedes second.

Olivier Panis drives 90 laps at Magny-Cours in an F3 Dallara, his first outing behind the wheel since breaking both legs in an accident during the Canadian GP.

Below: Take-off. Giancarlo Fisichella's Jordan becomes airborne as he takes a trip across Monza's unforgiving new kerbing during qualifying. His spectacular efforts were ultimately rewarded with third place in the starting line-up.

DAVID Coulthard scored the McLaren-Mercedes squad's second win of the season in the Italian Grand Prix at Monza after a well choreographed team effort which ended on an emotional note when the 26-year-old Scot dedicated the win to the memory of Diana, Princess of Wales, whose funeral had taken place in London the previous day.

After descending from the winner's rostrum, Coulthard was in a reflective frame of mind. 'I am very well aware of the mood in our country back home,' he said. 'I had the privilege of meeting her when I finished second in the 1995 British Grand Prix.

'I have a picture of her and the princes back home and it made me feel very emotional when the Union flag was being raised behind me. For the last ten laps of the race I found myself wondering whether I should be spraying champagne if I should get on the podium, but I got clarification of this and did so. Life goes on.'

Coulthard had qualified in sixth place on the starting grid after engine problems in practice, but a superb start saw him catapult through to third behind pole starter Jean Alesi's Benetton and the Williams of Heinz-Harald Frentzen by the time the pack reached the first corner.

His McLaren was carrying rather more fuel than the cars of his immediate rivals, which gave Coulthard extra tactical flexibility when it came to his crucial mid-race refuelling stop. The additional fuel meant that the car would spend less time stationary in the pit lane, offering a possible chance to leapfrog ahead of the opposition.

From the start, Alesi accelerated cleanly away from pole position to lead into the first chicane ahead of Frentzen and Coulthard. There were no dramas as the pack jostled through the turn, but Damon Hill's Arrows got badly squeezed out as he braked for the second chicane, losing several places as a result.

At the end of the opening lap Alesi led by 1.08s from Frentzen, Coulthard, Giancarlo Fisichella, Jacques Villeneuve, Mika Häkkinen, Michael Schumacher and Gerhard Berger.

Initially Alesi began to edge away. With five laps completed he had opened a 1.8s lead – about ten lengths – but Frentzen was under consistent pressure from Coulthard and the gap back to Fisichella in fourth place was

Below right: Photo opportunity. A lucky marshal grabs the chance to pose for a snapshot with Jan Magnussen and David Coulthard as the drivers wait for their cars to be recovered during practice.

Bottom right: Minardi had chalked up their 200th Grand Prix at Spa and the celebrations were still in full swing on home ground two weeks later.

also widening perceptibly. Further back, Pedro Diniz's Arrows had spun off at the Variante Ascari when its rear suspension broke, ending a troubled, albeit brief, afternoon's work for the young Brazilian.

'The start of the race was not very good as I had a problem with the dashboard which showed me in the wrong gear,' he said. 'I changed into third too soon, causing my engine to die at the start, so I lost a few places. Then I was closing the gap to Morbidelli's Sauber in front of me when I spun off.'

By lap nine Alesi was almost three seconds ahead. Meanwhile Ukyo Katayama's Minardi, running in last place, had picked up a stone between its left-front wheel rim and the brake caliper, holing the wheel and allowing the left-front tyre to deflate. He glanced the barrier at the second chicane, but gathered it all together sufficiently to limp back to the pits to retire.

Alesi was feeling confident enough at the head of the pack, but from lap 13 onwards his slight edge began to evaporate. He'd clipped a kerb and spun during the warm-up due, he explained, to a little too much oversteer in the slow corners. It wasn't a problem for the first dozen or so laps of the race, but then that slight imbalance reasserted itself.

'I wasn't too worried,' he admitted, 'because I wasn't under too much pressure as it's impossible to overtake anybody on this circuit unless they make a mistake.'

The high-speed deadlock for the first three places continued, Alesi's advantage gradually dwindling to 0.4s by lap 26, at which stage the gap between World Championship contenders Villeneuve and Schumacher, by now running in fifth and seventh, was 10.3s.

The procession continued until lap 29 when Frentzen made what he subsequently judged a premature 10.3s refuelling stop, dropping from second to eighth. On the previous lap Villeneuve had come in and dropped back to 11th.

On lap 30, Coulthard got into a huge 'tank slapper' as he exited the Variante Ascari. He didn't need to be reminded that this was the point on the Monza circuit where he'd made one of the biggest gaffes of his F1 career, spinning his pole-position Williams on the parade lap prior to the 1995 event.

'For a split-second, I thought a wheel had fallen off,' he grinned reflectively after the race. 'It looked as though it might be a mirror-image of that warm-up lap in 1995. These cars are *so* nervous!'

On lap 32 came the crucial moment

Ferrari's fans were dismayed after Michael Schumacher was unable to qualify better than ninth in the latest lightweight 'big tank' F310B. The Italian machines proved unexpectedly sensitive to increases in track temperature, losing grip progressively in fast corners throughout the day as the early haze gave way to fierce sunshine.

Michael was so frustrated that he took a long shot for qualifying, switching to the relatively untried spare car. It was his worst grid position of the season. The weekend began with a suspension breakage on Friday which saw him complete only 19 laps that day. You could say it set the tone for the weekend.

'I said last week during testing here that it would be difficult for us to get a good grid position at Monza,' he acknowledged. 'With so many competitive cars on the grid, a few tenths of a second costs you a lot of places. We have to accept that, and tomorrow I will do my best to rectify the situation.'

It looked as though Ferrari's problems would hand an overwhelming advantage to the Williams team, yet it was the consistently quick Jean Alesi who planted his Benetton B197 on pole position by less than a tenth of a second from Frank W's quickest car, driven by Heinz-Harald Frentzen.

'This is a beautiful moment for me, another pole position here at Monza where I had my last three years ago,' said Alesi.

'I did my best run quite early in the session, so I was a little concerned that I might have gone out too soon. But it all worked out OK.' In fact, once Ukyo Katayama and Tarso Marques had scattered gravel onto the racing line with

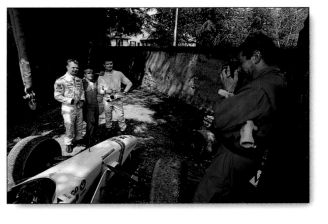

just over ten minutes of qualifying left, Alesi was home and dry.

Benetton benefited from revised rear suspension geometry while Williams used its variable brake balance system for the first time at a race, providing more precise adjustments for the drivers and a reassuringly firm feel to the brake pedal. Frentzen used the spare FW19 for Friday free practice after his race chassis developed a problem with a brake sensor barely half an hour before the start of the session, but switched back to his race chassis on Saturday.

Both he and team-mate Jacques Villeneuve squandered their best qualifying runs with slight driving errors, the Canadian ending up on the outside of the second row behind Giancarlo Fisichella's Jordan.

Fisichella began practice riding the crest of a wave of confidence after setting fastest time during the pre-race Monza test, although the on-going dispute between Benetton and Jordan over which team had the right to his services in 1998 could hardly have helped his mental equilibrium.

Yet third place in the final line-up was pretty satisfactory and Giancarlo was obviously very excited about his achievement. The Jordan also felt good with a heavy fuel load, which raised hopes for the race. He also diplomatically praised Alesi's achievement,

doubtless mindful that he might well end up at Benetton in 1998.

'I am a Benetton driver,' he said, referring to his contract, 'although I drive for Jordan, so I am very happy for Jean. If I have to drive for Benetton, then I am happy to do so. But I have been asked to stay out of the discussions between Benetton and Jordan. When I'm told what to do, that's OK!'

Giancarlo also found himself summoned in front of the stewards for failing to observe the yellow flag waved after Jarno Trulli's Prost spun off. His lap times from that run were disallowed and he was given a one-race suspended ban, effective for the remainder of the season. Thankfully, this did not affect his overall grid position.

Both Fisichella and team-mate Ralf Schumacher opted for the softer of the two Goodyear compounds, the latter having a difficult time and ending the session eighth fastest. From the start of Saturday free practice he was troubled with the car pulling to the right, so the steering was checked and the dampers changed. Then he hit a kerb and, since the precise problem could not be identified, it was

decided to change all the front suspension components. This work was still being completed when the qualifying hour began. Thereafter, Ralf was never able to make up for the time he had lost in the morning.

In the McLaren camp, Mika Häkkinen and David Coulthard emerged fifth and sixth fastest, Mika losing time with loss of oil pressure during the free practice session. He stopped on the circuit, but the car was retrieved at the mid-session break and a fresh engine was installed in time for him to complete an installation lap before the chequered flag finally fell.

Gerhard Berger was seventh in the other Benetton, moderately happy with his efforts despite losing a couple of tenths at the Ascari chicane on what he thought might be an even quicker lap.

Completing the top ten behind the Schumacher brothers came Eddie Irvine's Ferrari, the Ulsterman improving his time by 0.2s over the morning's free practice session. 'I had some understeer, but it was a little better than I expected,' he confessed.

In 11th place came Rubens Barrichello's Stewart SF1, the Brazilian running the P8 version of Ford's Zetec-R V10 and setting his best time on the second of four qualifying runs. 'I was a little unlucky following other cars,' he admitted. 'On my third run I got a little too close to Fisichella at the first chicane, lost downforce under braking behind him and went straight on.

'Then, on my last run, I got a little too close to Ralf Schumacher through the Lesmos and lost a bit of front downforce again. But overall it was a good effort.'

Jan Magnussen produced the best qualifying performance of his season with 13th-fastest time, the Dane using the spare car after sustaining slight damage to his race chassis during Friday free practice. On his second run he admitted to hitting a kerb pretty hard with the underside of his car: 'I still don't feel all that satisfied,' he admitted, 'but it is a good feeling to be up there in the middle of the grid.'

Splitting the two Stewarts was Johnny Herbert's Sauber, the Briton having crashed heavily at the Ascari chicane during the morning free practice session. It took quite a while to repair the damage, but he still managed his full allotment of laps in qualifying.

'My first run produced my best time,' he explained, 'after which the track temperature rose. The car was better than in the morning, but unfortunately the conditions were not, so that cancelled out the improvement.' Team-mate Gianni Morbidelli wound up a lowly 18th, troubled by bad understeer through Parabolica which lost him a lot of time.

Damon Hill lined up 14th, any possibility of further improvement by grabbing a tow from Frentzen's Williams being negated when the German driver backed off in front of him. 'I am not sure what he was doing as I am not particularly a threat to him,' said Hill crisply.

In 15th and 16th places were the Prost-Mugen Hondas, this time Shinji Nakano squeezing ahead of Jarno Trulli. The Italian had lost time when he damaged his fuel pump over a chicane kerb in free practice, then found his car unexpectedly nervous come qualifying. He switched to the spare for his final two runs, but this did not produce any meaningful improvement.

Diniz was 17th in the other Arrows ahead of Morbidelli and the Tyrrell twins, Mika Salo and Jos Verstappen. Mika ran wide onto the gravel on the first flying lap of his second run, thereafter switching to the spare 025 for the rest of the afternoon as there were so many stones in the cockpit and undertray of his race chassis. Both he and Verstappen did three sets of two flying laps, their only consolation being that they out-gunned the Minardi-Harts to keep off the back row of the grid.

Clive Mason/Allsport

Michael Cooper/Allsport

Peter Nygaard/GP Photo

Paul-Henri Cahier

of the race. Alesi (8.7s) and Coulthard (7.8s) made their refuelling stops from first and second positions and the McLaren accelerated back into the race ahead. Meanwhile Häkkinen had gone through in the lead with Schumacher's Ferrari up to second ahead of Berger's Benetton, Fisichella having stopped at the end of the previous lap and dropped from third to eighth.

'We believed we could run as long a first stint as anyone,' said Coulthard after the race. 'Once we saw Heinz-Harald had pitted, we decided to follow Jean in – and we were confident that we would not be stationary longer than he was.'

On lap 34 Schumacher took the Ferrari through into the lead – artificial though it may have been – as Häkkinen made a 9.2s refuelling stop, resuming in fourth. Next time round it was Schumacher's turn, a 7.2s stop dropping him back to seventh.

This left Coulthard firmly ahead of the game. Thereafter he drove with great composure and restraint, taking the chequered flag 2.4s ahead of Alesi with Frentzen another 1.5s adrift in third place.

For Häkkinen, only bitter disappointment was to follow. After his brief stint in the lead, he hoped to im-prove on fourth place after his tyre stop. Yet only three laps later he was back in the pit lane for an unscheduled stop after his right-front tyre delami-nated. The mechanics did their best, but he was down to 14th place when he resumed, any chance of even a single championship point now vanished.

It was a cruel blow, but Mika buck-led down to prove what he was made of over the remaining laps of the race. He would eventually finish ninth, posting a best lap 0.8s quicker than anybody else on the circuit.

'I am hugely disappointed for Mika,' said Ron Dennis sympathetically once the race was over. 'He posted so many fastest laps and so desperately wants to win.'

Not much happened in this proces-sional race thereafter, with the notable exception of a spectacular episode under braking for the first chicane as Ralf Schumacher's Jordan and Johnny Herbert's Sauber jousted for ninth place at the start of lap 39.

On the run down to the corner, Schu-macher Junior dived inside Herbert, but moved back onto his correct line before fully clear of the Sauber. With sickening inevitability, the Jordan's right-rear wheel clouted the Sauber's left-front, sending Herbert's mount skimming across the ineffectual gravel trap and into a tyre barrier. It was one hell of an impact, but Johnny happily walked away, emerging from the episode with some advice for his young rival.

'What he doesn't seem to under-stand is that at very high-speed places like that you need to give the other guy racing room,' he said. 'It was un-necessary and unacceptable, and the sign of an inexperienced driver who still has a lot to learn about the art of racing closely at high speeds.'

Subsequently the incident was ex-amined by the stewards, who eventu-ally concluded it was a racing accident. Yet on a day when Jacques Villeneuve was given a one-race ban, suspended somewhat severely for a re-markable nine races, for failing to slow for yellow caution flags during the race morning warm-up, and winner Coulthard was rewarded with a similar penalty suspended for five races after committing the same offence, many thought Ralf could count himself for-tunate to have got away without penalty. As for Villeneuve, it was the third time he had offended in this fashion during the course of the sea-son and he had no option but to grin and bear it.

Schumacher paid the price for his error when he was forced to retire with sus-pension damage soon after, leaving Fisichella to keep the Jordan flag flying through to the chequered flag. This he did magnificently, pounding home in fourth after another assured performance.

Despite being understandably ner-vous, Giancarlo had got away cleanly to run fourth from the start, looking very cool and composed as he fended off Vil-leneuve for lap after lap. His only real problem was a touch too much under-steer on his second set of tyres. 'I really had to anticipate the curves,' he said. 'I was hoping to finish on the podium today, but I still feel I did a good job and that fourth place is a good result.'

As far as the championship battle was concerned, Schumacher finished sixth, one place behind Villeneuve, which meant the German driver now led the title chase by ten points with four rounds remaining and 40 points still to race for.

Neither driver was overtly delighted with the outcome, but Michael could be said to have got away lightly. 'I re-ally pushed hard,' shrugged Vil-leneuve. 'The car was better than fifth, but my start was just average – I was between Fisichella and Coulthard braking for the first corner, but didn't want to get stuck in a sandwich, so I braked early and let them fight it out in front of me.'

Always quick at Monza, Jean Alesi claimed pole position for Benetton, but had to settle for second place on race day.

Below: Heinz-Harald Frentzen again made the podium, but the German's chances of victory were compromised by a poorly timed pit stop.

BMW confirms F1 with Williams

BMW signalled the end of more than a decade's absence from Formula 1 by unveiling its plans to start racing as the Williams team's engine partner from the 2000 season onwards.

The new deal, which extends for five years from the Williams-BMW's first race, was confirmed by BMW President and CEO Bernd Pischetsrieder on the eve of the Frankfurt motor show, barely 24 hours after arch-rivals Mercedes-Benz had propelled David Coulthard's McLaren to victory in the Italian Grand Prix at Monza.

'The fact that Mercedes has started to win is irrelevant,' claimed Pischetsrieder. 'We have always said that F1 must pay and be the right time for us corporately. That time has now come.

'It is the right time not because the public often puts pressure on us to come back, but because it is time to emphasise our brand values. Given the broad range of models that we are unveiling here [at Frankfurt], BMW must bring its face out more than in the past.'

The Munich car maker quit F1 at the end of the 1987 season after a long association with the Bernie Ecclestone-owned Brabham team, which used its BMW four-cylinder turbos to power Nelson Piquet to the 1983 World Championship. The hot tip was that Gerhard Berger might be recruited as Williams-BMW test driver.

The first BMW-engined Williams is expected to be testing by the start of 1999 and the team will use Mecachrome Renault V10s for the next two seasons, as previously announced. BMW was expected to make a substantial contribution to the £13 million annual lease fees for these engines while work continues on its own 3-litre V10 developed by a team headed by veteran engineer Paul Rosche.

The long-term deal with the German car maker also involves Williams building a BMW sports car which it intends to race at Le Mans in 1998. This will be designed and built at the old Williams premises at Didcot which, although now sold, have been leased back for the purpose.

---

his, so I lost that opportunity as well. With so many cars running at very similar speeds on the circuit, there was nothing to do.'

In eighth place, Irvine could console himself with the fact that he was only 6.2s behind Schumacher after 53 laps and actually posted a fastest race lap 0.1s quicker than his colleague. 'At the end, we were all doing the same times,' he pondered, 'but given my grid position, I could do no more.'

'Neither was it possible to come up with any special strategy to get past the others. I did not have any particular problems during the race, except just before my pit stop when I was pushing hard to close on Berger and blistered a front tyre.'

The flying Häkkinen was classified ninth ahead of Jarno Trulli and Shinji Nakano, both disappointed with their Prosts, while Morbidelli wound up a frustrated 12th. 'I had lots of understeer again,' said Gianni, 'and for me the kerbs seemed more like walls.'

The Stewart-Ford squad had a difficult race, opting for a two-stop strategy due to front tyre wear concerns. Barrichello added more rear downforce on the starting grid, much to the detriment of his car's handling balance. Team-mate Jan Magnussen ran two places ahead of him in 13th during the

opening stages of the race, and a bad first refuelling stop dropped Rubens to 17th. He made up only four places before the chequered flag.

Magnussen checked out of 16th place with transmission failure on lap 32. Mechanical problems also claimed Damon Hill's Arrows-Yamaha, which pulled off with engine failure six laps from the end while running ninth.

'The car was very difficult to drive and we paid the price for not testing here,' said Hill. 'If we had been here we would have maybe qualified a bit better, been running a little further up and could have been in the points. As far as the engine failure was concerned, I had no warning and then suddenly it just went bang.'

It was the third victory of Coulthard's three-and-a-half-year F1 career and the

second this season, even though he had waited a long time to repeat his Melbourne success. It also came as something of a relief after weeks of uncertainty over his future plans had been brought to an end only a fortnight earlier when his McLaren contract was renewed for 1998.

'That uncertainty certainly means that you have to compete under a degree of pressure which disrupts you from doing your job properly,' he admitted.

It was a result which suggested a degree of impending stalemate in the World Championship battle, which goes to show how wrong an observer of the F1 scene can be. What remained beyond doubt was that McLaren's position as a front-running force was gradually being consolidated. And this was only the start.

'Then I was stuck behind Fisichella. I could run quicker than him, but as soon as I got close I lost downforce and couldn't fight. Then we lost time in the pits, but the points I managed to win today are important.'

Schumacher added: 'Considering everything that happened this weekend, we can be really satisfied with this result. I have only lost one point in the championship, and it could have been a lot worse.' He followed that with the observation that the next two races took place on circuits where more downforce was needed, so he was confident the F310B would once again be competitive. Well . . .

Into seventh place came Berger, rather disappointed after an extremely difficult race in which he had given his all. 'I pushed from the first to the last lap,' said the Austrian. 'I was behind Michael's Ferrari, going at the same speed if not one-tenth quicker, but it was still not enough to overtake him.

'I was waiting for him to make a mistake in order to try and pass him. He made one, but then closed the door quickly and I did not want to run the risk of ending up on the grass. I had a second chance when he came into the pits, but my stop was not as good as

Bryn Williams

Race distance: 53 laps, 190.005 miles/305.785 km

Race weather: Dry, hot and sunny

ROUND 13

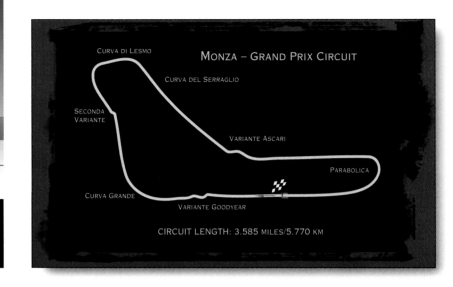

MONZA – GRAND PRIX CIRCUIT

CURVA DI LESMO
CURVA DEL SERRAGLIO
SECONDA VARIANTE
VARIANTE ASCARI
PARABOLICA
CURVA GRANDE
VARIANTE GOODYEAR

CIRCUIT LENGTH: 3.585 MILES/5.770 KM

Pos.	Driver	Nat.	No.	Entrant	Car/Engine	Tyres	Laps	Time/Retirement	Speed (mph/km/h)
1	David Coulthard	GB	10	West McLaren Mercedes	McLaren MP4/12-Mercedes FO110F V10	G	53	1h 17m 04.609s	147.908/238.036
2	Jean Alesi	F	7	Mild Seven Benetton Renault	Benetton B197-Renault RS9A V10	G	53	1h 17m 06.546s	147.846/237.936
3	Heinz-Harald Frentzen	D	4	Rothmans Williams Renault	Williams FW19-Renault RS9A V10	G	53	1h 17m 08.952s	147.770/237.813
4	Giancarlo Fisichella	I	12	B&H Total Jordan Peugeot	Jordan 197-Peugeot A14 V10	G	53	1h 17m 10.480s	147.721/237.734
5	Jacques Villeneuve	CDN	3	Rothmans Williams Renault	Williams FW19-Renault RS9A V10	G	53	1h 17m 11.025s	147.703/237.706
6	Michael Schumacher	D	5	Scuderia Ferrari Marlboro	Ferrari F310B 046/2 V10	G	53	1h 17m 16.090s	147.542/237.447
7	Gerhard Berger	A	8	Mild Seven Benetton Renault	Benetton B197-Renault RS9A V10	G	53	1h 17m 17.080s	147.511/237.396
8	Eddie Irvine	GB	6	Scuderia Ferrari Marlboro	Ferrari F310B 046/2 V10	G	53	1h 17m 22.248s	147.347/237.132
9	Mika Häkkinen	SF	9	West McLaren Mercedes	McLaren MP4/12-Mercedes FO110F V10	G	53	1h 17m 53.982s	146.346/235.522
10	Jarno Trulli	I	14	Prost Gauloises Blondes	Prost JS45-Mugen Honda MF301HB V10	B	53	1h 18m 07.315s	145.930/234.852
11	Shinji Nakano	J	15	Prost Gauloises Blondes	Prost JS45-Mugen Honda MF301HB V10	B	53	1h 18m 07.936s	145.911/234.821
12	Gianni Morbidelli	I	17	Red Bull Sauber Petronas	Sauber C16-Petronas V10	G	52		
13	Rubens Barrichello	BR	22	Stewart Ford	Stewart SF1-Ford Zetec-R V10	B	52		
14	Tarso Marques	BR	21	Minardi Team	Minardi M197-Hart 830 V8	B	50		
	Damon Hill	GB	1	Danka Arrows Yamaha	Arrows A18-Yamaha OX11A/D V10	B	46	Engine	
	Ralf Schumacher	D	11	B&H Total Jordan Peugeot	Jordan 197-Peugeot A14 V10	G	39	Collision damage	
	Johnny Herbert	GB	16	Red Bull Sauber Petronas	Sauber C16-Petronas V10	G	38	Accident	
	Mika Salo	SF	19	Tyrrell	Tyrrell 025-Ford ED5 V8	G	33	Engine	
	Jan Magnussen	DK	23	Stewart Ford	Stewart SF1-Ford Zetec-R V10	B	31	Transmission	
	Jos Verstappen	NL	18	Tyrrell	Tyrrell 025-Ford ED5 V8	G	12	Engine	
	Ukyo Katayama	J	20	Minardi Team	Minardi M197-Hart 830 V8	B	8	Suspension damage	
	Pedro Diniz	BR	2	Danka Arrows Yamaha	Arrows A18-Yamaha OX11A/D V10	B	4	Suspension damage	

Fastest lap: Häkkinen, on lap 49, 1m 24.808s, 152.192 mph/244.929 km/h (record).

Previous lap record: Michael Schumacher (F1 Ferrari F310 V10), 1m 26.110s, 149.891 mph/241.226 km/h (1996).

B – Bridgestone   G – Goodyear

Grid order	1	2	3	4	5	6	7	8	9	10	11	12	13	14	15	16	17	18	19	20	21	22	23	24	25	26	27	28	29	30	31	32	33	34	35	36	37	38	39	40	41
7 ALESI	7	7	7	7	7	7	7	7	7	7	7	7	7	7	7	7	7	7	7	7	7	7	7	7	7	7	7	7	7	7	7	7	9	9	5	10	10	10	10	10	10
4 FRENTZEN	4	4	4	4	4	4	4	4	4	4	4	4	4	4	4	4	4	4	4	4	4	4	4	4	4	4	4	4	10	10	10	5	5	10	7	7	7	7	7	7	7
12 FISICHELLA	10	10	10	10	10	10	10	10	10	10	10	10	10	10	10	10	10	10	10	10	10	10	10	10	10	10	10	10	12	12	9	8	9	8	4	4	4	4	4	4	4
3 VILLENEUVE	12	12	12	12	12	12	12	12	12	12	12	12	12	12	12	12	12	12	12	12	12	12	12	12	12	12	12	12	9	9	5	10	10	7	9	12	12	12	12	12	12
9 HÄKKINEN	3	3	3	3	3	3	3	3	3	3	3	3	3	3	3	3	3	3	3	3	3	3	3	3	3	3	3	3	9	5	8	7	7	4	12	13	3	3	3	3	3
10 COULTHARD	9	9	9	9	9	9	9	9	9	9	9	9	9	9	9	9	9	9	9	9	9	9	9	9	9	9	9	9	5	8	6	6	4	12	3	3	5	5	5	5	5
8 BERGER	5	5	5	5	5	5	5	5	5	5	5	5	5	5	5	5	5	5	5	5	5	5	5	5	5	5	5	5	8	4	12	4	12	3	5	8	8	8	8	8	8
11 R. SCHUMACHER	8	8	8	8	8	8	8	8	8	8	8	8	8	8	8	8	8	8	8	8	8	8	8	8	8	8	8	6	6	4	4	12	3		8	8	6	6	6	6	6
5 M. SCHUMACHER	6	6	6	6	6	6	6	6	6	6	6	6	6	6	6	6	6	6	6	6	6	6	6	6	6	6	6	16	16	11	11	3	6	6	6	6	1	1	1	1	
6 IRVINE	16	16	16	16	16	16	16	16	16	16	16	16	16	16	16	16	16	16	16	16	16	16	16	16	16	16	16	11	11	3	3	16	16	16	16	11	11	14	14	14	
22 BARRICHELLO	11	11	11	11	11	11	11	11	11	11	11	11	11	11	11	11	11	11	11	11	11	11	11	11	11	11	11	3	3	1	1	11	11	11	11	1	1	15	15	15	
16 HERBERT	14	14	14	14	14	14	14	14	14	14	14	14	14	14	14	14	14	14	14	14	14	14	14	14	1	16	15	1	1	1	1	14	14	9	9	9					
23 MAGNUSSEN	23	23	23	23	23	23	23	23	23	23	23	23	23	23	23	1	1	1	1	1	1	1	1	1	15	15	16	14	14	14	14	15	15	17	17						
1 HILL	1	1	1	1	1	1	1	1	1	1	1	1	1	1	1	15	15	15	15	15	15	15	15	15	17	17	17	15	15	15	15	9	9	22	22	22					
15 NAKANO	22	22	22	22	22	22	22	22	22	22	22	22	22	22	22	15	17	17	17	17	17	17	17	17	14	14	14	17	19	17	17	17	17	11	11	21					
14 TRULLI	19	19	19	19	19	19	19	19	19	19	19	19	19	15	17	23	23	23	23	23	23	23	23	23	23	23	19	17	17	22	22	22	22	22							
2 DINIZ	15	15	15	15	15	15	15	15	15	15	15	15	15	17	22	22	22	22	22	22	22	22	22	22	22	19	22	19	22	22	21	21	21	21							
17 MORBIDELLI	17	17	17	17	17	17	17	17	17	17	17	17	17	19	19	19	19	19	19	19	19	19	19	19	19	22	22	21	21												
19 SALO	2	2	2	18	18	18	18	18	18	18	18	18	18	21	21	21	21	21	21	21	21	21	21	21	21	21	21														
18 VERSTAPPEN	18	18	18	2	21	21	21	21	21	21	21																														
20 KATAYAMA	21	20	20	20	20	20	20	20																																	
21 MARQUES	20	21	21	21																																					

Pit stop
One lap behind leader

STARTING GRID

7 **ALESI** Benetton	4 **FRENTZEN** Williams
12 **FISICHELLA** Jordan	3 **VILLENEUVE** Williams
9 **HÄKKINEN** McLaren	10 **COULTHARD** McLaren
8 **BERGER** Benetton	11 **R. SCHUMACHER** Jordan
5 **M. SCHUMACHER** Ferrari	6 **IRVINE** Ferrari
22 **BARRICHELLO** Stewart	16 **HERBERT** Sauber
23 **MAGNUSSEN** Stewart	1 **HILL** Arrows
15 **NAKANO** Prost	14 **TRULLI** Prost
2 **DINIZ** Arrows	17 **MORBIDELLI** Sauber
19 **SALO** Tyrrell	18 **VERSTAPPEN** Tyrrell
20 **KATAYAMA** Minardi	21 **MARQUES** Minardi

42	43	44	45	46	47	48	49	50	51	52	53	
10	10	10	10	10	10	10	10	10	10	10	10	1
7	7	7	7	7	7	7	7	7	7	7	7	2
4	4	4	4	4	4	4	4	4	4	4	4	3
12	12	12	12	12	12	12	12	12	12	12	12	4
3	3	3	3	3	3	3	3	3	3	3	3	5
5	5	5	5	5	5	5	5	5	5	5	5	6
8	8	8	8	8	8	8	8	8	8	8	8	
6	6	6	6	6	6	6	6	6	6	6	6	
1	1	1	1	1	9	9	9	9	9	9	9	
14	14	14	14	14	14	14	14	14	14	14	14	
15	15	15	9	9	15	15	15	15	15	15	15	
9	9	15	15	15	17	17	17	17	17	17		
17	17	17	17	17	22	22	22	22	22	22		
22	22	22	22	22	21	21	21	21				
21	21	21	21	21								

TIME SHEETS

QUALIFYING

Weather: Dry, hot and sunny

Pos.	Driver	Car	Laps	Time
1	Jean Alesi	Benetton-Renault	10	1m 22.990s
2	Heinz-Harald Frentzen	Williams-Renault	11	1m 23.042s
3	Giancarlo Fisichella	Jordan-Peugeot	12	1m 23.066s
4	Jacques Villeneuve	Williams-Renault	11	1m 23.231s
5	Mika Häkkinen	McLaren-Mercedes	10	1m 23.340s
6	David Coulthard	McLaren-Mercedes	11	1m 23.347s
7	Gerhard Berger	Benetton-Renault	11	1m 23.443s
8	Ralf Schumacher	Jordan-Peugeot	11	1m 23.603s
9	Michael Schumacher	Ferrari	12	1m 23.624s
10	Eddie Irvine	Ferrari	12	1m 23.891s
11	Rubens Barrichello	Stewart-Ford	11	1m 24.177s
12	Johnny Herbert	Sauber-Petronas	11	1m 24.242s
13	Jan Magnussen	Stewart-Ford	11	1m 24.394s
14	Damon Hill	Arrows-Yamaha	12	1m 24.482s
15	Shinji Nakano	Prost-Mugen Honda	11	1m 24.553s
16	Jarno Trulli	Prost-Mugen Honda	12	1m 24.567s
17	Pedro Diniz	Arrows-Yamaha	12	1m 24.639s
18	Gianni Morbidelli	Sauber-Petronas	11	1m 24.735s
19	Mika Salo	Tyrrell-Ford	8	1m 25.693s
20	Jos Verstappen	Tyrrell-Ford	12	1m 25.845s
21	Ukyo Katayama	Minardi-Hart	10	1m 26.655s
22	Tarso Marques	Minardi-Hart	10	1m 27.677s

FRIDAY FREE PRACTICE

Weather: Sunny and hot

Pos.	Driver	Laps	Time
1	Heinz-Harald Frentzen	27	1m 23.991s
2	Jacques Villeneuve	28	1m 24.837s
3	Jean Alesi	24	1m 24.847s
4	David Coulthard	21	1m 25.050s
5	Giancarlo Fisichella	27	1m 25.050s
6	Mika Häkkinen	21	1m 25.096s
7	Jarno Trulli	29	1m 25.317s
8	Eddie Irvine	25	1m 25.340s
9	Ralf Schumacher	29	1m 25.422s
10	Jan Magnussen	23	1m 25.488s
11	Gerhard Berger	27	1m 25.559s
12	Johnny Herbert	30	1m 25.845s
13	Michael Schumacher	19	1m 26.224s
14	Pedro Diniz	29	1m 26.246s
15	Rubens Barrichello	26	1m 26.421s
16	Damon Hill	29	1m 26.502s
17	Mika Salo	23	1m 26.608s
18	Gianni Morbidelli	30	1m 26.696s
19	Shinji Nakano	30	1m 26.727s
20	Jos Verstappen	26	1m 26.755s
21	Ukyo Katayama	24	1m 26.891s
22	Tarso Marques	17	1m 28.388s

SATURDAY FREE PRACTICE

Weather: Dry, hot and sunny

Pos.	Driver	Laps	Time
1	Jacques Villeneuve	25	1m 23.194s
2	Jean Alesi	23	1m 23.262s
3	Giancarlo Fisichella	22	1m 23.329s
4	Mika Häkkinen	10	1m 23.346s
5	Ralf Schumacher	16	1m 23.387s
6	David Coulthard	19	1m 23.434s
7	Heinz-Harald Frentzen	28	1m 23.658s
8	Michael Schumacher	21	1m 23.815s
9	Gerhard Berger	27	1m 23.898s
10	Eddie Irvine	25	1m 24.236s
11	Johnny Herbert	22	1m 24.316s
12	Rubens Barrichello	20	1m 24.379s
13	Jan Magnussen	21	1m 24.436s
14	Jarno Trulli	9	1m 24.749s
15	Damon Hill	17	1m 24.892s
16	Shinji Nakano	27	1m 25.034s
17	Pedro Diniz	15	1m 25.243s
18	Gianni Morbidelli	28	1m 25.391s
19	Mika Salo	22	1m 25.561s
20	Jos Verstappen	24	1m 25.925s
21	Ukyo Katayama	23	1m 26.709s
22	Tarso Marques	27	1m 27.929s

WARM-UP

Weather: Dry, hot and sunny

Pos.	Driver	Laps	Time
1	Mika Häkkinen	12	1m 24.234s
2	Ralf Schumacher	16	1m 24.937s
3	David Coulthard	14	1m 25.093s
4	Giancarlo Fisichella	16	1m 25.118s
5	Jarno Trulli	13	1m 25.493s
6	Shinji Nakano	16	1m 25.608s
7	Jacques Villeneuve	14	1m 25.683s
8	Jean Alesi	8	1m 25.836s
9	Rubens Barrichello	13	1m 25.860s
10	Heinz-Harald Frentzen	12	1m 25.962s
11	Gerhard Berger	8	1m 26.028s
12	Mika Salo	14	1m 26.037s
13	Johnny Herbert	12	1m 26.115s
14	Michael Schumacher	13	1m 26.228s
15	Damon Hill	14	1m 26.364s
16	Pedro Diniz	14	1m 26.511s
17	Eddie Irvine	12	1m 26.907s
18	Gianni Morbidelli	11	1m 27.012s
19	Jan Magnussen	6	1m 27.343s
20	Jos Verstappen	12	1m 27.496s
21	Ukyo Katayama	13	1m 28.279s
22	Tarso Marques	3	1m 38.060s

RACE FASTEST LAPS

Weather: Dry, hot and sunny

Driver	Time	Lap
Mika Häkkinen	1m 24.808s	49
Heinz-Harald Frentzen	1m 25.600s	47
Gerhard Berger	1m 25.653s	47
Eddie Irvine	1m 25.655s	53
Jacques Villeneuve	1m 25.715s	20
Michael Schumacher	1m 25.863s	47
Ralf Schumacher	1m 25.909s	31
Giancarlo Fisichella	1m 25.960s	28
David Coulthard	1m 25.976s	31
Jean Alesi	1m 26.067s	52
Shinji Nakano	1m 26.383s	53
Johnny Herbert	1m 26.572s	27
Jarno Trulli	1m 26.718s	44
Damon Hill	1m 27.081s	27
Gianni Morbidelli	1m 27.257s	26
Jan Magnussen	1m 27.447s	21
Rubens Barrichello	1m 27.571s	20
Mika Salo	1m 28.004s	12
Jos Verstappen	1m 28.227s	9
Pedro Diniz	1m 28.569s	3
Tarso Marques	1m 29.116s	7
Ukyo Katayama	1m 29.133s	3

CHASSIS LOG BOOK

1	Hill	Arrows A18/5
2	Diniz	Arrows A18/4
	spare	Arrows A18/3
3	Villeneuve	Williams FW19/4
4	Frentzen	Williams FW19/5
	spare	Williams FW19/3
5	M. Schumacher	Ferrari F310B/180
6	Irvine	Ferrari F310B/179
	spare	Ferrari F310B/175
7	Alesi	Benetton B197/2
8	Berger	Benetton B197/4
	spare	Benetton B197/3
9	Häkkinen	McLaren MP4/12/7
10	Coulthard	McLaren MP4/12/4
	spare	McLaren MP4/12/5
11	R. Schumacher	Jordan 197/6
12	Fisichella	Jordan 197/5
	spare	Jordan 197/1
14	Trulli	Prost JS45/3
15	Nakano	Prost JS45/2
	spare	Prost JS45/1
16	Herbert	Sauber C16/3
17	Morbidelli	Sauber C16/6
	spare	Sauber C16/5
18	Verstappen	Tyrrell 025/4
19	Salo	Tyrrell 025/3
	spare	Tyrrell 025/1
20	Katayama	Minardi M197/4
21	Marques	Minardi M197/2
	spare	Minardi M197/1
22	Barrichello	Stewart SF1/2
23	Magnussen	Stewart SF1/3
	spare	Stewart SF1/1

POINTS TABLES

Drivers

1	Michael Schumacher	67
2	Jacques Villeneuve	57
3	Jean Alesi	28
4	Heinz-Harald Frentzen	27
5	David Coulthard	24
6	Gerhard Berger	21
7	Eddie Irvine	18
8	Olivier Panis	15
9	Giancarlo Fisichella	17
10 =	Mika Häkkinen	14
10 =	Johnny Herbert	14
12	Ralf Schumacher	11
13	Damon Hill	7
14	Rubens Barrichello	6
15	Alexander Wurz	4
16	Jarno Trulli	3
17 =	Mika Salo	2
17 =	Shinji Nakano	2
19	Nicola Larini	1

Constructors

1	Ferrari	85
2	Williams	84
3	Benetton	53
4	McLaren	38
5	Jordan	28
6	Prost	20
7	Sauber	15
8	Arrows	7
9	Stewart	6
10	Tyrrell	2

AUSTRIAN

Photos: Paul-Henri Cahier

VILLENEUVE

COULTHARD

FRENTZEN

FISICHELLA

R. SCHUMACHER

M. SCHUMACHER

Main photo: Jarno Trulli led the race in assured style and the young Italian was in a secure second place when his Prost suffered a major engine failure. Victory fell to Jacques Villeneuve *(above left)*, who was joined on the podium by his team-mate Heinz-Harald Frentzen.

grand prix

DIARY

Indianapolis boss Tony George reveals plans for a possible F1 circuit at the Brickyard on a 2.5-mile track inside the famous 2.5-mile banked oval.

Mika Salo named as Arrows replacement for Damon Hill in 1998.

Alexander Wurz confirmed as Benetton team driver for 1998.

Olivier Panis announces that he will make F1 return at the Luxembourg GP at the Nürburgring on 28 September after promising test for Prost at Magny-Cours.

JUST as it seemed Michael Schumacher was consolidating an almost impregnable advantage in the battle for the World Championship, Jacques Villeneuve kick-started the contest back into vibrant life with a superbly judged victory in the first Austrian Grand Prix to be held in a decade, its home now the brand-new A1-Ring circuit which occupies the site of the old Österreichring track of glorious memory.

Schumacher, who was confident his Ferrari could deliver second place despite a disappointing display in qualifying, had a catastrophic weekend and salvaged only sixth place for his efforts. Having qualified his F310B a lowly ninth, he battled his way up into the top three and actually led the race for two laps before making his sole refuelling stop on lap 42. He resumed in fifth place, but then had to come into the pits for a ten-second stop–go penalty after overtaking Heinz-Harald Frentzen at the uphill right-hand Remus Kurve when waved yellow flags were being displayed following a collision between, ironically, his teammate Eddie Irvine's Ferrari and the Benetton of Jean Alesi.

Thus with three Grands Prix remaining and 30 points to race for, Villeneuve came out of the weekend trailing his Ferrari rival by a single point as the F1 circus moved on to the Luxembourg Grand Prix the following Sunday at the Nürburgring, a track on which Villeneuve had scored his maiden F1 victory 16 months earlier with a split-second victory over the German driver.

'I made an average start and for the first two laps the tyres were not properly up to temperature, which is why [Rubens] Barrichello passed me on the first lap,' said Villeneuve.

'Once they warmed up to temperature, I was quicker than him, but I took my time passing him as I did not want to get involved in any wheel banging. It was vital for me to score points today.'

Villeneuve took the lead for good after 44 of the race's 71 laps and drove with great restraint and discipline to take the chequered flag 2.9s ahead of Italian GP winner David Coulthard, with Frentzen bringing the other Williams home third to consolidate the British team's lead in the constructors' championship table.

Villeneuve had managed to qualify on pole position, just squeezing out Mika Häkkinen's formidable McLaren-Mercedes, but it was the Finn who got away to the cleanest start. Villeneuve was slow off the mark, allowing Jarno Trulli's Prost-Mugen Honda and Rubens Barrichello's Stewart to slot into immediate second and third places.

Against all pre-race predictions, all the competitors managed to scramble through the worryingly tight first corner, although Gerhard Berger was spared the challenge as he started from the pit lane, having pulled in at the end of the final parade lap when a warning display on his Benetton's dashboard gave him cause for concern. He started behind the rest of the pack, beginning his race on a low note by spinning at the first corner.

At the end of the opening lap, even as Häkkinen came into view round the final right-hander in the lead, the McLaren driver was pulling over onto the grass on the left of the circuit. His Mercedes V10 had shown the first signs of tightening up and Mika wisely switched off before it suffered a major failure.

Thus Trulli, competing in only his 14th Grand Prix, completed the opening lap 0.6s ahead of Barrichello, with Villeneuve third from the impressive Jan Magnussen's Stewart, Frentzen's Williams, Schumacher's Ferrari, Coulthard, a well-placed Damon Hill, Ralf Schumacher, Irvine and Alesi.

Trulli was not going to squander his advantage or easily be pressured into a mistake. With four laps completed he had eased open his lead to 1.7s over Barrichello with Villeneuve apparently running just quickly enough in third place to keep Magnussen at bay. Behind this group, Frentzen was already dropping away slightly in fifth place.

By the ten lap mark, Trulli was 3.3s ahead of Barrichello, while Magnussen was falling back from Villeneuve and Schumacher's Ferrari was nibbling away at Frentzen's advantage, bringing Coulthard, Hill and brother Ralf closer with him. Magnussen by now had a serious problem and, by lap 14, had Frentzen's Williams almost tucked right under his wing.

'I made a really good start,' said Jan, 'but after three laps I had already blistered the rear tyres, so it was difficult to keep up the pace.' Yet he hung on doggedly and refused to be intimidated by the pressure from the Williams driver. The traffic quickly banked up into a long queue behind him, but he certainly wasn't worried about that.

It was lap 24 before Villeneuve finally managed to outbrake Barrichello to take over second place, by which time Trulli had expanded his advantage to 10.8s. Never did the young Italian put a wheel wrong, nor did he look flustered or concerned about his position at the head of the pack.

In many ways, Trulli's performance was the single most impressive aspect of the race. Even when Villeneuve had muscled ahead of Barrichello and began to make inroads into his lead, Trulli's concentration never wavered.

Jacques eventually hauled up to within three seconds of the Prost, then vaulted ahead at his refuelling stop. The Italian came in at the end of lap 37 for a 10.7s stop, with Jacques making a 9.7s stop three laps later and getting back into the race ahead of his rival once Schumacher's Ferrari, which went ahead on lap 41, came in for fuel and tyres at the end of lap 42.

However, by then, the damage had been done as far as Michael's prospects were concerned. On lap 38, Alesi, who had just accelerated back into the race in 12th place after his refuelling stop, came into the braking area for the uphill Remus Kurve with Irvine's Ferrari right on his tail. Irvine tried to run round the outside of the Benetton, but the two cars made very firm contact, Alesi's flying high over the Ferrari's right-front wheel and landing in the gravel on the outside of the corner.

Irvine managed to limp his car back to the pits where he immediately retired. He was in no doubt as to the precise cause of the accident.

'Running on soft tyres, I began to have handling problems around the 12th lap,' he said, 'so I backed off. Then after a few laps, the tyres started working again, which is why I was aiming for only one stop at the end of lap 41.

'Then Alesi came out of the pits and I got on the outside of him, but was running a lighter car than him. His car oversteered and he hit me on the right-rear wheel and on the right side. My car was too badly damaged for me to continue.' Needless to say, Alesi just dismissed Eddie as a 'madman', which was, all agreed, the response one might have expected from the volatile Frenchman.

Gerhard Berger endured a miserable weekend on home soil. Having qualified in a lowly 18th place, he started the race from the pit lane and contrived to spin at the tight first corner in his eagerness to catch the disappearing pack.

Left: Under control. Jacques Villeneuve passes the Stewart-Ford of Rubens Barrichello to move into second place. Once he had slipped ahead of Jarno Trulli during the course of their refuelling stops, the Williams driver was in complete command, convincingly re-establishing his World Championship credentials.

A1-RING QUALIFYING

As early as Thursday's acclimatisation testing on the new circuit, it had become apparent that the Bridgestone runners might have a worthwhile performance advantage at the A1-Ring. Damon Hill's Arrows was quickest ahead of the Stewart-Fords of Rubens Barrichello and Jan Magnussen.

Opinions about the new track were mixed and varied, but Gerhard Berger summed it up nicely. 'The old Österreichring was the greatest circuit in the world for me, but the new one fits to the new generation,' he said tactfully.

'Safety standards are completely different now. There is a very narrow line between going fast, and over-driving and going off.'

Yet by the end of Saturday morning free practice it seemed as though reality had been temporarily suspended with Pedro Diniz posting fastest time in his Arrows-Yamaha ahead of Magnussen.

Damon Hill, who wound up 11th fastest in this particular session, eventually qualified in seventh place – ironically having his best lap spoiled when he had to overtake one of Eddie Jordan's cars in the middle of a corner. He rounded off the session by spinning into a gravel trap.

Meanwhile, at the sharp end of the action, Jacques Villeneuve started his fight-back in the battle for the World Championship by qualifying his Williams-Renault on pole position. The Williams FW19s benefited from a further revised Renault RS9B engine, offering extra revs for qualifying, and Jacques certainly looked on pin-sharp form.

He shrewdly stayed in the pit lane garage until late in the hour-long session, realising that his hard-compound Goodyear tyres would work best as the track temperature crept up throughout the hour. Villeneuve achieved pole using a chassis set-up which was far closer to Patrick Head's suggestion than his traditional stiffly sprung configuration.

The Canadian eventually out-gunned Mika Häkkinen's McLaren-Mercedes by 0.094s with Jarno Trulli posting a sensational third-fastest time using his spare Prost-Mugen Honda after his original race car suffered an engine failure on the opening lap.

Häkkinen was delighted with the front-end bite offered by the latest Adrian Newey-inspired front wing which was being used on the McLaren MP4/12 for the first time. It was just disappointing that he would be unable to display its advantage come race day.

Heinz-Harald Frentzen qualified the second Williams in fourth place, having lost 15 minutes of the session when an electronic glitch unexpectedly activated the brake balance fail-safe mechanism. Behind him, Barrichello and Magnussen did a good job with the Stewart-Fords to line up fifth and sixth.

In the Ferrari camp, Eddie Irvine drove well to out-qualify World Championship points leader Michael Schumacher, the two Italian machines lining up in eighth and ninth places. Irvine used the softer

of the two available Goodyear compounds and also drove the latest lightweight version of the F310B chassis, but Schumacher preferred the older car and opted for hard tyres.

'My problem was that I was beginning to run out of fuel on my quickest lap,' said Schumacher, 'and although I set a decent time, I could have done better. Realistically, I think the best we could have done would have been to move up three or four places.'

For his part, Irvine, who had suffered a lot of understeer on new tyres during the morning, put on more frontal downforce for qualifying, which improved matters 'but not by much'. He spent a lot of the session trying to get the softer rubber to work in race trim.

Yet again, David Coulthard had a troubled time on Saturday. In the morning he hooked his McLaren MP4/12 over a kerb with about 20 minutes of the free practice session left, spinning across the road to remove his right-front wheel against a guard rail. In the afternoon David found himself unable to get a clear run in chaotically heavy traffic and had to settle for a distant tenth place.

The Jordan team's apparent elation at having secured Damon Hill's services for 1998 quickly evaporated when the time came for Ralf Schumacher and Giancarlo Fisichella to shape up to the hour-long qualifying session. Acute lack of grip and heavy traffic respectively were responsible for Schumacher Junior and Fisichella lining up 11th and 14th. It was less by far than they had been expecting.

Johnny Herbert was also struggling to get the Sauber up to 12th on the grid. 'Overall, the car is not too bad, but I still had too much understeer,' he shrugged. Gianni Morbidelli was right on his tail, happy to be close to his team-mate in 13th place after a session in which his car had performed well, despite a spin on the final corner on somebody else's gravel.

With Jean Alesi and Gerhard Berger in 15th and 18th places in the final line-up, Benetton had no answers either. 'We just didn't manage to get the best from the car,' said Berger. 'We opted for hard tyres, but we were simply unable to get a quick lap.'

Shinji Nakano's Prost was 16th, while Diniz was unable to duplicate his morning's performance after suffering engine failures with both his Arrows race chassis and the spare and had to be content with 17th-fastest time. Despite slight gearbox problems Ukyo Katayama qualified his Minardi 19th, split from team-mate Tarso Marques only by Jos Verstappen's Tyrrell.

As things transpired, the Brazilian's car was found to be below the minimum weight limit by 3 kg when pulled in for a random pit lane check. Minardi claimed it was because Marques had lost precisely that amount since his and his car's combined weight was last registered with the FIA. Nevertheless, that slip left Mika Salo's Tyrrell occupying the final row of the grid on its own.

215

Hill confirmed for Jordan

Lukas Gorys

THE way Eddie Jordan tells it, a chance meeting on a private jet led to Damon Hill signing the £10 million two-year contract to drive for his team which was formally announced in the paddock at the A1-Ring before free practice began on Friday morning.

On the evening after the Italian Grand Prix, Tom Walkinshaw, the Arrows team chief, apparently forgot to wait for his World Champion, leaving Hill standing on the tarmac at Milan's Linate airport. Conveniently, the HS125 furnished by one of the Jordan sponsors was waiting on the apron, ready to ferry the team hierarchy back to Oxford.

Hill hitched a lift and, by the time he stepped from the jet two hours later, had hammered out a deal to drive for the team. It was a tale Jordan recounted with a degree of well-practised relish, obviously delighted to have out-fumbled all the media speculation over Hill's future career plans.

'Jordan have really pushed themselves forward and established themselves as a very competitive package. That wasn't clear at this time last year,' said Hill, who turned down a Jordan offer at the start of 1997.

'I think without question they will be winning races, and if you can win races then you can challenge for the championship, and that's what I really want to do.'

However, the chronology of Jordan's tale left a trail of scepticism among some of the more hard-bitten members of the F1 community. If Hill had done his deal ten days earlier, they wondered, why did Jordan continue their High Court battle with Benetton over the services of Giancarlo Fisichella, a contest which they eventually lost in the run-up to the Austrian race?

Sutton Motorsport Images

Why did they allow the Arrows team to gain the PR initiative by effectively announcing that Mika Salo was replacing Hill? And why did Alain Prost take until the previous Thursday to announce that negotiations with the Hill camp had fallen through?

That last point certainly left Prost in a vexed frame of mind. In fact, Alain accused Hill of bad faith for apparently continuing to negotiate the terms of a contract long after he had seemingly signed the Jordan deal.

'I am very disappointed in the way that Damon has conducted himself,' said Prost. 'We had talked at length and I believed we had a firm deal. Then I was suddenly called to say he had been offered a drive with Jordan.

'It was as if he was expecting me to give him more money than we had already agreed. I felt his main motivation was money. We were great friends when we drove together at Williams, but I have now seen him in a different light.

'He did not prove to me that he was interested in my team and the challenge I offered him. You cannot only race for money. I had a budget limit and you can't put it all on a driver, even if he is one of the good ones. At the end of the day I think it is a good thing he is not coming.'

The Hill camp vigorously rebutted Prost's account of events. They explained that they advised the Frenchman quite properly that an offer had been accepted from Jordan and they were not in any way attempting to squeeze any additional money from Prost in doing so.

'Why does everyone think I'm so into money?' asked Hill. 'If that was the case, I would have taken Sauber's offer [the Swiss team reputedly bid £6.5 million].

'I'm driving for Jordan because that offers me the best chance of what I want to do, which is winning races.'

Below left: While Eddie Jordan and Damon Hill announce their engagement, the spurned suitor, Alain Prost, reads all about it in *L'Équipe.* C'est la vie!

Right: Come fly with me. Eddie Irvine and Jean Alesi tangle, with the Benetton being launched into the air, and the Frenchman into orbit.

'If I hadn't known it would have cost me $10,000, I would have put my fist in his face,' said Jean. 'I am very angry. Irvine tried to overtake me around the outside, and there was no room. I was taking my line and then suddenly the other car was there.'

On the following lap Schumacher found himself tempted into overtaking Frentzen at the same point after the Williams driver seemingly left the inside line wide open. A few laps later the Ferrari pit was notified that it should call Michael in for a ten-second stop-go penalty. This was duly done at the end of lap 50 so, with 21 laps to go, Ferrari's team leader found himself back in an unaccustomed ninth place.

'I think I could have finished second without that penalty,' he mused after the race, 'as after the pit stop I was right behind Villeneuve. Obviously I did not see the yellow flag because I was concentrating on my fight with Frentzen and Berger [who was being lapped at that point]. I think the flag was waved on the left-hand side of this right-hand corner. I think the flags should be made more visible and waved on both sides of the track. But I am not too unhappy, as I managed to pick up a point.'

Meanwhile, Trulli gamely slogged on in second place, increasingly aware that his refuelling rig had short-changed him in the pit lane, before his engine blew up spectacularly. There were only 13 laps to go.

'I led for all the first part of the race and I was in total control,' he reflected confidently. 'The gap over second place got bigger every lap and, psychologically, I wanted the others to see there was more to come if I wanted. Then, six or seven laps before my pit stop, I started to sense that there was a problem with the engine.

'That is why, instead of going after Villeneuve, it was a case of trying to hold on to second place. Without the engine problem, I could have gone harder and I think I could have won.'

Meanwhile, there had been some juggling about among the secondary placings as both Stewart-Fords had been on a two-stop schedule. Barrichello had made his first stop on lap 28, worried by front tyre wear, but launched himself back into the fray with undiminished enthusiasm in 11th place.

He climbed back to fourth before making his second stop on lap 50, rejoining in eighth and charging hard, confident that he could challenge for a place in the points before the end of the race. Unfortunately, Michael Schumacher had other ideas.

The Stewart and Ferrari were run-

ning in seventh and eighth places when Michael suddenly feinted dramatically for the inside line coming down to the last corner on lap 65. Rubens was momentarily distracted and, by the time he'd regained his concentration, his Stewart was flying across the gravel trap, shedding bits of bodywork and broken suspension. Michael, doubtless smiling to himself, moved up into seventh place.

Magnussen's early sprint had also ended in disappointment. After running fourth up to his first refuelling stop on lap 26, he resumed in 13th and then climbed back to fifth before stopping again on lap 47. He retired with engine failure on lap 59 while running tenth.

'My second and third sets of tyres were very good, but a two-stop strategy definitely didn't help us,' he said. 'It is a shame that the engine blew, be-

Publiracing Agency/Manfred Giet

cause I was already looking for a finish in the points.'

None of this detail could detract from Villeneuve's cool domination of the event. He eventually took the flag 2.9s ahead of Coulthard's McLaren, the Scot having run a good race and made worthwhile progress through his refuelling stops.

'The real pleasure today comes from taking nine points back from Michael,' grinned Villeneuve. 'In the early stages I was worried about Trulli's Prost because I thought it would be a strong car throughout the whole race. We planned to stay out for as long as the fuel would allow us before making our stop, and it worked out really well because that is how we got ahead of Trulli.'

Villeneuve also admitted that he was a little worried about Coulthard catching him in the closing stages of the race because he found himself

stuck in traffic behind Berger. 'I was taking it very easy then because I know from a recent experience how difficult he is to lap,' he noted wryly.

Coulthard was also happy with his performance. 'I had a lot of fun from the start,' he said. 'I gained a place during a pit stop, thanks to the mechanics, and I was certainly in better shape on the second set of tyres than on the first. But in terms of traffic, it was one of the worst races I have ever had. There were two Benettons in front of me, then a Prost which blew up, and there were not many blue flags being waved out there.'

Frentzen was quite happy with third, deriving some slight amusement from the fact Schumacher had lost so many points when he overtook him under the yellow flag. Fisichella was a good fourth ahead of Ralf Schumacher, the young German not feeling sufficiently generous to hand his fifth

place to brother Michael in the closing moments of the race.

Frustratingly for Damon Hill, Michael picked up that final point of the afternoon after diving through ahead of his Arrows at the Remus Kurve with just over a lap to go. 'The balance of the car was fantastic,' said Damon, 'but it was just hopeless on acceleration. We just don't have enough power. I also had a soft brake pedal in the closing stages, but even so I thought Michael was too far back to get past. I braked as late as I could, but he still slipped through.'

Eighth and ninth were the Saubers of Johnny Herbert and Gianni Morbidelli, both suffering with blistering of their softer-compound Goodyears. Morbidelli was particularly frustrated, having been forced to brake to a standstill in order to avoid being hit by debris from the Irvine/Alesi collision.

Berger finished tenth, the Benetton strategy being to run on the same set of tyres to the finish as they felt there was no evidence that fresh rubber offered an immediate advantage. It seemed a mixed blessing as he spun into the gravel at the very last corner of the race but he was able to extricate his B197 and continue to the flag.

Katayama's Minardi was 11th ahead of Verstappen's Tyrrell and Diniz's Arrows, while Barrichello was classified 14th despite the fact that his Stewart was off the road by the time the race ended.

Unquestionably, Villeneuve had seemed more capable than of late when it came to the task of unlocking the Williams FW19's potential. It was a good win, even though Trulli and Häkkinen had signalled opposition from other quarters.

Perhaps Ferrari's summer in the sun was coming to an end after all.

GROSSER PREIS VON ÖSTERREICH

19–21 SEPTEMBER 1997

A1-RING

Race distance: 71 laps, 190.719 miles/306.933 km

Race weather: Dry, hot and sunny

ROUND
14

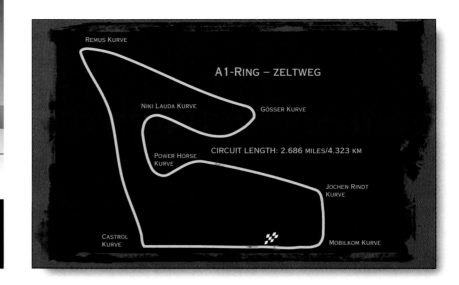

A1-RING – ZELTWEG

REMUS KURVE
NIKI LAUDA KURVE
GÖSSER KURVE
POWER HORSE KURVE
CASTROL KURVE
JOCHEN RINDT KURVE
MOBILKOM KURVE

CIRCUIT LENGTH: 2.686 MILES/4.323 KM

Pos.	Driver	Nat.	No.	Entrant	Car/Engine	Tyres	Laps	Time/Retirement	Speed (mph/km/h)
1	Jacques Villeneuve	CDN	3	Rothmans Williams Renault	Williams FW19-Renault RS9A V10	G	71	1h 27m 35.999s	130.629/210.228
2	David Coulthard	GB	10	West McLaren Mercedes	McLaren MP4/12-Mercedes FO110F V10	G	71	1h 27m 38.908s	130.557/210.111
3	Heinz-Harald Frentzen	D	4	Rothmans Williams Renault	Williams FW19-Renault RS9A V10	G	71	1h 27m 39.961s	130.531/210.069
4	Giancarlo Fisichella	I	12	B&H Total Jordan Peugeot	Jordan 197-Peugeot A14 V10	G	71	1h 27m 48.126s	130.329/209.744
5	Ralf Schumacher	D	11	B&H Total Jordan Peugeot	Jordan 197-Peugeot A14 V10	G	71	1h 28m 07.858s	129.842/208.961
6	Michael Schumacher	D	5	Scuderia Ferrari Marlboro	Ferrari F310B 046/2 V10	G	71	1h 28m 09.409s	129.804/208.900
7	Damon Hill	GB	1	Danka Arrows Yamaha	Arrows A18-Yamaha OX11A/D V10	B	71	1h 28m 13.206s	129.711/208.750
8	Johnny Herbert	GB	16	Red Bull Sauber Petronas	Sauber C16-Petronas V10	G	71	1h 28m 25.056s	129.421/208.284
9	Gianni Morbidelli	I	17	Red Bull Sauber Petronas	Sauber C16-Petronas V10	G	71	1h 28m 42.454s	128.998/207.603
10	Gerhard Berger	A	8	Mild Seven Benetton Renault	Benetton B197-Renault RS9A V10	G	70		
11	Ukyo Katayama	J	20	Minardi Team	Minardi M197-Hart 830 V8	B	69		
12	Jos Verstappen	NL	18	Tyrrell	Tyrrell 025-Ford ED5 V8	G	69		
13	Pedro Diniz	BR	2	Danka Arrows Yamaha	Arrows A18-Yamaha OX11A/D V10	B	67	Shock absorber	
14	Rubens Barrichello	BR	22	Stewart Ford	Stewart SF1-Ford Zetec-R V10	B	64	Accident	
	Jarno Trulli	I	14	Prost Gauloises Blondes	Prost JS45-Mugen Honda MF301HB V10	B	58	Engine	
	Jan Magnussen	DK	23	Stewart Ford	Stewart SF1-Ford Zetec-R V10	B	58	Engine	
	Shinji Nakano	J	15	Prost Gauloises Blondes	Prost JS45-Mugen Honda MF301HB V10	B	57	Engine	
	Mika Salo	SF	19	Tyrrell	Tyrrell 025-Ford ED5 V8	G	48	Transmission	
	Eddie Irvine	GB	6	Scuderia Ferrari Marlboro	Ferrari F310B 046/2 V10	G	38	Collision damage	
	Jean Alesi	F	7	Mild Seven Benetton Renault	Benetton B197-Renault RS9A V10	G	37	Collision with Irvine	
	Mika Häkkinen	SF	9	West McLaren Mercedes	McLaren MP4/12-Mercedes FO110F V10	G	1	Engine	
DNS	Tarso Marques	BR	21	Minardi Team	Minardi M197-Hart 830 V8	B		Excluded	

Fastest lap: Villeneuve, on lap 36, 1m 11.814s, 134.656 mph/216.709 km/h (establishes record).

B – Bridgestone   G – Goodyear

Grid order	1 2 3 4 5 6 7 8 9 10 11 12 13 14 15 16 17 18 19 20 21 22 23 24 25 26 27 28 29 30 31 32 33 34 35 36 37 38 39 40 41 42 43 44 45 46 47 48 49 50 51 52 53 54 55
3 VILLENEUVE	14 14 14 14 14 14 14 14 14 14 14 14 14 14 14 14 14 14 14 14 14 14 14 14 14 14 14 14 14 14 14 14 14 14 14 14 3 3 3 5 5 10 3 3 3 3 3 3 3 3 3 3 3 3 3
9 HÄKKINEN	22 22 22 22 22 22 22 22 22 22 22 22 22 22 22 22 22 22 22 22 23 3 3 3 3 3 3 3 3 3 3 3 3 4 5 5 4 10 3 14 12 14 14 14 14 14 14 14 14 14 14
14 TRULLI	3 3 3 3 3 3 3 3 3 3 3 3 3 3 3 3 3 3 3 3 22 22 22 22 22 4 4 4 4 4 4 4 5 4 4 10 4 14 12 14 5 5 5 5 5 10 10 10 10 10
4 FRENTZEN	23 23 23 23 23 23 23 23 23 23 23 23 23 23 23 23 23 23 23 23 23 23 4 4 5 5 5 5 5 5 5 5 10 10 10 3 3 12 5 5 22 22 22 22 22 4 4 4 4
22 BARRICHELLO	4 4 4 4 4 4 4 4 4 4 4 4 4 4 4 4 4 4 4 4 4 4 23 5 10 10 10 10 10 10 10 10 14 14 14 14 5 22 22 23 23 10 10 10 12 12 12 12 12
23 MAGNUSSEN	5 5 5 5 5 5 5 5 5 5 5 5 5 5 5 5 5 5 5 5 5 5 10 10 1 1 1 1 1 1 1 11 11 11 11 22 23 23 10 10 4 4 4 11 11 11 11 11
1 HILL	10 10 10 10 10 10 10 10 10 10 10 10 10 10 10 10 10 10 10 10 10 10 10 1 11 11 11 11 11 11 11 11 11 12 12 12 23 10 10 4 4 12 12 12 1 1 1 1 1
6 IRVINE	1 1 1 1 1 1 1 1 1 1 1 1 1 1 1 1 1 1 1 1 1 1 11 11 7 7 7 7 7 7 12 12 12 1 16 22 22 4 4 4 12 12 11 11 11 22 22 22 22
5 M. SCHUMACHER	11 11 11 11 11 11 11 11 11 11 11 11 11 11 11 11 11 11 11 11 11 11 7 7 12 12 12 12 12 12 7 16 16 16 22 23 23 11 11 11 11 11 1 1 1 5 5 5 5
10 COULTHARD	6 6 6 6 6 6 6 6 6 6 6 7 7 7 7 7 7 7 7 7 12 12 16 16 16 16 22 22 23 23 1 1 1 1 1 1 16 16 16 16 16 23 23 23
11 R. SCHUMACHER	7 7 7 7 7 7 7 7 7 7 7 12 12 12 12 12 12 12 12 12 16 22 22 22 22 22 22 23 23 1 17 16 16 16 16 16 23 23 23 16 16
16 HERBERT	12 12 12 12 12 12 12 12 12 12 12 6 6 6 6 6 6 16 16 16 16 16 2 2 2 23 23 23 23 23 7 17 17 17 16 17 17 17 17 17 17 17 17 17
17 MORBIDELLI	16 16 16 16 16 16 16 16 16 16 16 16 16 16 16 16 6 6 6 2 2 2 23 23 2 2 2 6 6 6 6 6 15 15 15 15 15 2 2 2 2 2 2 2 2
12 FISICHELLA	17 17 17 17 17 2 2 2 2 2 2 2 2 2 2 2 2 2 2 17 17 17 17 17 6 6 17 17 17 17 17 15 2 2 2 2 15 15 15 15 15 15 15 15 15
7 ALESI	2 2 2 2 17 17 17 17 17 17 17 17 17 17 17 17 17 6 6 6 6 6 17 17 15 15 19 19 15 2 8 8 8 8 8 8 8 8 8 8 8 8 8
15 NAKANO	15 15 15 15 15 15 15 15 15 15 15 15 15 15 15 15 15 15 15 15 15 15 15 2 19 15 15 2 8 19 19 19 8 19 19 20 20 20 20 20 20 20
2 DINIZ	20 20 20 20 20 20 20 20 20 20 20 20 20 20 20 20 20 20 20 20 8 8 8 8 8 19 2 2 8 19 2 2 2 8 19 20 20 20 20 20 18 18 18
8 BERGER	18 18 18 18 18 18 18 18 19 19 19 19 19 8 8 8 8 8 8 8 20 19 19 19 19 19 8 8 8 19 20 18 18 18 18 18
20 KATAYAMA	19 19 19 19 19 19 19 19 8 8 8 8 19 19 19 19 19 19 19 19 20 20 20 20 20 20 20 20 20 20 18
18 VERSTAPPEN	8 8 8 8 8 8 8 8 18 18 18 18 18 18 18 18 18 18 18 18 18 18 18 18 18 18 18 18 18 18
19 SALO		

Pit stop
One lap behind leader

STARTING GRID

3 VILLENEUVE Williams		**9** HÄKKINEN McLaren	
14 TRULLI Prost		**4** FRENTZEN Williams	
22 BARRICHELLO Stewart		**23** MAGNUSSEN Stewart	
1 HILL Arrows		**6** IRVINE Ferrari	
5 M. SCHUMACHER Ferrari		**10** COULTHARD McLaren	
11 R. SCHUMACHER Jordan		**16** HERBERT Sauber	
17 MORBIDELLI Sauber		**12** FISICHELLA Jordan	
7 ALESI Benetton		**15** NAKANO Prost	
2 DINIZ Arrows		**8** BERGER* Benetton	
20 KATAYAMA Minardi		**18** VERSTAPPEN Tyrrell	
19 SALO Tyrrell			

* started from pit lane

Excluded:
MARQUES (Minardi)

Lap chart (leaders)

56	57	58	59	60	61	62	63	64	65	66	67	68	69	70	71	
3	3	3	3	3	3	3	3	3	3	3	3	3	3	3	3	1
14	14	14	10	10	10	10	10	10	10	10	10	10	10	10	10	2
10	10	10	4	4	4	4	4	4	4	4	4	4	4	4	4	3
4	4	4	12	12	12	12	12	12	12	12	12	12	12	12	12	4
12	12	12	11	11	11	11	11	11	11	11	11	11	11	11	11	5
11	11	11	1	1	1	1	1	1	1	1	1	5	5	5	5	6
1	1	1	22	22	22	22	22	22	5	5	5	5	5	5	1	
22	22	22	5	5	5	5	5	16	16	16	16	16	16	16		
5	5	5	16	16	16	16	16	17	17	17	17	17	17	17		
23	23	23	17	17	17	17	17	2	2	8	8	8	8			
16	16	16	2	2	2	2	2	8	8	2	20	20				
17	17	17	8	8	8	8	20	20	20	18	18					
2	2	2	20	20	20	20	20	18	18							
15	15	15	8	18	18	18	18	18								
8	8	20														
20	20	18														
18	18															

TIME SHEETS

QUALIFYING

Weather: Dry, hot and sunny

Pos.	Driver	Car	Laps	Time
1	Jacques Villeneuve	Williams-Renault	12	1m 10.304s
2	Mika Häkkinen	McLaren-Mercedes	12	1m 10.398s
3	Jarno Trulli	Prost-Mugen Honda	12	1m 10.511s
4	Heinz-Harald Frentzen	Williams-Renault	11	1m 10.670s
5	Rubens Barrichello	Stewart-Ford	12	1m 10.700s
6	Jan Magnussen	Stewart-Ford	12	1m 10.893s
7	Damon Hill	Arrows-Yamaha	10	1m 11.025s
8	Eddie Irvine	Ferrari	11	1m 11.051s
9	Michael Schumacher	Ferrari	11	1m 11.056s
10	David Coulthard	McLaren-Mercedes	12	1m 11.076s
11	Ralf Schumacher	Jordan-Peugeot	12	1m 11.186s
12	Johnny Herbert	Sauber-Petronas	10	1m 11.210s
13	Gianni Morbidelli	Sauber-Petronas	12	1m 11.261s
14	Giancarlo Fisichella	Jordan-Peugeot	12	1m 11.299s
15	Jean Alesi	Benetton-Renault	11	1m 11.382s
16	Shinji Nakano	Prost-Mugen Honda	11	1m 11.596s
17	Pedro Diniz	Arrows-Yamaha	7	1m 11.615s
18	Gerhard Berger	Benetton-Renault	11	1m 11.620s
19	Ukyo Katayama	Minardi-Hart	12	1m 12.036s
20	Jos Verstappen	Tyrrell-Ford	12	1m 12.230s
21	Mika Salo	Tyrrell-Ford	6	1m 14.246s
	Tarso Marques	Minardi-Hart		Times disallowed

FRIDAY FREE PRACTICE

Weather: Sunny and bright

Pos.	Driver	Laps	Time
1	Heinz-Harald Frentzen	30	1m 11.527s
2	Jacques Villeneuve	26	1m 11.638s
3	Rubens Barrichello	29	1m 11.798s
4	Giancarlo Fisichella	30	1m 11.899s
5	Mika Häkkinen	15	1m 11.902s
6	David Coulthard	30	1m 11.967s
7	Michael Schumacher	30	1m 12.265s
8	Gerhard Berger	29	1m 12.283s
9	Pedro Diniz	30	1m 12.519s
10	Eddie Irvine	29	1m 12.548s
11	Damon Hill	24	1m 12.614s
12	Johnny Herbert	30	1m 12.751s
13	Jean Alesi	29	1m 12.820s
14	Jarno Trulli	30	1m 12.935s
15	Gianni Morbidelli	24	1m 12.966s
16	Ralf Schumacher	26	1m 13.041s
17	Shinji Nakano	29	1m 13.280s
18	Jan Magnussen	17	1m 13.286s
19	Ukyo Katayama	30	1m 13.348s
20	Mika Salo	30	1m 14.079s
21	Jos Verstappen	30	1m 14.188s
22	Tarso Marques	25	1m 14.739s

SATURDAY FREE PRACTICE

Weather: Warm and dry

Pos.	Driver	Laps	Time
1	Pedro Diniz	30	1m 10.782s
2	Jan Magnussen	27	1m 10.785s
3	Jacques Villeneuve	29	1m 10.798s
4	Jarno Trulli	30	1m 10.815s
5	Eddie Irvine	30	1m 10.824s
6	Mika Häkkinen	29	1m 10.872s
7	Michael Schumacher	26	1m 11.018s
8	Heinz-Harald Frentzen	19	1m 11.300s
9	Jean Alesi	30	1m 11.346s
10	Rubens Barrichello	27	1m 11.387s
11	Damon Hill	30	1m 11.471s
12	Johnny Herbert	28	1m 11.513s
13	Shinji Nakano	30	1m 11.698s
14	David Coulthard	21	1m 11.752s
15	Giancarlo Fisichella	30	1m 11.927s
16	Ralf Schumacher	26	1m 11.933s
17	Gerhard Berger	30	1m 12.109s
18	Ukyo Katayama	30	1m 12.285s
19	Gianni Morbidelli	30	1m 12.561s
20	Tarso Marques	30	1m 13.038s
21	Jos Verstappen	29	1m 13.187s
22	Mika Salo	30	1m 13.574s

WARM-UP

Weather: Cool and dry

Pos.	Driver	Laps	Time
1	Mika Häkkinen	18	1m 12.803s
2	Jarno Trulli	17	1m 12.868s
3	Michael Schumacher	18	1m 13.173s
4	Giancarlo Fisichella	19	1m 13.224s
5	David Coulthard	16	1m 13.227s
6	Rubens Barrichello	15	1m 13.509s
7	Ralf Schumacher	21	1m 13.510s
8	Gianni Morbidelli	17	1m 13.603s
9	Eddie Irvine	18	1m 13.621s
10	Pedro Diniz	8	1m 13.625s
11	Johnny Herbert	19	1m 13.692s
12	Jacques Villeneuve	16	1m 13.695s
13	Heinz-Harald Frentzen	11	1m 13.755s
14	Damon Hill	16	1m 13.929s
15	Gerhard Berger	14	1m 14.276s
16	Shinji Nakano	16	1m 14.466s
17	Jos Verstappen	16	1m 14.766s
18	Jean Alesi	12	1m 15.266s
19	Mika Salo	15	1m 15.340s
20	Jan Magnussen	10	1m 15.894s
21	Ukyo Katayama	12	1m 17.435s

RACE FASTEST LAPS

Weather: Dry, hot and sunny

Driver	Time	Lap
Jacques Villeneuve	1m 11.814s	36
Michael Schumacher	1m 12.169s	71
David Coulthard	1m 12.207s	65
Heinz-Harald Frentzen	1m 12.223s	55
Giancarlo Fisichella	1m 12.375s	64
Rubens Barrichello	1m 12.535s	55
Johnny Herbert	1m 12.574s	34
Jarno Trulli	1m 12.598s	30
Jan Magnussen	1m 12.605s	38
Gerhard Berger	1m 12.624s	66
Eddie Irvine	1m 12.704s	35
Gianni Morbidelli	1m 12.826s	71
Ralf Schumacher	1m 12.862s	65
Damon Hill	1m 12.903s	53
Jean Alesi	1m 12.953s	29
Shinji Nakano	1m 13.010s	57
Pedro Diniz	1m 13.074s	63
Jos Verstappen	1m 13.708s	69
Mika Salo	1m 13.862s	34
Ukyo Katayama	1m 14.394s	63
Mika Häkkinen	1m 31.574s	1

CHASSIS LOG BOOK

1	Hill	Arrows A18/5
2	Diniz	Arrows A18/4
	spare	Arrows A18/3
3	Villeneuve	Williams FW19/4
4	Frentzen	Williams FW19/5
	spare	Williams FW19/3
5	M. Schumacher	Ferrari F310B/180
6	Irvine	Ferrari F310B/179
	spare	Ferrari F310B/175
7	Alesi	Benetton B197/2
8	Berger	Benetton B197/4
	spare	Benetton B197/3
9	Häkkinen	McLaren MP4/12/7
10	Coulthard	McLaren MP4/12/4
	spare	McLaren MP4/12/5
11	R. Schumacher	Jordan 197/6
12	Fisichella	Jordan 197/4
	spare	Jordan 197/1
14	Trulli	Prost JS45/3
15	Nakano	Prost JS45/2
	spare	Prost JS45/1
16	Herbert	Sauber C16/7
17	Morbidelli	Sauber C16/6
	spare	Sauber C16/5
18	Verstappen	Tyrrell 025/4
19	Salo	Tyrrell 025/5
	spare	Tyrrell 025/1
20	Katayama	Minardi M197/4
21	Marques	Minardi M197/2
	spare	Minardi M197/1
22	Barrichello	Stewart SF1/2
23	Magnussen	Stewart SF1/3
	spare	Stewart SF1/1

POINTS TABLES

Drivers

1	Michael Schumacher	68
2	Jacques Villeneuve	67
3	Heinz-Harald Frentzen	31
4	David Coulthard	30
5	Jean Alesi	28
6	Gerhard Berger	21
7	Giancarlo Fisichella	20
8	Eddie Irvine	18
9	Olivier Panis	15
10 =	Mika Häkkinen	14
10 =	Johnny Herbert	14
12	Ralf Schumacher	13
13	Damon Hill	7
14	Rubens Barrichello	6
15	Alexander Wurz	4
16	Jarno Trulli	3
17 =	Mika Salo	2
17 =	Shinji Nakano	2
19	Nicola Larini	1

Constructors

1	Williams	98
2	Ferrari	86
3	Benetton	53
4	McLaren	44
5	Jordan	33
6	Prost	20
7	Sauber	15
8	Arrows	7
9	Stewart	6
10	Tyrrell	2

FIA WORLD CHAMPIONSHIP • ROUND 15

LUXEMBOURG
grand prix

In the lion's den. Following the early exit of local hero Michael Schumacher and the demise of the dominant Mercedes-powered McLarens, Jacques Villeneuve was able to strengthen his title challenge with a measured victory.

VILLENEUVE

ALESI

FRENTZEN

BERGER

DINIZ

PANIS

J ACQUES Villeneuve took another decisive stride towards the 1997 World Championship with a controlled run to victory in the Luxembourg Grand Prix – held at the Nürburgring – while Germany's motor racing fans watched in disbelief as their hopes of a home victory were reduced to dust, their only consolation being Heinz-Harald Frentzen's third-place finish behind Jean Alesi's Benetton.

Only seconds after the pack accelerated away from the grid, Ralf Schumacher distinguished himself by scoring a massive 'own goal', taking out his brother Michael's Ferrari as they jostled for position going into the first corner. The fast-starting Jordan driver also wiped out the Silverstone team's challenge in the process, having bounced off Giancarlo Fisichella's sister car before savaging Michael's front suspension. The younger Schumacher got off lightly with an official reprimand from the stewards – and that for crossing the circuit on foot, not for triggering the accident.

While the Jordan drivers were left to abandon their cars in the gravel trap, Schumacher's Ferrari lasted only two laps before stopping at the pits to retire with deranged right-front suspension. Meanwhile, the McLaren-Mercedes of Mika Häkkinen and David Coulthard initially dominated a processional race in commanding style, running away in first and second places in front of an approving crowd before stopping with engine failures.

Despite a brush with team-mate Frentzen on the sprint to the first corner, Villeneuve eventually crossed the line 11.7s ahead of Alesi, with Frentzen and Gerhard Berger's Benetton rounding off a decisive 1-2-3-4 grand slam for Renault-engined cars on a day when they had looked set to be humbled by Mercedes.

This victory left Villeneuve nine points ahead of Schumacher in the battle for the championship with only two races and 20 points remaining to be contested. However, he regarded himself as lucky to scrape home with a win as he was worried that his car might have been damaged in that first-corner collision.

From pole position, Häkkinen made a clean start to lead into the first corner with Coulthard re-enacting his Monza getaway to catapult through from sixth to second. As they went down to the first corner, Villeneuve and Frentzen momentarily banged wheels, resulting in Heinz-Harald accidentally switching off his ignition, which brought the second FW19 to a near-halt at the first corner as all hell erupted around him.

Despite Michael Schumacher's efforts to steer straight on across the gravel trap in a vain attempt to avoid contact, brother Ralf's car climbed over his right-front wheel and terminal damage was done to his chances. Ukyo Katayama's Minardi also found itself embroiled in the chaos, collecting the Jordans and retiring after a spin due to the resultant collision damage.

As for Villeneuve, he completed the opening lap third behind the two McLaren-Mercs, Häkkinen leading Coulthard by 1.3s as they crossed the timing line for the first time. But Jacques was definitely concerned.

'After the bump I was worried be-cause these cars aren't very strong when it comes to banging wheels with each other,' he said. 'My start was average, but I was very surprised to see David [Coulthard] alongside me even before I had changed into second gear.

'Heinz was on my left, but although I hit the brakes first, I ran wide and was unable to keep with David through the first corner.'

Behind Villeneuve at the end of the opening lap was Rubens Barrichello's Stewart, Alesi's Benetton, Jan Magnussen's Stewart, Damon Hill, Pedro Diniz, Johnny Herbert and the rest of the pack.

Frentzen was extremely frustrated to find himself back in 13th place at the end of the opening lap. 'It was pretty tight at the start,' he recalled. 'I had a better start than Jacques and I was alongside him and a nose ahead. But I was on the outside line and didn't want to take any risks going into that corner, and take somebody off – especially [not] Jacques.

'I had a lot of pressure around me and I tried to be tight on the inside, but I touched Jacques's left-rear wheel with my right-front, banged the dashboard and switched the ignition off.

'I didn't know what had happened. I was slowing down and looking quickly at my instruments to see what happened. I saw the ignition was switched off, managed to switch it on again and then had to wait for a second until everything was running. By then I found myself 15th!'

Thus the race settled down into a processional format. With ten laps gone, Häkkinen led Coulthard by 3.3s. Alesi was now pressuring Barrichello really hard while Magnussen had his work cut out keeping Hill at bay. Olivier Panis, who had been running a strong tenth, dropped two places as Berger and Frentzen went ahead of his Prost.

After that initial spate of collisions, there were no retirements until midway round lap 17 when Shinji Nakano's Prost retired from 14th place with another Mugen Honda engine failure. Three laps later, Alesi made a first 9.5s refuelling stop, dropping from fifth to 12th.

On lap 23 Eddie Irvine retired his Ferrari from tenth place with engine failure. 'Just as I went round a corner, my engine died on me,' he said. 'I had a heavy fuel load aboard at the start, which made the car difficult to drive, but I was confident that I would have been able to push hard after my pit stop.'

That was the official line, a précis of his true feelings. Later he told television viewers what he really thought of the car, as well as of Ferrari's chances for the championship.

From the start of free practice at the Nürburgring, Mika Häkkinen and his McLaren-Mercedes had looked formidably competitive. The Finn ended Friday's session by posting a best lap 0.3s ahead of Rubens Barrichello's Stewart-Ford, then sustained his advantage to see off the Williams-Renaults of Jacques Villeneuve and Heinz-Harald Frentzen in Saturday's hour-long qualifying session.

It was the first pole position of Häkkinen's 94-race career as well as the first for the McLaren-Mercedes alliance. It was certainly a close call, and Mika squeezed in only 0.089s ahead of the Canadian, relishing the front-end bite offered by the latest Adrian Newey-inspired front wing which had been fitted to the car for the first time in Austria. From the outset, he was upbeat and confident about the MP4/12's prospects.

'At the start of the session I found I needed two laps to get the best out of the tyres,' he explained, 'but as the conditions heated up it was necessary to do only a single flying lap. Even so, I think I made my final run too early, which made me nervous about being beaten.'

His team-mate David Coulthard was disappointed to take sixth on the grid, having suffered an engine failure on his 'out' lap at the start of Saturday free practice. During the mid-session break, the car was duly retrieved and the McLaren mechanics did a fantastic job installing a new engine in 34 minutes. He was back on the circuit with 20 minutes of track time left, but he never caught up that lost time before the end of qualifying.

Villeneuve, who went into the race trailing Schumacher by a single point, came to Germany fresh from an additional test session on Thursday at Silverstone where he practised starts and pit stop technique.

'With the championship so tight, we don't want to leave anything to chance,' he said. 'We have made several bad starts this season, and these have looked even worse because we have often started from the front row of the grid. It is also very difficult to differentiate between wheelspin and clutch slip, so we have been working hard on this. At least Michael is behind me on the grid, which is a good thing.'

Villeneuve improved his car slightly for Saturday free practice and again in qualifying. Happy with the race set-up, his main concern was that Schumacher's Ferrari F310B was firmly behind him on the grid, three places back in fact.

Third place fell to Frentzen's Williams FW19, the German driver having set the pace early in qualifying only to be displaced from the front row of the grid by Häkkinen and Villeneuve. Frentzen flat-spotted a tyre on his first run, had traffic on his second and complained about excessive dirt on the track when he made a third bid to grab pole.

Giancarlo Fisichella's Jordan qualified fourth; like team-mate Ralf Schumacher and Benetton's Gerhard Berger, he was using Goodyear's softer 'option' tyre compound. He achieved his time despite straight-lining the gravel trap going into the first corner at the start of his final run. Schumacher (R.) wound up a disappointed eighth, unable to cure his car's understeer and also making a mistake at the chicane before the pits.

From the outset, Schumacher Senior was playing his cards close to his chest, only too aware that his Ferrari lacked the fine handling edge so frequently displayed by the Williams FW19. To even up the battle, Michael would have liked a wet weekend, but the weather map resolutely promised nothing but bright skies and sunshine. He concentrated on the latest-spec lightweight F310B with the more powerful 046/2 version of the V10 engine.

Michael strained every sinew to improve on a third-row start. His final run came with barely a minute of the session left and, for the first two sectors of the lap, it looked as though he might just bump Fisichella. But the time just ebbed away on the last few corners and he ended up less than a tenth behind the Jordan.

'That was the most I could get out of the car,' he said, 'but, as usual, we should be quite competitive in race conditions when anything can happen. But as far as the championship is concerned, I would have preferred to be closer to Villeneuve and have a good fight on the track.'

Gerhard Berger was the quickest Benetton runner in seventh place, three positions ahead of Jean Alesi. Both men were disappointed. 'This was a normal qualifying session,' shrugged Berger. 'Unfortunately, I locked up the tyres on my first set and was therefore more conservative on my second, in order to stabilise my lap time. I was quite sure that I could have improved on my last run, but it did not happen.'

For his part, Alesi admitted that he was struggling with poor chassis balance throughout. 'It is not a long way off,' he said, 'but I was still missing that few tenths to get a good position on the grid.'

Splitting the two Benettons were Ralf Schumacher's Jordan and Rubens Barrichello's Stewart-Ford, the latter again emerging as the fastest Bridgestone contender. 'I think we might even have been in with a chance of seventh place on the grid, but I was a bit unlucky on my last two runs,' admitted Rubens.

'The track was pretty dirty at that stage and there was the usual late-session traffic. On the plus side, we did a lot of work for race day and that was really the most important thing.'

In the cockpit of the other Stewart SF1, Magnussen was pretty satisfied with 12th on the grid despite the fact that he took the spare car for his last two runs of the day after his race chassis suffered an engine failure. He posted his best time on the final run of the session.

Olivier Panis did very respectably to qualify 11th on his return to the Prost line-up. 'My car was quite good,' he reported, 'and had it not been for traffic on my final two runs, I think a place in the top five would have been possible.' Shinji Nakano managed to put the second Prost-Mugen Honda on the ninth row with 17th-fastest time, despite battling to get rid of more understeer than he would have liked.

Damon Hill was 13th fastest, disappointed that his Arrows's good handling balance had not translated into a better grid position. In 14th place, Eddie Irvine was definitely not satisfied, although he gained some consolation from the fact that he was only half a second away from team leader Schumacher's best.

'Because I went off the track in the morning, I was unable to decide which lap in my qualifying run would be the quickest,' he reflected. 'We decided it would be the first flying lap, and planned for that, but in fact I think the second would have been quicker.'

In 16th place, behind the Arrows of Pedro Diniz, Johnny Herbert was another to be bugged by understeer with his Sauber C16. 'I had what I felt was a good lap in practice this morning,' he said, 'but though the car was pretty similar this afternoon it was slower because of the rise in temperature and that, in turn, gave me even more understeer. I just don't seem to be able to get rid of it.'

Behind Nakano came a moderately optimistic Tarso Marques and a disappointed Gianni Morbidelli, while the Tyrrell-Fords of Mika Salo and Jos Verstappen edged out Katayama's Minardi at the tail of the starting order.

Richards takes over Benetton helm from Briatore

THE Luxembourg Grand Prix marked the final F1 race for Flavio Briatore in the role of Benetton F1 team boss, his position taken by Prodrive founder David Richards, who took over as chief executive in charge of the team's operations.

'It is a far simpler arrangement than anyone ever envisaged,' explained Richards. 'I always made no secret of the fact that we were trying to find our way into F1 and the routes into a commercially viable operation at the top level were very restrictive.'

Having been asked by BAT whether Prodrive might consider establishing an F1 team when the giant tobacco conglomerate began to assess plans for a Grand Prix involvement, Richards, whose BAT connections are well established through the 555 brand sponsorship of his Subaru rally cars, declined, but strongly recommended BAT to go with Benetton.

'Our proposal was rejected,' he reflected, 'but during those

discussions we found a certain synergy between our two organisations. So the Benetton family asked me to come aboard anyway.'

Richards admitted that his initial task in F1 would be to watch and learn. 'I have a total mandate to control the business,' he said, 'but I will draw a line between the commercial and technical sides and leave the engineers to get on and do their jobs.

'I am not underestimating the task ahead of me. It will be a big challenge.'

Briatore's future remained unclear, for the moment at least. There was speculation at the Nürburgring that he might go into business with Bernie Ecclestone, but Bernie issued a press release to say that he had never had any business associations with him or any of his companies 'other than through the Benetton team'.

Commented Briatore: 'My only definite plan is to take a three-month break.'

Paul-Henri Cahier

Allsport

Darren Heath

Paul–Henri Cahier

Above: David Coulthard locks a wheel during qualifying. Try as he might, the Scot was unable to match the pace of his team-mate Mika Häkkinen and had to be content with sixth place on the grid.

Left: In yer face. Michael Schumacher gets his retaliation in first as he shares the traditional cake with Bernie Ecclestone during celebrations to mark his 100th Grand Prix.

Jean Alesi *(right)* scored his fourth second place of the season as Renault achieved a crushing 1-2-3-4 grand slam.

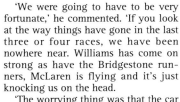

DIARY

Jan Magnussen reaches an agreement to stay with the Stewart-Ford team into the 1998 season.

BMW senior engineer Paul Rosche confirms that the Munich company's forthcoming F1 engine for the Williams team will be a V10.

The future of the French Grand Prix in 1998 is called into question as a provisional calendar is issued omitting the race from the schedule after a dispute between Bernie Ecclestone and the TV networks concerned.

Veteran CART engineer and former F1 team owner Morris Nunn announces his retirement.

Mark Blundell wins Marlboro 500 CART finale at Roger Penske's new California Speedway at Fontana.

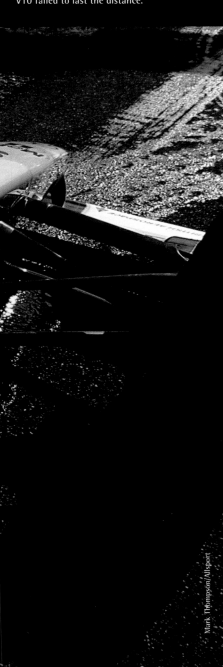

David Coulthard and Jacques Villeneuve head the pursuit of Mika Häkkinen as the multiple accident triggered by Ralf Schumacher continues to unfold in the background.

Having snatched the first pole position of his Grand Prix career, Häkkinen looked set to end his long winless streak but the unfortunate Finn was forced to abandon his McLaren *(below)* after its Mercedes V10 failed to last the distance.

Mark Thompson/Allsport

'We were going to have to be very fortunate,' he commented. 'If you look at the way things have gone in the last three or four races, we have been nowhere near. Williams has come on strong as have the Bridgestone runners, McLaren is flying and it's just knocking us on the head.

'The worrying thing was that the car was just atrocious. It's the worst I've ever had the car in the race. Normally the car is fantastic in race trim, but today it was just a joke. I couldn't turn in because of the oversteer. Once you get through the oversteer, it just understeers, and as you put the power on it snaps into oversteer. It was brick slow – so slow down the straights that it's unreal.'

By any standards, this was certainly a crisp *tour d'horizon* as far as Maranello's prospects were concerned – and an outburst which caused some sideways glances from the Italian media brigade, several of whom wondered whether Irvine was intent on committing career suicide. But what else was he to say if that was the truth?

On lap 28 Häkkinen (6.9s) and Villeneuve (8.8s) made their first refuelling stops, resuming in second and third behind Coulthard. Three laps later David was in for his own first refuelling stop and picked up again in second place behind Häkkinen. Villeneuve was third ahead of Barrichello with Hill now crawling all over Magnussen's fifth-place Stewart, the Dane suffering increasingly from massive understeer which had a dire effect on his front tyre wear.

Then on lap 36, Damon blotted his copybook in acutely embarrassing style. He came in from sixth place for his first refuelling stop, then stalled the Arrows's Yamaha V10. 'It was pathetic,' said Hill later with admirable candour. 'I am very upset about that, because afterwards the car was just going great. It was a real shame, because the car was again pretty competitive in the race, and I was able to fight back, but [otherwise] I would have been pretty well up in the points.'

By lap 37 Häkkinen was 12.8s ahead of Coulthard with Villeneuve still third but Barrichello coming in for his sole refuelling stop. He resumed after losing only one place, to Magnussen, and remained comfortably ahead of the impressive Diniz and Alesi's Benetton. Magnussen and Diniz both stopped at the end of lap 39, so now Barrichello was up to a confident fourth ahead of the Frenchman's Benetton, seemingly well placed for his second helping of points this season.

Returning to the race, Diniz neatly nipped ahead of Magnussen between the pit lane exit and the first corner. In fact, it wasn't as clever a move as it seemed, for Magnussen's car had broken a driveshaft as he accelerated back into the fray and that was the end of his race.

Then came disaster for McLaren. As Coulthard accelerated out of the final turn to complete lap 42, the silver-grey car emitted a puff of smoke and that was that. David pulled off at the end of the pit lane. Hardly had he released his seat harness and climbed from the cockpit than Häkkinen's sister car was rolling to a halt almost alongside, the Finn's machine having suffered an identical engine failure one lap later.

Mercedes director Jurgen Hubbert's face looked remarkably sanguine as he stepped down from his place on the McLaren pit wall. In some ways, the team could console itself by focusing on a genuinely promising performance. Only two years earlier, the McLaren-Mercs had been nothing more than a bad joke at the Nürburgring. This time they had been absolutely the class of the field. Only the reliability was missing.

Mercedes motorsport manager Norbert Haug did not stint when it came to apologising generously to the drivers. 'We knew that our speed was there, but our reliability could be a problem,' he said. 'I am really sorry for Mika and David and the whole team, which did a perfect job. The engine failures prevented a double victory and I apologise to the drivers and promise that we will sort out this problem very soon.'

On the same lap that Häkkinen pulled off, Rubens Barrichello's excellent run came to an end when his Stewart-Ford succumbed to loss of hydraulic pressure. Now the order was Villeneuve from Alesi and Berger, the Benetton drivers ducking in for their second stops on laps 44 and 45 respectively, which allowed Frentzen through into second place.

Frentzen made his second stop on lap 47, dropping back behind Alesi, while on lap 49 Villeneuve, now 56.4s ahead of Jean, had time to make his second refuelling stop without jeopardising his lead. With just under 20 laps left to run, the final finishing order had now been established.

In the closing stages, Jacques rolled off much of his speed to take the chequered flag 11.7s ahead of Alesi with Frentzen nibbling ever closer to the Benetton over the final laps, but still ending up just over a second shy of cementing the Williams team's long-overdue first 1-2 finish of the year.

Villeneuve admitted that the team had to wake him up slightly in the closing laps with a radio message reminding him that his advantage was dwindling quite fast.

'So I started pushing,' he explained, 'and on the next lap my engineer Jock Clear came on the radio again and said, "OK, point taken, you can relax again now." I had a huge gap, but when you start slowing down there is a danger of losing concentration and falling asleep. I started pushing again when I got bored; the faster you go, the sooner the race will be over.'

Alesi was justifiably delighted with second place while Frentzen could at least console himself with the knowledge that he had put in a fine recovery drive following his opening-lap problems, netting fastest lap of the race to boot.

In fourth place, Berger admitted he had mixed feelings about his result. 'I am obviously happy, but on the other hand I think I was a little unlucky,' he said. 'I managed to get around the first accident, but then the two Jordans collided and, with Michael's Ferrari in the middle, I had to go left to avoid a big crash and ended on the grass. It was very difficult to get back on the track, and in the meantime I lost a lot of positions. Slowly, I started to gain more, but the lap times were very close and I could not do better than I did.'

Diniz was simply elated with his fifth place, and rightly so. 'It was a great race with a lot of pressure from Panis behind me, who was very, very close for the last 30 laps,' he recalled. 'The balance of the car was not great in the race and at the end I got oversteer, but I did a good start and gained a lot of positions there. We also did a very late pit stop, which proved to be just the right strategy.'

In sixth place, Panis was also pleased to have proved that his stamina was not in any way a problem; it was a great result on his comeback drive following a three-month lay-off. Johnny Herbert finished seventh, reporting that his Sauber 'was never quite quick enough in the right places to let me challenge Panis or Diniz', while Hill trailed home eighth, quietly kicking himself and mentally speculating where he might have ended up had things gone to plan. Gianni Morbidelli and Mika Salo were the only other classified finishers.

In three races, Villeneuve had taken no fewer than 20 points off Michael Schumacher, translating an 11-point deficit after Spa into a nine-point lead with only two races to go. Had the advantage now swung irrevocably in the Canadian's favour? Or would there be another, unexpected change in the F1 tide before the season's end?

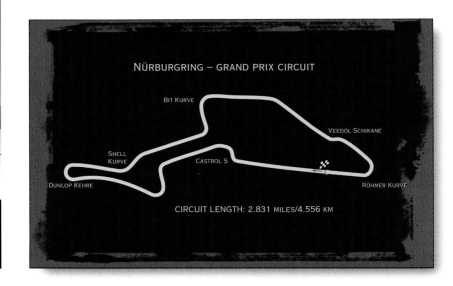

GROSSER PREIS VON
LUXEMBURG
26–28 SEPTEMBER 1997
NÜRBURGRING

NÜRBURGRING – GRAND PRIX CIRCUIT

Race distance: 67 laps, 189.664 miles/305.235 km

Race weather: Dry, warm and sunny

CIRCUIT LENGTH: 2.831 MILES/4.556 KM

ROUND
15

Pos.	Driver	Nat.	No.	Entrant	Car/Engine	Tyres	Laps	Time/Retirement	Speed (mph/km/h)
1	Jacques Villeneuve	CDN	3	Rothmans Williams Renault	Williams FW19-Renault RS9A V10	G	67	1h 31m 27.843s	124.418/200.232
2	Jean Alesi	F	7	Mild Seven Benetton Renault	Benetton B197-Renault RS9A V10	G	67	1h 31m 39.613s	124.152/199.804
3	Heinz-Harald Frentzen	D	4	Rothmans Williams Renault	Williams FW19-Renault RS9A V10	G	67	1h 31m 41.323s	124.114/199.742
4	Gerhard Berger	A	8	Mild Seven Benetton Renault	Benetton B197-Renault RS9A V10	G	67	1h 31m 44.259s	124.047/199.635
5	Pedro Diniz	BR	2	Danka Arrows Yamaha	Arrows A18-Yamaha OX11A/D V10	B	67	1h 32m 10.990s	123.448/198.670
6	Olivier Panis	F	14	Prost Gauloises Blondes	Prost JS45-Mugen Honda MF301HB V10	B	67	1h 32m 11.593s	123.435/198.649
7	Johnny Herbert	GB	16	Red Bull Sauber Petronas	Sauber C16-Petronas V10	G	67	1h 32m 12.197s	123.421/198.627
8	Damon Hill	GB	1	Danka Arrows Yamaha	Arrows A18-Yamaha OX11A/D V10	B	67	1h 32m 12.620s	123.412/198.612
9	Gianni Morbidelli	I	17	Red Bull Sauber Petronas	Sauber C16-Petronas V10	G	66		
10	Mika Salo	SF	19	Tyrrell	Tyrrell 025-Ford ED5 V8	G	66		
	Jos Verstappen	NL	18	Tyrrell	Tyrrell 025-Ford ED5 V8	G	50	Engine	
	Mika Häkkinen	SF	9	West McLaren Mercedes	McLaren MP4/12-Mercedes FO110F V10	G	43	Engine	
	Rubens Barrichello	BR	22	Stewart Ford	Stewart SF1-Ford Zetec-R V10	B	43	Hydraulics	
	David Coulthard	GB	10	West McLaren Mercedes	McLaren MP4/12-Mercedes FO110F V10	G	42	Engine	
	Jan Magnussen	DK	23	Stewart Ford	Stewart SF1-Ford Zetec-R V10	B	40	Driveshaft	
	Eddie Irvine	GB	6	Scuderia Ferrari Marlboro	Ferrari F310B 046/2 V10	G	22	Engine	
	Shinji Nakano	J	15	Prost Gauloises Blondes	Prost JS45-Mugen Honda MF301HB V10	B	16	Engine	
	Michael Schumacher	D	5	Scuderia Ferrari Marlboro	Ferrari F310B 046/2 V10	G	2	Accident damage	
	Tarso Marques	BR	21	Minardi Team	Minardi M197-Hart 830 V8	B	1	Engine	
	Ukyo Katayama	J	20	Minardi Team	Minardi M197-Hart 830 V8	B	1	Accident	
	Ralf Schumacher	D	11	B&H Total Jordan Peugeot	Jordan 197-Peugeot A14 V10	G	0	Collision with Fisichella	
	Giancarlo Fisichella	I	12	B&H Total Jordan Peugeot	Jordan 197-Peugeot A14 V10	G	0	Collision with R. Schumacher	

Fastest lap: Frentzen, on lap 32, 1m 18.805s, 129.324 mph/208.128 km/h (record).

Previous lap record: Michael Schumacher (F1 Benetton B195-Renault V10), 1m 21.180s, 125.540 mph/202.039 km/h (1995).

B – Bridgestone   G – Goodyear

Grid order	1	2	3	4	5	6	7	8	9	10	11	12	13	14	15	16	17	18	19	20	21	22	23	24	25	26	27	28	29	30	31	32	33	34	35	36	37	38	39	40	41	42	43	44	45	46	47	48	49	50	51	52
9 HÄKKINEN	9	9	9	9	9	9	9	9	9	9	9	9	9	9	9	9	9	9	9	9	9	9	9	9	9	9	9	9	9	10	10	10	9	9	9	9	9	9	9	9	9	9	9	3	3	3	3	3	3	3	3	3
3 VILLENEUVE	10	10	10	10	10	10	10	10	10	10	10	10	10	10	10	10	10	10	10	10	10	10	10	10	10	10	10	10	10	9	9	9	10	10	10	10	10	10	10	10	10	10	3	7	4	4	4	7	7	7	7	7
4 FRENTZEN	3	3	3	3	3	3	3	3	3	3	3	3	3	3	3	3	3	3	3	3	3	3	3	3	3	3	3	3	3	3	3	3	3	3	3	3	3	3	3	22	8	8	7	7	4	4	4	4
12 FISICHELLA	22	22	22	22	22	22	22	22	22	22	22	22	22	22	22	22	22	22	22	22	22	22	22	22	22	22	22	22	22	22	22	22	23	22	22	22	22	7	4	7	8	8	8	8	8	8
5 M. SCHUMACHER	7	7	7	7	7	7	7	7	7	7	7	7	7	7	7	7	7	7	7	7	7	7	23	23	23	23	23	23	23	23	23	23	23	23	23	23	22	23	7	7	7	8	2	2	2	2	2	2	2	2
10 COULTHARD	23	23	23	23	23	23	23	23	23	23	23	23	23	23	23	23	23	23	23	23	1	1	1	1	1	1	1	1	1	1	1	1	2	2	7	8	8	8	4	14	14	14	14	14	14	14
8 BERGER	1	1	1	1	1	1	1	1	1	1	1	1	1	1	1	1	1	1	1	1	8	4	4	4	4	4	4	4	4	2	2	2	2	2	7	14	4	4	2	16	16	16	16	16	16	16
11 R. SCHUMACHER	2	2	2	2	2	2	2	2	2	2	2	2	2	2	8	8	8	8	4	2	2	2	2	2	2	2	2	7	7	7	7	7	14	14	2	14	16	16	14	1	1	1	1	1	1	1
22 BARRICHELLO	16	16	16	16	16	16	16	16	16	16	16	16	16	16	8	2	2	2	2	14	14	14	7	7	7	7	7	14	14	14	14	14	8	8	8	16	2	2	16	17	17	17	17	17	17	17
7 ALESI	5	14	14	14	14	14	14	14	8	8	8	8	8	8	4	4	4	4	14	6	7	7	14	14	14	14	14	8	8	8	8	8	4	4	4	2	14	14	1	19	19	19	19	19	19	19
14 PANIS	14	6	6	6	6	6	6	8	8	4	4	4	4	16	14	14	14	6	7	17	8	8	8	8	8	8	8	4	4	4	4	16	16	16	17	1	1	17	18	18	18	18	18	18
23 MAGNUSSEN	6	4	4	4	4	4	4	4	14	14	14	14	14	14	6	6	6	7	17	8	18	16	16	16	16	16	16	16	16	16	16	16	17	17	1	19	19	19
1 HILL	4	8	8	8	8	8	8	6	6	6	6	6	6	6	17	17	17	17	8	18	16	17	17	17	17	17	17	17	17	17	17	17	1	1	1	19	17	17	18
6 IRVINE	21	15	15	15	15	15	15	15	15	15	15	15	15	15	19	19	19	19	19	16	17	19	19	19	19	19	19	19	19	19	19	19	23	18	18
2 DINIZ	8	5	19	19	19	19	19	19	19	19	17	17	17	17	18	18	18	18	18	19	19	18	18	18	18	18	18	18	18	18	18	18	18	18
16 HERBERT	15	19	17	17	17	17	17	17	17	17	19	19	19	19	16	16	16	16	16
15 NAKANO	19	17	18	18	18	18	18	18	18	18	18	18	18	18
21 MARQUES	18	18
17 MORBIDELLI	17
19 SALO	20
18 VERSTAPPEN		
20 KATAYAMA		

Pit stop

One lap behind leader

STARTING GRID

9 HÄKKINEN McLaren	**3** VILLENEUVE Williams
4 FRENTZEN Williams	**12** FISICHELLA Jordan
5 M. SCHUMACHER Ferrari	**10** COULTHARD McLaren
8 BERGER Benetton	**11** R. SCHUMACHER Jordan
22 BARRICHELLO Stewart	**7** ALESI Benetton
14 PANIS Prost	**23** MAGNUSSEN Stewart
1 HILL Arrows	**6** IRVINE Ferrari
2 DINIZ Arrows	**16** HERBERT Sauber
15 NAKANO Prost	**21** MARQUES Minardi
17 MORBIDELLI Sauber	**19** SALO Tyrrell
18 VERSTAPPEN Tyrrell	**20** KATAYAMA Minardi

53	54	55	56	57	58	59	60	61	62	63	64	65	66	67	
3	3	3	3	3	3	3	3	3	3	3	3	3	3	3	1
7	7	7	7	7	7	7	7	7	7	7	7	7	7	7	2
4	4	4	4	4	4	4	4	4	4	4	4	4	4	4	3
8	8	8	8	8	8	8	8	8	8	8	8	8	8	8	4
2	2	2	2	2	2	2	2	2	2	2	2	2	2	2	5
14	14	14	14	14	14	14	14	14	14	14	14	14	14	14	6
16	16	16	16	16	16	16	16	16	16	16	16	16	16	16	
1	1	1	1	1	1	1	1	1	1	1	1	1	1	1	
17	17	17	17	17	17	17	17	17	17	17	17	17	17	17	
19	19	19	19	19	19	19	19	19	19	19	19	19	19	19	

FOR THE RECORD

First Grand Prix pole position
Mika Häkkinen

100th Grand Prix start
Michael Schumacher

50th Grand Prix start
Mika Salo

TIME SHEETS

QUALIFYING

Weather: Sunny and bright

Pos.	Driver	Car	Laps	Time
1	Mika Häkkinen	McLaren-Mercedes	11	1m 16.602s
2	Jacques Villeneuve	Williams-Renault	10	1m 16.691s
3	Heinz-Harald Frentzen	Williams-Renault	12	1m 16.741s
4	Giancarlo Fisichella	Jordan-Peugeot	11	1m 17.289s
5	Michael Schumacher	Ferrari	11	1m 17.385s
6	David Coulthard	McLaren-Mercedes	12	1m 17.387s
7	Gerhard Berger	Benetton-Renault	9	1m 17.587s
8	Ralf Schumacher	Jordan-Peugeot	11	1m 17.595s
9	Rubens Barrichello	Stewart-Ford	12	1m 17.614s
10	Jean Alesi	Benetton-Renault	11	1m 17.620s
11	Olivier Panis	Prost-Mugen Honda	11	1m 17.650s
12	Jan Magnussen	Stewart-Ford	11	1m 17.722s
13	Damon Hill	Arrows-Yamaha	12	1m 17.795s
14	Eddie Irvine	Ferrari	12	1m 17.855s
15	Pedro Diniz	Arrows-Yamaha	11	1m 18.128s
16	Johnny Herbert	Sauber-Petronas	10	1m 18.303s
17	Shinji Nakano	Prost-Mugen Honda	12	1m 18.699s
18	Tarso Marques	Minardi-Hart	12	1m 19.347s
19	Gianni Morbidelli	Sauber-Petronas	12	1m 19.490s
20	Mika Salo	Tyrrell-Ford	12	1m 19.526s
21	Jos Verstappen	Tyrrell-Ford	12	1m 19.531s
22	Ukyo Katayama	Minardi-Hart	11	1m 20.615s

FRIDAY FREE PRACTICE

Weather: Sunny and bright

Pos.	Driver	Laps	Time
1	Mika Häkkinen	27	1m 17.998s
2	Rubens Barrichello	24	1m 18.339s
3	Gerhard Berger	30	1m 18.434s
4	Ralf Schumacher	20	1m 18.713s
5	Jean Alesi	24	1m 18.794s
6	David Coulthard	30	1m 18.912s
7	Heinz-Harald Frentzen	29	1m 18.926s
8	Michael Schumacher	29	1m 18.954s
9	Giancarlo Fisichella	29	1m 19.034s
10	Damon Hill	22	1m 19.091s
11	Olivier Panis	30	1m 19.412s
12	Jacques Villeneuve	30	1m 19.640s
13	Eddie Irvine	23	1m 19.708s
14	Pedro Diniz	14	1m 19.750s
15	Shinji Nakano	30	1m 20.073s
16	Johnny Herbert	26	1m 20.373s
17	Jan Magnussen	7	1m 20.592s
18	Jos Verstappen	27	1m 20.947s
19	Mika Salo	30	1m 21.118s
20	Gianni Morbidelli	30	1m 21.387s
21	Tarso Marques	26	1m 21.424s
22	Ukyo Katayama	6	1m 38.344s

SATURDAY FREE PRACTICE

Weather: Sunny and bright

Pos.	Driver	Laps	Time
1	Heinz-Harald Frentzen	30	1m 17.158s
2	Mika Häkkinen	21	1m 17.220s
3	Giancarlo Fisichella	30	1m 17.390s
4	Jacques Villeneuve	26	1m 17.395s
5	Michael Schumacher	26	1m 17.567s
6	Gerhard Berger	29	1m 17.778s
7	Rubens Barrichello	30	1m 17.778s
8	David Coulthard	12	1m 17.884s
9	Ralf Schumacher	28	1m 17.948s
10	Johnny Herbert	30	1m 17.953s
11	Olivier Panis	30	1m 18.106s
12	Jan Magnussen	24	1m 18.167s
13	Damon Hill	30	1m 18.180s
14	Jean Alesi	23	1m 18.233s
15	Pedro Diniz	29	1m 18.788s
16	Shinji Nakano	30	1m 19.031s
17	Eddie Irvine	16	1m 19.139s
18	Mika Salo	29	1m 19.490s
19	Tarso Marques	29	1m 19.609s
20	Ukyo Katayama	29	1m 19.883s
21	Jos Verstappen	29	1m 20.064s
22	Gianni Morbidelli	22	1m 20.256s

WARM-UP

Weather: Dry and bright

Pos.	Driver	Laps	Time
1	Mika Häkkinen	11	1m 17.959s
2	David Coulthard	17	1m 19.088s
3	Giancarlo Fisichella	17	1m 19.490s
4	Heinz-Harald Frentzen	14	1m 19.493s
5	Michael Schumacher	13	1m 19.512s
6	Jacques Villeneuve	12	1m 19.548s
7	Ralf Schumacher	17	1m 19.569s
8	Johnny Herbert	17	1m 19.754s
9	Jean Alesi	15	1m 19.918s
10	Olivier Panis	16	1m 19.970s
11	Eddie Irvine	13	1m 20.011s
12	Damon Hill	14	1m 20.051s
13	Gerhard Berger	14	1m 20.121s
14	Gianni Morbidelli	13	1m 20.291s
15	Rubens Barrichello	14	1m 20.377s
16	Jan Magnussen	16	1m 20.463s
17	Pedro Diniz	13	1m 20.558s
18	Ukyo Katayama	12	1m 21.251s
19	Mika Salo	16	1m 21.391s
20	Tarso Marques	16	1m 21.477s
21	Jos Verstappen	13	1m 21.695s
22	Shinji Nakano	3	1m 28.017s

RACE FASTEST LAPS

Weather: Dry, warm and sunny

Driver	Time	Lap
Heinz-Harald Frentzen	1m 18.805s	32
Mika Häkkinen	1m 19.576s	27
Jean Alesi	1m 19.716s	65
Jacques Villeneuve	1m 19.838s	31
David Coulthard	1m 19.920s	23
Gerhard Berger	1m 19.996s	61
Damon Hill	1m 20.407s	64
Johnny Herbert	1m 20.518s	33
Rubens Barrichello	1m 20.737s	25
Gianni Morbidelli	1m 20.865s	31
Olivier Panis	1m 21.086s	29
Pedro Diniz	1m 21.262s	25
Jan Magnussen	1m 21.448s	32
Eddie Irvine	1m 21.793s	13
Shinji Nakano	1m 21.969s	14
Mika Salo	1m 21.996s	26
Jos Verstappen	1m 22.455s	30
Michael Schumacher	1m 29.314s	2
Tarso Marques	1m 36.826s	1
Ukyo Katayama	3m 00.630s	1

CHASSIS LOG BOOK

1	Hill	Arrows A18/5
2	Diniz	Arrows A18/4
	spare	Arrows A18/3
3	Villeneuve	Williams FW19/4
4	Frentzen	Williams FW19/5
	spare	Williams FW19/3
5	M. Schumacher	Ferrari F310B/178
6	Irvine	Ferrari F310B/180
	spare	Ferrari F310B/175
7	Alesi	Benetton B197/2
8	Berger	Benetton B197/4
	spare	Benetton B197/3
9	Häkkinen	McLaren MP4/12/3
10	Coulthard	McLaren MP4/12/6
	spare	McLaren MP4/12/5
11	R. Schumacher	Jordan 197/6
12	Fisichella	Jordan 197/4
	spare	Jordan 197/1
14	Panis	Prost JS45/3
15	Nakano	Prost JS45/2
	spare	Prost JS45/1
16	Herbert	Sauber C16/7
17	Morbidelli	Sauber C16/6
	spare	Sauber C16/5
18	Verstappen	Tyrrell 025/4
19	Salo	Tyrrell 025/5
	spare	Tyrrell 025/1
20	Katayama	Minardi M197/4
21	Marques	Minardi M197/2
	spare	Minardi M197/1
22	Barrichello	Stewart SF1/2
23	Magnussen	Stewart SF1/3
	spare	Stewart SF1/1

POINTS TABLES

Drivers

1	Jacques Villeneuve	77
2	Michael Schumacher	68
3	Heinz-Harald Frentzen	35
4	Jean Alesi	34
5	David Coulthard	30
6	Gerhard Berger	24
7	Giancarlo Fisichella	20
8	Eddie Irvine	18
9	Olivier Panis	16
10 =	Mika Häkkinen	14
10 =	Johnny Herbert	14
12	Ralf Schumacher	13
13	Damon Hill	7
14	Rubens Barrichello	6
15	Alexander Wurz	4
16	Jarno Trulli	3
17 =	Mika Salo	2
17 =	Shinji Nakano	2
17 =	Pedro Diniz	2
20	Nicola Larini	1

Constructors

1	Williams	112
2	Ferrari	86
3	Benetton	62
4	McLaren	44
5	Jordan	33
6	Prost	21
7	Sauber	15
8	Arrows	9
9	Stewart	6
10	Tyrrell	2

JAPANESE
grand prix

Michael Schumacher demonstrates his spectacular car control as he heads for a vital victory that put him in a position to clinch the World Championship at the final round.

Bottom left: Schumacher celebrates his triumph with team-mate Eddie Irvine, whose support had played a crucial role in his success.

Bottom right: Jacques Villeneuve faces the media scrum after his interview with the stewards. The French-Canadian was excluded from the meeting but raced under appeal.

M. SCHUMACHER

FRENTZEN

IRVINE

HÄKKINEN

ALESI

HERBERT

THE unpredictable World Championship see-saw lurched back in Michael Schumacher's favour in the Japanese Grand Prix at Suzuka where the German driver scored a decisive win, aided by splendid support from his team-mate Eddie Irvine, who sacrificed his own chances of victory in the interests of helping Michael move closer to his third title.

However, Heinz-Harald Frentzen's run to second place clinched an all-time-record ninth constructors' championship for the Williams team at the end of a weekend when his team-mate Jacques Villeneuve fell foul of officialdom after being found guilty of failing to slow down under a waved yellow flag during free practice.

Villeneuve eventually finished fifth, having originally been excluded from the meeting and then racing under appeal. It was his fourth such offence this season, activating a one-race suspended ban which was originally imposed at the previous month's Italian Grand Prix.

Schumacher's victory was a triumph of Ferrari team tactics with Irvine collaborating perfectly to ensure Villeneuve was subjected to the maximum possible delay and inconvenience.

At the start, Villeneuve took an immediate lead and completed the first lap running as slowly as he dared in an attempt to wrong-foot Schumacher into a mistake or leave him vulnerable to attack from other drivers. Having moved right and left to cover Schumacher's second-place Ferrari as he accelerated away from pole position, Villeneuve did not pull away from the opposition but kept the pack crowded closely behind him as he negotiated the opening lap, braking early for the corners and then using his Renault power to squirt away quickly on the straights.

Going into the first corner of the second lap, Irvine swept round the outside of both Schumacher and Mika Häkkinen's third-place McLaren-Mercedes to move from fourth place to second at a stroke. On the following lap, Irvine outbraked Villeneuve to take the lead and pulled quickly away at the head of the field.

'When the chance presented itself, I was off and away,' he said. 'It was nice to be disappearing into the distance, but I was obviously waiting for the phone call to tell me what to do. Quite honestly, I was wondering what was going on back there.'

By the end of lap four Irvine was 5.3s clear of the pack and he was 12.6s ahead by the end of lap seven. Some observers simply couldn't understand what was happening, thinking that perhaps Irvine was on a three-stop strategy with an ultra-light fuel load. Yet a quick glance at the official TAG Heuer timing screens told the story: Villeneuve was lapping between four and five seconds slower than he had managed in the race morning warm-up and a string of a dozen cars was banked up behind him.

With Schumacher's Ferrari being shadowed closely by Häkkinen's McLaren, perhaps Villeneuve was counting on the Finn making an over-exuberant passing attempt and taking the Ferrari off. He was certainly hoping that his efforts would slow the pace sufficiently for somebody to at least attempt an overtaking move, yet for lap after lap the crocodile continued in an unchanging order, the drivers seemingly all hypnotised by the rear wings of the cars immediately ahead of them.

In the middle of all this, both Stewart-Ford drivers encountered disaster. Jan Magnussen made a good start to run 11th in the opening stages, but Rubens Barrichello went past on lap four and the Dane immediately lost downforce in the turbulence and spun off. Three laps later Rubens too spun off exiting the 130-R while chasing Damon Hill's Arrows, ending the team's brief foray on a disappointing note.

Being held up in this queue made little sense to the McLaren team, who called Häkkinen in for an early 6.9s stop on lap 13, dropping him to tenth. Berger also forfeited his place in the queue, his Benetton coming in for his first stop on the same lap and dropping from seventh to 13th.

Three laps later Irvine duly made the first of his two stops, the Ferrari being stationary for 7.6s and dropping from first to fourth. That left Villeneuve back at the front ahead of Schumacher, who made his first stop two laps later, dropping to fifth.

At the end of lap 20, Villeneuve made his first stop, resuming in fourth behind Frentzen, Irvine and Schumacher. He almost made it back onto the track ahead of Michael, who later admitted that he had been surprised by the Williams's refuelling strategy.

'For a while we thought they would be going for one stop only,' he said after the race. 'It was then a surprise when they went for two, and it was quite critical, because Jacques came right across the track in front of me and tried to close the door [after his first stop].

'I am not sure whether that was the correct thing to do, to come across the road and try to push someone. I was able to correct my own situation and took him on the inside, but it could have been very dangerous.'

Frentzen had meanwhile been running with a heavy fuel load and used rubber from the start and his low-downforce set-up had left him grappling with a touch too much understeer, preventing him from closing up on the leaders in the opening phase of the race.

The German driver duly made his own first stop at the end of lap 21, resuming in fourth place, which now put Irvine back ahead, 8.8s ahead of Schumacher and Villeneuve.

Now Ferrari put its master plan into effect. Over the radio link Ross Brawn told Eddie to ease his pace. By lap 23 he had slowed to just 6.5s ahead and the margin was down to three seconds as the number two Ferrari crossed the timing line next time round. Going through the fast swerves behind the paddock, Irvine moved out of the way to let Schumacher through into the lead before tucking neatly back into line before Villeneuve could follow him through.

Now the fun and games really started. After resuming the lead on lap 22, Irvine went round in 1m 40.864s. Easing back to let Schumacher catch up, he did one lap as gently as 1m 46.105s. Once through, Michael lapped in 1m 40.054s on lap 35. Irvine did 1m 45.422s. Having thrown Villeneuve off the trail, he then settled down to run about a second slower than Schumacher with the result that he was 7.9s behind when Villeneuve pulled into the pits at the end of lap 30, the earliest lap in the Williams driver's second refuelling 'window' on which he could make his second scheduled stop.

Unfortunately the fuel line proved reluctant to couple up to the car on this occasion, resulting in Jacques's being stationary for 13.4s. That dropped him back to seventh place and left the way clear for the two Ferraris to have untroubled second stops on laps 32 (Irvine) and 33 (Schumacher). Now Frentzen went ahead before making his second stop on lap 37, just squeezing back into the race ahead of Irvine to take second place.

Behind Irvine, Jean Alesi was now up to fourth ahead of Häkkinen, Villeneuve, Gerhard Berger, Johnny Herbert and a bitterly frustrated David Coulthard, who had been struggling with the balance of his McLaren virtually from the start of the race.

Alesi, like team-mate Berger, was on a three-stop strategy which he subsequently judged was too close to a two-stop option in terms of results achieved and he felt it was difficult to judge whether or not he gained any

Jacques Villeneuve *(right)* took pole position after a typically committed effort in qualifying but Minardi's Ukyo Katayama *(bottom left)* announced that he had decided to retire from F1. Meanwhile the team's engine supplier, Brian Hart *(bottom right)*, was left to ponder his plans for the future.

SUZUKA QUALIFYING

Qualifying at Suzuka was effectively overshadowed by the controversy stemming from Saturday free practice when Jacques Villeneuve – and several others – passed Jos Verstappen's abandoned Tyrrell at undiminished speed under waved yellow flags.

In addition to Villeneuve, Michael Schumacher, Heinz-Harald Frentzen, Rubens Barrichello, Johnny Herbert and Ukyo Katayama were all summoned to the stewards. They had recorded their fastest times while the yellow flag was being displayed, admittedly on the straight, while marshals attempted to move Verstappen's machine closer to the barrier.

Villeneuve, who had been handed a one-race ban suspended for nine races at Monza, was in deep trouble, with that suspension now being activated. He was thrown out of the Japanese GP. Frentzen received a one-race ban suspended until the fourth race of 1998, while Schumacher, Katayama, Herbert and Barrichello were admonished with one-race bans suspended to the end of the year.

Villeneuve's exclusion from the meeting produced an electrifying atmosphere on the eve of the race. It took the stewards almost four hours from the end of official qualifying to conclude that they had no choice but to exclude the French-Canadian from competing. Cynics suggested they had to wait until it was dawn in the UK in order to discuss the matter with FIA President Max Mosley before they could receive guidance as to what they should do in such a tricky situation.

After due consideration, Williams decided to appeal against the decision, so another lengthy stewards' meeting ensued. Eventually it was decided that Villeneuve could race subject to a decision by the FIA Court of Appeal, which everybody hoped would be convened before the final race at Jerez a fortnight later.

Although Villeneuve was pretty steamed up by his treatment, none of this controversy stood in the way of a no-holds-barred shoot-out between the two key title contenders. Villeneuve's Williams and Schumacher's Ferrari qualified together on the front row of the grid, separated by 0.062s.

Jacques was absolutely delighted with the feel of his FW19, which sported further detailed chassis modifications including longer aerodynamic side deflectors and an extended undertray to complement the 5 cm longer wheelbase which the team had used since the previous month's Austrian GP.

'I think we went out a bit too late, so we were going to get the chequered flag before I could start another flying lap,' said Jacques of his last run, 'and anyway, Michael didn't go out again. That lap was just a question of making sure we scrubbed in another set of tyres for the race.

'I am satisfied to be starting from pole position, because this is a track which suits us well. The car is competitive and we have made some worthwhile improvements in practice. I am a little surprised, though, to have the Ferraris so close behind us. But that means we are likely to have a good race tomorrow, and it looks as if Michael and I will actually be trying to beat each other on the track for once.'

Schumacher was using one of the latest lightweight F310Bs but, although Ferrari's uprated throttle control system was used in free practice, the flat torque curve of the Maranello V10 meant that it didn't offer much perceptible benefit. Perhaps more of the car's performance increment came from a new front wing which flexed very obviously at the outer extremities, closing the gap between the end plates and the track surface.

The need to conserve tyres also developed into a major theme from the start of the meeting. With nine sets of slicks allowed per car over the weekend, Villeneuve had consumed six sets by the end of qualifying, including one set discarded after a front tyre was cut badly by debris on the circuit.

For his part, Schumacher completed qualifying with six fresh sets still unused. In fact, he used only eight of his permitted 12 laps in qualifying, planned third and fourth qualifying runs being thwarted by red flags when Gianni Morbidelli crashed his Sauber and yellows after Eddie Irvine stopped the other Ferrari on the circuit, apparently out of fuel.

For Irvine, third place on the grid was certainly a welcome morale-booster at the end of a week in which fevered speculation in the Italian media had suggested that Austrian veteran Gerhard Berger might replace him as Schumacher's team-mate in 1998.

In reality, the Ulsterman need have had no such concerns. By the end of the weekend most Austrian F1 insiders correctly predicted that the 38-year-old veteran would announce his retirement in Vienna at the end of the following week. So it proved.

On the other hand, despite feeling groggy with his still-tender sinuses inflamed by the long flight to Japan, Berger made good use of the Benetton B197's latest front suspension revisions to qualify in fifth place. That set Gerhard wondering just what he might have achieved had he been feeling reasonably fit.

Irvine was obviously delighted with his performance. 'Yes, we have made some changes to the car since the Nürburgring that we needed to do,' he admitted, 'and those modifications have obviously helped us a lot. And if I can't be quick here, on a circuit I know so well, I am unlikely to go well anywhere!'

Mika Häkkinen remained in contention for pole position for much of the session, setting fastest time up to that point on his first run. Second time out his efforts were thwarted when he found a patch of oil dropped by Rubens Barrichello's expiring Stewart at the first corner and he was then caught by a Tyrrell leaving the pits and accelerating straight out onto the racing line on his third. As a result, he had to be satisfied with fourth place on the grid.

By contrast, David Coulthard was very disappointed to find himself seven places further back. He suffered hydraulic failure which cost him track time in Saturday free practice, then complained of a loose rear end in qualifying when Häkkinen had a more powerful version of the Merc V10 available to him.

'It made sense to give it to Mika under the circumstances,' said David stoically, 'although it would have helped me as well. It was probably the most frustrating qualifying session of the season. In the end I was 0.6s away from Mika, who probably got the most out of the car on this circuit. Last year I was three seconds from pole and eighth on the grid. F1 is so close now.'

Behind Berger came Heinz-Harald Frentzen's Williams and Jean Alesi in the other Benetton in seventh place on the grid. Jean suffered an oil leak on his race car and had to switch to the spare, which, although lacking in top speed, had reasonable chassis balance.

Next came Johnny Herbert, who turned out to be the lone Sauber driver in the race after Morbidelli crashed quite heavily on the up-hill section behind the pits, hurting his left wrist. The Italian was initially hopeful that he would be allowed to race, but on Sunday morning after a further medical examination he was advised that it would be prudent to stand down.

Thus Herbert was left alone to capitalise on the C16's new diffuser, the first major aerodynamic improvement applied to the car all season, and he immediately reported that the chassis balance was much better.

'On my last run I got the entry to the first corner just right, and carried a lot more speed into the esses,' he explained, 'but unfortunately I came across David [Coulthard] in the Dunlop Curve and lost the advantage. That was disappointing, but overall I'm pleased with eighth place on the grid.'

In the Jordan camp, Ralf Schumacher had been right on the pace from the start of the weekend, so it was disappointing when his qualifying efforts simply fell apart and he lined up 13th. Privately, the Jordan team felt that the pressure had got to him and he made a succession of mistakes as a result.

'I am not satisfied,' said Schumacher Junior. 'I was not on form this afternoon, and I lost time braking late into the hairpins. I am very disappointed.' By contrast, team-mate Giancarlo Fisichella, who freely admitted that he hadn't got to grips with the challenging Suzuka circuit, performed slightly better and squeezed onto the fifth row with ninth-fastest time.

Tenth place fell to a disappointed Olivier Panis in the Prost-Mugen Honda, which encountered too much traffic on its last run, the Frenchman having found oil on the track earlier in the session. Team-mate Shinji Nakano was down in 15th place, complaining that his understeer was accentuated as the temperature rose.

Leading the way for Stewart, Barrichello was moderately happy with 12th place on the grid, doing one run in his race before switching to the spare following an unexpected engine failure. 'That is a reasonably good position,' admitted Rubens, 'considering I made the wrong decision on the set-up, because at the end, with more wing, I just had a little touch of oversteer and the car was working very well.'

Jan Magnussen was two places further down, rather disappointed that his best lap had been spoiled by the red flag for Morbidelli's shunt. Pedro Diniz just out-gunned Damon Hill for 16th place on the grid, both Arrows drivers reporting that they were dramatically short of power. Morbidelli was eventually credited with 18th ahead of Ukyo Katayama and Tarso Marques in their Minardi-Harts.

The final row of the grid was shared by the two Tyrrell-Ford V8s of Jos Verstappen and Mika Salo. On a circuit with such a long lap as Suzuka, they were always going to struggle, but both men reported that the cars felt reasonably well balanced.

DIARY

Minardi secures deal to use Ford Cosworth Zetec-R V10 engines for the 1998 season.

Ukyo Katayama announces his retirement from F1 at the end of the season.

Honda President Nobuhiko Kawamoto confirms that the Japanese company will return to F1 with a works engine, but declines to put a firm date on their plans.

Toranosuke Takagi confirmed as full-time member of Tyrrell F1 line-up for 1998.

Paul Tracy dropped by Penske CART team for 1998 and replaced by Andre Ribeiro.

advantage from it. What he certainly did find was that he lost time behind Villeneuve in the closing stages of the race, having to be content with sixth at the chequered flag, although this would eventually turn out to be fifth after Villeneuve was excluded.

During his final stint, Frentzen was seriously pumped up and went after Schumacher with a purpose, trimming his old rival's advantage from 4.6s on lap 46 to 1.3s at the line, although he was helped when Hill's Arrows got in the Ferrari's way on lap 50, then moved aside swiftly to allow the Williams through.

Was Damon dozing? Certainly not. He had his hands full grappling with a gearshift mechanism which seemed to have developed a mind of its own and a head-rest which had fallen off and was pushing his head forward 'so I found it, pulled it off and threw it out – at Ralf Schumacher, I think!'

Despite this, Schumacher Senior whistled through to take the chequered flag ahead with Frentzen securing another constructors' championship for Williams with second place. Irvine just fended off Häkkinen for third with Villeneuve and Alesi completing the top half-dozen on the road.

Herbert finished seventh, bemoaning what he reckoned was his worst start of the season even though he was lucky not to lose any places. 'This was a very tough race where I just had to concentrate on being as steady as possible,' he said. 'Right at the end I was pushing as hard as I could after Villeneuve and Alesi, but I just couldn't get close enough to challenge either of them.'

Giancarlo Fisichella grappled with poor grip throughout to finish eighth ahead of Berger while Ralf Schumacher lost time during his final pit stop and had to be content with tenth. On the last lap, Coulthard's McLaren seized its engine and spun off hard, rounding off a bitterly disappointing weekend for the Scot, although he was still classified ahead of Hill, Pedro Diniz and Jos Verstappen.

So Michael Schumacher trailed Villeneuve by a single point going into the final race of the season. Nine days later the Williams team would withdraw its appeal against Villeneuve's disqualification with the FIA's agreement, so Jacques forfeited those two points for fifth place.

This reversed the situation, ensuring Schumacher led by a single point.

Right: Jacques Villeneuve leads the pack into the first corner. His tactic of slowing the field in the opening laps came unstuck when he was outgunned by Eddie Irvine *(below)*, who soon built up a commanding lead over the Canadian.

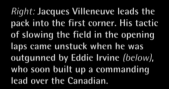

F1 teams consider legal action against FIA

THE spectre of a legal action between top F1 teams Williams and McLaren and the sport's governing body loomed over the Japanese Grand Prix weekend as the dispute over television and other income deriving from the FIA's alleged exploitation of the teams' 'intellectual rights' showed no signs of being resolved.

Under the terms of the new Concorde Agreement signed earlier this year by the Ferrari, Jordan, Sauber, Minardi, Arrows, Benetton and Prost teams, the exploitation of all commercial rights connected with their companies is relinquished to the FIA.

An early indication of the problems involved was given when electronics giant Sony found itself facing potential problems with its PlayStation F1 computer game because one team was objecting to the unauthorised use of its current car livery.

However, FIA Vice-President Bernie Ecclestone made it clear that the teams could think again if they imagined this argument might persuade him to expand the proposed flotation of his F1 Holdings empire to give them a stake in the equity or representation on the board.

'The teams can go to hell,' he told the *Sunday Times.* 'Some of them think they have me by the balls, but their hands aren't big enough. Under no circumstances will they get any free equity or a position on the board. I don't blame them for wanting it, but F1 is bigger than the teams and it could float without them.'

Williams and McLaren have made it plain that they will not sign up to the Concorde Agreement if it means, as they see it, giving the FIA *carte blanche* to exploit their team's image for any commercial purpose they see fit. To sustain this position, they are also prepared to relinquish the extra television income which would be theirs if they put their signatures on the document.

Ken Tyrrell also vigorously denied stories circulating at Suzuka that he had capitulated and signed the Concorde Agreement due to financial pressure.

All teams were also now concerned that Ecclestone was taking too big a share of the revenue generated from circuit advertising – particularly those seven who had belatedly realised what rights they have actually signed away.

Yet FIA President Max Mosley, who was re-elected for another five-year term by the FIA's General Assembly in the week before the Japanese race, hinted again that the Concorde Agreement might have outlived its usefulness and could yet be scrapped. It could be replaced by a simple rule book laying down technical, sporting and financial regulations and teams would be invited to submit entries to the championship on an individual basis.

FUJI TELEVISION
JAPANESE
GRAND PRIX
10–12 OCTOBER 1997
SUZUKA

Race distance: 53 laps, 192.995 miles/310.596 km

Race weather: Hot and sunny

ROUND 16

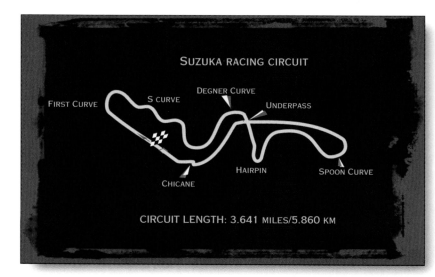

SUZUKA RACING CIRCUIT

FIRST CURVE · S CURVE · DEGNER CURVE · UNDERPASS · HAIRPIN · SPOON CURVE · CHICANE

CIRCUIT LENGTH: 3.641 MILES/5.860 KM

Pos.	Driver	Nat.	No.	Entrant	Car/Engine	Tyres	Laps	Time/Retirement	Speed (mph/km/h)
1	Michael Schumacher	D	5	Scuderia Ferrari Marlboro	Ferrari F310B 046/2 V10	G	53	1h 29m 48.446s	128.939/207.508
2	Heinz-Harald Frentzen	D	4	Rothmans Williams Renault	Williams FW19-Renault RS9A V10	G	53	1h 29m 49.824s	128.906/207.454
3	Eddie Irvine	GB	6	Scuderia Ferrari Marlboro	Ferrari F310B 046/2 V10	G	53	1h 30m 14.830s	128.310/206.496
4	Mika Häkkinen	SF	9	West McLaren Mercedes	McLaren MP4/12-Mercedes FO110F V10	G	53	1h 30m 15.575s	128.293/206.468
DQ	Jacques Villeneuve	CDN	3	Rothmans Williams Renault	Williams FW19-Renault RS9A V10	G	53	1h 30m 28.222s	127.994/205.987
5	Jean Alesi	F	7	Mild Seven Benetton Renault	Benetton B197-Renault RS9A V10	G	53	1h 30m 28.849s	127.979/205.963
6	Johnny Herbert	GB	16	Red Bull Sauber Petronas	Sauber C16-Petronas V10	G	53	1h 30m 30.076s	127.951/205.917
7	Giancarlo Fisichella	I	12	B&H Total Jordan Peugeot	Jordan 197-Peugeot A14 V10	G	53	1h 30m 45.271s	127.593/205.342
8	Gerhard Berger	A	8	Mild Seven Benetton Renault	Benetton B197-Renault RS9A V10	G	53	1h 30m 48.875s	127.509/205.206
9	Ralf Schumacher	D	11	B&H Total Jordan Peugeot	Jordan 197-Peugeot A14 V10	G	53	1h 31m 10.482s	127.006/204.396
10	David Coulthard	GB	10	West McLaren Mercedes	McLaren MP4/12-Mercedes FO110F V10	G	52	Engine	
11	Damon Hill	GB	1	Danka Arrows Yamaha	Arrows A18-Yamaha OX11A/D V10	B	52		
12	Pedro Diniz	BR	2	Danka Arrows Yamaha	Arrows A18-Yamaha OX11A/D V10	B	52		
13	Jos Verstappen	NL	18	Tyrrell	Tyrrell 025-Ford ED5 V8	G	52		
	Tarso Marques	BR	21	Minardi Team	Minardi M197-Hart 830 V8	B	46	Gearbox	
	Mika Salo	SF	19	Tyrrell	Tyrrell 025-Ford ED5 V8	G	46	Engine	
	Olivier Panis	F	14	Prost Gauloises Blondes	Prost JS45-Mugen Honda MF301HB V10	B	36	Engine	
	Shinji Nakano	J	15	Prost Gauloises Blondes	Prost JS45-Mugen Honda MF301HB V10	B	22	Wheel bearing	
	Ukyo Katayama	J	20	Minardi Team	Minardi M197-Hart 830 V8	B	8	Engine	
	Rubens Barrichello	BR	22	Stewart Ford	Stewart SF1-Ford Zetec-R V10	B	6	Spun off	
	Jan Magnussen	DK	23	Stewart Ford	Stewart SF1-Ford Zetec-R V10	B	3	Spun off	
DNS	Gianni Morbidelli	I	17	Red Bull Sauber Petronas	Sauber C16-Petronas V10	G		Qualifying accident	

Fastest lap: Frentzen, on lap 48, 1m 38.942s, 132.576 mph/213.361 km/h (record).

Previous lap record: Nigel Mansell (F1 Williams FW14B-Renault V10), 1m 40.646s, 130.332 mph/209.749 km/h (1992).

B – Bridgestone   G – Goodyear

Grid order	1	2	3	4	5	6	7	8	9	10	11	12	13	14	15	16	17	18	19	20	21	22	23	24	25	26	27	28	29	30	31	32	33	34	35	36	37	38	39	40	41
3 VILLENEUVE	3	3	6	6	6	6	6	6	6	6	6	6	6	6	6	6	3	3	3	3	4	6	6	6	5	5	5	5	5	5	5	5	5	4	4	4	4	5	5	5	5
5 M. SCHUMACHER	5	6	3	3	3	3	3	3	3	3	3	3	3	3	5	5	4	4	6	5	5	5	6	6	6	6	6	6	6	4	6	4	5	5	5	4	4	4	4	4	4
6 IRVINE	9	5	5	5	5	5	5	5	5	5	5	5	5	5	4	4	6	6	5	3	3	3	3	3	3	3	3	4	4	6	6	6	6	6	6	6	6	6	6	6	6
9 HÄKKINEN	6	9	9	9	9	9	9	9	9	9	9	9	9	9	9	4	4	4	6	6	16	16	3	4	4	4	4	4	4	4	4	16	16	16	16	16	16	7	7	7	7
8 BERGER	4	4	4	4	4	4	4	4	4	4	4	7	16	16	16	16	5	5	9	9	9	9	9	9	9	9	9	9	7	7	7	7	7	7	7	9	9	9	9	3	7
4 FRENTZEN	8	8	8	7	7	7	7	7	7	7	7	7	7	16	12	12	12	12	12	12	7	7	7	7	7	16	16	16	9	9	9	9	9	9	9	3	3	3	9	9	3
7 ALESI	7	7	7	8	8	8	8	8	8	8	8	8	8	10	1	1	9	9	9	7	8	8	8	8	16	7	7	7	3	3	3	3	3	3	3	8	16	16	16		
16 HERBERT	16	16	16	16	16	16	16	16	16	16	16	16	12	9	9	1	7	7	7	11	16	16	16	16	10	10	10	10	10	10	10	10	12	12	16	8	10	10			
12 FISICHELLA	10	10	10	10	10	10	10	10	10	10	10	10	1	14	7	7	11	11	11	11	10	10	12	12	12	12	12	12	12	8	8	10	10	12	12						
14 PANIS	12	12	12	12	12	12	12	12	12	12	12	12	9	11	11	11	8	8	16	10	12	12	14	14	14	14	14	8	8	10	10	12	12	8							
10 COULTHARD	23	23	23	22	22	1	1	1	1	1	1	1	7	8	8	10	10	10	12	14	14	14	1	1	1	1	8	1	1	1	11	11	1	11							
22 BARRICHELLO	22	22	22	1	1	14	14	14	14	14	14	11	8	15	10	21	14	14	14	1	1	1	11	11	11	11	1	11	11	11	1	1	11	11							
11 R. SCHUMACHER	1	1	1	11	11	11	11	11	11	11	11	8	15	10	15	2	1	1	1	11	11	11	11	11	1	14	14	14	2	2	2	2									
23 MAGNUSSEN	11	11	11	14	14	21	21	21	21	21	15	10	21	14	2	15	2	2	2	2	2	2	2	2	2	21	21	21	21	21	21	21									
15 NAKANO	14	14	14	21	21	15	15	15	15	15	21	21	2	1	15	2	21	21	21	21	21	21	21	21	21	2	19	19	19	19	19	19									
2 DINIZ	21	21	21	2	2	15	2	2	2	2	2	14	14	15	21	18	18	18	18	18	18	18	18	2	19	19	19	18	18	18	18	18									
1 HILL	2	2	2	15	15	2	18	18	18	18	18	2	18	2	18	18	19	19	19	19	19	19	18	18	18	18	18	18													
20 KATAYAMA	15	15	15	18	18	18	19	19	19	19	19	18	19	18	19	19	19	19	19	19	19	15																			
21 MARQUES	18	18	18	19	19	19	20	20																																	
18 VERSTAPPEN	19	19	19	20	20	20																																			
19 SALO	20	20	20																																						

Pit stop
One lap behind leader

STARTING GRID

3
VILLENEUVE
Williams

5
M. SCHUMACHER
Ferrari

6
IRVINE
Ferrari

9
HÄKKINEN
McLaren

8
BERGER
Benetton

4
FRENTZEN
Williams

7
ALESI
Benetton

16
HERBERT
Sauber

12
FISICHELLA
Jordan

14
PANIS
Prost

10
COULTHARD
McLaren

22
BARRICHELLO
Stewart

11
R. SCHUMACHER
Jordan

23
MAGNUSSEN
Stewart

15
NAKANO
Prost

2
DINIZ
Arrows

1
HILL
Arrows

20
KATAYAMA
Minardi

21
MARQUES
Minardi

18
VERSTAPPEN
Tyrrell

19
SALO
Tyrrell

Did not start:
MORBIDELLI (Sauber)

42	43	44	45	46	47	48	49	50	51	52	53	
5	5	5	5	5	5	5	5	5	5	5	5	1
4	4	4	4	4	4	4	4	4	4	4	4	2
6	6	6	6	6	6	6	6	6	6	6	6	3
9	9	9	9	9	9	9	9	9	9	9	9	4
3	3	3	3	3	3	3	3	3	3	3	3	
7	7	7	7	7	7	7	7	7	7	7	7	5
16	16	16	16	16	16	16	16	16	16	16	16	6
10	10	10	10	10	10	10	10	10	10	10	12	
12	12	12	12	12	12	12	12	12	12	12	8	
8	8	8	8	8	8	8	8	8	8	8	11	
11	11	11	11	11	11	11	11	11	11	11		
1	1	1	1	1	1	1	1	1	1	1		
2	2	2	2	2	2	2	2	2	2	2		
21	21	21	21	21	18	18	18	18	18	18		
19	19	19	19	19								
18	18	18	18	18								

TIME SHEETS

QUALIFYING
Weather: Warm and sunny

Pos.	Driver	Car	Laps	Time
1	Jacques Villeneuve	Williams-Renault	10	1m 36.071s
2	Michael Schumacher	Ferrari	8	1m 36.133s
3	Eddie Irvine	Ferrari	10	1m 36.466s
4	Mika Häkkinen	McLaren-Mercedes	10	1m 36.469s
5	Gerhard Berger	Benetton-Renault	11	1m 36.561s
6	Heinz-Harald Frentzen	Williams-Renault	12	1m 36.628s
7	Jean Alesi	Benetton-Renault	6	1m 36.682s
8	Johnny Herbert	Sauber-Petronas	11	1m 36.906s
9	Giancarlo Fisichella	Jordan-Peugeot	11	1m 36.917s
10	Olivier Panis	Prost-Mugen Honda	10	1m 37.073s
11	David Coulthard	McLaren-Mercedes	11	1m 37.095s
12	Rubens Barrichello	Stewart-Ford	11	1m 37.343s
13	Ralf Schumacher	Jordan-Peugeot	11	1m 37.443s
14	Jan Magnussen	Stewart-Ford	10	1m 37.480s
15	Shinji Nakano	Prost-Mugen Honda	10	1m 37.588s
16	Pedro Diniz	Arrows-Yamaha	10	1m 37.853s
17	Damon Hill	Arrows-Yamaha	12	1m 38.022s
18	Gianni Morbidelli	Sauber-Petronas	10	1m 38.556s
19	Ukyo Katayama	Minardi-Hart	12	1m 38.983s
20	Tarso Marques	Minardi-Hart	11	1m 39.678s
21	Jos Verstappen	Tyrrell-Ford	11	1m 40.259s
22	Mika Salo	Tyrrell-Ford	9	1m 40.529s

FRIDAY FREE PRACTICE
Weather: Bright and sunny

Pos.	Driver	Laps	Time
1	Eddie Irvine	30	1m 38.903s
2	Ralf Schumacher	28	1m 38.911s
3	Olivier Panis	26	1m 38.941s
4	Heinz-Harald Frentzen	26	1m 39.398s
5	Jean Alesi	19	1m 39.454s
6	Johnny Herbert	22	1m 39.840s
7	Damon Hill	27	1m 39.898s
8	David Coulthard	23	1m 39.945s
9	Gerhard Berger	25	1m 40.422s
10	Michael Schumacher	22	1m 40.460s
11	Jacques Villeneuve	27	1m 40.616s
12	Shinji Nakano	19	1m 40.653s
13	Giancarlo Fisichella	27	1m 40.720s
14	Mika Häkkinen	13	1m 40.724s
15	Rubens Barrichello	29	1m 40.937s
16	Ukyo Katayama	20	1m 41.158s
17	Jan Magnussen	26	1m 42.000s
18	Jos Verstappen	27	1m 42.290s
19	Mika Salo	28	1m 42.587s
20	Pedro Diniz	17	1m 42.893s
21	Gianni Morbidelli	14	1m 44.736s
22	Tarso Marques	15	1m 46.282s

SATURDAY FREE PRACTICE
Weather: Overcast and humid

Pos.	Driver	Laps	Time
1	Ralf Schumacher	22	1m 37.372s
2	Mika Häkkinen	23	1m 37.481s
3	Giancarlo Fisichella	28	1m 37.649s
4	Heinz-Harald Frentzen	22	1m 37.755s
5	Jacques Villeneuve	25	1m 37.758s
6	Jean Alesi	23	1m 37.905s
7	Johnny Herbert	23	1m 37.929s
8	Gerhard Berger	25	1m 38.147s
9	Shinji Nakano	21	1m 38.343s
10	Michael Schumacher	20	1m 38.403s
11	Damon Hill	27	1m 38.514s
12	Rubens Barrichello	23	1m 38.723s
13	Olivier Panis	22	1m 38.816s
14	Eddie Irvine	23	1m 38.910s
15	Jan Magnussen	15	1m 38.947s
16	David Coulthard	16	1m 39.537s
17	Gianni Morbidelli	23	1m 39.546s
18	Pedro Diniz	28	1m 39.702s
19	Ukyo Katayama	21	1m 39.995s
20	Mika Salo	15	1m 40.905s
21	Tarso Marques	26	1m 41.348s
22	Jos Verstappen	18	1m 41.370s

WARM-UP
Weather: Dry, hot and sunny

Pos.	Driver	Laps	Time
1	Mika Häkkinen	12	1m 38.113s
2	Ralf Schumacher	14	1m 38.547s
3	Heinz-Harald Frentzen	10	1m 39.084s
4	Michael Schumacher	12	1m 39.163s
5	Eddie Irvine	13	1m 39.233s
6	Olivier Panis	13	1m 39.370s
7	Johnny Herbert	13	1m 39.418s
8	Shinji Nakano	13	1m 39.553s
9	David Coulthard	10	1m 39.784s
10	Jacques Villeneuve	13	1m 40.061s
11	Damon Hill	11	1m 40.227s
12	Giancarlo Fisichella	13	1m 40.312s
13	Jan Magnussen	11	1m 40.345s
14	Pedro Diniz	13	1m 40.576s
15	Gerhard Berger	12	1m 40.685s
16	Tarso Marques	15	1m 41.480s
17	Ukyo Katayama	11	1m 41.685s
18	Rubens Barrichello	14	1m 41.983s
19	Mika Salo	13	1m 42.021s
20	Jos Verstappen	10	1m 42.835s
21	Jean Alesi	6	1m 44.098s

RACE FASTEST LAPS
Weather: Hot and sunny

Driver	Time	Lap
Heinz-Harald Frentzen	1m 38.942s	48
Michael Schumacher	1m 39.268s	48
Jean Alesi	1m 39.381s	29
Ralf Schumacher	1m 39.737s	46
David Coulthard	1m 39.771s	52
Eddie Irvine	1m 39.935s	15
Gerhard Berger	1m 39.998s	48
Mika Häkkinen	1m 40.151s	24
Jacques Villeneuve	1m 40.163s	22
Giancarlo Fisichella	1m 40.217s	45
Johnny Herbert	1m 40.266s	49
Olivier Panis	1m 40.430s	34
Damon Hill	1m 41.419s	35
Shinji Nakano	1m 41.608s	15
Pedro Diniz	1m 41.611s	33
Tarso Marques	1m 42.699s	34
Mika Salo	1m 42.996s	20
Jos Verstappen	1m 43.051s	49
Rubens Barrichello	1m 43.883s	3
Jan Magnussen	1m 44.089s	3
Ukyo Katayama	1m 44.403s	5

CHASSIS LOG BOOK

1	Hill	Arrows A18/5
2	Diniz	Arrows A18/4
	spare	Arrows A18/3
3	Villeneuve	Williams FW19/4
4	Frentzen	Williams FW19/5
	spare	Williams FW19/3
5	M. Schumacher	Ferrari F310B/178
6	Irvine	Ferrari F310B/180
	spare	Ferrari F310B/175
7	Alesi	Benetton B197/2
8	Berger	Benetton B197/4
	spare	Benetton B197/3
9	Häkkinen	McLaren MP4/12/4
10	Coulthard	McLaren MP4/12/6
	spare	McLaren MP4/12/7
11	R. Schumacher	Jordan 197/6
12	Fisichella	Jordan 197/5
	spare	Jordan 197/1
14	Panis	Prost JS45/3
15	Nakano	Prost JS45/2
	spare	Prost JS45/1
16	Herbert	Sauber C16/7
17	Morbidelli	Sauber C16/6
	spare	Sauber C16/5
18	Verstappen	Tyrrell 025/4
19	Salo	Tyrrell 025/5
	spare	Tyrrell 025/1
20	Katayama	Minardi M197/4
21	Marques	Minardi M197/2
	spare	Minardi M197/1
22	Barrichello	Stewart SF1/4
23	Magnussen	Stewart SF1/3
	spare	Stewart SF1/1

POINTS TABLES

Drivers

1	Michael Schumacher	78
2	Jacques Villeneuve	77
3	Heinz-Harald Frentzen	41
4	Jean Alesi	36
5	David Coulthard	30
6	Gerhard Berger	24
7	Eddie Irvine	22
8	Giancarlo Fisichella	20
9	Mika Häkkinen	17
10	Olivier Panis	16
11	Johnny Herbert	15
12	Ralf Schumacher	13
13	Damon Hill	7
14	Rubens Barrichello	6
15	Alexander Wurz	4
16	Jarno Trulli	3
17 =	Mika Salo	2
17 =	Shinji Nakano	2
17 =	Pedro Diniz	2
20	Nicola Larini	1

Constructors

1	Williams	118
2	Ferrari	100
3	Benetton	64
4	McLaren	47
5	Jordan	33
6	Prost	21
7	Sauber	16
8	Arrows	9
9	Stewart	6
10	Tyrrell	2

Results and points tables reflect
the position after the Williams
team withdrew its appeal against
Jacques Villeneuve's exclusion.

EUROPEAN

grand prix

HÄKKINEN

COULTHARD

VILLENEUVE

BERGER

IRVINE

FRENTZEN

The incident that settled the outcome of the 1997 World Championship. When Jacques Villeneuve slipped his Williams inside Michael Schumacher's Ferrari at Dry Sack on lap 48, the German turned into him but it was Schumacher who came off worst, having to abandon his stranded F310B in the gravel trap.

ANOTHER F1 World Championship ended in high drama and controversy at the European Grand Prix at Jerez when Michael Schumacher tried to barge Jacques Villeneuve's Williams off the road as the Canadian driver attempted a legitimate overtaking manoeuvre midway round lap 48 of the 69-lap title finale. The immediate result of this lapse was the end of the German driver's World Championship hopes; the Ferrari was left beached in the gravel trap, unable to drag itself back onto the tarmac. Despite concerns that his car had sustained quite serious damage, Villeneuve grappled confidently with poor handling and unpredictable tyre wear for the remainder of the distance, before easing his pace on the final lap to allow Mika Häkkinen and David Coulthard through to score a McLaren-Mercedes 1-2 as a 'thank you' for the apparent tacit help they had given him earlier in the event.

After the race both Schumacher and Villeneuve were summoned to the stewards to offer their explanations of the collision. It was eventually decided that this was a racing accident, but 24 hours later – after Schumacher had reaped a whirlwind of vitriolic criticism, particularly from the Italian and German media – the FIA stepped in to summon the Ferrari driver to appear before an extraordinary meeting of its World Council on 11 November, at which he was stripped of his second place in the World Championship.

Despite pre-race warnings from senior officials that the final round of the championship should be free of such aggressive confrontations, Schumacher turned into the Williams's left-hand side pod as the Canadian driver dived through on the inside to take the lead. It was widely perceived as a re-run of the controversial accident with Damon Hill at Adelaide in 1994 which Schumacher has since consistently denied was a deliberate attempt to force his rival off the track.

Unlike 1994, this time Schumacher came off second best as his car skidded into the gravel trap where it stopped, bogged down with its rear wheels spinning frantically as he tried in vain to extricate himself and return to the race. Eventually he abandoned his machine and walked back to the pits, knowing that Villeneuve now only had to score a single point to take the title.

The two championship rivals went to the line amidst a mood of enormous tension and expectancy. Villeneuve's pole position was on the cleaner left-hand side of the circuit, but many people predicted that Schumacher was more favourably placed on the right-hand side of the track, aiming for the first right-hander. And so it proved.

'I wasn't on new tyres from the start of the race and I had to struggle to keep up with Michael,' said Villeneuve. 'At the start he was simply glued to the asphalt – I don't know how he did it. I was impressed, because I was sliding everywhere.

'Then he was on the inside of me going into the first corner after the start and my team-mate Heinz-Harald Frentzen came up on the inside of me and I gave him room because I didn't want to risk banging wheels with him at this early stage in the race.'

By the end of the opening lap Schumacher was 1.9s ahead of Frentzen with Villeneuve third from Häkkinen, Coulthard, Damon Hill, Eddie Irvine, Jan Magnussen, Gerhard Berger and Rubens Barrichello. It was lap eight before Jacques went ahead of his team-mate to take second place, after which the Williams team leader immediately steadied the Ferrari's advantage at 4.2s, fading slightly to 4.7s by lap 12 as, further back, Pedro Diniz spun his Arrows into retirement from 13th place.

On lap 22 Schumacher made his first refuelling stop in 7.6s, resuming fourth behind Villeneuve, Frentzen and Häkkinen. For the final couple of corners he found himself inadvertently boxed in behind the Minardi of Tarso Marques. Coming down to the final hairpin, the young Brazilian kept well over to the left, thinking he was doing Michael a favour by leaving him room to pass on the racing line to the right. In fact, Michael wanted the left-hand line and a fast track to the pits. But it was an innocent misunderstanding. Hill also stopped the Arrows, dropping from sixth to eighth.

Now the race became acutely tactical. On lap 23 Villeneuve made his first refuelling stop, dropping down the order to fifth behind Coulthard. Frentzen, now leading, had been lapping in the mid-1m 24s bracket on laps 21 and 22. For three laps he now dropped his pace into the mid-1m 26s bracket to enable Villeneuve to catch up the bunch again.

On lap 25 Coulthard obligingly pulled in from fourth place to make his first refuelling stop (7.6s), which allowed Villeneuve to pull up onto Schumacher's Ferrari. On lap 26 Häkkinen made his first stop, then Frentzen headed for the pit lane on lap 28 and, hey presto, Schumacher and Villeneuve were back in first and second places, separated by only 0.9s.

With 30 laps completed the order was Schumacher, Villeneuve, Coulthard, Häkkinen, Frentzen, Irvine and Hill. As

Darren Heath

the two leaders crossed the start/finish line, Sauber stand-in Norberto Fontana accelerated back out of the pits into the first corner and quickly allowed Schumacher through. He then cut across in front of Villeneuve, dawdling around to the extent of costing Jacques 2.5s by the end of the following lap. The link was clearly Ferrari's engine deal with the Swiss team, although it could have been sheer inexperience. Incompetence, even.

Since his first stop, Villeneuve had been on fresh rubber and he was now piling on the pressure. From 3.1s behind the Ferrari after Fontana's intervention, the gap came down to 2.0s on lap 35, then 1.7s on lap 40. Ralf Schumacher, running the spare Jordan, did his bit to help big brother as they lapped the Peugeot-engined car on lap 40, but it cost Villeneuve only 0.4s. Now everybody was on tenterhooks

anticipating the second round of refuelling stops.

Schumacher made his second stop at the end of lap 43 followed by Villeneuve a lap later. Again the Williams driver got back into the race behind Coulthard, resuming in third place, but again the McLaren driver cleared the way, coming in for his second stop next time round.

Now Villeneuve was all over Schumacher's rear wing and lunged for the

inside line going into Dry Sack, the sixth corner of the lap. Then the two cars collided.

'I knew I had to make my move then, or else my tyres would go off a bit and I wouldn't be able to fight any more,' said Villeneuve. 'I just went for it, and just braked late. I was surprised that he hadn't closed the door yet, but it was only a matter of seconds before he decided to turn in on me. But he

Paul-Henri Cahier

Left: David Coulthard leads team-mate Mika Häkkinen before stepping aside as instructed to allow the Finn to head the pursuit of Jacques Villeneuve's Williams.

Bottom: Having let the McLarens through, Villeneuve punches the air as he crosses the line in third place just ahead of Gerhard Berger's Benetton.

didn't do it well enough, because he went out and I didn't.

'The impact was very hard. The way we banged wheels was hard enough to break my suspension. It was not a small thing, but the car felt strange and I took the next few laps pretty slowly. Once I was sure that the suspension was not touching the tyre I managed to press on intermittently, but the car felt odd on right-hand corners.'

On the same lap, Hill's Arrows-Yamaha blew up, ending the 1996 World Champion's unproductive season with Tom Walkinshaw's team on a disappointingly sterile note. Now it was a question of watching to see how Villeneuve handled the last 20 laps of the race with his odd-handling Williams, given the fact that there were two healthy McLaren-Mercs nibbling into his advantage.

However, all was not as it seemed. After an informal pre-race chat between Frank Williams and Ron Dennis, the McLaren lads had attempted to keep out of everybody's way in terms of the title battle, in particular not disrupting proceedings when Frentzen slowed the pace of the race after Villeneuve's first refuelling stop.

Now it was payback time on two fronts. Villeneuve was repeatedly reminded that he should remember their consideration while the McLaren management explained to Coulthard that

JEREZ QUALIFYING

F1's return to Jerez after an absence of three years was always going to represent something of an unknown quantity. 'It's a bit like Monaco without the barriers,' said David Coulthard. 'So you don't have any excuse to leave a little margin.'

Damon Hill had another viewpoint. 'Like Budapest, but a bit quicker,' he remarked, reflecting briefly on his third place on the grid for the Hungarian Grand Prix. He was about right there.

From the start of the weekend the circuit was understandably dusty and lacked grip. Friday free practice therefore was not truly representative, neither Jacques Villeneuve nor Michael Schumacher lifting the curtain on their possible qualifying form. They were left to play their cards close to their chest as Olivier Panis's Bridgestone-shod Prost-Mugen Honda set the early pace.

Panis finished the day only 0.16s ahead of Hill's Arrows-Yamaha, and, with Rubens Barrichello's Stewart-Ford making it three cars on Bridgestone rubber in the top four, the prospect of a first F1 win for the Japanese tyre company seemed a real possibility.

Villeneuve's Williams finished the day with third-fastest time, the Canadian surviving a lurid trip into a gravel trap after missing his braking point for one corner, yet there was no doubt he would be a strong pole-position contender in qualifying.

'I feel very good with how the session has gone today,' said Villeneuve. 'Usually we are not so quick in Friday practice, but here in Jerez our homework has come together well. It's important to be at the front of the grid, not just because it is difficult to overtake here but also because the tyres are likely to lose grip quickly once the race starts.'

Meanwhile Schumacher, who went into the race leading the World Championship by a single point, was content with ninth-fastest time in the Ferrari F310B. 'We concentrated on our race set-up today and the car generally feels good, so I am quite happy,' he said with a non-committal smile.

The build-up to Saturday's hour-long qualifying session was racked with tension. Free practice saw Eddie Irvine balk Villeneuve deliberately, so Jacques stormed down to the Ferrari pit and told Eddie just what he thought of him in unambiguous terms. Irvine, who had previously committed himself to putting his car in Villeneuve's way at every opportunity, wasn't in the slightest bit concerned.

Heinz-Harald Frentzen set the early qualifying pace with a 1m 22.022s, galvanising team-mate Villeneuve into prompt action. Despite the windy conditions slightly unsettling his FW19 in the fast corners, Jacques raised the stakes by posting a 1m 21.072s.

Then David Coulthard's McLaren moved up to second on 1m 21.476s followed by Schumacher's Ferrari on 1m 21.798s. Thereafter the action came thick and fast. Panis spoiled his second qualifying run with a lurid slide over a gravel trap, then Jean Alesi spun his Benetton out of the final left-hander onto the start/finish straight.

At 1.25 p.m. Schumacher's Ferrari began its second run just as brother Ralf spun his Jordan into the gravel trap at the chicane. The marshals hurried to remove the stricken car and Michael was lucky to find only stationary yellow flags when he arrived on his hot lap.

'Stationary yellows mean drive within your limits, and I can judge that very well,' he said loftily after finishing the lap to produce an amazing dead-heat with Villeneuve, recording precisely the same time to three decimal places. The destiny of second place on the starting grid was now resolved.

Yet this whole episode was marginal in the extreme. It certainly did not sit easily in comparison with Villeneuve's experience at Suzuka where he was penalised for passing a parked Tyrrell on the straight under a waved yellow flag.

The situation Schumacher experienced was potentially far more hazardous – there should have been waved yellow flags as a tractor was still pulling Ralf's Jordan back towards the tyre barrier. It was understandable that some of the Williams brigade reckoned this was another example of Ferrari's path to the World Championship being unexpectedly smoothed. Michael was certainly taking one hell of a risk.

In third place on the grid was Frentzen's Williams, which amaz-ingly produced exactly the same time as Villeneuve and Schumacher – an unprecedented occurrence in F1 championship history.

Quick qualifying times depended on how a driver used his tyres. The Goodyear runners needed to warm up their rubber very progressively with a very cautious 'out' lap. The Williams drivers were both notably circumspect and reaped the benefits. Perhaps the McLarens ran a little too hard too soon; both Mika Häkkinen and Coulthard produced laps that saw them ahead at the first timing split, but slower on the overall lap as the tenths ebbed away over the final sector.

The Bridgestone runners certainly seemed less prone to this slight performance drop-off with the steady rise in ambient temperature. In the closing moments of the session Hill came bounding into contention, grabbing fourth place on the grid – or second-fastest time, if you prefer – after a great performance with the Arrows.

'I really wanted to give them something special for this last race,' he said, 'and if it hadn't been for Katayama, who spun right in front of me on the last corner and cost me some time, I could have been on pole.'

Behind Hill, the two McLarens lined up with Häkkinen just ahead of Coulthard, both drivers encountering traffic during runs in the middle of the session and David taking a brief excursion across the chicane gravel trap.

'I don't usually like to complain about traffic, because it is the same for everybody,' said Coulthard, 'but it seemed to be particularly difficult out there today. My two middle runs had to be aborted because I caught the two Schumacher brothers on the first, and then Hill on the second. For my last run we made a small change to the car which I wasn't quite so happy with on the last section, so that restricted me to sixth place.'

Eddie Irvine lined up seventh, very disappointed that he had inadvertently scrambled his Ferrari's brake balance settings, while the Benettons of Gerhard Berger and Jean Alesi sandwiched Olivier Panis's Prost in eighth and tenth places. Gerhard, shaping up for his last Grand Prix, was disappointed that his B197's balance did not seem as good as it had during the morning free practice while Alesi, who had crashed his race car quite heavily in free practice, didn't like the set-up of the spare car he found himself obliged to use and spun twice.

In the Stewart-Ford camp there was a degree of optimism with Jan Magnussen and Rubens Barrichello both using the latest P9 version of the Zetec-R V10 engine to qualify in 11th and 12th respectively. Magnussen was pleased to have beaten the Brazilian fair and square, Barrichello having to use the spare car after sliding off into a tyre barrier and damaging his race chassis during the morning session.

Pedro Diniz admitted that he had improved the handling of his Arrows, but he had a disappointing time in traffic and could only line up 13th overall. Johnny Herbert was just behind in 14th place, four places ahead of team-mate Norberto Fontana, who had replaced Gianni Morbidelli for this final race of the season after the Italian injured an arm at Suzuka.

'On my first two runs I was very aggressive,' said Herbert,' as I think you should be in qualifying, but it just aggravated the tyres and made the rear end of the car very loose. We made some small changes, and on my last run I felt I was going better still, but in the final left-hander, the wind was pretty bad and when I felt the car understeering, I knew I'd lost out on a better lap.'

Behind the Prost of Shinji Nakano, the Jordan 197s of Ralf Schumacher and Giancarlo Fisichella qualified 16th and 17th, a disastrous note on which to round off the '97 season. Ralf spun off grappling with the abrupt transition from understeer to oversteer while Fisichella was simply at sea, unable properly to understand what on earth was happening with his machine.

Fontana was 18th ahead of the two Minardis of Ukyo Katayama and Tarso Marques while Mika Salo and Jos Verstappen brought up the rear for Tyrrell, Ken's two drivers running differing fuel loads. Verstappen complained of power understeer while Salo had too much oversteer.

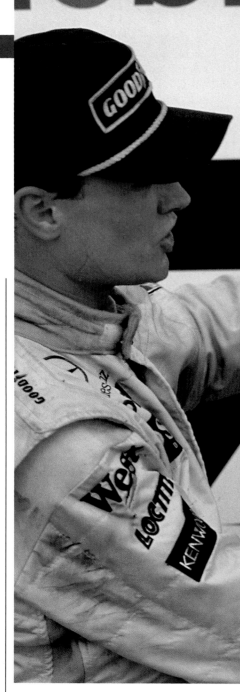

Moral race winner Jacques Villeneuve is about to be hoisted aloft by McLaren drivers David Coulthard and Mika Häkkinen, who filled the first two places.

Bottom left: It's good to talk. Häkkinen had finally achieved his long-overdue maiden Grand Prix win but in the circumstances the victory was somewhat hollow.

Bottom right: F1 said farewell to Gerhard Berger. He can always get a job driving one of Bernie's trucks!

he should drop back behind Häkkinen as Mika had sacrificed more than he had done in that early traffic jam.

There was also the frustration of having Giancarlo Fisichella's Jordan between Villeneuve and the two McLarens. With only two laps to go, Coulthard dutifully dropped back behind Häkkinen – then Fisichella suddenly responded to a waved blue flag and pulled out of the Finn's path.

Going into the chicane on the last lap, Häkkinen plunged past into the lead with Coulthard following through at the final hairpin to take second place. In fact, while all these theatricals were going on to reward the McLaren drivers, it seemed that nobody had noticed Gerhard Berger's Benetton – which had overtaken Irvine on the final lap – storming up behind and the Austrian veteran rounded off his F1 career by almost catching them all at the chequered flag, crossing the line just 1.9s behind Häkkinen, who had at last won a Grand Prix at his 96th attempt.

Mosley warns on tobacco ban

FIA President Max Mosley warned that European Grands Prix could be decimated if the European Union goes ahead with its proposed ban on tobacco advertising. Speaking at a press conference on the eve of the European Grand Prix, he made it clear that the F1 World Championship would shift its emphasis to the Far East if necessary, leaving once-classic European races to take place only once every three years.

'We would continue to have Grands Prix in Europe, but the number would be reduced to the same number which we already have without tobacco sponsorship,' he explained. 'At the moment we have three races where there is no tobacco sponsorship on the cars: the British, the German and – normally – the French GPs.

'At present we have nine races in EU countries, a figure which would be reduced to three, with each race being held once every third year in the countries where they are presently held every year. The races held in Europe which do not belong to the EU – for example Monaco and Hungary – would continue in the normal way on an annual basis.'

Mosley reminded his audience that there is talk of an EU ban on tobacco advertising being imposed within between three and five years, allowing the FIA adequate warning to implement its contingency plan. He insisted that this strategy did not reflect a willingness to endorse smoking, but stated that the FIA's best evidence was that cigarette sponsorship and the advertising of tobacco do not encourage people to take up smoking.

'There may be evidence to the contrary effect,' he continued, 'but if there is such evidence, nobody has yet produced it to us – despite many requests. We therefore find ourselves faced with a determination by governments to ban advertising because, they say, they oppose smoking, while all the evidence points to the fact that a ban on advertising will have exactly the opposite effect.'

However, Mosley explained that the FIA has an alternative strategy to offer. It has made approaches to a number of European governments offering an FIA-managed global reduction of the amount of tobacco advertising permitted within motorsport. Within ten days the British government had accepted this FIA proposal and announced that F1 would be exempt from tobacco advertising restrictions in the UK. Mosley has also told these governments that if they can produce evidence that the sponsorship on F1 cars increases smoking among young people, or increases the amount of tobacco consumed overall, the FIA will ban tobacco advertising on a worldwide basis.

On the issue of the continuing dispute over the Concorde Agreement, he confessed he was 'somewhat ambivalent' about the continued value of such a document and said he would be prepared to scrap this protocol which has governed the way in which F1 rules are implemented if all the competing teams agreed to do so.

'We don't want the Concorde Agreement,' he said. 'It is something which has always tied our hands and we received more disadvantages than advantages from it. We should just publish the regulations and if people wish to enter they are free to do so, or not, as they wish.'

However he did admit that the competing F1 teams seemed to want a Concorde Agreement as they feel it gives them a measure of stability and an influence over the rules and the evolution of F1.

Mosley added: 'It would be equally logical for us to reach a special agreement with teams that wish to make a long-term commitment to the championship. If they agreed to take part in the championship for, say, five years, it would be logical for those same teams to receive a greater financial reward for their greater commitment, and at the same time they should be allowed to have a role in making the rules for those five years.

'Why should someone be permitted to take part in forming the rules for 1999 when he has given no undertaking that he will be competing in 1999. It doesn't make sense.'

That said, Mosley added that he believed a revised agreement would be drawn up within weeks and signed by all competing teams. 'Everyone will sign, and there will be peace within our time,' he said confidently.

Fifth place fell to Irvine's Ferrari. 'I made a reasonable start and maintained my position,' he shrugged. 'I took it easy behind Hill, then I pushed before the pit stops and got ahead of him. I was then behind the McLarens for most of the race, but I could not pass them. I overtook Frentzen at the next pit stop, but then flat-spotted the right-front tyre and Fisichella held me up badly considering he was a lap down, chopped in front of me at both the chicane and the hairpin, and that let Berger pass me.'

Frentzen finished sixth after a chaotic second stop, initially losing five seconds as he slowed to stay behind Villeneuve as Jacques recovered from his incident with Schumacher, then losing another eight seconds running over two McLaren wheel guns and mistakenly turning into the Benetton pit before finally reaching his intended destination in front of the Williams garage.

Seventh place was taken by Olivier Panis's Prost, which had a steady run after a slow start, protected from the pursuing Sauber of Johnny Herbert when the British driver was balked by a Minardi as he lined up to challenge the French car.

Jan Magnussen ran confidently home to ninth place, the Dane's second top-ten finish of the season, in the sole surviving Stewart-Ford after team-mate Rubens Barrichello succumbed to a gearbox problem which caused his retirement after 30 laps.

Shinji Nakano completed the top ten ahead of Fisichella in the only Jordan to make the flag, Ralf Schumacher having called it a day with alternator problems. Mika Salo drove an energetic race to finish 12th, rounding off his Tyrrell career with an encouraging result after reporting that his car had felt good all weekend.

Jean Alesi trailed home in 13th after a spin, while Fontana, Marques, Jos Verstappen's Tyrrell and Ukyo Katayama's Minardi completed the large 17-strong list of classified finishers.

So Jacques Villeneuve became a worthy World Champion at the end of only his second F1 season. Häkkinen at last won his first Grand Prix, perhaps not in the manner he would have liked, while Coulthard finished the day in an extremely irked frame of mind, as his body language on the rostrum clearly proclaimed for all to see.

For Michael Schumacher it had been a very unhappy episode indeed. Whether Ferrari had now missed its window of opportunity as far as winning a World Championship was concerned was a matter to be resolved in 1998. Some feared this could be the case.

GRAND PRIX OF
EUROPE
24–26 OCTOBER 1997
JEREZ

Race distance: 69 laps, 189.819 miles/305.532 km

Race weather: Dry, warm and sunny

ROUND 17

PELUQUI · AYRTON SENNA CHICANE · EXPO 92 · MICHELIN · DUCADOS · DRY SACK

CIRCUITO DE JEREZ

CIRCUIT LENGTH: 2.751 MILES/4.428 KM

Pos.	Driver	Nat.	No.	Entrant	Car/Engine	Tyres	Laps	Time/Retirement	Speed (mph/km/h)
1	Mika Häkkinen	SF	9	West McLaren Mercedes	McLaren MP4/12-Mercedes FO110F V10	G	69	1h 38m 57.771s	115.103/185.240
2	David Coulthard	GB	10	West McLaren Mercedes	McLaren MP4/12-Mercedes FO110F V10	G	69	1h 38m 59.425s	115.070/185.188
3	Jacques Villeneuve	CDN	3	Rothmans Williams Renault	Williams FW19-Renault RS9A V10	G	69	1h 38m 59.574s	115.068/185.184
4	Gerhard Berger	A	8	Mild Seven Benetton Renault	Benetton B197-Renault RS9A V10	G	69	1h 38m 59.690s	115.065/185.180
5	Eddie Irvine	GB	6	Scuderia Ferrari Marlboro	Ferrari F310B 046/2 V10	G	69	1h 39m 01.560s	115.029/185.122
6	Heinz-Harald Frentzen	D	4	Rothmans Williams Renault	Williams FW19-Renault RS9A V10	G	69	1h 39m 02.308s	115.015/185.099
7	Olivier Panis	F	14	Prost Gauloises Blondes	Prost JS45-Mugen Honda MF301HB V10	B	69	1h 40m 04.916s	113.816/183.169
8	Johnny Herbert	GB	16	Red Bull Sauber Petronas	Sauber C16-Petronas V10	G	69	1h 40m 10.732s	113.705/182.991
9	Jan Magnussen	DK	23	Stewart Ford	Stewart SF1-Ford Zetec-R V10	B	69	1h 40m 15.258s	113.620/182.854
10	Shinji Nakano	J	15	Prost Gauloises Blondes	Prost JS45-Mugen Honda MF301HB V10	B	69	1h 40m 15.986s	113.606/182.832
11	Giancarlo Fisichella	I	12	B&H Total Jordan Peugeot	Jordan 197-Peugeot A14 V10	G	68		
12	Mika Salo	SF	19	Tyrrell	Tyrrell 025-Ford ED5 V8	G	68		
13	Jean Alesi	F	7	Mild Seven Benetton Renault	Benetton B197-Renault RS9A V10	G	68		
14	Norberto Fontana	RA	17	Red Bull Sauber Petronas	Sauber C16-Petronas V10	G	68		
15	Tarso Marques	BR	21	Minardi Team	Minardi M197-Hart 830 V8	B	68		
16	Jos Verstappen	NL	18	Tyrrell	Tyrrell 025-Ford ED5 V8	G	68		
17	Ukyo Katayama	J	20	Minardi Team	Minardi M197-Hart 830 V8	B	68		
	Michael Schumacher	D	5	Scuderia Ferrari Marlboro	Ferrari F310B 046/2 V10	G	47	Collision with Villeneuve	
	Damon Hill	GB	1	Danka Arrows Yamaha	Arrows A18-Yamaha OX11A/D V10	B	47	Hydraulics	
	Ralf Schumacher	D	11	B&H Total Jordan Peugeot	Jordan 197-Peugeot A14 V10	G	44	Alternator	
	Rubens Barrichello	BR	22	Stewart Ford	Stewart SF1-Ford Zetec-R V10	B	30	Gearbox	
	Pedro Diniz	BR	2	Danka Arrows Yamaha	Arrows A18-Yamaha OX11A/D V10	B	11	Spun off	

Fastest lap: Frentzen, on lap 30, 1m 23.135s, 119.145 mph/191.745 km/h (record).

Previous lap record: Michael Schumacher (F1 Benetton B194-Ford V8), 1m 25.040s, 116.429 mph/187.450 km/h (1994).

B – Bridgestone   G – Goodyear

Grid order	1	2	3	4	5	6	7	8	9	10	11	12	13	14	15	16	17	18	19	20	21	22	23	24	25	26	27	28	29	30	31	32	33	34	35	36	37	38	39	40	41	42	43	44	45	46	47	48	49	50	51	52	53	54
3 VILLENEUVE	5	5	5	5	5	5	5	5	5	5	5	5	5	5	5	5	5	5	5	5	5	5	3	4	4	4	4	4	5	5	5	5	5	5	5	5	5	5	5	5	5	3	3	5	5	5	3	3	3	3	3	3	3	3
5 M. SCHUMACHER	4	4	4	4	4	4	4	3	3	3	3	3	3	3	3	3	3	3	3	3	3	4	9	9	9	5	5	3	3	3	3	3	3	3	3	3	3	3	3	3	5	5	3	3	3	10	10	10	10	10	10	10	10	10
4 FRENTZEN	3	3	3	3	3	3	4	4	4	4	4	4	4	4	4	4	4	4	4	4	4	9	5	5	5	3	3	8	10	10	10	10	10	10	10	10	10	10	10	10	4	4	4	9	9	9	9	9	9	9	9	9	9	9
1 HILL	9	9	9	9	9	9	9	9	9	9	9	9	9	9	9	9	9	9	9	9	9	5	10	10	3	8	8	10	9	9	9	9	9	9	9	9	9	9	9	9	4	8	8	10	6	6	6	6	6	6	6	6		
9 HÄKKINEN	10	10	10	10	10	10	10	10	10	10	10	10	10	10	10	10	10	10	10	10	10	3	3	8	9	10	4	4	4	4	4	4	4	4	4	4	4	4	4	4	8	10	10	9	8	8	8	8	8	8	8	8		
10 COULTHARD	1	1	1	1	1	1	1	1	1	1	1	1	1	1	1	1	1	1	1	1	6	6	8	10	10	9	9	6	6	6	6	6	6	6	6	6	6	6	6	6	1	9	9	6	4	4	4	4	4	4	4	4		
6 IRVINE	6	6	6	6	6	6	6	6	6	6	6	6	6	6	6	6	6	6	6	6	8	8	6	6	6	6	6	1	1	1	1	1	1	1	1	1	8	8	8	8	8	6	6	8	14	14	14	14	14	14	14	14		
8 BERGER	23	23	23	23	23	23	23	23	23	23	23	23	23	23	23	23	8	8	8	1	1	1	1	1	1	8	8	8	8	8	8	8	8	8	1	1	1	1	1	6	1	1	1	16	16	16	16	16	16	16			
14 PANIS	8	8	8	8	8	8	8	8	8	8	8	8	8	8	8	8	22	22	22	22	22	22	22	22	22	23	23	23	23	23	23	23	23	23	23	23	23	23	23	16	14	14	23	23	23	23	23	23	23	23			
7 ALESI	22	22	22	22	22	22	22	22	22	22	22	22	22	22	22	14	7	7	7	7	7	16	16	23	23	14	14	14	14	14	14	14	14	14	7	7	7	23	16	16	19	19	19	19	15	15	15	15						
23 MAGNUSSEN	7	7	7	7	7	14	14	14	14	14	14	14	14	14	14	7	16	16	16	16	23	23	14	14	14	7	7	7	7	7	7	7	7	7	14	16	16	7	23	23	15	15	12	12	12	12								
22 BARRICHELLO	2	2	2	14	14	14	14	7	7	7	7	7	7	7	7	23	23	23	23	23	14	14	7	7	7	22	16	16	16	16	16	16	16	16	16	14	14	16	16	23	15	12	12	19	19	19								
2 DINIZ	14	14	14	2	2	2	2	2	2	2	16	16	16	16	16	16	12	12	12	12	15	7	7	16	16	16	19	19	11	11	11	11	11	11	11	11	11	15	15	15	12	19	7	7	7	7	7	7						
16 HERBERT	16	16	16	16	16	16	16	16	16	16	11	11	11	11	12	12	15	15	15	14	19	19	19	19	11	11	15	15	15	15	15	15	15	15	12	12	19	12	21	21	21	17	17	17										
15 NAKANO	11	11	11	11	11	11	11	11	11	12	12	12	12	15	15	15	18	14	17	20	11	11	11	11	19	11	11	15	15	12	12	12	12	12	19	19	7	7	17	17	17	21	21	21										
11 R. SCHUMACHER	12	12	12	12	12	12	12	12	15	15	15	15	15	18	14	18	14	18	14	18	12	12	15	12	12	19	19	19	19	19	19	11	11	21	21	21	18	18	18	18	18	18	18	18										
12 FISICHELLA	19	19	19	19	19	19	19	19	19	15	15	15	18	14	18	14	20	20	20	15	20	20	20	15	15	15	12	12	12	21	17	17	17	17	17	17	21	21	18	18														
17 FONTANA	15	15	15	15	15	15	15	15	18	18	18	17	20	20	20	19	19	12	21	21	21	21	12	20	20	12	18	18	18	18	18	21	20	20	17	18																		
20 KATAYAMA	18	18	18	18	18	18	18	18	18	18	21	21	21	20	11	19	19	11	19	11	11	21	21	21	20	17	20	20	21	21	21	20	17	17	18	20	20																	
21 MARQUES	21	21	21	21	21	21	21	21	21	17	17	17	19	19	19	11	11	11	11	18	21	17	17	17	17	18	20	20	20	20	20	17	18	18																				
19 SALO	20	20	17	17	17	17	17	17	20	20	20	20	21	21	21	21	21	18	18	20	20	20	20	20																														
18 VERSTAPPEN	17	20	20	20	20	20	20	20	20	20	20																																											

Pit stop

One lap behind leader

3
VILLENEUVE
Williams

5
M. SCHUMACHER
Ferrari

4
FRENTZEN
Williams

1
HILL
Arrows

9
HÄKKINEN
McLaren

10
COULTHARD
McLaren

6
IRVINE
Ferrari

8
BERGER
Benetton

14
PANIS
Prost

7
ALESI
Benetton

23
MAGNUSSEN
Stewart

22
BARRICHELLO
Stewart

2
DINIZ
Arrows

16
HERBERT
Sauber

15
NAKANO
Prost

11
R. SCHUMACHER
Jordan

12
FISICHELLA
Jordan

17
FONTANA
Sauber

20
KATAYAMA
Minardi

21
MARQUES
Minardi

19
SALO
Tyrrell

18
VERSTAPPEN
Tyrrell

55	56	57	58	59	60	61	62	63	64	65	66	67	68	69	
3	3	3	3	3	3	3	3	3	3	3	3	3	3	9	1
10	10	10	10	10	10	10	10	10	10	10	10	10	9	9	10	2
9	9	9	9	9	9	9	9	9	9	9	9	9	10	10	3	3
6	6	6	6	6	6	6	6	6	6	6	6	6	6	6	8	4
8	8	8	8	8	8	8	8	8	8	8	8	8	8	8	6	5
4	4	4	4	4	4	4	4	4	4	4	4	4	4	4		6
14	14	14	14	14	14	14	14	14	14	14	14	14	14			
16	16	16	16	16	16	16	16	16	16	16	16	16	16			
23	23	23	23	23	23	23	23	23	23	23	23	23	23			
15	15	15	15	15	15	15	15	15	15	15	15	15	15			
12	12	12	12	12	12	12	12	12	12	12	12	12	12			
19	19	19	19	19	19	19	19	19	19	19	19	19	19			
7	7	7	7	7	7	7	7	7	7	7	7	7				
17	17	17	17	17	17	17	17	17	17	17	17	17	17			
21	21	21	21	21	21	21	21	21	21	21	21	21	21			
18	18	18	18	18	18	18	18	18	18	18	18	18	18			
20	20	20	20	20	20	20	20	20	20	20	20	20	20			

FOR THE RECORD

First Grand Prix win

Mika Häkkinen

QUALIFYING

Weather: Overcast, becoming bright and warm

Pos.	Driver	Car	Laps	Time
1	Jacques Villeneuve	Williams-Renault	11	1m 21.072s
2	Michael Schumacher	Ferrari	11	1m 21.072s
3	Heinz-Harald Frentzen	Williams-Renault	12	1m 21.072s
4	Damon Hill	Arrows-Yamaha	12	1m 21.130s
5	Mika Häkkinen	McLaren-Mercedes	11	1m 21.369s
6	David Coulthard	McLaren-Mercedes	10	1m 21.476s
7	Eddie Irvine	Ferrari	11	1m 21.610s
8	Gerhard Berger	Benetton-Renault	11	1m 21.656s
9	Olivier Panis	Prost-Mugen Honda	11	1m 21.735s
10	Jean Alesi	Benetton-Renault	11	1m 22.011s
11	Jan Magnussen	Stewart-Ford	11	1m 22.167s
12	Rubens Barrichello	Stewart-Ford	12	1m 22.222s
13	Pedro Diniz	Arrows-Yamaha	11	1m 22.234s
14	Johnny Herbert	Sauber-Petronas	12	1m 22.263s
15	Shinji Nakano	Prost-Mugen Honda	12	1m 22.351s
16	Ralf Schumacher	Jordan-Peugeot	11	1m 22.740s
17	Giancarlo Fisichella	Jordan-Peugeot	12	1m 22.804s
18	Norberto Fontana	Sauber-Petronas	12	1m 23.281s
19	Ukyo Katayama	Minardi-Hart	12	1m 23.409s
20	Tarso Marques	Minardi-Hart	12	1m 23.854s
21	Mika Salo	Tyrrell-Ford	9	1m 24.222s
22	Jos Verstappen	Tyrrell-Ford	12	1m 24.301s

FRIDAY FREE PRACTICE

Weather: Bright and sunny

Pos.	Driver	Laps	Time
1	Olivier Panis	28	1m 22.735s
2	Damon Hill	29	1m 22.898s
3	Jacques Villeneuve	29	1m 22.922s
4	Rubens Barrichello	26	1m 22.964s
5	Mika Häkkinen	20	1m 23.024s
6	Heinz-Harald Frentzen	30	1m 23.124s
7	Jean Alesi	21	1m 23.174s
8	David Coulthard	15	1m 23.440s
9	Michael Schumacher	24	1m 23.532s
10	Ralf Schumacher	22	1m 23.678s
11	Jan Magnussen	20	1m 23.685s
12	Eddie Irvine	25	1m 23.695s
13	Gerhard Berger	22	1m 23.923s
14	Giancarlo Fisichella	25	1m 24.263s
15	Ukyo Katayama	23	1m 24.329s
16	Johnny Herbert	29	1m 24.507s
17	Shinji Nakano	28	1m 24.735s
18	Pedro Diniz	28	1m 24.797s
19	Mika Salo	25	1m 25.025s
20	Norberto Fontana	28	1m 25.134s
21	Jos Verstappen	20	1m 25.327s
22	Tarso Marques	9	1m 26.816s

SATURDAY FREE PRACTICE

Weather: Cool and overcast

Pos.	Driver	Laps	Time
1	David Coulthard	22	1m 20.738s
2	Mika Häkkinen	20	1m 20.856s
3	Heinz-Harald Frentzen	26	1m 21.263s
4	Olivier Panis	26	1m 21.364s
5	Gerhard Berger	21	1m 21.525s
6	Jacques Villeneuve	23	1m 21.593s
7	Jan Magnussen	24	1m 21.605s
8	Shinji Nakano	28	1m 21.671s
9	Damon Hill	30	1m 21.780s
10	Jean Alesi	10	1m 21.814s
11	Ralf Schumacher	28	1m 21.881s
12	Johnny Herbert	28	1m 22.065s
13	Rubens Barrichello	21	1m 22.117s
14	Michael Schumacher	29	1m 22.120s
15	Norberto Fontana	30	1m 22.404s
16	Giancarlo Fisichella	30	1m 22.438s
17	Ukyo Katayama	19	1m 22.512s
18	Pedro Diniz	27	1m 22.750s
19	Eddie Irvine	29	1m 22.820s
20	Tarso Marques	28	1m 23.369s
21	Jos Verstappen	27	1m 23.742s
22	Mika Salo	27	1m 24.429s

WARM-UP

Weather: Cool and overcast

Pos.	Driver	Laps	Time
1	Mika Häkkinen	14	1m 23.016s
2	Gerhard Berger	13	1m 23.160s
3	Olivier Panis	18	1m 23.166s
4	David Coulthard	12	1m 23.359s
5	Jacques Villeneuve	13	1m 23.849s
6	Johnny Herbert	14	1m 24.012s
7	Michael Schumacher	16	1m 24.063s
8	Heinz-Harald Frentzen	15	1m 24.089s
9	Shinji Nakano	15	1m 24.125s
10	Damon Hill	11	1m 24.231s
11	Jan Magnussen	12	1m 24.309s
12	Ralf Schumacher	17	1m 24.386s
13	Jean Alesi	10	1m 24.540s
14	Eddie Irvine	15	1m 24.560s
15	Norberto Fontana	7	1m 24.795s
16	Pedro Diniz	12	1m 25.103s
17	Ukyo Katayama	15	1m 25.159s
18	Rubens Barrichello	13	1m 25.275s
19	Giancarlo Fisichella	16	1m 25.377s
20	Mika Salo	15	1m 25.419s
21	Tarso Marques	12	1m 25.707s
22	Jos Verstappen	12	1m 26.307s

RACE FASTEST LAPS

Weather: Dry, warm and sunny

Driver	Time	Lap
Heinz-Harald Frentzen	1m 23.135s	30
Gerhard Berger	1m 23.361s	31
Michael Schumacher	1m 23.692s	42
Jacques Villeneuve	1m 23.906s	42
Olivier Panis	1m 23.941s	45
Jean Alesi	1m 23.975s	27
David Coulthard	1m 24.006s	27
Mika Häkkinen	1m 24.072s	28
Eddie Irvine	1m 24.266s	37
Damon Hill	1m 24.274s	40
Shinji Nakano	1m 24.679s	45
Norberto Fontana	1m 25.154s	32
Johnny Herbert	1m 25.159s	30
Mika Salo	1m 25.237s	37
Jan Magnussen	1m 25.370s	31
Giancarlo Fisichella	1m 25.434s	45
Ralf Schumacher	1m 25.895s	34
Tarso Marques	1m 25.947s	55
Rubens Barrichello	1m 26.169s	13
Ukyo Katayama	1m 26.215s	27
Jos Verstappen	1m 26.369s	40
Pedro Diniz	1m 26.434s	3

CHASSIS LOG BOOK

1	Hill	Arrows A18/5
2	Diniz	Arrows A18/4
	spare	Arrows A18/3
3	Villeneuve	Williams FW19/4
4	Frentzen	Williams FW19/5
	spare	Williams FW19/3
5	M. Schumacher	Ferrari F310B/178
6	Irvine	Ferrari F310B/180
	spare	Ferrari F310B/175
7	Alesi	Benetton B197/2
8	Berger	Benetton B197/5
	spare	Benetton B197/4
9	Häkkinen	McLaren MP4/12/5
10	Coulthard	McLaren MP4/12/6
	spare	McLaren MP4/12/7
11	R. Schumacher	Jordan 197/6
12	Fisichella	Jordan 197/5
	spare	Jordan 197/1
14	Panis	Prost JS45/3
15	Nakano	Prost JS45/2
	spare	Prost JS45/1
16	Herbert	Sauber C16/7
17	Fontana	Sauber C16/2
	spare	Sauber C16/5
18	Verstappen	Tyrrell 025/3
19	Salo	Tyrrell 025/5
	spare	Tyrrell 025/1
20	Katayama	Minardi M197/4
21	Marques	Minardi M197/2
	spare	Minardi M197/1
22	Barrichello	Stewart SF1/2
23	Magnussen	Stewart SF1/3
	spare	Stewart SF1/4

POINTS TABLES

Drivers

1	Jacques Villeneuve	81
2	Michael Schumacher	78
3	Heinz-Harald Frentzen	42
4 =	David Coulthard	36
4 =	Jean Alesi	36
6 =	Gerhard Berger	27
6 =	Mika Häkkinen	27
8	Eddie Irvine	24
9	Giancarlo Fisichella	20
10	Olivier Panis	16
11	Johnny Herbert	15
12	Ralf Schumacher	13
13	Damon Hill	7
14	Rubens Barrichello	6
15	Alexander Wurz	4
16	Jarno Trulli	3
17 =	Mika Salo	2
17 =	Pedro Diniz	2
17 =	Shinji Nakano	2
20	Nicola Larini	1

Constructors

1	Williams	123
2	Ferrari	102
3	Benetton	67
4	McLaren	63
5	Jordan	33
6	Prost	21
7	Sauber	16
8	Arrows	9
9	Stewart	6
10	Tyrrell	2

Michael Schumacher was subsequently stripped of his second place in the World Championship when he appeared before the FIA World Motor Sports Council on Tuesday 11 November.

DRIVERS' POINTS TABLE

Compiled by Nick Henry

Place	Driver	Nationality	Date of birth	Car	Australia	Brazil	Argentina	San Marino	Monaco	Spain	Canada	France	Britain	Germany	Hungary	Belgium	Italy	Austria	Luxembourg	Japan	Europe	Points total
1	Jacques Villeneuve	CDN	9/4/71	Williams-Renault	Rp	1pf	1psb	Rp	R	1ps	R	4	1p	R	1	5pfs	5	1pf	1	DQpb	3p	81
	Michael Schumacher	D	3/1/69	Ferrari	2b	5	R	2	1fs	4b	1pb	1pf	Rfb	2b	4pb	1	6b	6	R	1s	R	78
2	Heinz-Harald Frentzen	D	18/5/67	Williams-Renault	8fs*	9	R	1fs	Rpb	8	4	2	R	Rfs	3	3	3	3f	2f	6f	42
3=	David Coulthard	GB	27/3/71	McLaren-Mercedes	1	10	R	R	R	6	7fs	7b*	4	R	R	R	1	2	Rbs	10*	2	36
3=	Jean Alesi	F	11/6/64	Benetton-Renault	R	6	7	5	R	3	2	5	2	6	11	8	2ps	R	2	5	13	36
5=	Gerhard Berger	A	27/8/59	Benetton-Renault	4	2	6f	R	9	10	–	–	1pf	8	6b	7	10	4	8	4	27
5=	Mika Häkkinen	SF	28/9/68	McLaren-Mercedes	3	4b	5	6	R	7	R	R	Rs	3s	R	DQ	9f	R	Rp	4	1s	27
7	Eddie Irvine	GB	10/11/65	Ferrari	R	16	2	3	3	12	R	3	R	R	9*	10*	8	R	R	3	5	24
8	Giancarlo Fisichella	I	14/1/73	Jordan-Peugeot	R	8s	R	4	6	9f	3	9	7	11*	R	2	4	4s	R	7	11	20
9	Olivier Panis	F	2/9/66	Prost-Mugen Honda	5	3	R	8	4	2	11*	–	–	–	–	–	–	6	R	7	16
10	Johnny Herbert	GB	25/6/64	Sauber-Petronas	R	7	4	R	R	5	5	8	R	R	3	4	R	8	7	6	8	15
11	Ralf Schumacher	D	30/6/75	Jordan-Peugeot	R	R	3	R	R	R	R	6s	5	5	5	R	R	5	R	9	R	13
12	Damon Hill	GB	17/9/60	Arrows-Yamaha	DNS	17*	R	R	R	R	9	12	6	8	2	13*	R	7	8	12	R	7
13	Rubens Barrichello	BR	23/5/72	Stewart-Ford	R	R	R	R	2	R	R	R	R	R	R	R	13	14*	R	R	R	6
14	Alexander Wurz	A	15/2/74	Benetton-Renault	–	–	–	–	–	R	R	3	–	–	–	–	–	–	–	–	–	4
15	Jarno Trulli	I	13/7/74	Minardi-Hart	9	12	9	DNS	R	15	R	–	–	–	–	–	–	–	–	–	–	
				Prost-Mugen Honda	–	–	–	–	–	–	–	10	8	4	7	15	10	R	–	–	–	3
16=	Mika Salo	SF	30/11/66	Tyrrell-Ford	R	13	8	9	5	R	R	R	R	R	13	11	R	R	10	R	12b	2
16=	Pedro Diniz	BR	22/5/70	Arrows-Yamaha	10	R	R	R	R	R	R	8	R	R	R	R	7	R	13*	5	13	R	2
16=	Shinji Nakano	J	1/4/71	Prost-Mugen Honda	7	14	R	R	R	R	6	R	11*	7	6	R	11	R	R	R	10	2
19	Nicola Larini	I	19/3/64	Sauber-Petronas	6	11	R	7b	R	–	–	–	–	–	–	–	–	–	–	–	–	1
	Norberto Fontana	RA	20/1/75	Sauber-Petronas	–	–	–	–	–	–	–	R	9	9	–	–	–	–	–	–	14	0
	Ukyo Katayama	J	29/5/63	Minardi-Hart	R	18	R	11	10	R	R	11	R	R	R	10	14*	R	11	R	17	0
	Jan Magnussen	DK	4/7/73	Stewart-Ford	R	DNS	10*	R	7	13	R	R	R	R	R	R	12	R	R	R	9	0
	Tarso Marques	BR	19/1/76	Minardi-Hart	–	–	–	–	–	–	–	R	10	R	12	R	14	EXC	R	R	15	0
	Gianni Morbidelli	I	31/1/68	Sauber-Petronas	–	–	–	–	–	14	10	–	–	–	R	9	12	9	9	DNS	–	0
	Ricardo Rosset	BR	27/7/68	Lola-Ford	DNQ	DNP	–	–	–	–	–	–	–	–	–	–	–	–	–	–	–	0
	Vincenzo Sospiri	I	7/10/66	Lola-Ford	DNQ	DNP	–	–	–	–	–	–	–	–	–	–	–	–	–	–	–	0
	Jos Verstappen	NL	4/3/72	Tyrrell-Ford	R	15	R	10	8	11	R	R	R	10	R	R	R	12b	R	13	16	0

KEY

p	pole position	R	retired	*	not running at finish	DQ	disqualified	DNS	did not start	DNQ did not qualify
EXC	excluded	DNP	did not practise	f	fastest lap	b	fastest pit stop (time in pit lane)	s	fastest speed through start/finish line

POINTS & PERCENTAGES

Compiled by David Hayhoe

GRID POSITIONS: 1997

Pos.	Driver	Races	Best	Worst	Average
1	Jacques Villeneuve	17	1	9	2.12
2	Heinz–Harald Frentzen	17	1	8	3.59
3	Michael Schumacher	17	1	9	3.65
4	Mika Häkkinen	17	1	17	5.82
5	David Coulthard	17	3	12	7.59
6	Jean Alesi	17	1	15	8.18
7	Giancarlo Fisichella	17	2	17	8.29
8	Olivier Panis	10	3	12	8.50
9	Ralf Schumacher	17	3	16	8.59
10	Alexander Wurz	3	7	11	8.67
11	Gerhard Berger	14	1	18	9.07
12	Eddie Irvine	17	3	17	9.35
13	Johnny Herbert	17	7	16	10.88
14	Rubens Barrichello	17	3	21	11.06
15	Damon Hill	17	3	20	12.29
16	Nicola Larini	5	11	19	13.80
17	Jarno Trulli	14	3	20	14.50
18	Gianni Morbidelli	8	13	19	15.57
19	Jan Magnussen	17	6	22	15.76
20	Shinji Nakano	17	12	21	16.35
21	Pedro Diniz	17	8	22	16.65
22	Mika Salo	17	14	22	18.82
23	Norberto Fontana	3	18	22	19.50
24	Jos Verstappen	17	14	22	19.59
25	Ukyo Katayama	17	15	22	19.88
26	Tarso Marques	9	18	22	20.67

Note: Ricardo Rosset and Vincenzo Sospiri did not qualify.

CAREER PERFORMANCES: 1997 DRIVERS

Driver	Nationality	Races	Championships	Wins	2nd places	3rd places	4th places	5th places	6th places	Pole positions	Fastest laps	Points
Jean Alesi	F	135	–	1	16	14	11	12	6	2	4	225
Rubens Barrichello	BR	81	–	–	2	1	8	4	4	1	–	52
Gerhard Berger	A	210	–	10	17	21	26	8	13	12	21	*386
David Coulthard	GB	58	–	3	8	4	4	4	4	3	5	117
Pedro Diniz	BR	50	–	–	–	–	–	1	2	–	–	4
Giancarlo Fisichella	I	25	–	1	1	3	–	1	–	1	20
Norberto Fontana	RA	4	–	–	–	–	–	–	–	–	–
Heinz–Harald Frentzen	D	65	–	1	2	5	5	3	8	1	6	71
Mika Häkkinen	SF	96	–	1	3	12	7	8	5	1	1	118
Johnny Herbert	GB	113	–	2	1	3	10	5	4	–	–	82
Damon Hill	GB	84	1	21	15	5	3	1	2	20	19	333
Eddie Irvine	GB	65	–	–	1	6	3	5	3	–	–	52
Ukyo Katayama	J	95	–	–	–	–	–	2	1	–	–	5
Nicola Larini	I	49	–	–	1	–	–	–	1	–	–	7
Jan Magnussen	DK	18	–	–	–	–	–	–	–	–	–	–
Tarso Marques	BR	11	–	–	–	–	–	–	–	–	–	–
Gianni Morbidelli	I	67	–	–	–	1	–	1	3	–	–	8.50
Shinji Nakano	J	17	–	–	–	–	–	2	–	–	2
Olivier Panis	F	59	–	1	3	1	3	4	5	–	–	54
Ricardo Rosset	BR	16	–	–	–	–	–	–	–	–	–	–
Mika Salo	SF	52	–	–	–	–	–	5	2	–	–	12
Michael Schumacher	D	102	2	27	17	10	6	3	4	17	28	440
Ralf Schumacher	D	17	–	–	–	4	1	–	1	–	–	13
Vincenzo Sospiri	I	–	–	–	–	–	–	–	–	–	–	–
Jarno Trulli	I	14	–	–	–	1	–	–	–	–	–	3
Jos Verstappen	NL	48	–	–	2	–	1	1	–	–	–	11
Jacques Villeneuve	CDN	33	1	11	5	3	1	2	–	13	9	159
Alexander Wurz	A	3	–	–	1	–	–	–	–	–	–	4

* includes 1 point from 1984 that was not valid for the championship.

Note: Drivers beginning the formation lap are deemed to have made a start.

UNLAPPED: 1997

Number of cars on same lap as leader

Grand Prix	Starters	at ¼ distance	at ½ distance	at ¾ distance	at full distance
Australia	22	14	9	7	6
Brazil	22	18	14	11	9
Argentina	22	19	11	7	7
San Marino	22	16	13	6	4
Monaco	22	10	8	4	4
Spain	22	20	15	11	10
Canada	22	17	16	8	7
France	22	15	9	4	6
Britain	22	20	14	11	6
Germany	22	16	15	9	7
Hungary	22	17	11	8	8
Belgium	22	19	14	12	10
Italy	22	19	18	13	11
Austria	21	19	15	14	9
Luxembourg	22	16	13	8	8
Japan	21	18	17	12	10
Europe	22	21	15	9	10

LAP LEADERS: 1997

Grand Prix	Jacques Villeneuve	Michael Schumacher	David Coulthard	Heinz–Harald Frentzen	Damon Hill	Mika Häkkinen	Gerhard Berger	Jarno Trulli	Jean Alesi	Eddie Irvine	Giancarlo Fisichella	Total
Australia	–	–	34	24	–	–	–	–	–	–	–	58
Brazil	69	–	–	–	–	3	–	–	–	–	–	72
Argentina	66	–	–	–	–	–	–	–	6	–	–	72
San Marino	25	1	–	36	–	–	–	–	–	–	–	62
Monaco	–	62	–	–	–	–	–	–	–	–	–	62
Spain	62	1	–	–	–	–	–	1	–	–	–	64
Canada	–	34	20	–	–	–	–	–	–	–	–	54
France	–	70	–	2	–	–	–	–	–	–	–	72
Britain	36	15	–	–	–	8	–	–	–	–	–	59
Germany	–	–	–	–	–	38	–	–	–	7	45
Hungary	1	10	–	4	62	–	–	–	–	–	–	77
Belgium	4	40	–	–	–	–	–	–	–	–	–	44
Italy	–	1	19	–	–	2	–	31	–	–	–	53
Austria	31	2	1	–	–	–	37	–	–	–	–	71
Luxembourg	24	–	3	–	40	–	–	–	–	–	–	67
Japan	6	25	–	5	–	–	–	–	17	–	53
Europe	24	39	–	–	–	1	–	–	–	–	–	69
Total	348	300	77	76	62	51	41	37	32	23	7	1054
(Per cent)	33.0	28.5	7.3	7.2	5.9	4.8	3.9	3.5	3.0	2.2	0.7	(100)

RETIREMENTS: 1997

Number of cars to have retired

Grand Prix	Starters	at ¼ distance	at ½ distance	at ¾ distance	at full distance	percentage
Australia	22	7	7	11	13	59.1
Brazil	22	3	3	4	5	22.7
Argentina	22	4	7	11	13	59.1
San Marino	22	5	7	10	11	50.0
Monaco	22	7	10	12	12	54.5
Spain	22	1	2	5	7	31.8
Canada	22	5	6	9	12	54.5
France	22	4	6	7	11	50.0
Britain	22	2	3	9	12	54.5
Germany	22	6	6	8	12	54.5
Hungary	22	3	5	7	10	45.5
Belgium	22	2	5	6	8	36.4
Italy	22	3	3	7	8	36.4
Austria	21	1	1	4	9	40.9
Luxembourg	22	6	7	12	12	54.5
Japan	21	3	4	5	8	36.4
Europe	22	1	2	5	5	22.7

ZONTA'S ZENITH?

by Tom Alexander

Above: A happy trio on the podium at Pau with winner Juan Pablo Montoya flanked by Tom Kristensen *(left)* and Jamie Davies.

Brazilian Ricardo Zonta took the title in convincing style in his Super Nova Lola *(left)* but, despite a win in front of the Grand Prix teams at Hockenheim *(below far left)*, is by no means certain of graduating to F1.

Bottom: Montoya secured second place in the championship with victory in the final round at Jerez.

Sutton Motorsport Images

Martyn Elford/LAT Photographic

Sutton Motorsport Images

CHAMPION with one round to go: that was quite an achievement for a driver who had a nice round zero to his name after the first three races of the year.

Ricardo Zonta became the 13th FIA F3000 title-holder in 1997 – and rightfully so. Generally the Brazilian was the most consistent performer and his sluggish start wasn't entirely of his own making.

He won the opening race at Silverstone on merit – but was later deprived of the points because of an alleged gearbox irregularity. The stewards were unable to locate first gear on Zonta's Super Nova Lola during qualifying and accepted the explanation that it was simply broken; the FIA later over-ruled them and excluded him on the grounds that there was no proof his car had conformed to the regulations. Similarly, there was none that it hadn't. This set the tone for a season in which the frequent excellence of the racing was tarnished by persistent bickering beneath the formula's friendly surface.

If the stewards had ordered Zonta's gearbox to be stripped down in the first place – a task which takes barely 20 minutes – all of this could have been avoided.

The decision didn't so much shatter the 21-year-old's confidence as his faith in perceived justice. After making rash errors of judgement on the street circuits in Pau and Helsinki he cut a forlorn figure and he admits he considered going off to do something else.

But then he won the accident-shortened race at the Nürburgring and started to claw his way back into contention, aided by the closeness and the inconsistency of his competition: the first five races produced five different winners.

Zonta followed up with two second places, one fifth and further victories at Hockenheim and Mugello, the latter of which was by far his best drive of the season. Fittingly, it was there that he clinched the title. If he felt he had been unfortunate to be thrown out at Silverstone, perhaps Mugello provided the antidote. He arrived at the mandatory drivers' briefing only two minutes before it ended – and then only because Jason Watt of sister team Den Blå Avis had alerted him via portable phone! On that occasion the FIA forgave him so on balance he can't complain: but for Watt, Zonta would once again have been excluded.

There were some basic errors: Zonta was lucky to win at Hockenheim after throwing away most of his 30-second lead trying to find his way out of a gravel trap and he spun off while leading in Jerez. But his rivals made more and the well-drilled Super Nova team collected its second title in three years.

In his second F3000 season, Zonta was pursued by a clutch of impressive newcomers and his three-win tally was matched by Juan Pablo Montoya, likely to become Colombia's first Grand Prix driver since Roberto Guerrero in 1983.

After winning the Jerez finale Montoya admitted that it was entirely his own fault that he hadn't won the championship, a rare concession from a man blessed with an uncommon degree of self-confidence. Some of his exploratory laps on circuits he had never seen before – particularly Pau and Helsinki – were just awesome. Such balls-out commitment often got him into trouble, however, and of the four races he didn't finish he should arguably have won two and certainly have been on the podium in the others. With a bit of careful polishing he'll make it.

Jamie Davies looked a likely contender to be the first Briton to lift the F3000 title. He was walking away in Helsinki when he hit the wall but bounced back to make amends at Enna. However, after taking the championship lead at mid-season he failed to score again. His DAMS team suffered a little from running a combined GT and F3000 programme and the impressive Davies was never quite sure who was going to be engineering him from one weekend to the next. His drive from 24th to third at Silverstone showcased his patient racecraft – but if his methods were less spectacular than Montoya's the end results were no less so.

The same is true of Jason Watt. The Dane arrived in F3000 via Formula Opel and the now-defunct International Touring Car Championship. At the start of the year he struggled to shake off a few tin-top habits though it didn't take him long to re-adapt. His Den Blå Avis team was affiliated to Super Nova and benefited from free availability of technical information: the net result was a splendid victory at Spa, Watt withstanding intense pressure every inch of the way in perhaps the race of the year.

He eventually finished third in the championship and his emergence has given Denmark something of an embarrassment of riches, what with Jan Magnussen in F1 and Tom Kristensen winning the Le Mans 24 Hours. Kristensen – a comparative veteran at 30 – was supposed to be an F3000 title-contender, too, but his season slumped alarmingly. He inherited Zonta's Silverstone win and followed Montoya home in Pau, at which point it appeared his experience and consistency would be valuable assets in the midst of impetuous youth.

However, the three Grand Prix support races encapsulated Kristensen's season in a nutshell. He qualified his ASR Lola on pole for the first two but failed to complete a racing lap in either: at Hockenheim he was bundled off the road at almost 160 mph and at Spa he crashed violently at similar speed, an accident from which he was fortunate to escape with no more than bruising. He thought qualifying only second at Jerez might mark an ironic turning point: he duly led after five laps but was then forced to restart from pole when the race was red-flagged. Almost inevitably, he had been knocked off the track before a further lap was completed.

In reality the turning point in his year came at Le Mans: he won the endurance classic at his first attempt and simply nothing went right thereafter.

The sixth winner was Soheil Ayari, but victory in Helsinki was a solitary beacon in a difficult first season for the highly rated 1996 French F3 Champion. He pulled off one of the overtaking manoeuvres of the year to secure his success in Finland – scraping around the outside of a surprised Oliver Tichy in a flurry of tyre smoke, late braking and opposite lock. Such flair was never again apparent, though that wasn't entirely Ayari's fault. He was set fair to end the year on the podium until (lapped) Astromega team-mate Boris Derichebourg elbowed him off the track. The two Frenchmen didn't get along even before that and their lack of co-operation was unquestionably a hindrance given their shortage of previous experience.

Last but not least of the leading players, diminutive Brazilian Max Wilson proved himself one of the most effective racers of the year – which was just as well as he didn't always do himself justice in qualifying. Twice second and once third, Wilson was responsible for keeping Watt on his toes at Spa. To his credit, he never once threatened to take up any of numerous opportunities to shove his rival off the track, even though he was in a position to do so. He never gave up trying, but he was always scrupulously clean. The Edenbridge team is keen to hold on to him; unsurprisingly it could have a fight on its hands.

Others who showed flashes of inspiration included Cyrille Sauvage, Gonzalo Rodriguez, Tichy, Laurent Redon, Rui Aguas, Gareth Rees, Derichebourg, Patrick Lemarié, Craig Lowndes, Pedro Couceiro, Werner Lupberger, Stephen Watson and Dino Morelli. Ulsterman Morelli scored the best result of his career when he finished third in Helsinki but was lucky to escape with his life after crashing in the blinding spray at the Nürburgring.

After slamming into Rees's slowing and hidden car on the main straight Morelli's DKS Lola continued at unabated speed all the way to the first corner where it flattened three tyre walls and a guard rail before coming to rest. The initial impact with Rees had left Morelli's lower legs exposed yet, by October, the resourceful Dino was talking cheerfully about racing again having made an almost complete recovery.

It was an uplifting tale in a generally uplifting year, petty protests notwithstanding.

The formula was oversubscribed once again and the future just south of Formula 1 looks bright, with several Grand Prix teams – notably McLaren – suddenly showing interest in F3000 as a means of keeping their F1 test drivers sharp.

All that still remains to be found is a means of securing promotion to Formula 1 for the overall champion. The main purpose of the one-make series (Lola chassis, Zytek engines, Avon tyres) is, after all, to cultivate the Grand Prix racing stars of the future. By the time Zonta had clinched the title in September there were virtually no F1 seats left to be negotiated and the fact remains that 1993 F3000 champion Olivier Panis is the last to have established a foothold in Formula 1.

As good a benchmark of driver ability as this formula is, that's still a worrying statistic.

by Jaimes Baker

POWERPLAY

Sutton Motorsport Images

OR the first time in 23 years Formula 3 took a step forward at the start of the 1997 season. For so long the cars had been criticised for having too much grip and too little power, and something had to be done, as the gap to Formula 3000 was becoming a significant step. With the opening of the air restrictor the power was increased by 35 bhp to around 212 bhp. It was a step in the right direction – and essential if the category was to remain as a meaningful springboard to Formula 1.

Jarno Trulli's jump from winning the German F3 Championship straight to F1 with Minardi and Prost did immeasurable good to F3. It showed that the category is not only a fertile seedbed for future talent, but that in some cases that talent can flourish and prosper on the Grand Prix stage straight away.

Looking to the future, it would seem that the first of this season's crop to arrive in F1 will be German champion Nick Heidfeld.

The 20-year-old Mönchengladbach driver was taken into the Mercedes young driver programme and, as expected, won the German title. But after some stunning early results, including a dominant victory in the prestigious Monaco Grand Prix F3 support race, the Opel Team BSR youngster experienced a wobble which developed into mid-season freefall, and he only tied up the title at the final race of the season.

There were many differing explanations for Heidfeld's problems, but the most likely was that during the season he put in an extraordinary 3500 miles of testing with Mercedes' F1 partner McLaren. It was almost impossible to remain focused while regularly switching from his Dallara F397-Opel to a 750 bhp Grand Prix car.

The problems manifested themselves as poor starts, poor qualifying and the odd indifferent race. But whatever, from his Monaco win in early May it was not until late August that he won again.

Heidfeld's main competition came from the reigning champion KMS Opel team. Eighteen-year-old Timo Scheider had begun the season pretty much unfancied, but wins at the Nürburgring and the Sachsenring (two in one day), sent him to the top of the table.

In F3, qualifying counts for a great deal, and Scheider's lack of experience meant that he was slower to set up his car on new circuits than his rival, and was forced to fight back from a lowly grid position on too many occasions. He ultimately lost out to Heidfeld by only six points.

The major shock of the season was Wolf Henzler. The German finally broke Dallara's three-year stranglehold on world F3 when he took his French-built Josef Kaufmann Racing Martini MK73 to victory at the Nürburgring in round three. The Martini seemed to have better traction and aerodynamics than the Dallara, and a further win at Zweibrücken helped Henzler to a fine fourth in the table behind Scheider's team-mate, four-times winner Alex Müller.

The five main F3 championships in Britain, Germany, France, Italy and Japan produced a staggering 29 different race winners this year, but once again it was the British series that stood head and shoulders above the rest in terms of the level of competition, the depth of talent on the grid and the number of manufacturers involved.

Two years ago, the Paul Stewart Racing team walked away from the British F3 Championship shaking their heads. Its driver Ralph Firman had won seven of the 16 races and still lost the title due to his 'win or spin' attitude. Since then PSR has drummed into its drivers that the championship, not individual race glory, is the goal, and that consistency is the way to win it. It may not be exciting, but it's effective. Northern Irishman Jonny Kane took the PSR philosophy and embraced it wholeheartedly this season to claim the team's sixth championship in eight years.

The 24-year-old had ended 1996 as the man to beat with a stunning run of three wins and three seconds from the final six races. At the start of the '97 season, he picked up where he had left off, winning three of the first five races – two of them stunning drives in the wet where he looked on a different level to the rest of the field.

For most of the season, though, Kane was put well and truly in the shade by Frenchman Nicolas Minassian. In its second year in Britain, Renault had ironed out all the engine gremlins that had hampered the Promatecme team last year and Minassian enjoyed by far the best power unit in the championship. That counts for a lot in a category that is so reliant on power.

There are many lessons that F3 teaches a driver, and one of the most important is how to work with your engineer to rapidly fine-tune suspension geometry and dampers, and in his fourth year in F3 Minassian had almost perfected the skill. The Marseilles-born driver demonstrated all the fire, flair and electrifying pace needed to win championships. Ultimately,

however, his total commitment probably cost him the title when he assaulted another driver on the slowing-down lap in the third round at Thruxton. He believed that the back-marker had blocked him on the final lap, allowing Kane to sweep past to victory. The resulting 30-day ban meant that he missed three races. In the meantime Kane picked up 53 points. The fact that Minassian, 60 points adrift after seven rounds, took the title to the final round with seven victories and closed to within 16 points says a good deal.

One can only speculate as to whether Kane would have been able to raise his game had he been under pressure all season. Those wet-race victories suggest that he could, but when the pressure did build at the end of the season he was less than impressive until the final round. One has to say that, of the two, the flamboyant Frenchman looks to have the momentum to take him all the way to F1.

The revelation of the season was 1996 Formula Ford Festival winner Mark Webber. Having arrived in Britain only a week before the first race, the Australian took a shock win at Brands Hatch in round four and looked one of the most exciting drivers in the championship. His move around the outside of Kane at Stowe in the British Grand Prix support race at Silverstone was arguably the best of the season.

The other two really exciting prospects were Brazilians Mario Haberfeld and Enrique Bernoldi. Haberfeld won the prestigious Grand Prix support race and at Snetterton. His aggressive style, however, got him into too many unnecessary tangles when he started down the grid. Once

Left: Mercedes protégé Nick Heidfeld won the German series in his Opel Team BSR Dallara and also took the spoils at the prestigious Monaco F3 race *(bottom left).*

Right: Nicolas Minassian threw away his chances of winning the British F3 championship when he incurred a 30-day ban. During his absence Jonny Kane *(below right)* built up the advantage he needed to secure yet another title for Paul Stewart Racing.

Top right: Patrice Gay emerged as the French champion, while Aussie Mark Webber *(bottom right)* marked himself out as another man to watch in the UK.

eighteen-year-old European Formula Renault Champion Bernoldi had recovered from a serious road accident early in the season he showed flashes of brilliance, and took a dominant win at Spa-Francorchamps.

That Spa race brought some of the French teams over for a visit to the British series and showed once again that the accepted view of the French as the poor relations simply did not hold water. In open combat on the challenging Ardennes circuit the La Filière team Martinis of Franck Montagny and Oriol Servia and the year-old ASM Dallara of David Saelens took three of the top five positions.

Had it not been for a ponderous start back home for Montagny and his team he may have taken the French title in his first season, his four wins being one more than champion Patrice Gay recorded. If the French series fell down, it was in the depth of talent, not the level of the top drivers.

That was demonstrated at Monaco when Gay and Saelens took third and fourth, and proved at the Marlboro Masters at Zandvoort, where Sébastien Philippe's ASM car had not only taken pole, but led most of the race.

That Japanese F3 Champion Tom Coronel eventually triumphed was – perhaps unfairly – attributed largely to his intimate knowledge of the Bridgestone control rubber (as used in Japan) that was completely new to the rest of the field. The Dutchman had destroyed all opposition in the Far East, and had he not been shunted out in Monaco, he may well have won there too. His victory at Zandvoort would have increased the standing of the Japanese championship in worldwide F3, but for the fact that no other driver had really come close to him in the series.

All the F3 championships went to the pre-season favourites, except the Italian. Oliver Martini, brother of former Grand Prix driver Pierluigi, emerged as champion at his fourth attempt. Several on-track clashes with favourite Andre Couto put him ahead, and when Couto faded from mid-season Martini was left unchallenged.

In terms of international F3 this season, Coronel's utter dominance in Japan, coupled to his Zandvoort win, look to have stolen the title of top dog for the 25-year-old. The newly increased power has re-established the category where it belongs, as a true breeding ground for F1. A handful of this season's drivers have every right to expect to go to the very top. Some of them will return to F3 next year, and if they do, they will return to a formula that is in very rude health indeed.

Photos: Sutton Motorsport Images

by Gary Watkins

BLITZKRIEG!

Shutterspeed Photografik

Unveiled shortly before the start of the season, the magnificent Mercedes CLK-GTR *(left)* redefined the concept of the GT racing car. Once it had achieved reliability, the new design predictably set the pace, allowing Bernd Schneider to add the drivers' title to his CV.

Below left: The main opposition was provided by JJ Lehto and Steve Soper in the factory McLaren-BMW F1 GTR.

The Joest team's venerable TWR-built Porsche WSC95 *(right)* triumphed at Le Mans in the hands of Michele Alboreto, Stefan Johansson and Tom Kristensen.

THE revived discipline of GT racing came of age in 1997. The Global Endurance GT Series turned into the FIA GT Championship, and with what was essentially a take-over by the governing body came the factory big guns: BMW threw its deutschmarks at motorsport partner McLaren, which built a new version of the F1 GTR; Porsche made a last-minute commitment to run the full series with its controversial 911 GT1; and then Mercedes ended months of speculation by unveiling its CLK-GTR just three weeks before the 11-round series began.

With the American Panoz marque represented by three of its front-engined GTRs, designed by leading race car constructor Reynard, and a new state-of-the-art chassis from Lotus, the FIA GT series promised close racing, a variety of winners and a healthy future. In reality, however, the racing was seldom close, only two marques took the top step of the podium and, as the season drew to a close with two October fixtures in the US, the prospects for 1998 looked bleak.

The writing was already on the wall when what was the world's premier sports car series kicked off at Hockenheim in the second week of April. Bernd Schneider's CLK-GTR may have been finished only at 7.00 a.m. on Friday, yet the German was still able to claim pole position, the best part of a second ahead of JJ Lehto in the first of the factory McLaren-BMW F1 GTRs, which had been pounding around the test tracks of Europe since November.

The CLK-GTR, which had been designed and built in just four months, leap-frogged the existing generation of GT cars, just as Porsche's 911 GT1 had done in 1996. Whereas the F1 GTR and, to a lesser extent, the Porsche homologation special had their origins in road-going supercars, the Mercedes was a bespoke racer. But what angered Mercedes' rivals most was that it was only allowed into the series by an eleventh-hour rule change.

McLaren, Porsche and Lotus had already gone through the time-consuming and expensive process of gaining the necessary type approval for the road-going versions of their respective racers, as originally demanded by the regulations. Then, days before the CLK-GTR hit the track for the first time, it was announced that type approval would only be required by the end of the year, ostensibly to enhance the grids of the fledgling series.

Although the two CLK-GTRs didn't prove reliable enough to make an impression after one-quarter distance in the Hockenheim four-hour event, by race two at Silverstone the car was already a contender for victory. In fact, Schneider and team-mate Alex Wurz thought they were victorious when the red flag brought a premature halt to the race when two cars crashed on the flooded circuit. Only when the results were back-dated a lap as per the regulations was the win handed to Roberto Ravaglia and Peter Kox in the second BMW McLaren.

When the CLK notched up its first victory at round four on home ground at the Nürburgring in late June, few doubted that the championship would go the way of Mercedes. After all, the 12-point lead enjoyed by Lehto and team-mate Steve Soper, who had won two of the opening three rounds in their factory McLaren-BMW and finished third in the other, hardly looked insurmountable.

The series, however, was kept alive until the final rounds by virtue of a brilliant display of wet-weather driving by Lehto at Spa-Francorchamps two weeks later and then a freak accident which deprived Schneider of certain victory at Mugello in early September and handed maximum points to the Finn and Soper, who all the while had been consistently notching up points behind the Mercedes squad.

Schneider and his AMG Mercedes team, however, needed to take advantage of a bizarre rule that allowed drivers to swap cars at any stage of the race and still score championship points, the German switching to Klaus Ludwig's and Bernd Maylander's car at the A1-Ring in Austria and to the CLK-GTR of Alessandro Nannini and Marcel Tiemann at Suzuka.

Mercedes remarkably agreed to a late-season rule change to rid the series of this anomaly, preventing Schneider from salvaging any points from the Mugello weekend. Yet if the pendulum of fortune had swung in favour of the Anglo-Finnish McLaren pairing in Italy, three weeks later it veered just as dramatically the other way at Sebring.

While Schneider, this time sharing with veteran Klaus Ludwig, notched up a fifth victory of the year, Lehto and Soper retired just minutes from the end of the three-hour race, their McLaren seriously damaged by an engine fire after a storming comeback drive by the Finn. A week later at Laguna Seca on the other side of the USA, the Schnitzer McLaren team was completely at sea, Schneider wrapping up a drivers' and teams' title double with yet another victory.

Laguna Seca marked the most competitive display of the year from Porsche, a marque that had dominated three end-of-season outings in the Global series in 1996. For the factory team, a 2-3 finish behind Schneider and Ludwig was the culmination of a long and hard slog to mount a competitive challenge in the FIA series. After intending to be represented by the half-dozen customer teams that had forked out £600,000 for one of its 911 GT1s, Porsche made a late decision to enter a factory team when the intentions of Mercedes and BMW became clear, and it has to be said that it was totally unprepared. The solo '96-spec 911 GT1 it entered at Hockenheim was run as it had finished the previous season, right down to the Le Mans scrutineering sticker on its flanks. Only after the Le Mans 24 Hours, when the 'evo' version of the 911 GT1 came on stream in the FIA GT series, did Porsche begin to make progress. But Porsche's late run of three podiums didn't allow it to leap-frog the Gulf-backed GTC Motorsport McLaren squad, which was the leading privateer team throughout the season, for third place in the teams' classification.

Panoz ended the year with a podium in wet conditions at Sebring, but until that point barely looked like troubling the scorers. The cars – two for the factory-backed David Price Racing squad and one for the French DAMS team – were finished late and engine problems meant they showed little form until the second half of the year.

Lotus was the financial minnow of the series, the independent Lotus Racing team that had developed the Elise-based GT1 receiving little financial input from the car manufacturer and its owner, Proton. An eighth place in the wet at Spa was the best result for the factory team, although the Benetton-backed GBF customer squad proved the worth of the Lotus's nimble chassis with fifth place against a depleted field in Helsinki in May.

If Soper wasn't able to claim the overall title, Britain could still boast an FIA GT Champion, Justin Bell going some of the way to emulating his famous father, double World Sports Car Champion and five-times Le Mans winner Derek, by claiming honours in the GT2 division with a Chrysler Viper.

Mercedes may have done the double in the FIA GT Championship, but the Three-Pointed Star wasn't present for what remains the jewel in the crown of sports car racing. The fiercely chauvinistic organiser of the Le Mans 24 Hours maintained its independence, remaining outside the FIA series, retaining its own rules and, crucially as it turned out, receiving open-top sports racing cars with open arms.

Porsche's decision to concentrate on Le Mans looked as though it was going to bear fruit. Not only did the factory have the new 'evo' version of the 911 GT1, which was much more stable than the car that had come close to victory the year before, but Le Mans engine rules gave it an extra 30 bhp over FIA series levels.

The factory team appeared on course for its second Le Mans victory in four years, even after the number one car driven by veterans Hans Stuck, Thierry Boutsen and Bob Wollek crashed out of the lead just after sunrise on Sunday morning. As the race entered its 23rd hour, the second car, driven by three-times Le Mans winner Yannick Dalmas and young guns Emmanuel Collard and Ralf Kelleners, had a lead of more than one lap when an engine fire brought the factory team's challenge to a fiery end.

But when the official Porsche entries hit problems, waiting to pick up the pieces was the car that had beaten the original 911 GT1 to victory in 1996. Joest Racing's Porsche WSC95, this time driven by ex-Ferrari Formula 1 drivers Michele Alboreto and Stefan Johansson and Dane Tom Kristensen, wasn't quite the competitive proposition that it had been the year before. But the car, built by sports car specialist TWR back in 1994, did have the legs of the two McLaren-BMW F1 GTRs which filled the remaining places on the podium, the privateer GTC car of Jean-Marc Gounon, Pierre-Henri Raphanel and Anders Olofsson leading home the sole remaining factory entry.

Although the FIA GT Championship looked headed for a winter of uncertainty, there seemed little doubt that the rise and rise of the Le Mans classic would continue into 1998, not least because Toyota had long since announced that it would be joining arch-rival and 1997 returnee Nissan on the grid for the most important sports car race of them all.

HORSES FOR COURSES

by Paul Fearnley

THE notion of the two-litre Super Touring category acting as a worldwide saloon car formula was dented in 1997. This racing remains cheap in the overall motorsport scheme of things; even so, its financial implications became too burdensome for some of the lesser nations that had originally been swept along on a tide of euphoria.

This phenomenon has indubitably ebbed: Aussie petrol-heads have still to be weaned off their spectacular, five-litre V8 autosaurs; the North American series has not taken off as had been hoped; Belgium's Procar series eked out a final year of Super Touring before following South Africa's lead by pulling the plug on it in favour of a more affordable formula; Spain has struggled on without manufacturer support; the French series is a shadow of its former self.

For the big hitters, however, Super Touring remains global thanks to the televisual reach of the British and German championships. Along with Japan, these European motorsport giants are the only federations that can sustain championships which still generate far-reaching impacts. And all three look set to go their separate ways within a rough envelope based upon the FIA-mandated technical regulations. The category is clearly at a crossroads.

That is not necessarily a bad thing. More than ever, this form of racing is led by marketing demands, so it stands to reason that the remaining series should bend to the whim of their host nations. If the average Japanese boy racer arrives at a meeting in a turbocharged, four-wheel drive Nissan Skyline, why should he be excited by two-litre, front-wheel drive racers? If the run-of-the-mill *autobahn*-burner boasts flared wheel arches, a whale-tail wing and ABS, shouldn't its owner expect his track heroes to race something more hi-tech and visually potent?

Japan veered from the FIA's chosen path this season, allowing competitors to utilise flared wheel arches and bigger rear wings – not, it must be said, with much success. For this series is in direct competition with a very strong national GT series that bristles with Skylines and the like.

Outwardly, Germany adheres to the Super Touring rule book. But it is known that a number of 'developments' that would be stamped on by BTCC scrutineers are allowed to ride in a country that still yearns for the over-the-top Class One – the ultimate, hi-tech, high-cost 'touring car' series that imploded at the end of 1996. Lessons have been learned from its demise but there still needs to be an element of horses for courses.

World and European touring car series have come and gone. For one reason or another, they didn't work. So why attempt to enforce a cross-boundary formula? The original idea was a good one – it still is, in theory – but national motorsport constantly evolves. The governing body should be flexible with it. Or, at the very least, be bent into shape.

The cancellation of the 1996 FIA World Cup was the first sign of manufacturer power in action. The clarion call of the governing body was ignored. The proposed TV coverage of the event wasn't good enough and that was that. Manufacturers flexed their muscles further when a clutch of them railed against plans to alter the technical regulations for 1999. The basic idea was to reduce aerodynamic and mechanical grip in an effort to spice up some increasingly turgid racing. A vocal faction from the German series was vehemently opposed to this – admittedly perhaps more to the FIA's

252

Sutton Motorsport Images

Sutton Motorsport Images

John Overton

Main photo: Renault dominated the British Touring Car Championship with the Williams-prepared Laguna, allowing Swiss driver Alain Menu *(inset left)* to shed the bridesmaid tag at last.

Popular ex-champions Gabriele Tarquini, returning to the series with Honda *(below left)*, and Frank Biela, again leading the Audi effort *(bottom left)*, were unable to keep pace with Menu.

Derek Warwick *(below right)* and John Cleland struggled to bring their Vauxhall Vectras to a competitive pitch, hamstrung by an unsuitable aerodynamic package.

before beginning frantic, orgiastic build programmes for their new partners, the marriage of Renault and Williams remained as solid as a rock. This stability allowed the Didcot outfit to produce the car of the season. Meanwhile, its engine preparers, Sodemo, based at Magny-Cours, eradicated the bugs that had put the kibosh on the previous season's Laguna campaign. Add to this the final, telling ingredient of the undoubted talents of Menu and this recipe proved unpalatable to all but Renault. Menu didn't mind. He came back for seconds. And thirds. And fourths. By the end of June, he had had his fill, winning ten of the 14 races so far run. It would

have been 12 out of 14 had it stayed dry at Thruxton in May. He cantered to the title thereafter, although his pass of rookie team-mate Jason Plato in the penultimate round showed that the hunger remains – a steely ruthless streak born of, and hardened by, a penniless scrabble to the top.

This move was the only blot on Renault's escutcheon, for it ended hopes that Plato would finish as the series runner-up. This distinction fell to Audi's Frank Biela, although the 1996 champion was powerless to prevent the French manufacturer and Williams from completing a clean sweep of the titles, taking both the manufacturer and team honours.

VECTRA

88

Auto Trader

Mobil 1 **VAUXHALL** Mobil 1

MICHELIN

TOSHIBA **TOSHIBA**

John Overton

control than to the changes to the cars. And it got its way. What was eventually passed by the World Council in early October was little more than a tidying-up of what had gone before.

This will hit hard the smaller nations and those manufacturers still considering a plunge into the fray. The entry level is becoming increasingly high. Hopes that the likes of Hyundai, Proton and Daewoo would eventually bolster the manufacturer count have waned in the past 12 months. Two almost unnoticed casualties of this year's political war of words could return to haunt the formula. Increased freedom of suspension and cylinder heads was bundled in with the proposed aerodynamic changes and thrown out. Road-going suspensions of the average family buzzbox are becoming increasingly simplified, while ever-more-stringent emission controls are militating against high-

performance evolutions of the base power unit. This failure to implement two of the more sensible suggestions of recent times could, in theory, reduce the number of potentially competitive models. As the number of truly valid championships dwindles, it is vital that those remaining series maintain the current variety in their entries. For if rising costs force manufacturers to narrow their field of vision, such continued diverse support will be vital if reasonable-sized – and interesting - grids are to be maintained.

The BTCC is still the leader in this respect – eight different marques jostling for success in 1997. Yet there was only one man, one car and one team in the final reckoning. Swiss star Alain Menu ended a bizarre run of three consecutive runner-up slots in convincing style. While the rest of the manufacturers threw their keys into the centre of the silliest of silly seasons

BMW reduced its touring car commitments in favour of the FIA GT series but still enjoyed plenty of success. Former Grand Prix motor cycle racer Didier de Radiguès, pictured leading the pack at Spa, claimed the Belgian Procar title while Italy's Superturismo championship fell to Emanuele Naspetti *(bottom)*.

This was a difficult season for Audi. In 1996, its Quattro had swept all before it, winning all seven championships that it contested. This dominance was, however, the straw that broke the FIA's back and it prohibited the use of the four-wheel drive as of 1998. It also bumped up the car's base weight for its swan-song year by 30 kilos, forcing it to run 95 kilos heavier than its front-wheel drive rivals and 70 more than the rear-wheel drive cars – basically its perennial enemy, BMW.

These decisions left Audi languishing between the devil and the deep, blue sea. It adopted the long-term view and decided to concentrate upon the development of its front-wheel drive challenger during the winter. Its old warhorse, therefore, was somewhat neglected and was, unsurprisingly, off the pace at the season's start. Once some developments for it came on stream in the second half of the season, the car proved competitive in the BTCC, which was the only championship that allowed it to remove that extra ballast.

Of its many titles, Audi retained only one, the relatively minor Central European series. There is hope for the future, though: its singleton front-wheel drive car, driven throughout the season by Frenchman Yvan Muller, has shown considerable promise and should return the Ingolstadt marque to the winner's circle next season.

As the four-wheel drive horseman of the apocalypse was put out to grass, its underlings made hay. The German series was won by Peugeot's Laurent Aïello. The Frenchman is possibly Menu's only true rival in terms of front-wheel drive pace. He dominated the early stages of the Supertourenwagen Cup and survived a couple of late hiccoughs to fend off the BMWs of Joachim Winkelhock and Johnny Cecotto.

Aïello's triumph was the product of a huge effort by Peugeot France. Its success was in marked contrast to the, admittedly improving, efforts of its Peugeot UK cousin. There were a number of reasons for this anomaly. Part of it can be laid at the door of the current aerodynamic regulations. A manufacturer must homologate a single wing kit at the start of the season. It will, therefore, tailor it to suit the circuits of its premier programme. German tracks tend to be faster, wider and less undulating than their British counterparts. They thus make different downforce demands. The 'British' Peugeots suffered as a result. As did the BTCC Vauxhall Vectras. The latter concern's circumstance was doubly frustrating in that its German brethren, who had come up with a next-to-useless package, were allowed to switch back to the previous season's package,

an option not provided for by the British championship's regulations. Would it not make sense to allow a manufacturer to homologate a specific aero package for each series? There's that flexibility thing again.

BMW has always stated that the current aerodynamic regulations favour the front-wheel drive cars, which generate the bulk of their downforce via drag-free frontal underbody tweaks instead of a boot-mounted rear wing dragging tiresomely through the airstream. The Munich marque has been a stalwart of this category. Without its support, it might never have got off the ground. But this season, it throttled back its involvement, concentrating its effort instead on a GT campaign. The Team Bigazzi-run cars in Germany were thus the only Three Series to benefit from official works backing. Despite this, BMW still hoovered up its fair share of titles: former bike star Didier de Radiguès

mounted a late charge to win the Belgian title, while ex-Formula 1 racer Emanuele Naspetti dominated Italy's Superturismo series. Also, as AUTOCOURSE went to press, Paul Morris lay in pole position for Australia's two-litre honours with one round remaining. BMW also continued to dominate long-distance saloon car racing, prevailing in the Spa 24 Hours and Down Under at Bathurst.

The latter event is destined to become the mecca for Super Touring. Snaffled from under the noses of Australia's V8 brigade by BTCC czar Alan Gow, it is the only non-championship race with sufficient kudos and, more importantly, a wide enough TV net, to cajole the ever-so-slightly diverse series to bury their self-interests and unite for a weekend. One such occasion would be beneficial, allowing the championships to touch base. For the basic category is not a million miles away from the ideal. The current regulations have been the most successful in tin-top history. Manufacturer support may have stagnated recently but it remains at an all-time high. That should not be thrown carelessly away. There is nothing fundamentally wrong with a formula that is now seven years old – hundreds of millions of a dozen manufacturers' pounds can't all be wrong.

This stability, investment and white-hot development fuelled by so many feverish marques desperate to see a return has, however, dulled the on-track excitement. The cars have become increasingly 'pure', exhibiting single-seater-like responses and a distaste for door-handling excesses. To undo these developments would cost more than the so-called cost-cutting measures originally proposed by the FIA's Touring Car Commission. If the racing is to be enlivened, then the category must solve an ethical dilemma: should the race always go to the swift? Formula 1 is the pinnacle of the sport. As such, it can seemingly absorb any number of dull races. Touring car racing cannot. The dominance demonstrated by the likes of Menu can only be bad – even, in the longer term, for Renault. Telegenic, all-action entertainment is an absolute must for its continued survival, much more so than the adherence to regulatory minutiae. And if that requires contrived grids or 'success ballast' to be employed, then so be it.

Touring car racing has come a long way in the last seven years; it must not be allowed to mark time now. If the technical side is deemed as near as damn it spot on, then it's time to look elsewhere within the sphere to ensure that it continues to evolve and revolve.

THE POWER OF MOTORSPORT

AT SILVERSTONE

Silverstone

In 1998 Silverstone celebrates its 50th year by hosting another action-packed season of first class motor sport. From Formula 1 to British Touring Cars, from World Rally to British Superbikes - there are meetings to suit all tastes:

- RAC British Grand Prix
- Coys International Historic Festival presented by Chrysler
- Network Q RAC Rally
- British Empire Trophy (FIA GT Championship)
- Auto Trader RAC Touring Car Championship, 2 meetings (inc finals)
- MCN British Superbikes
- Mobil 1 British Rally Championship
- Silverstone Spring Trophy and Autumn Gold Cup
- Numerous national, marque and club meetings

To book in advance or order your copy of the 1998 Yearbook please call now on: **01327 857273**

Silverstone Driving Centre

Choose from single seaters, race saloons, 4x4, rally or road skills for yourself or as a memorable gift for friends and family. You can also choose the venue, Silverstone or Croft Circuit (North Yorkshire), at which to introduce someone else to the world's most dynamic sport or to fulfil your own long-held ambition. For details of all gifts and courses at both locations, for individuals, groups and corporate enquiries, please call now on **01327 857788.**

Marketing through Motorsport

Marketing through Motorsport is a unique concept developed to enable any company to maximise the valuable corporate communication and incentive opportunities offered by association with motor sport and with Silverstone, The Home of British Motor Racing. For details of hospitality, driving days, sponsorship, advertising, conferences and exhibitions, please call now on **01327 320330.**

Silverstone™
THE HOME OF BRITISH MOTOR RACING

SILVERSTONE
50 YEARS YOUNG

SILVERSTONE is 50 years old. Yes, 50 years of wonderful racing have passed since Luigi Villoresi, driving a Maserati, won the first British Grand Prix held at the Home of British Motor Racing back in 1948. And what started on a rudimentary circuit along the runways and perimeter roads of a former airfield grew like topsy, with both the circuit and the racing becoming better and better as the years advanced. Highlights include the time that Peter Collins headed home Mike Hawthorn in a Ferrari 1-2 in 1958, topping the 100 mph race average for the first time; Jackie Stewart dicing with Jochen Rindt in 1969; Nigel Mansell versus Nelson Piquet in 1987; and Damon Hill winning the race his father never won, in 1994. And Silverstone's dedication to being the world's premier motorsport facility will ensure that many more great races are added to these layers of memories.

As Silverstone celebrates its golden anniversary, it is a very, very different place to the one that welcomed 100,000 fans in 1948. Back then it was little more than a temporary track marked out by hay bales and oil drums. Now it's a high-tech, super-safe, multi-million pound development offering much more than just a race track. Indeed, not only does Silverstone host the most highly respected Grand Prix on the Formula 1 calendar, but its ultra-modern facilities are far beyond the wildest dreams of the thousands who were there 50 years ago.

While the fans thrilled to the sights and sounds of the early post-war racers in 1948, today's fans have so much more to make their day at the races a memorable one. Not only are there more regular race meetings blessed with packed fields of closely matched cars, but the viewing is now safer and the commentary both easier to hear and more informative. Added to this, the advent of the circuit's own television station - Silverstone TV - has led to the introduction of giant viewing screens that not only permit you to see the action all the way around the circuit from almost any vantage point, but also to keep up with driver interviews both before and after each race, combining all the advantages of television with the thrills of being there.

Another advantage enjoyed by the fans of today is that everyone can have a go. If you fancy emulating the stars of the track, it's easy, as all you have to do is visit the Silverstone Driving Centre. They can offer you everything from both indoor and outdoor karting to 4 x 4 off-road driving, to trying your hand at the skid-control cars, to the full racing school course in both saloons and single-seaters. From family and corporate days out to the first steps in the careers of the budding stars of the future, the Silverstone Driving Centre has something for everyone.

Silverstone isn't only about racing, as rallying too is now firmly on the agenda, with the world famous RAC Rally making its historic return in 1997. Fittingly, the Silverstone Driving Centre also has a rally school as well as its own rally stage.

While other circuits stand still, Silverstone is constantly updating its facilities. Particular care has been lavished in adapting the circuit to include the extra safety modifications required as the cars become capable of ever greater speeds. But Silverstone alone also alters its layout to ensure that the circuit keeps its flow and has points at which drivers can overtake. Safe racing is one thing, but it must be exciting too. Ever looking to new ideas, there's now a separate circuit on the infield - the Stowe circuit - that can be used even when races are being held on the full Grand Prix track. The Grand Prix circuit itself can be split into two separate circuits - the

National and the South circuits - and there is also now the new International circuit using the southern link from Becketts to Abbey providing an exciting 2.27-mile track for a number of events including F3 and BTCC.

So, whether you're coming to Silverstone for the Spring Trophy meeting in April, the British Grand Prix in July, the British Touring Car Championship finale in September, or the RAC Rally in November, welcome, as there is something for everyone and everything for the motorsport enthusiast.

Main picture: Jacques Villeneuve wins the 1997 RAC British Grand Prix.

Far left: Greats from the past. Mike Hawthorn and Jackie Stewart, just two British World Champions who have graced Silverstone with their talents.

Left: The all-action British Touring Car Championship. Thrills and spills for the spectators.

Right: Ferrari's fifty this year - Silverstone's turn next!

Silverstone™
THE HOME OF BRITISH MOTOR RACING

EVER INCREASING CIRCLES

by Gordon Kirby

Oval racing appears set to regain its traditional position as the dominant form of motorsport in the USA. While the NASCAR Winston Cup, long associated with established short ovals such as Martinsville *(top)* and Richmond *(right)*, continues to enjoy booming popularity, the favourable economic climate has fuelled the construction of a spate of new tracks such as Roger Penske's breathtaking California Speedway at Fontana *(below)*, which hosted the final round of the CART series.

Arie Luyendyk won the Indianapolis 500, the IRL's flagship race, but for the second consecutive year CART's teams and drivers pursued their business elsewhere.

Photos: Nigel Kinrade

Michael C. Brown

Allsport USA

THERE'S an old saying in the sport that if the economy is in good shape, motor racing will be healthy, and if the economy is flat or takes a downturn, racing gets sick. In the USA, the economy is booming like never before and motorsport as a whole is growing by leaps and bounds. Every segment and variety of racing is enjoying full fields and bountiful interest from fans and sponsors, but the growth is measured best by an unprecedented boom in the last few years in the building of superspeedway oval tracks.

In the last two years no fewer than seven brand-new ovals have opened for business with at least three more in the planning stages scheduled to open in 1999 or 2000. The new tracks range from the rather basic $5 million Disney World oval in Orlando, Florida to palatial $100 million-plus high-banked monuments to 200-plus mph lap speeds like those built in California, close to Los Angeles, by Roger Penske, and outside Dallas/Ft Worth, Texas by one of Penske's track-building rivals, Bruton Smith.

Penske, Smith and NASCAR President Bill France Jr have been the prime motivators of this superspeedway-building binge. Through their three competing, publicly traded track-owning and building companies, Penske, France and Smith own or control no fewer than 16 major race tracks in the USA.

Of the three, NASCAR and Daytona boss France may be the most powerful. The son of NASCAR founder Bill France Sr, Bill Jr followed in his father's footsteps and has dictatorially run NASCAR for more than a quarter of a century. 'Billy', as he's known to his closest friends, is Mr France to everyone else.

The France family also owns the Daytona and Talladega superspeedways, as well as the Watkins Glen road course in upstate New York. The Frances' race track-owning company is known as the International Speedway Corporation (ISC). Since going public, the company has acquired a ten per cent interest in Penske's California Speedway, a forty per cent stake in Ralph Sanchez's Homestead Motorsports Complex south of Miami, and a seven per cent interest in Chris Pook's Grand Prix Association of Long Beach, which operates the Long Beach GP and new ovals near St Louis (called Gateway) and Memphis. Also, ISC is building a 1.5-mile superspeedway outside Kansas City due for completion in 1999.

Then there's Penske, whose Indy car team has won a record 99 races, three

this year. In addition to very successful CART and NASCAR teams, and world-wide business interests in commercial diesel engine-building and fleet truck leasing, Penske also operates a publicly owned and traded race track business known as Penske Motorsports Inc. (PMI).

PMI owns the brand-new California Speedway in addition to Michigan and Nazareth Speedways as well as a controlling interest in the North Carolina Motor Speedway (Rockingham), a forty per cent share in the Homestead Motorsports Complex, and a seven per cent share in Chris Pook's GPALB. Penske is also building a brand-new high-banked 2.0-mile superspeedway, similar to his California and Michigan tracks, outside Denver, Colorado, and he and France appear to have forged a strong business partnership, sharing ownership interests in five different racing facilities.

Bruton Smith is a contemporary of Bill France Sr who promoted races and built a string of automobile dealerships across the American South. Thirty years ago he built the Charlotte Motor Speedway, located right in the heart of NASCAR country. Smith lost and then regained control of Charlotte, and, with partner and promoter 'Humpy' Wheeler, transformed the track into the biggest, slickest modern racing facility in the South. Smith then bought the Atlanta Motor Speedway, which has gone through a series of renovations, and then launched Speedway Motorsports Inc. (SMI), his own publicly traded company.

With the income from selling shares, Smith has bought the Sears Point road course in central California as well as the Bristol Motor Speedway in North Carolina. This past summer he opened his new jewel, the Texas Motor Speedway near Dallas/Ft Worth. Smith is also planning another new oval for Atlantic City, New Jersey. It's easy to imagine that all this Stateside track-building and cash-generating captured Bernie Ecclestone's attention, and further fuelled his own dreams of floating F1. If France, Penske and Smith can do it, you can almost hear Bernie saying to himself, why can't I?

Meanwhile, the sudden appearance of so many new oval tracks has created tremendous pressure for major NASCAR and CART race dates. If any of these spiffy and expensive new tracks is unable to attract a NASCAR Winston Cup race or two, and a CART Indy car race as well, it will soon face serious financial problems, particularly as they must perform to the bottom line as publicly owned corporations.

White elephants, you ask? The most

likely of the new tracks to struggle for survival appear to be those in Las Vegas, Colorado Springs (known as Pike's Peak) and Disney World. None of these has been able to establish a strong schedule of major races, or attract large audiences. With more tracks coming on-line in the next couple of years the quest for major events will continue, however, and some of the older, more established NASCAR and CART tracks that are located in smaller markets will also face questions of survival.

Bear in mind that NASCAR ran 32 Winston Cup races this year with 33 scheduled for 1998 and as many as 35 races expected in '99. CART ran 17 races in 1997 with 19 scheduled for '98, and both organisations face additional requests for races in 1999 and beyond. From the teams' point of view this escalation in the number of races is pushing up costs and making any kind of family life impossible if not intolerable for the mechanics, technicians, engine-builders and engineers who give the sport life. Thus lurks the dark side of success.

History's Second Indy Car Split

While the sport's popularity reaches new heights in America, with NASCAR leading the way thanks to thirty years of political stability and strong management, Indy car racing has been torn apart for the second time in twenty years, resulting in a sharp drop in domestic TV ratings if not in trackside ticket sales.

After squabbling with CART for a couple of years, young Indianapolis Motor Speedway owner Tony George set up his own, separate Indy car series in 1996, breaking the Indy 500 away from CART's Indy Car World Series. George called his series the Indy Racing League (IRL), but was able to attract only the smaller or less successful teams, many of them used to running, or more correctly attempting to qualify for, just one race each year – the Indy 500.

George's IRL teams raced 1995-spec CART cars and engines in 1996, but an entirely new formula was debuted in '97. Despite Indy car racing's steady growth under CART, George wanted a cheaper, slower formula, creating a 4.0-litre naturally aspirated, stock-block engine formula and more restrictive aerodynamics and car construction rules with a $385,000 price cap. Engines were supposed to cost no more than $75,000, although prices soon doubled.

A loan scheme was developed to

help the many impoverished IRL teams buy cars, and Dallara and G-Force jumped in to build chassis. Engines were supplied by Oldsmobile thanks to General Motors' motorsports boss Herb Fishel, who helped devise the engine formula to suit Oldsmobile's new, road-going four-cam V8 Aurora engine. Nissan America also got in on the act with a production-based atmo V8 of its own, but the Nissan was way down on power and only a handful of teams, sometimes only a single starter, raced the engine.

There were seven IRL races in 1997, all on ovals, in accordance with Mr George's philosophy, with the Indy 500 as the big draw. Crowds were down a little at Indianapolis on race day, and substantially smaller over the course of 'the month of May', but a good 81st Indy 500, without CART's stars and cars for the second year in a row, was won by Arie Luyendyk, the IRL's most acclaimed and experienced driver.

The IRL title was won, however, by the series 'poster boy' Tony Stewart, who graduated to the IRL from Mid-Western midget and sprint car racing where he was a multiple champion. Driving for the IRL's big-buck team owned by Wisconsin lumber and building magnate John Menard, young Stewart led most races, but won only once. He took the championship with a disappointing 11th-place finish, three laps down, in the season-closer, beating one of A.J. Foyt's drivers, Davey Hamilton, who finished seventh in the final race.

Some IRL rounds drew reasonable crowds, notably the inaugural races at Bruton Smith's Charlotte Motor Speedway and new Texas track. Others played to famously empty houses with fewer than 15,000 fans at Phoenix, including many giveaways, and a shocking low of just 700 tickets sold in New Hampshire. Both these tracks previously ran CART races and it's very clear that the IRL can't draw flies at any venue where CART used to race.

So far, the IRL hasn't created the critical mass in fan interest, ticket sales and sponsorship that's required to support a modern, professional automobile racing series. In fact, the total sponsorship attracted by the IRL and its teams in 1997 was reckoned by an independent financial analyst to be around $30 million versus $385 million spent by sponsors in CART.

TV ratings have been disappointing too, for CART as well as the IRL. Many races drew less than a 1.0 rating, roughly a million households in a country of 100 million households. Prior to the split, CART was getting

Italy's Alex Zanardi built on his impressive 1996 rookie season to deservedly become the new CART champion in Target/Chip Ganassi Racing's Reynard-Honda but his forceful tactics made him less than popular with many of his rivals.

Providing further confirmation that there is life after F1, former McLaren driver Mark 'Billy' Blundell *(below right)* responded to the encouragement of his supporters by scoring three wins for the ambitious PacWest team.

solid 2 ratings with an occasional 3 or slightly more. The Indy 500 has also suffered from the split, falling to a 6 the past two years, 2–3 points less than it used to draw with CART. This rating is well short of NASCAR's keynote race, the Daytona 500, and smaller in fact than many other NASCAR races.

Despite the damage inflicted by the split, George persists with the IRL. He's added four more races for 1998, all on ovals, of course, but has yet to attract any major new teams or drivers, relying on the same sad sack of has-beens and also-rans who have supported the IRL through its first two years. Not one CART team or major sponsor has shown any interest in the IRL, and the situation seems set to carry on at least through to 1999.

Two truly amazing things did happen to the IRL in 1997. First of all, after a disastrously officiated race at Texas in June where A.J. Foyt punched Luyendyk in Victory Circle as a result of a scoring squabble, the IRL divested itself of USAC and took over its own officiating, using many former USAC people. USAC was created by Tony George's grandfather Tony Hulman, and had sanctioned and officiated at the Indy 500 since 1955. A key to the IRL's gestation and creation, USAC continued to run the Indy 500 through CART's 1979 breakaway until the past year. Nobody involved in any way with CART ever believed USAC would lose its prestigious and lucrative grip on the Indy 500, and most CART veterans view Tony George's mid-season axing of USAC for incompetence as something of an irony.

The other amazing thing was George's decision in September to shorten 'the month of May', cutting one week of practice and one weekend of qualifying from the traditional schedule. Over the years, many CART team owners had quietly complained about the costs of being at Indianapolis for three weeks, but George declared two years ago that he would never permit the traditions of the month of May to be changed and the month shortened. In the face of pleas last summer, however, from his threadbare IRL teams that they simply couldn't afford two weeks of practice, George has cut seven days of practice and two of qualifying out of the month of May for 1998. Remarkable irony, yet again.

Finally, there's the safety issue that IRL constructors G-Force and Dallara will try to solve this winter. No fewer than 18 drivers were injured in IRL crashes in 1997, many of them receiv-

ing some type of head injury as a result of rearward crashes into a wall, an inevitability in oval racing.

Among those badly injured were Davy Jones, whose career seemed to be in jeopardy after a bad crash at Disney World early in the year. Also injured were '96 IRL co-champions Scott Sharp and Buzz Calkins, with Sharp sitting out the last few months of the season after two separate accidents resulted in two brain injuries. Late in the year, Indy winner Luyendyk called for a fix to be mandated, threatening not to compete in the IRL series in '98 if a solution to the problem isn't found.

Zanardi Wins CART Title

As the IRL struggled for survival, CART continued to roll along, barely affected, other than for TV ratings, by the loss of the Indy 500. Ticket and corporate sales at most races were up over 1996. Unhappy as they are over flagging TV ratings, most sponsors remain solidly committed to CART, which provides a much wider demographic reach than NASCAR, both nationally and around the world.

For 1998, rapid package and freight handler FedEx comes on board as CART's new series sponsor. FedEx takes over as the title sponsor from paint and glass manufacturer PPG, although the latter will continue with its pace car programme as well as awarding the PPG Cup to each year's champion. FedEx is expected to give the CART series a much higher profile, tying the series into its national and international advertising and marketing programmes.

Also, with the split between Indianapolis and CART appearing to be irrevocable, CART has decided to renounce the Indy car name. Instead, starting in 1998, CART reverts to calling its cars 'championship cars', the traditional name for Indy cars used through the 1950s, '60s and '70s.

The first half of the 1997 PPG Cup season was wide open as Michael Andretti, Scott Pruett and then Paul Tracy led the points standings. The first four races were won by four different drivers – Andretti, Pruett, Alex Zanardi and Tracy – and after ten of seventeen races the top five were covered by just 16 points. But it was there at the year's tenth race, in Cleveland, that the tide began to turn very clearly in Zanardi's direction.

The 30-year-old Italian scored a superb win in Cleveland, coming from more than half a lap behind after a stop–go penalty for pitting when the pits were closed. Lapping almost a full

second quicker than anyone else, Zanardi caught and passed leader Gil de Ferran with just six laps to go to win his second race of the year, his first since Long Beach three months earlier.

Zanardi was second to Mark Blundell in Toronto the next weekend, then won three straight races – the US 500, and the Mid-Ohio and Road America road races – emerging as an irresistible force. He was far enough ahead by the end of August to be in a position to wrap up the title in Vancouver, but after qualifying on the pole and leading the early laps Zanardi twice went down the same escape road because of braking problems, then indulged in a shoving match with Bryan Herta that earned him a $25,000 fine and put him on probation for the year's last two races.

At Laguna Seca the next weekend Zanardi drove a slightly conservative race to put the championship in his pocket, finishing third behind teammate Jimmy Vasser and Blundell. Rookie of the Year in 1996, Zanardi became the first resident of Italy ever to win America's national driving championship and only the third overseas resident in the sport's eighty-year history to do so.

It was also the first time in ten years, since Bobby Rahal won a pair of championships with TrueSports in 1986 and '87, that a team has won back-to-back PPG Cup titles, and the first time since Penske did it with Rick Mears and Al Unser in 1982 and '83 that a team has done so with two different drivers. Hats off to Chip Ganassi and his Target Reynard-Honda/Firestone team.

For his part, Zanardi's confidence, always considerable, grew as the year wore on. 'I never doubted my talent or the talent and skill of the whole Target/Chip Ganassi Racing team,' he commented. 'I have had plenty of support all the time from Chip, from our PR man Michael Knight, my engineer Morris Nunn, my chief mechanic Rob Hill and all the mechanics. That's my family, and, of course, my wife Daniela. She always washes my brain every night before we close our eyes and she's always happy for the following day. I knew we could do it. I never doubted we could do it.'

Zanardi's powerful run to the title certainly wasn't without controversy as he made himself increasingly unpopular with most of the other drivers by lecturing them in drivers' meetings to get out of the way of faster cars – his in particular. Things came to a head at the race in Vancouver when he had a number of close calls as he charged

Diana Burnett

Michael C. Brown

back through the field, bulling his way by under braking, then forcing Herta into a tyre barrier after hitting him in the previous corner.

'In Italy they say, "A lot of enemies, a lot of honour," ' Alex says about his unpopularity. 'I understand that it's hard to accept, when you have talent, that just because somebody has a little bit more luck than you he gets a better result. But eventually people are going to understand that I worked very hard and I deserve this championship. All I had to do was do my job consistently day by day, and I think I did that.'

Zanardi reflected on the satisfaction of winning a major racing championship after the hardships he went through recovering from his terrible accident at Spa aboard an F1 Lotus in 1993, an accident from which he was lucky to escape without serious brain injuries.

'My life is not going to change,' he said at Laguna Seca after winning the title. 'I'm obviously a much happier man. It's a great accomplishment for me. It just feels great. This week I'm going to think of all the pain I went through a few years ago after my accident at Spa in 1993.

'I'm a very optimistic person and I felt like that when I was going through the recovery from that accident, but now that I'm here as the champion it feels so good. I don't think there is anything good in life without the bad. If you haven't experienced the bad, it's tough to realise how good a moment like this is.'

Gil de Ferran split Zanardi and team-mate and outgoing champion Jimmy Vasser in the points table, taking second in the championship in his first year with Derrick Walker's team. De Ferran failed to win a race but was on the podium seven times with two seconds and five thirds, and also led seven races – as many as Zanardi.

Defending champion Vasser made a slow start to the season but came on strong at the end of the year. Jimmy scored his first win in 15 months on home turf at Laguna Seca in September, and was first or second in the year's last three races. Zanardi, de Ferran and Vasser gave Honda a 1-2-3 sweep in the PPG Cup drivers' championship.

CART's Manufacturers' Championship went to Mercedes-Benz, however, with four Mercedes drivers

261

Photos: Michael C. Brown

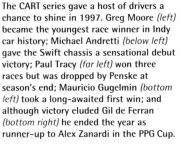

The CART series gave a host of drivers a chance to shine in 1997. Greg Moore *(left)* became the youngest race winner in Indy car history; Michael Andretti *(below left)* gave the Swift chassis a sensational debut victory; Paul Tracy *(far left)* won three races but was dropped by Penske at season's end; Mauricio Gugelmin *(bottom left)* took a long-awaited first win; and although victory eluded Gil de Ferran *(bottom right)* he ended the year as runner-up to Alex Zanardi in the PPG Cup.

Right: Frantic action as the pit crews go to work at a round of NASCAR's Winston Cup. Heading the line-up is Jeff Gordon, currently the series' outstanding driver.

Diana Burnett

combining to score nine wins for Mercedes versus Honda's six. Paul Tracy (3), Mark Blundell (3), Greg Moore (2) and Mauricio Gugelmin (1) won races for Mercedes with Gugelmin beating his M-B mates to fourth in the championship. Ford/Cosworth won two races, both at the beginning of the year, with Michael Andretti and Scott Pruett. Reynard was a runaway winner of CART's constructors' title with 13 wins, including the last 11 straight. Firestone shared Reynard's record of 11 straight wins from June through to season's end, and 13 wins in all, rather eclipsing Goodyear.

Tracy won three short-oval races in a row in April and May and led the championship for ten weeks through mid-season. On the street and road circuits the Penske PC26 wasn't much good, however, and the team seemed to go backwards as the year wore on. Tracy faded to fifth by season's end while team-mate and twice champion Al Unser Jr had a terrible year, failing to finish half the races and ending the season 13th in the points standings. Unser has high hopes that next year's PC27, designed by new chief engineer John Travis, will turn the tables.

Tracy was fired at the end of the season, jumping to Barry Green's team. He will be partnered in 1998 and '99 by Dario Franchitti in a pair of Reynard-Hondas on Firestones and may be in a position to embarrass Team Penske. To everyone's surprise, Penske's choice to replace Tracy was Andre Ribeiro, a fast but inconsistent and sometimes wild Brazilian who won one race in 1995 and two in '96 with Steve Horne's Honda/Firestone Tasman team. Future sponsorship and business connections were the key factors, Penske admitted, in his decision to hire Ribeiro.

A team that really made its mark in 1997 was PacWest. Mark Blundell scored the first victory for Bruce McCaw's organisation in a tricky wet–dry race in Portland at the end of June. It was the first CART win for driver and team but by season's end there were three more victories to savour, two for Blundell and one for Gugelmin. 'Big Mo's' long-deserved, ice-breaking win at Vancouver at the end of August and Blundell's first oval track and 500-mile win for the team at the season-closing Marlboro 500 put PacWest among the series' big dogs.

Greg Moore scored the first win of his career at Milwaukee in June, becoming, at 22 years, one month and ten days old, the youngest driver in history to win an Indy car race. Moore won again in Detroit after Gugelmin and Blundell ran out of fuel on the last lap, and was very competitive in many races but failed to finish too many times, often with engine failures. A championship contender early in the year, poor reliability meant that Moore fell to seventh at season's end behind Tracy and Blundell.

A storybook debut win for Swift in the season-opener at Homestead did not presage the tough season that followed for Newman-Haas. Michael Andretti was very quick in many races, struggled in others, and also fought reliability problems with engines and transmissions. He finished the year an undistinguished eighth in the points table, but the potential of the Swift is there for all to see. Next year will be interesting.

Team-mate Christian Fittipaldi made an excellent comeback from a terrible early-season crash in Australia and at the end of the year he and Michael each signed long-term contracts. Roberto Moreno was drafted in to substitute for Fittipaldi in six races and did a great job, running near the front in most of the events he contested. Later in the year, Moreno was called in to sub for injured rookie Patrick Carpentier in Tony Bettenhausen's entry.

Scott Pruett made a strong start to the year with one of Pat Patrick's Reynard-Ford/Firestones, winning in Australia and finishing third in Long Beach, but, fast as he was in many subsequent

races, results were few and far between. Pruett faded to ninth in the championship at the end of the year with team-mate Raul Boesel tenth.

Eleventh and twelfth in the points standings just ahead of Al Jr were Bryan Herta and Bobby Rahal, teammates, of course, *chez* Team Rahal. Both Bryan and Bobby had their moments, both leading races and Herta taking two poles, but neither took anything more than a single trip to the podium from the year.

Most CART races were accompanied by a round of the Indy Lights championship, now CART's 'official support series'. Eleven years after its birth, Indy Lights has truly come of age with full fields and fierce, extremely competitive races, much more so than the IRL which the Lights series thoroughly outshines for competition, sponsors and professionalism. The '97 Lights title was won by young Brazilian Tony Kanaan, who beat Tasman Motorsports team-mate Helio Castro-Neves to the title.

Also running at many CART races was a round of the Toyota/Atlantic championship, which was swept in 1997 by the big-buck Lynx Racing operation and rookie drivers Alex Barron and Memo Gidley. Long-time kart racer Barron was particularly impressive, winning the Atlantic title at his first try at 24 years of age after only a half-season of FF2000 in 1996.

The thriving Barber/Dodge series saw a pitched championship battle between rapid Italian Rino Mastronardi and Derek Hill, son-of-Phil, while the very healthy US FF2000 series saw fifty cars at many races with the title going to Brazilian teenager Zak Morioka, who nosed out 19-year-old Chicagoan Matt Sielsky.

The Jeff Gordon Era Arrives

As everyone knows, by far the most popular form of motorsport in America is NASCAR's Winston Cup series. NASCAR has grown steadily over the past quarter-century, helped immensely by series sponsor Winston cigarettes and without any of the long-term political in-fighting which has savaged Indy car racing, thanks to Bill France's iron-fisted control. Ticket sales and TV ratings for NASCAR continue to set new records for the sport, and it is NASCAR's booming success that has fuelled the building of so many new tracks.

A good indicator of NASCAR's strength in the marketplace is the earning power of seven-times NASCAR champion Dale Earnhardt. Thanks to considerable income from

Nigel Kinrade

Nigel Kimrade

Dale Earnhardt has encountered a number of setbacks in the last couple of years but The Intimidator has no intention of quitting this side of the Millennium.

Below: NASCAR fans come to the races ready to really enjoy the show and make no secret of their allegiances.

licensed Earnhardt products and collectables, the good Dale is reputed to earn around $700,000 per week, or $35 million per year, possibly out-earning even Michael Schumacher!

The past couple of years have been tough ones for Earnhardt. For one thing, with two races to go in the '97 Winston Cup championship as AUTO-COURSE closed for press, he hadn't won in 56 starts. For another, he had survived a huge, multi-car accident in a mid-season race at Talladega in 1996, breaking a collarbone but refusing to miss the next weekend's or any subsequent races in NASCAR's unremitting, week-in, week-out schedule. Then, in the summer of '97, 46-year-old Earnhardt had to pull out of a race because he was badly disoriented, somehow 'in an altered mental state', one doctor later reported.

Earnhardt was subjected to a battery of different medical tests but was pronounced entirely fit and continued to race, week-in, week-out. Although at the time of writing he hadn't won in 1997, nobody could call Earnhardt uncompetitive. He had finished second four times and was sixth in the championship, a pretty good year for most drivers. Near season's end Earnhardt declared he had no thoughts of retiring and hoped to race into the next century.

The Winston Cup championship battle was pretty tight for much of the year but turned out to be almost a cakewalk for 1995 champion Jeff Gordon. The 26-year-old is NASCAR's youngest driver, and easily the series' most successful over the last three years, winning 27 races over that time span. Driving for Rick Hendrick's three-car team, Gordon won the Winston Cup title for the first time in 1995, scoring seven wins. He was second to team-mate Terry Labonte in '96, despite winning ten races to Labonte's two, and was almost irre-sistible in '97. He had won ten more races as this was written, beating veterans Mark Martin and Dale Jarrett to his second championship.

Gordon has become so successful that he is now booed just as roundly as he is cheered at pre-race driver introductions. He is disliked because he is too much Mr Nice Guy in image and appearance, as well as being married to a former Miss Winston, the pair of them squeaky-clean. On the track, however, he is as tough as they come, and has survived and won his share of bumping matches, a rite of passage in stock car racing.

As good as the year was for Gordon and his DuPont-sponsored 'Rainbow Warriors' team, it was a very difficult year for team owner Hendrick. While fighting a life-threatening attack of leukemia, Hendrick also encountered difficulties with his business affairs. Because of his poor health, he was unable to attend any races in 1997.

With two rounds remaining, defending champion Labonte had won only once for Hendrick's Chevrolet team, and was no better than fifth in the points standings. Gordon's stiffest competition for the title came from Dale Jarrett in one of Robert Yates's Fords and Mark Martin aboard Jack Roush's lead Ford. Jarrett was very strong in many races, and had won six times, while Martin was equally quick in most races, scoring four wins. Fourth in the championship was Martin's Roush team-mate Jeff Burton, who had enjoyed his best year to date with three wins and many strong runs.

It used to be rare to see two-car teams in NASCAR but multi-car operations are now all the rage. Hendrick's team has run three cars for ten years, while Yates expanded to two cars two years ago and Roush moved up to running three cars in 1997 and plans to run no fewer than five in '98! Further proof, if needed, that sponsorship abounds in NASCAR.

Another Split!

American GT and sports car racing has been in turmoil for some time and the tepid soup leaked out of the pot this year after the redoubtable Andy Evans bought IMSA. Driver, team owner, entrepreneur, Evans said he believed he was walking in the footsteps of Bernie Ecclestone, Bill France and Roger Penske, but seemed only to fall foul of almost everyone in the business. Evans renamed his organisation Professional SportsCar Racing (PSR), but found himself in a deepening squabble with many of his entrants, as well as other promoters and manufacturers.

In October, a breakaway group was established by NASCAR boss Bill France working in partnership with the SCCA, original IMSA founder John Bishop, most of the USA's road racing promoters and most major IMSA teams represented by owner/driver Rob Dyson. Initially, Evans threatened to sue, claiming that France, the SCCA and others had created an illegal cartel and violated American anti-trust laws, but as this story was written he appeared to be trying to work out a compromise with his opponents, possibly even selling out to them. If Evans agreed to acquiesce, he will have given sports car racing a much-needed chance for revival in the USA.

Nigel Kimrade

BUILDING FOR THE FUTURE

A STRONG business is built from the bottom up. Without a strong foundation, the pinnacle is weak and vulnerable.

When Brown & Williamson Tobacco became involved in motorsports, it realized a strong base was necessary to achieve its marketing goals and support the continued growth of the sport in the United States.

That's why it took a proactive role in developing opportunities for individuals and series to prosper through its support of the grassroots level of development of American drivers and open-wheel development series.

Right: Barry Green, President of Team KOOL Green.

Below: The KOOL Indy Lights pair of Chris Simmons and Mark Hotchkis.

Bottom: KOOL partners Toyota in support of the Formula Atlantic series.

What began as a two-car Team KOOL Green effort in the 1996 PPG Firestone Indy Lights Championship, blossomed in 1997 into a comprehensive program that impacts all phases of open-wheel racing in this country.

At the peak is the high profile CART program, featuring races in the global markets of Australia, Brazil, the United States and Canada (and Japan in 1998). Almost 2.5 million spectators attended the 17 races in 1997 and more than 1 billion fans in 100 countries were exposed to the sport.

A level below CART was the three-car Team KOOL Green Indy Lights effort in the CART official development series – the PPG Firestone Indy Lights Series. In 1997, the Indy Lights effort was complemented by co-sponsorship – with Toyota Motor Sales of America – of the Formula Atlantic series, one of the longest-running open-wheel racing series anywhere and a series recognized world-wide as the proving ground for many of the sport's top drivers. Another building block to stabilize the foundation!

Jacques Villeneuve and his late father, Gilles, made their initial mark in Atlantic cars. So too, did CART Indy car stars such as Bobby Rahal, Greg Moore and a host of others.

Complementing the driver development efforts in Indy Lights and Atlantics was the Team Green Academy, operated in conjunction with the Derek Daly SpeedCentre at the Las Vegas Motor Speedway. Barry and Kim Green created the Academy to provide opportunities for aspiring American drivers who might not otherwise have the financial resources to learn their trade and move up through the open-wheel ranks. Over time, this program coupled with KOOL's driver development efforts will undoubtedly yield a stable of American drivers vying for seats in the premier open-wheel class of racing – the CART World Series.

Right: Part of the KOOL hospitality program includes in depth pit and paddock tours for the VIP guest.

Far right: The KOOL Balloon, a distinctive sight at race meetings and competitor in the KOOL Balloon Racing Series (inset below).

OTHER foundation elements of KOOL's program included the Reporter's Club and the KOOL Balloon Racing Series. The Reporter's Club focused on providing the media with the necessary support to perform their critical role of keeping fans apprised of the latest news about open-wheel racing in the United States. The KOOL Balloon Racing Series, a ten event series of hot-air balloon races at major CART race events, provided a new and unique method of entertaining fans and building interest in the sport.

Rounding out KOOL's program was its world-class hospitality program at each CART event, which exposes KOOL's business partners, a new set of influential corporate executives, to the sport.

ON THE RIGHT TRACK

T HE 17 race PPG CART World Series featured stops in Brazil, Australia and Canada as well as 13 events in the United States.

1997 saw Team KOOL Green field a Reynard-Honda for three-time IMSA champion Parker Johnstone in all 17 rounds of the PPG CART World Series. The combination was a promising one, bringing together the team that won the 1995 PPG Cup with Johnstone, one of IMSA's winningest drivers and a man who won the pole position for the 1995 Michigan 500 in the first oval race of his career.

The season got off to a promising start, with Johnstone running competitively throughout the opening round at the Homestead Motor Sports Complex only to finish eighth after losing a couple of laps to the leaders as a result of a cut tire.

However, Homestead proved to be a precursor to a season in which the Team KOOL Green Reynard-Honda earned just 5 top ten finishes as Johnstone and Team KOOL Green were unable to match the pace of championship leaders Alex Zanardi, Gil de Ferran, Jimmy Vasser, Michael Andretti and Paul Tracy with any regularity. As was the case at Homestead, on those occasions when the KOOL Reynard-Honda was in a position for a top finish, misfortune usually intervened. Despite the intervention of misfortune, the KOOL Reynard-Honda prevailed to finish 10 of the 17 races in the points, and 16th overall in the championship.

Triple IMSA champion Parker Johnstone headed the CART challenge in Team KOOL Green's Reynard-Honda.

But while victory on the track is the ultimate goal of every race team and an integral element of most racing sponsorships, it is not the ultimate litmus test of KOOL's multi-faceted program. The scope of KOOL's racing efforts extends well beyond the boundaries of the PPG CART World Series program to Indy Lights, Atlantics, and the ancillary efforts designed to support and enhance the overall initiative.

KOOL's multi-faceted involvement in the PPG Fire-stone Indy Lights Championship is emblematic of this two-fold approach to racing, as represented by Team KOOL Green's entries for drivers Mark Hotchkis (below), Naoki Hattori and Chris Simmons as well as the

KOOL Rookie Challenge, Race Challenge, and KOOL Move of the Race contingency awards.

1997 was the second year of Team KOOL Green's Indy Lights effort, with Simmons returning for his sophomore season with the team, joined by Indy Lights veteran Hotchkis and exciting newcomer Hattori with support from Brown & Williamson Tobacco of Japan. The trio enjoyed a successful campaign with at least one driver finishing in the top 10 in 12 out of the 13 races in addition to 5 podium finishes. Mark Hotchkis earned 1 pole on the way to 7th in the Indy Lights points standings, while Chris Simmons earned his first career pole and a total of 2 poles en route to 6th in the points race, and Naoki Hattori enjoyed a solid rookie campaign that netted 16th in the points standings.

Team KOOL Green ran a three-car Indy Lights team in 1997. Drivers were (from left to right) Chris Simmons, Mark Hotchkis and Naoki Hattori.

I N addition to the impact of Hotchkis, Simmons and Hattori's on-track efforts, KOOL's impact on the Indy Lights series was manifested in its contingency awards. Over the course of the season, KOOL distributed some $65,000 in its Rookie Challenge, Move of the Race and Race Challenge awards. Following the final round of the championship at California Speedway, impressive rookie Cristiano da Matta took home the KOOL Racing and KOOL Rookie Challenge seasonal awards totaling $25,000.

That pattern was repeated in the KOOL/Toyota Atlantic Championship where KOOL served as the co-title series sponsor and also awarded some $24,000 over the course of the 12 race season to winners of the KOOL Rookie Challenge and KOOL Move of the Race competitions. That sum was augmented by the $25,000 presented to Alex Barron as winner of both the KOOL "Series Cup Award" and "Rookie Challenge Winner" as well as the $15,000 KOOL "Racing Challenge Award" presented to Alex Tagliani as the non-rookie with the highest points total.

Never viewing their Team KOOL Green Indy Lights program and ancillary support programs for Indy Lights and the KOOL/Toyota Atlantic Championship as substantially different, KOOL considers all involvement as part of an integrated American driver development program. The Team KOOL Green sponsorship is a direct sponsorship of American driving talent providing a stepping stone for that talent to rise into Indy car racing, whereas sponsorship of Atlantics and involvement in Indy Lights contingency programs is a broad-brush approach of supporting two series that have as their objective developing drivers for the future of Indy car racing. Different elements – but all part of the driver development vision and methodology.

KOOL's multi-faceted sponsorship program extended into numerous innovative awards and incentives for both the Indy Lights and the KOOL/Toyota Atlantic series.

TEAM GREEN ACADEMY

P ERHAPS the most innovative element of the driver development initiative is Team Green's own Team Green Academy. Team Green owner Barry Green has long been known for his ability to develop some of racing's finest young talents including Michael Andretti and Jacques Villeneuve. Working in concert with Derek Daly SpeedCentre (DDS) driving school, the Team Green Academy identifies 25 of America's most promising racing drivers from a variety of disciplines and invites them to participate in a comprehensive training and development program at the Las Vegas Motor Speedway. Five finalists are then selected from the initial group for a final competition with the outstanding talent selected for ongoing support from the Academy in the subsequent racing season, including financial backing from KOOL and coaching and tutoring support from DDS.

The Class of '97 saw drivers Matt Sielsky and Jeff Shafer selected to drive KOOL-sponsored cars in the U.S. National Formula Ford 2000 Championship. Sielsky earned 4 poles and finished second in the championship, while Shafer won the Phoenix round of the series as well as one pole position and finished 12th in the points race.

Above: Jeff Shafer (foreground) and Matt Sielsky, Team Green Academy graduates, were selected to drive in the U.S. National Formula Ford 2000 Championship with KOOL sponsorship support.

Sielsky (left) finished second in the championship.

Below: The final five. New racing talent chosen by the Team Green Academy pose with Parker Johnstone and the Team KOOL Green Reynard–Honda.

The Team Green Academy is a fresh and unique approach to grassroots development of open-wheel drivers in the United States. The program includes advanced on-track driving training and evaluation, technical training, physical and mental evaluation by Human Performance International (HPI) in Daytona Beach, Florida, and media training conducted by Aviva Diamond.

"There's a huge reservoir of driving talent in this country," Barry Green says. "But due to the tremendous diversity in the sport, developing drivers have a tough time making a name for themselves, because team owners face a difficult task of identifying new talent. The goal of the Team Green Academy is to support the development of American driving talent for the benefit not only of the drivers and Team Green, but also for the benefit of motor racing in general."

Four-time Indy car champion and former F1 titleist Mario Andretti lauds Green's efforts, "I have never seen as comprehensive a driver development program. Team Green and Derek Daly will give a huge boost to the future of American motorsports. I applaud and support them."

BEHIND THE SCENES

K OOL entered into motorsports realizing there were a lot of other people participating in the sport, many for quite some time. Responding to the challenge of "How do we get noticed?" KOOL focused on doing new and innovative things.

One of KOOL's most visible trackside presences during the past two seasons has been the Reporter's Club, a full service motorcoach facility for use by the writers and photographers who cover the CART, Indy Lights and Atlantic series. The coach has work stations, meeting rooms, telephones, fax and copy machines as well as computers with access to Speednet Pro available to working journalists. Breakfast and lunch are served during the three day weekends at the track, and Sunday mornings feature the unique "Stars of Tomorrow" breakfasts in which drivers from the Indy Lights and Atlantics series, together with other rising stars, are invited to meet with the media.

"Sure, at the end of the day we're hoping to get exposure out of that," says Bert Kremer, Manager, Sponsorships for Brown & Williamson Tobacco. "But we don't expect every journalist who comes into the motorcoach to walk away and write an article about KOOL. What we would like to happen – and I think there's enough indication that it is happening – if we facilitate the job the media has to do, if we help them to do their job more effectively, then it helps grow the sport and we benefit too."

Above: Oasis of calm. Luxurious state-of-the-art meeting rooms allow for business meetings to be conducted away from the whirlwind of activity that is naturally a part of race weekends.

Top: The Elkhart Lake KOOL barbecue served host to many members of the racing community.

Left: Full media service available to journalists from within the KOOL motorcoach.

Another less apparent dimension to the KOOL Racing Program is symbolized by Brown & Williamson's state-of-the-art hospitality unit featuring meeting rooms, marble floors, hardwoods, 2 full bathrooms, a shower, a full commercial kitchen, a 12' x 12' deck, three 70" and one 50" built-in big screen televisions.

The hospitality unit is the centerpiece to KOOL's ability to utilize its racing program to enhance its business-to-business relationships with suppliers, retailers and other business partners. Less visible to the racing fan, but still an important aspect of a sponsorship program, KOOL again sought to break out of the pack. Looking around the paddock, they saw what was being done and decided to set a new benchmark.

Says Kremer, "Our trade program focuses objectively, on being better than anyone else in that paddock. Brown & Williamson and KOOL are first class and very quality-driven. So when we bring our VIP customers to an event, we want to ensure everyone walks away with an experience that clearly communicates a world-class image.

Above: KOOL hospitality area caters to VIP guests both in the open and under cover.

Left: Sunday morning means "Stars of Tomorrow" at the Reporter's Club.

RISING ABOVE
THE CROWD

T HE newest and most unique element to the KCOL Racing Program has been the 1997 KCOL Balloon. At 10 races throughout the United States, balloons entered by approximately 20 corporate sponsors, from a range of industries, competed for a total of $120,000 in seasonal prize funds.

Working to devise promotion programs that would help KCOL "surround" the series, the awesome 15 story tall KCOL Indy car balloon and the KCOL Balloon Racing Series was yet another interesting way to do something fun and innovative and something that had not existed in CART in any way, shape or form.

Indeed, one could say much the same thing about the whole KCOL Racing Program. From the PPG CART World Series to the PPG Firestone Indy Lights Championship, KCOL/Toyota Atlantic Championship, Team Green Academy to the contingency awards, KCOL Reporter's Club, KCOL Balloon Racing Series and its many supporting programs, KCOL's racing effort is arguably the most ambitious sponsorship and marketing program ever seen in American open-wheel racing.

OTHER MAJOR RESULTS

Compiled by David Hayhoe

International Formula 3000 Championship

1996 Results

Kenny Bräck's appeal was rejected, confirming his disqualification from Hockenheim and Jörg Müller winning the championship.

1997 Results

All cars are Lola T96/50-Zytek Judd.

AUTOSPORT INTERNATIONAL TROPHY, Silverstone Grand Prix Circuit, Towcester, Northamptonshire, Great Britain, 11 May. Round 1. 40 laps of the 3.194-mile/5.140-km circuit, 127.903 miles/205.840 km.
1 Tom Kristensen, DK, 1h 21m 22.689s, 94.299 mph/151.760 km/h.
2 Pedro Couceiro, P, 1h 21m 27.037s; 3 Jamie Davies, GB, 1h 21m 27.289s; 4 Jason Watt, DK, 1h 21m 30.381s; 5 Dino Morelli, GB, 1h 21m 31.896s; 6 Patrick Lemarié, F, 1h 21m 32.730s; 7 Cyrille Sauvage, F, 1h 21m 33.368s; 8 Oliver Tichy, A, 1h 21m 40.515s; 9 Jean-Philippe Belloc, F, 1h 21m 53.151s; 10 Gaston Mazzacane, RA, 1h 21m 58.156s; 11 Werner Lupberger, ZA, 1h 22m 14.977s; 12 Boris Derichebourg, F, 1h 22m 27.069s; 13 Marc Gene, E, 1h 22m 53.583s; 14 Craig Lowndes, AUS, 39 laps; 15 Stephen Watson, ZA, 39; 16 Christian Horner, GB, 39; 17 Soheil Ayari, F, 29 (DNF – accident); 18 Laurent Redon, F, 27 (DNF – handling); 19 Juan-Pablo Montoya, CO, 20 (DNF – accident damage); 20 Max Wilson, BR, 19 (DNF – spin); 21 Gareth Rees, GB, 11 (DNF – accident); 22 Rui Aguas, P, 7 (DNF – spin); 23 David Cook, GB, 0 (DNF – accident); 24 Anthony Beltoise, F, 0 (DNF – accident); 25 Fabrizio Gollin, I, 0 (DNF – accident).
Ricardo Zonta, BR, finished 1st in 1h 21m 15.501s, 99.442 mph/151.990 km/h, but was disqualified the following month for gearbox irregularities.
Fastest race lap: Gene, 1m 53.745s, 101.084 mph/162.680 km/h.
Fastest qualifying lap: Zonta, 1m 40.463s, 114.449 mph/184.187 km/h.
Did not qualify:
Markus Freisacher, A; Thomas Biagi, I; Grégoire de Galzain, F; Oliver Gavin, GB; Gonzalo Rodriguez, U; Emiliano Spataro, I; Thomas Schie, N.
Did not start: Kurt Mollekens, B (excluded for not attending a drivers' briefing).
Championship points: 1 Zonta, 10; 2 Kristensen, 6; 3 Couceiro, 4; 4 Davies, 3; 5 Watt, 2; 6 Morelli, 1.

57th GRAND PRIX AUTOMOBILE DE PAU, Circuit de Pau, France, 19 May. Round 2. 75 laps of the 1.715-mile/2.760-km circuit, 128.624 miles/207.000 km.
1 Juan-Pablo Montoya, CO, 1h 32m 44.230s, 83.218 mph/133.927 km/h.
2 Tom Kristensen, DK, 1h 33m 19.303s; 3 Jamie Davies, GB, 1h 33m 21.430s; 4 Laurent Redon, F, 1h 33m 32.085s; 5 Cyrille Sauvage, F, 1h 33m 32.792s; 6 Soheil Ayari, F, 1h 33m 53.950s; 7 Max Wilson, BR, 1h 33m 56.122s; 8 Oliver Tichy, A, 1h 33m 59.367s; 9 Rui Aguas, P, 74 laps; 10 Kurt Mollekens, B, 74; 11 Dino Morelli, GB, 74; 12 Jason Watt, DK, 74; 13 Patrick Lemarié, F, 74; 14 Thomas Schie, N, 74; 15 Boris Derichebourg, F, 74; 16 Gareth Rees, GB, 57 (DNF – accident); 17 Fabrizio Gollin, I, 45 (DNF – steering); 18 Craig Lowndes, AUS, 39 (DNF – accident); 19 Anthony Beltoise, F, 37 (DNF – steering); 20 Jean-Philippe Belloc, F, 15 (DNF – accident); 21 Pedro Couceiro, P, 2 (DNF – accident); 22 Ricardo Zonta, BR, 2 (DNF – accident).
Did not qualify:
David Cook, GB; Gaston Mazzacane, RA; Stephen Watson, ZA; Marc Gene, E; Werner Lupberger, ZA; Markus Freisacher, A; Christian Horner, GB; Thomas Biagi, I; Oliver Gavin, GB; Emiliano Spataro, I; Grégoire de Galzain, F.
Fastest race lap: Montoya, 1m 12.697s, 84.927 mph/136.677 km/h.
Fastest qualifying lap: Montoya, 1m 12.607s, 85.032 mph/136.846 km/h.
Championship points: 1 Kristensen, 12; 2= Zonta, 10; 2= Montoya, 10; 4 Davies, 7; 5 Couceiro, 4; 6 Redon, 3.

FIA INTERNATIONAL FORMULA 3000 CHAMPIONSHIP, Grand Prix Center of Helsinki, Finland, 25 May. Round 3. 65 laps of the 1.976-mile/3.180-km circuit, 128.437 miles/206.700 km.
1 Soheil Ayari, F, 1h 38m 32.881s, 78.198 mph/125.847 km/h.
2 Oliver Tichy, A, 1h 38m 52.205s; 3 Dino Morelli, GB, 1h 38m 57.056s; 4 Patrick Lemarié, F, 1h 38m 59.256s; 5 Rui Aguas, P, 1h 39m 40.160s; 6 Stephen Watson, ZA, 1h 39m 56.579s; 7 David Cook, GB, 64 laps; 8 Boris Derichebourg, F, 64; 9 Anthony Beltoise, F, 63; 10 Gareth Rees, GB, 56 (DNF – accident); 11 Gaston Mazzacane, RA, 55 (DNF – accident); 12 Laurent Redon, F, 21 (DNF – accident); 13 Fabrizio Gollin, I, 21 (DNF – accident); 14 Tom Kristensen, DK, 17 (DNF – accident); 15 Gonzalo Rodriguez, U, 17 (DNF – accident); 16 Max Wilson, BR, 17 (DNF – accident); 17 Kurt Mollekens, B, 15 (DNF – accident); 18 Jamie Davies, GB, 12 (DNF – accident); 19 Craig Lowndes, AUS, 12 (DNF – driveshaft); 20 Jean-Philippe Belloc, F, 9 (DNF – spin); 21 Pedro Couceiro, P, 6 (DNF – accident); 22 Juan-Pablo Montoya, CO, 5 (DNF – accident); 23 Ricardo Zonta, BR, 1 (DNF – accident); 24 Cyrille Sauvage, F, 0 (DNF – accident).
Fastest race lap: Montoya, 1m 25.466s, 83.231 mph/133.948 km/h.
Fastest qualifying lap: Montoya, 1m 23.968s, 84.716 mph/136.338 km/h.
Did not start: Jason Watt, DK (accident during qualifying).
Did not qualify: Thomas Schie, N; Emiliano Spataro, I; Markus Freisacher, A; Christian Horner, GB; Werner Lupberger, ZA; Thomas Biagi, I; Grégoire de Galzain, F; Oliver Gavin, GB.
Championship points: 1 Kristensen, 12; 2 Ayari, 11; 3= Montoya, 10; 3= Zonta, 10; 5 Davies, 7; 6 Tichy, 6.

FIA INTERNATIONAL FORMULA 3000 CHAMPIONSHIP, Nürburgring, Nürburg/Eifel, Germany, 29 June. Round 4. 4 laps of the 2.831-mile/4.556-km circuit, 11.324 miles/18.224 km.
Stopped prematurely due to torrential rain. Half points awarded.
1 Ricardo Zonta, BR, 7m 57.334s, 85.403 mph/137.444 km/h.
2 Jason Watt, DK, 7m 59.522s; 3 Tom Kristensen, DK, 8m 02.206s; 4 Juan-Pablo Montoya, CO, 8m 15.156s; 5 Max Wilson, BR, 8m 16.667s; 6 Gonzalo Rodriguez, U, 8m 18.057s; 7 Rui Aguas, P, 8m 18.997s; 8 Jamie Davies, GB, 8m 22.697s; 9 Oliver Tichy, A, 8m 24.572s; 10 Gaston Mazzacane, RA, 8m 29.369s; 11 Emiliano Spataro, I, 8m 33.218s; 12 Emmanuel Clérico, F, 8m 41.312s; 13 Patrick Lemarié, F, 8m 51.764s; 14 Anthony Beltoise, F, 8m 52.178s; 15 Pedro Couceiro, P, 8m 52.517s; 16 Stephen Watson, ZA, 8m 52.741s; 17 Grégoire de Galzain, F, 8m 58.693s; 18 Werner Lupberger, ZA, 8m 59.836s; 19 Soheil Ayari, F, 9m 00.338s; 20 Jean-Philippe Belloc, F, 9m 00.938s; 21 Laurent Redon, F, 9m 40.440s; 22 Gareth Rees, GB, 3 laps (DNF – accident); 23 Cyrille Sauvage, F, 3 (DNF – accident); 24 Dino Morelli, GB, 3 (DNF – accident); 25 Craig Lowndes, AUS, 3 (DNF – spin); 26 Boris Derichebourg, F, 1 (DNF – gear linkage).
Fastest race lap: Zonta, 1m 56.523s, 87.463 mph/140.758 km/h.
Fastest qualifying lap: Zonta, 1m 31.294s, 111.634 mph/179.657 km/h.
Did not qualify: Thomas Biagi, I; Thomas Schie, N; Markus Freisacher, A; David Cook, GB; Marc Gene, E; Kurt Mollekens, B; Christian Horner, GB; James Taylor, GB.
Championship points: 1 Kristensen, 18; 2 Montoya, 11.5; 3 Ayari, 11; 4 Davies, 8; 5= Tichy, 6; 5= Morelli, 6; 5= Couceiro, 6; 5= Watt, 6.

35th GRAN PREMIO del MEDITERRANEO, Ente Autodromo di Pergusa, Enna-Pergusa, Sicily, Italy, 20 July. Round 5. 41 laps of the 3.076-mile/4.950-km circuit, 126.107 miles/202.950 km.
1 Jamie Davies, GB, 1h 04m 48.310s, 116.757 mph/187.902 km/h.
2 Ricardo Zonta, BR, 1h 05m 12.572s; 3 Max Wilson, BR, 1h 05m 20.311s; 4 Craig Lowndes, AUS, 1h 05m 21.297s; 5 Kurt Mollekens, B, 1h 05m 30.141s; 6 Laurent Redon, F, 1h 05m 36.323s; 7 Stephen Watson, ZA, 1h 05m 45.169s; 8 Cyrille Sauvage, F, 1h 06m 22.203s; 9 Boris Derichebourg, F, 1h 06m 24.329s; 10 Marc Gene, E, 40 laps (DNF – spin); 11 Juan-Pablo Montoya, CO, 40; 12 Anthony Beltoise, F, 40; 13 Emiliano Spataro, I, 40; 14 Thomas Biagi, I, 40; 15 Gaston Mazzacane, RA, 40; 16 Gareth Rees, GB, 40; 17 Markus Freisacher, A, 40; 18 Soheil Ayari, F, 22 (DNF – accident); 19 David Cook, GB, 21 (DNF – accident); 20 Tom Kristensen, DK, 17 (DNF – accident); 21 Gonzalo Rodriguez, U, 14 (DNF – accident); 22 Grégoire de Galzain, F, 9 (DNF – accident); 23 Werner Lupberger, ZA, 5 (DNF – accident); 24 Oliver Tichy, A, 5 (DNF – accident); 25 Jason Watt, DK, 0 (DNF – accident); 26 Rui Aguas, P, 0 (DNF – accident).
Fastest race lap: Davies, 1m 33.500s, 118.426 mph/190.588 km/h.
Fastest qualifying lap: Davies, 1m 32.846s, 119.260 mph/191.931 km/h.
Did not start: Pedro Couceiro, P (accident in warm-up).
Did not qualify:
Thomas Schie, N; James Taylor, GB; Christian Horner, GB.
Championship points: 1= Kristensen, 18; 1= Davies, 18; 3 Montoya, 11.5; 4= Ayari, 11; 4= Zonta, 11; 6= Tichy, 6; 6= Morelli, 6; 6= Couceiro, 6; 6= Watt, 6.

FIA INTERNATIONAL FORMULA 3000 CHAMPIONSHIP, Hockenheimring, Heidelberg, Germany, 26 July. Round 6. 31 laps of the 4.240-mile/6.823-km circuit, 131.428 miles/211.513 km.
1 Ricardo Zonta, BR, 1h 04m 33.262s, 122.156 mph/196.591 km/h.
2 Max Wilson, BR, 1h 04m 36.688s; 3 Jamie Davies, GB, 1h 04m 38.694s; 4 Jason Watt, DK, 1h 04m 46.683s; 5 Juan-Pablo Montoya, CO, 1h 04m 52.926s; 6 Kurt Mollekens, B, 1h 05m 21.671s; 7 Oliver Tichy, A, 1h 05m 23.644s; 8 Marc Gene, E, 1h 05m 24.039s; 9 Grégoire de Galzain, F, 1h 05m 25.629s; 10 Gaston Mazzacane, RA, 1h 05m 27.901s; 11 Gareth Rees, GB, 1h 05m 30.477s; 12 Stephen Watson, ZA, 1h 05m 30.969s; 13 Anthony Beltoise, F, 1h 05m 31.339s; 14 Werner Lupberger, ZA, 1h 05m 35.183s; 15 Thomas Schie, N, 1h 05m 41.377s; 16 Emiliano Spataro, I, 1h 05m 41.799s; 17 Gonzalo Rodriguez, U, 1h 05m 42.455s; 18 Thomas Biagi, I, 1h 05m 43.816s; 19 Laurent Redon, F, 28 laps (DNF – handling); 20 Pedro Couceiro, P, 16 (DNF – handling); 21 Soheil Ayari, F, 10 (DNF – spin); 22 Patrick Lemarié, F, 8 (DNF – accident); 23 Craig Lowndes, AUS, 3 (DNF – accident); 24 Cyrille Sauvage, F, 0 (DNF – spin); 25 Tom Kristensen, DK, 0 (DNF – accident).
Rui Aguas, P, completed 13 laps before being disqualified for dangerous driving.
Fastest race lap: Montoya, 2h 03.508s, 123.576 mph/198.876 km/h.
Fastest qualifying lap: Kristensen, 2m 01.579s, 125.537 mph/202.032 km/h.
Did not qualify:
Boris Derichebourg, F; Markus Freisacher, A; Christian Horner, GB; David Cook, GB; James Taylor, GB.
Championship points: 1 Davies, 22; 2 Zonta, 21; 3 Kristensen, 18; 4 Montoya, 13.5; 5= Ayari, 11; 5= Wilson, 11.

FIA INTERNATIONAL FORMULA 3000 CHAMPIONSHIP, A1-Ring, Knittelfeld, Austria, 3 August. Round 7. 48 laps of the 2.684-mile/4.319-km circuit, 128.818 miles/207.312 km.
1 Juan-Pablo Montoya, CO, 1h 12m 39.794s, 106.369 mph/171.183 km/h.
2 Ricardo Zonta, BR, 1h 12m 40.263s; 3 Laurent Redon, F, 1h 13m 17.414s; 4 Rui Aguas, P, 1h 13m 21.284s; 5 Oliver Tichy, A, 1h 13m 22.944s; 6 Tom Kristensen, DK, 1h 13m 40.253s; 7 Gonzalo Rodriguez, U, 1h 13m 40.504s; 8 Max Wilson, BR, 1h 13m 43.165s; 9 Jamie Davies, GB, 1h 13m 48.256s; 10 Soheil Ayari, F, 1h 13m 54.334s; 11 Pedro Couceiro, P, 47 laps; 12 Emiliano Spataro, I, 47; 13 Boris Derichebourg, F, 47; 14 David Cook, GB, 47; 15 Grégoire de Galzain, F, 47; 16 Christian Horner, GB, 47; 17 Gaston Mazzacane, RA, 46; 18 Werner Lupberger, ZA, 21 (DNF – gearbox); 19 Cyrille Sauvage, F, 21 (DNF – spin); 20 Thomas Biagi, I, 0 (DNF – accident); 21 Jason Watt, DK, 0 (DNF – accident); 22 Craig Lowndes, AUS, 0 (DNF – accident); 23 Kurt Mollekens, B, 0 (DNF – accident); 24 Anthony Beltoise, F, 0 (DNF – accident); 25 Gareth Rees, GB, 0 (DNF – accident); 26 Stephen Watson, ZA, 0 (DNF – accident).
Fastest race lap: Zonta, 1m 24.161s, 114.796 mph/184.746 km/h.
Fastest qualifying lap: Montoya, 1m 24.225s, 114.709 mph/184.606 km/h.
Did not qualify:
Thomas Schie, N; Markus Freisacher, A; James Taylor, GB; Mario Waltner, A.
Championship points: 1 Zonta, 27; 2 Montoya, 23.5; 3 Davies, 22; 4 Kristensen, 19; 5= Ayari, 11; 5= Wilson, 11.

FIA INTERNATIONAL FORMULA 3000 CHAMPIONSHIP, Circuit de Spa-Francorchamps, Stavelot, Belgium, 23 August. Round 8. 29 laps of the 4.330-mile/6.968-km circuit, 125.562 miles/202.072 km.
1 Jason Watt, DK, 1h 05m 19.036s, 115.331 mph/185.608 km/h.
2 Max Wilson, BR, 1h 05m 19.322s; 3 Boris Derichebourg, F, 1h 05m 39.915s; 4 Cyrille Sauvage, F, 1h 05m 40.995s; 5 Ricardo Zonta, BR, 1h 05m 49.462s; 6 Stephen Watson, ZA, 1h 05m 51.693s; 7 Pedro Couceiro, P, 1h 05m 51.882s; 8 Jamie Davies, GB, 1h 05m 52.097s; 9 Rui Aguas, P, 1h 05m 59.062s; 10 Thomas Schie, N, 1h 06m 02.405s; 11 Gaston Mazzacane, RA, 1h 06m 03.721s; 12 James Taylor, GB, 1h 06m 34.479s; 13 Werner Lupberger, ZA, 28 laps; 14 Laurent Redon, F, 27; 15 Oliver Tichy, A, 19 (DNF – handling); 16 Gareth Rees, GB, 10 (DNF – accident); 17 Grégoire de Galzain, F, 9 (DNF – clutch); 18 Soheil Ayari, F, 8 (DNF – wing); 19 Markus Freisacher, A, 1 (DNF – accident); 20 Craig Lowndes, AUS, 1 (DNF – accident); 21 Tom Kristensen, DK, 0 (DNF – accident); 22 Emiliano Spataro, I, 0 (DNF – accident); 23 Kurt Mollekens, B, 0 (DNF – accident); 24 David Cook, GB, 0 (DNF – accident); 25 Thomas Biagi, I, 0 (DNF – accident).
Juan-Pablo Montoya, CO, completed 12 laps before being disqualified for holding up the field with his damaged car.
Fastest race lap: Aguas, 2m 13.517s, 116.741 mph/187.877 km/h.
Fastest qualifying lap: Krtistensen, 2m 29.405s, 104.327 mph/167.898 km/h.
Did not qualify: Christian Horner, GB; Maro Waltner, A.
Championship points: 1 Zonta, 29; 2 Montoya, 23.5; 3 Davies, 22; 4= Watt, 19; 4= Kristensen, 19; 6 Wilson, 17.

FIA INTERNATIONAL FORMULA 3000 CHAMPIONSHIP, Autodromo Internazionale del Mugello, Scarperia, Firenze (Florence), Italy, 28 September. Round 9. 40 laps of the 3.259-mile/5.245-km circuit, 130.364 miles/209.800 km.
1 Ricardo Zonta, BR, 1h 09m 03.576s, 113.262 mph/182.277 km/h.
2 Jason Watt, DK, 1h 09m 19.080s; 3 Juan-Pablo Montoya, CO, 1h 09m 20.956s; 4 Max Wilson, BR, 1h 09m 34.793s; 5 Laurent Redon, F, 1h 09m 34.919s; 6 Soheil Ayari, F, 1h 09m 39.608s; 7 Gareth Rees, GB, 1h 09m 42.329s; 8 Gonzalo Rodriguez, U, 1h 09m 44.943s; 9 Cyrille Sauvage, F, 1h 09m 47.630s; 10 Gaston Mazzacane, RA, 1h 09m 56.141s; 11 Werner Lupberger, ZA, 1h 10m 00.129s; 12 Rui Aguas, P, 1h 10m 04.587s; 13 Fabrizio Gollin, I, 1h 10m 21.219s; 14 Patrick Lemarié, F, 1h 10m 22.501s; 15 Stephen Watson, ZA, 1h 10m 22.687s; 16 Thomas Biagi, I, 1h 10m 27.250s; 17 Christian Horner, GB, 1h 10m 29.403s; 18 Thomas Schie, N, 1h 10m 45.464s; 19 Markus Freisacher, A, 39 laps; 20 Gianluca Paglicci, I, 39; 21 Craig Lowndes, AUS, 39; 22 Boris Derichebourg, F, 38; 23 David Cook, GB, 14 (DNF – spin); 24 Kurt Mollekens, B, 8 (DNF – fuel pressure); 25 Emiliano Spataro, I, 3 (DNF – accident); 26 Pedro Couceiro, P, 2 (DNF – throttle).
Fastest race lap: Zonta, 1m 42.448s, 114.524 mph/184.308 km/h.
Fastest qualifying lap: Zonta, 1m 40.372s, 116.892 mph/188.120 km/h.
Did not start: Tom Kristensen, DK (excluded – illegal spacer fitted); Jamie Davies, GB, (excluded – missed drivers' briefing); Grégoire de Galzain, F (excluded – missed drivers' briefing).
Did not qualify: James Taylor, GB.
Championship points: 1 Zonta, 39; 2 Montoya, 27.5; 3 Watt, 25; 4 Davies, 22; 5 Wilson, 20; 6 Kristensen, 19.

FIA INTERNATIONAL FORMULA 3000 CHAMPIONSHIP, Circuito de Jerez, Spain, 25 October. Round 10. 44 laps of the 2.751-mile/4.428-km circuit, 121.063 miles/194.832 km.
1 Juan-Pablo Montoya, CO, 1h 13m 47.224s, 98.442 mph/158.428 km/h.
2 Oliver Tichy, A, 1h 14m 13.144s; 3 Gareth Rees, GB, 1h 14m 18.272s; 4 Werner Lupberger, ZA, 1h 14m 30.585s; 5 Rui Aguas, P, 1h 14m 36.630s; 6 Christian Horner, GB, 1h 14m 45.683s; 7 David Cook, GB, 1h 15m 02.843s; 8 Grégoire de Galzain, F, 1h 15m 07.814s; 9 Craig Lowndes, AUS, 43 laps; 10 Max Wilson, BR, 43; 11 Laurent Redon, F, 43; 12 Thomas Biagi, I, 43; 13 Kurt Mollekens, B, 39 (DNF – fuel pressure); 14 Soheil Ayari, F, 36 (DNF – accident); 15 Boris Derichebourg, F, 35 (DNF – accident); 16 Gonzalo Rodriguez, U, 33 (DNF – accident); 17 Marc Gene, E, 28 (DNF – accident); 18 Stephen Watson, ZA, 5 (DNF – spin); 19 Ricardo Zonta, BR, 4 (DNF – spin); 20 Tom Kristensen, DK, 4 (DNF – accident); 21 Jason Watt, DK, 4 (DNF – accident); 22 Gaston Mazzacane, RA, 4 (DNF – spin); 23 Pedro Couceiro, P, 4 (DNF – accident); 24 Thomas Schie, N, 4 (DNF – accident); 25 Jamie Davies, GB, 0 (DNF – driveshaft).
Cyrille Sauvage, F, finished 2nd in 1h 13m 52.493s, but was excluded because a member of his team entered parc fermé after the race.

Fastest race lap: Zonta, 1m 39.010s, 100.042 mph/161.001 km/h.
Fastest qualifying lap: Zonta, 1m 36.473s, 102.673 mph/165.236 km/h.
Did not qualify: Patrick Lemarié, F; Markus Freisacher, A; Miguel Angel de Castro, E; James Taylor, GB.

Final championship points
1 Ricardo Zonta, BR, 39; **2** Juan-Pablo Montoya, CO, 37.5; **3** Jason Watt, DK, 25; **4** Jamie Davies, GB, 22; **5** Max Wilson, BR, 21; **6** Tom Kristensen, DK, 19; **7** Oliver Tichy, A, 14; **8** Soheil Ayari, F, 12; **9** Laurent Redon, F, 10; **10** Rui Aguas, P, 7; **11=** Pedro Couceiro, P, 6; **11=** Dino Morelli, GB, 6; **13** Cyrille Sauvage, F, 5; **14=** Boris Derichebourg, F, 4; **14=** Patrick Lemarié, F, 4; **14=** Gareth Rees, GB, 4; **17=** Craig Lowndes, AUS, 3; **17=** Kurt Mollekens, B, 3; **17=** Werner Lupberger, ZA, 3; **20** Stephen Watson, ZA, 2; **21** Christian Horner, GB, 1.

FIA International Touring Car Series (ITC)

1996 Results

The two Suzuka races were run after Autocourse 1996/97 *went to press.*

FIA INTERNATIONAL TOURING CAR SERIES, Suzuka International Racing Course, Suzuka City, Mie-Ken, Japan, 10 November. 2 x 18 laps of the 3.644-mile/5.864-km circuit.
Round 25 (65.587 miles/105.552 km)
1 Dario Franchitti, GB (AMG Mercedes C-Klasse), 38m 23.290s, 102.511 mph/164.976 km/h.
2 Christian Danner, D (Alfa Romeo 155 V6 Ti), 38m 25.628s; **3** Bernd Schneider, D (AMG Mercedes C-Klasse), 38m 26.052s; **4** Giancarlo Fisichella, I (Alfa Romeo 155 V6 Ti), 38m 26.221s; **5** Stefano Modena, I (Alfa Romeo 155 V6 Ti), 38m 26.711s; **6** Nicola Larini, I (Alfa Romeo 155 V6 Ti), 38m 28.725s; **7** Jan Magnussen, DK (AMG Mercedes C-Klasse), 38m 29.176s; **8** Bernd Mayländer, D (AMG Mercedes C-Klasse), 38m 31.081s; **9** Uwe Alzen, D (Opel Calibra V6), 38m 32.715s; **10** Alessandro Nannini, I (Alfa Romeo 155 V6 Ti), 38m 38.067s.
Fastest race lap: Danner, 2m 05.278s, 104.706 mph/168.508 km/h.
Fastest qualifying lap: Danner, 2m 02.737s, 106.874 mph/171.997 km/h.

Round 26 (65.587 miles/105.552 km)
1 Bernd Schneider, D (AMG Mercedes C-Klasse), 37m 43.447s, 104.316 mph/167.880 km/h.
2 Giancarlo Fisichella, I (Alfa Romeo 155 V6 Ti), 38m 02.497s; **3** Jan Magnussen, DK (AMG Mercedes C-Klasse), 38m 03.044s; **4** Stefano Modena, I (Alfa Romeo 155 V6 Ti), 38m 11.604s; **5** Alessandro Nannini, I (Alfa Romeo 155 V6 Ti), 38m 11.674s; **6** Nicola Larini, I (Alfa Romeo 155 V6 Ti), 38m 11.676s; **7** Christian Danner, D (Alfa Romeo 155 V6 Ti), 38m 19.470s; **8** JJ Lehto, SF (Opel Calibra V6), 38m 21.325s; **9** Yannick Dalmas, F (Opel Calibra V6), 38m 28.566s; **10** Klaus Ludwig, D (Opel Calibra V6), 38m 28.944s.
Fastest race lap: Schneider, 2m 03.886s, 105.883 mph/170.402 km/h.

Final championship points
Drivers
1 Manuel Reuter, D, 218; **2** Bernd Schneider, D, 205; **3** Alessandro Nannini, I, 180; **4** Dario Franchitti, GB, 171; **5** JJ Lehto, SF, 148; **6** Giancarlo Fisichella, I, 139; **7** Klaus Ludwig, D, 130; **8** Uwe Alzen, D, 119; **9** Hans-Joachim Stuck, D, 112; **10** Jan Magnussen, DK, 97; **11** Nicola Larini, I, 95; **12** Stefano Modena, I, 92; **13** Jörg van Ommen, D, 87; **14** Gabriele Tarquini, I, 60; **15** Christian Danner, D, 48; **16** Alexander 'Alex' Wurz, A, 43; **17** Yannick Dalmas, F, 33; **18** Kurt Thiim, DK, 22; **19=** Bernd Mayländer, D, 17; **19=** Jason Watt, DK, 17; **19=** Max Wilson, BR, 17; **22=** Michael Bartels, D, 16; **22=** Oliver Gavin, GB, 16; **22=** Alexander 'Sandy' Grau, D, 16; **25** Ellen Lohr, D, 7; **26** Christian Fittipaldi, BR, 1.

Manufacturers
1 Opel, 349; **2** Alfa Romeo, 340; **3** Mercedes-Benz, 305.

British Formula 3 Championship

AUTOSPORT BRITISH FORMULA 3 CHAMPIONSHIP, Donington Park Grand Prix Circuit, Derbyshire, Great Britain, 23 March. Round 1. 20 laps of the 2.500-mile/4.023-km circuit, 50.000 miles/80.467 km.
1 Jonny Kane, GB (Dallara F397-Mugen Honda), 29m 57.893s, 100.117 mph/161.123 km/h.
2 Guy Smith, GB (Dallara F397-Opel), 30m 06.602s; **3** Enrique Bernoldi, BR (Dallara F397-Renault), 30m 06.871s; **4** Nicolas Minassian, F (Dallara F397-Renault), 30m 07.173s; **5** Peter Dumbreck, GB (Dallara F397-Mugen Honda), 30m 19.059s; **6** Mark Webber, AUS (Dallara F397-Mugen Honda), 30m 20.336s; **7** Kevin McGarrity, GB (TOM'S 037F-Toyota), 30m 20.601s; **8** Simon Wills, NZ (Dallara F397-Opel), 30m 25.195s; **9** Mario Haberfeld, BR (Dallara F397-Opel), 30m 26.494s; **10** Darren Manning, GB (Dallara F396-Mugen Honda), 30m 29.242s.
Fastest race lap: Kane, 1m 29.130s, 100.976 mph/162.505 km/h.
National Class winner: Martin O'Connell, GB (Dallara F395/6-TOM'S Toyota), 4 laps (DNF).
Fastest qualifying lap: Smith (Guy), 1m 41.842s, 88.372 mph/142.221 km/h.
Championship points. 1 Kane, 20; **2** Smith (Guy), 15; **3** Bernoldi, 12; **4** Minassian, 10; **5** Dumbreck, 8; **6** Webber, 6.

AUTOSPORT BRITISH FORMULA 3 CHAMPIONSHIP, Silverstone International Circuit, Towcester, Northamptonshire, Great Britain, 6 April. Round 2. 17 laps of the 2.252-mile/3.624-km circuit, 38.331 miles/61.688 km.
1 Nicolas Minassian, F (Dallara F397-Renault), 21m 26.364s, 107.273 mph/172.639 km/h.
2 Peter Dumbreck, GB (Dallara F397-Mugen Honda), 21m 30.666s; **3** Jonny Kane, GB (Dallara F397-Mugen Honda), 21m 34.324s; **4** Darren Manning, GB (Dallara F396-Mugen Honda), 21m 34.748s; **5** Ben Collins, GB (Dallara F397-HKS Mitsubishi), 21m 39.145s; **6** Mark Webber, AUS (Dallara F397-Mugen Honda), 21m 41.923s; **7** Brian Smith, RA (Dallara F397-HKS Mitsubishi), 21m 45.195s; **8** Giovanni Anapoli, I (TOM'S 037F-Toyota), 21m 45.571s; **9** Mark Shaw, GB (Dallara F397-Opel), 21m 50.790s; **10** Guy Smith, GB (Dallara F397-Opel), 21m 51.803s.
Fastest race lap: Minassian, 1m 14.929s, 108.191 mph/174.117 km/h.
National Class winner: Martin O'Connell, GB (Dallara F395/6-TOM'S Toyota), 0 laps (DNF).
Fastest qualifying lap: Minassian, 1m 14.145s, 109.335 mph/175.958 km/h.
Championship points. 1 Kane, 33; **2** Minassian, 31; **3** Dumbreck, 23; **4** Smith (Guy), 16; **5=** Bernoldi, 12; **5=** Webber, 12.

AUTOSPORT BRITISH FORMULA 3 CHAMPIONSHIP, Thruxton Circuit, Andover, Hampshire, Great Britain, 13 April. Round 3. 20 laps of the 2.356-mile/3.792-km circuit, 47.170 miles/75.832 km.
1 Jonny Kane, GB (Dallara F397-Mugen Honda), 23m 19.723s, 121.190 mph/195.036 km/h.
2 Martin O'Connell, GB (Dallara F396-TOM'S Toyota), 23m 25.382s (1st National Class); **3** Peter Dumbreck, GB (Dallara F397-Mugen Honda), 23m 27.817s; **4** Brian Smith, RA (Dallara F397-HKS Mitsubishi), 23m 33.201s; **5** Mark Shaw, GB (Dallara F397-Opel), 23m 43.221s; **6** Ricardo Mauricio, BR (Dallara F397-Mugen Honda), 23m 51.647s; **7** Mario Haberfeld, BR (Dallara F397-Opel), 23m 52.264s; **8** Ben Collins, GB (Dallara F397-HKS Mitsubishi), 23m 55.633s; **9** Simon Wills, NZ (Dallara F397-Opel), 23m 56.403s; **10** Guy Smith, GB (Dallara F397-Opel), 23m 56.506s.
Nicolas Minassian, F (Dallara F397-Renault), finished 2nd but was disqualified for forcing Bentwood off the track on the slowing-down lap.
Fastest race lap: Smith (Guy), 1m 09.063s, 122.810 mph/197.643 km/h.
Fastest qualifying lap: Minassian, 1m 08.252s, 124.269 mph/199.991 km/h.
Championship points. 1 Kane, 53; **2** Dumbreck, 38; **3** Minassian, 31; **4** Smith (Guy), 19; **5** Smith (Brian), 16; **6=** Bernoldi, 12; **6=** Webber, 12; **6=** Collins, 12. **National Class: 1** O'Connell, 22.

AUTOSPORT BRITISH FORMULA 3 CHAMPIONSHIP, Brands Hatch Grand Prix Circuit, Dartford, Kent, Great Britain, 27 April. Round 4. 20 laps of the 2.600-mile/4.184-km circuit, 52.000 miles/83.686 km.
1 Mark Webber, AUS (Dallara F397-Mugen Honda), 26m 17.607s, 118.661 mph/190.996 km/h.
2 Peter Dumbreck, GB (Dallara F397-Mugen Honda), 26m 19.561s; **3** Jonny Kane, GB (Dallara F397-Mugen Honda), 26m 35.212s; **4** Martin O'Connell, GB (Dallara F395-TOM'S Toyota), 26m 35.528s (1st National Class); **5** Mario Haberfeld, BR (Dallara F397-Opel), 26m 35.650s; **6** Ben Collins, GB (Dallara F397-HKS Mitsubishi), 26m 36.167s; **7** Brian Smith, RA (Dallara F397-HKS Mitsubishi), 26m 42.318s; **8** Guy Smith, GB (Dallara F397-Opel), 26m 43.467s; **9** Darren Manning, GB (Dallara F397-Renault), 27m 00.180s; **10** Michael Bentwood, GB (Dallara F397-Mugen Honda), 27m 02.670s.
Fastest race lap: Webber, 1m 18.085s, 119.869 mph/192.911 km/h.
Fastest qualifying lap: Webber, 1m 27.410s, 107.082 mph/172.331 km/h.
Championship points. 1 Kane, 65; **2** Dumbreck, 53; **3** Webber, 33; **4** Minassian, 31; **5** Smith (Guy), 23; **6** Smith (Brian), 22. **National Class: 1** O'Connell, 44.

AUTOSPORT BRITISH FORMULA 3 CHAMPIONSHIP, Silverstone Grand Prix Circuit, Towcester, Northamptonshire, Great Britain, 11 May. Round 5. 15 laps of the 3.194-mile/5.140-km circuit, 47.957 miles/77.179 km.
1 Jonny Kane, GB (Dallara F397-Mugen Honda), 29m 41.504s, 96.909 mph/155.961 km/h.
2 Martin O'Connell, GB (Dallara F396-TOM'S Toyota), 30m 06.697s (1st National Class); **3** Mario Haberfeld, BR (Dallara F397-Opel), 30m 10.428s; **4** Peter Dumbreck, GB (Dallara F397-Mugen Honda), 30m 23.871s; **5** Darren Manning, GB (Dallara F397-Renault), 30m 30.250s; **6** Enrique Bernoldi, BR (Dallara F397-Renault), 30m 32.690s; **7** Jamie Spence, GB (TOM'S 037F-Toyota), 30m 36.984s; **8** Mark Webber, AUS (Dallara F397-Mugen Honda), 30m 37.738s; **9** Simon Wills, NZ (Dallara F397-Opel), 30m 45.115s; **10** Andy Priaulx, GB (Dallara F396-Mugen Honda), 31m 04.669s.
Fastest race lap: Kane, 1m 56.561s, 98.642 mph/158.749 km.
Fastest qualifying lap: Webber, 1m 41.629s, 113.136 mph/182.074 km.
Championship points. 1 Kane, 86; **2** Dumbreck, 65; **3** Webber, 37; **4** Haberfeld, 33; **5** Minassian, 31; **6** Manning, 24. **National Class: 1** O'Connell, 65.

AUTOSPORT BRITISH FORMULA 3 CHAMPIONSHIP, Croft Circuit, North Yorkshire, Great Britain, 18 May. Round 6. 25 laps of the 2.100-mile/3.380-km circuit, 52.500 miles/84.491 km.
1 Nicolas Minassian, F (Dallara F397-Renault), 33m 50.671s, 93.073 mph/149.786 km/h.
2 Jonny Kane, GB (Dallara F397-Mugen Honda), 33m 51.378s; **3** Peter Dumbreck, GB (Dallara F397-Mugen Honda), 33m 51.854s; **4** Mark Webber, AUS (Dallara F397-Mugen Honda), 33m 58.573s; **5** Enrique Bernoldi, BR (Dallara F397-Renault), 34m 16.460s; **6** Martin O'Connell, GB (Dallara F396-TOM'S Toyota), 34m 17.082s (1st National Class); **7** Ben Collins, GB (Dallara F397-HKS Mitsubishi), 34m 18.511s; **8** Brian Smith, RA (Dallara F397-HKS Mitsubishi), 34m 25.137s; **9** Kevin McGarrity, GB (TOM'S 037F-Toyota), 34m 43.810s; **10** Simon Wills, NZ (Dallara F397-Opel), 34m 44.545s.
Fastest race lap: Dumbreck, 1m 19.548s, 95.037 mph/152.947 km/h.
Fastest qualifying lap: Kane, 1m 19.376s, 95.243 mph/153.279 km/h.
Championship points. 1 Kane, 101; **2** Dumbreck, 78; **3** Minassian, 51; **4** Webber, 47; **5** Haberfeld, 34; **6=** Smith (Brian), 26; **6=** Collins, 26. **National Class: 1** O'Connell, 85.

AUTOSPORT BRITISH FORMULA 3 CHAMPIONSHIP, Oulton Park International Circuit, Tarporley, Cheshire, Great Britain, 22 June. Round 7. 18 laps of the 2.775-mile/4.466-km circuit, 49.950 miles/80.387 km.
1 Peter Dumbreck, GB (Dallara F397-Mugen Honda), 31m 30.66s, 95.110 mph/153.064 km/h.
2 Ben Collins, GB (Dallara F397-HKS Mitsubishi), 31m 55.09s; **3** Kevin McGarrity, GB (TOM'S 037F-Toyota), 31m 56.87s; **4** Jonny Kane, GB (Dallara F397-Mugen Honda), 31m 57.01s; **5** Mario Haberfeld, BR (Dallara F397-Opel), 31m 57.62s; **6** Guy Smith, GB (Dallara F397-Opel), 31m 57.93s; **7** Brian Smith, RA (Dallara F397-HKS Mitsubishi), 31m 58.20s; **8** Mark Webber, AUS (Dallara F397-Mugen Honda), 32m 19.37s; **9** Mark Shaw, GB (Dallara F397-Opel), 32m 33.87s; **10** Paula Cook, GB (Dallara F397-Opel), 32m 49.77s.
Fastest race lap: Dumbreck, 1m 42.75s, 97.226 mph/156.471 km/h.
Fastest qualifying lap: Kane, 1m 39.973s, 99.927 mph/160.817 km/h.
Championship points. 1 Kane, 111; **2** Dumbreck, 99; **3** Minassian, 51; **4** Webber, 50; **5** Haberfeld, 42; **6** Collins, 41. **National Class: 1** O'Connell, 85.

AUTOSPORT BRITISH FORMULA 3 CHAMPIONSHIP, Silverstone Grand Prix Circuit, Towcester, Northamptonshire, Great Britain, 12 July. Round 8. 15 laps of the 3.194-mile/5.140-km circuit, 47.910 miles/77.104 km.
1 Mario Haberfeld, BR (Dallara F397-Opel), 26m 06.705s, 110.089 mph/177.171 km/h.
2 Mark Webber, AUS (Dallara F397-Mugen Honda), 26m 10.480s; **3** Nicolas Minassian, F (Dallara F397-Renault), 26m 13.356s; **4** Kevin McGarrity, GB (TOM'S 037F-Toyota), 26m 13.813s; **5** Brian Smith, RA (Dallara F397-HKS Mitsubishi), 26m 14.728s; **6** Guy Smith, GB (Dallara F397-Opel), 26m 15.855s; **7** Ricardo Mauricio, BR (TOM'S 037F-Toyota), 26m 20.710s; **8** Ben Collins, GB (Dallara F397-HKS Mitsubishi), 26m 23.373s; **9** Jamie Spence, GB (TOM'S 037F-Toyota), 26m 23.966s; **10** Enrique Bernoldi, BR (Dallara F397-Renault), 26m 24.334s.
Fastest race lap: Bernoldi, 1m 43.143s, 111.475 mph/179.401 km.
National Class winner: Martin O'Connell, GB (Dallara F396-TOM'S Toyota), 26m 42.897s (15th).
Fastest qualifying lap: Minassian, 1m 43.395s, 111.203 mph/178.964 km.
Championship points. 1 Kane, 111; **2** Dumbreck, 99; **3** Webber, 65; **4** Minassian, 63; **5** Haberfeld, 62; **6** Collins, 44. **National Class: 1** O'Connell, 106; **2** Jeremy Gumbley, GB, 15.

AUTOSPORT BRITISH FORMULA 3 CHAMPIONSHIP, Pembrey Circuit, Llanelli, Dyfed, Great Britain, 17 August. 20 and 12 laps of the 1.456-mile/2.343-km circuit.
Round 9 (29.120 miles/46.864 km)
1 Brian Smith, RA (Dallara F397-HKS Mitsubishi), 18m 50.673s, 92.716 mph/149.213 km/h.
2 Jonny Kane, GB (Dallara F397-Mugen Honda), 18m 51.427s; **3** Peter Dumbreck, GB (Dallara F397-Mugen Honda), 18m 52.221s; **4** Mark Webber, AUS (Dallara F397-Mugen Honda), 18m 54.859s; **5** Ricardo Mauricio, BR (TOM'S 037F-Toyota), 18m 55.745s; **6** Kevin McGarrity, GB (TOM'S 037F-Toyota), 18m 56.570s; **7** Paula Cook, GB (Dallara F397-Opel), 19m 02.114s; **8** Enrique Bernoldi, BR (Dallara F397-Renault), 19m 02.214s; **9** Mark Shaw, GB (Dallara F397-Opel), 19m 03.284s; **10** Haruki Kurosawa, J (Dallara F397-Mugen Honda), 19m 04.427s.
Fastest race lap: Smith (Brian), 50.079s, 104.667 mph/168.445 km/h.
National Class winner: Martin O'Connell, GB (Dallara F396-TOM'S Toyota), 0 laps (DNF – spin).
Fastest qualifying lap: Kane, 49.379s, 106.150 mph/170.832 km/h.

Round 10 (17.472 miles/28.118 km)
1 Nicolas Minassian, F (Dallara F397-Renault), 12m 35.579s, 83.246 mph/133.972 km/h.
2 Enrique Bernoldi, BR (Dallara F397-Renault), 12m 37.283s; **3** Mark Webber, AUS (Dallara F397-Mugen Honda), 12m 37.891s; **4** Mario Haberfeld, BR (Dallara F397-Opel), 12m 38.705s; **5** Martin O'Connell, GB (Dallara F396-TOM'S Toyota), 12m 40.436s (1st National Class); **6** Jonny Kane, GB (Dallara F397-Mugen Honda), 12m 40.890s; **7** Simon Wills, NZ (Dallara F397-Opel), 12m 41.479s; **8** Ben Collins, GB (Dallara F397-HKS Mitsubishi), 12m 41.821s; **9** Guy Smith, GB (Dallara F397-Opel), 12m 49.721s; **10** Brian Smith, RA (Dallara F397-HKS Mitsubishi), 12m 50.446s.
Fastest race lap: Minassian, 50.231s, 104.350 mph/167.935 km/h.
Fastest qualifying lap: Mauricio, 48.944s, 107.094 mph/172.351 km/h.
Championship points. 1 Kane, 134; **2** Dumbreck, 111; **3** Webber, 87; **4** Minassian, 84; **5** Haberfeld, 72; **6** Smith (Brian), 61. **National Class: 1** O'Connell, 127; **2** Gumbley, 15.

AUTOSPORT BRITISH FORMULA 3 CHAMPIONSHIP, Donington Park Club Circuit, Derbyshire, Great Britain, 24 August. Round 11. 20 laps of the 1.957-mile/3.150-km circuit, 39.140 miles/62.990 km.
1 Nicolas Minassian, F (Dallara F397-Renault), 24m 47.018s, 94.756 mph/152.495 km/h.
2 Jonny Kane, GB (Dallara F397-Mugen Honda), 24m 47.533s; **3** Martin O'Connell, GB (Dallara F396-TOM'S Toyota), 24m 47.610s (1st National Class); **4** Mark Webber, AUS (Dallara F397-Mugen Honda), 24m 48.790s; **5** Peter Dumbreck, GB (Dallara F397-Mugen Honda), 25m 07.129s; **6** Guy Smith, GB (Dallara F397-Opel), 25m 11.645s; **7** Brian Smith, RA (Dallara F397-HKS Mitsubishi), 25m 17.593s; **8** Enrique Bernoldi, BR (Dallara F397-Renault), 25m 19.168s; **9** Warren Hughes, GB (Dallara F397-HKS Mitsubishi), 25m 25.205s; **10** Henry Stanton, GB (Dallara F397-Mugen Honda), 25m 25.321s.
Fastest race lap: O'Connell, 1m 09.761s, 100.991 mph/162.528 km/h.
Fastest qualifying lap: Minassian, 1m 14.885s, 94.080 mph/151.407 km/h.
Championship points. 1 Kane, 149; **2** Dumbreck, 121; **3** Minassian, 104; **4** Webber, 99; **5** Haberfeld, 72; **6** Smith (Brian), 67. **National Class: 1** O'Connell, 148; **2** Gumbley, 15.

AUTOSPORT BRITISH FORMULA 3 CHAMPIONSHIP, Snetterton Circuit, Norfolk, Great Britain, 14 September. 2 x 20 laps of the 1.952-mile/3.141-km circuit.
Round 12 (39.040 miles/62.829 km)
1 Mario Haberfeld, BR (Dallara F397-Opel), 22m 18.388s, 105.010 mph/168.997 km/h.
2 Enrique Bernoldi, BR (Dallara F397-Renault), 22m 18.646s; **3** Jonny Kane, GB (Dallara F397-Mugen Honda), 22m 23.656s; **4** Nicolas Minassian, F (Dallara F397-Renault), 22m 25.391s; **5** Jamie Spence, GB (Dallara F397-Mugen Honda), 22m 30.000s; **6** Peter Dumbreck, GB (Dallara F397-Mugen Honda), 22m 30.313s; **7** Brian Smith, RA (Dallara F397-HKS Mitsubishi), 22m 30.794s; **8** Ricardo Mauricio, BR (TOM'S 037F-Toyota), 22m 31.681s; **9** Simon Wills, NZ (Dallara F397-Opel), 22m 32.483s; **10** Darren Turner, GB (TOM'S 037F-Toyota), 22m 33.441s.
Fastest race lap: Bernoldi, 1m 02.436s, 112.550 mph/181.132 km/h.
National Class winner: Damon Wellman, GB (Dallara F396-Mugen Honda), 23m 14.155s (15th).
Fastest qualifying lap: Haberfeld, 1m 02.111s, 113.139 mph/182.080 km/h.

Round 13 (39.040 miles/62.829 km)
1 Nicolas Minassian, F (Dallara F397-Renault), 21m 00.001s, 111.543 mph/179.511 km/h.
2 Jonny Kane, GB (Dallara F397-Mugen Honda), 21m 04.578s; **3** Enrique Bernoldi, BR (Dallara F397-Renault), 21m 05.578s; **4** Guy Smith, GB (Dallara F397-Opel), 21m 09.760s; **5** Peter Dumbreck, GB (Dallara F397-Mugen Honda), 21m 10.369s; **6** Mark Webber, AUS (Dallara F397-Mugen Honda), 21m 10.745s; **7** Mario Haberfeld, BR (Dallara F397-Opel), 21m 11.765s; **8** Warren Hughes, GB (Dallara F397-HKS Mitsubishi), 21m 12.543s; **9** Jamie Spence, GB (Dallara F397-Mugen Honda), 21m 14.908s; **10** Brian Smith, RA (Dallara F397-HKS Mitsubishi), 21m 20.817s.
Fastest race lap: Minassian, 1m 02.278s, 112.836 mph/181.592 km/h.
National Class winner: Martin O'Connell, GB (TOM'S 037F-Toyota), 21m 28.491s (14th).
Fastest qualifying lap: Minassian, 1m 02.270s, 112.850 mph/181.615 km/h.
Championship points. 1 Kane, 176; **2=** Dumbreck, 135; **2=** Minassian, 135; **4** Webber, 105; **5** Haberfeld, 96; **6** Bernoldi, 80. **National Class: 1** O'Connell, 148; **2** Wellman, 42; **3** Gumbley, 15.

AUTOSPORT BRITISH FORMULA 3 CHAMPIONSHIP, Circuit de Spa-Francorchamps, Stavelot, Belgium, 28 September. Round 14. 10 laps of the 4.330-mile/6.968-km circuit, 43.297 miles/69.680 km.
1 Enrique Bernoldi, BR (Dallara F397-Renault), 23m 04.463s, 112.585 mph/181.188 km/h.
2 David Saelens, B (Dallara F396-Opel), 23m 06.381s; **3** Franck Montagny, F (Martini MK73-Opel), 23m 06.734s; **4** Mark Webber, AUS (Dallara F397-Mugen Honda), 23m 07.745s; **5** Oriol Servia, E (Martini MK73-Opel), 23m 09.634s; **6** Nicolas Minassian, F (Dallara F397-Renault), 23m 11.706s; **7** Mario Haberfeld, BR (Dallara F397-Opel), 23m 15.564s; **8** Ben Collins, GB (Dallara F397-HKS Mitsubishi), 23m 20.985s; **9** Ricardo Mauricio, BR (TOM'S 037F-Toyota), 23m 25.660s; **10** Bas Leinders, B (Dallara F397-Opel), 23m 26.125s.
Fastest race lap: Minassian, 2m 17.445s, 113.405 mph/182.508 km/h.
National Class winner: Martin O'Connell, GB (TOM'S 037F-Toyota), 23m 26.792s (11th).
Fastest qualifying lap: Montagny, 2m 16.765s, 113.969 mph/183.415 km/h.
Championship points. 1 Kane, 176; **2** Minassian, 142; **3** Dumbreck, 135; **4** Webber, 115; **5=** Haberfeld, 100; **5=** Bernoldi, 100. **National Class: 1** O'Connell, 148; **2** Wellman, 42; **3** Gumbley, 15.

AUTUMN GOLD CUP, Silverstone International Circuit, Towcester, Northamptonshire, Great Britain, 5 October. Round 15. 25 laps of the 2.252-mile/3.624-km circuit, 56.300 miles/90.606 km.
1 Nicolas Minassian, F (Dallara F397-Renault), 32m 04.118s, 105.337 mph/169.523 km/h.
2 Enrique Bernoldi, BR (Dallara F397-Renault), 32m 05.624s; **3** Mark Webber, AUS (Dallara F397-Mugen Honda), 32m 13.067s; **4** Ben Collins, GB (Dallara F397-HKS Mitsubishi), 32m 15.520s; **5** Jonny Kane, GB (Dallara F397-Mugen Honda), 32m 20.158s; **6** Warren Hughes, GB (Dallara F397-HKS Mitsubishi), 32m 20.614s; **7** Peter Dumbreck, GB (Dallara F397-Mugen Honda), 32m 31.258s; **8** Guy Smith, GB (Dallara F397-Opel), 32m 34.332s; **9** Darren Manning, GB (Dallara F396-Mugen Honda), 32m 34.545s; **10** Ricardo Mauricio, BR (TOM'S 037F-Toyota), 32m 37.443s.
Fastest race lap: Minassian, 1m 16.199s, 106.395 mph/171.226 km/h.
National Class winner: Martin O'Connell, GB (TOM'S 036F-Toyota), 32m 46.308s (15th).
Fastest qualifying lap: Minassian, 1m 15.682s, 107.122 mph/172.396 km/h.
Championship points. 1 Kane, 184; **2** Minassian, 163; **3** Dumbreck, 139; **4** Webber, 127; **5** Bernoldi, 115; **6** Haberfeld, 100. **National Class: 1** O'Connell, 148; **2** Wellman, 57; **3** James, 21.

AUTOSPORT BRITISH FORMULA 3 CHAMPIONSHIP, Thruxton Circuit, Andover, Hampshire, Great Britain, 12 October. Round 16. 20 laps of the 2.356-mile/3.792-km circuit, 47.120 miles/75.832 km.
1 Nicolas Minassian, F (Dallara F397-Renault), 23m 15.624s, 121.546 mph/195.609 km/h.
2 Jonny Kane, GB (Dallara F397-Mugen Honda), 23m 20.415s; **3** Enrique Bernoldi, BR (Dallara F397-Renault), 23m 22.075s; **4** Peter Dumbreck, GB (Dallara F397-Mugen Honda), 23m 22.735s; **5** Mario Haberfeld, BR (Dallara F397-Opel), 23m 23.695s; **6** Warren Hughes, GB (Dallara F397-HKS Mitsubishi), 23m 24.518s; **7** Mark Webber, AUS (Dallara F397-Mugen Honda), 23m 31.206s; **8** Ben Collins, GB (Dallara F397-HKS Mitsubishi), 23m 31.487s; **9** Martin O'Connell, GB (Dallara F396-TOM'S Toyota), 23m 31.979s (1st National Class); **10** Paula Cook, GB (Dallara F397-Opel), 23m 42.958s.
Fastest race lap: Guy Smith, GB (Dallara F397-Opel), 1m 08.794s, 123.290 mph/198.416 km/h.
Fastest qualifying lap: Kane, 1m 08.355s, 124.082 mph/199.690 km/h.

Final championship points
1 Jonny Kane, GB, 199; **2** Nicolas Minassian, F, 183; **3** Peter Dumbreck, GB, 148; **4** Mark Webber, AUS, 131; **5** Enrique Bernoldi, BR, 127; **6** Mario Haberfeld, BR, 108; **7** Brian Smith, RA, 72; **8** Ben Collins, GB, 64; **9** Guy Smith, GB, 60; **10** Kevin McGarrity, GB, 36; **11=** Ricardo Mauricio, BR, 26; **11=** Darren Manning, GB, 26; **13** Simon Wills, NZ, 22; **14=** Jamie Spence, GB, 18; **14=** Warren Hughes, GB, 18; **16** Mark Shaw, GB, 16; **17** David Saelens, B, 15; **18** Frank Montagny, F, 12; **19** Oriol Servia, E, 8; **20** Paula Cook, GB, 7; **21** Giovanni Anapoli, I, 3; **22=** Michael Bentwood, GB, 2; **22=** Andy Priaulx, GB, 2; **22=** Henry Stanton, GB, 2; **22=** Darren Turner, GB, 2; **26=** Haruki Kurosawa, J, 1; **26=** Bas Leinders, B, 1.

National Class
1 Martin O'Connell, GB, 148; **2** Damon Wellman, 78; **3** Ian James, GB, 21; **4** Jeremy Gumbley, GB, 15.

French Formula 3 Championship

COUPES DE PAQUES DE NOGARO, Circuit Automobile Paul Armagnac, Nogaro, France, 30/31 March. 2 x 14 laps of the 2.259-mile/3.636-km circuit.
Round 1 (31.630 miles/50.904 km)
1 Patrice Gay, F (Dallara F396-Opel), 19m 50.164s, 95.675 mph/153.974 km/h.
2 David Saelens, B (Dallara F396-Opel), 19m 52.743s; **3** Steeve Hiesse, F (Dallara F396-Honda Seymaz), 19m 54.811s; **4** Oriol Servia, E (Martini MK73-Opel), 19m 56.731s; **5** Sébastien Philippe, F (Dallara F396-Opel), 19m 57.326s; **6** Franck Montagny, F (Martini MK73-Opel), 19m 57.528s; **7** Pascal Hernandez, F (Dallara F395-Fiat), 20m 02.623s; **8** Marcel Fässler, CH (Dallara F396-Fiat), 20m 03.230s; **9** David Terrien, F (Dallara F396-Opel), 20m 03.741s; **10** Thierry Glas, F (Dallara F395-Fiat), 20m 17.233s.
Fastest race lap: Stéphane Sarrazin, F (Dallara F396-Fiat), 1m 23.944s, 96.892 mph/155.933 km/h.

Round 2 (31.630 miles/50.904 km)
1 Stéphane Sarrazin, F (Dallara F396-Fiat), 19m 45.454s, 96.055 mph/154.586 km/h.
2 Fabrice Walfisch, F (Dallara F397-Opel), 19m 49.651s; **3** Stéphane Sallaz, F (Dallara F396-Opel), 19m 53.621s; **4** Sébastien Philippe, F (Dallara F396-Opel), 19m 54.581s; **5** Marcel Fässler, CH (Dallara F396-Fiat), 19m 58.238s; **6** David Saelens, B (Dallara F396-Opel), 19m 58.674s; **7** Patrice Gay, F (Dallara F396-Opel), 19m 59.117s; **8** Steeve Hiesse, F (Dallara F396-Honda Seymaz), 20m 08.409s; **9** Pascal Hernandez, F (Dallara F395-Fiat), 20m 09.192s; **10** Sébastien Enjolras, F (Dallara F396-Fiat), 20m 10.249s.
Fastest race lap: Gay, 1m 23.527s, 97.376 mph/156.711 km/h.

GRAND PRIX DE LA VILLE DE NIMES, Circuit de Lédenon, Remoulins, Nimes, France, 13 April. 2 x 15 laps of the 1.957-mile/3.150-km circuit.
Round 3 (29.360 miles/47.250 km/h)
1 Fabrice Walfisch, F (Dallara F396-Opel), 20m 07.327s, 87.545 mph/140.890 km/h.
2 Patrice Gay, F (Dallara F396-Opel), 20m 08.114s; **3** Stéphane Sarrazin, F (Dallara F396-Fiat), 20m 21.519s; **4** Sébastien Philippe, F (Dallara F396-Opel), 20m 24.480s; **5** David Saelens, B (Dallara F396-Opel), 20m 25.550s; **6** Stéphane Sallaz, F (Dallara F396-Opel), 20m 26.510s; **7** Franck Montagny, F (Martini MK73-Opel), 20m 26.804s; **8** David Terrien, F (Dallara F396-Opel), 20m 28.614s; **9** Pascal Hernandez, F (Dallara F395-Fiat), 20m 31.086s; **10** Marcel Fässler, CH (Dallara F396-Fiat), 20m 31.197s.
Fastest race lap: Walfisch, 1m 19.739s, 88.368 mph/142.214 km/h.

Round 4 (29.360 miles/47.250 km/h)
1 Fabrice Walfisch, F (Dallara F396-Opel), 20m 14.274s, 87.044 mph/140.084 km/h.
2 Patrice Gay, F (Dallara F396-Opel), 20m 15.710s; **3** David Saelens, B (Dallara F396-Opel), 20m 23.660s; **4** Sébastien Philippe, F (Dallara F396-Opel), 20m 24.898s; **5** David Terrien, F (Dallara F396-Opel), 20m 26.022s; **6** Franck Montagny, F (Martini MK73-Opel), 20m 27.128s; **7** Stéphane Sarrazin, F (Dallara F396-Fiat), 20m 33.274s; **8** Sébastien Enjolras, F (Dallara F396-Fiat), 20m 36.227s; **9** Marcel Fässler, CH (Dallara F396-Fiat), 20m 37.052s; **10** Stéphane Sallaz, F (Dallara F396-Opel), 20m 39.435s.
Fastest race lap: Gay, 1m 20.299s, 87.751 mph/141.222 km/h.

TROPHÉES DE PRINTEMPS, Circuit de Nevers, Magny-Cours, France, 26/27 April. 2 x 14 laps of the 2.641-mile/4.250-km circuit.
Round 5 (36.972 miles/59.500 km)
1 Stéphane Sarrazin, F (Dallara F396-Fiat), 26m 48.247s, 82.759 mph/133.188 km/h.
2 Patrice Gay, F (Dallara F396-Opel), 26m 57.285s; **3** Sébastien Philippe, F (Dallara F396-Opel), 26m 59.788s; **4** Fabrice Walfisch, F (Dallara F396-Opel), 27m 00.004s; **5** Steeve Hiesse, F (Dallara F396-Fiat), 27m 00.332s; **6** David Saelens, B (Dallara F396-Opel), 27m 04.920s; **7** Marcel Fässler, CH (Dallara F396-Fiat), 27m 20.002s; **8** Sébastien Enjolras, F (Dallara F396-Fiat), 27m 26.849s; **9** Franck Montagny, F (Martini MK73-Opel), 27m 28.832s; **10** David Terrien, F (Dallara F396-Opel), 27m 37.745s.
Fastest race lap: Hiesse, 1m 51.822s, 85.019 mph/136.825 km/h.

Round 6 (36.972 miles/59.500 km)
1 Fabrice Walfisch, F (Dallara F396-Opel), 25m 44.863s, 86.155 mph/138.653 km/h.
2 Patrice Gay, F (Dallara F396-Opel), 25m 46.511s; **3** David Saelens, B (Dallara F396-Opel), 25m 47.096s; **4** Franck Montagny, F (Martini MK73-Opel), 25m 54.777s; **5** Sébastien Enjolras, F (Dallara F396-Fiat), 26m 02.501s; **6** Steeve Hiesse, F (Dallara F396-Fiat), 26m 04.347s; **7** Damien Bianchi, F (Dallara F396-Fiat), 26m 06.336s; **8** Oriol Servia, E (Martini MK73-Opel), 26m 07.893s; **9** David Terrien, F (Dallara F396-Opel), 26m 08.555s; **10** Stéphane Sallaz, F (Dallara F396-Opel), 26m 14.439s.
Fastest race lap: Saelens, 1m 46.198s, 89.521 mph/144.071 km/h.

FRENCH FORMULA 3 CHAMPIONSHIP, Circuit de Pau Ville, France, 18 May. Round 7. 28 laps of the 1.715-mile/2.760-km circuit, 48.020 miles/77.280 km.
1 David Saelens, B (Dallara F396-Opel), 35m 33.54s, 81.025 mph/130.397 km/h.
2 Patrice Gay, F (Dallara F396-Opel), 35m 34.21s; **3** Sébastien Philippe, F (Dallara F396-Opel), 35m 45.41s; **4** Fabrice Walfisch, F (Dallara F396-Opel), 35m 46.60s; **5** Stéphane Sarrazin, F (Dallara F396-Fiat), 35m 46.86s; **6** Stéphane Sallaz, F (Dallara F396-Opel), 35m 52.22s; **7** Damien Bianchi, F (Dallara F396-Fiat), 35m 57.20s; **8** Franck Montagny, F (Martini MK73-Opel), 36m 00.26s; **9** Pascal Hernandez, F (Dallara F395-Fiat), 36m 01.11s; **10** Steeve Hiesse, F (Dallara F396-Fiat), 36m 01.59s.
Fastest race lap: Sarrazin, 1m 14.29s, 83.106 mph/133.746 km/h.

GRAND PRIX DIJON-BOURGOGNE, Circuit de Dijon-Prenois, Fontaine-les-Dijon, France, 1 June. Round 8. 20 laps of the 2.361-mile/3.800-km circuit, 47.224 miles/76.000 km.
1 Franck Montagny, F (Martini MK73-Opel), 24m 57.653s, 113.516 mph/182.686 km/h.
2 Stéphane Sarrazin, F (Dallara F396-Fiat), 25m 01.628s; **3** Sébastien Philippe, F (Dallara F396-Opel), 25m 08.288s; **4** David Saelens, B (Dallara F396-Opel), 25m 12.946s; **5** Marcel Fässler, CH (Dallara F396-Fiat), 25m 13.800s; **6** Steeve Hiesse, F (Dallara F396-Fiat), 25m 14.659s; **7** David Terrien, F (Dallara F396-Opel), 25m 15.762s; **8** Oriol Servia, E (Martini MK73-Opel), 25m 16.801s; **9** Damien Bianchi, F (Dallara F396-Fiat), 25m 17.901s; **10** Pascal Hernandez, F (Dallara F395-Fiat), 25m 21.294s.
Fastest race lap: Montagny, 1m 14.107s, 114.704 mph/184.598 km/h.

37th TROPHÉES D'AUVERGNE, Circuit de Charade, Clermont-Ferrand, France, 8 June. 2 x 12 laps of the 2.470-mile/3.975-km circuit.
Round 9 (29.639 miles/47.700 km)
1 Franck Montagny, F (Martini MK73-Opel), 21m 12.040s, 83.882 mph/134.996 km/h.
2 Stéphane Sarrazin, F (Dallara F396-Fiat), 21m 13.039s; **3** David Terrien, F (Dallara F396-Opel), 21m 17.561s; **4** Steeve Hiesse, F (Dallara F396-Fiat), 21m 25.476s; **5** Oriol Servia, E (Martini MK73-Opel), 21m 26.056s; **6** Patrice Gay, F (Dallara F396-Opel), 21m 27.105s; **7** Marcel Fässler, CH (Dallara F396-Fiat), 21m 27.547s; **8** Stéphane Sallaz, F (Dallara F396-Opel), 21m 29.130s; **9** Sébastien Philippe, F (Dallara F396-Opel), 21m 30.141s; **10** Fabrice Walfisch, F (Dallara F396-Opel), 21m 33.381s.
Fastest race lap: Montagny, 1m 45.451s, 84.322 mph/135.703 km/h.

Round 10 (29.639 miles/47.700 km)
1 Patrice Gay, F (Dallara F396-Opel), 21m 06.132s, 84.274 mph/135.626 km/h.
2 Stéphane Sarrazin, F (Dallara F396-Fiat), 21m 07.519s; **3** Oriol Servia, E (Martini MK73-Opel), 21m 12.954s; **4** Sébastien Philippe, F (Dallara F396-Opel), 21m 19.851s; **5** Franck Montagny, F (Martini MK73-Opel), 21m 20.253s; **6** Steeve Hiesse, F (Dallara F396-Fiat), 21m 21.751s; **7** Marcel Fässler, CH (Dallara F396-Fiat), 21m 22.145s; **8** Fabrice Walfisch, F (Dallara F396-Opel), 21m 22.524s; **9** David Saelens, B (Dallara F396-Opel), 21m 23.526s; **10** David Terrien, F (Dallara F396-Opel), 21m 23.841s.
Fastest race lap: Gay, 1m 44.847s, 84.808 mph/136.485 km/h.

6th COUPE DU VAL DE VIENNE, Circuit du Val de Vienne, Le Vigeant, France, 22 June. 2 x 13 laps of the 2.334-mile/3.757-km circuit
Round 11 (30.348 miles/48.841 km)
1 Sébastien Philippe, F (Dallara F396-Opel), 24m 37.973s, 73.922 mph/118.965 km/h.
2 Stéphane Sarrazin, F (Dallara F396-Fiat), 24m 39.289s; **3** Fabrice Walfisch, F (Dallara F396-Opel), 24m 40.464s; **4** Patrice Gay, F (Dallara F396-Opel), 24m 43.731s; **5** David Terrien, F (Dallara F396-Opel), 24m 50.264s; **6** Franck Montagny, F (Martini MK73-Opel), 24m 54.642s; **7** David Saelens, B (Dallara F396-Opel), 24m 59.742s; **8** Damien Bianchi, F (Dallara F396-Fiat), 25m 02.903s; **9** Marcel Fässler, CH (Dallara F396-Fiat), 25m 31.420s; **10** Cyril Prunet, F (Elise-Fiat), 25m 38.802s.
Fastest race lap: Sarrazin, 1m 51.206s, 75.573 mph/121.623 km/h.

Round 12 (30.348 miles/48.841 km)
1 Patrice Gay, F (Dallara F396-Opel), 20m 41.154s, 88.026 mph/141.665 km/h.
2 Stéphane Sarrazin, F (Dallara F396-Fiat), 20m 44.327s; **3** David Saelens, B (Dallara F396-Opel), 20m 46.914s; **4** Marcel Fässler, CH (Dallara F396-Fiat), 20m 53.389s; **5** Fabrice Walfisch, F (Dallara F396-Opel), 20m 53.625s; **6** Franck Montagny, F (Martini MK73-Opel), 20m 57.590s; **7** Oriol Servia, E (Martini MK73-Opel), 20m 59.264s; **8** Stéphane Sallaz, F (Dallara F396-Opel), 21m 01.226s; **9** Steeve Hiesse, F (Dallara F396-Fiat), 21m 02.785s; **10** Damien Bianchi, F (Dallara F396-Fiat), 21m 04.447s.
Fastest race lap: Gay, 1m 34.657s, 88.786 mph/142.886 km/h.

23rd PRIX DU PAS-DE-CALAIS, Circuit Auto-Moto de Croix-en-Ternois, France, 6 July. Round 13. 45 laps of the 1.181-mile/1.900-km circuit, 53.127 miles/85.500 km.
1 Stéphane Sarrazin, F (Dallara F396-Fiat), 38m 07.561s, 83.608 mph/134.554 km/h.
2 Fabrice Walfisch, F (Dallara F396-Opel), 38m 11.272s; **3** Sébastien Philippe, F (Dallara F396-Opel), 38m 18.429s; **4** Steeve Hiesse, F (Dallara F396-Fiat), 38m 20.424s; **5** Franck Montagny, F (Martini MK73-Opel), 38m 21.504s; **6** Stéphane Sallaz, F (Dallara F396-Opel), 38m 22.124s; **7** David Saelens, B (Dallara F396-Opel), 38m 25.768s; **8** David Terrien, F (Dallara F396-Opel), 38m 26.960s; **9** Marcel Fässler, CH (Dallara F396-Fiat), 38m 27.474s; **10** Damien Bianchi, F (Dallara F396-Fiat), 38m 27.991s.
Fastest race lap: Walfisch, 52.107s, 81.566 mph/131.268 km/h.

FRENCH FORMULA 3 CHAMPIONSHIP, Circuit ASA Paul Ricard, Le Beausset, France, 20 July. Round 14. 22 laps of the 2.361-mile/3.800-km circuit, 51.947 miles/83.600 km.
1 Franck Montagny, F (Martini MK73-Opel), 29m 25.729s, 105.910 mph/170.445 km/h.
2 David Saelens, B (Dallara F396-Opel), 29m 38.354s; **3** Oriol Servia, E (Martini MK73-Opel), 29m 38.772s; **4** Sébastien Philippe, F (Dallara F396-Opel), 29m 39.274s; **5** Stéphane Sallaz, F (Dallara F396-Opel), 29m 39.519s; **6** Patrice Gay, F (Dallara F396-Opel), 29m 40.526s; **7** Stéphane Sarrazin, F (Dallara F396-Fiat), 29m 43.535s; **8** David Terrien, F (Dallara F396-Opel), 29m 45.610s; **9** Fabrice Walfisch, F (Dallara F396-Opel), 29m 45.652s; **10** Damien Bianchi, F (Dallara F396-Fiat), 29m 45.995s.
Fastest race lap: Montagny, 1m 19.589s, 106.803 mph/171.883 km/h.

55th GRAND PRIX D'ALBI, Circuit d'Albi, France, 7 September. 12 and 15 laps of the 2.206-mile/3.551-km circuit. Round 15 (26.478 miles/42.612 km)
1 David Saelens, B (Dallara F396-Opel), 14m 13.578s, 111.671 mph/179.718 km/h.
2 Steeve Hiesse, F (Dallara F396-Fiat), 14m 15.884s; **3** Patrice Gay, F (Dallara F396-Opel), 14m 16.566s; **4** Franck Montagny, F (Martini MK73-Opel), 14m 16.837s; **5** Sébastien Philippe, F (Dallara F396-Opel), 14m 18.354s; **6** Stéphane Sarrazin, F (Dallara F396-Fiat), 14m 18.705s; **7** Fabrice Walfisch, F (Dallara F396-Opel), 14m 19.408s; **8** Marcel Fässler, CH (Dallara F396-Fiat), 14m 20.747s; **9** Stéphane Sallaz, F (Dallara F396-Opel), 14m 21.620s; **10** Pascal Hernandez, F (Dallara F395-Fiat), 14m 26.879s.
Fastest race lap: Oriol Servia, E (Martini MK73-Opel), 1m 09.479s, 114.328 mph/183.992 km/h.

Round 16 (33.097 miles/53.265 km)
1 Oriol Servia, E (Martini MK73-Opel), 17m 49.157s, 111.443 mph/179.351 km/h.
2 David Saelens, B (Dallara F396-Opel), 17m 50.047s; **3** Franck Montagny, F (Martini MK73-Opel), 17m 52.604s; **4** Stéphane Sallaz, F (Dallara F396-Opel), 17m 55.276s; **5** David Terrien, F (Dallara F396-Opel), 17m 56.697s; **6** Steeve Hiesse, F (Dallara F396-Fiat), 17m 57.421s; **7** Patrice Gay, F (Dallara F396-Opel), 17m 59.564s; **8** Marcel Fässler, CH (Dallara F396-Fiat), 18m 01.673s; **9** Damien Bianchi, F (Dallara F396-Fiat), 18m 02.299s; **10** Yann Goudy, F (Dallara F396-Fiat), 18m 21.618s.
Fastest race lap: Montagny, 1m 10.117s, 113.287 mph/182.318 km/h.

COUPES D'AUTOMNE, Circuit Le Mans-Bugatti, France, 21 September. Round 17. 17 laps of the 2.753-mile/4.430-km circuit, 46.795 miles/75.310 km).
1 Franck Montagny, F (Martini MK73-Opel), 28m 27.745s, 98.647 mph/158.757 km/h.
2 Fabrice Walfisch, F (Dallara F396-Opel), 28m 28.806s; **3** Stéphane Sallaz, F (Dallara F396-Opel), 28m 36.134s; **4** Sébastien Philippe, F (Dallara F396-Opel), 28m 45.961s; **5** Patrice Gay, F (Dallara F396-Opel), 28m 46.300s; **6** Steeve Hiesse, F (Dallara F396-Fiat), 28m 46.881s; **7** Stéphane Sarrazin, F (Dallara F396-Fiat), 28m 47.374s; **8** David Terrien, F (Dallara F396-Opel), 28m 48.116s; **9** Oriol Servia, E (Martini MK73-Opel), 28m 48.470s; **10** David Saelens, B (Dallara F396-Opel), 28m 50.323s.
Fastest race lap: Walfisch, 1m 39.805s, 99.290 mph/159.972 km/h.

Final championship points
Class A
1 Patrice Gay, F, 151; **2** Stéphane Sarrazin, F, 141; **3** David Saelens, B, 131; **4** Franck Montagny, F, 129; **5** Fabrice Walfisch, F, 126; **6** Sébastien Philippe, F, 117; **7** Steeve Hiesse, F, 76; **8** Oriol Servia, E, 62; **9** Stéphane Sallaz, F, 59; **10** David Terrien, F, 50; **11** Damien Bianchi, F, 48; **12** Marcel Fässler, CH, 18; **13** Pascal Hernandez, F, 12; **14=** Cyril Prunet, F, 1; **14=** Yann Goudy, F, 1; **14=** Thierry Glas, F, 1.

Class B
1 Pascal Hernandez, F, 185; **2** Benjamin Alvaro, B, 135; **3** Yann Goudy, F, 124; **4** Bruno Laffite, F, 110; **5** Thierry Glas, F, 97.

German Formula 3 Championship

ADAC-PREIS-HOCKENHEIM, Hockenheimring, Heidelberg, Germany, 26/27 April. 12 and 11 laps of the 4.240-mile/6.823-km circuit.
Round 1 (50.875 miles/81.876 km)
1 Nick Heidfeld, D (Dallara F397-Opel), 25m 53.838s, 117.870 mph/189.694 km/h.
2 Tim Verbergt, B (Dallara F397-Opel), 25m 59.793s; **3** Timo Scheider, D (Dallara F397-Opel), 26m 10.616s; **4** Bas Leinders, B (Dallara F397-Opel), 26m 15.609s; **5** Pierre Kaffer, D (Dallara F396-Opel), 26m 16.890s; **6** Luciano Crespi, I (Dallara F396-Opel), 26m 17.482s; **7** Tomas Enge, CZ (Dallara F397-Opel), 26m 19.869s; **8** Tim Coronel, NL (Dallara F397-Opel), 26m 21.512s; **9** Sascha Bert, D (Dallara F397-Opel), 26m 31.603s; **10** Johan Stureson, S (Dallara F397-Opel), 26m 31.903s.
Fastest race lap: Heidfeld, 2m 07.663s, 119.554 mph/192.403 km/h.

Round 2 (46.636 miles/75.053 km)
1 Nick Heidfeld, D (Dallara F397-Opel), 26m 29.154s, 105.647 mph/170.022 km/h.
2 Bas Leinders, B (Dallara F397-Opel), 26m 49.844s; **3** Wolf Henzler, D (Martini MK73-Opel), 27m 01.811s; **4** Tim Verbergt, B (Dallara F397-Opel), 27m 02.570s; **5** Dominik Schwager, D (Dallara F397-Opel), 27m 06.623s; **6** Tim Coronel, NL (Dallara F397-Opel), 27m 11.471s; **7** Yves Olivier, B (Dallara F397-Opel), 27m 15.291s; **8** Sascha Bert, D (Dallara F397-Opel), 27m 15.544s; **9** Timo Scheider, D (Dallara F397-Opel), 27m 18.069s; **10** Michael Stelzig, D (Dallara F395-Opel), 27m 22.300s.
Fastest race lap: Heidfeld, 2m 22.066s, 107.433 mph/172.897 km/h.

ADAC-EIFELRENNEN NÜRBURGRING, Nürburgring, Nürburg/Eifel, Germany, 24/25 May. 2 x 18 laps of the 2.831-mile/4.556-km circuit.
Round 3 (50.957 miles/82.008 km)
1 Timo Scheider, D (Dallara F397-Opel), 28m 52.732s, 105.871 mph/170.383 km/h.
2 Nick Heidfeld, D (Dallara F397-Opel), 28m 54.960s; **3** Alexander 'Alex' Müller, D (Dallara F397-Opel), 28m 57.238s; **4** Wolf Henzler, D (Martini MK73-Opel), 28m 57.739s; **5** Sascha Bert, D (Dallara F397-Opel), 29m 05.046s; **6** Bas Leinders, B (Dallara F397-Opel), 26m 06.868s; **7** Tim Verbergt, B (Dallara F397-Opel), 29m 08.142s; **8** Pierre Kaffer, D (Dallara F396-Opel), 29m 08.626s; **9** Norman Simon, D (Dallara F397-Opel), 29m 16.435s; **10** Tomas Enge, CZ (Dallara F397-Opel), 29m 25.491s.
Fastest race lap: Heidfeld, 1m 35.134s, 107.128 mph/172.405 km/h.

Round 4 (50.957 miles/82.008 km)
1 Wolf Henzler, D (Martini MK73-Opel), 29m 03.109s, 105.241 mph/169.369 km/h.
2 Alexander 'Alex' Müller, D (Dallara F397-Opel), 29m 03.497s; **3** Nick Heidfeld, D (Dallara F397-Opel), 29m 04.828s; **4** Timo Scheider, D (Dallara F397-Opel), 29m 05.515s; **5** Norman Simon, D (Dallara F397-Opel), 29m 12.078s; **6** Bas Leinders, B (Dallara F397-Opel), 29m 14.563s; **7** Tim Verbergt, B (Dallara F397-Opel), 29m 15.186s; **8** Pierre Kaffer, D (Dallara F396-Opel), 29m 16.237s; **9** Dominik Schwager, D (Dallara F397-Opel), 29m 24.945s; **10** Steffen Widmann, D (Dallara F397-Opel), 29m 37.614s.
Fastest race lap: Schwager, 1m 35.609s, 106.595 mph/171.549 km/h.

ADAC-PREIS-SACHSENRING, Sachsenring, Germany, 14/15 June. 2 x 23 laps of the 2.185-mile/3.517-km circuit.
Round 5 (50.263 miles/80.891 km)
1 Timo Scheider, D (Dallara F397-Opel), 37m 06.207s, 81.281 mph/130.809 km/h.
2 Nick Heidfeld, D (Dallara F397-Opel), 37m 08.854s; **3** Bas Leinders, B (Dallara F397-Opel), 37m 09.124s; **4** Alexander 'Alex' Müller, D (Dallara F397-Opel), 37m 10.188s; **5** Wolf Henzler, D (Martini MK73-Opel), 37m 10.625s; **6** Tomas Enge, CZ (Dallara F397-Opel), 37m 25.643s; **7** Dominik Schwager, D (Dallara F397-Opel), 37m 46.972s; **8** Johan Stureson, S (Dallara F397-Opel), 37m 50.849s; **9** Pierre Kaffer, D (Dallara F396-Opel), 38m 01.525s; **10** Andreas Scheld, D (Dallara F397-Opel), 38m 01.652s.
Fastest race lap: Heidfeld, 1m 32.187s, 85.341 mph/137.343 km/h.

Round 6 (50.263 miles/80.891 km)
1 Timo Scheider, D (Dallara F397-Opel), 36m 52.713s, 81.777 mph/131.607 km/h.
2 Bas Leinders, B (Dallara F397-Opel), 36m 53.040s; **3** Wolf Henzler, D (Martini MK73-Opel), 37m 02.313s; **4** Dominik Schwager, D (Dallara F397-Opel), 37m 12.125s; **5** Pierre Kaffer, D (Dallara F396-Opel), 37m 14.952s; **6** Nick Heidfeld, D (Dallara F397-Opel), 37m 22.448s; **7** Andreas Scheld, D (Dallara F397-Opel), 37m 26.372s; **8** Yves Olivier, B (Dallara F397-Opel), 37m 26.821s; **9** Steffen Widmann, D (Dallara F397-Opel), 37m 27.018s; **10** Luciano Crespi, I (Dallara F396-Opel), 37m 31.453s.
Fastest race lap: Scheider, 1m 24.416s, 93.197 mph/149.986 km/h.

ADAC-NORISRING-TROPHÄE, Norisring, Nürnberg, Germany, 28/29 June. 2 x 35 laps of the 1.429-mile/2.300-km circuit. Round 7 (50.020 miles/80.500 km)
1 Dominik Schwager, D (Dallara F397-Opel), 30m 01.737s, 99.944 mph/160.845 km/h.
2 Sascha Bert, D (Dallara F397-Opel), 30m 14.853s; **3** Wolf Henzler, D (Martini MK73-Opel), 30m 16.313s; **4** Tim Verbergt, B (Dallara F397-Opel), 30m 17.147s; **5** Timo Scheider, D (Dallara F397-Opel), 30m 25.330s; **6** Pierre Kaffer, D (Dallara F396-Opel), 30m 35.362s; **7** Johan Stureson, S (Dallara F397-Opel), 30m 38.957s; **8** Ronny Melkus, D (Dallara F396-Opel), 30m 44.529s; **9** Luciano Crespi, I (Dallara F396-Opel), 30m 45.958s; **10** Tim Coronel, NL (Dallara F397-Opel), 30m 46.312s.

Fastest race lap: Alexander 'Alex' Müller, D (Dallara F397-Opel), 50.671s, 101.536 mph/163.407 km/h.

Round 8 (50.020 miles/80.500 km)
1 Dominik Schwager, D (Dallara F397-Opel), 30m 06.941s, 99.656 mph/160.382 km/h.
2 Sascha Bert, D (Dallara F397-Opel), 30m 16.260s; **3** Wolf Henzler, D (Martini MK73-Opel), 30m 19.938s; **4** Timo Scheider, D (Dallara F397-Opel), 30m 23.607s; **5** Tim Verbergt, B (Dallara F397-Opel), 30m 25.182s; **6** Norman Simon, D (Dallara F397-Opel), 30m 25.257s; **7** Alexander 'Alex' Müller, D (Dallara F397-Opel), 30m 25.855s; **8** Nick Heidfeld, D (Dallara F397-Opel), 30m 31.703s; **9** Johan Stureson, S (Dallara F397-Opel), 30m 43.170s; **10** Pierre Kaffer, D (Dallara F396-Opel), 30m 50.837s.
Fastest race lap: Simon, 50.823s, 101.233 mph/162.918 km/h.

ADAC-FLUGPLATZRENNEN WUNSTORF, Wunstorf Airfield Circuit, Germany, 12/13 July. 2 x 16 laps of the 3.138-mile/5.050-km circuit.
Round 9 (50.207 miles/80.800 km)
1 Alexander 'Alex' Müller, D (Dallara F397-Opel), 26m 52.263s, 112.106 mph/180.417 km/h.
2 Ronny Melkus, D (Dallara F397-Opel), 26m 53.529s; **3** Timo Scheider, D (Dallara F397-Opel), 26m 53.961s; **4** Pierre Kaffer, D (Dallara F396-Opel), 27m 00.567s; **5** Tim Verbergt, B (Dallara F397-Opel), 27m 01.795s; **6** Johan Stureson, S (Dallara F397-Opel), 27m 02.500s; **7** Steffen Widmann, D (Martini MK73-Opel), 27m 03.087s; **8** Bas Leinders, B (Dallara F397-Opel), 27m 10.965s; **9** Sascha Bert, D (Dallara F397-Opel), 27m 12.391s; **10** Tomas Enge, CZ (Dallara F397-Opel), 27m 23.201s.
Fastest race lap: Leinders, 1m 39.07s, 114.026 mph/183.507 km/h.

Round 10 (50.207 miles/80.800 km)
1 Alexander 'Alex' Müller, D (Dallara F397-Opel), 26m 50.735s, 112.212 mph/180.588 km/h.
2 Ronny Melkus, D (Dallara F397-Opel), 26m 50.893s; **3** Timo Scheider, D (Dallara F397-Opel), 26m 51.804s; **4** Nick Heidfeld, D (Dallara F397-Opel), 26m 53.164s; **5** Steffen Widmann, D (Martini MK73-Opel), 26m 58.810s; **6** Tim Verbergt, B (Dallara F397-Opel), 27m 04.017s; **7** Tomas Enge, CZ (Dallara F397-Opel), 27m 05.058s; **8** Sascha Bert, D (Dallara F397-Opel), 27m 07.121s; **9** Dominik Schwager, D (Dallara F397-Opel), 27m 07.878s; **10** Yves Olivier, B (Dallara F397-Opel), 27m 10.099s.
Fastest race lap: Scheider, 1m 39.140s, 113.945 mph/183.377 km/h.

ADAC-RACE-CHALLENGE ZWEIBRÜCKEN, Zweibrücken Circuit, Germany, 9/10 August. 2 x 29 laps of the 1.740-mile/2.800-km circuit.
Round 11 (50.455 miles/81.200 km)
1 Pierre Kaffer, D (Dallara F396-Opel), 30m 19.530s, 99.828 mph/160.657 km/h.
2 Timo Scheider, D (Dallara F397-Opel), 30m 22.453s; **3** Wolf Henzler, D (Martini MK73-Opel), 30m 23.009s; **4** Norman Simon, D (Dallara F397-Opel), 30m 26.580s; **5** Nick Heidfeld, D (Dallara F397-Opel), 30m 28.026s; **6** Tim Verbergt, B (Dallara F397-Opel), 30m 36.735s; **7** Alexander 'Alex' Müller, D (Dallara F397-Opel), 30m 37.206s; **8** Bas Leinders, B (Dallara F397-Opel), 30m 38.152s; **9** Tomas Enge, CZ (Dallara F397-Opel), 30m 44.692s; **10** Yves Olivier, B (Dallara F397-Opel), 30m 45.495s.
Fastest race lap: Kaffer, 1m 02.013s, 101.002 mph/162.547 km/h.

Round 12 (50.455 miles/81.200 km)
1 Wolf Henzler, D (Martini MK73-Opel), 30m 23.822s, 99.593 mph/160.279 km/h.
2 Timo Scheider, D (Dallara F397-Opel), 30m 27.718s; **3** Norman Simon, D (Dallara F397-Opel), 30m 30.196s; **4** Nick Heidfeld, D (Dallara F397-Opel), 30m 31.017s; **5** Steffen Widmann, D (Martini MK73-Opel), 30m 37.112s; **6** Alexander 'Alex' Müller, D (Dallara F397-Opel), 30m 37.863s; **7** Ronny Melkus, D (Dallara F397-Opel), 30m 49.753s; **8** Yves Olivier, B (Dallara F397-Opel), 30m 50.080s; **9** Sascha Bert, D (Dallara F397-Opel), 30m 53.831s; **10** Lucas Luhr, D (Dallara F397-Opel), 30m 54.196s.
Fastest race lap: Heidfeld, 1m 02.224s, 100.659 mph/161.995 km/h.

ADAC-ALPENTROPHÄE SALZBURGRING, Salzburgring, Austria, 23/24 August. 2 x 15 laps of the 2.630-mile/4.232-km circuit.
Round 13 (39.445 miles/63.480 km)
1 Nick Heidfeld, D (Dallara F397-Opel), 18m 37.583s, 127.061 mph/204.484 km/h.
2 Timo Scheider, D (Dallara F397-Opel), 18m 38.316s; **3** Norman Simon, D (Dallara F397-Opel), 18m 45.477s; **4** Sascha Bert, D (Dallara F397-Opel), 18m 46.620s; **5** Pierre Kaffer, D (Dallara F396-Opel), 18m 47.199s; **6** Bas Leinders, B (Dallara F397-Opel), 18m 47.253s; **7** Wolf Henzler, D (Martini MK73-Opel), 18m 47.511s; **8** Johan Stureson, S (Dallara F397-Opel), 18m 47.814s; **9** Dominik Schwager, D (Dallara F397-Opel), 18m 48.141s; **10** Lucas Luhr, D (Dallara F397-Opel), 18m 48.229s.
Fastest race lap: Scheider, 1m 13.684s, 128.477 mph/206.764 km/h.

Round 14 (39.445 miles/63.480 km)
1 Nick Heidfeld, D (Dallara F397-Opel), 18m 41.122s, 126.659 mph/203.839 km/h.
2 Timo Scheider, D (Dallara F397-Opel), 18m 46.627s; **3** Norman Simon, D (Dallara F397-Opel), 18m 47.165s; **4** Wolf Henzler, D (Martini MK73-Opel), 18m 48.181s; **5** Sascha Bert, D (Dallara F397-Opel), 18m 48.904s; **6** Pierre Kaffer, D (Dallara F396-Opel), 18m 54.519s; **7** Tomas Enge, CZ (Dallara F397-Opel), 18m 54.920s; **8** Johan Stureson, S (Dallara F397-Opel), 18m 56.736s; **9** Steffen Widmann, D (Martini MK73-Opel), 18m 57.756s; **10** Tim Verbergt, B (Dallara F397-Opel), 18m 58.296s.
Fastest race lap: Heidfeld, 1m 14.043s, 127.854 mph/205.762 km/h.

ADAC-REGIO-PREIS LAHR, Lahr Circuit, Germany, 6/7 September. 2 x 24 laps of the 2.085-mile/3.355-km circuit. Round 15 (50.033 miles/80.520 km)
1 Alexander 'Alex' Müller, D (Dallara F397-Opel), 29m 46.901s, 100.799 mph/162.221 km/h.
2 Nick Heidfeld, D (Dallara F397-Opel), 29m 51.422s; **3** Wolf Henzler, D (Martini MK73-Opel), 29m 55.707s; **4** Bas Leinders, B (Dallara F397-Opel), 29m 56.579s; **5** Lucas Luhr, D (Dallara F397-Opel), 30m 05.960s; **6** Norman Simon, D (Dallara F397-Opel), 30m 08.583s; **7** Pierre Kaffer, D (Dallara F396-Opel), 30m 10.028s; **8** Tim Bergmeister, D (Dallara F397-Opel), 30m 26.126s; **9** Ronny Melkus, D (Dallara F397-Opel), 30m 26.305s; **10** Steffen Widmann, D (Martini MK73-Opel), 30m 36.499s.
Fastest race lap: Simon, 1m 13.213s, 102.508 mph/164.971 km/h.

Round 16 (50.033 miles/80.520 km)
1 Alexander 'Alex' Müller, D (Dallara F397-Opel), 29m 31.821s, 101.657 mph/163.601 km/h.
2 Nick Heidfeld, D (Dallara F397-Opel), 29m 31.941s; **3** Bas Leinders, B (Dallara F397-Opel), 29m 35.131s; **4** Norman Simon, D (Dallara F397-Opel), 29m 39.165s; **5** Timo Scheider, D (Dallara F397-Opel), 29m 47.455s; **6** Ronny Melkus, D (Dallara F397-Opel), 29m 48.596s; **7** Pierre Kaffer, D (Dallara F396-Opel), 29m 49.572s; **8** Sascha Bert, D (Dallara F397-Opel), 29m 57.388s; **9** Tomas Enge, CZ (Dallara F397-Opel), 29m 57.806s; **10** Tim Bergmeister, D (Dallara F397-Opel), 30m 10.188s.
Fastest race lap: Simon, 1m 13.113s, 102.648 mph/165.196 km/h.

ADAC-SUPERSPRINT NÜRBURGRING, Nürburgring Short Circuit, Nürburg/Eifel, Germany, 4/5 October. 2 x 27 laps of the 1.888-mile/3.038-km circuit.
Round 17 (50.969 miles/82.026 km)
1 Nick Heidfeld, D (Dallara F397-Opel), 29m 05.891s, 105.096 mph/169.136 km/h.
2 Norman Simon, D (Dallara F397-Opel), 29m 18.679s; **3** Timo Scheider, D (Dallara F397-Opel), 29m 20.686s; **4** Pierre Kaffer, D (Dallara F396-Opel), 29m 21.355s; **5** Alexander 'Alex' Müller, D (Dallara F397-Opel), 29m 27.552s; **6** Tomas Enge, CZ (Dallara F397-Opel), 29m 31.906s; **7** Johan Stureson, S (Dallara F397-Opel), 29m 32.708s; **8** Sascha Bert, D (Dallara F397-Opel), 29m 33.497s; **9** Bas Leinders, B (Dallara F397-Opel), 29m 34.019s; **10** Tim Bergmeister, D (Dallara F397-Opel), 29m 36.239s.
Fastest race lap: Heidfeld, 1m 03.849s, 106.436 mph/171.292 km/h.

Round 18 (50.969 miles/82.026 km)
1 Norman Simon, D (Dallara F397-Opel), 29m 22.515s, 104.105 mph/167.541 km/h.
2 Nick Heidfeld, D (Dallara F397-Opel), 29m 22.868s; **3** Timo Scheider, D (Dallara F397-Opel), 29m 23.355s; **4** Pierre Kaffer, D (Dallara F396-Opel), 29m 25.249s; **5** Alexander 'Alex' Müller, D (Dallara F397-Opel), 29m 32.039s; **6** Sascha Bert, D (Dallara F397-Opel), 29m 36.970s; **7** Yves Olivier, B (Dallara F397-Opel), 29m 41.580s; **8** Ronny Melkus, D (Dallara F397-Opel), 29m 43.216s; **9** Andreas Scheld, D (Dallara F397-Opel), 29m 49.379s; **10** Tim Bergmeister, D (Dallara F397-Opel), 29m 49.752s.
Fastest race lap: Kaffer, 1m 03.254s, 107.437 mph/172.903 km/h.

Final championship points
1 Nick Heidfeld, D, 224; **2** Timo Scheider, D, 218; **3** Alexander 'Alex' Müller, D, 147; **4** Wolf Henzler, D, 144; **5** Norman Simon, D, 113; **6** Pierre Kaffer, D, 103; **7** Bas Leinders, B, 100; **8** Sascha Bert, D, 80; **9** Tim Verbergt, B, 72; **10** Dominik Schwager, D, 68; **11** Ronny Melkus, D, 48; **12** Tomas Enge, CZ, 30; **13=** Johan Stureson, S, 26; **13=** Steffen Widmann, D, 26; **15** Yves Olivier, B, 16; **16=** Tim Coronel, NL, 10; **16=** Lucas Luhr, D, 10; **18** Luciano Crespi, I, 9; **19** Andreas Scheld, D, 7; **20** Tim Bergmeister, D, 6; **21** Michael Stelzig, D, 1.

Italian Formula 3 Championship

ITALIAN FORMULA 3 CHAMPIONSHIP, Autodromo di Magione, Perugia, Italy, 31 March. Round 1. 39 laps of the 1.616-mile/2.600-km circuit, 63.007 miles/101.400 km.
1 André Couto, P (Dallara F397-Fiat), 44m 19.013s, 85.304 mph/137.284 km/h.
2 Oliver Martini, I (Dallara F397-Opel), 44m 30.003s; **3** Alfredo Melandri, I (Dallara F396-Fiat), 44m 30.996s; **4** Paolo Ruberti, I (Dallara F396-Fiat), 44m 33.054s; **5** Nikolaos 'Nico' Stremmenos, GR (Dallara F395-Fiat), 45m 01.113s; **6** Miguel Angel Perez, RA (Dallara F396-Fiat), 45m 13.230s; **7** Marco Barindelli, I (Dallara F395/396-Opel), 45m 13.683s; **8** Michel Rangoni, I (Dallara F396-Fiat), 38 laps; **9** Davide Uboldi, I (Dallara F396-Fiat), 38; **10** Michelangelo 'Michele' Segatori, I (Dallara F396-Fiat), 37.
Fastest race lap: Ruberti, 1m 07.108s, 86.667 mph/139.477 km/h.
Fastest qualifying lap: Couto, 1m 06.619s, 87.303 mph/140.500 km/h.

ITALIAN FORMULA 3 CHAMPIONSHIP, Autodromo Internazionale del Mugello, Scarperia, Firenze (Florence), Italy, 13 April. Round 2. 23 laps of the 3.259-mile/5.245-km circuit, 74.959 miles/120.635 km.
1 Oliver Martini, I (Dallara F396-Opel), 40m 35.165s, 110.815 mph/178.339 km/h.
2 Nicola 'Niki' Cadei, I (Dallara F396-Fiat), 40m 43.676s; **3** Maurizio Mediani, I (Dallara F396-Fiat), 40m 45.580s; **4** André Couto, P (Dallara F397-Fiat), 40m 46.286s; **5** Michele Gasparini, I (Dallara F396-Alfa Romeo), 40m 54.020s; **6** Paolo Ruberti, I (Dallara F396-Fiat), 40m 59.412s; **7** Marco Barindelli, I (Dallara F396-Opel), 41m 03.883s; **8** Alfredo Melandri, I (Dallara F396-Fiat), 41m 12.195s; **9** Nikolaos 'Nico' Stremmenos, GR (Dallara F396-Fiat), 41m 19.617s; **10** Miguel Angel Perez, RA (Dallara F396-Fiat), 41m 20.288s.

Fastest race lap: Martini, 1m 44.550s, 112.221 mph/180.603 km/h.
Fastest qualifying lap: Martini, 1m 42.794s, 114.138 mph/183.688 km/h.

GRAN PREMIO CAMPAGNANO – TROFEO IGNAZIO GIUNTI, Autodromo di Vallelunga, Campagnano di Roma, Italy, 4 May. Round 3. 38 laps of the 1.988-mile/3.200-km circuit, 75.559 miles/121.600 km.
1 Oliver Martini, I (Dallara F397-Opel), 44m 42.669s, 101.396 mph/163.181 km/h.
2 Paolo Ruberti, I (Dallara F396-Fiat), 44m 55.397s; **3** André Couto, P (Dallara F397-Fiat), 45m 00.699s; **4** Alfredo Melandri, I (Dallara F396-Fiat), 45m 01.400s; **5** Ananda Mikola, RI (Dallara F397-Fiat), 45m 22.700s; **6** Gabriele Gardel, I (Dallara F396-Fiat), 45m 29.160s; **7** Nikolaos 'Nico' Stremmenos, GR (Dallara F396-Fiat), 45m 31.244s; **8** Marco Barindelli, I (Dallara F396-Opel), 45m 35.016s; **9** Guido Pedrini, I (Dallara F396-Fiat), 45m 49.792s; **10** Miguel Angel Perez, RA (Dallara F396-Fiat), 45m 54.265s.
Fastest race lap: Martini, 1m 09.631s, 102.802 mph/165.444 km/h.
Fastest qualifying lap: Martini, 1m 08.593s, 104.358 mph/167.947 km/h.

41st GRAN PREMIO PERGUSA, Ente Autodromo di Pergusa, Enna-Pergusa, Sicily, 1 June. Round 4. 25 laps of the 3.076-mile/4.950-km circuit, 76.895 miles/123.750 km.
1 André Couto, P (Dallara F396-Fiat), 45m 36.497s, 101.159 mph/162.799 km/h.
2 Nicola 'Niki' Cadei, I (Dallara F396-Fiat), 45m 59.404s; **3** Marco Barindelli, I (Dallara F396-Opel), 46m 01.360s; **4** Maurizio Mediani, I (Dallara F396-Fiat), 46m 11.883s; **5** Alfredo Melandri, I (Dallara F396-Fiat), 46m 13.752s; **6** Michele Gasparini, I (Dallara F396-Alfa Romeo), 46m 20.000s; **7** Ananda Mikola, RI (Dallara F396-Fiat), 46m 24.697s; **8** Davide Campana, I (Dallara F396-Opel), 46m 26.522s; **9** Sébastian Mordillo, F (Dallara F396-Fiat), 46m 52.980s; **10** Davide Uboldi, I (Dallara F396-Fiat), 46m 55.261s.
Fastest race lap: Oliver Martini, I (Dallara F396-Opel), 1m 47.278s, 103.216 mph/166.110 km/h.
Fastest qualifying lap: Couto, 1m 37.414s, 113.668 mph/182.930 km/h.

36th TROFEO AUTOMOBILE CLUB PARMA, Autodromo Riccardo Paletti, Varano, Parma, Italy, 15 June. Round 5. 56 laps of the 1.118-mile/1.800-km circuit, 62.634 miles/100.800 km.
1 Maurizio Mediani, I (Dallara F396-Fiat), 42m 09.591s, 89.138 mph/143.454 km/h.
2 Oliver Martini, I (Dallara F397-Opel), 42m 15.740s; **3** Nicola 'Niki' Cadei, I (Dallara F396-Fiat), 42m 17.816s; **4** Michele Gasparini, I (Dallara F396-Alfa Romeo), 42m 18.337s; **5** Alfredo Melandri, I (Dallara F396-Fiat), 42m 18.833s; **6** Paolo Ruberti, I (Dallara F397-Fiat), 42m 22.815s; **7** Davide Campana, I (Dallara F397-Opel), 42m 23.597s; **8** Roberto Carta, I (Dallara F396-Fiat), 42m 41.217s; **9** Donny Crevels, NL (Dallara F396-Fiat), 42m 41.955s; **10** Riccardo Moscatelli, I (Dallara F397-Fiat), 42m 42.810s.
Fastest race lap: Mediani, 44.620s, 90.239 mph/145.226 km/h.
Fastest qualifying lap: André Couto, P (Dallara F397-Fiat), 44.123s, 91.256 mph/146.862 km/h.

38th GRAN PREMIO LOTTERIA DI MONZA, Autodromo Nazionale di Monza, Milan, Italy, 29 June. Round 6. 21 laps of the 3.585-mile/5.770-km circuit, 75.292 miles/121.170 km.
1 Nicola 'Niki' Cadei, I (Dallara F396-Fiat), 39m 16.040s, 115.045 mph/185.146 km/h.
2 Michele Gasparini, I (Dallara F396-Alfa Romeo), 39m 19.480s; **3** Marco Barindelli, I (Dallara F396-Opel), 39m 21.639s; **4** Maurizio Mediani, I (Dallara F396-Fiat), 39m 21.111s; **5** Davide Campana, I (Dallara F397-Opel), 39m 31.709s; **6** Sébastian Mordillo, F (Dallara F396-Fiat), 39m 37.887s; **7** Nikolaos 'Nico' Stremmenos, GR (Dallara F396-Opel), 39m 54.498s; **8** Oliver Martini, I (Dallara F397-Opel), 40m 00.562s; **9** Gabriele Gardel, I (Dallara F396-Fiat), 40m 02.998s; **10** Alessandro Manetti, I (Dallara F396-Fiat), 40m 09.796s.
Fastest race lap: Mediani, 1m 48.125s, 119.372 mph/192.111 km/h.
Fastest qualifying lap: Martini, 1m 45.751s, 122.052 mph/196.424 km/h.

ITALIAN FORMULA 3 CHAMPIONSHIP, Autodromo di Magione, Perugia, Italy, 20 July. Round 7. 39 laps of the 1.616-mile/2.600-km circuit, 63.007 miles/101.400 km.
1 Oliver Martini, I (Dallara F397-Opel), 44m 21.111s, 85.237 mph/137.176 km/h.
2 Paolo Ruberti, I (Dallara F396-Fiat), 44m 26.225s; **3** Marco Barindelli, I (Dallara F397-Opel), 44m 26.843s; **4** Nicola 'Niki' Cadei, I (Dallara F396-Fiat), 44m 32.474s; **5** Nikolaos 'Nico' Stremmenos, GR (Dallara F396-Opel), 44m 56.148s; **6** Ananda Mikola, RI (Dallara F397-Fiat), 44m 59.509s; **7** Gabriele Gardel, I (Dallara F396-Fiat), 45m 34.899s; **8** André Couto, P (Dallara F397-Fiat), 38 laps; **9** Maurizio Mediani, I (Dallara F396-Fiat), 38; **10** Riccardo Moscatelli, I (Dallara F397-Fiat), 28.
Fastest race lap: Martini, 1m 07.346s, 86.361 mph/138.984 km/h.
Fastest qualifying lap: Martini, 1m 06.831s, 87.026 mph/140.055 km/h.

ITALIAN FORMULA 3 CHAMPIONSHIP, Autodromo del Levante, Binetto, Italy, 21 September. Round 8. 63 laps of the 0.980-mile/1.577-km circuit, 61.734 miles/99.351 km.
1 Paolo Ruberti, I (Dallara F396-Fiat), 46m 23.520s, 79.842 mph/128.493 km/h.
2 Maurizio Mediani, I (Dallara F396-Fiat), 46m 23.919s; **3** Nikolaos 'Nico' Stremmenos, GR (Dallara F396-Opel), 46m 49.537s; **4** André Couto, P (Dallara F397-Fiat), 46m 49.827s; **5** Alfredo Melandri, I (Dallara F396-Fiat), 46m 53.125s; **6** Oliver Martini, I (Dallara F397-Opel), 47m 07.910s; **7** Nicola 'Niki' Cadei, I (Dallara F396-Fiat), 62 laps; **8** Marco Barindelli, I (Dallara F396-Fiat), 62; **9** Tom Schwister (Dallara F397-Opel), 62; **10** Gabriele Gardel, I (Dallara F396-Fiat), 62.
Fastest race lap: Mediani, 41.925s, 84.142 mph/135.413 km/h.
Fastest qualifying lap: Mediani, 43.101s, 81.846 mph/131.719 km/h.

ITALIAN FORMULA 3 CHAMPIONSHIP, Autodromo Enzo e Dino Ferrari, Imola, Italy, 5 October. Round 9. 25 laps of the 3.063-mile/4.930-km circuit, 76.584 miles/123.250 km.
1 Oliver Martini, I (Dallara F397-Opel), 45m 37.394s, 100.717 mph/162.088 km/h.
2 Paolo Ruberti, I (Dallara F396-Fiat), 45m 46.446s; **3** Maurizio Mediani, I (Dallara F396-Fiat), 45m 53.712s; **4** André Couto, P (Dallara F397-Fiat), 45m 54.663s; **5** Nikolaos 'Nico' Stremmenos, GR (Dallara F396-Opel), 46m 06.025s; **6** Ananda Mikola, RI (Dallara F397-Fiat), 46m 06.288s; **7** Fabrizio de Pace, I (Dallara F396-Opel), 46m 07.896s; **8** Alfredo Melandri, I (Dallara F396-Fiat), 47m 06.614s; **9** Michelangelo 'Michele' Segatori, I (Dallara F396-Fiat), 24 laps; **10** Sébastian Mordillo, F (Dallara F396-Fiat), 23.
Fastest race lap: Martini, 1m 48.173s, 101.949 mph/164.071 km/h.
Fastest qualifying lap: Martini, 1m 45.980s, 104.058 mph/167.466 km/h.

ITALIAN FORMULA 3 CHAMPIONSHIP, Autodromo Santamonica, Misano Adriatico, Rimini, Italy, 19 October. Round 10. 29 laps of the 2.523-mile/4.060-km circuit, 73.160 miles/117.740 km.
1 Oliver Martini, I (Dallara F397-Opel), 42m 35.122s, 103.078 mph/165.888 km/h.
2 André Couto, P (Dallara F396-Fiat), 42m 42.536s; **3** Sascha Bert, D (Dallara F397-Opel), 42m 46.766s; **4** Donny Crevels, NL (Dallara F396-Fiat), 42m 48.001s; **5** Alfredo Melandri, I (Dallara F396-Fiat), 42m 54.035s; **6** Marco Barindelli, I (Dallara F396-Fiat), 42m 54.835s; **7** Nicola 'Niki' Cadei, I (Dallara F396-Fiat), 42m 55.658s; **8** Sébastian Mordillo, F (Dallara F396-Fiat), 42m 55.829s; **9** Fabrizio de Pace, I (Dallara F396-Opel), 43m 11.350s; **10** Andra Cammarone, I (Dallara F396-Fiat), 43m 24.641s.
Fastest race lap: Martini, 1m 27.373s, 103.945 mph/167.283 km/h.
Fastest qualifying lap: Couto, 1m 26.530s, 104.957 mph/168.913 km/h.

Final championship points
1 Oliver Martini, I, 139; **2** André Couto, P, 100; **3** Paolo Ruberti, I, 87; **4** Maurizio Mediani, I, 81; **5** Nicola 'Niki' Cadei, I, 80; **6** Alfredo Melandri, I, 60; **7** Marco Barindelli, I, 56; **8** Nikolaos 'Nico' Stremmenos, GR, 46; **9** Michele Gasparini, I, 39; **10** Ananda Mikola, RI, 34; **11** Davide Campana, I, 15; **12** Gabriele Gardel, I, 13; **13** Sébastian Mordillo, F, 12; **14** Sascha Bert, D, 12; **15** Donny Crevels, NL, 12; **16** Miguel Angel Perez, RA, 8; **17** Fabrizio de Pace, I, 6; **18=** Michel Rangoni, I, 3; **18=** Davide Uboldi, I, 3; **18=** Roberto Carta, I, 3; **18=** Michelangelo 'Michele' Segatori, I, 3; **22=** Andrea Pedrini, I, 2; **22=** Riccardo Moscatelli, I, 2; **22=** Tom Schwister, 2; **25=** Andrea Cammarone, I, 1; **25=** Alessandro Manetti, I, 1.

Major Non-Championship Formula 3 Results

1996 Result

The Macau Formula 3 race was run after Autocourse *1996/97 went to press.*

FIA F3 WORLD CUP, 43rd MACAU GP, Circuito Da Guia, Macau, 17 November. 27 laps of the 3.801-mile/6.117-km circuit, 102.625 miles/165.159 km.
1 Ralph Firman, GB (Dallara F396-Mugen Honda), 1h 03m 14.79s, 97.357 mph/156.681 km/h.
2 Massimiliano 'Max' Angelelli, I (Dallara F396-Opel), 1h 03m 19.33s; **3** Jarno Trulli, I (Dallara F396-Opel), 1h 03m 20.17s; **4** Soheil Ayari, F (Dallara F396-Opel), 1h 03m 22.98s; **5** Tom Coronel, NL (TOM'S 035F-Toyota), 1h 03m 24.84s; **6** Nick Heidfeld, D (Dallara F396-Opel), 1h 03m 34.94s; **7** Pedro de la Rosa, E (Dallara F396-Mugen Honda), 1h 04m 00.25s; **8** André Couto, P (Dallara F396-Fiat), 1h 04m 02.66s; **9** Darren Manning, GB (Dallara F396-Mugen Honda), 1h 04m 05.36s; **10** Guy Smith, GB (TOM'S 036F-Toyota), 1h 04m 20.14s.
Fastest race lap: Coronel, 2m 18.598s, 98.727 mph/158.885 km/h.
Fastest qualifying lap: Heidfeld, 2m 19.082s, 98.383 mph/158.332 km/h.

1997 Results

39th GRAND PRIX DE 'MONACO FORMULA 3', Monte Carlo Street Circuit, Monaco, 11 May. 24 laps of the 2.068-mile/3.328-km circuit, 49.630 miles/79.872 km.
1 Nick Heidfeld, D (Dallara F397-Opel), 37m 35.297s, 79.222 mph/127.495 km/h.
2 Wolf Henzler, D (Martini MK73-Opel), 37m 57.694s; **3** Patrice Gay, F (Dallara F396-Opel), 37m 58.593s; **4** David Saelens, B (Dallara F396-Opel), 37m 59.414s; **5** Sébastien Philippe, F (Dallara F396-Opel), 38m 07.350s; **6** Sascha Bert, D (Dallara F397-Opel), 38m 08.537s; **7** Bas Leinders, B (Dallara F397-Opel), 38m 10.967s; **8** Maurizio Mediani, I (Dallara F396-Fiat), 38m 11.330s; **9** Nicola 'Niki' Cadei, I (Dallara F396-Fiat), 38m 12.340s; **10** Paolo Ruberti, I (Dallara F396-Fiat), 38m 12.978s.
Fastest race lap: Heidfeld, 1m 32.935s, 80.105 mph/128.916 km/h.
Fastest qualifying lap: Heidfeld, 1m 32.564s, 80.426 mph/129.433 km/h.

7th MARLBORO MASTERS OF FORMULA 3, Circuit Park Zandvoort, Holland, 3 August. 32 laps of the 1.565-mile/2.519-km circuit, 50.087 miles/80.608 km.

1 Tom Coronel, NL (Dallara F397-TOM'S Toyota), 35m 52.569s, 83.767 mph/134.810 km/h.
2 Sébastien Philippe, F (Dallara F396-Opel), 35m 53.680s; **3** Mark Webber, AUS (Dallara F397-Mugen Honda), 35m 54.687s; **4** Nicolas Minassian, F (Dallara F397-Renault), 35m 54.963s; **5** Brian Smith, RA (Dallara F397-HKS Mitsubishi), 35m 55.521s; **6** Norman Simon, D (Dallara F397-Opel), 35m 56.550s; **7** Nick Heidfeld, D (Dallara F397-Opel), 35m 57.144s; **8** Donny Crevels, NL (Dallara F397-Fiat), 35m 57.261s; **9** David Saelens, B (Dallara F396-Opel), 35m 58.278s; **10** Patrice Gay, F (Dallara F396-Opel), 35m 58.447s.
Fastest race lap: Philippe, 1m 03.188s, 89.176 mph/143.515 km/h.
Fastest qualifying lap: Philippe, 1m 02.001s, 90.883 mph/146.262 km/h.

Result of Macau Formula 3 race will be given in Autocourse 1998/99.

FIA Grand Touring Championship

FIA GT CHAMPIONSHIP, Hockenheimring, Heidelberg, Germany, 13 April. Round 1. 83 laps of the 4.240-mile/6.823-km circuit, 351.888 miles/566.309 km.
1 JJ Lehto/Steve Soper, SF/GB (McLaren F1 GTR-BMW), 2h 57m 21.061s, 119.048 mph/191.589 km/h (1st GT1 class).
2 Jean-Marc Gounon/Pierre-Henri Raphanel, F/F (McLaren F1 GTR-BMW), 2h 58m 22.894s; **3** John Nielsen/Thomas Bscher, DK/D (McLaren F1 GTR-BMW), 82 laps; **4** Hans Stuck/Thierry Boutsen, D/B (Porsche 911 GT1), 82; **5** Ralf Kelleners/Yannick Dalmas, D/F (Porsche 911 GT1), 81; **6** Bob Wollek/Pedro Lamy, F/P (Porsche 911 GT1), 81; **7** Pierluigi Martini/Christian Pescatori, I/I (Porsche 911 GT1), 81; **8** Christophe Bouchut/Klaus Ludwig/Carl Rosenblad, F/D/S (Porsche 911 GT1), 81; **9** Emmanuel Collard/Jurgen von Gartzen, F/D (Porsche 911 GT1), 80; **10** Olivier Beretta/Philippe Gache, MC/F (Chrysler Viper GTS-R), 77 (1st GT2 class).
Fastest race lap: Lehto, 2m 01.711s, 125.400 mph/201.812 km/h.
Fastest qualifying lap: Bernd Schneider, D (Mercedes CLK-GTR), 1m 59.099s, 128.151 mph/206.239 km/h.

BRITISH EMPIRE TROPHY, Silverstone Grand Prix Circuit, Towcester, Northamptonshire, Great Britain, 11 May. Round 2. 87 laps of the 3.194-mile/5.140-km circuit, 277.865 miles/447.180 km.
1 Peter Kox/Roberto Ravaglia, NL/I (McLaren F1 GTR-BMW), 3h 20m 27.077s, 83.172 mph/133.852 km/h (1st GT1 class).
2 Bernd Schneider/Alexander 'Alex' Wurz, D/A (Mercedes-Benz CLK-GTR), 3h 20m 27.702s; **3** JJ Lehto/Steve Soper, SF/GB (McLaren F1 GTR-BMW), 3h 21m 46.116s; **4** Andrew Gilbert-Scott/Pierre-Henri Raphanel/Ray Bellm, GB/F/GB (McLaren F1 GTR-BMW), 3h 22m 05.919s; **5** Hans Stuck/Thierry Boutsen, D/B (Porsche 911 GT1), 3h 22m 08.717s; **6** Chris Goodwin/Gary Ayles, GB/GB (McLaren F1 GTR-BMW), 3h 22m 24.043s; **7** Pedro Lamy/Bob Wollek, P/F (Porsche 911 GT1), 84 laps; **8** Tommy Archer/Justin Bell, USA/GB (Chrysler Viper GTS-R), 83 (1st GT2 class); **9** John Nielsen/Thomas Bscher, DK/D (McLaren F1 GTR-BMW), 83; **10** Bruno Eichmann/Claudia Hurtgen/Ni Amorin, CH/D/P (Porsche 911 GT2), 83.
Fastest race lap: Lamy, 1m 45.946s, 108.526 mph/174.655 km/h.
Fastest qualifying lap: Schneider, 1m 41.193s, 113.623 mph/182.858 km/h.

THUNDER IN HELSINKI, Grand Prix Center of Helsinki, Finland, 25 May. Round 3. 113 laps of the 1.227-mile/1.975-km circuit, 138.675 miles/223.175 km.
1 JJ Lehto/Steve Soper, SF/GB (McLaren F1 GTR-BMW), 3h 00m 31.711s, 46.090 mph/74.174 km/h (1st GT1 class).
2 Ralf Kelleners/Stéphane Ortelli, D/F (Porsche 911 GT1), 110 laps; **3** John Nielsen/Thomas Bscher, DK/D (McLaren F1 GTR-BMW), 110; **4** Andrew Gilbert-Scott/Pierre-Henri Raphanel, GB/F (McLaren F1 GTR-BMW), 109; **5** Andrew Boldrini/Mauro Martini, I/I (Lotus GT1), 109; **6** Pierluigi Martini/Christian Pescatori, I/I (Porsche 911 GT1), 108; **7** Mauro Baldi/Massimiliano 'Max' Angelelli, I/I (Porsche 911 GT1), 108; **8** Bernd Schneider/Alexander 'Alex' Wurz, D/A (Mercedes-Benz CLK-GTR), 107; **9** Bruno Eichmann/Claudia Hurtgen/Ni Amorin, CH/D/P (Porsche 911 GT2), 106 (1st GT2 class); **10** Cor Euser/Harald Becker, NL/D (Marcos LM600), 106.
Fastest race lap: Schneider, 1m 27.901s, 50.261 mph/80.886 km/h.
Fastest qualifying lap: Lehto, 1m 26.097s, 51.314 mph/82.581 km/h.

FIA GT CHAMPIONSHIP, Nürburgring, Nürburg/Eifel, Germany, 29 June. Round 4. 147 laps of the 2.822-mile/4.542-km circuit, 414.873 miles/667.674 km.
1 Bernd Schneider/Klaus Ludwig, D/D (Mercedes-Benz CLK-GTR), 4h 00m 11.517s, 103.635 mph/166.785 km/h (1st GT1 class).
2 Alessandro Nannini/Marcel Tiemann, I/D (Mercedes-Benz CLK-GTR), 147 laps; **3** JJ Lehto/Steve Soper, SF/GB (McLaren F1 GTR-BMW), 146; **4** Peter Kox/Roberto Ravaglia, NL/I (McLaren F1 GTR-BMW), 146; **5** Jean-Marc Gounon/Pierre-Henri Raphanel, F/F (McLaren F1 GTR-BMW), 146; **6** Chris Goodwin/Gary Ayles, GB/GB (McLaren F1 GTR-BMW), 144; **7** John Nielsen/Thomas Bscher, DK/D (McLaren F1 GTR-BMW), 144; **8** Emmanuel Collard/Jurgen von Gartzen, F/D (Porsche 911 GT1), 143; **9** Christophe Bouchut/Carl Rosenblad, F/S (Porsche 911 GT1), 143; **10** Hans Stuck/Thierry Boutsen, D/B (Porsche 911 GT1), 142.
GT2 class winner: Claudia Hurtgen/Bruno Eichmann/Ni Amorim, D/CH/P (Porsche 911 GT2), 133 laps (16th).
Fastest race lap: Schneider, 1m 33.614s, 108.533 mph/174.666 km/h.
Fastest qualifying lap: Schneider, 1m 31.488s, 111.055 mph/178.725 km/h.

FIA GT CHAMPIONSHIP, Circuit de Spa-Francorchamps, Stavelot, Belgium, 20 July. Round 5. 101 laps of 4.330-mile/6.968-km circuit, 437.301 miles/703.768 km.
1 JJ Lehto/Steve Soper, SF/GB (McLaren F1 GTR-BMW), 4h 01m 54.816s, 108.460 mph/174.550 km/h (1st GT1 class).
2 Bernd Schneider/Alexander 'Alex' Wurz, D/A (Mercedes-Benz CLK-GTR), 101 laps; **3** Thierry Boutsen/Yannick Dalmas/Bob Wollek, B/F/F (Porsche 911 GT1), 99; **4** Peter Kox/Roberto Ravaglia, NL/I (McLaren F1 GTR-BMW), 99; **5** Klaus Ludwig/Ralf Schumacher, D/D (Mercedes-Benz CLK-GTR), 99; **6** Chris Goodwin/Gary Ayles, GB/GB (McLaren F1 GTR-BMW), 98; **7** Ralf Kelleners/Pedro Chaves, D/P (Porsche 911 GT1), 98; **8** Fabien Giroix/Jean-Denis Deletraz, F/CH (Lotus GT1), 96; **9** Andy Wallace/James Weaver, GB/GB (Panoz GTR), 96; **10** Pierluigi Martini/Christian Pescatori, I/I (Porsche 911 GT1), 94.
GT2 class winner: Marc Duez/Justin Bell, B/GB (Chrysler Viper GTS-R), 93 laps (11th).
Fastest race lap: Schneider, 2m 12.058s, 118.031 mph/189.953 km/h.
Fastest qualifying lap: Lehto, 2m 08.984s, 120.844 mph/194.480 km/h.

FIA GT CHAMPIONSHIP, A1-Ring, Knittelfeld, Austria, 3 August. Round 6. 161 laps of the 2.686-mile/4.323-km circuit, 432.476 miles/696.003 km.
1 Klaus Ludwig/Bernd Mayländer/Bernd Schneider, D/D/D (Mercedes-Benz CLK-GTR), 4h 00m 55.815s, 107.702 mph/173.329 km/h (1st GT1 class).
2 Alessandro Nannini/Marcel Tiemann, I/D (Mercedes-Benz CLK-GTR), 161 laps; **3** JJ Lehto/Steve Soper, SF/GB (McLaren F1 GTR-BMW), 160; **4** Bernd Schneider/Alexander 'Alex' Wurz, D/A (Mercedes-Benz CLK-GTR), 159; **5** PierreHenri Raphanel/Anders Olofsson, F/S (McLaren F1 GTR-BMW), 159; **6** Bob Wollek/Thierry Boutsen, F/B (Porsche 911 GT1), 159; **7** Yannick Dalmas/Allan McNish, F/GB (Porsche 911 GT1), 158; **8** Pierluigi Martini/Christian Pescatori, I/I (Porsche 911 GT1), 156; **9** Eric Bernard/Franck Lagorce, F/F (Panoz GTR), 156; **10** Emmanuel Collard/Mauro Baldi, F/I (Porsche 911 GT1), 155.
GT2 class winner: Stéphane Ortelli/Bruno Eichmann/Claudia Hurtgen, F/CH/D (Porsche 911 GT2), 148 laps (13th).
Fastest race lap: Schneider, 1m 24.601s, 114.305 mph/183.955 km/h.
Fastest qualifying lap: Nannini, 1m 22.990s, 116.523 mph/187.526 km/h.

1000 KM OF SUZUKA, Suzuka International Racing Course, Suzuka City, Mie-Ken, Japan, 24 August. Round 7. 171 laps of the 3.644-mile/5.864-km circuit, 623.076 miles/1002.744 km.
1 Alessandro Nannini/Marcel Tiemann/Bernd Schneider, I/D/D (Mercedes-Benz CLK-GTR), 5h 59m 31.003s, 103.986 mph/167.349 km/h (1st GT1 class).
2 Klaus Ludwig/Bernd Mayländer, D/D (Mercedes-Benz CLK-GTR), 171 laps; **3** Jean-Marc Gounon/Pierre-Henri Raphanel/Anders Olofsson, F/F/S (McLaren F1 GTR-BMW), 171; **4** JJ Lehto/Steve Soper, SF/GB (McLaren F1 GTR-BMW), 171; **5** Hans Stuck/Thierry Boutsen/Bob Wollek, D/B/F (Porsche 911 GT1), 169; **6** Geoff Lees/John Nielsen/Andrew Gilbert-Scott/Pierre-Henri Raphanel, GB/DK/GB/F (McLaren F1 GTR-BMW), 169; **7** Bernd Schneider/Alexander 'Alex' Wurz/Aguri Suzuki, D/A/J (Mercedes-Benz CLK-GTR), 169; **8** Peter Kox/Roberto Ravaglia, NL/I (McLaren F1 GTR-BMW), 169; **9** Keiichi Tsuchiya/Masanori Sekiya/Akahiko Nakaya, J/J/J (McLaren F1 GTR-BMW), 168; **10** Yannick Dalmas/Allan McNish/Pedro Lamy, F/GB/P (Porsche 911 GT1), 164.
GT2 class winner: Philippe Gache/Olivier Beretta, F/MC (Chrysler Viper GTS-R), 156 laps (14th).
Fastest race lap: Ludwig, 2m 00.019s, 109.294 mph/175.892 km/h.
Fastest qualifying lap: Ludwig, 1m 56.023s, 113.059 mph/181.950 km/h.

FIA GT CHAMPIONSHIP, Donington Park Grand Prix Circuit, Derbyshire, Great Britain, 14 September. Round 8. 160 laps of the 2.481-mile/3.993-km circuit, 396.982 miles/638.880 km.
1 Bernd Schneider/Alexander 'Alex' Wurz, D/A (Mercedes-Benz CLK-GTR), 4h 00m 01.691s, 99.234 mph/159.701 km/h (1st GT1 class).
2 Alessandro Nannini/Marcel Tiemann, I/D (Mercedes-Benz CLK-GTR), 159 laps; **3** JJ Lehto/Steve Soper, SF/GB (McLaren F1 GTR-BMW), 159; **4** Klaus Ludwig/Bernd Mayländer, D/D (Mercedes-Benz CLK-GTR), 158; **5** Peter Kox/Roberto Ravaglia, NL/I (McLaren F1 GTR-BMW), 158; **6** Jean-Marc Gounon/Pierre-Henri Raphanel, F/F (McLaren F1 GTR-BMW), 157; **7** Geoff Lees/Anders Olofsson, GB/S (McLaren F1 GTR-BMW), 156; **8** David Brabham/Perry McCarthy, AUS/GB (Panoz GTR), 155; **9** James Weaver/Andy Wallace, GB/GB (Panoz GTR), 154; **10** Pierluigi Martini/Christian Pescatori, I/I (Porsche 911 GT1), 152.
GT2 class winner: Philippe Gache/Olivier Beretta, F/MC (Chrysler Viper GTS-R), 146 laps (15th).
Fastest race lap: Schneider, 1m 26.075s, 103.771 mph/167.003 km/h.
Fastest qualifying lap: Schneider, 1m 23.854s, 106.520 mph/171.427 km/h.

FIA GT CHAMPIONSHIP, Autodromo Internazionale del Mugello, Scarperia, Firenze (Florence), Italy, 28 September. Round 9. 132 laps of the 3.259-mile/5.245-km circuit, 430.200 miles/692.340 km.
1 JJ Lehto/Steve Soper, SF/GB (McLaren F1 GTR-BMW), 4h 01m 36.747s, 106.832 mph/171.930 km/h (1st GT1 class).
2 Alessandro Nannini/Marcel Tiemann, I/D (Mercedes-Benz CLK-GTR), 132 laps; **3** Yannick Dalmas/Bob Wollek, F/F (Porsche 911 GT1), 132; **4** Thierry Boutsen/Ralf Kelleners, B/D (Porsche 911 GT1), 132; **5** Peter Kox/Roberto Ravaglia, NL/I (McLaren F1 GTR-BMW), 131; **6** Jean-Marc Gounon/Pierre-Henri Raphanel, F/F (McLaren F1 GTR-BMW), 131; **7** Franck Lagorce/Eric Bernard, F/F (Panoz GTR), 131; **8** Geoff Lees/Anders Olofsson, GB/S (McLaren F1 GTR-BMW), 130; **9** Klaus Ludwig/Bernd Mayländer, D/D (Mercedes-Benz CLK-GTR), 130; **10** David Brabham/Perry McCarthy, AUS/GB (Panoz GTR), 129.
GT2 class winner: Luca Drudi/Justin Bell, I/GB (Chrysler Vipe GTS-R), 122 laps (14th).
Fastest race lap: Schneider, 1m 45.013s, 111.726 mph/179.806 km/h.
Fastest qualifying lap: Schneider, 1m 41.865s, 115.179 mph/185.363 km/h.

SEBRING OKTOBERFEST, Sebring International Raceway, Florida, USA, 19 October. Round 10. 70 laps of the 3.700-mile/5.955-km circuit, 259.000 miles, 416.821 km.
1 Bernd Schneider/Klaus Ludwig, D/D (Mercedes-Benz CLK-GTR), 3h 00m 19.227s, 86.180 mph/138.693 km/h (1st GT1 class).
2 Peter Kox/Roberto Ravaglia, NL/I (McLaren F1 GTR-BMW), 70 laps; **3** David Brabham/Perry McCarthy, AUS/GB (Panoz GTR), 69; **4** Yannick Dalmas/Bob Wollek, F/F (Porsche 911 GT1), 69; **5** Jean-Marc Gounon/Pierre-Henri Raphanel, F/F (McLaren F1 GTR-BMW), 68; **6** Hans Stuck/Thierry Boutsen, D/B (Porsche 911 GT1), 68; **7** Greg Moore/Alexander 'Alex' Wurz/Klaus Ludwig, CDN/A/D (Mercedes-Benz CLK-GTR), 68; **8** Franck Lagorce/Eric Bernard, F/F (Panoz GTR), 67; **9** Emmanuel Collard/Mauro Baldi, F/I (Porsche 911 GT1), 67; **10** Geoff Lees/Anders Olofsson, GB/S (McLaren F1 GTR-BMW), 67.
GT2 class winner: Olivier Beretta/Philippe Gache, MC/F (Chrysler Viper GTS-R), 67 laps (11th).
Fastest race lap: Schneider, 1m 59.290s, 111.661 mph/179.700 km/h.
Fastest qualifying lap: Steve Soper, GB (McLaren F1 GTR), 1m 55.929s, 114.898 mph/184.910 km/h.

FIA GT CHAMPIONSHIP, Laguna Seca Raceway, Monterey, California, USA, 26 October. Round 11. 130 laps of the 2.238-mile/3.602-km circuit, 290.940 miles/468.223 km.
1 Bernd Schneider/Klaus Ludwig, D/D (Mercedes-Benz CLK-GTR), 3h 00m 46.987s, 96.560 mph/155.398 km/h (1st GT1 class).
2 Yannick Dalmas/Bob Wollek, F/F (Porsche 911 GT1), 130 laps; **3** Allan McNish/Ralf Kelleners, GB/D (Porsche 911 GT1), 130; **4** Pierre-Henri Raphanel/Jean-Marc Gounon, F/F (McLaren F1 GTR-BMW), 130; **5** Thierry Boutsen/Hans Stuck, B/D (Porsche 911 GT1), 129; **6** David Brabham/Andy Wallace, AUS/GB (Panoz GTR), 128; **7** Geoff Lees/Anders Olofsson, GB/S (McLaren F1 GTR-BMW), 128; **8** Alexander 'Alex' Wurz/Greg Moore, A/CDN (Mercedes-Benz CLK-GTR), 127; **9** Alessandro Nannini/Marcel Tiemann, I/D (Mercedes-Benz CLK-GTR), 127; **10** Jan Lammers/Mike Hezemans, NL/NL (Lotus GT1), 127.
GT2 class winner: Bruno Eichmann/Stéphane Ortelli, CH/F (Porsche 911 GT2), 121 laps (16th).
Fastest race lap: Dalmas, 1m 19.713s, 101.073 mph/162.661 km/h.
Fastest qualifying lap: Wurz, 1m 17.941s, 103.370 mph/166.359 km/h.

Final championship points
GT1 Drivers
1 Bernd Schneider, D, 72; **2=** JJ Lehto, SF, 59; **2=** Steve Soper, GB, 59; **4** Klaus Ludwig, D, 51; **5=** Alessandro Nannini, I, 34; **5=** Marcel Tiemann, D, 34; **7** Pierre-Henri Raphanel, F, 27; **8=** Roberto Ravaglia, I, 26; **8=** Peter Kox, NL, 26; **10** Alexander 'Alex' Wurz, A, 25; **11** Jean-Marc Gounon, F, 22; **12** Bob Wollek, F, 21; **13=** Yannick Dalmas, F, 19; **13=** Bernd Mayländer, D, 19; **15** Thierry Boutsen, B, 18.

GT1 Teams
1 AMG Mercedes, 110; **2** Team BMW Motorsport (Schnitzer), 85; **3** Gulf Team Davidoff, 37; **4** Porsche AG, 35; **5** Roock Racing, 8.

GT2 Drivers
1 Justin Bell, GB, 66; **2** Bruno Eichmann, CH, 65; **3=** Philippe Gache, F, 60; **3=** Olivier Beretta, MC, 60; **5** Claudia Hurtgen, D, 55.

GT2 Teams
1 Viper Team ORECA, 126; **2** Roock Racing, 83; **3** Konrad, 15; **4=** Marcos Racing, 13; **4=** Krauss, 13.

Other Sports Car Race

65th 24 HEURES DU MANS, Circuit de la Sarthe, Le Mans, France, 14-15 June. 361 laps of the 8.451-mile/13.600-km circuit, 3050.684 miles/4909.600 km.
1 Michele Alboreto/Stefan Johansson/Tom Kristensen, I/S/DK (Porsche WSC95), 24h 02m 40.875s, 126.876 mph/204.186 km/h (1st Prototype Category).
2 Pierre-Henri Raphanel/Jean-Marc Gounon/Anders Olofsson, F/F/S (McLaren F1 GTR-BMW), 360 laps (1st GT1 Category); **3** Peter Kox/Roberto Ravaglia/Eric Hélary, NL/I/F (McLaren F1 GTR-BMW), 358; **4** Didier Cottaz/Jérôme Policand/Marc Goossens, F/F/B (Courage C41), 336; **5** Armin Hahne/Pedro Lamy/Patrice Gouselard, D/P/F (Porsche 911 GT1), 331; **6** Didier Theys/Giampiero Moretti/Massimiliano 'Max' Papis, B/I/I (Ferrari 333SP), 321; **7** Emmanuel Clérico/Henri Pescarolo/Jean-Philippe Belloc, F/F/F (Courage C36), 319; **8** Pierluigi Martini/Christian Pescatori/Antonio Hermann, I/I/BR (Porsche 911 GT1), 317; **9** Michel Neugarten/Jean-Claude Lagniez/Guy Martinolle, B/F/F (Porsche 911 GT2), 307 (1st GT2 Category); **10** Bruno Eichmann/Andy Pilgrim/Andre Ahrle, CH/USA/D (Porsche 911 GT2), 306; **11** Manuel Breyner/Pedro Breyner/Tomaz Breyner, P/P/P (Porsche 911 GT2), 295; **12** Kazuyoshi Hoshino/Erik Comas/Masahiko Kageyama, J/F/J (Nissan R390 GT1), 294; **13** Claudia Hurtgen/Hugh Price/John Robinson, D/GB/GB (Porsche 911 GT2), 287; **14** Justin Bell/John Morton/Pierre Yver, GB/USA/F (Chrysler Viper GTS-R), 278; **15** Jari Nurminen/Chris Gleason/Hans Hugenholtz, SF/USA/NL (Chrysler Viper GTS-R), 269; **16** Fredrik Ekblom/Jean-Louis Ricci/Jean-Paul Libert, S/F/F (Courage C36), 265; **17** Franck Fréon/Yojiro Terada/Jim Downing, F/J/USA (Mazda Kudzu MS97), 263; **18** Emmanuel Collard/Yannick Dalmas/Ralf Kelleners, F/F/D (Porsche 911 GT1), 327 (DNF – fire); **19** Ray Bellm/Andrew Gilbert-Scott/Masanori Sekiya, GB/GB/J (McLaren F1 GTR-BMW), 326 (DNF – fire); **20** Philippe Gache/Olivier Beretta/Dominique Dupuy, F/MC/F (Chrysler Viper GTS-R), 263 (DNF – accident); **21** Bob Wollek/Hans Stuck/Thierry Boutsen, D/D/B (Porsche 911 GT1), 238 (DNF – accident); **22** JJ Lehto/Steve Soper/Nelson Piquet, SF/GB/BR (McLaren F1 GTR-BMW), 238 (DNF – accident); **23** Alain Ferté/Olivier Thévenin/Jurgen von Gartzen, F/F/D (Porsche 911 GT1), 236 (DNF – engine); **24** Andy Wallace/James Weaver/Butch Leitzinger, GB/GB/USA (Panoz GTR), 236 (DNF – engine); **25** Christophe Bouchut/Bertrand Gachot/Andy Evans, F/F/USA (Porsche 911 GT1), 207 (DNF – engine); **26** Patrick Bourdais/Andre Lara-Resende/Peter Kitchak, F/BR/USA (Porsche 911 GT2), 205 (DNF – gearbox); **27** Mario Andretti/Michael Andretti/Olivier Grouillard, USA/USA/F (Courage C36), 197 (DNF – accident); **28** Franck Lagorce/Eric Bernard/Jean-Christophe Boullion, F/F/F (Panoz GTR), 149 (DNF – oil pump); **29** David Brabham/Perry McCarthy/Doc Bundy, AUS/GB/USA (Panoz GTR), 145 (DNF – fire); **30** Martin Brundle/Jörg Müller/Wayne Taylor, GB/D/ZA (Nissan R390 GT1), 139 (DNF – accident); **31** Mauro Baldi/Robert Nearn/Franz Konrad, I/GB/A (Porsche 911 GT1), 138 (DNF – suspension); **32** Steve Saleen/Price Cobb/Carlos Palau, USA/USA/E (Saleen Mustang RRR), 133 (DNF – suspension); **33** Michel Ligonnet/Larry Schumacher/Toni Seiller, F/USA/CH (Porsche 911 GT1), 126 (DNF – engine); **34** Eric van de Poele/Aguri Suzuki/Riccardo Patrese, B/J/I (Nissan R390 GT1), 121 (DNF – gearbox); **35** Jan Lammers/Mike Hezemans/Alexander 'Sandy' Grau, NL/NL/D (Lotus GT1), 121 (DNF – oil pump); **36** Tomas Saldana/Carl Rosenblad/Jurgen Lässig, E/S/D (Kremer K8), 103 (DNF – engine); **37** Enzo Calderai/Lilian Bryner/Angelo Zadra, CH/CH/I (Porsche 911 GT2), 98 (DNF – engine); **38** Keiichi Tsuchiya/Gary Ayles/Akihiko Nakaya, J/GB/J (McLaren F1 GTR-BMW), 81 (DNF – accident); **39** Jean-Pierre Jarier/Jean-Luc Chereau/Jack Leconte, F/F/F (Porsche 911 GT2), 77 (DNF – gearbox); **40** Julian Bailey/Mark Skaife/Thomas Erdos, GB/AUS/BR (Lister Storm GTL), 77 (DNF – gearbox); **41** Tommy Archer/Soheil Ayari/Marc Duez, USA/F/B (Chrysler Viper GTS-R), 76 (DNF – accident); **42** Almo Coppelli/Rocky Agusta/Eric Graham, I/I/F (Callaway Corvette LMGT2), 45 (DNF – out of fuel); **43** Rob Schirle/David Warnock, GB/GB (Saleen Mustang RRR), 28 (DNF – electrics); **44** Geoff Lees/Tiff Needell/George Fouché, GB/GB/ZA (Lister Storm GTL), 21 (DNF – accident); **45** Michel Ferté/Adrian Campos/Charles Nearburg, F/E/USA (Ferrari 333SP), 18 (DNF – out of fuel); **46** Cor Euser/Harald Becker/Takaji Suzuki, NL/D/J (Marcos 600LM), 15 (DNF – engine); **47** Allan McNish/Karl Wendlinger/Stéphane Ortelli, GB/A/F (Porsche 911 GT1), 8 (DNF – accident); **48** Harri Toivonen/Jesus Pareja/Eliseo Salazar, SF/E/RCH (BRM P301), 6 (DNF – engine).
Fastest race lap: Kristensen, 3h 45.068s, 135.170 mph/217.534 km/h.
Fastest qualifying lap: Alboreto, 3m 41.581s, 137.297 mph/220.958 km/h.
Did not start: John Nielsen/Thomas Bscher/Chris Goodwin, DK/D/GB (McLaren F1 GTR-BMW) (fire damage); Giovanni Lavaggi/Jean-Luc Maury-Laribiere/Bernard Chauvin, I/F/F (Kremer K8); Fabien Giroix/Jean-Denis Deletraz, F/CH (Lotus GT1); Dominic Chappell/François Migault/Henri Maunoir, GB/F/F (Marcos 600LM).

PPG CART World Series

MARLBORO GRAND PRIX OF MIAMI PRESENTED BY TOYOTA, Metro-Dade Homestead Motorsports Complex, Florida, USA, 2 March. Round 1. 147 laps of the 1.517-mile/2.441-km circuit, 222.999 miles/358.882 km.
1 Michael Andretti, USA (Swift 007i-Ford Cosworth XD), 1h 38m 45.666s, 135.478 mph/218.030 km/h.
2 Paul Tracy, CDN (Penske PC27-Mercedes Benz IC 108D), 1h 38m 49.067s; **3** Jimmy Vasser, USA (Reynard 97I-Honda HRR), 147 laps; **4** Greg Moore, CDN (Reynard 97I-Mercedes Benz IC 108D), 147; **5** Scott Pruett, USA (Reynard 97I-Ford Cosworth XD), 147; **6** Mauricio Gugelmin, BR (Reynard 97I-Mercedes Benz IC 108D), 147; **7** Alessandro 'Alex' Zanardi, I (Reynard 97I-Honda HRR), 147; **8** Parker Johnstone, USA (Reynard 97I-Honda HRR), 146; **9** Patrick Carpentier, CDN (Reynard 97I-Mercedes Benz IC 108D), 146; **10** Bryan Herta, USA (Reynard 97I-Ford Cosworth XD), 146.
Most laps led: Andretti, 73.
Fastest qualifying lap: Zanardi, 28.000s, 195.043 mph/313.891 km.h.
Championship points: **1** Andretti, 21; **2** Tracy, 16; **3** Vasser, 14; **4** Moore, 12; **5** Pruett, 10; **6** Gugelmin, 8.

SUNBELT INDYCARNIVAL AUSTRALIA, Surfers Paradise Street Circuit, Queensland, Australia, 6 April. Round 2. 57 laps of the 2.795-mile/4.498-km circuit, 159.315 miles/256.393 km.
1 Scott Pruett, USA (Reynard 97I-Ford Cosworth XD), 2h 01m 04.678s, 78.948 mph/127.055 km/h.
2 Greg Moore, CDN (Reynard 97I-Mercedes Benz IC 108D), 2h 01m 05.362s; **3** Michael Andretti, USA (Swift 007i-Ford Cosworth XD), 57 laps; **4** Alessandro 'Alex' Zanardi, I (Reynard 97I-Honda HRR), 57; **5** Gil de Ferran, BR (Reynard 96I-Honda HRR), 57; **6** Andre Ribeiro, BR (Lola T97/00-Honda HRR), 57; **7** Raul Boesel, BR (Reynard 97I-Ford Cosworth XD), 57; **8** Mark Blundell, GB (Reynard 97I-Mercedes Benz IC 108D), 57; **9** Dario Franchitti, GB (Reynard 97I-Mercedes Benz IC 108D), 57; **10** Bobby Rahal, USA (Reynard 97I-Ford Cosworth XD), 57.

Most laps led: Paul Tracy, CDN (Penske PC27-Mercedes Benz IC 108D), 21.
Fastest qualifying lap: Zanardi.
Championship points: 1 Andretti, 35; 2 Pruett, 30; 3 Moore, 28; 4 Zanardi, 20; 5 Tracy, 17; 6 Vasser, 15.

TOYOTA GRAND PRIX OF LONG BEACH, Long Beach Street Circuit, California, USA, 13 April. Round 3. 105 laps of the 1.586-mile/2.552-km circuit, 166.530 miles/268.004 km.
1 Alessandro 'Alex' Zanardi, I (Reynard 97I-Honda HRR), 1h 46m 17.792s, 93.999 mph/151.277 km/h.
2 Mauricio Gugelmin, BR (Reynard 97I-Mercedes Benz IC 108D), 1h 46m 21.612s; 3 Scott Pruett, USA (Reynard 97I-Ford Cosworth XD), 105 laps; 4 Al Unser Jr, USA (Penske PC27-Mercedes Benz IC 108D), 105; 5 Parker Johnstone, USA (Reynard 97I-Honda HRR), 105; 6 Bryan Herta, USA (Reynard 97I-Ford Cosworth XD), 105; 7 Paul Tracy, CDN (Penske PC27-Mercedes Benz IC 108D), 105; 8 Raul Boesel, BR (Reynard 97I-Ford Cosworth XD), 105; 9 Jimmy Vasser, USA (Reynard 97I-Honda HRR), 105; 10 Bobby Rahal, USA (Reynard 97I-Ford Cosworth XD), 105.
Most laps led: Zanardi, 41.
Fastest qualifying lap: Gil de Ferran, BR (Reynard 96I-Honda HRR), 51.293s, 111.313 mph/179.142 km/h.
Championship points: 1 Pruett, 47; 2 Zanardi, 41; 3 Andretti, 35; 4 Moore, 28; 5 Gugelmin, 24; 6 Tracy, 23.

BOSCH SPARK PLUG GRAND PRIX PRESENTED BY TOYOTA, Nazareth Speedway, Pennsylvania, USA, 27 April. Round 4. 225 laps of the 1.000-mile/1.609-km circuit, 225.000 miles/362.102 km.
1 Paul Tracy, CDN (Penske PC27-Mercedes Benz IC 108D), 1h 53m 31.337s, 118.919 mph/191.382 km/h.
2 Michael Andretti, USA (Swift 007i-Ford Cosworth XD), 1h 53m 31.846s; 3 Al Unser Jr, USA (Penske PC27-Mercedes Benz IC 108D), 225 laps; 4 Gil de Ferran, BR (Reynard 97I-Honda HRR), 225; 5 Jimmy Vasser, USA (Reynard 97I-Honda HRR), 224; 6 Bobby Rahal, USA (Reynard 97I-Ford Cosworth XD), 224; 7 Bryan Herta, USA (Reynard 97I-Ford Cosworth XD), 224; 8 Raul Boesel, BR (Reynard 97I-Ford Cosworth XD), 224; 9 Mauricio Gugelmin, BR (Reynard 97I-Mercedes Benz IC 108D), 224; 10 Scott Pruett, USA (Reynard 97I-Ford Cosworth XD), 224.
Most laps led: Tracy, 186.
Fastest qualifying lap: Tracy, 18.831s, 191.174 mph/307.665 km/h.
Championship points: 1 Andretti, 51; 2 Pruett, 47; 3 Tracy, 45; 4 Zanardi, 43; 5 Vasser, 29; 6 Gugelmin, 28.

HOLLYWOOD RIO 400, Emerson Fittipaldi Speedway at Nelson Piquet International Raceway, Rio de Janeiro, Brazil, 11 May. Round 5. 133 laps of the 1.864-mile/3.000-km circuit, 247.912 miles/398.976 km.
1 Paul Tracy, CDN (Penske PC26-Mercedes Benz IC 108D), 2h 10m 47.996s, 113.721 mph/183.016 km/h.
2 Greg Moore, CDN (Reynard 97I-Mercedes Benz IC 108D), 2h 10m 49.801s; 3 Scott Pruett, USA (Reynard 97I-Ford Cosworth XD), 133 laps; 4 Alessandro 'Alex' Zanardi, I (Reynard 97I-Honda HRR), 133; 5 Raul Boesel, BR (Reynard 97I-Ford Cosworth XD), 133; 6 Bryan Herta, USA (Reynard 97I-Ford Cosworth XD), 133; 7 Al Unser Jr, USA (Penske PC27-Mercedes Benz IC 108D), 133; 8 Mark Blundell, GB (Reynard 97I-Mercedes Benz IC 108D), 133; 9 Jimmy Vasser, USA (Reynard 97I-Honda HRR), 133; 10 Bobby Rahal, USA (Reynard 97I-Ford Cosworth XD), 132.
Most laps led: Rahal, 102.
Fastest qualifying lap: Mauricio Gugelmin, BR (Reynard 97I-Mercedes Benz IC 108D), 39.034s, 171.912 mph/276.665 km/h.
Championship points: 1 Tracy, 65; 2 Pruett, 61; 3 Zanardi, 55; 4 Andretti, 51; 5 Moore, 44; 6 Vasser, 43.

MOTOROLA 300, Gateway International Raceway, Madison, Illinois, USA, 24 May. Round 6. 236 laps of the 1.270-mile/2.044-km circuit, 299.720 miles/482.353 km.
1 Paul Tracy, CDN (Penske PC26-Mercedes Benz IC 108D), 2h 37m 54.496s, 113.884 mph/183.278 km/h.
2 Patrick Carpentier, CDN (Reynard 97I-Mercedes Benz IC 108D), 2h 37m 56.887s; 3 Gil de Ferran, BR (Reynard 97IHonda HRR), 236 laps; 4 Alessandro 'Alex' Zanardi, I (Reynard 97I-Honda HRR), 236; 5 Jimmy Vasser, USA (Reynard 97I-Honda HRR), 236; 6 Mauricio Gugelmin, BR (Reynard 97I-Mercedes Benz IC 108D), 236; 7 Parker Johnstone, USA (Reynard 97I-Honda HRR), 236; 8 Adrian Fernandez, MEX (Lola T97/00-Honda HRR), 236; 9 Richie Hearn (Lola T97/00-Ford Cosworth XD), 236; 10 Andre Ribeiro, BR (Lola T97/00-Honda HRR), 236.
Most laps led: Michael Andretti, USA (Swift 007i-Ford Cosworth XD), 66.
Fastest qualifying lap: Raul Boesel, BR (Reynard 97I-Ford Cosworth XD), 24.324s, 187.963 mph/302.496 km/h.
Championship points: 1 Tracy, 85; 2 Zanardi, 67; 3 Pruett, 61; 4 Andretti, 54; 5 Moore, 44; 6 Vasser, 43.

MILLER 200, The Milwaukee Mile, Wisconsin State Fair Park, West Allis, Milwaukee, USA, 1 June. Round 7. 200 laps of the 1.032-mile/1.661-km circuit, 206.400 miles/332.169 km.
1 Greg Moore, CDN (Reynard 97I-Mercedes Benz IC 108D), 1h 43m 32.873s, 119.597 mph/192.472 km/h.
2 Michael Andretti, USA (Swift 007i-Ford Cosworth XD), 1h 43m 33.221s; 3 Jimmy Vasser, USA (Reynard 97I-Honda HRR), 200; 4 Raul Boesel, BR (Reynard 97I-Ford Cosworth XD), 200; 5 Mauricio Gugelmin, BR (Reynard 97I-Mercedes Benz IC 108D), 200; 6 Paul Tracy, CDN (Penske PC26-Mercedes Benz IC 108D), 200; 7 Gil de Ferran, BR (Reynard 97I-Honda HRR), 200; 8 Patrick Carpentier, CDN (Reynard 97I-Mercedes Benz IC 108D), 200; 9 Scott Pruett, USA (Reynard 97I-Ford Cosworth XD), 200; 10 Roberto Moreno, BR (Swift 007i-Ford Cosworth XD), 200.
Most laps led: Moore, 104.
Fastest qualifying lap: Tracy, 20.160s, 184.286 mph/296.579 km/h.
Championship points: 1 Tracy, 94; 2 Andretti, 70; 3 Zanardi, 67; 4= Moore, 65; 4= Pruett, 65; 6 Vasser, 57.

ITT AUTOMOTIVE DETROIT GRAND PRIX, The Raceway on Belle Isle, Detroit, Michigan, USA, 8 June. Round 8. 77 laps of the 2.100-mile/3.380-km circuit, 161.700 miles/260.231 km.
1 Greg Moore, CDN (Reynard 97I-Mercedes Benz IC 108D), 1h 52m 45.143s, 86.047 mph/138.479 km/h.
2 Michael Andretti, USA (Swift 007i-Ford Cosworth XD), 1h 52m 46.961s; 3 Gil de Ferran, BR (Reynard 97I-Honda HRR), 77 laps; 4 Jimmy Vasser, USA (Reynard 97I-Honda HRR), 77; 5 Roberto Moreno, BR (Swift 007i-Ford Cosworth XD), 77; 6 Raul Boesel, BR (Reynard 97I-Ford Cosworth XD), 77; 7 Bryan Herta, USA (Reynard 97I-Ford Cosworth XD), 77; 8 Al Unser Jr, USA (Penske PC27-Mercedes Benz IC 108D), 77; 9 Bobby Rahal, USA (Reynard 97I-Ford Cosworth XD), 77; 10 Juan Fangio II, RA (Reynard 96I-Toyota), 77.
Most laps led: de Ferran, 27.
Fastest qualifying lap: de Ferran, 1m 09.052s, 109.483 mph/176.195 km/h.
Championship points: 1 Tracy, 94; 2 Andretti, 86; 3 Moore, 85; 4 Vasser, 69; 5 Zanardi, 67; 6 Pruett, 65.

BUDWEISER/G.I.JOE'S 200 PRESENTED BY TEXACO/HAVOLINE, Portland International Raceway, Oregon, USA, 22 June. Round 9. 78 laps of the 1.967-mile/3.166-km circuit, 153.426 miles/246.915 km.
Scheduled for 98 laps, but stopped prematurely due to bad weather bringing the two hour rule into effect.
1 Mark Blundell, GB (Reynard 97I-Mercedes Benz IC 108D), 2h 00m 12.982s, 76.575 mph/123.235 km/h.
2 Gil de Ferran, BR (Reynard 97I-Honda HRR), 2h 00m 13.009s; 3 Raul Boesel, BR (Reynard 97I-Ford Cosworth XD), 78 laps; 4 Christian Fittipaldi, BR (Swift 007i-Ford Cosworth XD), 78; 5 Greg Moore, CDN (Reynard 97I-Mercedes Benz IC 108D), 1h 52m 45.143s, 78; 6 Mauricio Gugelmin, BR (Reynard 97I-Mercedes Benz IC 108D), 78; 7 Paul Tracy, CDN (Penske PC26-Mercedes Benz IC 108D), 78; 8 Michael Andretti, USA (Swift 007i-Ford Cosworth XD), 78; 9 Parker Johnstone, USA (Reynard 97I-Honda HRR), 78; 10 Adrian Fernandez, MEX (Lola T97/00-Honda HRR), 78.
Most laps led: Gugelmin, 38.
Fastest qualifying lap: Scott Pruett, USA (Reynard 97I-Ford Cosworth XD), 59.383s, 119.246 mph/191.908 km/h.
Championship points: 1 Tracy, 100; 2 Moore, 95; 3 Andretti, 91; 4 de Ferran, 77; 5= Vasser, 69; 5= Zanardi, 69.

MEDIC DRUG GRAND PRIX OF CLEVELAND PRESENTED BY DAIRY MART, Burke Lakefront Airport Circuit, Cleveland, Ohio, USA, 13 July. Round 10. 90 laps of the 2.106-mile/3.389-km circuit, 189.540 miles/305.035 km.
1 Alessandro 'Alex' Zanardi, I (Reynard 97I-Honda HRR), 1h 41m 40.661s, 111.848 mph/180.001 km/h.
2 Gil de Ferran, BR (Reynard 97I-Honda HRR), 1h 41m 41.942s; 3 Bryan Herta, USA (Reynard 97I-Ford Cosworth XD), 90 laps; 4 Al Unser Jr, USA (Penske PC26-Mercedes Benz IC 108D), 90; 5 Bobby Rahal, USA (Reynard 97I-Ford Cosworth XD), 90; 6 Christian Fittipaldi, BR (Swift 007i-Ford Cosworth XD), 90; 7 Paul Tracy, CDN (Penske PC26-Mercedes Benz IC 108D), 90; 8 Scott Pruett, USA (Reynard 97I-Ford Cosworth XD), 90; 9 Mark Blundell, GB (Reynard 97I-Mercedes Benz IC 108D), 90; 10 Parker Johnstone, USA (Reynard 97I-Honda HRR), 90.
Most laps led: de Ferran, 49.
Fastest qualifying lap: Zanardi, 56.984s, 133.048 mph/214.120 km/h.
Championship points: 1 Tracy, 106; 2 Moore, 95; 3 de Ferran, 94; 4 Andretti, 91; 5 Zanardi, 90; 6 Pruett, 71.

MOLSON INDY TORONTO, Exhibition Place Circuit, Toronto, Ontario, Canada, 20 July. Round 11. 95 laps of the 1.721-mile/2.770-km circuit, 163.495 miles/263.120 km.
1 Mark Blundell, GB (Reynard 97I-Mercedes Benz IC 108D), 1h 45m 43.936s, 92.779 mph/149.313 km/h.
2 Alessandro 'Alex' Zanardi, I (Reynard 97I-Honda HRR), 1h 45m 44.595s; 3 Andre Ribeiro, BR (Reynard 97I-Honda HRR), 95 laps; 4 Michael Andretti, USA (Swift 007i-Ford Cosworth XD), 95; 5 Scott Pruett, USA (Reynard 97I-Ford Cosworth XD), 95; 6 Mauricio Gugelmin, BR (Reynard 97I-Mercedes Benz IC 108D), 95; 7 Jimmy Vasser, USA (Reynard 97I-Honda HRR), 95; 8 Raul Boesel, BR (Reynard 97I-Ford Cosworth XD), 95; 9 Bobby Rahal, USA (Reynard 97I-Ford Cosworth XD), 95; 10 Paul Tracy, CDN (Penske PC26-Mercedes Benz IC 108D), 95.
Most laps led: Blundell, 93.
Fastest qualifying lap: Dario Franchitti, GB (Reynard 97I-Mercedes Benz IC 108D), 58.618s, 105.694 mph/170.099 km/h.
Championship points: 1 Tracy, 109; 2 Zanardi, 106; 3 Andretti, 103; 4 Moore, 95; 5 de Ferran, 94; 6 Pruett, 81.

U.S. 500 PRESENTED BY TOYOTA, Michigan Speedway, Brooklyn, Michigan, USA, 27 July. Round 12. 250 laps of the 2.000-mile/3.219-km circuit, 500.000 miles/804.672 km.
1 Alessandro 'Alex' Zanardi, I (Reynard 97I-Honda HRR), 2h 59m 35.579s, 167.044 mph/268.832 km/h.
2 Mark Blundell, GB (Reynard 97I-Mercedes Benz IC 108D), 3h 00m 07.316s; 3 Gil de Ferran, BR (Reynard 97I-Honda HRR), 249 laps; 4 Paul Tracy, CDN (Penske PC26-Mercedes Benz IC 108D), 249; 5 Bryan Herta, USA (Reynard 97I-Ford Cosworth XD), 248; 6 Mauricio Gugelmin, BR (Reynard 97I-Mercedes Benz IC 108D), 244; 7 Dennis Vitolo, USA (Lola T97-Ford Cosworth XD), 242; 8 Massimiliano 'Max' Papis, I (Reynard 97I-Toyota), 241; 9 Hiro Matsushita, J (Reynard 97I-Toyota), 241; 10 Gualter Salles, BR (Reynard 97I-Ford Cosworth XD), 240.
Most laps led: Zanardi, 104.
Fastest qualifying lap: Scott Pruett, USA (Reynard 97I-Ford Cosworth XD), 30.788s, 233.857 mph/376.357 km/h.
Championship points: 1 Zanardi, 127; 2 Tracy, 121; 3 de Ferran, 108; 4 Andretti, 103; 5 Moore, 95; 6 Pruett, 82.

MILLER 200, Mid-Ohio Sports Car Course, Lexington, Ohio, USA, 10 August. Round 13. 83 laps of the 2.258-mile/3.634-km circuit, 186.446 miles/300.056 km.
1 Alessandro 'Alex' Zanardi, I (Reynard 97I-Honda HRR), 1h 41m 16.682s, 110.456 mph/177.762 km/h.
2 Greg Moore, CDN (Reynard 97I-Mercedes Benz IC 108D), 1h 41m 21.553s; 3 Bobby Rahal, USA (Reynard 97I-Ford Cosworth XD), 83 laps; 4 Raul Boesel, BR (Reynard 97I-Ford Cosworth XD), 83; 5 Jimmy Vasser, USA (Reynard 97I-Honda HRR), 83; 6 Gil de Ferran, BR (Reynard 97I-Honda HRR), 83; 7 Mauricio Gugelmin, BR (Reynard 97I-Mercedes Benz IC 108D), 83; 8 Michael Andretti, USA (Swift 007i-Ford Cosworth XD), 83; 9 Scott Pruett, USA (Reynard 97I-Ford Cosworth XD), 83; 10 Andre Ribeiro, BR (Reynard 97I-Honda HRR), 83.
Most laps led: Zanardi, 56.
Fastest qualifying lap: Bryan Herta, USA (Reynard 97I-Ford Cosworth XD), 1m 06.277s, 122.649 mph/197.384 km/h.
Championship points: 1 Zanardi, 148; 2 Tracy, 121; 3 de Ferran, 116; 4 Moore, 111; 5 Andretti, 108; 5 Pruett, 86.

TEXACO/HAVOLINE 200, Road America Circuit, Elkhart Lake, Wisconsin, USA, 17 August. Round 14. 50 laps of the 4.048-mile/6.515-km circuit, 202.400 miles/325.731 km.
1 Alessandro 'Alex' Zanardi, I (Reynard 97I-Honda HRR), 1h 57m 54.544s, 102.995 mph/165.754 km/h.
2 Mauricio Gugelmin, BR (Reynard 97I-Mercedes Benz IC 108D), 1h 58m 00.692s; 3 Gil de Ferran, BR (Reynard 97I-Honda HRR), 50 laps; 4 Christian Fittipaldi, BR (Swift 007i-Ford Cosworth XD), 50; 5 Scott Pruett, USA (Reynard 97I-Ford Cosworth XD), 50; 6 Bobby Rahal, USA (Reynard 97I-Ford Cosworth XD), 50; 7 Al Unser Jr, USA (Penske PC26-Mercedes Benz IC 108D), 50; 8 Jimmy Vasser, USA (Reynard 97I-Honda HRR), 50; 9 Richie Hearn, USA (Lola T97/00-Ford Cosworth XD), 50; 10 Juan Fangio II, RA (Reynard 97I-Toyota), 50.
Most laps led: Mark Blundell, GB (Reynard 97I-Mercedes Benz IC 108D), 23.
Fastest qualifying lap: Gugelmin, 1m 42.379s, 142.342 mph/229.077 km/h.
Championship points: 1 Zanardi, 168; 2 de Ferran, 130; 3 Tracy, 121; 4 Moore, 111; 5 Andretti, 108; 6 Pruett, 96.

MOLSON INDY VANCOUVER, Vancouver Street Circuit, Concord Pacific Place, Vancouver, British Columbia, Canada, 31 August. Round 15. 100 laps of the 1.703-mile/2.741-km circuit, 170.300 miles/274.071 km.
1 Mauricio Gugelmin, BR (Reynard 97I-Mercedes Benz IC 108D), 1h 47m 17.995s, 95.228 mph/153.255 km/h.
2 Jimmy Vasser, USA (Reynard 97I-Honda HRR), 1h 47m 20.867s; 3 Gil de Ferran, BR (Reynard 97I-Honda HRR), 100 laps; 4 Alessandro 'Alex' Zanardi, I (Reynard 97I-Honda HRR), 100; 5 Al Unser Jr, USA (Penske PC26-Mercedes Benz IC 108D), 100; 6 Raul Boesel, BR (Reynard 97I-Ford Cosworth XD), 100; 7 Mark Blundell, GB (Reynard 97I-Mercedes Benz IC 108D), 100; 8 Bryan Herta, USA (Reynard 97I-Ford Cosworth XD), 100; 9 Christian Fittipaldi, BR (Swift 007i-Ford Cosworth XD), 99; 10 Andre Ribeiro, BR (Reynard 97I-Honda HRR), 99.
Most laps led: Vasser, 46.
Fastest qualifying lap: Zanardi, 54.025s, 113.481 mph/182.630 km/h.
Championship points: 1 Zanardi, 181; 2 de Ferran, 144; 3 Tracy, 121; 4 Gugelmin, 115; 5 Moore, 111; 6 Andretti, 108.

TOYOTA GRAND PRIX OF MONTEREY, Laguna Seca Raceway, Monterey, California, USA, 7 September. Round 16. 83 laps of the 2.238-mile/3.602-km circuit, 185.754 miles/298.942 km.
1 Jimmy Vasser, USA (Reynard 97I-Honda HRR), 1h 41m 38.813s, 109.647 mph/176.459 km/h.
2 Mark Blundell, GB (Reynard 97I-Mercedes Benz IC 108D), 1h 41m 39.356s; 3 Alessandro 'Alex' Zanardi, I (Reynard 97I-Honda HRR), 83 laps; 4 Andre Ribeiro, BR (Reynard 97I-Honda HRR), 83; 5 Gil de Ferran, BR (Reynard 97I-Honda HRR), 83; 6 Bryan Herta, USA (Reynard 97I-Ford Cosworth XD), 83; 7 Gualter Salles, BR (Reynard 97I-Ford Cosworth XD), 83; 8 Raul Boesel, BR (Reynard 97I-Ford Cosworth XD), 83; 9 Mauricio Gugelmin, BR (Reynard 97I-Mercedes Benz IC 108D), 82; 10 Roberto Moreno, BR (Reynard 97I-Mercedes Benz IC 108D), 82.
Most laps led: Vasser, 58.
Fastest qualifying lap: Herta, 1m 07.895s, 118.666 mph/190.974 km/h.
Championship points: 1 Zanardi, 195; 2 de Ferran, 154; 3 Vasser, 128; 4 Tracy, 121; 5 Gugelmin, 119; 6 Moore, 111.

MARLBORO 500 PRESENTED BY TOYOTA, California Speedway, Fontana, California, USA, 28 September. Round 17. 250 laps of the 2.029-mile/3.265-km circuit, 507.250 miles/816.340 km.
1 Mark Blundell, GB (Reynard 97I-Mercedes Benz IC 108D), 3h 02m 42.620s, 166.575 mph/268.077 km/h.
2 Jimmy Vasser, USA (Reynard 97I-Honda HRR), 3h 02m 45.467s; 3 Adrian Fernandez, MEX (Lola T97/00-Honda HRR), 249 laps; 4 Mauricio Gugelmin, BR (Reynard 97I-Mercedes Benz IC 108D), 249; 5 Bobby Rahal, USA (Reynard 97I-Ford Cosworth XD), 249; 6 Gil de Ferran, BR (Reynard 97I-Honda HRR), 249; 7 Scott Pruett, USA (Reynard 97I-Ford Cosworth XD), 248; 8 Robby Gordon, USA (Reynard 97I-Ford Cosworth XD), 247; 9 Christian Fittipaldi, BR (Swift 007i-Ford Cosworth XD), 247; 10 P.J. Jones (Reynard 97I-Toyota), 244.
Most laps led: Andre Ribeiro, BR (Reynard 97I-Honda HRR), 114.
Fastest qualifying lap: Gugelmin, 30.316s, 240.942 mph/387.759 km/h.

Final championship points
1 Alessandro 'Alex' Zanardi, I, 195; 2 Gil de Ferran, BR, 162; 3 Jimmy Vasser, USA, 144; 4 Mauricio Gugelmin,

BR, 132; 5 Paul Tracy, CDN, 121; 6 Mark Blundell, GB, 115; 7 Greg Moore, CDN, 111; 8 Michael Andretti, USA, 108; 9 Scott Pruett, USA, 102; 10 Raul Boesel, BR, 45; 15 Christian Fittipaldi, BR, 42; 16 Parker Johnstone, USA, 36; 17= Patrick Carpentier, CDN, 27; 17= Adrian Fernandez, MEX, 27; 19 Roberto Moreno, BR, 16; 20= Gualter Salles, BR, 10; 20= Dario Franchitti, GB, 10; 20= Richie Hearn, USA, 10.

Nations' Cup
1 United States, 252; 2 Brazil, 238; 3 Italy, 198; 4 Canada, 190; 5 England, 115; 6 Mexico, 27; 7 Scotland, 10; 8 Argentina, 9; 9 Japan, 4; 10 Germany, 2.

Manufacturers' Championship (engines)
1 Mercedes-Benz, 316; 2 Honda, 290; 3 Ford Cosworth, 230; 4 Toyota, 15.

Constructors' Championship
1 Reynard, 346; 2 Penske, 156; 3 Swift, 143; 4 Lola, 45.

Rookie of the Year
1 Patrick Carpentier, CDN, 27; 2= Gualter Salles, BR, 10; 2= Dario Franchitti, GB, 10; 4 Arnd Meier, D, 1.

Marlboro Pole Award
1 Alessandro 'Alex' Zanardi, I, 4; 2 Mauricio Gugelmin, BR, 3; 3= Paul Tracy, USA, 2; 3= Gil de Ferran, BR, 2; 3= Bryan Herta, USA, 2; 3= Scott Pruett, USA, 2; 7= Dario Franchitti, GB, 1; 7= Raul Boesel, BR, 1.

Indy Car race

81st INDIANAPOLIS 500, Indianapolis Motor Speedway, Speedway, Indiana, USA, 26/27 May. 200 laps of the 2.500-mile/4.023-km circuit, 500.000 miles/804.672 km.
Delayed by two days of rain with 15 laps being run on Monday 26 May and 185 laps on Tuesday 27 May.
1 Arie Luyendyk, NL (G-Force-Aurora), 3h 25m 43.388s, 145.827 mph/234.686 km/h.
2 Scott Goodyear, CDN (G-Force-Aurora), 3h 25m 43.958s; 3 Jeff Ward (G-Force-Aurora), 200 laps; 4 Buddy Lazier, USA (Dallara-Aurora), 200; 5 Tony Stewart, USA (G-Force-Aurora), 200; 6 Davey Hamilton, USA (G-Force-Aurora), 199; 7 Billy Boat, USA (Dallara-Aurora), 199; 8 Robbie Buhl, USA (G-Force-Aurora), 199; 9 Robbie Groff, USA (G-Force-Aurora), 197; 10 Fermin Velez, E (Dallara-Aurora), 195; 11 Buzz Calkins, USA (G-Force-Aurora), 188 (DNF – right halfshaft); 12 Mike Groff, USA (G-Force-Infiniti), 188; 13 Lyn St James, USA (Dallara-Infiniti), 186 (DNF – accident); 14 Steve Kinser, USA (Dallara-Aurora), 185 (DNF – accident); 15 Dennis Vitolo, USA (Dallara-Infiniti), 173; 16 Marco Greco, BR (Dallara-Aurora), 166 (DNF – gearbox); 17 Vincenzo Sospiri, I (Dallara-Aurora), 163; 18 Johnny Unser, USA (Dallara-Infiniti), 158 (DNF – oil pressure); 19 Tyce Carlson, USA (Dallara-Aurora), 156 (DNF – accident); 20 Dr Jack Miller, USA (Dallara-Infiniti), 131 (DNF – accident); 21 Paul Durant, USA (G-Force-Aurora), 111 (DNF – accident); 22 Billy Roe, USA (G-Force-Aurora), 110 (DNF – accident); 23 Eddie Cheever, Jr, USA (G-Force-Aurora), 84 (DNF – timing chain); 24 Eliseo Salazar, RCH (Dallara-Aurora), 70 (DNF – accident); 25 Greg Ray, USA (G-Force-Aurora), 48 (DNF – water pump); 26 Jim Guthrie, USA (Dallara-Aurora), 43 (DNF – engine); 27 Roberto Guerrero, USA (Dallara-Infiniti), 25 (DNF – steering gear); 28 Mark Dismore, USA (Dallara-Aurora), 24 (DNF – accident); 29 Robby Gordon, USA (G-Force-Aurora), 19 (DNF – fire); 30 Claude Bourbonnais, CDN (Dallara-Aurora), 9 (DNF – engine); 31 Stéphan Grégoire, F (G-Force-Aurora), 0 (DNF – accident); 32 Alfonso Giaffone, BR (Dallara-Aurora), 0 (DNF – accident); 33 Kenny Bräck, S (G-Force-Aurora), 0 (DNF – accident); 34 Sam Schmidt, USA (Dallara-Aurora), 0 (DNF – engine); 35 Alessandro Zampedri, I (Dallara-Aurora), 0 (DNF – oil leak).
Most laps led: Stewart, 64.
Fastest race lap: Stewart, 41.738s, 215.631 mph/347.024 km/h.
Pole Position/Fastest qualifying lap: Luyendyk, 2m 44.940s, 218.263 mph/351.260 km/h (over four laps).

Rookie of the Year: Jeff Ward.

NASCAR Winston Cup

1996 Result

The Atlanta race was run after Autocourse 1996/97 went to press.

NAPA 500, Atlanta Motor Speedway, Hampton, Georgia, USA, 10 November. Round 31. 328 laps of the 1.522-mile/2.449-km circuit, 499.216 miles/803.410 km.
1 Bobby Labonte, USA (Chevrolet Monte Carlo) 3h 39m 13s, 136.636 mph/219.895 km/h.
2 Dale Jarrett, USA (Ford Thunderbird), 3h 39m 13.41s; 3 Jeff Gordon, USA (Chevrolet Monte Carlo), 328 laps; 4 Dale Earnhardt, USA (Chevrolet Monte Carlo), 328; 5 Terry Labonte, USA (Chevrolet Monte Carlo), 328; 6 Bobby Hamilton, USA (Pontiac Grand Prix), 328; 7 Mark Martin, USA (Ford Thunderbird), 328; 8 Ricky Rudd, USA (Ford Thunderbird), 328; 9 Jeff Burton, USA (Ford Thunderbird), 328; 10 Rusty Wallace, USA (Ford Thunderbird), 328.
Fastest qualifying lap: Labonte (Bobby), 29.476s, 185.887 mph/299.156 km/h (record).

Final championship points
Drivers
1 Terry Labonte, USA, 4657; 2 Jeff Gordon, USA, 4620; 3 Dale Jarrett, USA, 4568; 4 Dale Earnhardt, USA, 4327; 5 Mark Martin, USA, 4278; 6 Ricky Rudd,